AF656827

An International Text in

MICRO & MACROECONOMICS

An International Text in MICRO & MACROECONOMICS

Sunil Bhaduri
Former Senior Lecturer of Economics
Middlesex University, London

John Cole
Former Senior Lecturer of Economics
Middlesex University, London

New Central Book Agency (P) Ltd

LONDON
HYDERABAD ERNAKULAM BHUBANESWAR
NEW DELHI KOLKATA PUNE GUWAHATI

NCBA

REGD OFFICE
8/1 Chintamoni Das Lane, Kolkata 700 009, India
email: ncbapvtltd@eth.net

OVERSEAS
NCBA (UK) Ltd, 149 Park Avenue North, Northampton, NN3 2HY, UK
email: ncbauk@yahoo.com

EXPORT
NCBA Exports Pvt. Ltd, 212 Shahpur Jat, New Delhi 110 049
email: ncbaexports@ncbapvtltd.com

BRANCHES

2/27 Ansari Road, 1st Floor
Daryaganj, **New Delhi** 110 002
email: ncbadel@ncbapvtltd.com

Shop Nos. 3 & 4, Vinayak Towers
681/B Budhwar Peth, Appa Balwant Chowk
Pune 411 002
email: ncbapune@ncbapvtltd.com

Shop No. 15, Bharati Towers, Ground Floor
Forest Park
Bhubaneswar 751 001
email: ncbabub@ncbapvtltd.com

House No. 3-1-315, 1st Floor
Nimboliadda, Kachiguda, **Hyderabad** 500 027
email: ncbahydb@ncbapvtltd.com

GSS Shopping Complex, 1st Floor
Opposite College Post Office, Convent Road
Ernakulam 682 035
0484-4021054 / 53

Radhamayee Complex [Second Floor]
Opp. Axis Bank, Panbazar, Jaswanta Road
Guwahati 781 001
email: ncbaguwahati@ncbapvtltd.com

AN INTERNATIONAL TEXT IN MICRO AND MACROECONOMICS • Sunil Bhaduri and John Cole

© Copyright reserved by the Authors

Publication, Distribution, and Promotion Rights exclusively reserved by the Publisher

All rights reserved. No part of the text in general, and the figures, diagrams, page layout, and cover design in particular, may be reproduced or transmitted in any form or by any means—electronic, mechanical, photocopying, recording, or by any information storage and retrieval system—without the prior written permission of the Publisher

First Published: 2011
Reprinted: 2019

PUBLISHER AND TYPESETTER
New Central Book Agency (P) Ltd
8/1 Chintamoni Das Lane, Kolkata 700 009

PRINTER
New Central Book Agency (P) Ltd
Web-Offset Division, Dhulagarh, Sankrail, Howrah

PROJECT TEAM
Swapan Sarkar and Sarab Chatterjee

ISBN: 978 81 7381 667 3

Price ₹ 950.00
£ 20.00
$ 34.00

Dedicated

to

Theodora

and

Kalpana

Contents

Preface

The goal of this text is simple: to help readers understand Micro and Macroeconomics, so that they might do better in studies and business, and to do this as concisely and clearly as possible.

The subject is, for some students, not quite easy to comprehend. Its foremost requirement is for a student to grasp the intricacies of an economic model before that model can be usefully applied to real world problems. With this in mind, we have tried to keep the number of diagrams down to minimum. The aim is to relate theories to some of the practical problems faced by modern economies and try to explain recent approaches to all such economic problems.

Apart from the usual topics, the book also covers factors affecting autonomous consumption, post-Keynesian economics, detecting inflationary pressures, effects of interest rate changes on the economy, supply side policies, speculation, overshooting exchange rates, economic problems associated with deflation, the origins of the 'credit crunch', and modern monetary theory.

We profusely thank the staff of New Central Book Agency (P) Ltd in general, and Mr Amitabha Sen in particular, for generous cooperation and help.

However, the authors bear full responsibility for all errors and omissions in the text.

John Cole
Sunil Bhaduri
London, UK

PART I

MICROECONOMICS

CHAPTER 1

INTRODUCTION

KEY TERMS

Economics: The study of how people choose among alternative uses of scarce resources.

Resources: Labour (quantity and quality), Capital (quantity and quality), and land (quantity and quality).

Scarcity: A condition that exists when current resources are inadequate to provide (goods and services) for all of society's wants.

Opportunity Cost: The quantity of other goods sacrificed to get another unit of a particular good.

Production Possibility Frontier (curve): The PPF shows the maximum combinations of output (goods) that the economy can produce using all available resources.

As a discipline 'Economics' is more than two centuries old. The study of economics as a separate subject started after the publication of Adam Smith's 'Wealth of Nations' in 1776. The Classical Economists like Smith, J.S. Mill and others defined economics as 'the science of wealth'. This definition did not cover the major problems faced by human society in solving its economic problems. Moreover, it laid the entire emphasis on the material side of life and ignored the quality of life. This was, thus, criticised and rejected by later economists as well as philosophers.

In 1890 Alfred Marshall published his 'Principles of Economics' where his definition of economics shifted from wealth to human being. He defined Economics as 'a study of mankind in their money getting and money spending activity'. This definition also did not indicate why economic activities—such as production, consumption and exchange—are undertaken. In other words, his definition is somewhat wide.

In the 1930s Lionel Robbins offered another definition of Economics, which is more precise than other definitions. He defined Economics as 'the science which studies human behaviour as a relationship between ends (the production of goods and services) and scarce means (resources—also known as the factors of production) which have alternative uses'.

Services are such things as transport, insurance, banking services etc. Goods can be defined as physical commodities—food, clothing etc. Items such as cars, TVs, washing machines are durable goods—they are not immediately consumed, they provide a stream of services over time.

The output of goods and service of any country are dependent upon the resources (labour, capital and land) available. Land (the factor of production that nature supplies) is not only the amount of physical land available but also includes raw materials (iron ore, natural gas, oil etc.).

When measuring the resources available to any society we are not only interested in the quantity of the resources available but also the quality of the available resources. So we are interested in both the quantity and the quality of labour, capital and land.

By capital we mean the stock of tangible capital assets (factories, plant, machinery, office buildings etc.), not financial capital. The stock of capital is an accumulation of investment over a long period of time. Investment is a flow variable. Net investment is an addition to (positive net investment) or a reduction in (negative net investment) the stock of capital. Thus, we see that the central economic problems are overall problems of scarcity of resources (labour, land and capital), which cannot satisfy fully the unlimited wants of society (goods and services).

It is, therefore, necessary to decide which of them are going to be satisfied. Thus, economics is about scarcity and choice. As P. Samuelson said that every society has to answer three fundamental problems: What to produce? How to produce them? And, for whom to produce them?

This definition has also been considered as too narrow as it did not consider economics as the study of welfare, which is an end in itself. Thus, K.E. Boulding defined economics 'as a body of general principles which may be applied to the interpretation of all economic problems, past and present. It rests on a broad foundation of the study of human nature, and its most fundamental propositions can be applied to all conditions of mankind.'

All said, Robbins' definition remains by far more popular. However, it was modified by other economists, such as Milton Friedman, who defined: 'Economics is a science of how a particular society solves its economics problem. An economic problem exists whenever scarce means are used to satisfy alternative ends. If the means are not scarce, there is no problem at all; there is nirvana.'

Economics is too much interesting to be left to economists alone. It affects almost everything we do. It influences the future we leave for our children, the extent to which we care for the disadvantaged, and resources we have for enjoying ourselves. These issues are discussed daily everywhere. The formal study of economics is important and exciting as it gives us tools that allow us a better understanding of the problem we face everyday.

This book is designed to give you the tools of analysis and provide you practice in using it. With practice, it would be helpful to analyse the environment in which we live.

* * * *

Economics is the study of how society decides what, how, and for whom, to produce. Every society must solve these three problems of living—what goods and services to produce, how to produce them, and, for whom to produce them.

By emphasizing the role of society, we place economics within the social sciences that study and explain human behaviour. Economics studies behaviour in the production, exchange and use of goods and services. Society has to reconcile the conflict between limitless desires for goods and services, and the scarcity of resources with which to produce them. Economics analyses these decisions. Its subject matter is human behaviour and its method is to develop theories and test them against facts.

Although economics is about human behaviour, we consider it a science. This reflects the method of analysis, not the subject matter of economics. We can afford the necessities of life—food, shelter, education, health and some extras such as education and entertainment. We are richer than some people and poorer than others. Income distribution is closely linked to what, how, and for whom questions. Table 1.1 shows income per person in different countries. In rich countries, income per person is £18,340 a year, and in poor countries it is £280 a year. For whom does the world economy produce? Mainly for the 15% of the world population living in the high income countries. What is produced? What do people in these countries want?

Why are there big differences in incomes between different groups of countries? This reflects how goods and services are made in different countries. Poor countries have little capital (machinery etc.), and their people have less access to other amenities. Workers in poor countries are, thus, less productive than rich countries as they work in less favourable conditions.

Income is also unequally distributed within each country and between countries. The degree to which income is unequally distributed affects what goods and services to be produced.

In developed countries, agriculture is only 2% of GDP and industry is about 30% and the rest is services, which include banking, transport, entertainment, communication, tourism and public services (such as defence, education, health). Most output comes from services, and the share of this sector in GDP continues to grow.

Economists develop theories of human behaviour and test them against facts. We discuss later the tools economists use and explain the senses in which their approach is scientific.

Economics does not ignore people as individuals. It is the individual consumer that purchases final goods and services. Consumers purchase goods and services because they receive utility (satisfaction) or benefit (the desirable attribute of a good or service, which a customer perceives she/he will get from purchasing the good or service). We assume that any extra good or service consumed will increase a person's benefit/utility. However, we also assume diminishing marginal utility (benefit). Diminishing marginal benefit occurs when the extra benefit received from the extra unit is less than the extra benefit received from the previous unit. People will continue to

Table 1.1: World Population and their Incomes in 2005

	Country Group		
	Low	Middle	High
Income per head ($'s)	578	2,872	37,566
% of world population	36.5	47.75	15.7
% of world income	5	41	54

Source: World Bank, World Development Report

Table 1.2: Percentage National Output Produced in Different Countries

Percentage of National Output in	UK	USA	France	Japan
Agriculture	2	2	2	3
Industry	30	28	27	38
Services	68	70	71	60

Source: World Bank, World Development Report

purchase a particular good until the extra (private) benefit they receive from purchasing the extra unit is just equal to the cost of the good.

In economic jargon, people will continue to purchase a particular good until their marginal private benefit (MPB) is just equal to the price of the good (P). i.e. MPB = P. Marginal means 'additional'. Hence, marginal private benefit is the change in total benefit that occurs when an additional unit of a good is purchased.

If MPB > P then the individual will purchase more of the good and this will increase their utility.

If MPB < P then the individual will purchase less of the good and this will increase their utility. If the marginal social benefit (MSB) is equal to MPB then, in equilibrium, MSB = P, where MSB is the incremental benefit of an activity as viewed by society.

• Economic Issues

To try to understand economics by studying definition is like trying to learn swimming by reading an instruction manual. Formal analysis makes sense once you have some practical experience. Here we discuss examples of how society allocates scarce resources between competing ends and see the importance of the questions what, how, and for whom, to produce.

• Oil Price Shocks

We know oil provides fuel for heating, transport, machinery and so on. Energy is a key input. When inputs become more expensive, costs rise, profits drop. Firms begin to go out of business. People are sacked. The price of oil matters both directly and indirectly—because of its indirect importance in determining the prices of plastics, medicines, clothing, pesticides, paint, and thousands of other things we take for granted. Petroleum is also the lifeblood of transport and delivery. The largest user of energy in Britain is now the transport sector. Transport energy use has shot up: *today the sector consumes as much energy as the whole of industry and services combined.*

Its price shapes all energy prices. A graph of the price of natural gas and of coal looks like a smoother version of the graph for the price of petroleum, so oil prices govern electricity prices too.

Trebling of oil prices will increase the price level of consumer products and will reduce real disposable earnings. If people are poorer, they cut back on the rest of their spending. A cinema or bookshop is not as immune from oil as its owners may think.

The consequences of oil price movements reach deep into the economy. As a group the industrial nations burn more oil than ever before. And, because everything in the world is made using energy and people, when energy becomes dearer something has to give up. It is true that we use energy more efficiently (2008). Compared with 1980, our economy gets 25 per cent more output for each unit of energy. That is useful; *but it is a relatively small gain in the face of, say, a trebling of the price of petroleum.*

In 2000 and 2008 many European countries were brought to a halt by blockades of lorry drivers protesting about high fuel prices. Similar protests occurred when oil prices rose sharply in 1973-74 and again in 1979-80.

Fig. 1.1 shows the average annual price of crude oil between 1970 and 2008 and the logarithm of the average annual price of crude oil between 1970 and 2008. (We can use the logarithm of price so that a rise in the price of oil from, say, \$5 to \$10 (100%) is the same vertical distance on the diagram as a rise in the price of oil from \$50 to \$100 (also 100%).

Until 1973 use of oil increased steadily. Oil was cheaper and abundant. Then Organisation of Petroleum Exporting Countries (OPEC) cartel became active in 1973. It organised a production cutback by its members, making oil so scarce that the price tripled in 1973-74. Users could not quickly do without oil. Making oil scarce was very profitable for OPEC members.

The oil price doubled again in 1979-80. High oil prices did not last long because markets found ways to overcome the oil

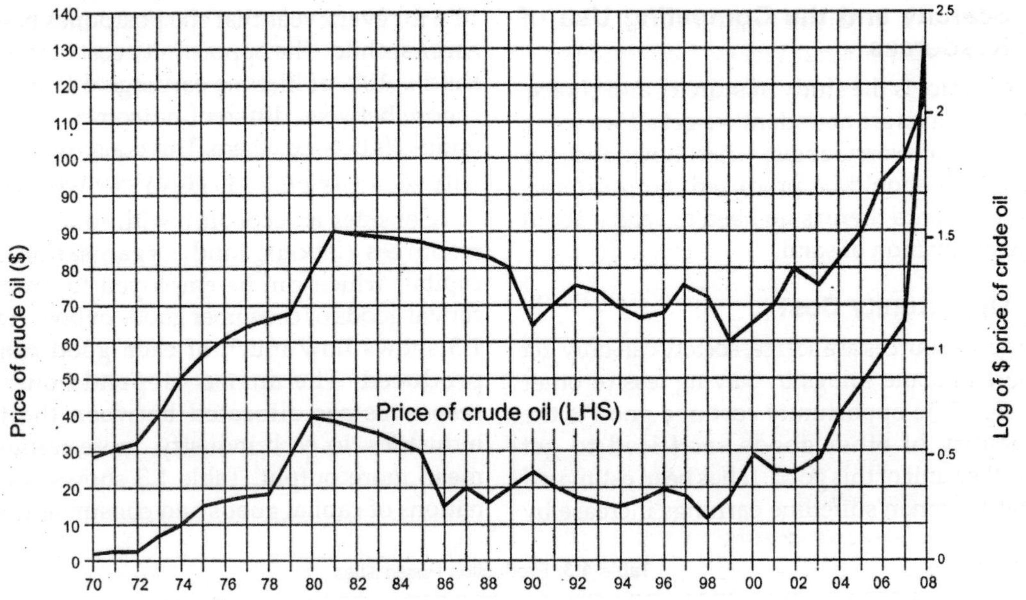

Fig. 1.1: The Price of Crude Oil (LHS) and the Log of the Crude Oil Price (RHS)

shortage in the long-run. Given time, the high oil price induced consumers of oil to use less oil and non-OPEC producers to sell more. These responses, guided by prices, are part of the way many societies determine what, how, and for whom, to produce.

Consider now how things are produced. When the oil price jumped, firms cut their use of oil-based products. Chemical firms developed artificial substitutes for petroleum inputs; airlines ordered more oil-efficient aircraft; electricity was produced from gas-fired generators. High oil prices make the economy produce using less oil.

How about what is being produced? Households switch to gas-friendly central heating (although gas prices will also increase) and buy smaller cars, which use less petrol.

High prices choke off the demand for oil-related commodities, but also encourage consumers to purchase substitute commodities. Higher demand for these commodities bids up their prices and encourages their production.

The 'for whom' question had a clear answer. OPEC revenue from oil sales increased from $35 billion in 1973 to nearly $300 billion in 1980. Much of their increased revenue was spent on goods produced in the industrialised countries of the West. In contrast, oil-importing countries had to give their own production in exchange for oil imports. In terms of goods as a whole, the rise of oil prices increased the purchasing power of OPEC and reduced the buying power of oil-importing countries such as Germany and Japan. The world economy was producing more for OPEC and less for oil importing countries.

After 1980 there was a large fall in oil prices. OPEC power diminished as other oil suppliers came to the market, and users developed substitutes. However, OPEC got its act together again in 1999, cut supply, forced up oil prices, and prompted another oil crisis in 2000. There are conflicting explanations of the very large oil shock of 2007-08.

These oil shocks illustrate how society allocates scarce resources between competing ends. The high oil price reflected its great scarcity when OPEC reduced production level. A resource is scarce if the demand at a zero price would exceed the available supply.

• Scarcity and the Competing Use of Resources

Economics is the study of scarcity and choice. When things are abundant we get all we want, we do not worry about what, how, and, for whom, it should be produced. For example, in the Sahara there is no need to worry about the production of sand.

• Opportunity Cost

When resources are scarce, society can only get more of some things by having less of other things. The opportunity cost of a good is the quantity of other goods sacrificed to get another unit of this good. It has been estimated that a woman's lifetime earnings increase by 10% for every year that she postpones having her first child. The opportunity cost of the first child is 10% of lifetime earnings. We need to choose between different outcomes, or make trade-offs between them. This is also the reason why we are required to study economics.

Consider an economy with four units of resources (labour, land, organisation and capital) which can be employed to produce capital goods or consumer goods or both. Table 1.3 shows how much of each good can be produced. The answer depends on how resources are allocated between the two industries. In each industry, more resources mean more output. Table 1.3 shows combinations of capital goods and consumer goods

Table 1.3: Production Possibilities

Capital Goods		Consumer Goods		
Resources	Output	Resources	Output	Point
0	0	4	25	A
1	9	3	22	B
2	17	2	17	C
3	24	1	10	D
4	30	0	0	E

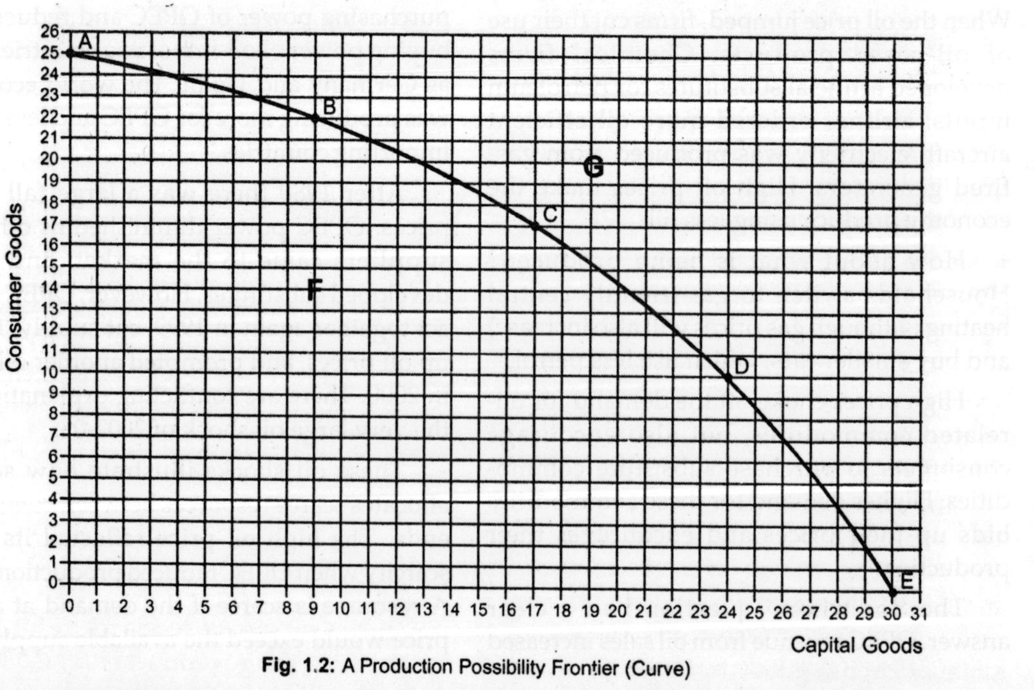

Fig. 1.2: A Production Possibility Frontier (Curve)

that can be produced if all resources are fully employed. By moving resources from one sector to another, the economy can make more of one good, but less of the other good. There is a trade-off between the output of capital goods and consumer goods.

Table 1.3 also shows the maximum combinations of the two goods that the economy can produce. Point A plots the first row of Table 1.3, where the resources devoted to the output of capital goods is zero and all four resources are devoted to the production of consumer goods (in this case the output of consumer goods will be 25 units).

Points B, C, D and E correspond to the other rows of the table. The curve joining points A to E in Fig. 1.2 is the production possibility frontier (PPF)—also known as a production possibility curve (PPC).

The PPF shows: for each output of one good, the maximum amount of other good that can be produced when all resources are fully employed.

Definition: The PPF shows the maximum combinations of outputs (in this case consumer goods and capital goods) that the economy can produce using all the available resources.

The PPF displays a trade-off; more of one commodity implies less of the other. Points above the frontier need more resources than the economy has available (for example, point G).

Points inside the frontier are inefficient (for example, point F). By using all the available inputs (resources) the economy can expand output to the frontier.

When resources are scarce, society can get more of some things only by having less of other things. We can choose between different outcomes, or make trade-off between them.

The slope of PPF tells us the opportunity cost of a good: how much one good (consumption) has to be sacrificed to make more of another (capital). If we start at point B and move to point C then we are gaining 8 units of capital goods but losing 5 units of consumer goods. The opportunity cost of producing 8 units of capital goods is 5 units of consumer goods. On average we are sacrificing 5/8th of a unit of consumer goods to gain 1 unit of capital goods. If we start at point C and move to point D, then we are gaining 7 units of capital goods but losing 7 units of consumer goods. The opportunity cost of producing 7 units of capital goods is 7 units of consumer goods. On average we are sacrificing 1 unit of consumer goods to gain 1 unit of capital goods. Fig. 1.2 also illustrates the phenomena of increasing opportunity cost. As a country produces more of one good (capital) it has to sacrifice more and more (1 instead of 5/8th) of the other good (consumer). This is because the different factors of production have different properties. People have different skills; land differs in different parts of the country. Thus, as a country concentrates more and more on the production of one good (capital), it has to use resources that are less and less suitable—resources that would be more efficiently employed in producing the other good (consumer).

The PPF shows the points at which society is producing efficiently. Points such as F inside the boundary are inefficient because society is wasting resources. At point F, more output of one good would not require less output of another good.

Production efficiency means more output of one good can be obtained only by sacrificing output of other goods.

Points outside the PPF, such as G, are unattainable given the available resource; this output combination cannot be produced. Scarce resources limit society to a choice of points on (or within) the PPF. Society must choose how to allocate these scarce resources between different goods.

Since society wants to produce efficiently, they must choose between the different points on the PPF.

How does society decide where to produce on the PPF? The government may make these tough decisions, but markets can also play a key role.

Is there a practical alternative to market economy?

The answer to the above question is no in one sense and yes in another sense. At the broad level we can distinguish mainly 4 types of economic system; traditional economic system, free market system, command or planned system, and mixed system.

- **Traditional Economic System**

A traditional system is one in which behaviour is primarily based on tradition, custom and habit. Young men follow their fathers' occupations and women do what their mothers did. There are few changes in the pattern of goods produced from year to year, other than those imposed by the vagaries of nature. The technique of production also follows traditional patterns, except when effects of an occasional new invention are felt.

The concept of private property is often not well-defined, and property is often held in common.

Finally, production is allocated among the members of society according to tradition. In short, the answers to the economic questions of what to produce, how to produce, and for whom to produce, are guided by traditions.

Such a system works best in an unchanging environment. Under static conditions, a system that does not continually require people to make choices can prove effective in meeting economic and social needs.

Traditional systems were common in earlier times. The feudal system under which most people lived in medieval Europe was a largely traditional society. Today only a few small, isolated, self-sufficient communities still live in the traditional system.

- **The Free Market System**

A market uses prices to reconcile decisions between consumption and production. Prices of goods and services adjust to ensure that scarce resources are used to make the goods and services that society wants. Markets and prices are one way society can decide what, how, and for whom, to produce.

Prices guide us to decide to buy a sandwich, McDonald's decision to sell burger, and the student's decision to work for McDonald. Society allocates resources through the price system. If people do not want sandwich or burgers, their sales revenue would not cover their costs. Society would devote no resources to produce burgers. Peoples desire to buy hamburgers guide resources into hamburger production.

These individual decisions collectively determine the allocation of resources in the economy and the distribution of its output among individual citizens. In a pure market economy, buyers and sellers acting through the markets make all of these decisions. The state provides the background of defining property right and protecting them from enemies but, beyond that, markets determine all resource allocation and income distribution.

- **The Command or Planned System**

How resources would be allocated if market did not exist. In a planned economy government planners decide what, how and for whom, to produce. Households, firms and resources are then told what to do. Central planning is a difficult job. No country has ever made all decisions by central command. However, in some socialist countries, there used to be a lot of central direction and planning. The state owned land and factories may make key decisions about what people should consume, how goods should be produced, and how much people should work.

Imagine a society in which you had to run the city where you live. Think of the food, clothing and housing allocation decisions you would have to make. How would you decide what things were to be made, and who got what? These decisions are being made every day in our city, but mainly through the mechanism of markets and prices. The opposite extreme of central planning is a reliance on markets in which prices can freely adjust. In 1776, Adam Smith, in his 'Wealth of

Nations', argued that people pursuing their self-interest would be led 'by an invisible hand' to do things in the interest of the society as a whole.

In a market economy, prices adjust to reconcile desires and scarcity. Markets in which governments do not intervene are called the free market and the invisible hand does the trick. In a planned economy decisions are taken by the state. Between the two extremes is the mixed economy.

- **Mixed Economy**

Fully traditional, fully central-controlled and fully free market economies are useful concepts for studying the basic principles of resource allocation. When we look in detail at any real economy, however, we find that its economic behaviour is the result of some mixture of central control and market determined, with a certain amount of traditional behaviour as well. The term mixed economy refers to an economy in which both governments and free markets have significant effects on the allocation of resources and distribution of income.

In practice, every economy is a mixed economy in the sense that it combines some elements of all three systems in determining economic behaviour and solving economic problems. The government influences decisions through taxation, subsidies and government expenditure to make provisions of free services such as defence, the police and so on. It also regulates the extent to which individuals may pursue their own self-interest. All countries are mixed economies. The degree of the mixture of free market determination and government control varies from economy to economy and over time. There is more free market determination in the UK and USA than in France and South Korea. There is more free market determination in the UK today than there was 25 years ago. The degree to mix also varies from sector to sector within any one economy. For example, European agricultural markets have a substantial amount of government intervention. Under market determination, the average size of the farm would have to be much larger and agricultural prices much lower than they are now. In contrast, the markets for information and computer technologies are largely free from government intervention.

Thus, the first answer to the question posed at the outset of this section is "No". There is no real alternative to a mixed system with major reliance on markets but a substantial government presence in most aspects of the economy. The second answer is "Yes". Within the framework of a mixed economy there are substantial alternatives among many different and complex mixes of free market and government determination of economic life.

- **Government in the Modern Mixed Economy**

Modern market economies are based primarily on market transactions between people who voluntarily decide whether or not to engage in them. Private individuals have the right to buy and sell what they wish, to accept or refuse work that is offered to them, and to move to where they want when they want.

Key characteristics of a market economy are the right of individuals to own private property and to freely enter into business contracts, both of which must be maintained by active government policies. The government creates laws of ownership and contract and then empowers the courts to enforce these laws.

In modern mixed economies governments go well beyond these important basic functions. They intervene in market transactions to correct what are called 'market failures'. These are situations where free markets do not work well. Governments intervene to prevent monopolies using their power to 'overcharge' the consumer. Resources such as fishing grounds and common pastureland tend to be over-exploited to the point of destruction under free market conditions. Some products, called public goods, are not provided by markets because, once produced no one can be prevented from consuming them. Thus their use cannot be restricted to those who are willing to pay for them. Defence and police protection are public goods. In other cases, private transactions imposed costs such as externalities (an externality is an action by either a producer or a consumer that affects other producers or consumers, yet is not accounted for in the market price) on those who have no say in the transaction. This is the case where factories pollute the air and rivers. The public is harmed who have no part in the decisions—what and how to make it. These are some of the reasons why free markets fail to function. They also explain why people wish governments to intervene and alter the allocation of resources instead of leaving everything to the market forces.

There are also important equity issues that arise from letting free markets determine people's incomes. Some people lose their jobs because firms are reorganizing to become more efficient in the face of new technology. Others keep their jobs, but the market values their services so poorly that they face economic deprivation. The old and chronically ill may suffer if they failed to save enough to support themselves. Thus we support government intervention to redistribute income by taking from the haves and to give it to the have-nots.

• Positive and Normative Economies

Microeconomics deals with both positive and normative questions. Positive questions have to do with explanation and prediction, normative economies deal with what ought to be. A positive question is a statement capable of proof and disproof. For example, inflation is currently running at 3%, the UK's economic growth is higher than Germany; the US has a huge deficit on her balance of payments. These are positive statements because they can be tested by reference to the facts. Positive analysis is central to microeconomics. Theories are developed to explain phenomena, are tested against observations, and are used to construct models from which predictions are made. A normative statement is a statement of values which cannot be tested by reference to facts. For example, a 3% rate of inflation is not very high; old-age pension 'ought' to be raised. Such statements are normative. Some economists claim that economics should be concerned with positive economies only. The argument is that, as a science, economics is concerned with constructing theories which can be proved or disproved. It is the role of the economists to find out how the economy operates and not to concern one's self with value judgements. That should be left to the politicians.

Another school of thought, including A. Smith, regards economics as a study of 'political economy'. These economists consider that economics is not only concerned with facts and testable theories, but also with value judgement. For instance, it is the role of the economists not merely to say that unemployment is 1 million, but also to say whether it is too high or not (a normative statement). When value judgements (normative statements) are involved, microeconomics cannot tell us what the best policy is. However, it can clarify the trade-off and thereby help to illuminate and help to sharpen the debate.

• Microeconomic and Macroeconomic Models

Microeconomics offers a detailed treatment of individual decisions about particular commodities. Macroeconomics emphasises interactions in the economy as a whole. It deliberately simplifies the individual building blocks of the analysis in order to retain a manageable analysis of the complete interaction of the economy. For example, the Keynesian consumption function is a macroeconomic model which attempts to predict how much all consumers in an economy will consume. The marginal utility theory is a microeconomic model which attempts to explain how an individual consumer allocates his or her consumption. Similarly, there are other macroeconomic concepts-GDP is the value of total output of an economy in a given period, say a year. The aggregate price level measures the average price of goods and services in the economy. The unemployment rate is the fraction of the labour force without a job.

In terms of their Greek roots, 'micro' implies a close-up look at small objects, 'macro' a broader, less magnified, view over a large field. The distinction used to be described as that between a detailed study of the behaviour of individual decision-makers in the economy (microeconomics) and the behaviour of the broad aggregates (macroeconomics). Although there remains some truth in this simple distinction, it is no longer entirely valid. Many macroeconomists consider some parts of the economy—such as banking system and the money and securities markets—in far more detail than are studied in microeconomics.

The economy is a complex system. In order to study it, some degree of simplification is required. The real distinction between microeconomics and macroeconomics lies in the type of simplifications that are made, and the particular aim of those simplifications. Microeconomics remains primarily concerned about economics in general, which are intended to be the principles underlying all economics at all times. Macroeconomics, on the other hand, descends directly from analysis designed to influence public policy at particular times and particular places—Keynes was concerned with unemployment in an advanced industrial country during the 1930s.

The difference in outlook has made macroeconomics more empirically oriented than microeconomics. If it can be shown that consumers in a country during the current decade behave in a certain way, this is prime data for a macroeconomist interested in providing information for decisions on next year's economic policy. It may be of much less interest to a microeconomic economist concerned with the general principles of consumers' behaviour unless it seems to run contrary to his expectations based on his theory. In other words, data are used in macroeconomics primarily for predicting the behaviour of a particular economy at a particular time, in microeconomics for testing the generality of his theoretical apparatus.

It should be made clear that modern microeconomics, like macroeconomics, is also concerned with the economy as a whole, not just with the behaviour of isolated components. Modern microeconomics is "general equilibrium" economics, as is macroeconomics. The general equilibrium approach has greatly changed the orientation of microeconomics. It is not the study of individual components and how they fit together. The claim of microeconomics to be an important intellectual system lies in its success in showing how individual components, each behaving in its own way, fit together in a complete system, and, further, that this system is optimal in a certain sense. Next we turn to the representation of economic data and show how an economist might develop a theoretical model of an economic relationship. Finally, we discuss how actual data might be used to test the theory that has been developed.

• Economic Data

We gather evidence to study changes over time, or changes across groups or regions at the same point in time. Table 1.4 shows a cross-section of unemployment rates in different countries in 2008, and Table 1.5 shows a time-

Table 1.4: Standardised Unemployment Rate by Country (% of Labour force) March 2008

US	UK	Japan	France	Germany
5.1	5.3	3.8	7.8	7.4

Source: UK Treasury

series of UK house prices between 1960 and 2000.

• Real (Relative) Versus Nominal Prices

We often want to compare the price of a good today with what it was in the past or is likely to be in the future. To make such a comparison meaningful, we need to measure prices relative to the overall price level. In nominal terms, the price of a dozen eggs is many times higher today than it was 50 years ago, but relative to prices overall, it is actually lower. Thus, we must be careful to correct for inflation when comparing prices across time. This means measuring prices in real rather than nominal (money) terms. The nominal price of a good is just its current market price. The real price of a good is the price relative to an aggregate measure of prices or constant pound price. Table 1.5 will give us some idea about nominal and real variables.

To calculate the real price of houses in 1975, by expressing them at 2008 prices, we take the nominal price of houses in 1975, divide it by the RPI in 1975, and multiply it by 100 (£10,800/15.8 × 100 = £68,600). Real prices have increased by approximately 154% (2.54 times) since 1975. Most of the increase in nominal house prices was due to inflation. The average price of a house rose from £10,800 in 1975 to £174,500 in 2008 (151%). Are houses really 16 times as expensive as in 1975? No. Once we allow for inflation we see that they rose by about 2.5 times (150%). Nominal values are measured in current prices. Real values are nominal values adjusted for changes in the general price level.

In the UK, the RPI and the consumer price index (CPI) measure the price of a basket of goods bought by a typical household. Inflation caused a big rise in the RPI during 1975-2008 (over 500%).

Table 1.5: UK House Price (Average Price of All Houses)

	1975	1990	2008
House price (000)	10.8	57.7	174.5
RPI (2008 = 100)	15.8	58.6	100
Real Price of houses (2008)	68.6	98.6	174.5

Source: ONS, Economic Trend

The first row of the Table 1.5 shows the average price of a housing, which rose from £10,800 in 1975 to £ 174,500 in 2008. Are houses really 16 times as expensive as in 1975? Not when we allow for inflation.

Nominal values are measured in the prices ruling at the time of measurement. Real values are obtained by adjusting nominal values for changes in the aggregate price level. The 2nd row gives the retail price index (RPI), using 2008 as the base year (2008=100). Inflation led to substantial increases in the RPI, during 1975-2008 (533%). The third row calculates an index of real house prices, expressed in 2008 prices. Since we are using 2008 as the base year, the nominal value of house prices in 2008 is the same as the real values of houses in 2008.

• The CPI and Other Indices

To keep track of the prices faced by consumers, countries construct a consumer price index. In the UK this is called the consumer price index (CPI). The CPI is used to measure changes in the cost of living, the money that must be spent to purchase the typical bundle of goods by a representative household. The inflation rate is the annual rate of change of the price index. The CPI is constructed in two stages. First, index numbers are calculated for each category of commodity purchased by households. Then the CPI is constructed by taking a weighted average of the different commodity grouping. Other examples of indices include the index of wages in manufacturing, a weighted average of wages in different manufacturing industries. The FTSE, is the Financial Times-

Stock Exchange index of share prices quoted on the London Stock Exchange. The index of industrial production is a weighted average of the quantity of goods produced by industry.

The procedure by which the index numbers are calculated is always the same. We choose a base year at which to set the index equal to 100, then calculate the other values relative to this base period. Where the index refers to more than one commodity, we have to choose weights by which to average across the different commodities that the index describes.

• Real and Relative Prices

The distinction between nominal and real variables applies to all variables measured in money values. The argument carries over to prices themselves. The nominal price of houses has risen a lot since 1960. To calculate an index of the real price of houses, divide an index of nominal house prices by the retail price index and multiply by 100. Real prices indicate economic scarcity. They show whether the price of a commodity rose faster than prices in general. Thus, real prices are sometimes called relative prices.

Consider the price of television over the last 20 years. TV prices, measured in pounds, have hardly changed. The RPI has increased by a large amount. The real (relative) price of TVs have, in fact, fallen. Advances in technology reduced the cost of producing TVs. Because the real price has fallen, many consumers now have several sets. It is misleading to base your analysis on nominal values of variables.

• The Purchasing Power of Money

When the price of goods rises, the purchasing power of money falls because £1 buys fewer goods.

The purchasing power of money is an index of the quantity of goods that can be bought for £1.

To distinguish real and nominal variables we say that real variables measure nominal variables as if the purchasing power of money has remained unchanged. Another way to express this idea is to distinguish between nominal variables in current prices and real variables in constant prices.

• Measuring Changes in Economic Variables

The percentage change is the absolute change divided by the original number, then multiplied by 100.

Percentage change = absolute change $(P_t - P_{t-1})$ divided by original number (P_{t-1}) times 100. The growth rate is the % change per period = $100 \times (P_t - P_{t-1})/P_{t-1}$, usually a year. In the case of real house prices; $P_t = 174.5$, $P_{t-1} = 68.6$. $(100 \times [174.5 - 68.6]/68.6) = 154.37\%$. Negative growth rates are shown as percentage falls. Economists usually define economic growth as the positive percentage annual change in the national income.

• Economic Models

Suppose you are asked to determine the London Underground fare that will reduce the losses. How do you analyse the problem?

To build a model, you will need to simplify reality, picking out the key elements of the problem. You begin with the simple equation

Revenue = fare multiplied by the number of passengers ... (1)

London underground sets the fare, but influences the number of passengers through the fare that is set.

Economists will take the view that it is possible to travel by cars, buses, taxi or tube. Decisions about how to travel will depend on the relative costs of different modes of transport. Equation (1) requires a model or theory of what determines the number of passengers. We need a model which expresses the demand for tube journeys.

First, tube fare matters. Other things equal, higher tube fares reduce the quantity of the journeys demanded.

Second, if there are price rises for competing modes of journeys, more people will use tube journeys at any given tube fare.

Third, if passengers have higher income, they are likely to take more tube journeys at any given fare.

Number of passengers =

f(tube fare, taxi fare, bus fares, petrol prices, passenger incomes) ... (2)

Writing down a model forces us to look for all the relevant effects; combining equations (1) and (2) we get

Tube revenue =

Tube fare × number of passengers =

Tube fare × f(tube fare, taxi fare, bus fares, petrol prices, passenger incomes) ... (3)

Models are simple devices to ensure that we think clearly about problems; clear thinking requires simplification. The real world is too complicated for us to think about everything at once. Learning to use model is more of an art than a science. Again, too much simplification may omit a crucial factor from the analysis.

Sometimes data guide us where factors are crucial and even where they are not so crucial. At other times, as with tube fares, it is not enough to understand the forces at work. We need to quantify them. For both reasons, we turn now to the interaction of economic models and data.

• Models and Data

Equation (3) gives us our model of tube revenue determination. High fares give more revenue per passenger, but reduce the number of passengers. Theory cannot tell us which effect dominates. This is an empirical issue. We need some empirical research to establish the fact. Experimental science conduct controlled experiments in a laboratory, varying one factor at a time while holding all other relevant factors constant. Like astronomy, economics is primarily a non-experimental science. Astronomers cannot suspend planetary motion to examine the relation between the earth and the sun in isolation; similarly economists cannot suspend the laws of economic activity to conduct controlled experiments.

Most empirical research in economics must deal with data collected over a period of time in which many of the relevant factors were simultaneously changing. The problem is how to disentangle the separate influences on observed behaviour. We approach this in two stages. First, we proceed by examining the

Table 1.6: The Tube Fare (1989/90 to 1999/2000) and Real Revenue

	(1)	(2)	(3)
Year	Real Fare (£)	No. of trips per kilometer (billion)	Real Revenue (£million)
1989-90	0.109	6.0	655
1990-91	0.111	6.2	686
1991-92	0.117	5.9	690
1992-93	0.121	5.8	704
1993-94	0.129	5.8	749
1994-95	0.135	6.1	822
1995-96	0.134	6.3	848
1996-97	0.139	6.2	863
1997-98	0.145	6.5	942
1998-99	0.148	6.7	993
1999-2000	0.149	7.1	1060

Source: Department of Environment, Transport and Region, Transport for London relationship between revenue and fares, neglecting the possibilities that other relevant factors were changing. Then we indicate how economists deal with the harder problems in which variations of other factors are also included in the analysis.

Table 1.6 shows data on tube fares and passengers, when annual data is measured over calendar years from 1989-90 to 1999-2000. Column (1) shows the real tube fare per passenger kilometre, column (2) shows demand for tube journeys, in billions of passenger kilometre a year, and column (3) shows real revenue. It is useful to present the evidence in a scatter diagram plotted in Fig. 1.3.

The vertical axis measures the real fare per passenger kilometre. The horizontal axis measures real revenue in constant billion pounds. Real revenue can be obtained by multiplying real fare per passenger and the number of passenger travelled. The years of lowest real revenue are also the years in which the real tube fares are the lowest. Yet the effect of changes in real fares cannot be the whole story. Other things being equal, a higher fare reduces the number of tube journeys. In fact, column (2) shows that tube use rose despite higher tube fares. In that case, something else must have changed.

• Diagrams, Lines and Equations

A scatter diagram plots pairs of values simultaneously observed for two different variables.

If we draw line or curve through all these points, this suggests, but does not prove, an underlying (positive) relationship between the two variables. When the points are plotted, they lie all over the place; this suggests, but does not prove relationships between them. Only if economics were an experimental science, we could interpret scatter diagrams unambiguously. Nevertheless, they often provide helpful clues.

• Fitting Lines through Scatter Diagram

In Fig. 1.3, if we drew a line through the scatter points we plotted, the line would show the average relation between fare and revenue between 1989-90 and 1999-2000. We could then quantify the average relation between fare and usage. Given a particular scatter of points, how do we decide where to draw the line, given that it cannot fit all points exactly?

Econometrics uses mathematical statistics to measure relationship in economic data. Having plotted the points describing the data, a computer works out where to draw the line to minimise the dispersion of points around

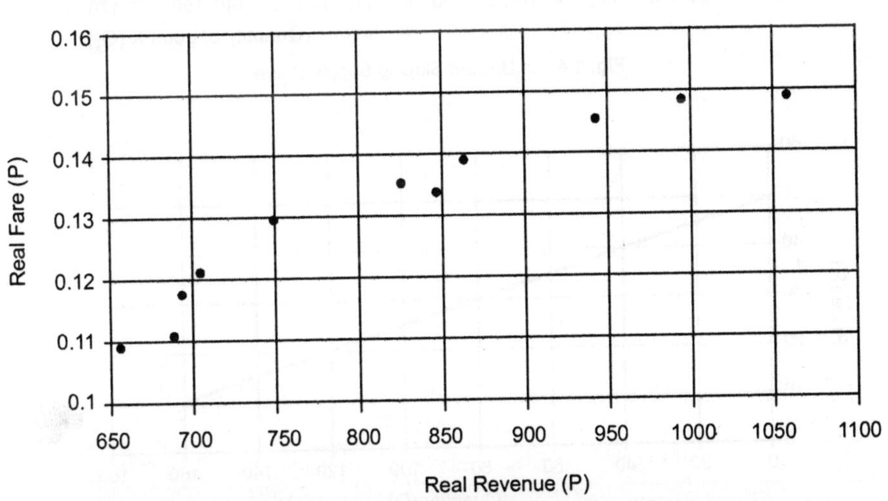

Fig. 1.3: A Scatter Diagram of Tube Fares and Revenues 1989-2000

the line. Fortunately, computers can work many dimensions at once. Conceptually, it is simply an extension of fitted lines through scatter diagrams. By disentangling separate influences from data where many different things move simultaneously, econometricians conduct empirical research even though economics is not an experimental science like Physics or Chemistry. Here we are not going to use anything more complicated than two-dimensional diagrams.

• Reading Diagrams

We need to read diagrams and understand what they represent. Fig. 1.4 shows a hypothetical relationship between two variables: Price and Quantity. The diagram plots Q = Q(P). The quantity is a function of price. Knowing the value of P we can tell the corresponding value of Q. In Fig. 1.4, Q is a positive function of P. Higher values of P imply higher values of Q. When the function is a straight line, only two pieces of information are needed to draw the entire relationship between Q and P. We need to know intercept and slope. The intercept is the height of the line when measured on the vertical axis. In Fig. 1.4 the intercept is 10, which means P = 10, when Q = 0.

Lots of line could pass through the point at which Q = 0 and P = 0. The other characteristic is the slope (gradient) of the line, measuring its steepness. The slope tells how much Q changes when we change P. Fig. 1.4 shows a positive relationship between Q and P. Since higher P values are associated with

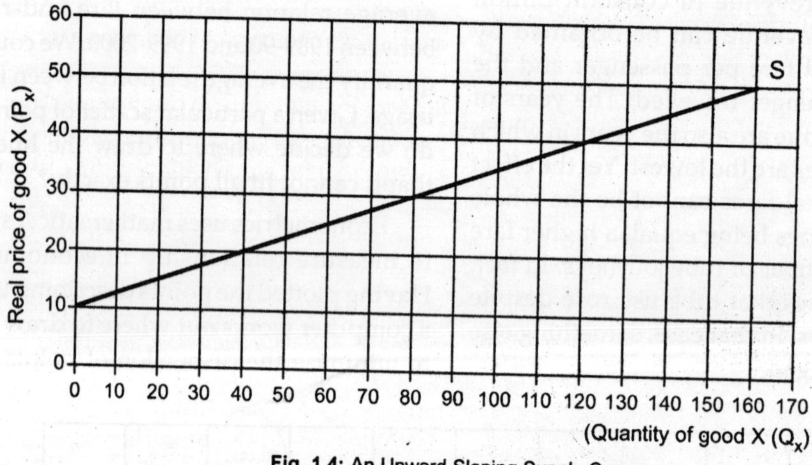

Fig. 1.4: An Upward Sloping Supply Curve

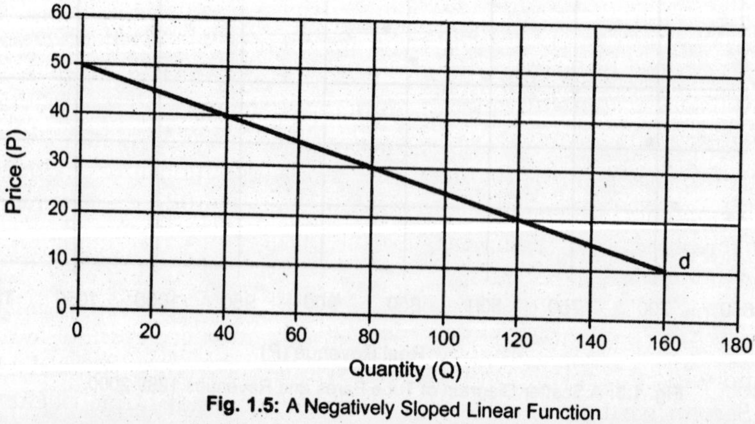

Fig. 1.5: A Negatively Sloped Linear Function

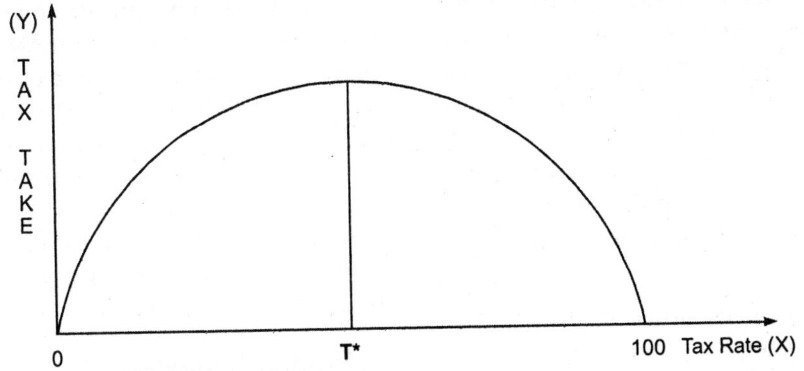

Fig. 1.6: A Non-Linear Relationship

higher Q values, the line slopes upward. The line has a positive relationship. Fig. 1.5 shows a case where Q is a negative function of P. A negative slope is when a higher (lower) P values have a lower (higher) Q value.

Economic relationships may not always be straight line or linear. Fig. 1.6 shows a non-linear relationship between two variables, say X and Y. The slope keeps changing. Each time we raise X by 1 unit we get a different rise (or fall) in Y. Consider the relationship between the income tax rate X and tax take Y.

When the tax rate is zero, no revenue is raised. When the tax rate is 100%, revenue is again zero (no-one will work). Beginning from X = 0, increases in X initially raise tax revenue. Beyond T*, further rises in tax rates reduce tax take, which becomes zero at X = 100%.

• Theories and Evidence

A theory consists of a set of assumptions and a set of definitions. We must not worry about unrealistic assumptions in economics. However, it is important to remember that every theory is an abstraction from reality.

We analyse a problem in three distinct stages. First, a phenomenon is observed or contemplated and the problem is formulated. May be by an armchair reasoning, or cursory inspection of the data, we decide that tube fares have something to do with revenues. We want to understand what this relationship is and why it exists. Second, we develop a theory or model to capture the essence of the phenomenon. By thinking about incomes and the decision about the type of transport to use, we identify the things relevant to tube usage and, hence, tube revenue. Third, we test the predictions of the theory by confronting it with data. We can then see if, on average, they work on the direction that our model suggests. Indeed, by including in our investigation some extra factors, deliberately left out of our model in the quest for simplicity, we can observe that those extra factors were sufficiently unimportant and it makes sense to omit them from our analysis.

Suppose we confront our theory with the data and the two seem compatible. We do not reject our theory. If our model is rejected we have to start again. If it is not rejected by the data, this does not mean that we have found the correct model. There may be a better model that has escaped our attention but would be compatible with our data. As time elapses, we acquire new data. We can also use data from other countries. The more we confront different data and find that they are still not rejected, the more confident we become about our model. Relationships in which we have become very confident are sometimes called economic laws.

• Scientific Theories

Economics is concerned with human behaviour which is often predictable. We have also evidence that human behaviour does show stable response patterns. Theories grow up in response to questions—'Why?' A theory attempts to explain this 'Why?' The main consequence of a theory is that it enables us to predict unobserved events. For example, National Income Theory predicts that an increase in tax rates will raise unemployment and increase in government expenditure is likely to reduce it.

Suppose we advance another idea—demand for a good is a function of price. We may say further that, as the price increases, so the demand decreases and, when price decreases, the demand increases. This gives us a hypothesis which may be tested on observed behaviour. The testing of ideas is known as empiricism, on the basis of our observations we may either: (a) confirm the theory, or (b) reject the theory, or amend it in the light of fresh evidence.

Assumption behind the theory is that "all other things are remaining constant, or ceteris paribus". For example, if we wish to examine the effect of price on demand we do not change simultaneously income, prices of other commodities, tastes, etc. Thus, when formulating economic principles, we are careful to state that such and such things will happen, *ceteris paribus*. This process is shown diagrammatically in Chart 1.1.

- **Human Behaviour**

Economics is concerned with human behaviour which is often unpredictable. We seem to obey Aristotle's dictum: 'Man is a reasoning, but not a reasonable animal'. Naturally it is impossible to reach any firm conclusions. This is so if we consider the behaviour of one person. However, while individuals are unpredictable, people in large number are not. For example, if we increase

Chart 1.1: Scientific Method

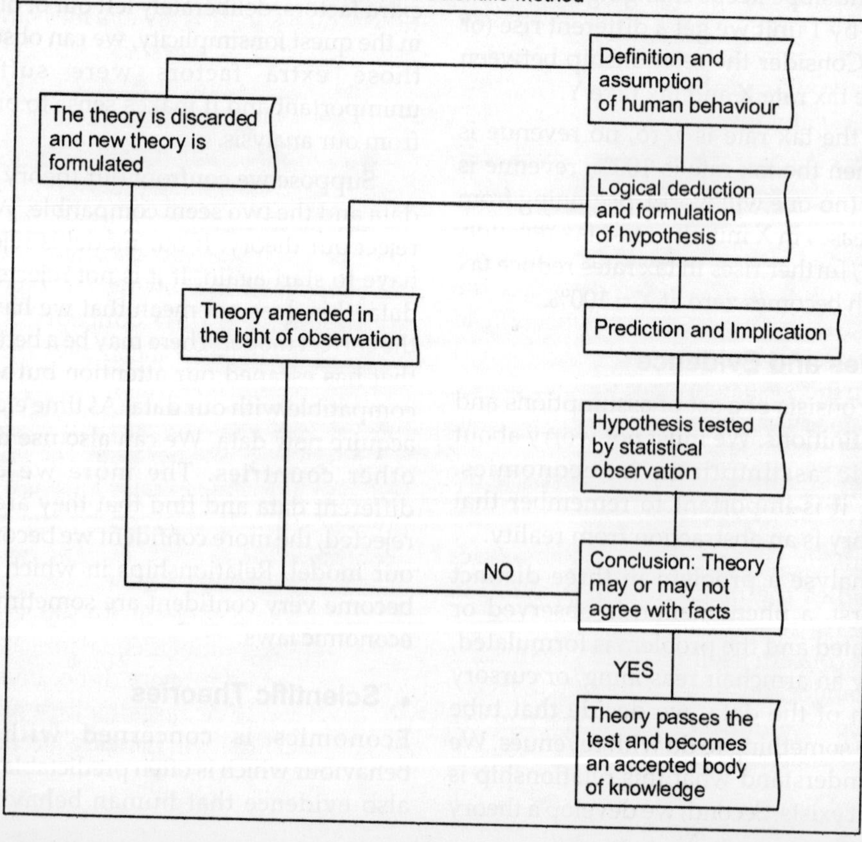

peoples' income any particular individual may, or may not, spend more. But what happens to a million people when their incomes increase? It is not impossible to conlude that, in general, their expenditure will also increase. Thus, examining the behaviour of a large number, it may be possible to take advantage of the law of large numbers. This law, therefore, predicts that the random behaviour of one person in a large group will be offset by the random behaviour of another, so that it would be possible for us to make a definite prediction about the behaviour of the group as a whole.

• Free and Economic Goods

A good produced from scarce resources is also scarce and is known as economic good. Since economic goods are scarce in relation to demand, we are faced with decisions how best to use them. All goods are not economic goods; some are free goods. Of course, in modern society, there are very few free goods. We used to call air and water free goods. But they are not really free goods in modern society. Air in many cities is polluted and we pay a large sum of money as water taxes.

In mountain areas, clean air is still a free good; you can have as much as you want at a zero price. There is no scarcity involved. If all goods were free, there would be no need for economists. Economists only step in when the problem of scarcity arises and allocation of scarce resources is needed. As population and production increase many free goods become economic goods, such as water, land, air, etc.

• Statics, Comparative Statics and Dynamic Analysis

Static analysis is the branch of economics which studies the properties of position of equilibrium in the economic system. However, it does not concern itself with the time it takes to reach equilibrium, or with the path to follow to reach the equilibrium. This is the concern of dynamic analysis.

Dynamic analysis is necessary for the following reasons: First, dynamic analysis is necessary to consider the stability of the system. An equilibrium is known as a stable equilibrium if any disturbance from the equilibrium brings the system back to the equilibrium. For example, if we start from a dis-equilibrium position and then want to know whether the system moves towards equilibrium or not, we require to analyse the time path of the relevant variable. This is known as dynamic analysis. Second, since the adjustment of one variable takes time to cause a change in another variable, there are lags in many functions. The presence of these lags requires dynamic analysis. Third, there are certain variables which depend on the rate of growth of other variables. Such problems also require dynamic analysis.

• Stocks and Flows

Stock and flow variables are an important distinction in economics. A flow variable has a time dimension. It is always measured over a period of time. A stock variable has no time dimension. It is measured at a given point in time. The stock variable is just a number at a point in time, not a flow rate. For example, the concepts like total money supply, capital stock, etc. are stock concepts whereas the concepts such as national income, net investment (investment after allowing for depreciation), saving, etc. are flow concepts. When we measure the national income we consider the amount produced over a period of time—usually one year. Thus, national income is measured as a flow per year. The relationship between a stock (capital = K) and a flow (net investment = I) is given by the following equation:

$\frac{\Delta K}{\Delta t} = I_t$ The change in the stock of capital (over time) is equal to the amount of net investment. If net investment is positive [*negative*] then the stock capital will increase [*decrease*].

QUESTIONS

1. How are the problems, what, how and for whom, settled with your own family?
2. Which of the following are scarce?
   (a) Water in a desert.
   (b) Water in a rainforest.
   (c) Economic textbooks.
   (d) Hours a day for work, rest and play.
3. An economy has 5 workers. Each worker can make 8 cakes and 6 shirts.
   (a) How many cakes can society get if it decides not to have shirts?
   (b) How many shirts can it get if it decides not to have cakes?
   (c) What is the opportunity cost of making a shirt?
4. Which of the following statements are positive and which are normative?
   (a) Taxing cigarettes reduces the quantity sold.
   (b) Cigarettes should be highly taxed.
   (c) The British earn more than the Indians.
   (d) Indians should work harder.
   (e) All Europeans earn high salaries.
5. Society abolishes higher education. Students have to find jobs immediately. If there are no jobs available, how do wages and prices adjust so those who want jobs can find them?
6. Why are these statements wrong?
   (a) Since some economists are right but others are left, economics can justify anything.
   (b) There is no such thing as a free lunch. To have more of one thing you have to give up something else.
7. Which statements refer to microeconomics, which to macroeconomics?
   (a) Inflation is lower then in the 1980s.
   (b) Food prices fell this month.
   (c) Good weather means a good harvest.
   (d) Unemployment in London is below the UK average.
8. What is the difference between scarcity and poverty? If everyone in the world had enough to eat, could we say that food is no longer scarce?
9. How are specialisation, division of labour, market economies, and money related to each other?
10. List some of the things you can easily do, or actually do, that are the characteristic of behaviour in (a) Market economy, (b) a planned economy, and (c) traditional economy.
11. The table below shows UK consumer spending and household income in £billion at 1995 prices:
   (a) Plot a scatter diagram;
   (b) Draw a fitted line through these points;
   (c) Suggest a relation between consumption and income.

	Income	Consumption
1993	476	434
1994	482	447
1995	495	454
1996	505	471
1997	525	489
1998	539	509
1999	550	530
2000	657	548

12. You are a consultant to advice whether the level of crime is affected by the unemployment rate.
   (a) How would you test this idea? What data would you want?
   (b) What, other things being equal, would you bear in mind?
13. Why are these statements incorrect?
   (a) The purpose of a theory is to let you ignore the facts.
   (b) Economics cannot be a science since it cannot conduct controlled experiments.

ANSWERS

1. Sometimes by hierarchy or command, sometimes by negotiation, and sometimes using money and prices.
2. All are scarce except (b).
3. (a) 40 cakes, (b) 30 shirts and (c) 1.33 cakes.
4. (a), (c) and (e) are positive; and (b) and (d) are normative.
5. Wages fall in jobs that students want to do. With lower wages, firms can cut their prices, raising the quantity sold and, hence, demand for workers in these jobs also increases.
6. (a) The hypothesis in positive economics can be tested against evidence. Support for different political parties may reflect different normative value judgements. (b) Beginning from an inefficient point, moving to an efficient point yields more of some things and no less of others, a free lunch. Only at an efficient point no further lunch is available.
7. (a) Macroeconomics, (b) Microeconomics (c) Microeconomics, and (d) Macroeconomics.
8. Scarcity implies the existence of a limit to the quantity of a resource or a good. Even if all have enough to eat, food will still be scarce because its supply is not unlimited. Poverty implies a more than trivial degree of deprivation; it is a relative concept and indicates lack of the means to buy a share of commodities that deemed adequate. People considered poor in a wealthy economy may be far better off materially than the poor in a developing economy. Interestingly, the UN Development Programme distinguishes between the 'food poor', who do not have enough money to buy the minimum quantity of food necessary for a healthy diet, and the 'non-food poor', who have enough to eat but lack adequate income for expenditure on education, health, etc.
9. Division of labour is possible if people specialize in doing particular forms of work, rather than trying to be self-sufficient. However, if not self-sufficient, people need to exchange goods and services and this is most efficiently done in a market where information is available about choices and comparisons can be made. The use of money as a medium of exchange makes markets work more easily.
10. This question is designed to explore the differences between these ways of organizing economic activity. There are many possible answers; we give one answer in each case. (a) We see job advertisement, apply for the job, negotiate the salary at the time of interview, and have a contract of employment, (b) We are trained for a particular job and are sent to work in a particular place, and we are not in a position to influence our remuneration, (c) From childhood we know that we will follow the same occupation as our parents, much of the properties will be held in common, and our social position will be well-defined.
11. Plot an upward-sloping line with the time-series data.
12. (a) This idea would be tested by collecting cross-section data on crimes and unemployment. (b) Collect other data on income, policing, inequality, rural and urban areas and use econometrics to analyse them.
13. (a) Theory organizes facts by providing a simple framework in which to interpret them. (b) Many sciences including economics cannot conduct laboratory experiments, still it is a science. For example, Political Science.

CHAPTER 2

DEMAND, MARGINAL UTILITY AND INDIFFERENCE CURVE ANALYSIS

KEY TERMS

Utility (benefit): The desirable attribute of a good or service, which a customer perceives. She/he will get that from purchasing the good or service.

Marginal Utility: The change in total utility from an additional unit of a good.

Diminishing Marginal Utility: The extra utility received from the extra unit of a good is less than the extra utility received from the previous unit of the good.

Util: A unit of utility.

Indifference Curve: A locus of points showing combinations of goods that will give an individual the *same level* of utility.

Budget Line: A locus of points showing combinations of goods that can be purchased from a given money income (M).

In his chapter we are more concerned with individual demand, that is, the demand for particular products by a single consumer. We assume that the individual demands, goods and services ($q_1, q_2, q_2, \dots, q_n$) in order to obtain maximum satisfaction (utility [U]) given their limited money income (M). Consumers purchase goods and services because they receive utility (satisfaction) or benefit (the desirable attribute of a good or service, which a customer perceives she/he will get from purchasing the good or service). In brief:

$$U = U(q_1, q_2, q_3, \dots, q_n)$$

where $U = U(q_1, q_2, q_3, \dots, q_n)$ indicates that an individuals satisfaction (utility [U]) is a function of (depends upon) the quantity of goods ($q_1, q_2, \dots, q_n$) consumed.

We assume that any extra good or service consumed will increase a person's utility (benefit).

However, we also assume diminishing marginal utility.

Marginal means 'additional'. Hence marginal utility is the increase in total utility received by the individual from an additional unit of a good.

Diminishing marginal utility occurs when the extra utility received from an extra unit of a good is less than the extra utility received from the previous unit of the good. For example, we might say that a consumer derives 20 units of utility (20 utils) from the consumption of the first unit of a commodity, 18.6 utils from the second, 17.5 utils from the third and so on. In fact, it is impossible to measure utility in this manner since it is a matter of subjective judgement how much utility a person is deriving from her/his consumption. However, we will follow this concept a little further and, hopefully, learn something from it.

People will continue to purcahse a particular good until the extra (private) utility they receive from purchasing the extra unit is just equal to the cost of the good. In economic jargon people will continue to purcahse a particular good until their marginal utility is just equal to the price of the good (P). i.e. MU = P.

If MU > P, then the individual will purchase more of the good and this will decrease their marginal utility.

If MU < P, then the individual will purchase less of the good and this will increase their marginal utility.

Until now, we have treated the law of demand inductively, in the sense that we have based it upon observation of how consumers generally respond to price changes. Here we examine how the law of demand can be based on a 'theoretical' footing, and then arrive at the conclusion that demand curves will usually slope downwards from left to right. There are basically two major approaches of consumer behaviour that are available, neither presents a complete picture. The first approach is the marginal utility or cardinalist approach. Second, is the indifference curve approach. At the end of this chapter we shall consider Samuelson's revealed preference approach.

For over 200 years economists have assumed that there is a pleasure at every act of consumption which they called utility. J. Bentham was the founder of the branch of philosophy known as utilitarianism, which was influenced by several eminent economists of the time, particularly his idea that the satisfaction gained from consuming a commodity could be measured in numbers.

Table 2.1 gives some hypothetical figures showing the total and marginal utility derived by a consumer from the consumption of the product $q_1(q_x)$. When the individual consumes one unit of the commodity, she/he derives 20 units of satisfaction. When she/he consumes two units in the same week, his total utility rises to 50 and so on. The figures for marginal utility eventually decline as each successive unit is consumed. This is called the law of diminishing marginal utility.

Total utility increases with consumption, but it rises at a decreasing rate, showing diminishing marginal utility. This observation led early economists to formulate the law of downward-sloping demand curve. The fact

Table 2.1: Diminishing Marginal Utility

Units of q_1 (q_x) consumed (per week)	Total Utility (per week)	Marginal Utility (Utils)
0	0	
1	20	20
2	50	30
3	60	10
4	62	2
5	63	1

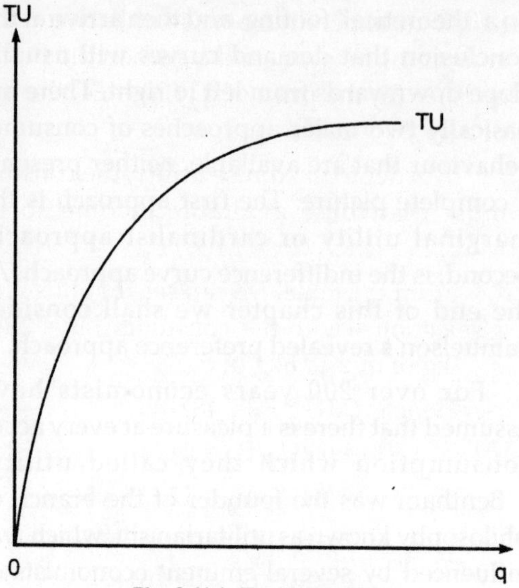

Fig. 2.1(a): Total Utility (TU)

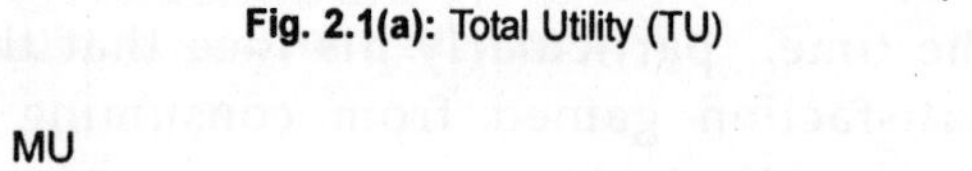

Fig. 2.1(b): Marginal Utility (MU)

that utility increases at a decreasing rate is shown in Fig. 2.1(b) by the declining marginal utility curve though the total utility is increasing as in Fig. 2.1(a).

Economists know that consumers choose amongst different commodities (goods and services) depending on the satisfaction they are likely to derive. From the notion of utility, we derive a demand curve and explain its properties.

Utility refers to how consumers rank different commodities. If basket A has a higher utility than basket B for a consumer, this ranking indicates his preferences for A over B. Often it is convenient to think of utility as usefulness that a person derives from consuming a commodity. Utility is not a psychological concept that can be observed or measured. Rather, it is a scientific construct that economists use to understand how rational consumers divide their limited resources among different commodities that provide them with satisfaction.

In the demand theory, we say that people maximise their satisfaction, which means that they choose the bundle of consumption goods that they prefer most.

• Marginal Utility and the Law of Diminishing Marginal Utility

How does utility apply to the theory of demand?

When we consume an additional unit of a commodity, we will get additional utility. This increment to our utility is called marginal utility. Marginal utility denotes the additional utility we get from the consumption of an additional unit of a commodity.

The law of diminishing marginal utility means that the amount of extra utility declines as a person consumes more and more of a good in the same period. According to the law of diminishing marginal utility, as we consume more and more, our total utility will grow at a slower and slower rate. Growth in the total utility slows because marginal utility diminishes as more of the good is consumed. The diminishing marginal utility results from the fact that our enjoyment of the goods drops off as more and more of it is consumed.

If we assume that consumers are utility-maximisers, i.e., they wish to obtain as much utility as they can, subject to no other constraints, the consumer in Table 2.1, would consume 5 units of q_1 where total utility is the greatest. However, two complicating factors need to be considered.

(a) The consumer's income is limited,
(b) The consumer must distribute expenditure among many different commodities.

Let us assume that the consumer has a choice between two goods, q_1 (q_x) and q_2(q_y). If good q_x and good q_y both cost £1 each, and the consumer has £1 to spend, then the commodity which yields the greatest utility will be bought. If we were to apply this principle to each successive unit of the consumer's spending, then we could conclude that utility will be maximised when income has been allocated in such a way that the utility derived from one extra pound's worth of q_1 is equal to the utility derived from the consumption of one extra pound's worth of q_2. If this condition is not satisfied then the consumer could obviously increase the total utility by switching expenditure from q_1 to q_2, or vice versa.

The extra satisfaction derived from the consumption of one more unit of q_1 is its marginal utility which we can write as MU_1 and that of q_2 as MU_2, etc. We must consider the relative price of good q_x and good q_y which we can write as P_1 and P_2. We can see that the utility maximising condition is fulfilled when

$$\frac{MU_1}{P_1} = \frac{MU_2}{P_2}$$

Any number of commodities may then be added to the equation. Table 2.2 gives marginal utility figures for a consumer who wants to distribute expenditure of £44.00 between three commodities, q_1, q_2 and q_3, when the price of $q_1(P_1)$ = £8, the price of q_2 (P_2) = £4, the price of q_3 (P_3) = £2.

In order to maximise utility, the consumer must distribute available income so that $MU_1/P_1 = MU_2/P_2 = MU_3/P_3$.

From the table, we can see that this yields a selection where the consumer buys 2kg of q_1, 4kg of q_2 and 6kg of q_3.

Hence, $(MU_1/P_1 = 48/8)$
$= (MU_2/P_2 = 24/4)$
$= (MU_3/P_3 = 12/2 = 6)$.

This gives the consumer greatest total utility by spending all the £44.00. It is impossible to distribute it in any other way to increase his utility.

• The Demand Curve

The marginal utility approach gives us a rationalisation of the demand curve. We start from a condition of equilibrium, where $MU_1/P_1 = MU_2/P_2$, and the price of q_1 falls relative to the price of q_2. We now have a condition where the utility from the last pound spent on q_1 will be greater than the utility from the last pound spent on q_2. This can be written as $MU_1/P_1 > MU_2/P_2$.

The consumer can now increase his total utility by consuming more of q_1. This will have the effect of decreasing the marginal utility of q_1 and she/he will continue increasing his

Table 2.2: Marginal Utility

Consumed	MU derived from each kg of		
	q_1 (£8/kg)	q_2 (£4/kg)	q_3 (£2/kg)
1	72	60	64
2	**48**	44	46
3	40	32	40
4	36	**24**	28
5	32	20	16
6	20	8	**12**
7	12	4	8

expenditure on q_1 until the equality is restored. We now have the result we have been seeking that a fall in the price of a good will, *ceteris paribus*, give rise to an increase in a consumer's demand for it – that is to say, the demand curve slopes downwards from left to right. Suppose initially we have $MU_1 = 20$ utils, $MU_2 = 25$ utils, $P_1 = 4$ and $P_2 = 5$ so that the condition of utility is satisfied $20/4 = 25/5$ or $MU_1/P_1 = MU_2/P_2$.

Now, let the price of q_1 fall to £2 with the consumption unchanged, MU per £ of q_1 rises to 10 utils > MU per £ of q_2. How will the consumer respond to this? By spending an extra pound on good q_1, she/he derives 10 utils of utility; by spending an extra pound on q_2, she/he derives only 5 utils. Thus, she/he will buy more of q_1, reducing MU_1 until the marginal utility per pound for good q_1 and good q_2 are once again equal. Thus, we have attained the normal demand relationship that, other things being equal, as the price of q_1 falls, more of it is bought, we have, thus, a normal downward-sloping demand curve. The demand curve we have derived is the individual's demand curve for a product. The market demand curve can then be obtained by aggregating horizontally all the individual demand curves.

This gives us the price (or substitution) effect.

• Indifference Curve Analysis

The marginal utility approach is subject to the major criticism that we have never found a satisfactory way of quantifying utility. In the 1930s, a group of economists came to believe that the cardinal measurement of utility was unnecessary. They argued that demand behaviour could be explained with oridnal numbers because individuals are able to rank their preferences, saying that they would prefer this bundle to that bundle, and so on. Finite measurement of utility becomes unnecessary and it is sufficient simply to know consumers' preferences. Indifference curve analysis can explain this. An indifference curve represents all combinations of baskets that provide the same level of satisfaction to a person. The theory of consumer behaviour begins with three basic assumptions regarding peoples' preference for one basket over another. The first assumption is that preferences are complete, which means that consumers can compare and rank all baskets. The second assumption is that preferences are transitive, which means that if a consumer prefers basket A to basket B and prefers B to C, then she/he also prefers A to C. The third assumption is that all goods are "good", so consumers always prefer more of any good to less. These three assumptions form the basis of the consumer theory. They do not explain consumers' preferences, but they do impose a degree of rationality and reasonableness on them. We add another one to these three assumptions – the indifference curve is convex to the origin.

In order to explain indifference curves, we will make simplifying assumptions that the consumer only buys two goods or two baskets of goods – good q_1 and good q_2 and that the consumer's satisfaction (utility) depends upon the quantity of goods (q_1, q_2) consumed.

To simplify $U = U(q_1, q_2)$.

The consumer's preference for good 1 and good 2 are represented by the indifference map in Fig. 2.2. In Fig. 2.2 the vertical axis measures

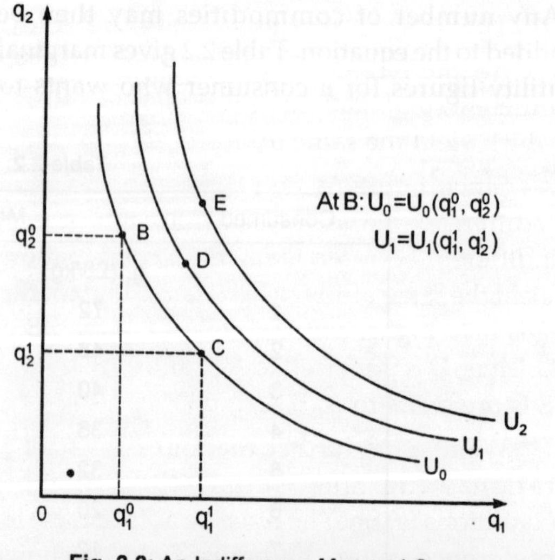

Fig. 2.2: An Indifference Map and Curves

the quantity of good q_2 and the horizontal axis measures the quantity of good q_1. Thus, every point on the graph represents some combination of good q_1 and good q_2. We assume that the consumer can rank his preference over the entire field of choice. This means that the consumer must be able to consider any two possible combinations of good q_1 and good q_2 and say either that she/he prefers one to the other, or she/he is indifferent between them.

A point very close to the origin, like A*, represents very small quantities of good q_1 and good q_2. Points further away from the origin represent bigger quantities where U_0, U_1, and U_2 are three indifference curves representing 3 (ordinal) levels of utility.

An indifference map is a complete set of indifference curves that describes a person's preferences (in Fig. 2.2 we have just highlighted 3). Any combinations on indifference curve 3, such as point E, is preferred to any market basket on curve U_1, (point D), which, in turn, is preferred to any basket on U_0, such as points B or C.

At point B the individual is consuming q_1^0 of good q_1 and q_2^1 of good q_2 and receiving utility (satisfaction) of U_0. If we move to point C the individual will consume less of good q_2^1 (q_2^1) and more of q_1 (q_1^1) but receive the same level of utility (satisfaction) U_0.

An indifference curve joins together all the different combinations of two baskets of goods which yield the same utility to the consumer.

Since points B and C are on the same indifference curve, the consumer is said to be indifferent between them. Both combinations yield the same utility to him/her. Combination D is on a higher indifference curve than B or C. Thus, D is preferred to A, B and C. Similarly, E is preferred to A, B, C and D.

We assume further that our consumer is rational and must satisfy the following conditions (a) She/he must be able to raise his preferences over the entire field of choice facing him/her. (b) His/her behaviour must be transitive: this means that if she/he prefers combination A to B and combination B to C, then she/he must also prefer A to C. (c) She/he must never have all she/he wants of all goods she/he must always want some more of at least one good.

We must consider several important features of indifference curves.

- **Indifference Curves Slope Downwards from Left to Right**

If both good q_1 and good q_2 are goods and if the consumer is rational, then we must conclude that if consumers give up some of good q_1, they will want more of good q_2 to remain at the same level of utility. Consider Fig. 2.3; In moving from B to C, as units of good 2 are given up, more units of good 1 are obtained and the utility derived is unchanged. For this to be true, the indifference curve must slope downwards from left to right (it has to have a negative slope).

- **Indifference Curves are Convex to the Origin**

As more and more units of one good, say q_2, are given up, it is reasonable to suppose that successively bigger quantities of q_1 must be

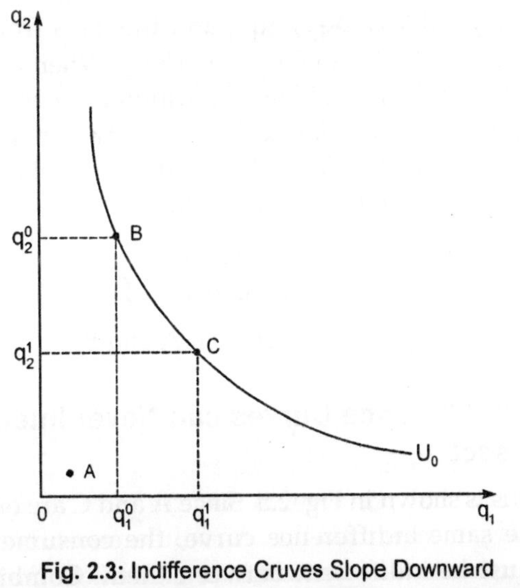

Fig. 2.3: Indifference Cruves Slope Downward

obtained to compensate the consumer for his loss and leave him at the same level of utility. In Fig. 2.3, this proposition is considered. Since the slope of an indifference curve is called the marginal rate of substitution (MRS), the proposition is sometimes summed up as the diminishing marginal rate of substitution.

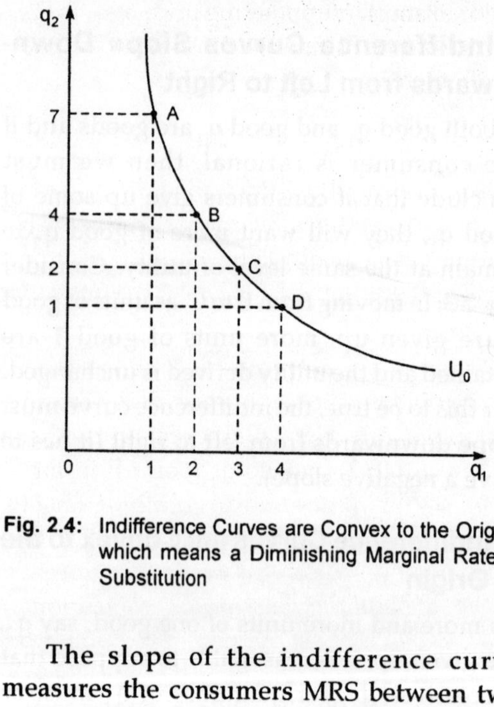

Fig. 2.4: Indifference Curves are Convex to the Origina which means a Diminishing Marginal Rate of Substitution

The slope of the indifference curve measures the consumers MRS between two goods. In Fig. 2.4, the MRS between good 2 and good 1 is $\Delta q_2 / \Delta q_1$, and this falls from 3(A to B) to 2(B to C) to 1(C to D). When the MRS diminishes along an indifference curve, preferences are convex. The MRS at any point is equal, in absolute value, to the slope of the indifference curve at that point:

$$\text{MRS for } q_2 = \frac{\text{change in } q_2}{\text{change in } q_1} = \frac{3}{1}$$

$$= 3 \text{ (between A and B)}$$

- **Indifference Curves can Never Intersect**

This is shown in Fig. 2.5. Since A and C are on the same indifference curve, the consumer must be indifferent between them. Combination, B and C are also on the same indifference curve, so the consumer must be indifferent between them as well. If a consumer is indifferent between A and C, and between B and C, she/he must (by the rule of transitivity) be indifferent between A and B. This is absurd and illogical because A contains more q_2 and the same amount of q_1 as B and so A must be preferred to it. This kind of absurd result occurs whenever indifference curves intersect. We conclude, thus, that indifference curves can never intersect each other.

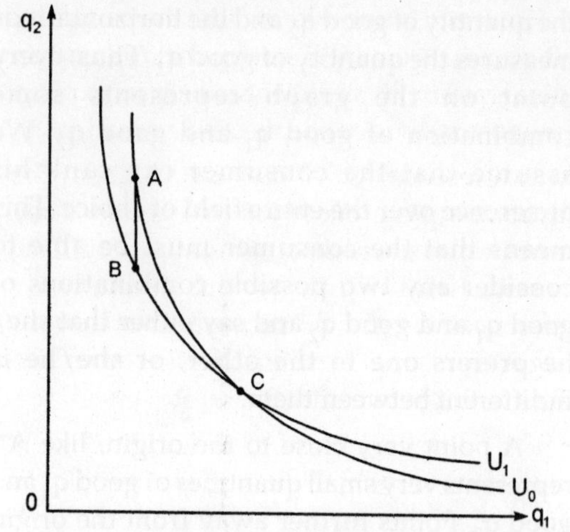

Fig. 2.5: Indifference Curves Never Intersect

- **Ordinal Versus Cardinal Rankings**

We have shown only 3 indifference curves in Fig. 2.2. The three curves provide an oridinal ranking of baskets of goods. Ordinal ranking places baskets of goods in the order of most preferred to least preferred, but it does not indicate by how much one basket is preferred to another. For example, we know that consumption of any basket on U_2, such as E, is preferred to consumption of any basket on indifference curve U_1 such as D. However, the amount by which E is preferred to D is not revealed by the indifference map. By contrast, when economists first studied utility, they assumed that individual preference could easily measure in terms of basic units and could, therefore, provide a cardinal measurement.

However, we now know that the particular unit of measurement is not important, and an ordinal ranking is sufficient to help us explain how most individual decisions are made.

Indifference curves only tell us about the consumer's preferences for two goods. They cannot tell us which combinations will be chosen. In addition to the consumer's preferences, we need to know the individual's budget constraint, i.e., income (M) and the prices of the two goods (P_1 and P_2). Given this information, and assuming that the combination of two goods chosen which will yield the greatest utility, we can find the combination of q_1 and q_2 that the consumer will choose.

We assume that the individual will spend all her/his income on the two goods. In this case:

$$M = P_1q_1 + P_2q_2 \quad \text{... (1)}$$

where

P_1q_1 is the total expenditure on good 1

and,

P_2q_2 is the total expenditure on good 2

To plot equation (1) on a diagram like Fig. 2.3 it is more convenient to rearrange equation (1).

Rearranging, we obtain a general equation for the budget line:

$$q_2 = \frac{M}{P_2} - \frac{P_1}{P_2} \cdot q_1 \quad \text{... (2)}$$

Equation (2) is a linear equation with an intercept (on the q_2 axis) of M/P_2 and a (negative) gradient (slope) of P_1/P_2 $(= \Delta q_2 / \Delta q_1)$.

For example, suppose the price of q_1 is £2, the price of q_2 is £1, and the consumer's income is £100, then

$$q_2 = \frac{100}{1} - \frac{2}{1}q_1 = 100 - 2q_1$$

Now we can draw the budget line which shows all the combinations of two goods which can be purchased with a given level of income when the price of good 1 is P_1 and the price of good 2 is P_2.

At the two extremes we can either consume 100 units of q_2(M/P_2 = £100/1) and no q_1 [point A in Fig. 2.6(a)] or 50 units of q_1 (M/P_2 = £100/2) and no q_2 [point F in Fig. 2.6(a)] or we can consume any combination of q_1 and q_2 that can be purchased for £100. This is illustrated in Fig. 2.6(a), where the straight line AF (the budget line) shows combinations of two goods that can be purchased with an

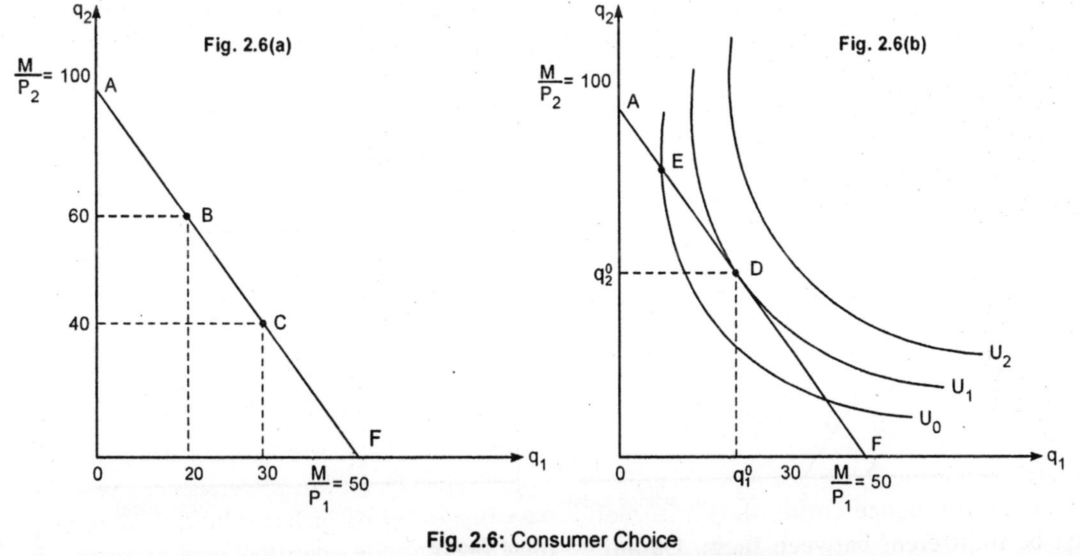

Fig. 2.6: Consumer Choice

income of £100 when the price of q_2 is £2 and the price of q_1 is £1.

For example, at point B the consumption of good q_1 is 20 and the consumption of good q_2 is 60. At point C the consumption of good q_1 is 30 and the consumption of good q_2 is 40.

The slope of the budget line $-P_1/P_2 = -2 = \left(\frac{q_1}{q_2}\right)$ measures the relative price of q1 in terms of q_2, that is 1/2 a unit of q_2 must be given in order to buy one unit of q_1; q_1 is twice as expensive as q_2. The slope of the budget line measures the relative cost of q_1 in terms of q_2.

The AF line shows the budget associated with an income of £100, given that the price of q_2, P_2 = £1, and the price of q_1, P_1 = £2. The slope of the budget line is $-P_1/P_2 = -0.5$.

- **Consumer Choice**

Given preferences and budget constrains, we can choose how much of each good to buy. We assume that consumers make this choice to maximize the satisfaction, given budget constraint. Now we draw indifference map on the graph which shows that if one spends all his income on good q_1 and good q_2 he will choose the combination 2.6(b). Assuming that the consumer represented by D (the consumer will purchase q_1^0 units of good 1 and q_2^0 units of good 2). This is the point where the budget line is tangential to an indifference curve – the indifference curve U_2 is the highest one that can be reached. Point D is called the consumer equilibrium point where she/he maximises his utility subject to his budget constraint. At point D, the slope of the indifference curve (MRS) is equal to the slope of the budget line at that point. Thus, we can write that, at the consumer equilibrium point, slope of the budget line $-P_1/P_2$ = MRS.

It may be noted that point E on U_0 is not the most preferred choice, because a reallocation of income in which more is spend on q_1 and less on q_2 can increase the consumer's satisfaction. In particular, by moving to point D, the consumer spends the same amount but achieves a higher level of satisfaction associated with U_1. U_2 will give a still higher level of satisfaction but cannot be reached with the available income. Thus, D maximises the consumer's satisfaction.

- **Perfect Substitute and Perfect Complement**

In Fig. 2.7(a) the consumer views orange juice and apple juice as perfect substitutes; the consumer is indifferent between a glass of one

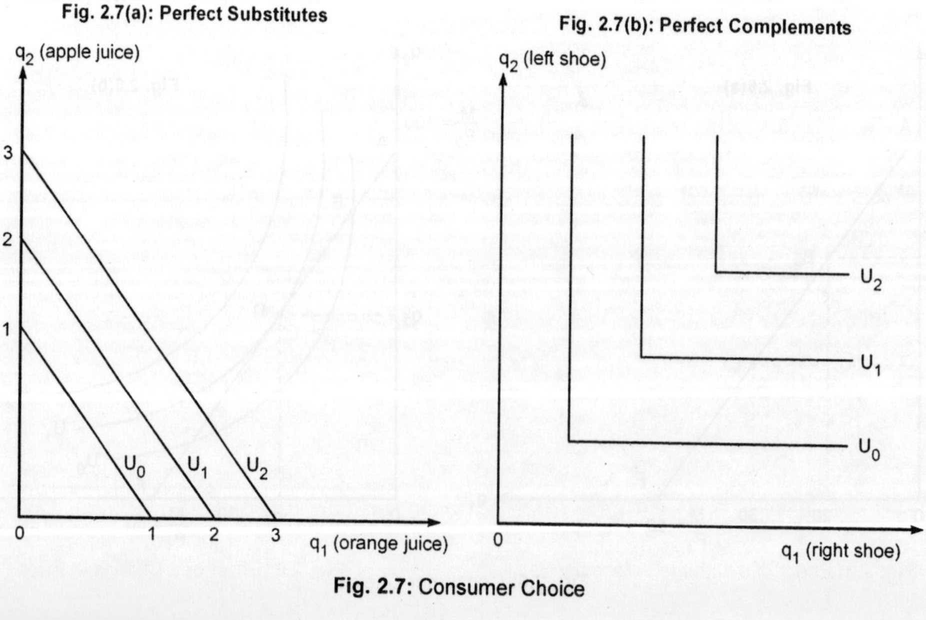

Fig. 2.7: Consumer Choice

and the other. The indifference curves with perfect substitute have a constant slope. In Fig. 2.7(b), consumer views left shoes and right shoes as perfect complements. An additional left shoe gives the consumer no extra satisfaction unless consumer also obtains the matching right shoe.

• Effect of a Change in Income

If the consumer's income increases, her/his budget line will shift upwards remaining parallel to the original one. Similarly, if his/her income falls, his budget line will shift downwards remaining parallel.

Starting at point C in Fig. 2.8 where the consumer's income is £100, the price of q_1 is £2, the price of q_2 is £1 and the utility maximising purchase of good 1 is q_1^C. Suppose that the consumer's income increases from £100 to £200. The new budget line is A'F' and the new utility maximising purchase of good 1 is q_1^B. Now suppose that income falls to £50 and the new budget line, A"F". The new utility maximising purchase of good 1 is q_1^B.

With an income of £200, the consumer equilibrium point is shown as point B in Fig. 2.8. With an income of only £50, the consumer's equilibrium point is D. The important result to remember is that when income changes, the budget line shifts but remains parallel. DCB is called the Income Consumption Curve (ICC). It shows what happens to the consumer's demand for the two goods as income changes.

• Effect of Price Change

We now examine the effect of a price change. Suppose the price of q_1 falls, *ceteris paribus*, from q_1^0 to q_1^1. The new budget line AF' is drawn together with the original one AF in Fig. 2.9. Income is still £100, the price of q_2 is still £1 as before and the price of q_1 has fallen to £1. When the price of one of the goods falls, the budget line does not shift, but pivots and so does not remain parallel to the original one. It becomes less steep reflecting the fall in the relative price of q_1. The effect of the price falls on the consumer equilibrium point is shown in Fig. 2.9, it moves from point C to point B. The line CB is called the Price Consumption curve (PCC). The fall in the price of q_1 causes the consumer's demand for it to increase from q_1^0 to q_1^1. There are two possible reasons for this:

(a) As the price of q_1 falls, it becomes relatively cheaper and q_2 becomes relatively more expensive. The consumer is, thus, induced to substitute q_1

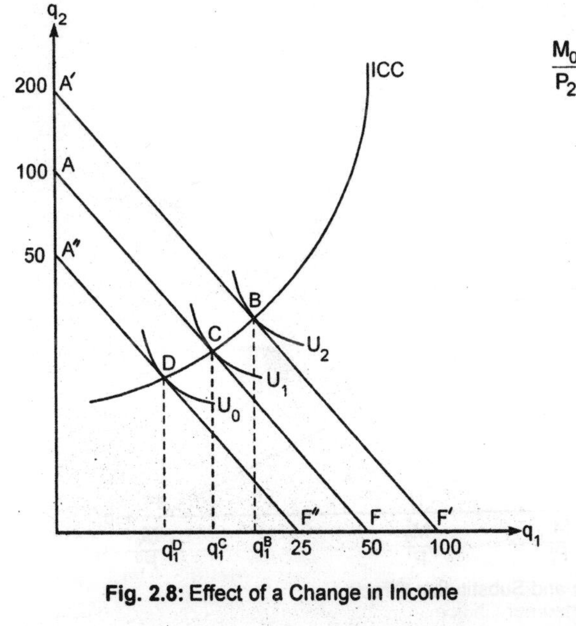

Fig. 2.8: Effect of a Change in Income

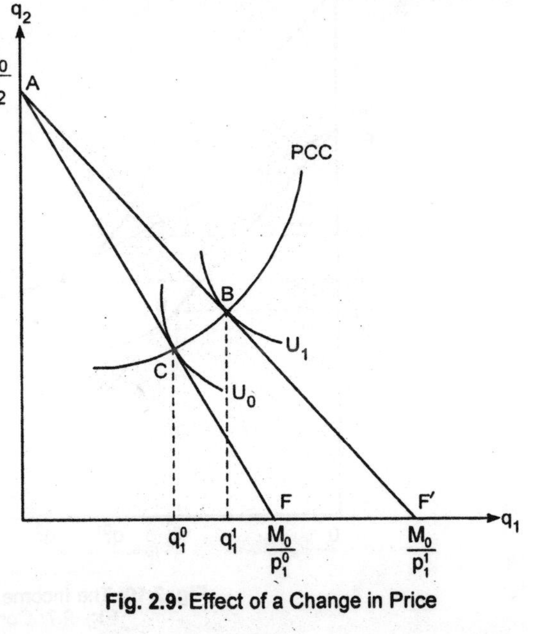

Fig. 2.9: Effect of a Change in Price

for q_2. This is called the substitution-effect of the price change.

(b) As the price of q_1 falls, the consumer is now better-off – he experiences an increase in his real income (M/P increases). This may allow him to buy more q_1 and more of q_2. This is called the income effect of the price change. It is possible to identify these two effects graphically and this is done in Fig. 2.10. If we start at point A on indifference curve U_0 when the original level of income is M_0, the price of q_1 is q_1^0 and the price of q_2 is P_2. The original budget line is AF.

We then assume that the price of q_1 increases from P_1^0 to P_1^1. The budget line will shift from AF to AF′ and the new equilibrium position will be at point B on U_1 and AF′. The overall fall in the quantity of q_1 is from q_1^0 to q_1^1 and q_2 falls from q_2^0 to q_2^1.

The first step is to eliminate the income effect and, to do this, we assume that, accompanying the fall in the price of q_1, there is a compensating variation in income which leaves the consumer at the same level of utility (the consumer remains on U_0) as he was before the price change. In Fig. 2.10 the original budget line is labelled AF whilst the new budget line after the price change is labelled AF′. To make the compensating variation in income, we draw a new budget line parallel to AF until it becomes tangential to the original indifference curve U_0. If the new budget line is GH (theoretically money income has been increased from M_0 to M_0^1) then the new consumer's equilibrium point is at point C; the point of tangency of GH and U_0. You should note that point C must be to the left of point A.

We can now split up the movement from A to B into 2 parts. We can identify the movement from A to C as substitution effect: the consumer is no better-off, but the fall in the consumption of good q_1 from q_0^1 to q_1^{01} has been substituted by an increase in good q_2 from q_2^0 to q_2^{01}. This substitution has been brought about because of the change in relative prices; the price of good q_1 has risen relative to the price of good q_2.

The movement from C to B can be identified as the income effect; in this case the consumer buys less of good q_1(q_1^{01} to q_1^1) because of the decrease in real income.

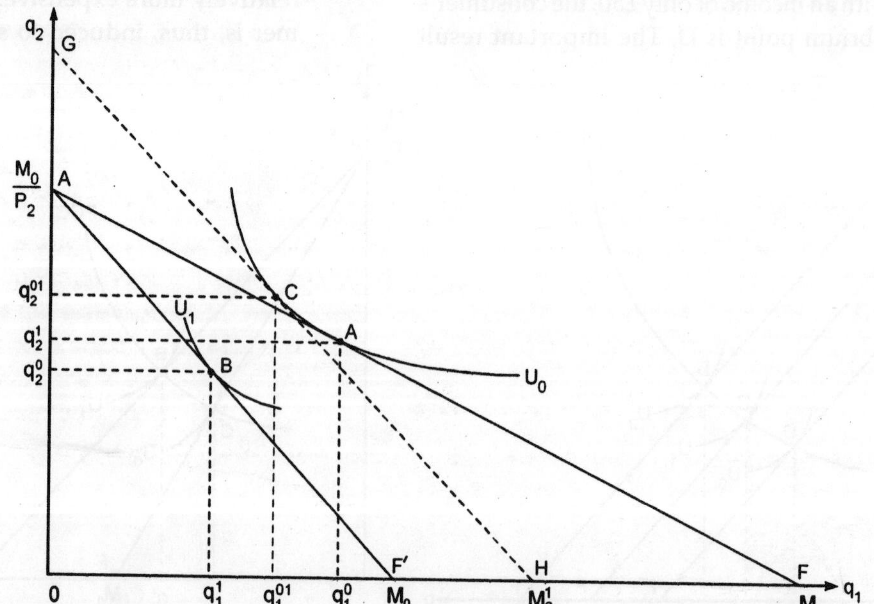

Fig. 2.10: The Income and Substitution Effects

Total effect of a rise = in the price of q_1	Substitution Effect +	Income Effect
A to B	A to C	C to B
q_1^0 to q_1^1	q_1^0 to q_1^{01}	q_1^{01} to q_1^1

• Normal, Inferior and Giffen Goods and Indifference Curves

The substitution effect always acts in such a way that when the relative price of a good increases [falls] (real income remaining constant), more [less] of it is purchased. The income effect can work either way when the consumer's real income falls [rises], she/he may buy less or more of q_1. If less is purchased when real income falls, it is a normal good. This situation is shown in Fig. 2.10, where both good q_1 (q_1^{01} to q_1^1) and good q_2(q_2^{01} to q_2^1) are normal goods.

If more is purchased when real income falls, then the good is an inferior good: this is shown in Fig. 2.11, where the movement from B to C is the negative income effect.

If less is purchased, and the income effect is actually bigger than the substitution effect so that the overall effect of the price increase is an increase in consumption, then the good is a Giffen good. This is shown in Fig. 2.12, where the negative income effect (B to C) is larger than the substitution effect (A to C).

• The Derivation of the Demand Curve for a Normal Good

From the previous analysis we can derive a consumer's demand curve. The price consumption curve in Fig. 2.9 shows the different points of 'consumer's equilibrium' as the price of q_1 is varied, *ceteris paribus*. It gives sufficient information to draw consumers demand curve from indifference curve.

This is done in Fig. 2.13 where q_1 is a normal good as the price of q_1 is reduced from q_1^0 to q_1^1 to q_1^2, the quantity of q_1 demanded expands from q_1^0 to q_1^1 to q_1^2. The resulting demand curve (d) is downward-sloping from left to right.

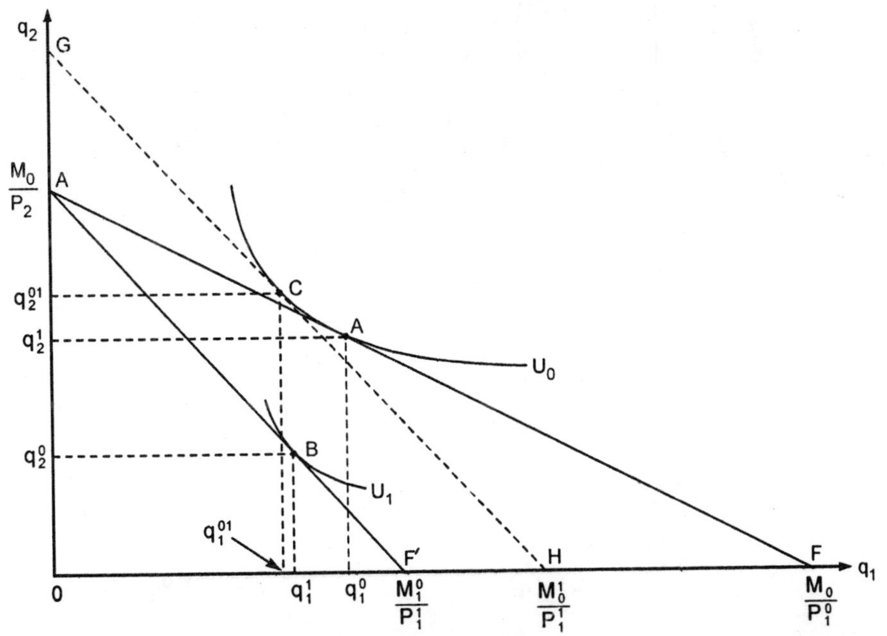

Fig. 2.11: An Inferior Good

Fig. 2.12: A Giffen Good

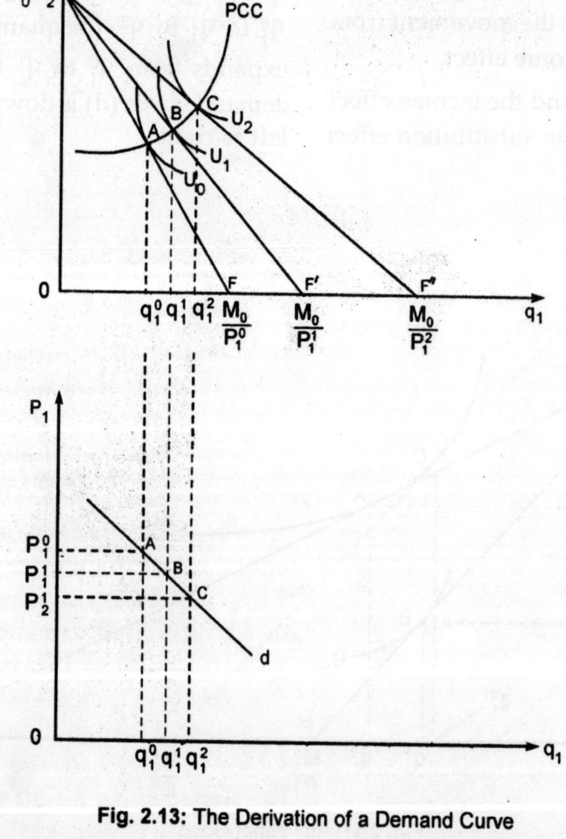

Fig. 2.13: The Derivation of a Demand Curve

We have completed a full circle. Having started by considering an individual consumer's demand curve in isolation, we have looked at the concept of utility and the theory of consumer behaviour which underlies demand. Moreover, we have also seen that by making certain assumptions about the consumer's preferences and assuming *ceteris paribus*, we can derive a demand curve which slopes downwards from left to right. Under certain exceptional circumstances a demand curve which slopes upwards from left to right can be constructed.

• Consumer Surplus

We now consider individual demand curve for good q_1 as shown in Fi.g 2.14 and suppose that the prevailing market price is £6. Since people continue to purchase a particular good until the extra (private) benefit (utility) they receive from purchasing the extra unit is just equal to the price of the good, then this individual's marginal private benefit is equal to £6.

It is clear from the Fig. 2.14 that the individual will buy 6 units of the good per week, paying £36 and, from the foregoing analysis, we know that she/he will maximise his utility by these purchases. Consider also that the first unit of q_1, that she/he yields him so much utility that she/he would have been prepared to pay as much as £11 for it. Similarly, she/he would have been prepared to pay £10 for the second unit, £9 for the third

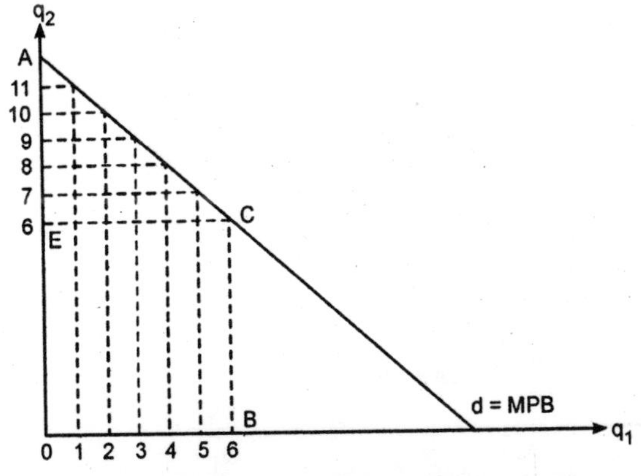

Fig. 2.14: Consumer Surplus

unit, and so on. Since a single price of £6 prevails in the market, she/he has only had to pay £36 (£6 × 6) for the six units (area OBCE). Since the area under the marginal private benefit (utility) curve (MPB) is equal to total private benefit (TPB), then the individual will receive £54 of TSB (the area OACB). The difference (£54 - £36 = £18) of £18 is the individual's consumer surplus.

Consumer surplus is represented by the area under a (inverse) demand curve above the price line, the area ECA.

• Engel Curves

Income-consumption curves can be used to construct Engel curves, which relate the quantity of a good consumed to income. Fig. 2.15 shows how Engel Curves can be constructed for two different goods. Fig. 2.15(a) shows an upward sloping Engel curve, which is derived directly from Fig. 2.8. In both figures, as income increases, the consumption of q_1 also increases. The upward-sloping Engel curve applies to all normal goods. Fig. 2.15(b) shows the Engel curve for rice. We see that rice consumption increases initially as income increases. As income increases further, consumption falls. The portion of the Engel curve that is 'downward-sloping' in the income range is where rice is an inferior good.

• Market Demand

So far we have discussed the demand curve for an individual consumer. But here we show how market demand curves can be derived as the sum of the individual demand curves of all consumers in a particular market.

For simplicity, let us assume that there are only three consumers for coffee in the market. Table 2.3 presents several points on each of these consumers' demand carves. The market demand column (5), is found by adding columns (2), (3) and (4) to determine the total quantity demanded at each price. For example, when the price is £3, the total quantity demanded is 2 + 6 + 10 = 18. Fig. 2.16 shows these three consumers' demand curves for

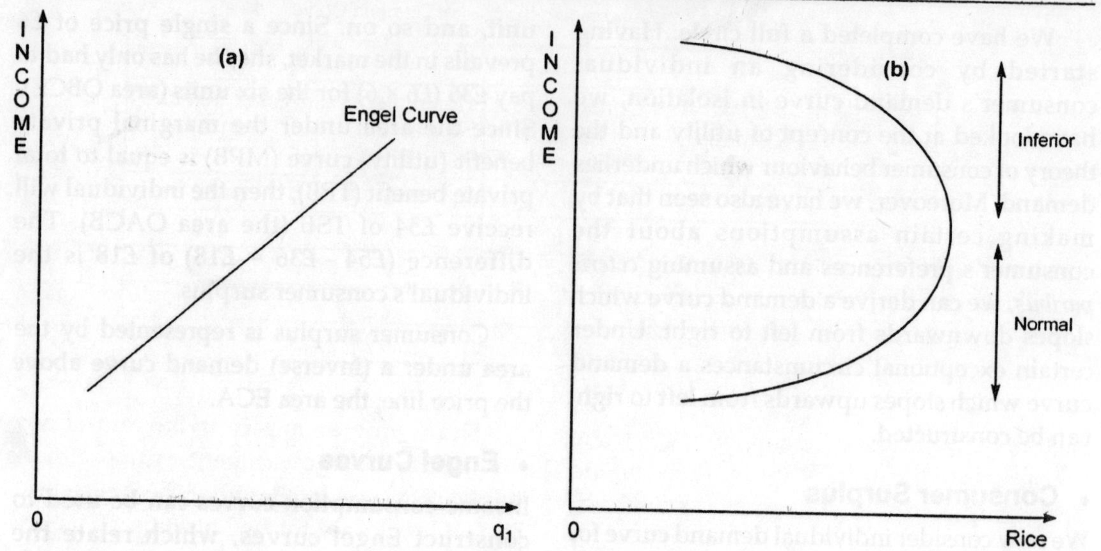

Fig. 2.15: Engel Curves

coffee (labelled dA, dB and dC). In the figure, the market demand curve (D) is the horizontal summation of the demands of each of the consumers. We sum horizontally to find the total amount that the three consumers will demand at any given price. For example, when the price is £4, the quantity demanded by the market (11 units) is the sum of the quantity demanded by A (no units), by B (4 units) and by C (7 units). Because all the individual demand curves slope downward, the market demand curve will also slope downward. However, the market demand curve need not be a straight line, even though each of the individual demand curves is. In Fig. 2.16 for example, the market demand curve is kinked, as one consumer makes no consumption at a price of 4. However, we always draw demand curves as continuous lines.

Two points should be noted here. First, the market demand curve will shift to the right as more consumers enter the market. Second,

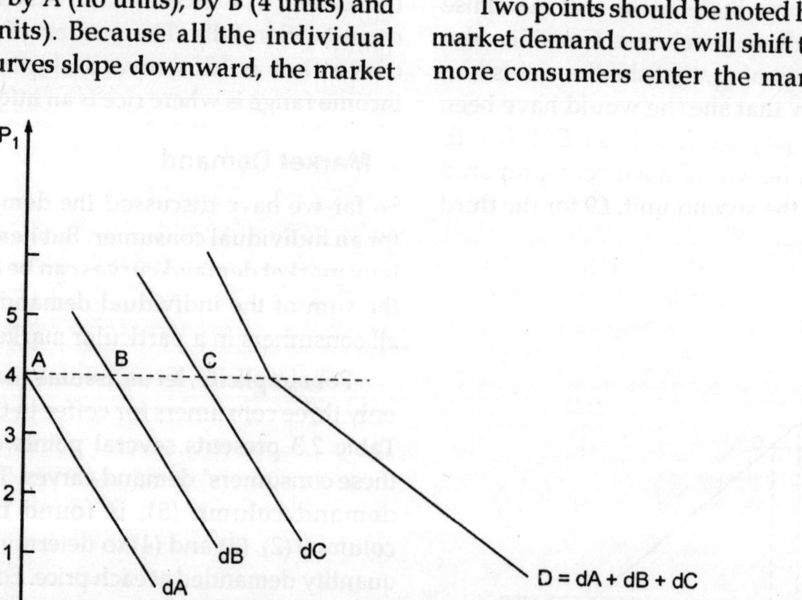

Fig. 2.16: From Individual to Market Demand

Table 2.3: Determining the Market Demand Curve

(1)	(2)	(3)	(4)	(5)
Price £s	Consumer A's demand (units)	Consumer B's demand (units)	Consumer C's demand (units)	Market demand (units)
1	6	10	16	32
2	4	8	13	25
3	2	6	10	18
4	0	4	7	11
5	0	2	4	6

factors that influence the demands for many consumers will also affect the market demand. For example, suppose that most consumers in a particular market have more income and as a result, increase their demand for coffee. Since each consumer's demand curve shifts to the right, so will the market demand curve.

The aggregation of individual demands into a market demand is not just a theoretical exercise, but also important in practice. For example, we can obtain information about the demand for home computers by adding independently the demands of: (i) households with children, (ii) households without children, and (iii) single individuals.

• Some Useful Examples

Example 1. The Decision-making of a Local Public Official

Grant programmes from the central government to local governments suppose that a public official is in charge of the police budget, which is paid for by local taxes. His preferences reflect what she/he believes should be allocated for police spending and what she/he feels citizens would prefer to have available for private consumption. Before the introduction of the grant programmes, the city's buget line is PQ, as in Fig. 2.17. This budget line represents the total amount of resources available for public police spending (on the horizontal axis) and private spending (on the vertical axis). The preference-maximising point A on indifference curve U_0 shows that 0R is spent on private spending and 0S on police expenditure. Since public expenditures are paid for by local taxes, these private expenditures represent spending after local taxes have been paid.

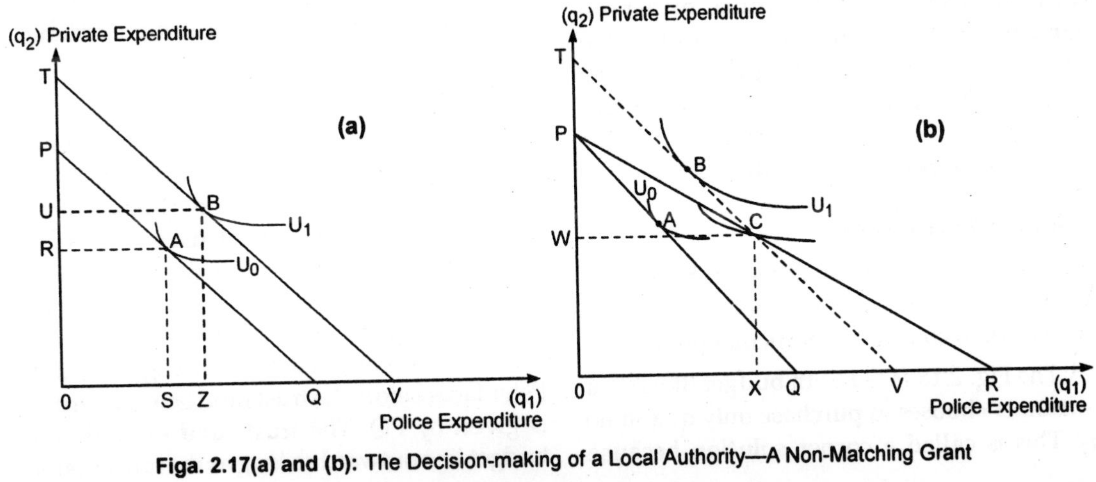

Figa. 2.17(a) and (b): The Decision-making of a Local Authority—A Non-Matching Grant

There are two types of grants: non-matching grant and matching grant.

A non-matching grant from the central government to a local government acts just like an increase in income in the traditional consumer analysis. The local government official moves from A to B, thereby allocating a portion of the grant to public expenditures and a portion to lower taxes and, therefore, to increase private expenditures. An unconditional grant shifts the community budget line outward from PQ to TV, where PT = QV, as in Fig. 2.17(a). The response to this grant is to move to a higher indifference curve by selecting point B, with more of both goods.

A matching grant acts like a price decrease in the traditional consumer analysis. For example, the central government might offer to pay £1 for every £2 that the local government raises to pay for police. As a result, a matching grant lowers the relative cost of the publicly provided goods. In Fig. 2.17(a) the matching grant shifts the budget line from PQ to PR. If no local money is spent on police, the budget line remains unchanged.

However, if they decide to spend money on the public sector, the budget increases. In response to the matching grant, the official chooses point C rather than A which involves an increase in both police and private expenditures. At C, 0W is allocated to private expenditures and 0X on police expenditures. However, the spending effects of the matching grant are different from those of a non-matching grant. The diagram shows that the matching grant leads to greater police spending then does the non-matching grant when the two grant programmes involve identical government expenditure.

• A Corner Solution

The indifference curve analysis can be used to show conditions under which consumers choose not to consume a particular good.

The Fig. 2.18 faced with budget line AB, a consumer chooses to purchase only q_1 and no q_2. This is called a corner solution because when one of the goods is not consumed, the consumption bundle appears at the corner of the graph that describes the consumer's budget line. At B, which is the point of 'maximum satisfaction', the MRS of q_1 for q_2 is greater than the slope of the budget line.

When a corner solution arises, the consumer's MRS is greater than the price ratio for all levels of consumption. The consumer maximises satisfaction by consuming only one of the two goods. Given budget line AB; the highest level of satisfaction is achieved at B on indifference curve U_0, and only q_1 is consumed.

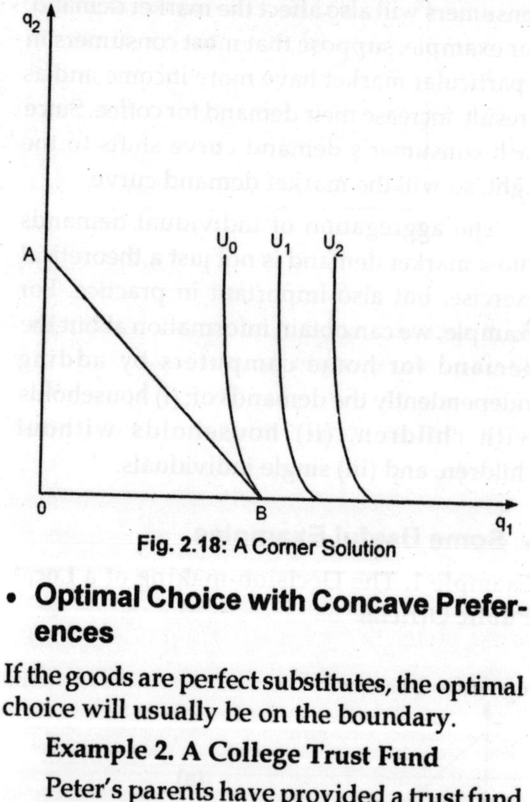

Fig. 2.18: A Corner Solution

• Optimal Choice with Concave Preferences

If the goods are perfect substitutes, the optimal choice will usually be on the boundary.

Example 2. A College Trust Fund

Peter's parents have provided a trust fund for his college education. The trust fund is a welcome gift to Peter but perhaps not as welcome as an unrestricted trust would be. In Fig. 2.19 pounds per year spent on education are shown on the horizontal axis, and pounds spent on other forms of consumption are shown on the vertical axis. The budget line that Peter faces before the trust fund being awarded is given by PQ. The trust fund expands the budget line outward so long as the full amount,

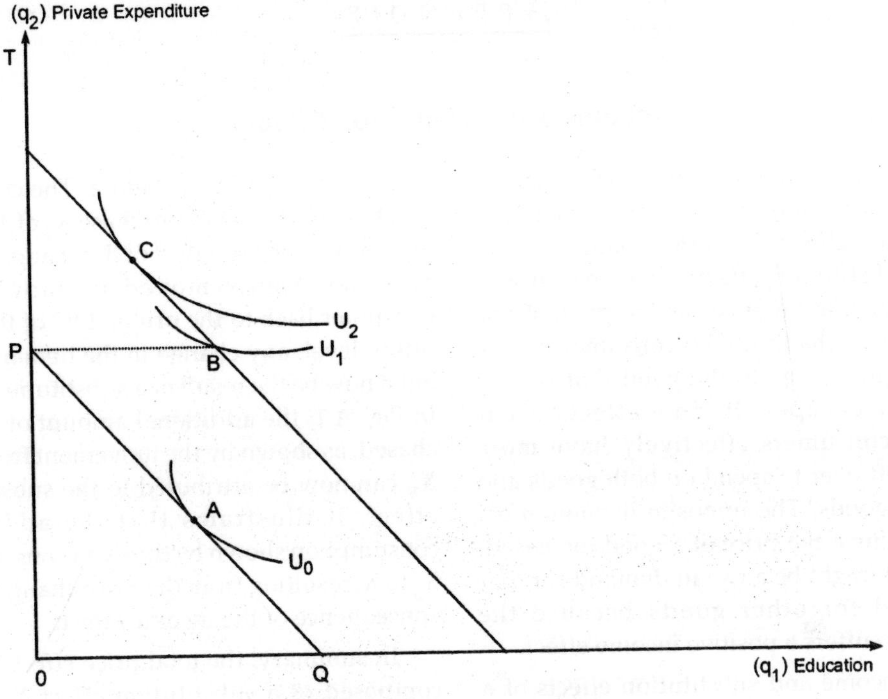

Fig. 2.19: A College Trust Fund

PB, is spent on education. By accepting the trust fund and going to college, Peter increases his satisfaction, moving from point A on indifference curve U_0 to point B on indifference curve U_1.

It may be noted that point B represents a corner solution because Peter's MRS of other consumption for education is lower than the relative price of other consumption. Peter would prefer to spend a portion of the trust fund on other goods as well as on education. Without the restriction on trust fund, she would move to point C on U_2, decreasing his spending on education but increasing his spending on other goods.

For the trust recipient, a restricted trust would be less beneficial than an unrestricted trust. Restricted trusts are popular because they enable parents to control their children's expenditures.

Appendix

Income and Substituton Effects

By adopting indifference curve (IC) analysis it is possible to identify clearly the income and substitution effects of a price change. As we know, substitution effects occur because of changes in relative prices as the price of one of the goods changes. The consumer can be expected to change to the good that is now relatively cheaper. Income effects occur because consumers effectively have more income left over to spend on both goods and on other goods. The opposite income effect would occur if the price of a good increased. The result might be a rise in demand for that good and for other goods because the consumer suffers a positive income effect.

The income and substitution effects of a price change can be easily identified using IC analysis – this is one of the important benefits of this approach to analysing consumer demand. Suppose the price of good X falls from P_1 to P_2 while the consumer's money income remains the some. This is shown by the line M/P_x^1, M/P_y^1 of the consume buys X_1 of X and Y_1 of Y, as determined by the budget line of the IC_1, with the reduction in the price of X the budget lines becomes M/P_x^2, M/P_y^1. The result is that the consumer can buy a larger combination of goods because X is now cheaper. In other words, the consumer can now operate on the IC_2. The individual now consumes X_2 of X and Y_2 of Y. The increase consumption of X, shown by the distance X_1 to X_2, is the total effect of the price change.

To identify the separate income and substitution effects within this total effect, suppose that the consumer loses the maximum amount of income compatible with him/her being able to obtain the original level of utility given by the new price line. This is shown by a new budget line, SR, tangential to the original IC_1. The consumer is constrained to operate on the original IC and, therefore, obtain the same level of utility as before. The consumer would now choose to purchase X_3 of X and Y_3 of Y. As the income effect of the change in price of X has been removed by moving the consumer back to the original IC of the same utility level, any change in the demand for X must now be the result of a substitution effect. In Fig. A.1 the additional amount of X_1 purchased, as shown by the movement from X_1 to X_3, can now be attributed to the substitution effect. It illustrates that the additional consumption shown by the extra consumption X_3 to X_2 resulting from the price changes is the consequence of the income effect.

In summary, the total price effect X_1X_2, is composed of a substitution effect X_1X_3 and income effect X_3X_2. Income and substitution effects will be found for all goods and services when there is a price change. In this example, X is a normal good – more is bought when price falls. However, some goods may be inferior goods, where the income effect reduces the effect of a price change by offsetting some of the substitution effect. This is shown in Fig. A.2. The approach to identify the income and substitution effects is the same as discussed so far in Fig. A.1, but in this case the total price effect is X_1X_2, the substitution effect X_1X_3 of the income effect reduces the consumption of X. The income effect is X_2X_3. If the income effect were sufficient to lead to an overall fall in the demand for X when the price of the good was reduced (if $X_2X_3 > X_1X_3$), the result is a Giffen good. The income effect is negative and larger then the positive substitution effect.

Thus, the demand for good X falls as the price of X is reduced. As it is obvious from the above while the substitution effect of price change is always positive, the income effect can be positive or negative, depending on the nature of the good. Normal goods always have a positive income effect, whereas inferior goods and especially Giffen goods have a negative income effect.

The above discussion of ICs has dealt with the IC of an individual. Through a full understanding of income and substitution effects provided by IC analysis, the reasons why total consumer spending changes with price changes can be better understood. IC analysis confirms that an induvidual's demand curves, normally slope downwards. Market demand curves, also slopes downwards because they result from combining the spending patterns of all individuals in the market.

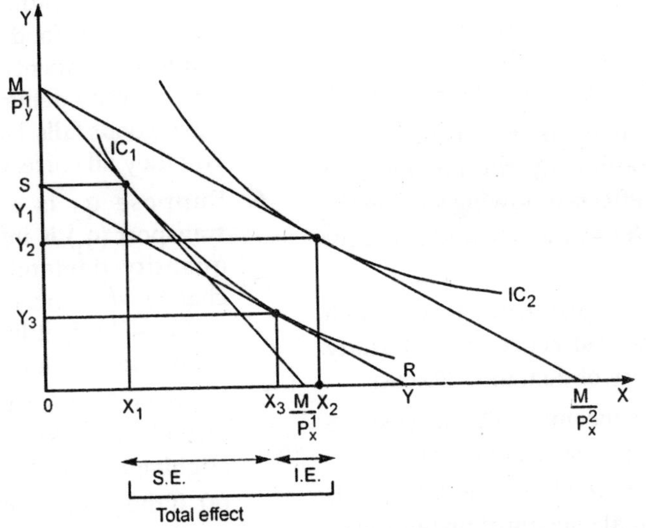

Fig. A.1: Substituion and Income Effects of a Price Change for a Normal Good

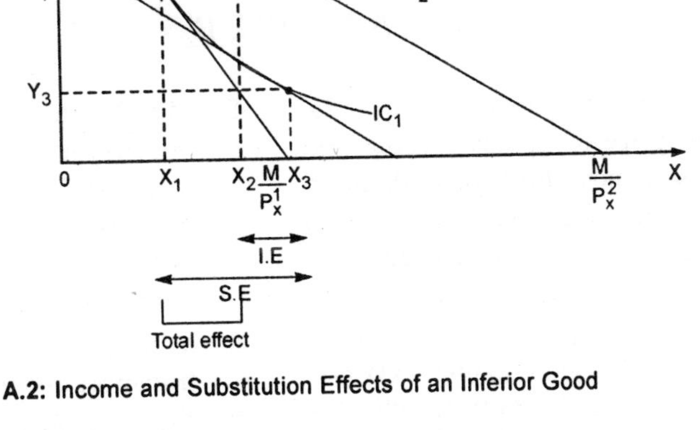

Fig. A.2: Income and Substitution Effects of an Inferior Good

QUESTIONS

1. Suppose an individual spends all his weekly income on two goods, q_1 and q_2. Draw the individual's budget line if his income is £150 per week the price of q_1 is £5 per unit and price of q_2 is £10 per unit. Draw the new budget lines
   (a) if the price of q_1 doubles;
   (b) if the price of q_2 halves;
   (c) if the individual's income rises to £200.
2. Suppose that q_1 is a normal good. Illustrate graphically the income and substitution effects following a fall in the price of q_1. Derive the demand curve for q_1.
3. 'The revealed preference approach eliminates the abstract concept of utility from the theory of demand.' Discuss.
4. A consumer's income is £50, q_1 costs £5 per unit and q_2 costs £2 per unit:
   (a) Draw the budget line and let point E be the initial consumption bundle.
   (b) The price of q_1 falls to £2.50. Draw the new budget line. What can be said about the new consumption point E' if both goods are normal?
   (c) The price of q_2 also falls to £1. Draw the new budget line and show the chosen point E".
   (d) How does E" differ from E? Why?
5. The own-price elasticity of demand for q_1 is negative. The demand for q_1 is inelastic. A higher price of q_1 varies spending on food. Higher prices of q_1 imply less is spent on all the other goods. The quantity demanded of each of these other goods falls. Discuss each statement. Are they all correct?
6. Suppose q_2 is a normal good but transport (q_1) is inferior. How does the quantity demand for the two goods change when income rises. Draw the old and new budget lines and illustrate the change in demand.
7. Suppose Scottish people have a given income, and like a weekend trip to the Highlands, a 3 hr drive:
   (a) If the price of petrol doubles, what is the effect on the demand for trips to the Highland? Discuss both income and substitution effects.
   (b) Use a demand and supply diagram to show what happens to the price of Highland hotel rooms.

ANSWERS

4. Budget line joins points $q_1 = 10$, $q_2 = 25$. Fall in the price of q_1 has income and substitution effects. Both raise demand for q_1. For q_2, income effect raises demand, substitution effect reduces it. Where price of q_2 falls, demand for q_2 rises, demand for q_1 could go either way. Putting two price cuts together, between E and E" there is no substitution effect–the relative prices are the same. Since both goods are normal, E" is north-east of E since real income is higher.
5. First 3 statements are correct, but the 4th one may not be so. For other goods, there is a substitution towards them, but since real income is lower, demand for normal goods can go either way. Demand for inferior goods must rise.
6. q_2 increases as budget line moves out, transport declines.
7. Cross-elasticities need to be symmetric.

CHAPTER 3

DEMAND AND SUPPLY

KEY TERMS

Equilibrium Price (market clearing price): At the equilibrium price, the amount sellers wish to sell is exactly equal to the amount buyers wish to buy.

Law of Demand: There is negative (inverse) relation between price and quantity. They move in opposite directions. If one increases the other falls. The quantity demanded of good X increases when its real price falls. The converse is also true, the quantity demanded falls when the price rises (*ceteris paribus*).

Law of Supply: There is positive (direct) relation between price and quantity. They move in the same direction. If one increases the other increases. The quantity demanded of good X increases when its real price increases. The converse is also true—the quantity demanded increases when the price rises (*coteris paribus*).

Quantity Demanded (Q_d): Maximum quantity of a good that buyers are willing to buy at a given price (over a fixed period of time).

Quantity Supplied (Q_s): Maximum quantity of a good that sellers are willing to supply at a given price (over a fixed period of time).

The basic economic problem faced by all societies is that of the allocation of the scarce resources of labour, capital and land among competing uses in an attempt to satisfy the unlimited wants of consumers. In a free market economy, the price mechanism plays an important role in allocating resources.

Before looking in detail at the working of the price mechanism, however, we need to examine how the economic forces of demand (buyers) and supply (sellers) interact with each other to determine the market prices of goods and services. Whenever we talk about demand and supply curves we are implicity assuming a perfectly competitive market structure.

• Demand

In this section we concentrate on the determination and measurement of demand—one of the most important concepts in economics.

As a first step, consider the main factors which influence an individual consumer's demand (q_d) for a particular good (from now on, for brevity, we shall use the term 'good' to mean good or service), say good X. An individual's demand for a good may be defined as the maximum quantity of that good that the individual wishes to buy at a particular price (over a fixed period of time). Strictly speaking we are talking about effective demand. Effective demand is demand that is backed by income. No income, no demand.

We see the interaction between two groups of people in every market, viz., buyers and sellers. In a free market (where there is no government intervention) the price of a good is determined by such interactions.

The market price is also known as equilibrium price. At the equilibrium price the amount sellers wish to sell is exactly equal to the amount buyers wish to buy. Each good has a price, and, if we consider all good markets we can see numerous such prices. These prices help to allocate resources, and changes in prices lead to reallocation of such resources. In the first part of this chapter we propose to study the theory of consumer demand, which means the behaviour of buyers. After this we will study the theory of supply and the behaviour of sellers. Our main objective is to bring the demand and supply together and determine the equilibrium price and quantity of a particular good.

• Consumer Demand

We will, in this chapter, consider two groups that are part of any society: households (consumer) and firms (industry). We shall first study the behaviour of households or consumers. We use the term consumers to refer to those who buy goods and services for their ultimate use. Suppose we list some of the factors which may be expected to influence the individual consumer's demand for good X over a given time period (qdx):

1. The price of good X (P_x).
2. The price of other goods which are related to good X (complementary and substitute goods {P_c and P_s respectively}).

   A complementary good is a good that is usually consumed at the same time as good X. For example—petrol and cars, salad and mayonnaise.

   A substitute good is a good that can be used in place of good X. For example—margarine and butter, the London tube and cars.
3. The consumer's income (M).
4. The consumer's taste and preference for good X (T).
5. The consumer's expectations about future prices (E).
6. Other relevant factors (Z). This could be, for example, the weather.

Using functional notation, we can write the following demand *function*:

$$qdx = f(P_x, P_c, P_s, M, T, E, Z)$$

demand function

This states that the individual's demand for good X is a function of (determined by) all the factors listed in the brackets. Although all the factors are undoubtedly important, the price of a good in many cases is the most important factor influencing an individual's demand for the good. Economists analyse the relationship between a consumer's demand for good X and the price of good X by assuming that all the other influencing factors remain unchanged: this is the important *ceteris paribus* assumption (which means 'other things being equal').

We can write the individual's demand *curve* as:

$$qdx = f(P_x) \text{ demand curve.}$$

This simply states that an individual's demand for good 'X' (qdx) is determined by the price of good X (P_x), assuming that all other factors that could affect demand (P_c, P_s, M, T, E, Z) are unchanged.

Consider Table 3.1 where different prices of good X are listed together with a consumer's weekly demand for good X, *ceteris paribus*. As prices rise from 10p per unit to 20p per unit, weekly demand for good X falls from 160 units to 120 units. As prices rise from 20p to 30p, demand falls from 120 units to 80 units. If the price rose from 40p to 50p, the consumer would choose to buy no units at all.

Table 3.1: An Individual's Demand for Good X

Real price per unit of good X	Quantity demanded
10p	160
20p	120
30p	80
40p	40
50p	0

An individual's demand curve can be represented most conveniently by the use of graphs. Conventionally, the relative (real) price of the good is represented on the vertical axis and the quantity demanded per time period on the horizontal axis. (Even though price is the independent variable and the quantity demanded is the dependent variable !). Thus, in Fig. 3.1, the vertical axis represents the real (relative) price of good 'X' and the horizontal axis measures the quantity demanded of good 'X' per week. By real price we mean the price of the good relative to the prices of all other goods. Thus, for example, if the price of good X increases (*decreases*) by 5% and the prices of all other goods increase (decrease) by 10% then the relative price of good X has fallen (*increased*) by, approximately, 5%.

The line marked **'d'** is an individual's demand curve for good 'X'. Demand is a flow concept, so in measuring the quantity of a good demanded, it is imperative to refer to some time period. A demand for 80 units has no meaning whatever unless it is expressed over some specified period of time.

The demand curve for 'X' represented in Fig. 3.1 is a straight line and slopes downwards from left to right(that is, it is negatively sloped). It is not required to be a straight line—it is only a straight line in Fig. 3.1 because of the simple numbers used in our example but it is, with a few exceptions, negatively sloped. The negative slope of the demand curve reflects the reasonable expectation that, as the price of X

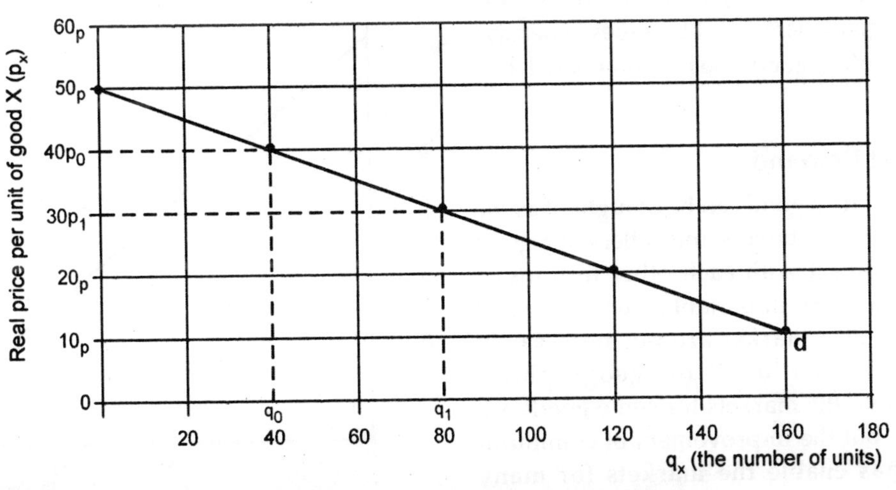

Fig. 3.1: An Individual's Demand Curve (d)

falls (for example from P_0 {= 40} to P_1 {= 30}), *ceteris paribus*, there will be *a change in the quantity demanded* by a consumer (from q_0 {= 40} to q_1{= 80}) along the demand curve. A movement along the demand curve is referred to as *a change in the quantity demanded.* This is in contrast to a shift in the demand curve which is referred to as *a change in demand.*

This proposition will be discussed in greater detail later on where we will deal with the theory of consumer behaviour and where we introduce the important concepts of utility and indiffernce curve analysis.

The demand curve shows the relationship between the real (relative) price of a good and the quantity demanded of the good. The demand curve illustrates the Law of Demand which states that the change in the quantity demanded of good X increases when its real price falls. The converse is also true; the change in the quantity demanded of good X falls when the price rises. Thus, there is a negative (inverse) relation between price and quantity. They move in opposite directions. If one increases the other falls.

The reason is simple. When the price of a good falls it becomes cheaper relative to other goods. This encourages consumers to buy more of it and less of others (its substitutes) whose prices remain unchanged. Similarly, as the price of a good increases it becomes expensive relative to other goods. So consumers will buy less of it.

- **Market Demand**

The market for a good can be thought of as the area in which all buyers and sellers of a good come in contact with each other to transact their business. It is important to remember that the limits of a market are not necessarily defined by national or geographical boundaries—the markets for some goods are localized, but the improvement of communications has enable the markets for many commodities to become worldwide.

We assume here, just for simplicity, that the market for good X is restricted to the home economy. Thus, the market demand (Qdx) for good X is the sum of the demand of all the individuals in the economy. As with individual's demand, we may expect the market demand also be influenced by the price of X (P_x) and the prices of other related goods, substitutes and complements (P_s and P_c). A single consumer's income will not have much effect on market demand; so we will take into account the income of the whole economy—that is to say, national income (Y). If T represents society's taste for X, and Z represents other relevant factors, we can write the following market demand *function* for X:

$$Qdx = f(P_x, P_s, P_c, Y, T, Z)$$

demand function

Again, making the *ceteris paribus* assumption we can write the demand *curve* as:

$$Qdx = (Px), \textit{ ceteris paribus}$$

demand curve

Representing this on a graph, and assuming that a fall in the real price of X (P_x) will cause an increase in the total quantity demanded (Q_x), we will have the downward sloping (inverse) market demand curve, D shown in Fig. 3.2.

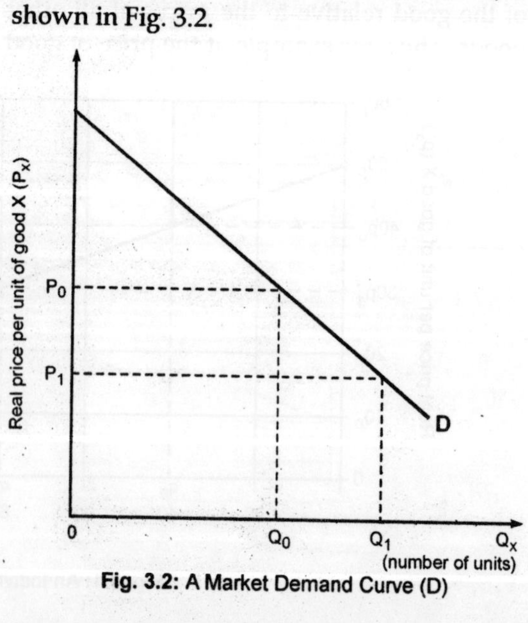

Fig. 3.2: A Market Demand Curve (D)

As the real price falls from P_0 to P_1, the change in the quantity demanded in the market rises from Q_0 to Q_1; if price should rise back to P_0, quantity demanded would fall back to Q_0.

This inverse relationship between the price of a good and the quantity of good demanded in the market is summed up in the Law of Demand, which states that: A rise in the price of a good leads to a fall in the total quantity demanded. A fall in the price of a good leads to a rise in the total quantity demanded.

This law is not an unassailable truth. There are some rare exceptions to it.

Giffen goods: A Giffen good is a very inferior good for which demand increases as price rises, and demand decreases as price falls. This is possible when consumers in some poor countries are so poor that most of their income is spent on a good necessary for subsistence, like rice or bread. If the price of rice or bread falls, consumer may reduce their demand for rice and use their surplus income to purchase egg or meat or some other nutritious food.

Veblen goods: A Veblen good is a luxury good, like jewellery, which is in great demand at a high price than a low price. Thus, if a diamond is put up for sale at a low price, it may lack snob-appeal and demand for it may be low. As the price is raised, the good gains snob-value and the demand for it increases again.

The market demand curve for Giffen goods and for Veblen goods will be upward-sloping (that is, positively sloped) as Fig. 3.3 shows.

• Movements Along and Shifts of the Demand Curve

Consider the market demand curve for good X in Fig. 3.4. Suppose the price of X is 40p per unit and the quantity demanded is 500 units: this combination is represented as point A in the curve. If the price goes down to 30p per unit, *ceteris paribus*, there will be a change in the quantity demanded of good X from 500 to 600 units, which means that we have simply moved along the same demand curve from point A to point B. If price goes up from 40p to 50p per unit, there will be a change in the quantity demanded of good X from 500 to 400

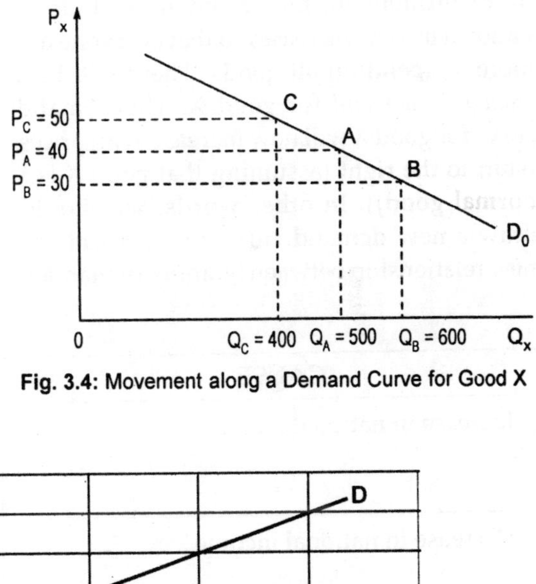

Fig. 3.4: Movement along a Demand Curve for Good X

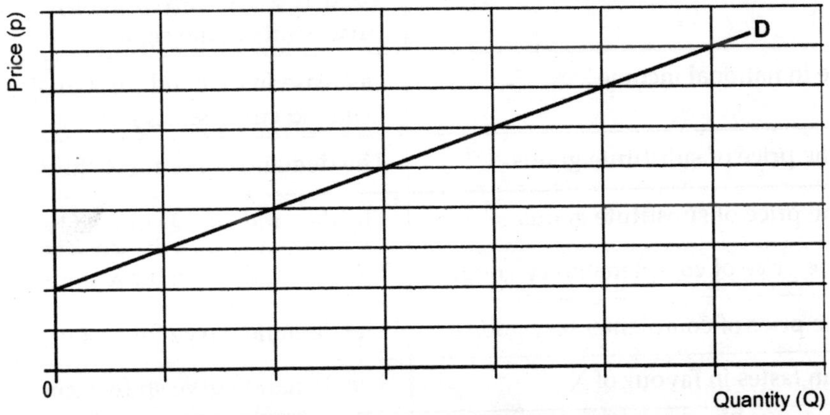

Fig. 3.3: The Demand Curve for a Giffen or Veblen good

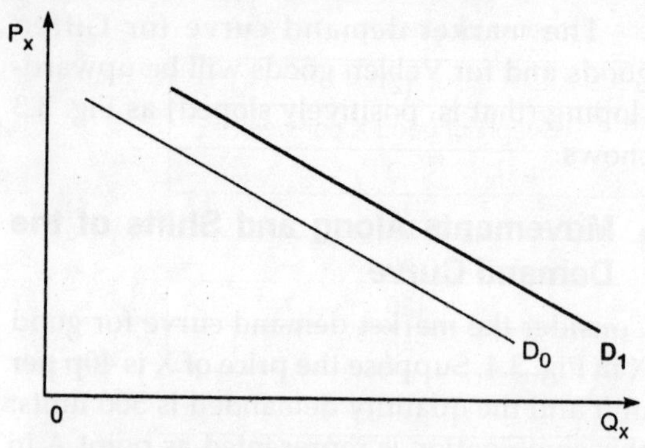

Fig. 3.5: A Shift in the Demand Curve for Good X

units. Again, we have moved along the same demand curve from A to C.

The effect of a change in the price of good X, *ceteris paribus*, can be traced along the demand curve for good X as Fig. 3.4 shows.

Again, starting from point A on the demand curve, suppose now that one of the other influencing factors changes, that is, national income increases so that everyone has more to spend on all goods. There will be *a change in demand* for good X. The demand curve for good X will now increase at all prices (shift to the right {assuming that good X is a normal good}). In other words, we should draw a new demand curve to represent the new relationship between quantity demanded and price. Fig. 3.5 shows the original demand curve, D_0, and the new demand curve D_1. D_1 lies to the right of D_0. A change in any of the influencing factors (P_s, P_c, M, E, T, Z) except the price of X causes a shift in the demand curve for X.

It must be emphasized that the stability of a given market demand curve depends on the reasonableness of the *ceteris paribus* assumption.

• Supply

We now turn to the other side of the market, the determination of the supply of a good. The quantity supplied is the maximum quantity of a good that sellers (a firm or an industry) wish to sell at each possible price (over a fixed period of time).

Supply is not a particular quantity but a complete description of the quantity the sellers want to sell at each possible price. Table 3.2 shows how much sellers wish to sell at 5 different prices. Plotting the data in table 3.2 we obtain Fig. 3.6.

A good cannot be produced for nothing. Nobody would supply at a zero price. In our example, a price above 10p is required before there is any incentive to supply the good. At

CAUSE	EFFECT
Increase in national income	Increase in demand for X (assuming the good is a NORMAL good). The demand curve shifts to the right
Decrease in national income	Decrease in demand for X at all prices. The Demand curve shifts left
Rise in the price of substitute goods	The demand curve for X shifts to the right
Fall in the price of substitute goods	The demand curve shifts to the left
Rise in the price of complementary goods	The demand curve for X shifts to the left
Fall in the price of complementary goods	The demand curve for X shifts to the right
Change in tastes in favour of X	The demand curve shifts right
Change in taste against X	The demand curve shifts left.

Table 3.2: The Market Supply Schedule for Good X

(1)	(2)
Price of good X per unit	Supply of good X per week
10p	0
20p	40
30p	80
40p	120
50p	160

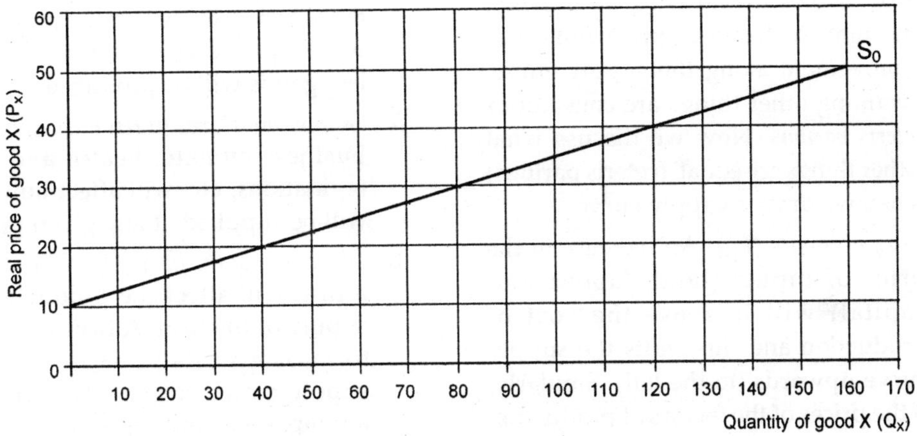

Fig. 3.6: An Upward Sloping Supply Curve

higher prices it is more attractive to supply more of the good and there is a rise in the quantity supplied. Together columns (1) and (2) describe the supply of X as a function of their prices – they describe a supply curve. The higher the price, the greater the quantity the suppliers will wish to supply. The lower the price, the lower the quantity the suppliers will wish to supply. If the price goes on decreasing there will be a price at which suppliers are not willing to supply at all because they cannot cover the cost of production at this price. The supply curve slopes upward because the higher the price, the more firms are usually able and willing to produce and supply. Other things being equal, the industry can increase output in the short-run by hiring extra labour, and, in the long-run, by increasing the input of other factors.

We can now state that the main factor which can influence the supply of a good is its real price. We can say that a greater quantity will be supplied at a higher price because, as the price increases, firms which could not be in a position to produce profitably at a lower price would be able to do so at a higher price. For example, North Sea oil – which costs four times as much to extract as Saudi Arabian oil. The lower price of oil in the 1960s would not have allowed the UK to obtain North Sea oil profitably but, as the price rocketed in 1970s, it became profitable to extract North Sea oil.

• The Market Supply Curve

As with demand, the market supply curve can be drawn as Fig. 3.6 shows. The supply curve slopes upwards (direct or positive relation), i.e. as price goes up from 30p to 40p, the change in the quantity supplied also goes up from 80 units to 120 units. This movement along the supply curve is called a change in the quantity supplied. As with demand, an extension or contraction of the quantity of the good supplied is brought about by a change in the price only.

- **Determinants of Supply**

Just as we listed the factors that determined the demand for good X we can also list the other factors which can influence the supply of good X:

1. *Price* (P_x): In general, a higher real price is needed to induce the industry (businesses) to supply more of the good, other things equal. So the supply curve slopes upwards as we move to the right. A change in price will cause a movement along the supply curve, assuming other things are constant or *ceteris paribus*. Now we discuss what 'other things are equal' (ceteris paribus) when we draw a supply curve.
2. *Price of inputs* (P_m): An increase in the price of inputs (land, labour and capital) will increase the cost of production and this shifts the supply curve upwards (to the left). Similarly, if the prices of the factors of production go down the cost of production will fall and this will shift the supply curve downwards (to the right).
3. *The price of other commodities* (P_0): If there is a rise in the price of barley but not wheat, this will tend to decrease the supply of wheat because farmers will switch from wheat to barley production. Economic theory envisages resources switch from one type of production to another in response to price changes. In fact, this may be a slow and painful process.
4. *Technology* (*Tech*): Improvement of technology also affects supply. An improvement of technology allows more goods to be produced with same factors of production or same quantity of goods will less factors of production. This will have the effect of shifting the supply curve downwards (to the right).
5. *Tastes of producers* (T_p): In theory, producers are perfectly rational beings interested in obtaining the highest return for their efforts. However, producers may have preferences and be willing to tolerate lower returns if they find a business otherwise preferable. Conversely, businesses may avoid unpleasant lines of work.
6. *Special factors* (S_f): Supply may be affected by conditions outside market forces. Perhaps the most obvious example of this would be weather. If the weather is favourable more goods will be produced and if unfavourable less goods will be produced.
7. *Government regulation* (G_r): Taxes, business climate, health and safety regulations, etc. will affect how much will be supplied at any given price.
8. *Objectives of the firm* (O_f): Objectives of a firm will affect the production and supply of the firm. A firm which aims to maximise its sales revenue will supply a greater quantity than a firm aiming to maximise profits.

Using functional notation, we can write the following supply *function:*

$$Qsx = f(P_x, P_m, P_o, Tech, T_p, S_f, G_r, O_f)$$

Supply function

This states that the industry's supply of good X is a function of (determined by) all the factors listed in the brackets. Although all the factors are undoubtedly important, the real price of a good is, in many cases, the most important factor influencing the supply of an individual good. Economists analyse the relationship between an industry's supply of good X and the price of X by assuming that all the other influencing factors remain unchanged: this is the important *ceteris paribus* assumption (which means 'other things being equal').

We can write the market supply *curve* as:

$Qsx = Qs(P_x)$ Supply curve

This simply states that the market supply of good 'X' (Qs_x) is determined by the price of X (P_x), assuming that all other factors that could affect supply (P_m, P_0, Tech, T_p, S_f, G_r, O_f) are unchanged.

As the other determinants of supply change, supply will increase or decrease, which means supply curve will shift either to the right or the left. There will be a change in the quantity supplied. For example, bad weather condition would have the effect of decreasing the supply of agricultural product and this will shift the supply curve to the left from S_0 to S_1. Conversely, good weather condition will shift the curve rightwards from S_0 to S_2. Fig. 3.7 shows this change of supply.

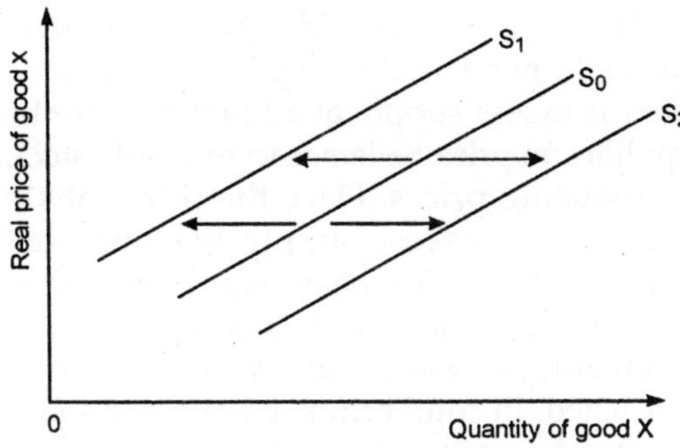

Fig. 3.7: A Shift in the Supply Curve

• Equilibrium Price and Quantity

We often show the market equilibrium through a demand and supply diargram like the one in Fig. 3.8. This figure combines the supply curve with the demand curve. Combining the two graphs is possible because they are drawn with exactly the same units on each axis.

Fig. 3.8 measures real price per unit of good X (Px) on the vertical axis and the number of units (quantity) of good X (Q_x) on the horizontal axis. This demand curve 'D_0' happens to be a straight line, though it need not be. The straight line demand curve has a negative slope. Large quantities are demanded at lower prices. The supply curve shows the relation between the real price per unit and the quality supplied, holding other things constant. In this particular case, the supply curve happens to be a straight line, although it may not be the case everywhere. It always slopes upwards because suppliers only wish to increase the quantity supplied, if they receive a higher price.

Market equilibrium is at point E, where, at P_0, the amount sellers wish to sell is exactly equal to the amount buyers wish to buy. The quantity demanded (Q_0), the quantity supplied (Q_0) and the equilibrium price (P_0) comes at the intersection of the supply and demand curves, S and D_0, at point E.

How do we know that the intersection of the supply and demand curves is the market equilibrium P_0?

Let us repeat our experiment. At price above the equilirbrium price, P_1, the market demand for the good is 'F' and the amount the industry (firms) wish to supply is 'G'. There is an excess supply of FG at the price P_1. This

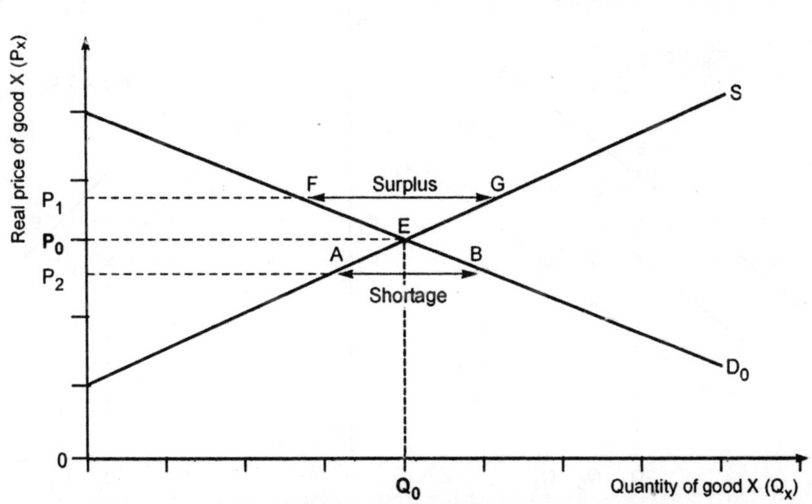

Fig. 3.8: The Market for Good X

means that suppliers wish to sell more than demanders want to buy, so there is market surplus of good X—an excess supply of good X. We will assume that, when there is an excess supply of a good, its price will fall. As the price falls demand will increase and supply will decrease. There will be a movement, to the right, along the demand curve from point 'F' towards point 'E' and a movement, to the left, along the supply curve from point 'G' towards point 'E'. The market will be back in equilibrium when $P = P_0$ and $Q = Q_0$.

At prices below the equilibrium price there is excess demand.

At the price P_2: AB shows the excess demand for good X. Under condition of excess demand or shortage, the competition among buyers causes the price to rise until $P = P_0$ and $Q = Q_0$.

We can now see that the equilibrium of demand and supply comes at point E, where the demand and supply intersect. At point E, where the price is P_0 the amount sellers wish to sell is exactly equal to the amount buyers wish to buy (q_0 units); there are no shortages or surpluses, and thus there is no tendency for price to rise or fall. At E alone, the forces of demand and supply are in balance and the price has settled at a sustainable level.

Participation in a market is voluntary. Buyers are not forced to buy and sellers are not forced to sell. When markets are not in equilibrium, the quantity that the industry wishes to sell (point G) is greater than the amount buyers wish to buy (point F) or is smaller (point A) than the quantity demanded (point B). Thus, in a competitive market, the equilibrium price and quantity come at point E, where the price is P_0 and the amount sellers wish to sell is exactly equal to the amount buyers wish to buy (Q_0 units). There are no shortages or surpluses. In a competitive market, this equilibrium is found at the intersection of the demand and supply curves.

We can now reconsider price determination in the good market. Fig. 3.8 illustrates that there is excess supply at all prices above the equilibrium price. Sellers react to unsold stocks by reducing prices. Once the price falls to equilibrium, excess supply is eliminated. Conversely, at prices below equilibrium there is excess demand, which bids up the price, eliminating excess demand until equilibrium is reached. In equilibrium, buyers and sellers can trade as much as they wish at the equilibrium price. There is no incentive for further price changes.

• Effect of a Shift in Demand and Supply Schedule

The analysis of the demand and supply can do much more than informing us about the equilibrium price and quantity. It can be used to predict the impact of changes in economic conditions on prices and quantities.

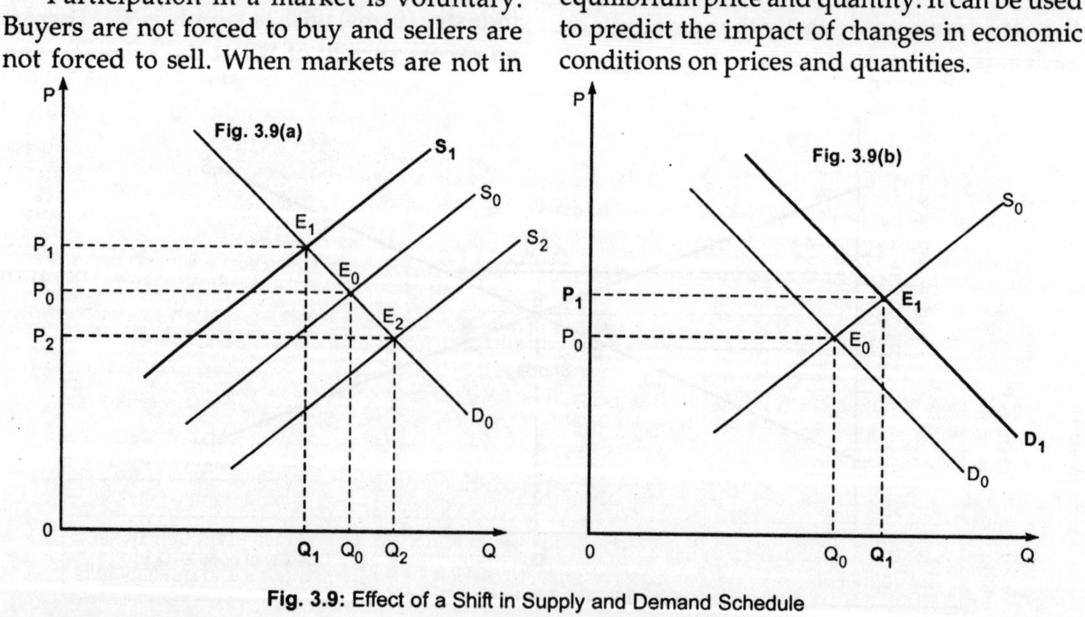

Fig. 3.9: Effect of a Shift in Supply and Demand Schedule

Let us take the example of bread. Suppose that a spell of bad weather raises price of wheat, a key ingredients of bread. That shifts the supply curve for bread upwards (to the left). Starting at E_0 in Fig. 3.9(a) the supply curve of bread will shift from S_0 to S_1. In contrast, the demand curve has not shifted— it has remained unchanged.

Now let us consider what happens in the bread market. The increase in the price of wheat causes bakers to produce less bread at the old price, so the quantity demanded exceeds the quantity supplied. The price of bread thus rises, encouraging producers to increase production and supply, while simultaneously discouraging consumption and lowering quantity demanded. The price of bread continues to rise until, at the new equilibrium price (P_1), and the amount sellers wish to sell is exactly equal to the amount buyers wish to buy. This is shown in Fig. 3.9(a), at the intersection of the new supply curve S_1 and the original demand curve (D_0)—point E_1. Thus bad weather raises prices (from P_0 to P_1) and, by the law of a downward sloping demand curve, lowers quantity demanded (from Q_0 to Q_1).

Now, staring at E_0 in Fig. 3.9(a), suppose that new baking technologies lower costs and thus increase supply. That means that the supply curve shifts to the right. The new supply curve is S_2, and the new equilibrium is E_2. The equilibrium price is lower and the equilibrium quantity is higher.

We can also use our supply-demand analysis to examine how changes in demand affect the market equilibrium. This is represented in Fig. 3.9(b), where a shift in demand at every price increases consumer's demand for bread. The demand curve shifts to the right from D_0 to $\mathbf{D_1}$. The demand shift produces a shortage of bread at the old price. Prices are bid upward until demand and supply come back into balance at a higher price ($\mathbf{P_1}$). Graphically, the increase in demand has changed the market equilibrium from E_0 to E_1 in Fig. 3.9(b). For both examples of shifts, a variable underlying the demand or supply curve has changed.

In general, a shift in supply might have been brought about by a change in technology or input prices, etc. For the demand shift, one of the influences affecting demand (incomes, population, etc.) changes and thereby shifts the demand schedule.

When other elements underlying demand (P_s, P_c, Y, T, Z) or supply (P_m, P_0, Tech, T_p, S_f, G_r, O_f) change, this leads to shifts in demand or supply and also changes the market equilibrium price and quantity.

• Interpreting Changes in Price and Quantity

Again, we go back to our bread example. Suppose the price of bread has doubled. Does the increase in prices mean that the demand for bread has risen, or does it mean that bread has become more expensive to produce? The correct answer is that without more information, we do not know—it could be either, or both. Let us take another example. If fewer airline tickets are sold, is it because of the fact that airline fares have gone up or because of the fact that demand for air travel has gone down? Airlines will be more

Table 3.3: The Effect on Price and Quantity of Different Demand and Supply Shifts

Change in Demand Or supply	Demand (D) or Supply (S) shifts	Effect on Price & Quantity
If demand rises	D curve shifts to the right	Price and quantity rise
If demand falls	D curve shifts to the left	Price and quantity fall
If supply rises	S curve shifts to the right	Price falls and quantity rises
If supply falls	S curve shifts to the left	Price rises and quantity falls

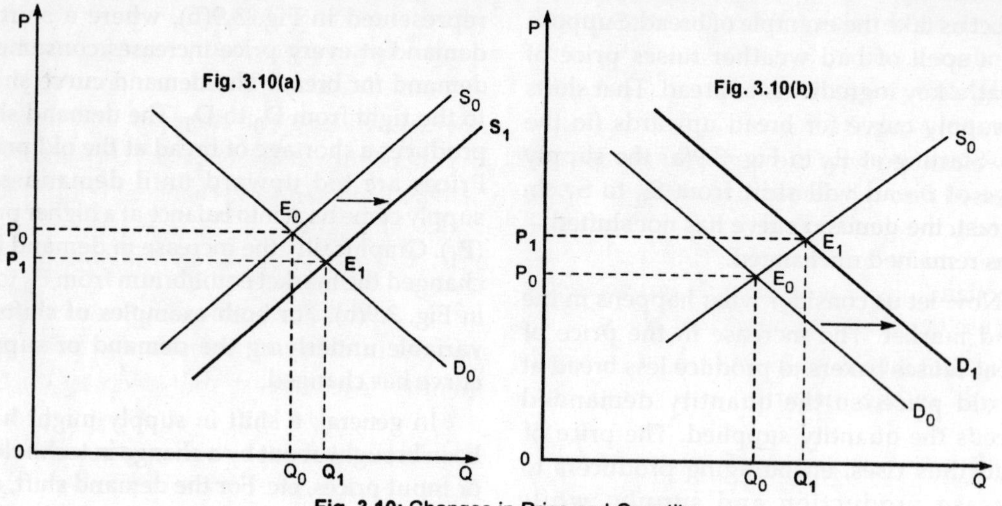

Fig. 3.10: Changes in Price and Quantity

interested in answer to this question. Economists deal with these sorts of questions all the time: when prices and quantities change in a market, does the situation reflect a change on the supply side or the demand side? Sometimes, in simple situations, looking at price and quantity simultaneously we obtain a clear idea whether it is the supply curve that is shifted or the demand curve. For example, a rise in the price of bread accompanied by a decrease in quantity suggests that the supply curve has shifted to the left (a decrease in supply). A rise in price accompanied by an increase in quantity indicates that the demand curve for bread has shifted to the right (an increase in demand).

This point is illustrated in Fig. 3.10. In both panels (a) and (b), quantity goes up. But, in 3.10(a), the price falls and in 3.10(b), the price rises. Fig. 3.10(a) shows the case of an increase in supply and a movement along the demand curve. In this case, a supply shift changes the market equilibrium from E_0 to E_1. As a result quantity demanded increases.

But demand does not change in this case; rather, quantity demanded increases as consumers move along the demand curve from E_0 to E_1 in response to a price change. Fig. 3.10(b) shows an increase in demand, or a shift in the demand curve to the right. As a result of the shift, the equilibrium quantity demanded increases.

• Rationing by Prices

Let us now take stock of what the market mechanism achieves. By determining equilibrium price and quantity, the market allocates or rations out scarce resources amongst their competing uses. Who does the rationing? It is the market, through the interaction of demand and supply, which does the rationing. This is rationing by the money vote. Those who have the highest money votes have the greatest influence on what goods should be produced.

What goods should be produced? This question is answered by signals of market prices. High oil prices stimulate oil production—resources flow into the oil production industry. Low food prices drive productive resources out of food industry. Those who have the highest money votes have the greatest influence on what goods should be produced.

For whom are the goods to be produced? The power of the money vote dictates the type of goods to be produced. Those with the higher incomes end up with larger houses and more of everything. When backed up by money (effective demand), the most urgently felt needs get fulfilled through the demand curve.

Even the how question is decided by demand and supply. When good prices are low, it is not profitable to use the most expensive productive technology. When prices are high, oil producers drill in deep offshore waters and use high technology to find oil.

With the introduction of demand and supply, we can see how the desire for goods, as expressed through demand, interact with cost of producing goods, as reflected in supplies. Further study will, hopefully, increase our understanding of these concepts and will help us to use these tools in important areas.

Fig. 3.11 illustrates the difference between changes in the quantity demanded and supplied versus changes in demand and changes in supply. Changes in the quantity demanded and supplied are shown by a movement along the demand and supply curves as shown by Figs. 3.11(a) and (c). Changes in demand and changes in supply are shown by a shift in the demand and supply curves as shown by Figs. 3.11(b) and (d).

Fig. 3.12 illustrates the difference between changes in demand and supply, price and quantity. An increase and decrease in the

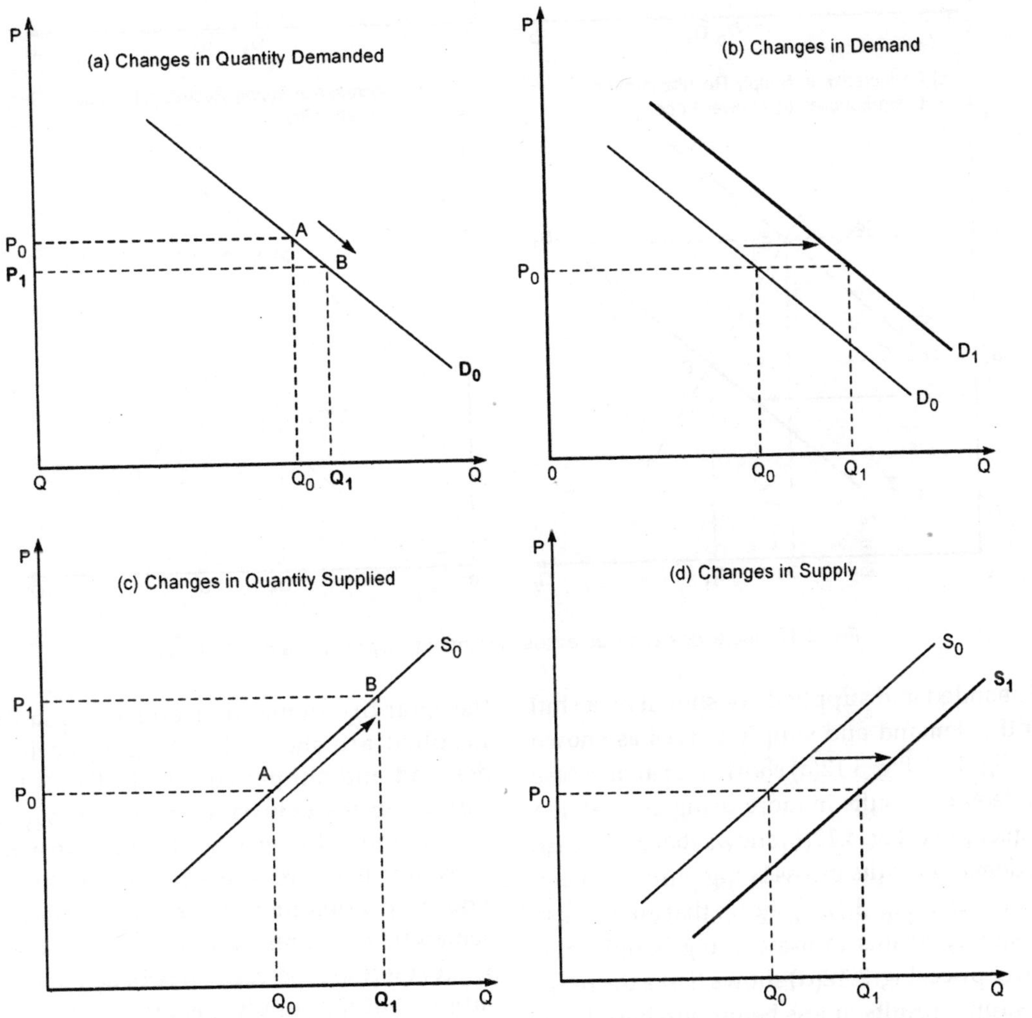

Fig. 3.11: Changes in the Quantity Demanded and Supplied versus Changes in Demand and Changes in Supply

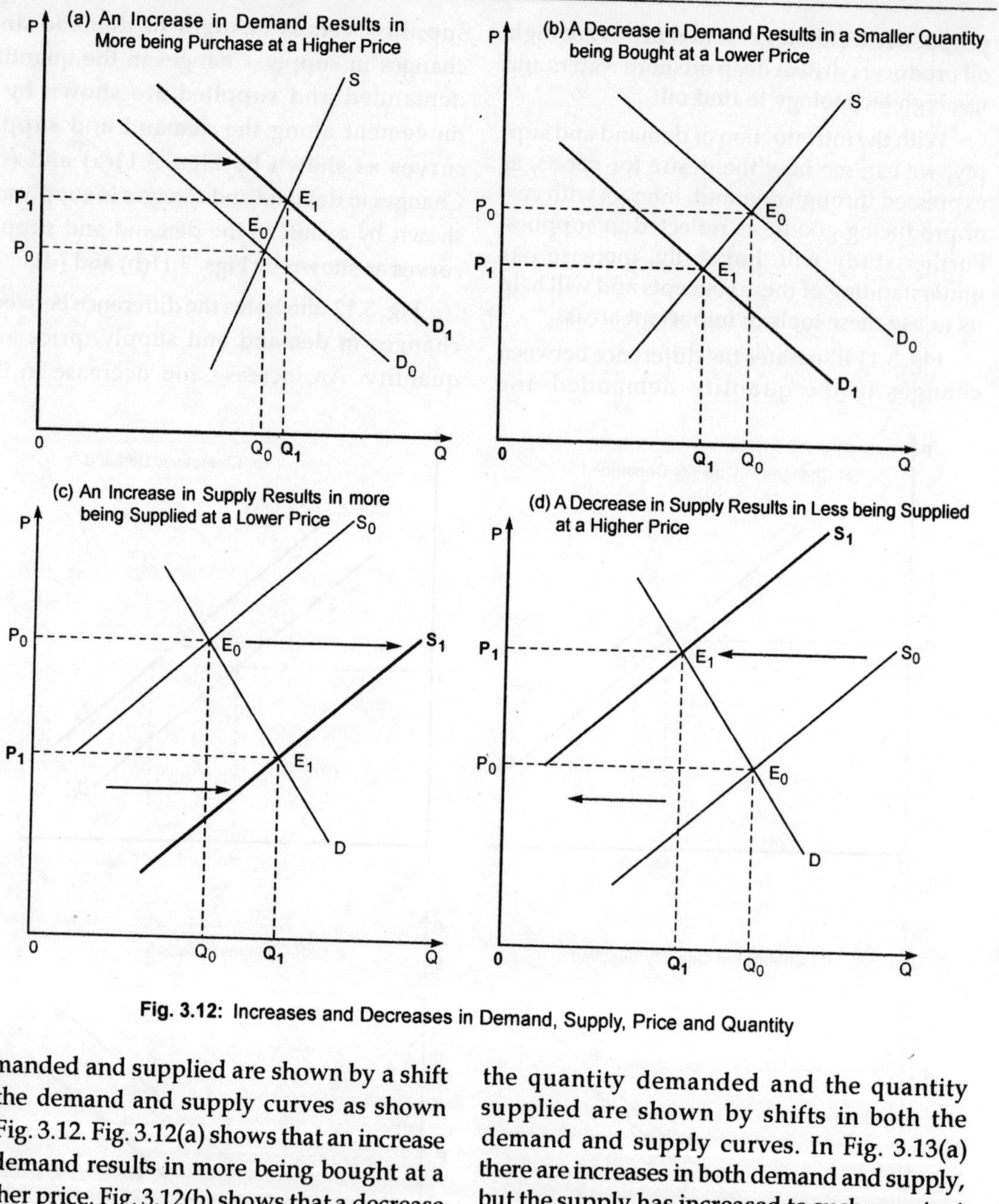

Fig. 3.12: Increases and Decreases in Demand, Supply, Price and Quantity

demanded and supplied are shown by a shift in the demand and supply curves as shown by Fig. 3.12. Fig. 3.12(a) shows that an increase in demand results in more being bought at a higher price. Fig. 3.12(b) shows that a decrease in demand results in less being purchased at a lower price. Fig. 3.12(c) shows that an increase in supply results in more being bought at a lower price. Fig. 3.12(d) shows that a decrease in supply results in less being purchased at a higher price.

Fig. 3.13 illustrates the effect of changes in both demand and supply. An increase in both the quantity demanded and the quantity supplied are shown by shifts in both the demand and supply curves. In Fig. 3.13(a) there are increases in both demand and supply, but the supply has increased to such an extent (offsetting the increase in price {E_0 to A} which would be brought about by an increase in demand) that the result is a fall in price. In Fig. 3.13(b) there are increases in both demand and supply, but the supply has increased to such an extent (just offsetting the increase in price {E_0 to A} that would be brought about by an increase in demand) that the result is no change in price.

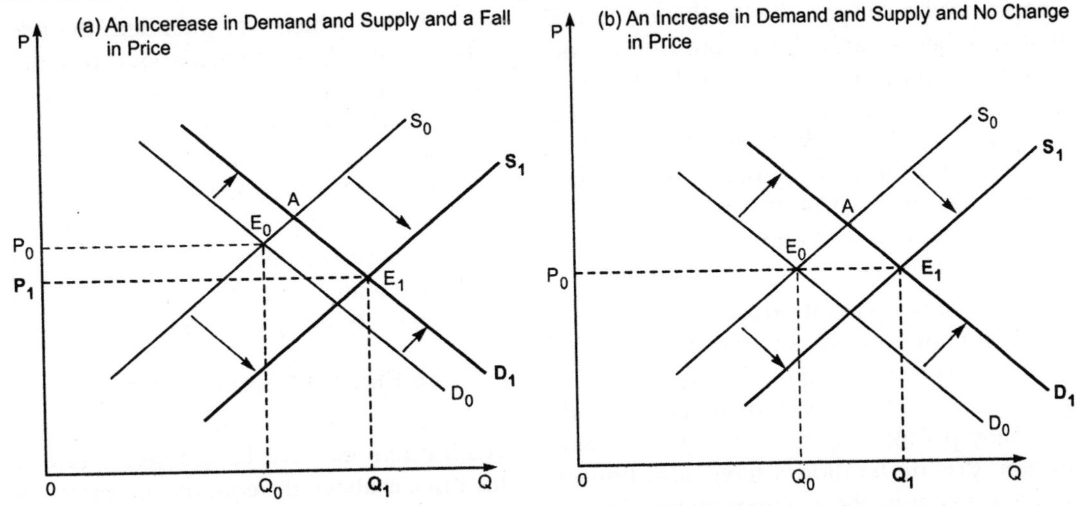

Fig. 3.13: Complex Changes in Demand and Supply

• Price Ceiling (Maximum Prices)

Governments have often considered it prudent to fix the price of a basic good below its equilibrium price. If the price of a basic good had been left to find its own level it would have been very high and beyond the means of most ordinary people.

In Fig. 3.14, equilibrium price is shown as price P_0. A celing (maximum) price is shown as P_m. At this price, consumers will wish to buy $Q^D{}_{max}$, but suppliers are only willing to supply $Q^S{}_{max}$. There is, therefore, an excess demand of $Q^S{}_{max}$ to $Q^D{}_{max}$. Thus, price is failing to fulfil its rationing function and some other method will have to be used. In some cases this is often dealt with by allowing some commodities, such as meat, to be sold only one day of the week, thus, decreasing demand. Governments sometimes adopt the rationing device to the problem of excess demand.

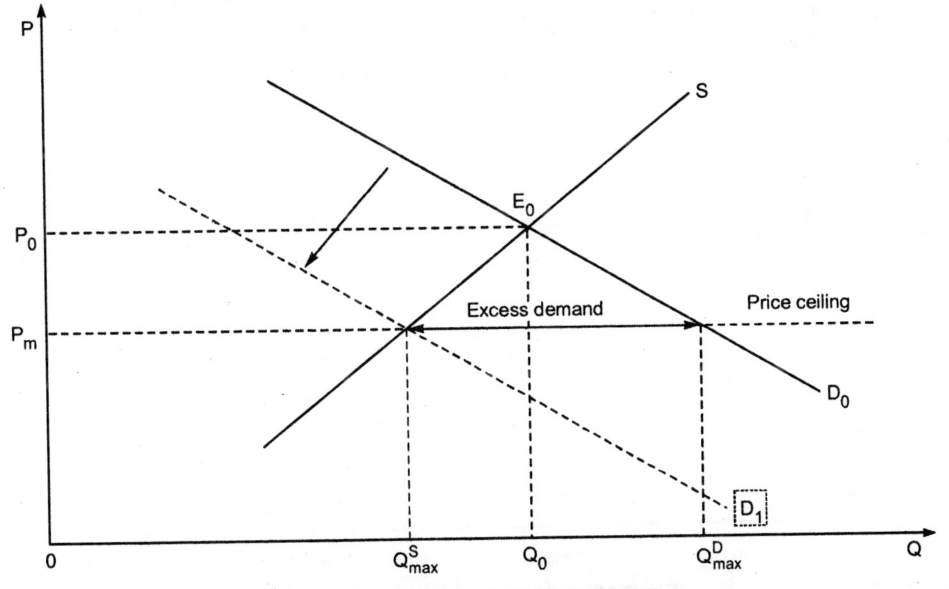

Fig. 3.14: A Price Ceiling (a Maximum Price)

People need a coupon as effective as money that specifies a particular amount of a good that can be purchased. Thus, in effect, a new money-plus-coupon has been created. Demand could be effectively decreased to equate with supply by regulating the number of coupons. In Fig. 3.14, this is shown by the new demand curve D_1 and, thus, equilibrium is arrived at P_m.

Rent control was introduced in the private sector in many countries to try and solve the problem of cheap accommodation for all. The problem is that this has made it very difficult for many people to even find any accommodation. Private landlords have sold houses rather than letting them at uneconomically low rents. This rent control has had the opposite effect of that which was intended. Rent controls in many places led to massive distortions in the housing market. They were, it is claimed, the reasons for high level of owner-occupation in the UK. The Government in the UK has abolished most of the controls in housing. Now it remains to be seen what the long-term results would be. The present let-to-buy demand has created shortages of supply and high prices in the housing market in the UK.

- **Price Floor (Minimum Price)**

If the government establishes a floor below which prices may not be allowed to fall, and this price is above the equilibrium price, then excess supply will be created. This is shown in Fig. 3.15.

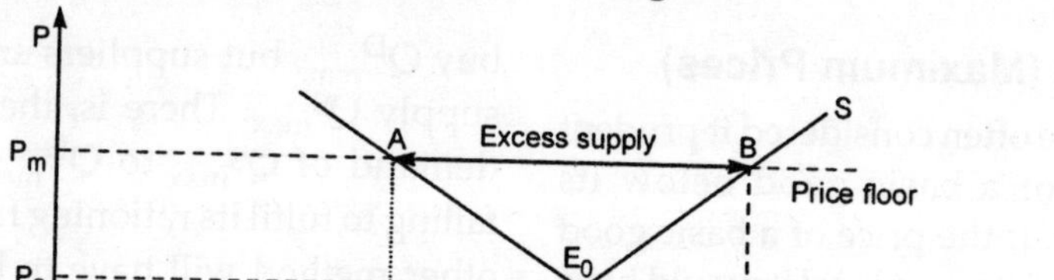

Fig. 3.15: A price Floor (a Minimum Price)

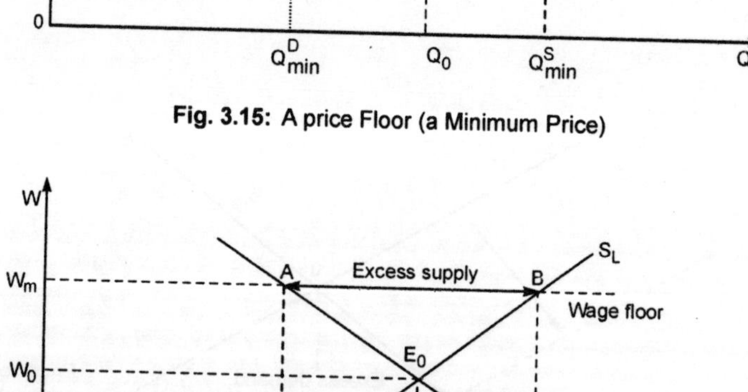

Fig. 3.16: A Wage Floor (a Minimum Wage)

Many countries set floor prices for agricultural products. Fig. 3.15 shows a floor price for wheat or rice. In the previous example, we have seen quantity traded would be the smaller of the quantity supplied and quantity demanded at the controlled price since private individual cannot be forced at participating in a market. There is another possibility: the government may intervene not only to set the price but also to buy up the excess supply A to B.

Another market in which the government may 'intervene' is the labour market. In many countries (including the UK, the USA and France) the government sets a minimum wage. Consider Fig. 3.16: D_L and S_L are the demand and supply of labour, respectively.

A competitive market price for labour would be at W_0. If this is considered to be too low then the government may pass laws that make it illegal for employers to pay less than W_m. W_m is the minimum wage.

At W_m the available jobs are L^D_{min}, but the number requiring jobs are L^S_{min}; there is an excess supply of labour of an amount A to B. Individuals who wish to work but cannot find a job are involuntarily unemployed.

• Free Market Equilibrium

The free market is one way for solving the basic economic problems. What, how, and for whom to produce. We have already seen how the market allocates scarce resources among competing users.

In Fig. 3.17, we see the market equilibrium position E_0. The market decides how much of a good should be produced by finding the price at which the quantity demanded equals quantity supplied. Other things being equal, more a good would be produced at market equilibrium, the higher the quantity demanded at each price, and the higher the quantity supplied at each price.

The market also tells us for whom the good is produced: in equilibrium, the good is produced by all those consumers willing to pay P_0 per unit for the good. The market also tells us who is producing: all those willing to supply at a price P_0 per unit. Markets also tell us how goods would be produced.

Finally, the market determines what goods are to be produced. In Fig. 3.17, the equilibrium price P_0 persuades producers to produce an amount Q_0.

Fig. 3.18, gives an example of a good that will not be produced. The consumers are willing to pay not more than P_1, which is sufficient to persuade the producers to produce. Technological progress may, in the long-run, shift the supply curve sufficiently to the right, to intersect the demand curve at positive quantity—and the good may be produced.

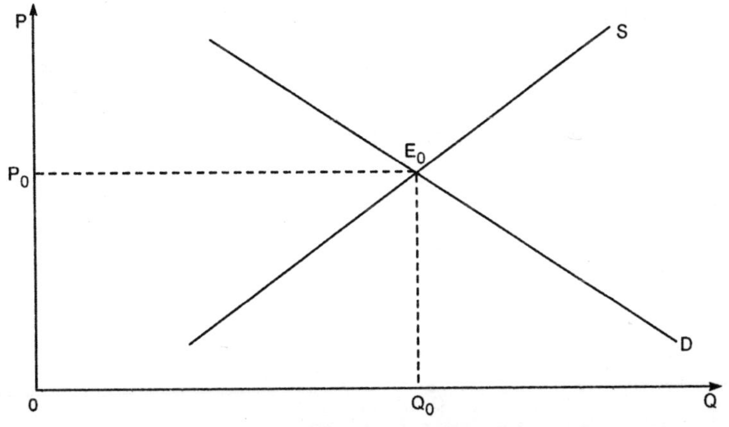

Fig. 3.17: Free Market Equilibrium

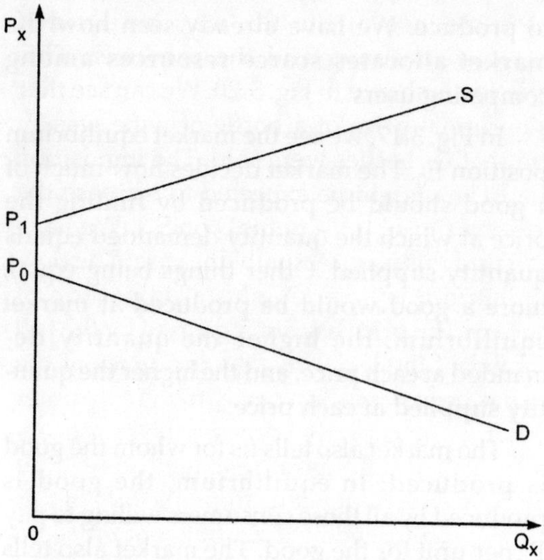

Fig. 3.18: It is Not Economic to Produce Good

Conversely, changes in taste may shift the demand curve to the right; that will induce the producer to produce the good because demand now interesects supply at positive price and quantity.

It is possible that the society may not like the answers the market provides. Free markets do not provide food or medical care for everyone. They provide food or medical care for those who are willing and able to pay equilibrium price. Society may apply a normative judgment that the poor should enjoy better food and medical care than free market provides for them. Few societies allow unrestricted free markets for all commodities and wish for the government to intervene through regulation, taxation and transfer payments to correct the market provision.

• Government Intervention through Taxes

There are two main types of taxes – direct and indirect. Direct taxes are those which are levied directly on incomes – income and profit tax. Indirect taxes are those which are levied on expenditure. We are concerned here on expenditure taxes and their effect on demand and supply. The most important indirect taxes are VAT (Value Added Tax) and excise duty. VAT is an *ad valorem* tax, i.e., it is a percentage of the selling price of the commodities. Excise duty is a specific tax which is levied per unit of the good; for example, it is levied per packet of cigarettes or per bottle of wine.

• Effect of a Tax

The effect of a tax can be shown by shifting the supply curve upward by the amount of the tax. This may be treated as a cost of production. The effect of indirect taxes is shown in Fig. 3.19.

In Fig. 3.19(a) the specific tax has raised the supply curve from S_0 to S_0 + tax, and in Fig. 3.19(b) the effect of an *ad valorem* tax is shown by the new supply curve, S_1, that diverges from the old one, S_0, ($S_1 = S_0 \times \{1.175\}$)

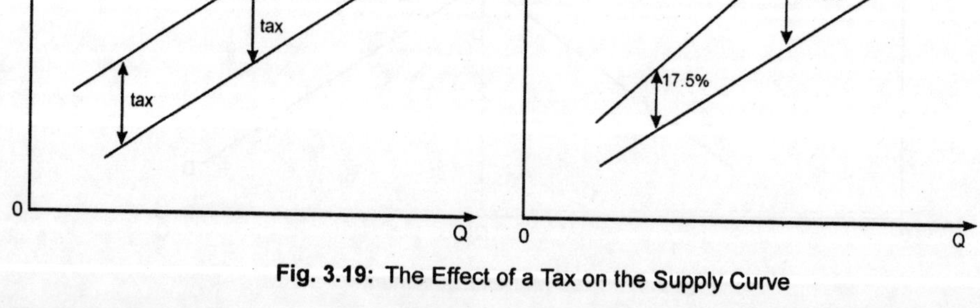

Fig. 3.19: The Effect of a Tax on the Supply Curve

when the rate of VAT (value added tax) is 17.5%.

• The (short-run) Incidence of a Specific Tax

The incidence of taxation means whom the tax falls upon. The formal (legal) incidence of a tax is upon the person who is legally responsible for paying it. In the case of alcohol, for example, the tax is legally paid by the producer or importer. But, since the demand for alcohol it is possible that some or all of the tax may be passed on to the consumer, in which case the incidence is said to be shifted wholly or partly to the consumer.

It is often thought that if the government imposes a tax upon a good, the price of that good will immediately rise by the amount of the tax. This may not always be true.

Consider what might happen if a tax of £1 per bottle were imposed on wine. If the price were to be put up by £1 then the producer would *wish* to sell output Q_0 at a price of P_{01} (point D on S_1); where $P_{01} = P_0 + £1$. But, at P_{01}, there is a fall in demand for wine to point C on the demand curve D (consumer may substitute wine for beer or soft drinks). At a price of P_{01} there is an excess supply of wine (points C to D) in Fig. 3.20. The new equilibrium price is at P_1.

The wine seller may partly absorb the tax and increase the price by less than £1. Thus, the incidence of the tax may be divided between consumer and the producer. This situation is shown in Fig. 3.20. We can see that the original price of a bottle of wine was P_0 and that Q_0 bottles were sold. The imposition of a £1 tax might be expected to increase the price by £1 (to P_{0_1} - point D on S_1). We have seen that this is not actually the case. The new equilibrium is P_1 = (P_0 plus a proportion of the tax). The price has not increased by the full amount of the tax. Thus, the incidence of the tax has been passed on partly to the consumer (B to E_1) and is partly borne by the producers (A to B). The amount of revenue received by the government depends upon the tax, in this case £1, multiplied by the number of unit sold (Q_1).

The extent of the tax that will be passed on to the consumer will be determined by the elasticity of demand and supply—the more inelastic the demand, the greater will be the incidence upon the consumer. If the demand curve was vertical, the entire tax would be passed on to the consumer. But the more elastic is the demand, greater will be the incidence on the producer. For example, if the demand is perfectly elastic the entire tax will have to be borne by the producer.

• Subsidies

If the government subsidizes a product by giving an amount of money to the producers

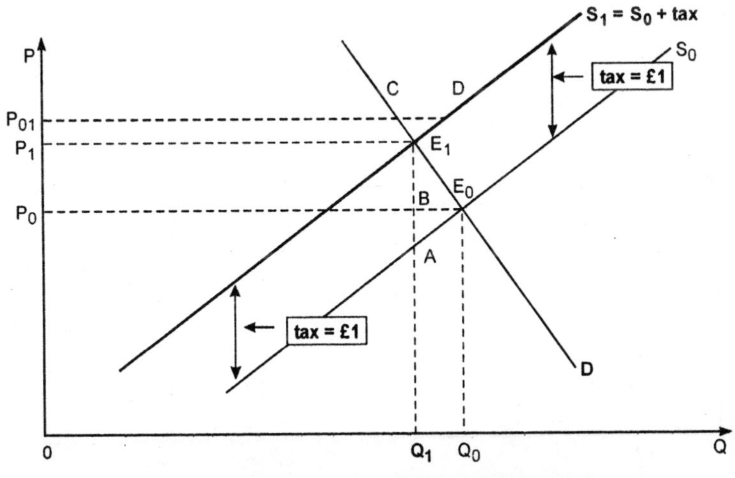

Fig. 3.20: The Incidence of an Indirect Tax

then, for each unit they sell, the supply curve will shift down by the amount of the tax. The benefit of the subsidy will be split between the producer and consumer. The division will, again, depend on the elasticity of demand. It is the opposite situation to the one illustrated in Fig. 3.20 (we would start at E_1 and end up at E_0).

- **Government Tax Revenue**

If the government wishes to raise the tax revenue, it will increase taxes on those commodities which have inelastic demands. If the government were to increase the tax on those products with elastic demands the revenue it collects will actually decline. To increase revenue from those products with elastic demand curves it would do best to lower the tax.

- **Demand, Supply Analysis and Comparative Static**

The demand and supply analyses developed so far has been concerned with the formation of an equilibrium price. Any change in market condition has moved us to a new equilibrium. For example, the analysis predicts that an increase in supply will lead to a new equilibrium at a lower price with a greater quantity supplied. We arrived at this conclusion by comparing one static equilibrium with another. This method of analysis is known as comparative static.

If a time element is introduced into the analysis, we need a theory which will explain the movement of prices with respect to time. Such a study is called a dynamic analysis. We may indeed find when we use dynamic analysis that a market may never be in a state of equilibrium. This does not mean that we should give up comparative static analysis. Comparative static is a useful way to explain changes in market and is the basis for our understanding of the forces involved.

- **Towards a Dynamic Theory of Market Prices**

A simple dynamic theory of market prices will be developed by considering the Cobweb theorem. We would normally say that supply is a function of market price which is written as: $Q_t^s = f(P_t)$, where t is the time period we are considering. However, it may be pointed out that for some products, especially agricultural ones, it is the price in the previous period which determines the supply. For example, farmers will look at this year's price in determining how much crop to plant next year. This can be written as: $Q_t^s = f(P_{t-1})$, which means that the supply in the present period (Q_t^s) is a function of the price in the previous period (P_{t-1}).

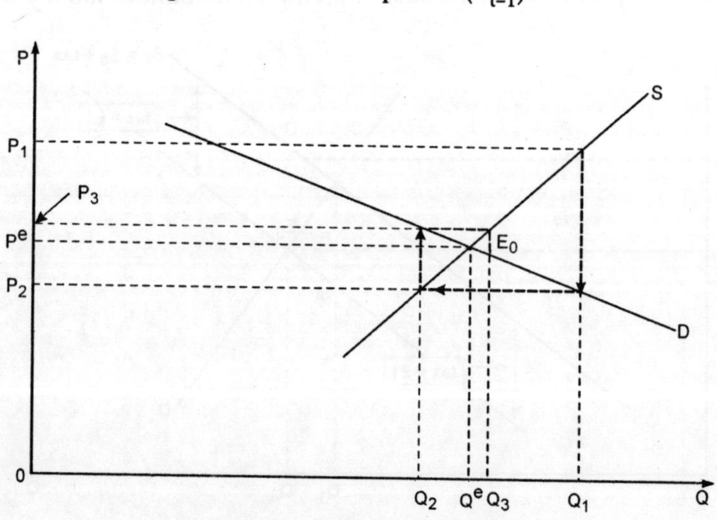

Fig. 3.21: A Converging (Stable) Cobweb

Let us consider the effect of this in the market situation as in Fig. 3.21, where P^e and Q^e represent the equilibrium situtation for barley. Suppose we start in year 1 with disequilibrium price of P_1. The quantity supplied in year 2 (which depends on the price in year 1) will be Q_1. To sell an amount Q_1, the price in year 2 has to be P_2—determined by the demand for quantity Q_1. This price will bring forth a supply of Q_2 in year 3. This quantity can be sold at the price P_3 and this will bring forth a supply of Q_3 in year 4. This process will continue year after year, tracing out a cobweb pattern on the figure, with the market slowly approaching the equilibrium position (P^e, Q^e) as in Fig. 3.21. This is an example of stable cobweb. In this situation, other things being equal, equilibrium will eventually be reached. This is brought about when the demand curve is flatter than the supply curve. As price changes, the absolute quantity demanded changes more than the absolute quantity supplied.

Fig. 3.22 shows a divergent or unstable Cobweb. This is brought about because the supply curve is flatter than the demand curve; the quantity supplied responds more to price changes than the quantity demanded. When there is an excess supply, a large price fall is necessary to call forth the required demand. This price fall causes a larger reduction in the next year's supply (because supply is more responsive to price). Next year, there is a large shortage and a very sharp price increase is necessary to reduce quantity demanded to the level of the available supply. This process again causes a very large increase in quantity supplied the following year, and so it goes on, in a series of alternating periods of ever-increasing surpluses and shortages.

In the case of an unstable equilibrium, the oscillations get larger and larger. There is nothing in the theory, so far, to say that these oscillations will not become infinitely large. In practice, it is unlikely to happen; the oscillation will tend to reach limits. A full theory of such a market would require an analysis of these limits, which we are not discussing here. We have established the following: Although, the price system does allocate resources, it does not cause adjustments to occur smoothly. Where supply shortages are long and delayed, reactions are large, fluctuations around equilibrium are possible with alternatively too much and too little being produced.

The Cobweb model can be difficult and much more complicated. To handle any difficulties and complications mathematical analysis is required.

• Government and Markets

We have seen that the forces of demand and supply acting through the market system can

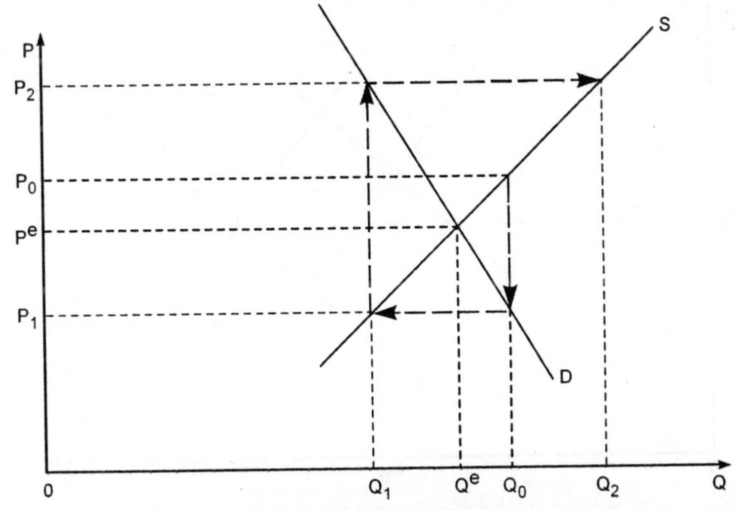

Fig. 3.22: A Divergent (Unstable) Cobweb

solve the basic economic problems. We also know that no country is a pure private market economy. In addition to market forces, there are many other forces that affect the allocation of resources. One of the most important non-market forces is government intervention. We will look at the impact on markets of various forms of governmental intervention. In doing so, we shall show some application of supply and demand analysis. Agriculture, even in developed countries, is not left to unregulated market forces because, in the absence of any intervention, the operation of market forces results in a low and unstable income situtation for the farming community.

We shall then show that the concept of price elasticity of demand and supply are helpful in understanding the intervention of the government.

Finally, we considered the impact of government policies which control free market prices.

• The Agricultural Problem

It seems that agriculture approximates to a perfectly competitive market situation where there are:

1. A large number of producers producing a relatively
2. homogeneous products for which
3. world price is the ruling market price
4. No individual producer and consumer can influence the market price
5. and, thus, are pricetakers

Yet we can see that agriculture is an industry in which governments (of any persuasion) have consistently intervened in order to support farm prices and agricultural incomes. Here we examine the causes of fluctuating prices and incomes, and compare some of the ways in which governments can intervene to create greater stability.

Agriculture has experienced two closely related problems. Firstly, there has been a long-run downward trend in agricultural prices relative to the prices of manufactures and services (although there have been large increases in 2007-08), and secondly, agricultural prices and incomes have been unstable. The long-run trend is explained by shifts in agricultural demand and supply curves through time, while the short-run instability results from the inelastic nature of agricultural demand and supply.

• The Long-run Downward Trend in the Relative Price of Agricultural Commodities

In Fig. 3.23, the equilibrium price and output

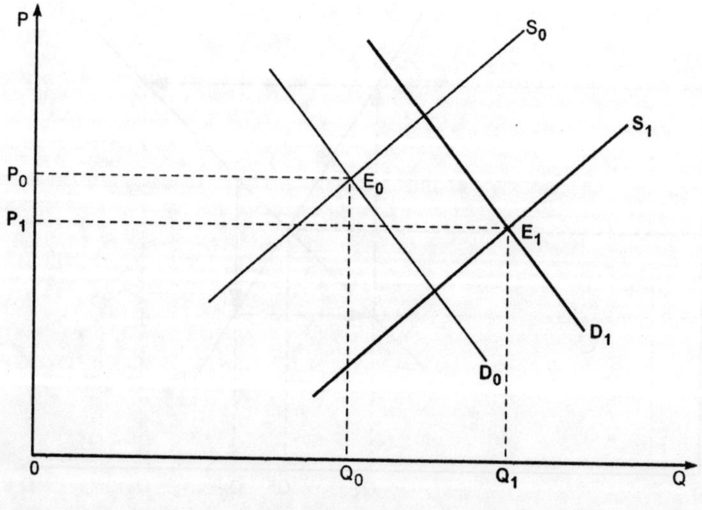

Fig. 3.23: The Long-Term Downward Trend in the Relative Price of Agricultural Products

of food in an earlier period is shown at E_0. Over time, both the supply and the demand have increased, but the supply curve has shifted further to the right. Thus the new equilibrium at E_1 represents a higher output at a lower price. The shift in the demand curve is explained mainly by an increase in the populaton and higher incomes. Improvements in technology, such as the introduction of machinery and fertilizers, have rapidly increased farm yields, thereby causing much greater long-run increase in supply.

• Price Instability

The instability of farm prices is caused by low short-run elasticities of supply and demand together with random fluctuations in harvest. The short-run supply curve is almost vertical or completely inelastic. We know that, once the crop is harvested, it will be sold for whatever price it will bring. The short-run supply curve S_0, as in Fig. 3.24(a), represents supply curve in a normal year. However, the supply curve can shift from year to year depending on weather conditions and other factors outside the control of farmers. The size of resulting price fluctuations will depend upon the elasticity of demand. Demand for food is price and income-inelastic because food is a necessity. So significant fluctuation in price will occur as the supply curve shifts up and down the relatively inelastic demand curve.

• Fluctuation in Agricultural Incomes

If the demand for agricultural products is elastic, then, a fall in price causes a rise in farm income, but when the demand is inelastic—the usual case, a rise in price causes a rise in farm income. Thus income falls when price falls.

Following a bad harvest, the supply curve (S_0) in Fig. 3.24(a) shifts to S_2 and agricultural incomes ($P_2 \times Q_2$) increase as they are represented by the area $0P_2BQ_2 > 0P^*YQ^*$ (assuming an inelastic demand curve {D}). In the event of a good harvest, the supply curve shifts to the right to S_1 and farm income declines to the area $0P_1AQ_1$. Thus, paradoxically, a farmer may benefit more from a bad harvest than from a good one, when demand is inelastic.

• Government Policy to Stabiliaze Prices

If the government wishes to stabilize the price of food at P*, then the government must buy up the amount $Q_1 - Q^*$ in the event of the good

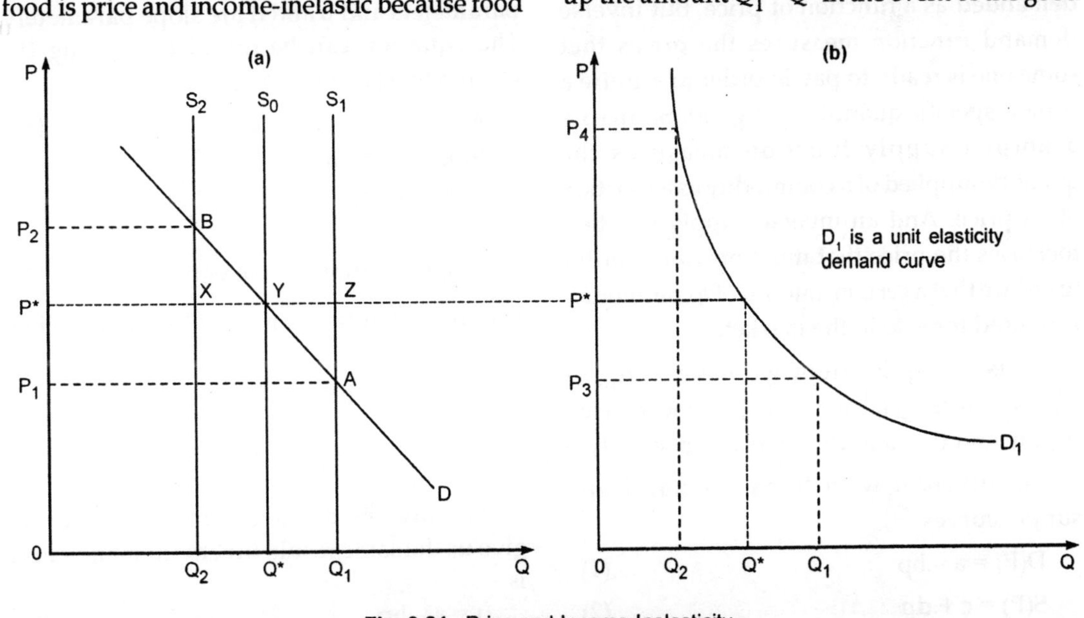

Fig. 3.24: Price and Income Inelasticity

harvest, to prevent price falling to P_1.If in the following year, a bad harvest occurs, the government will supplement supply by releasing food into the market from its stocks of an amount $Q^* - Q_2$. This will prevent the price from rising to P_2. Provided that agricultural products can be stored, and that the government is prepared to meet the cost of storage, and the good and bad harvests can be evenly divided – then the price can be stabilized at P*. If the government wanted to make the policy self-financing, it could buy at a lower price and sell at a higher price. Price would now be stabilized within a range and the costs of storage could be met from the difference between buying and selling prices.

- **Stabilization of Agricultural Income**

The policy described above is an example of buffer stock scheme. Although such a policy successfully stabilizes price, it does not necessarily stabilise the incomes of farmers. Consider Fig. 3.24(b). If the target income of farmers is $P^*Q^* = TR^*$, then a unit elastic demand curve (D_1) will tell us what price the government will have to pay farmers to stabilize their incomes. (Along a unit elasticity demand curve $|\%\Delta P| = |\%\Delta Q|$. {where '|' is the absolute value operator}). If the quantity produced falls to Q_2 the unit elastic demand curve tells us that the price paid should be P_4: Then $P_4.Q_2 = TR^*$. In a similar way if the quantity rises to Q_1 the price paid should be P_3:Then $P_3 \times Q_1 = TR^*$.

APPENDIX

Inverse Demand and Supply Curves

Demand curve indicate the optimum quantity demanded as a function of price. But inverse demand function measures the prices that some one is ready to pay in order to acquire a certain specific quantity of a good. Similarly, a normal supply function measures the quantity supplied of a commodity as a function of its price. And an inverse supply function increases the price that must prevail in order to ensure that a certain amount of a commodity is offered for sale in the market.

Thus, in equilibrium we have: $P_s(q_0) = P_d(q_0)$, where $P_s(q_0)$ and $P_d(q_0)$ are the increase supply and demand functions, respectively.

Equilibrium with linear demand and supply curves:

$$D(P) = a - bp \quad ....(1)$$

$$S(P) = c + dp \quad ....(2)$$

The coefficient a and c are intercept parameters and b and d are slope parameters. The equation can be found by solving the following equation:

$$a - bp = C + dp \quad ....(3)$$

Since in equation

$$D(P) = S(P) \quad ....(4)$$

From equation (4) we get: $P_s = \frac{a-c}{d+b}$. The equation quantity demanded (and supplied) is

$$D(P_0) = a - bP_0$$

$$= a - b\frac{a-c}{d+b} = \frac{ad+bc}{b+d} \quad ...(5)$$

The inverse demand and supply curves give us the same result. Inverse demand curve is

$$q = a - bp \quad ....(6)$$

which indicates at what price is quantity q demand. Equation (6) is obtained by substituting q for D(P) and solving for P. From equation (6) we derive $P_d(q) = \frac{q-c}{b}$. Similarly, from equation (6) we also get inverse supply curve, $P_s(q) = \frac{q-c}{b}$. Equating the demand and supply prices and solving for equation quantity we get

$$P_d(q) = \frac{a-q}{b} = \frac{q-c}{d} = P_s(q)$$

$$\text{or} \quad q = \frac{ad+bc}{b+d} \quad ...(7)$$

This equation gives the same values for both the equation price and quantity as equation (5).

For example Demand function and Supply function and the determination of equation price and quantity.

Demand function: $q_d = 80 - 2P$ ....(1)

Supply function: $q_s = 8 + 6P$ ....(2)

Equilibrium condition: $q_d = q_s$ ....(3)

This system of simultaneous equations can be solved to give us the following results.

Using demand and supply function, we get (1) + (2)

$q_d = q_s$

or, $80 - 2P = 8 + 6P$ or, $8P = 72$

or, $P = 9$, $\therefore P = 9$

$\therefore q_d = 80 - 2 \times 9 = 62$

Similarly using supply function (2)

$q_s = 8 + 6 \times 9 = 62$

In general, the demand and supply can be expressed as:

$q_d = a - bp$; $q_s = c + dp$;

$b < 0, d > 0$. $q_d = q_s$.

So find the equation price, we require that: $a - bp = c + dp$.

Rearranging gives us $a - c = p(b+d)$

or, $P = \frac{a-c}{b+d}$. Now equation quantity can be found using demand equation, we get

$$q_d = a - b\left[\frac{a-c}{b+d}\right]$$

$$= \frac{ab+ad-ab+bc}{b+d} = \frac{ad+bc}{b+d}.$$

QUESTIONS

1. (a) Demand and supply data for Washing Machine are given below. Plot the supply and demand curves and find the equilibrium price and quantity.

Price	10	12	14	16	18	20
Quantity: demanded	10	9	8	7	6	5
Quantity: supplied	3	4	5	6	7	8

(b) What is the excess demand and supply when price is (i) 12; and (ii) 20? Describe the price movements induced by position (i) and (ii).

(c) What happens to the demand curve for washing machine if the price of washing powder rises? Show in a demand-supply diagram how the equilbrium price and quantiy of washing machine changes.

2. Suppose you are a sheep farmer. Give three examples of a change that would reduce the supply of wool. Did you use a fall in the price of wool as one of your example? Is it a valid example?

ANSWERS

1. (a) Equilibrium price is £17 and quantity is 6.5.

   (b) Excess demand = 5, and price rises
   (ii) Excess supply = 3, and price falls.

   (c) Demand curve for washing machines shifts downwards. The equilibrium price and quantity of washing machines fall.

2. Drought, disease, wild dogs – all can shift supply curve down.

   Price falls move farmers down a given supply curve, not a fall in supply.

CHAPTER 4

ELASTICITY

KEY TERMS

Elasticity: The responsiveness of one variable (Q) to the change in another (P), both changes expressed in percentages. The elasticity of Q with respect to P is the percentage change in Q for every 1% change in P.

Own Price Elasticity of Demand (Ed): The responsiveness of quantity demanded of good X (Q_x) to a change in the price of good X (P_x).

Income Elasticity of Demand: The responsiveness of the quantity demanded to a change in income.

Cross-elasticity of Demand: The responsiveness of the quantity demanded to a change in the price of another good.

Price Elasticity of Demand: The responsiveness of the quantity demanded to a change in the price.

Price Elasticity of Supply: The responsiveness of the quantity supplied to a change in the price.

We would now like to extend and deepen our analysis of markets, and devote this chapter to an understanding of another important tool of economic analysis: that of elasticity. In this chapter we are going to examine various types of elasticity.

Elasticity is defined as the responsiveness of one variable (Q) to the change in another (P), both change expressed in percentages. The elasticity of Q with respect to P is the percentage change in Q for every 1% change in P.

The own price elasticity of demand of good

$$Z\ (Edz) = \frac{\%\Delta \text{ in quantity of good Z } (Q_z)}{\%\Delta \text{ in price of good Z } (P_z)}.$$

Demand and supply theory is essential for an understanding of economics. It has been argued that certain relationships exist between price and quantity demanded and supplied, other things remaining constant. But if price changes, by how much does quantity demanded or supplied change? It could be that a large change in prices would have more or less effect on quantity demanded or supplied. Theoretically it is impossible to say exactly what will happen in cases like these. Each product may have a different price-quantity reaction. It is a matter for economists to collect evidence and calculate this relationship.

- **Own Price Elasticity of Demand (Ed)**

Is a measure of the sensitivity of the quantity demanded of good Z to the change in price of good Z. Consider Fig. 4.1:

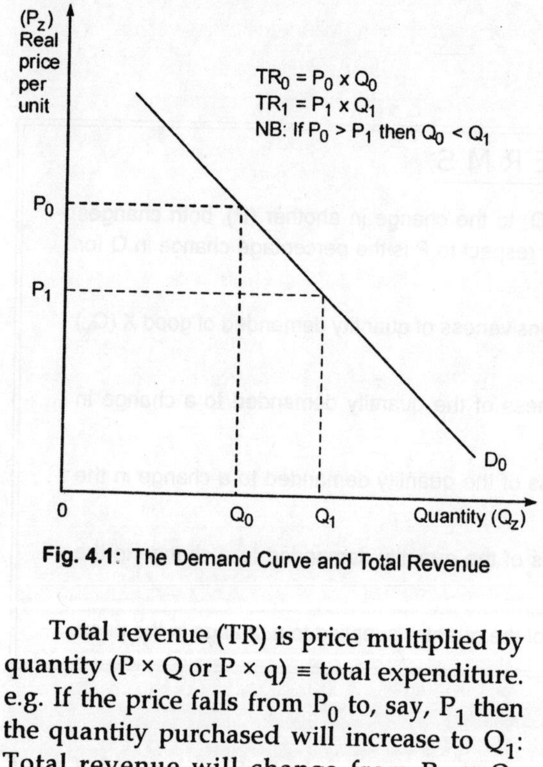

Fig. 4.1: The Demand Curve and Total Revenue

Total revenue (TR) is price multiplied by quantity (P × Q or P × q) ≡ total expenditure. e.g. If the price falls from P_0 to, say, P_1 then the quantity purchased will increase to Q_1: Total revenue will change from $P_0 \times Q_0$ (= TR_0) to $P_1 \times Q_1$ (= TR_1).

Consider the effect of a fall in price:

1. Revenue will fall when price falls, *but*
2. Since the quantity sold will always increase (except, in extremely rare occasions, when we consider a positively sloped demand curve) then this will increase revenue.

The relationship between the percentage change in quantity and the percentage change in price is known as elasticity.

We are interested in percentage change because taking 5p off a loaf of bread costing 50p is of a very different magnitude than taking 5p off a washing machine costing £300 (10% versus 0.017%).

Since TR = P × Q

then, %ΔTR = %ΔP + %ΔQ

N.B: If %ΔP < 0, then %ΔQ > 0, and vice-versa.

Consider a price fall:

Will the loss in revenue from a fall in price be:

1. Less than the increase in revenue brought about by an increase in quantity?
2. Greater than the increase in revenue brought about by an increase in quantity?
3. Equal to the increase in revenue brought about by an increase in quantity?

If TR increases when price falls then this part of a demand curve is elastic: $TR_1 > TR_0$.

If TR decrease when price falls then this part of a demand curve is **inelastic**: $TR_1 < TR_0$.

If TR is unchanged when price falls then this part of a demand curve has an **elasticity** of one and $TR_1 = TR_0$.

Since %ΔTR = %ΔP + %ΔQ

If TR increases when price falls then

%ΔQ > %ΔP and

$$\frac{|\%\Delta \text{ in quantity}|}{|\%\Delta \text{ in price}|} > 1 \text{ and } |E_d| > 1.$$

If $|E_d| > 1$, then the demand curve is elastic.

If TR decreases when price falls then

%ΔQ < %ΔP and

$$\frac{|\%\Delta \text{ in quantity}|}{|\%\Delta \text{ in price}|} < 1 \text{ and } |E_d| < 1.$$

If $|E_d| < 1$, then the demand curve is inelastic.

The own price elasticity of demand of good Z (Ed_z)

$$= \frac{\%\Delta \text{ in quantity of good Z } (Q_z)}{\%\Delta \text{ in price of good Z } (P_z)}$$

If $|E_d| > 1$ then $|\%\Delta Q| > |\%\Delta P|$ along an arc of the demand curve or at a point on the demand curve, then the demand for a product is ELASTIC.

If $|E_d| < 1$ then $|\%\Delta Q| < |\%\Delta P|$ along an arc of the demand curve or at a point on the demand curve, then the demand for a product is INELASTIC.

If $|E_d| = 1$ then $|\%\Delta Q| = |\%\Delta P|$ along an arc of the demand curve or at a point on the demand curve, then the demand for a product has UNIT ELASTICITY. The price elasticity of demand is always negative but we put an extra negative sign to make it positive for methematical use of concept.

• Total Expenditure and Price Elasticity

If we multiply the price of a good by the number of units consumed, then we measure the total expenditure of consumers. The total expenditure of consumers will have the same value as the total revenue received by the suppliers of the good.

There is an important relationship between total expenditure on a good and price elasticity of demand. Ths relationship is summarized thus:

$E_d > 1$ a rise in price leads to a fall in total expenditure and, hence, total revenue.

$E_d > 1$ a fall in price leads to a rise in total expenditure and, hence, total revenue.

$E_d < 1$ a rise in price leads to a rise in total expenditure and, hence, total revenue.

$E_d < 1$ a fall in price leads to a fall in total expenditure and, hence, total revenue.

$E_d = 1$ a rise or fall in price leaves total expenditure and revenue unchanged.

This tells us that if we look at the total expenditure or revenue before and after a price change, we can say whether demand is elastic (P falls TR increases), inelastic (P falls, TR decreases), or unit elastic (P falls TR is unchanged). Conversely, if we know the elasticity of demand, we can predict whether a price change will increase or decrease total revenue or expenditure.

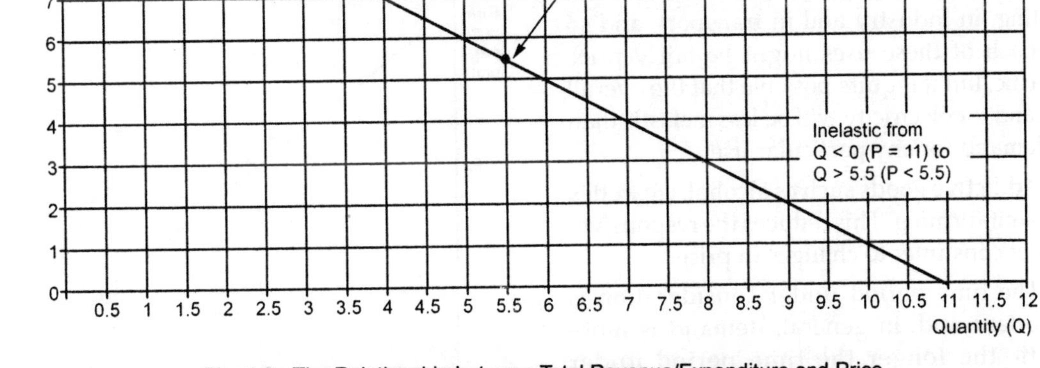

Fig. 4.2: The Relationship between Total Revenue/Expenditure and Price

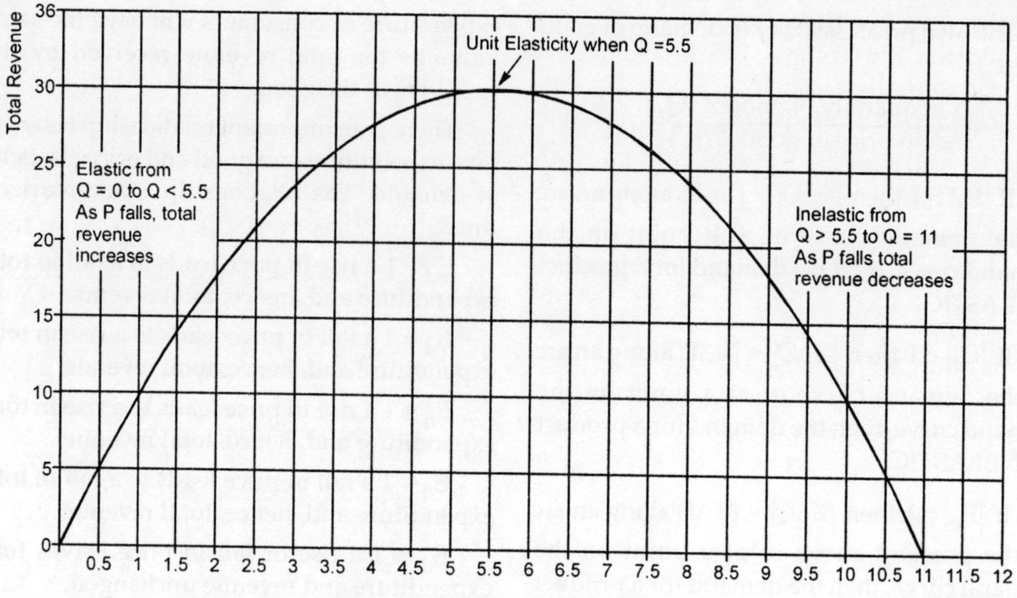

Fig. 4.3: Total Revenue and Elasticity

The main determinant of price elasticity is the number of substitutes. The greater the number of substitutes, the greater the elasticity of demand. Another important determinant of elasticity is the proportion of income spent on a good. A family holiday takes up a more substantial part of a family income than a box of matches. The durability of a good might affect demand in some cases.

The number of uses for a good is an important determinant of elasticity in some cases. Where a good has many uses, it is possible that small reaction by consumers purchasing for a particular use can add up to a large overall reaction. For example, electricity has a number of uses. It is used in the home for heating and lighting, in industry and in transport, and so on. Each of these uses might be fairly price inelastic, but it is quite possible that the overall demand for electricity will be less inelastic than its demand for any particular use.

Addictive goods such as alcohol, cigarettes are habit-forming. This reduces the responsiveness of consumer to changes in price.

The time period under consideration is important and, in general, demand is more elastic the longer the time period under consideration. During the oil shocks of the 1970s, the demand for Middle East oil products was fairly inelastic, and the industrialised countries suffered due to their inability to react quickly to price changes. However, since this time alternative sources of energy have been developed, and in the long run, demand has proved to be more elastic than in the short run.

These influences are offered as possibilities, and for many commodities it would be very difficult to define precisely what affects price elasticity of demand. Some of these influences will tend to counteract each other; a very durable good might have a very few substitutes, for instance.

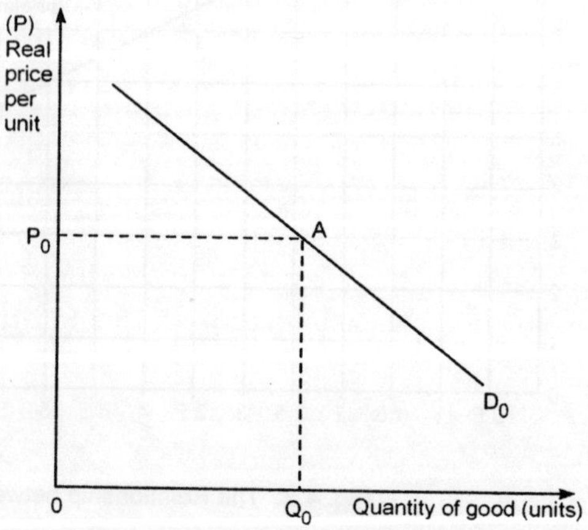

Fig. 4.4: Point Elasticity of Demand

- **Point and Arc Elasticity**
  1. **Point Elasticity:** Point elasticity measures the elasticity at a point. In this case it is measured at point 'A'. At point 'A' the elasticity of demand is

     $$\frac{\Delta Q.P_0}{\Delta P.Q_0}$$

     Note: The slope of the (inverse) demand curve is $\frac{\Delta P}{\Delta Q}$.
  2. **Arc Elasticity:** Arc elasticity measures the elasticity between two point. In this case, between points 'A' and 'B'

     $$E_d = \frac{\%\Delta Q}{\%\Delta P}$$

     where $\%\Delta Q = \frac{Q_1 - Q_0}{Q_0} \times 100$

     $\%\Delta P = \frac{P_1 - P_0}{P_0} \times 100$

     Along a straight-line demand curve (D_0) elasticity varies from infinity to zero.

     At point 'A' Ed = ∞

     At point 'B' Ed = 0

     Halfway along AB the elasticity of demand is 1.

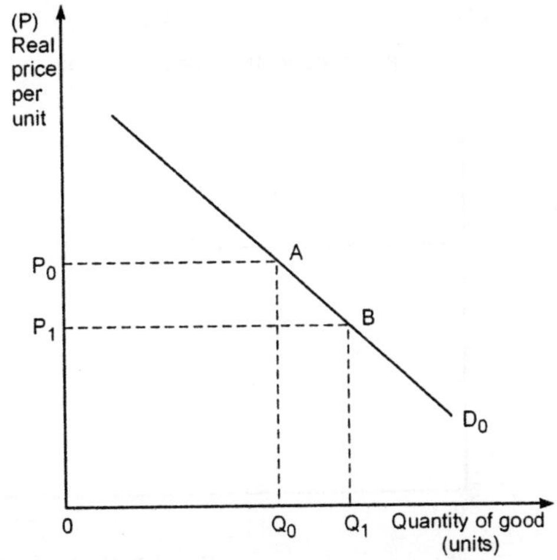

Fig. 4.5: Arc Elasticity of Demand

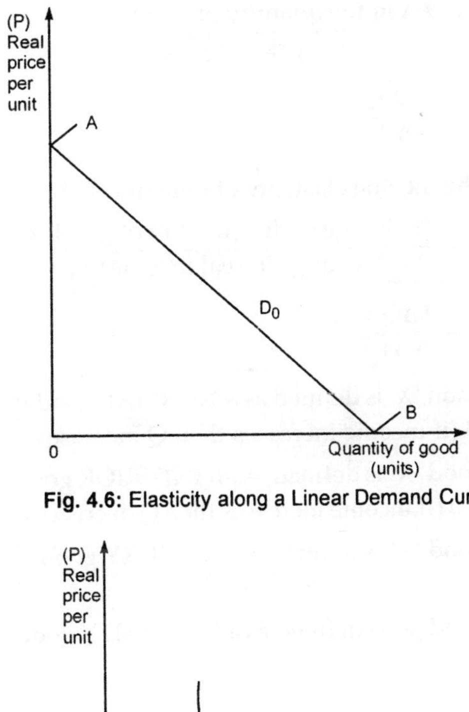

Fig. 4.6: Elasticity along a Linear Demand Curve

- **Unitary Price Elasticity of Demand**

All areas under D_0 have the same value. Line D_0 is known as a rectangular hyperbola [Fig. 4.7]

For example the area $0P_0AQ_0$ is equal to the area $0P_1BQ_1$. A 5% change in price will lead to a 5% change in quantity.

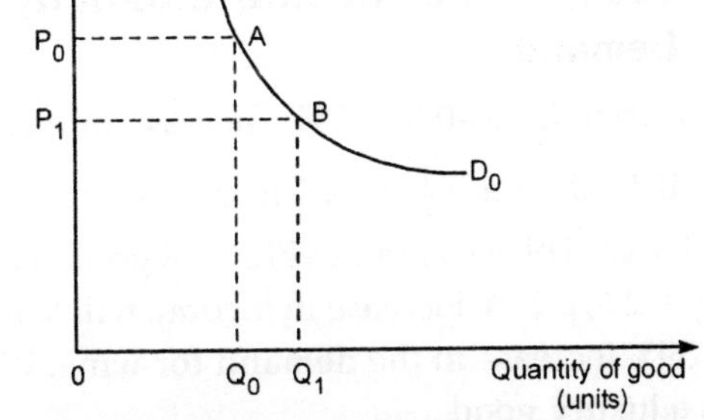

Fig. 4.7: Unit Elastic Demand

- **The Importance of Price Elasticity**

Suppose that the E_d for a company's product is 1.8. If the price is reduced by, say, 10%, then the quantity demanded will increase by 18% and revenue will increase by 8%. As long as costs do not increase by more 8% then profit will increase.

Profit = TR (total revenue) less TC (total cost).

Other Elasticities:

Cross-price elasticity

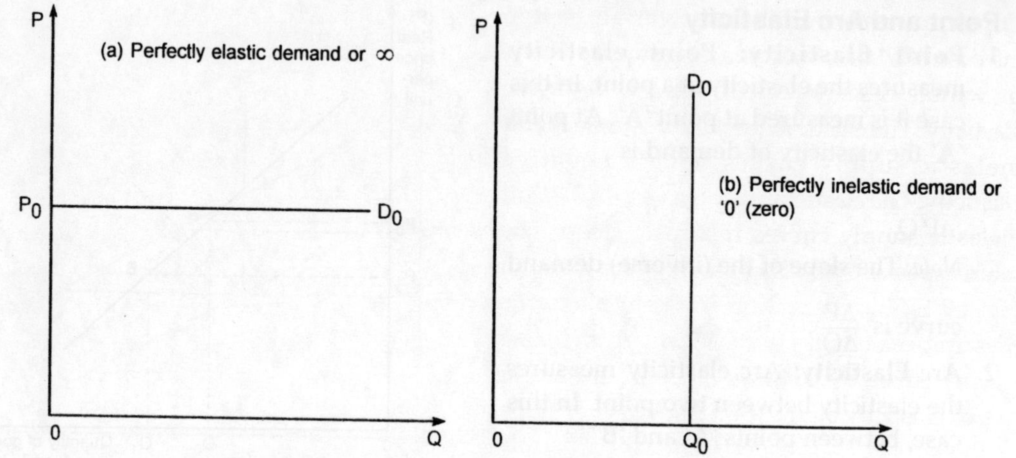

Fig. 4.8: Perfectly Elastic and Inelastic Demand

$$= \frac{\%\Delta \text{ in the quantity of good 'x'}}{\%\Delta \text{ in the price of good 'y'}}$$

$$= \frac{\%\Delta Q_x}{\%\Delta P_y}$$

The income elasticity of demand (E_y)

$$= \frac{\%\text{ change in the quantity of good 'x'}}{\%\text{ change in real income (Y)}}$$

$$= \frac{\%\Delta Q_x}{\%\Delta Y}$$

Good 'X' is defined as a NORMAL good if $E_y > 0$ (if income increases then Q increases)

Good 'X' is defined as an INFERIOR good if $E_y < 0$ (If income increases then Q decreases)

Good 'X' is defined as a LUXURY good if $E_y > 1$

Good 'X' is defined as a NECESSITY good if $E_y < 1$.

- **Uses of the Income Elasticity of Demand**

Tobacco: $E_y = -0.5$; a 15% increase in income will lead to a $7\frac{1}{2}$ % fall in the demand for tobacco. Tobacco is an INFERIOR good. Wine: Ey = 2.6; a 15% increase in income will lead to a 39% increase in the demand for wine. Wine is a luxury good.

- **Inflation and Demand**

If all prices and nominal incomes increase by, say, 'x' percent, then there should be no change in the quantity demanded. There is no money illusion. The relationship between quantity demanded and the variables that affect demand is a homogeneous function of degree zero.

It is only changes in REAL (RELATIVE) prices and real INCOMES that affect the quantity demanded.

- **Elasticity of Supply**

Unlike the demand side, economists consider only one type of supply elasticity, measuring the responsiveness of market supply to changes in the price of the product. The elasticity of supply, E_s, is measured using the formulae:

E_s = Percentage change in quantity supplied/percentage change in price

Or, $E_s = (P \times \Delta Q)/(Q \times \Delta P)$, where P = original price, Q = original quantity supplied, ΔP = change in price, ΔQ = change in quantity.

This appears that the elasticity of supply is identical with the formula of elasticity of demand. However, you will recall that price elasticity of demand is always negative, whereas the price elasticity of supply is normally positive since the supply curve slopes upwards from left to right—except in the case of a backward-bending supply curve, in which case it would have a negative elasticity. The elastic supply curves are flat and inelastic supply curves have a negative elasticity. The elastic supply curves are flat and inelastic supply curves relatively steep. The main types of elasticity of supply are given in Fig. 4.9 'S_0' is a perfectly inelastic supply curve. S_1 is unit-elastic supply curve (any straight line supply curve that passes through the origin has an elasticity of unity—irrespective of slope of the curve). S_2 is a perfectly elastic supply curve.

• Classifying Supply Elasticity

Just as with demand, there are different ranges of elasticity of supply. There are similar ranges of definition of demand elasticity.

If 1% increase in price elicits more than 1% increase in the quantity supplied, we call this elastic supply. The most extreme elastic supply is called perfectly elastic supply. If, conversely, 1% increase in price elicits less than 1% increase in the quantity of goods supplied, we call that an inelastic supply. The most extreme inelastic supply is called perfectly inelastic supply or zero elastic supply.

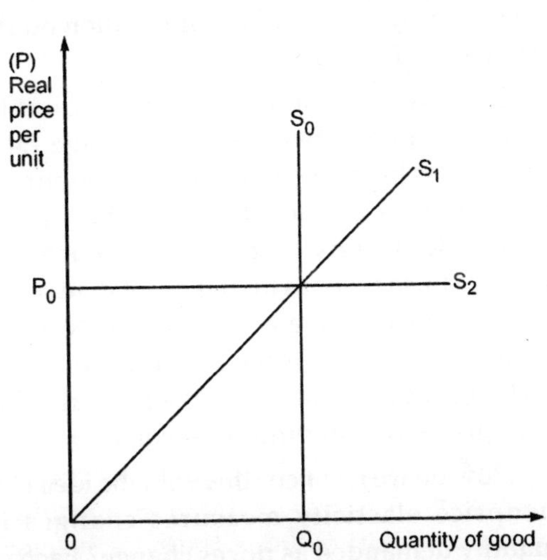

Fig. 4.9: Supply Curves with Different Elasticities

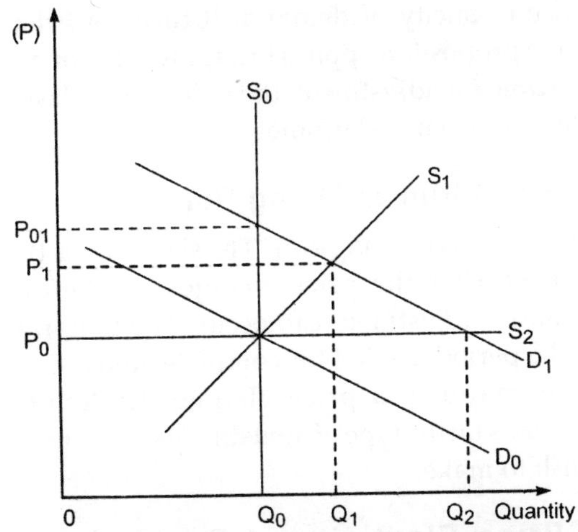

Fig. 4.10: Supply Curves with Different Elasticities

If the percentage change in the quantity supplied is just equal to the percentage change in the price, we call this unit-elastic supply.

In Fig. 4.10, we draw different supply schedules with different elasticities; 'S_0' is a perfectly inelastic supply curve. S_1 is unit-elastic supply curve (any straight line supply curve that passes through the origin has an elasticity of unity—irrespective of slope of the curve). S_2 is a perfectly elastic supply curve. For supply curve S_2 any price increase above the price P_0 leads to an infinite increase in quantity supplied.

The elasticity of supply tells us how the equilibrium price and quantity will change when there is a shift in demand. Fig. 4.10 shows a demand shift from D_0 to D_1. Beginning from equilibrium at P_0, Q_0, a demand shift from D_0 to D_1 leads to a new equilibrium at P_{01}, Q_0 or P_1, Q_1 or P_0, Q_2 depending on the elasticity of supply. The more inelastic is supply, the more the demand increase leads to a higher price rather than higher quantity. In extreme cases, the move from P_0 to P_{01} reflects only a price increase and the move from Q_0 to Q_2 reflects only a quantity increase.

• Price Elasticity of Supply and Length of Time for Adjustment

We pointed out earlier that the longer the time period allowed for adjustment, the greater the price elasticity of demand. It turns out that same propositon applies to supply. The longer the time for adjustment, the more price-elastic the supply curve becomes:

• Short-Run and Long-Run

How long is the long-run? The short-run is the period after the price changes but before quantity adjustment can occur. The long-run is the period needed for complete adjustment of demand to a price change. Its length depends on the type of adjustments consumers wish to make.

• Price Elasticity of Demand and Supply

Short-run and long-run: The price elasticity of demand varies with time in which consumer can adjust their spending patterns with price changes. The most dramatic price change of the last 40 years, the oil price rise of 1973-74, caught many households with a new but fuel-inefficient car. At first, they expected that the higher oil price would not be sustained. When they found that it would not be of a temporary nature, they then started to plan for fuel-efficient cars. But in countries like the US, few small cars were yet available. In the short-run, households were stuck. Unless they could rearrange their lifestyles to reduce car use, they had to pay the higher petrol prices.

Over the longer period, consumers had time to sell their large cars and buy cars with a better fuel economy, or to move from the distant suburbs closer to their place of work. Over this period of time, they could reduce the quantity of petrol demanded much more than their initial savings. The price elasticity of demand is lower in the short-run than in the long-run when there is more scope to substitute other goods. This result is very general. Even if addicted smokers cannot adjust to a rise in the price of cigarettes fewer young people start smoking and gradually the number of smokers fall.

How long is the long-run: Demand responses to a change in the price of chocolate should be completed within a few months, but the full adjustment to changes in the price of petrol or cigarettes may take many years.

• Using Income Elasticity of Demand

Income elasticity helps us forecast the pattern of consumer demand as the economy grows and people get richer. Suppose real income grows by 15% over the next five years. The estimates of demand imply that it is likely that demand for tobacco will fall, but the demand for wines and spirits will rise substantially. The growth prospects of these two industries would be very different. These forecasts will affect decisions by firms about whether to build new factories and government projections of tax revenue from cigarettes and alcohol.

Similarly, as poor countries get richer, they demand more luxuries such as televisions, washing machines, and cars.

• Inflation and Demand

Elasticity measures the response of quantity demanded to separate variations in three factors – the own price, the price of related goods, and income.

We know the distinction between nominal variables, measured in market prices, and in real variables, which adjusts for inflation when comparing measurements at different dates. We now examine the effect of inflation on the behaviour of demand.

Suppose all nominal variables double. Every good costs twice as much, wage rates are twice as high, and so on. Whatever bundle of goods was previously affordable is still affordable. Goods cost twice as much but income is also twice as high. The relative prices between goods remain unchanged. Nothing has really changed. Demand behaviour will be unchanged by a doubling of the normal value of all prices and all forms of income.

How do we reconcile this with the idea that ownprice elasticity measures changes in quantity demanded as prices change? Each of the elasticities (own price, cross-price and income) measures the effect of changing that variable holding constant all other determinants of demand. When all income and all prices are simultaneously changing, the definition of elasticity warns us that it is incorrect to examine the effect of one variable, such as own price elasticity on quantity demanded. We can decompose the change in quantity demanded into three components – the effect of changes in the own price alone plus the effect of changes in the price of related goods, and the effect of changes of incomes. When all nominal variables change by the same proportion, the sum of these three effects is exactly zero.

• Who Pays the Tax

By spending and taxing, the government affects the resource allocation in the economy. By taxing cigarettes, the government can reduce smoking and thereby improve health and also increase revenue – which is one of the objectives of imposing taxes. By taxing fuel it can discourage pollution, by taxing income earned from work, the government affects the amount of time people want to work. Taxes loom large in the working of the mixed economy and have a profound effect on the way society allocates its scarce resources.

There are two types of commodity taxes: specific and ad-valorem taxes. First we discuss what is called specific taxes, those that specify a particular amount, such as £5 per bottle of vodka. We show how the effect of a specific tax is related to the slopes of supply and demand curves. Secondly, we show how this argument is related to ad-valorem taxes that are measured as a percentage of the commodity value. For example, VAT is levied at the UK at 17.5% of the value of the good or services. Just as specific taxes are related to slopes of demand and supply curves in particular units, so ad-valorem taxes are related to elasticities of demand and supply, which are expressed in percentages. Either way, what we want to know is who ends up paying the tax. Suppose for simplicity we imagine a packet of cigarettes costs £1 (P_0 = £1) and the government imposes a specific tax of 50p per packet. D_0 smokers end up paying the tax, or is it borne by cigarette producers? How much of the tax can producers pass on to the consumer? We will show that this depends on the slopes (elasticities) of the demand and supply curves.

The incidence of a tax describes who eventually bears the burden of it. Fig. 4.11 and 4.12 below plot the (after-tax) price to the consumer on the vertical axis. D_0 shows the demand curve, which determines the price smokers have to pay for a particular quantity. Since the price received by the producers is

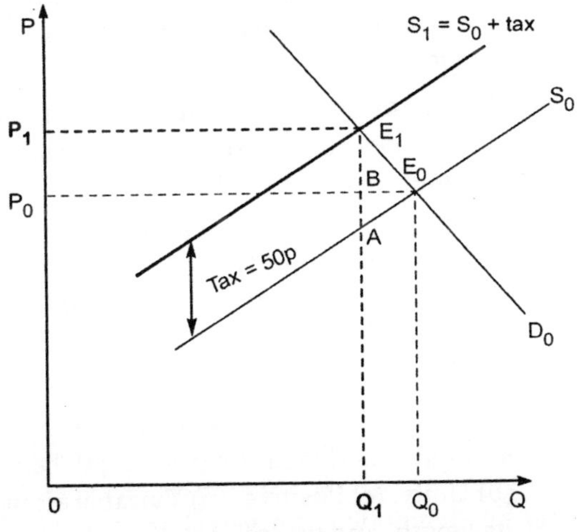

Fig. 4.11: The Incidence of an Indirect Tax

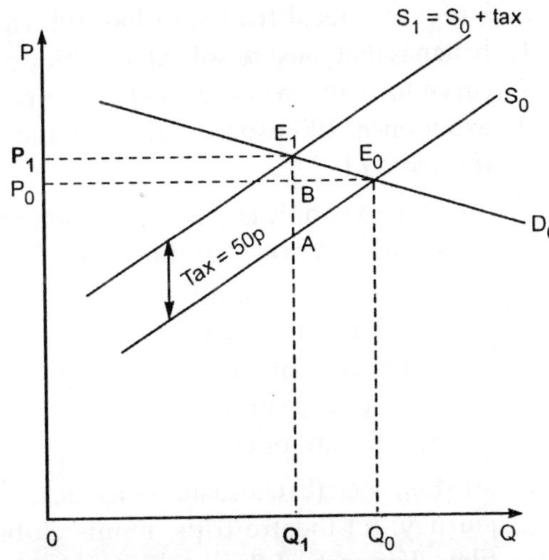

Fig. 4.12: The Incidence of Indirect Taxation

the price consumers pay minus the 50p tax per packet, the effect of the tax is to shift the supply curve from S_0 to S_1 (= S_0 + tax) in both diagrams.

Each possible quanity supplied depends upon the price received by the producer, which will be the same as before only if consumer prices are 50p higher, that is why we must shift the supply curve up by 50p.

In Fig. 4.10, with a flat supply curve and steep demand curve, the tax is borne mainly by consumers. Point E_1 is *nearly* 50p higher than point E_0. Since the demand is price inelastic producers can pass on most of the tax in the form of higher prices. Supply is price-elastic, so the price received by producers cannot fall much. We will assume that P_1 = £1.45 and this is the price paid by consumers.

Producers have to pay the government 50p in tax so they will receive 95p a packet (£1.45 less 50p). Prior to the imposition of the tax they were receiving £1 per packet. Effectively, they are paying 0.05p in tax (points A to B in Fig. 4.10). The government will be receiving £0.5 × Q_1.

In Fig. 4.11, with a flat demand and steep supply curves, most of the tax is born by cigarette producers. Demand is price-elastic, so it is difficult to pass on the tax in higher prices. Supply is price inelastic, producers hardly cut back even though the price they receive has fallen substantially (by nearly 50p). Consumers pay a price of P_1(= £1.05) per packet and 5p per packet in tax (B to E_1 in Fig. 4.11). Producers pay £0.45p a packet in tax (points A to B in Fig. 4.11). The government will be receiving £0.5 × Q_1. The key implication is that the incidence of a tax has nothing to do with who initially hands over the tax to the government. The imposition of a specific tax has affected the equilibrium price and quantity (from P_0, Q_0 to P_1, Q_1). These induced effects may be large or small, depending on the slope of the supply and demand curves.

However, since Q_1 in Fig. 4.11 is less than Q_1 in Fig. 4.10 it is the government's interest (if they wish to maximize their tax income) to tax goods that have a low price elasticity of demand (goods that have a demand curve that is price inelastic).

QUESTIONS

1. Suppose a local fruit stall has 100 ripe bananas that must be sold at once. Supply curve for bananas is vertical. From past experience, 100 bananas are demanded if price is £1.
   (a) Draw a supply and demand diagram, showing market equilibrium.
   (b) The demand elasticity is 0.5. Fruit stall has found that 10 bananas are rotten and cannot be sold. Draw the new supply curve. What is the new equilibrium price?
2. (a) Milk, beer; (b) chocolate, chicken, train journey; (c) theatre trips, tennis clubs, films. For each of the categories do you expect demand to be elastic or inelastic? Then rank the elasticities within each category. Explain your answer.
3. Where, along a straight-line demand curve, does consumer spending reach a maximum? Explain why?
4. In 1974 the UK consumers spent £1.3 million on bread and cereals. In 2001 they spent over £5 million on bread and cereals, yet bread is an inferior good. Explain.
5. The elasticity of a downward sloping straight line demand curve is: (a) Zero, (b) Unity, (c) Positive, (d) Variable along its length, and (e) Infinity.

ANSWERS

1. (a) Vertical supply curve, and downward-slopping demand curve. (b) To sell 10% less, raise price by 20% to £120. Supply curve is vertical and the equilibrium price now is £0.90.
2. (a) Inelastic, (b) More elastic, and (c) more elastic still.
3. Where demand elasticity is 1. Below this point on the demand curve, demand is inelastic: high prices add to high revenue. Above this point, demand is elastic, and lower prices add to revenue. If the stadium is free to operate, maximizing profits means maximizing revenue.
4. These data are for nominal—not real—spending on bread, which fell as real income rose.
5. The elasticity of a downward-sloping demand curve is variable along its length, infinity where it hit the vertical axis, and zero where it hit the horizontal axis.

CHAPTER 5

RISK AND UNCERTAINTY

KEY TERMS

- Risk Aversion and Diminishing Marginal Utility
- Risk pooling and Risk spreading
- How inside information leads to Moral Hazard and Adverse Selection
- How an asset return reflects its cash income and capital gain (loss)
- How correlation of asset returns affect risk pooling
- Asset Market efficiency
- Spot and Forward Markets
- How Hedging shift the burden of risk

In an uncertain environment, whenever an act is decided upon, the consequence is not certain—various consequences may follow with different probabilities. Therefore, every act is like a gamble or a lottery. A lottery may be defined more formally as follows: Suppose an act a is chosen. This has consequences/ Payoffs C(a, 1), C(a, 2),..., with associate probabilities P_1, P_2 ... when we couple these consequences with their associated probabilities, we have a lottery or a gamble; $L(a) = [\{P_1, C(a, 1)\}), \{P_2, C(a, 2)\}....]$.

Thus, in an uncertain situation, the individual in essence has to choose between lotteries. Example 1 gives an illustration of a lottery involving a toss of a coin.

Example 1. There are 2 possibilities when tossing a coin: If the coin comes up heads, you win £1, if it comes up tails, you lose £0.50.

If the first action is taken (not tossing a coin), there is only one consequence with certainty, a payment of 0. If the coin is tossed, there are two possibilities, head or tail, with associated probabilities 0.5 of Consequence/ Payoffs £1 to –£0.50.

One important property of a lottery is its expected value (EV), which is the weighted average of all its possible outcomes, with the weight being the respective probabilities. In Example 1, the EV if the coin is tossed is EV = (0.5)1 + (0.5) (–0.5) = 0.25

One way of choosing between lotteries would be to select the lottery that has the highest EV. In Example 1, it would seem that the decision should be to toss the coin, because this gives the expected value of 0.25, whereas not tossing the coin gives 0.

However, the EV criterion suffers from the weakness that it does not distinguish between consequences and utilities from consequences. The formal economic theory of choice in situations of uncertainty is due to Neumam and Morgenotem. The central assumption of this theory is that people choose the alternative that provides the highest expected utilities, not the highest EV. To explain the theory simply, let us assume that the outcome of a lottery is determined uniquely by the amount of total wealth W to which it corresponds. If certain conditions are fulfilled, then the agent will have a utility function U(W), called the von Neumann–Morgenstern (vNM) utility function. If the agent takes an action, various outcomes are possible, each characterised by a different W_1, hence a different $U(W_1)$ having associated Probabilities (P_i). The expected utility (EU) is taken; $EU = P_1U(W_1) + P_2U(W_2) + ... + P_sU(W5_s) = \Sigma P_iU(W_i)$.

According to the expected utility theory, the individual will take that action which maximises her EU.

Note that if $U(W_i) = W_i$, then the expected utility becomes identical with the EV.

Example 2. The vNM utility function of an individual is $v = \sqrt{W}$ or $W^{0.5}$, and her initial wealth is 36. Will she accept a gamble in which she wins 13 with a probability $\frac{2}{3}$ + loses of 11 with probability $\frac{1}{3}$?

The EU of the gamble s given by

$$EU = \left(\frac{2}{3}\right)\sqrt{(36+13)} + \frac{1}{3}\sqrt{(36-11))}$$

$$= \left(\frac{2}{3}\right)7 + \left(\frac{1}{3}\right)5 = \frac{14}{3} + \frac{5}{3}$$

$$= \frac{19}{3} > \sqrt{36} = 6$$

(which is what individual will get if she does not gamble). Hence the gamble should be accepted.

Suppose that the consumer's preference under uncertainty can be represented by a utility function U(.). Different people have different attitudes towards risk. How can we categorize these risks?

Definition: The consumer is said to be risk-averse if she strictly prefers a certain consequence to a risky prospect when mathematical expectation of consequences equal the certain consequence.

That is, consumer is risk-averse if U(v) > EU(c), where r = EC, U U(EC) > EU(c) written out more fully, this means that $U(\Sigma P_sC_s) > \Sigma P_sU(C_s)$, when $C_s = C(a, s)$ for some act a and P_s are the probabilities, $\Sigma P_s = 1$.

The consumer is risk-lowing if U(EC) < EU(c), and is risk-neutral if U(EC) = EU(c).

If U is a twice continuously differentiable function, then it can be shown that $U''(C) < 0$ => $EU(C) < U(EC)$, i.e. concavity of U denotes risk-averse behaviour. If U is linear, then the individual is risk-neutral, and if it is converse, then she is risk-loving. So to simplify matters, from now on we assume that the consequence function is denominated in terms of just one variable – wealth W. Moreover, the individual always prefers more wealth to less, i.e. U(W) > 0.

The utility function of a risk-averse individual is shown below. Suppose that there are 2 possible outcomes $W_1 + W_2$ with associated probabilities P + (1 – P). Then expected utility $PU(W_1) + (1 - P)U(W_2)$, $0 \leq P \leq 1$, will be represented by the point D on the chord AB in Fig. 5.1. The chord joining 2 points on the curve always lies below the curve. Hence $U(PW_1) + (1 - P) \equiv (W_1)$, utility function, will always lie above the point D.

Example 3. Suppose that an individual's $PU(W_1) + (1 - P)W_2\ U(W) = W^2$. Then $U''(W) = 2 > 0$, and the person is a risk-lover. Will the

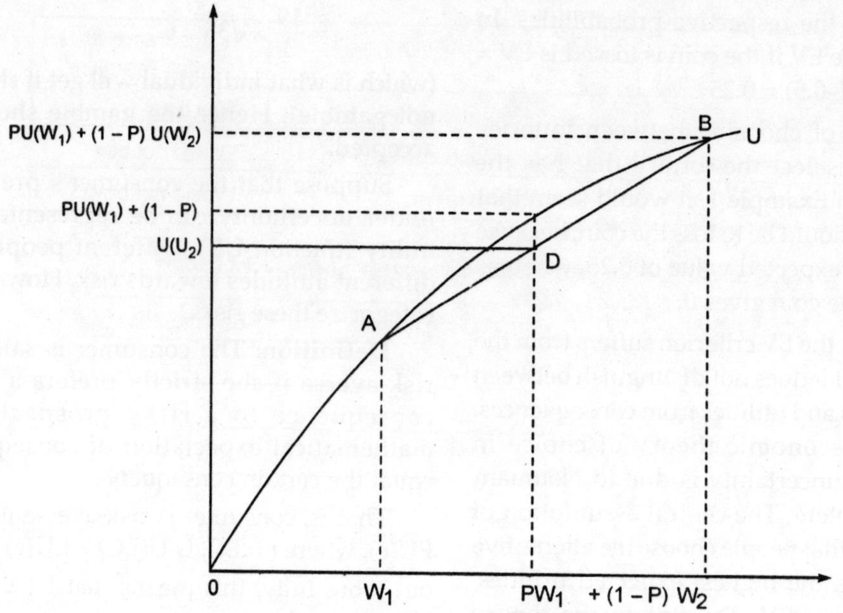

Fig. 5.1: Risk-Premium

person accept a gamble where is a 50% chance of wining 20 and a 50% chance of losing 20, if the person's initial wealth is 100?

If the person does not accept the gamble, then utility is 100^2 = 10,000. If the gamble is accepted, the expected utility is 0.5 $(120)^2$ + $0.5(80^2)$ = 0.5 (14,400 + 6,400) = 10,400. Hence the gamble will be accepted.

It can be shown that if U = W, the person is risk - neutral and will be indifferent between accepting or rejecting the gamble.

Insurance is the opposite of gambling. Suppose we own a £200,000 worth of property. There is a 10% chance it may burn down by accident. We have 90% chance of continuing to have the property but a 10% chance of having nothing. Our risky world forces us to take this bet. On average, we end up with £180,000, which is 90% of £200,000. Plus 10% of nothing.

An insurance company offers to insure the full value of our property for a premium of £30,000. Whether or not our property burns down, we pay the insurance company the £30,000 premium. They pay us £200,000 if it burns down. Whatever happens, we end up with £170,000.

Is it worth insuring? The insurance company is offering unfavourable odds, this is how they earn their income. Uninsured, our property is worth £180,000, insured it, worth only £17,000. A risk-neutral person would not insure on these terms. The mathematical calculation says, it is, on average, better to stand the risk. The risk-lover will also decline insurance. Not only are the odds poor, there is added enjoyment of standing the risk. But a risk-averse will accept the offer, happy to give up money to avoid the probability of catastrophe. Table 5.1 summarises the attitude towards risk.

• Insurance and Risk

A farmer and an actor have uncertain or risky income. Each get, 20 in a good month, and 0 in a bad month. But the risks are independent. Their good months are not in any way connected. Individually, their incomes are risky. Collectively they are less risky. In Table 5.2, they pool their incomes and risks, each

Table 5.1: Attitude Towards Risk

Tastes	Betting	Insurance at unfair Premium
Risk-averse	Needs favourable odds	May buy
Risk-neutral	Except at unfavourable odds	Would not buy
Risk-lover	Even if odds against	Would not buy

Table 5.2: Risk-pooling of Income or Sharing Joint Income

Farmer	Good months	Bad months
	10	0
Actor Good month 10	10	5
Bad month 0	5	0

getting half of their joint income. If they both have a good month or both have a bad month, pooling arrangement make no difference. They each get what they would have got on their own. In other two cases, the success of one partner offsets the failure of other partners. Together, their income is more stable than as individuals. If they are risk-averse, they gain by pooling. If it were not so hard to set up such deals (expenses of lawyers fee, tax, etc.), we would see them more. Pooling independent risk is the key to insurance.

Now let us choose randomly any 1000 people aged 55 knowing nothing about their health. Throughout the country, 1% of such people will die in the next year. In our sample of 1,000 people, it could be 0, 10%, 20% or even more. The larger the sample, the more likely it is that around 1% will die in the next year. With 1 million 55 year-olds we could be pretty confident that around 10,000 would die, though it is difficult to say which ones. By putting together more and more people we reduce the risk or dispersion of the aggregate outcome.

Life assurance companies take in premium in exchange for a promise to pay big amount to the family if the insured person dies. The company can makes this promise with certainty because it pools risks over many clients. Since the company cannot guarantee that exactly 1% of its many 55-years-olds will die in any one year, there is a small element of residual risk for the company to bear, and it makes a small change for this in calculating its premiums. However, its ability to pool the risk means that it will make only a small charge for this. If companies want to charge more, new entrants join the industry knowing that it is trying to make more profits for the small residual risk to be borne.

Risk-pooling does not work when all individuals face the same risk. Suppose there is a 10% risk of a nuclear war in the US in the next 10 years. If it happens, everyone in the US dies, leaving money to their surviving relative in the rest of the world. Ten million Americans offer to buy insurance from a British company.

Despite the number of people, the risk cannot be pooled. If everybody in the US dies, the company either pays out everybody's relatives or it pays nothing. In the aggregate there is still 10% chance of having to pay out, just as individual American faces a 10% of disaster. When the same thing happens to everybody if it happens at all, the aggregate behave like the individual. There is no risk reduction from pooling.

Many companies do not insure against the 'acts of god'. Such disasters are no more natural or unnatural than a heart attack. But they affect large number of company's clients if they happen at all. The risk cannot be reduced by pooling. Companies cannot quote the low premium as in the case of heart attacks, where risks are independent and the aggregate outcome is fairly certain. Risk-pooling aggregates independent risks to make the aggregate more certain.

Another way of reducing the cost of risk-bearing is known as risk-sharing, and the example is the Lloyd's insurance market in London. Risk-sharing is necessary when it is impossible to reduce risk by pooling.

To understand risk-sharing we need to explain diminishing marginal utility. It may be argued that the utility benefit from an extra £10,000 is less than the utility sacrificed when £10,000 is given up. However, this difference in marginal utility from equivalent monetary gains and losses is tiny if the size of the stake is also tiny. The marginal utility from an extra £1 is only fractionally less than the utility lost by sacrificing £1. For small stakes, people are almost risk-neutral. The larger the stake, the more diminishing marginal utility bites.

• Risk-sharing Works by Reducing the Stake

If we go to Lloyd's to insure an aeroplane for £2 billion, a big risk. Only part of this risk can be pooled as part of a larger portfolio of risks. It is too big for anyone to take on at a reasonable premium.

The Lloyd's market in London has hundreds of syndicates, each a group of 20 or so individuals who have each put up £100,000. Each syndicate takes about 1% of £2 billion deal and then resells this risk to other people in the insurance industry. By the time the deal has been subdivided again and again, each syndicate or insurance company holds a tiny share of the total. And each syndicate risk is further subdivided among its 20 members. The risk is shared out until each individual's stake is so small that there is a tiny difference between the marginal utility from a gain and the marginal loss of utility in the event of a disaster. The package can be sold to the client at a premium low enough to attack the business.

By pooling and sharing risks, insurance allows individuals to deal with many risks at affordable premiums. These two things inhibit the operation of the insurance markets, reducing the extent to which individuals can use insurance to buy their way out of risky situations.

• Moral Hazard

Insurance companies calculate the statistical chances of particular events happening. They work out how many cars are stolen each year. Since different thefts are independent risks, insurance company pools the risk over many clients and charges low premium for car theft.

Suppose we are in a restaurant taking our meal, we remember all on a sudden that your car is unlocked. Do we rush outside to lock it? May not be if your car is fully insured against theft. If the act of insurance changes the odds, we call this moral hazard. Moral hazard is the use of inside information to exploit the other party to the contract.

Statistical averages for the whole population, some of whom may not be insured and take greater care, are no longer a reliable guide to the risks the insurance company faces and the premium it should charge. Moral hazard makes it hard to get insurance, and more expensive when you get it. Insurance company insure your car only up to a certain percentage of its replacement cost. They take over a great part of the risk, but we are worse off if something happens. The company gives out an incentive to hold down the chance of bad thing happening. By limiting moral hazard, they pay out less frequently and charge a lower premium.

• Adverse Selection

Some people are smokers but others are not. People who smoke are likely to die early.

Individuals know whether they are smokers or not, but the insurance company are unlikely to know the difference and must charge the same premium to all clients for life assurance.

Suppose the premium is based on mortality rates for the nation as a whole. People who do not smoke know that they have an above-average life expectancy and find the premium too expensive. Smokers know their life expectancy is low and realize that premium is a bargain. Even though the insurance company cannot tell the difference between the two groups, it knows the premium based on the national average will only attract the high risk individuals. Adverse selection takes place when an individual uses the inside information to accept or reject a contract. Those who accept are not an average sample of the population.

One solution is to assume that all clients smoke and charge high premium to all. Non-smokers cannot get insruance at a reasonable price. They might pay for a medical examination to try to prove that they are low-risk clients who should be charged a lower price. Medical examination are now compulsory for almost all insurance contracts.

• Uncertainty and Asset Returns

There are many ways to carry wealth from the present to the future. People can hold money, government bond or bills, company shares, housing and so on. We now compare the rates of return on Treasury bonds and shares—two types of holding wealth.

The real return on Treasury bills is not very risky because it is guaranteed by the government. Company shares offer a return in two different ways.

Dividends and the capital gains (loss). If the share is bought at a low price and later sold at a high price, this is the return in capital gain (loss). The rate of return is the percentage of the money initially invested in shares. Hence, Rate of return = Dividend + Capital gains divided by initial purchase price.

To compute the real rate of return, we subtract the inflation rate from the nominal rate of return. The annual rate of return on company shares was much more variable than that on Treasury bills. Treasury bills vary very little, but the return on shares is volatile. Thus, shares are much more risky than Treasury bills.

The average real return on Treasury bills is close to zero, whereas shares on average yield nearly 10% a year in real terms.

Shares are riskier than the Treasury bills. this larger risk is compensated by a higher return. Since the risk is big it needs a large real return, on average, to induce people to take this risk.

Shares are riskier for two reasons. First, nobody is sure what dividend the firm will give. It depends on what profit the firm makes and how confident it is about the future. When firms anticipate tough times in the future, they cut dividends in order to keep contingency reserves. Second, views about the likely capital gains change radically.

• Portfolio Selection

The portfolio selection of a financial investor is the bundle of financial and real assets. How does a risk-averse investor select his portfolio? Indifference curve analysis may be used to choose the bundle of the highest possible indifference curve given the budget constraint describing which bundle was affordable, indifference curve approach will be used to choose the portfolio. Instead of a choice between two goods, we now focus on the choice between the average or expected return on the portfolio and the risk that the portfolio embodies.

• The Risk-Return Choice

The risk-averse person prefers a higher average return on the portfolio but dislikes higher risk. To take more risk he needs a higher than average return. By risk we mean variability of return on portfolios. We know that a portfolio composed exclusively of industrial shares is riskier than a portfolio composed of Treasury bills.

To highlight the problem of portfolio selection, we assume that there are only two assets in which to invest. Bank deposits are quite a safe asset whose return is predictable. The other asset is company shares—much riskier—whose return is variable. The investor has a given wealth to invest. If all assets are put in the bank, the whole portfolio would earn a small but risk-less return. The higher the fraction of the portfolio held in shares, the larger the average return on the whole portfolio but greater its risk.

Portfolio Choice: The risk-averse investor will put the whole portfolio into the safe asset. For him to buy risky asset, he must believe the average return on the risky asset is much higher than on the safe asset. If this is case, how much of the portfolio will he put into the risky assets? Generally, the fraction of the portfolio held in the risky asset will be higher: (1) the higher the average return on the risky compared to safe asset, (2) the less risky is the risky asset, and (3) the less risk-averse is the investor.

Diversification: When there are several risky assets the investor may be able to reduce the risk on the whole portfolio without having to accept a lower average return. The Table 5.3 shows this. Suppose there are two risky assets—oil shares and bank shares. Each has two possible returns: £8 if things go well and £4 if things go badly. Each industry has a 50 : 50 chance of good and bad times. Finally, we assume that returns in the two industries are independent.

Suppose we have £2 pounds to invest, and in two shares. Each share cost the £1. Which portfolio gives the best risk-return combination? Two shares have the same risk and, thus, same expected return. We are indifferent between buying the two shares. But the superior strategy is to buy one each and thus to diversify the portfolio.

This means pooling risk across several assets whose individual returns behave differently from one another. Diversification means not putting all your eggs in one basket; if we put all our eggs in one basket, buying, say, oil shares for £2, we have 50 : 50 chance of getting £8 or £4. It depends on whether the oil industry has a good or bad time. The average return is £6, but the actual return will be either £8 or £4.

Table 5.3 shows a diversified portfolio with two shares—Bank and Oil shares. If both industries do well we will make £8, but this is only a 25% chance. There is 50% chance of oil doing well, and also a 50% chance that bank will do well—since they are independent industries. Similarly, there is 25% chance of both industries doing badly at the same time. There is also a 25% chance that one industry does well while the other one does badly. Each of the four portfolios' returns shown in Table 5.3 is a 25% chance.

The average return is still £6, as if we put our £2 in one basket, but the variability of returns is smaller. Instead of 50 : 50 chance of £4 or £8, we now have only 25% chance of each extreme, and a 50% chance of earning the average return of £6.

Diversification reduces the risk by pooling it without altering the average rate of return. It offers us a better deal. As before, the greater the number of risky assets with independent returns across which the portfolio pools the risk, the lower will be the total risk of the portfolio.

Fig. 5.2 shows the typical relationship between the total portfolio risk and the number of independent assets in the portfolio. Portfolio risk declines as the number of independent risky assets is increased. However, most of the risk reduction through

Table 5.3: A Diversified Portfolio

		Oil Shares	
		Good	Bad
Bank Shares	Good	£8	£6
	Bad	£6	£4

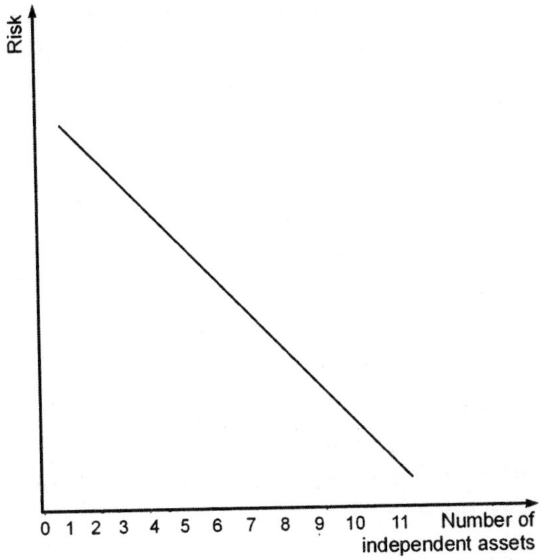

Fig. 5.2: Diversifying risk

diversificaton comes very quickly. Even a few assets cut the total risk a lot. For example, our car has one spare tyre, not five. Because it is more expensive to buy in small quantities, small investors hold a dozen different shares rather than a 100. They get most of the benefits of diversification without needing lots of small packages of shares. People who are more risk-averse and want a large number of shares can buy shares in a mutual fund or unit trust, professional fund managers who buy large quantities of shares in many firms, and the retails stake in the fund to small investors.

The riskiness of portfolio, the variability of its total return, can be reduced through diversification but the gains to further diversification diminishes quite rapidly.

- **Diversification When Asset Returns Are Correlated**

Risk-pooling works because asset returns are independent of each other. When asset returns are correlated—means move together in the same direction—we call them as positively correlated. When they move in opposite direction we call them negatively correlated. Positive and negative correlations affect the way in which diversification changes risk. Suppose the two shares rise or fall together, buying one each is like putting all our money in either share. Diversificaton achieves nothing when returns are perfectly positively correlated, risk-pooling does not work, just as it fails in the insurance industry.

Conversely, diversification is a complete success when returns are negatively correlated. Suppose bank shares do well only when gold shares do badly, and vice versa. Buying one each, we earn either £4 from bank and £2 from gold or £2 from bank or £4 from gold.

On the diversified portfolio, we earn £6 for certain. We have diversified away all the risk, even when individually they are risky.

In practice, returns on different shares are never perfectly correlated. Some tend to vary together and some tend to vary in opposite directions, but over any particular period actual return on two shares may not exhibit their usual correlation. Thus it is impossible to completely diversify away all portfolio risk. But fund managers are always on the lookout for an asset that tends to have a negative correlation with the assets on the existing portfolio. On average, extending the portfolio to include that asset will improve risk-retrun characteristics.

- **Beta**

It measures how much an asset's return moves with the return on the whole stock market. Table 5.4 gives some examples. The first row shows returns on the market as a whole in booms, normal times, and slumps. A share with beta = 1 moves the same way as the whole market. A high bets share does even better when the market is up, even worse when market is down. A low beta share moves in the same general direction as the market but more sluggishly than the market. Negative beta shares move against the market.

Most shares moves pretty much with the market and have beta close to 1. There are not too many negative beta shares, but some gold shares have beta close to zero. Most people should have some gold shares in their portfolio.

Beta is calculated from the past behaviour of individual shares and the whole stock market. Ideally, they are looking for negative beta shares that greatly reduce the risk of a portfolio whose other components vary with the market as a whole. Even low beta shares are partly independent of the rest of the whole market and allow some risks to be pooled. High beta shares are undesirable. Including them in the porfolio adds to its total risk.

A share with low (or negative) beta will be in high demand. Risk-averse purchasers are anxious to buy low beta shares whose inclusion in their portfolos reduce the total portfolio risk. High demand bids up the share price and reduce the average return; since it costs more to buy shares, people get less per pound invested. However, investors are happy to trade-off lower return for the fast that low beta shares reduce the total risk of their portfolio.

In stock market equilibrium, low beta shares have high prices and low rates of return on average. Conversely, high beta shares add to investors' portfolio risk and are bought only because they have low prices and, on average, offer high rates of return that compensate for their undesirable risk characteristics. Fig. 5.4 shows the result. Average return on individual shares rise steadily with the beta share—as the theory predicts.

Each share's risk is measured by its beta, which shows how that share's returns move with returns in the market as a whole. The higher the beta, the more the inclusion of the share in a portfolio will increase the total portfolio risk. The data show that risky shares with higher betas must offer higher return on average to compensate for the disadvantage.

To sum up, individual share prices depend both on expected or average returns, and on risk characteristics. The risk characteristics of a firm's shares determine the expected return its shares must offer to compete with other shares. For a given required return, higher anticipated income means a higher current share price.

• Diversification in Other Situtation

Risk is all around us, and diversification happens all the time. Countries diversify their sources of raw materials. Otherwise, if anything disrupts the sole supplier's ability or willingness to sell, the country may face disaster. Similarly, a farmer is reluctant to rely on a single crop.

• Efficient Asset Markets

There are two views about the stock market: one is that of casino, without any rational basis for speculation; it is a matter of luck. The other view—the theory of efficient markets is that the stock market—is a sensitive processor of information, quickly responding to new information to adjust share prices.

An efficient asset market already incorporates existing information properly in asset prices. The second view recognises that

Table 5.4: Share Retruns and Beta

Asset	Return (%)		
	Boom	Normal	Slump
Whole market	14	6	22
High Beta	20	10	28
Beta = 1	14	6	22
Low Beta	5	4	3
Negative Beta	2	3	5

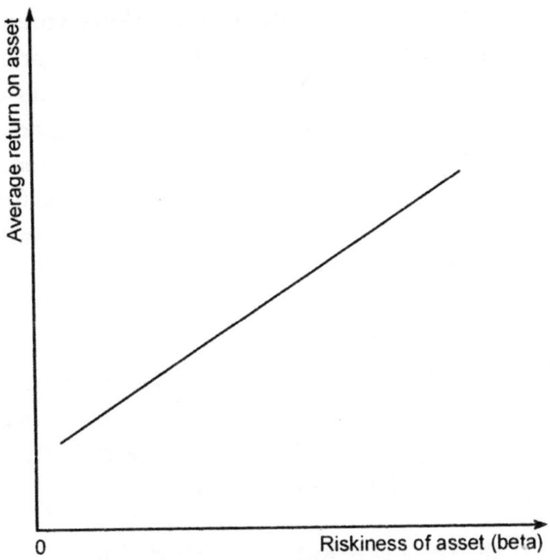

Fig. 5.3: The risk-return relationship for shares

share prices fluctuate a lot but argues that these fluctuations are the appropriate response to new information. ·

Companies with higher than average returns and low betas should be valued both by society and by the stock market. The higher the share prices, the more money a company raises from new share issue. High share prices are guiding the right firms to invest. Companies with low average returns and high beta are valued neither by financial investor nor by society. Low share prices make it harder for them to finance new investment and they are likely to contract. It matters which of the two views is correct. If share prices correctly reflect prospective dividends and risk characteristics, the efficient market view, a free market in industrial shares is guiding society's scarce resources towards the right firms. But if share prices are purely a matter of luck, as in casinos, the wrong firm may expand just incorporated because their share prices are high.

The crucial implication of the efficient market theory is that asset prices correctly reflect all existing information. It is unforeseen new information that changes share prices as the market quickly incorporates this unanticipated development to restore expected development to the required level.

• Speculative Bubbles

Economic life is a risky business. Speculation is a risky activity. Even experienced speculators sometimes lose their fortune by making bad guesses. Speculation could sometimes be beneficial to society. The economic function of speculators is to move goods from period of abundance to period of scarcity. Speculative activity can even out the price differences of commodities among regions and over time. They do this by buying goods when they are abundant and prices are low and selling when they are scarce and prices are high.

• Arbitrage and Geographical Price Pattern

The simplest case is one in which speculative activity reduces and eliminates regional price differences by buying and selling the same commodity. This activity is known as arbitrage, which is the purchase of a good or asset in one market for resale in another market in order to make profit from price differences. Generally, as a result of arbitrage, the price difference between markets will be less than the cost of moving the good from one market to the other.

A well-informed corn speculator knows that if all the corn is put on the market after the autumn harvest, it will fetch a very low price because there will be a glut on the market. Several months later, when corn is running short, the price will tend to rise. In this case, the speculator can make a profit by (1) buying some of the autumn crop while it is cheap, (2) keeping it into storage, (3) selling it later when the price has risen.

Thus, we can see, as a result of speculative activities, the autumn price of corn increases, the spring supply of corn increases and the spring price declines. The process of speculative buying and selling tends to even out the supply and price over the years.

Moreover, if there is brisk competition among the well-informed speculators, none of them will make excess profits. The return to the speculators will include the interest on their capital, the appropriate earnings for their time, plus the risk premium to compensate them for whatever risks they incur with their funds. The speculators will not see the corn nor will they know the technology of storage or delivery. They merely buy and sell pieces of paper.

Speculation reveals the invisible-hand principle at work. By evening out supply and prices, speculation actually increases economic efficiency. By moving goods over time from period of abundance to period of scarcity, the speculator is buying where the price and marginal utility of the good are low and selling where the price and marginal utility are high.

By pursuing their private interests (profits), speculators are also increasing the public interest (total utility).

In such markets all depend on what people today think and people tomorrow will expect. Such a market is vulnerable to speculative bubbles. If everyone believes the price will rise tomorrow, it makes sense to purchase the asset today. For example, the South-sea bubble of 1720. A company was formed to sell British goods to people in the South sea and to bring home the goods produced there. The shares were issued long before any attempt was made to trade these goods. It was considered a good idea and people bought the shares. The price rise quickly, and soon people were buying not in anticipation of dividends but to resell the shares at a profit once the price had gone even higher. The price rose even faster, till one day it became apparent that the company's proposal was a fiasco with no chance of success and the bubble burst.

Keynes argued that the share market is like a casino, dominated by short-term gain from the resell value. Since next period's share price depends on what people think the following period's share price will be, Keynes compare the share market to a beauty competition in a newspaper, where the winner is the reader who guesses the beauty getting most votes from all readers. Share prices reflect what average opinion expects average opinion to be.

Undoubtedly, financial markets sometimes exhibit temporary bubbles. The overpricing of shares in dot.com companies was a recent example. Nevertheless, bubbles are normally temporary, when it cannot be justified by fundamentals. Bubbles are less likely for assets whose income is mainly from dividends or interests and not from capital gains.

• More on Risk

Risk is central to economic life. There are two aspects to this risk, individuals want to reduce risk, and those who take over the risk must have be compensated for doing so.

• Forward Markets and Hedging

A spot market deals in contracts for delivery immediately. A forward market is for contract made today for goods to be delivered at a specific data in the future according to agreement entered today. There are forward markets for many goods and assets—especially in foreign currencies.

Suppose the current price for copper is £800 a ton and people expect the price to rise to £880 a ton after a year. Some people will hold copper in their portfolios. The expected capital gain is 10% of the purchase price.

We own a copper mine and will have a ton of copper to sell in a year's time. The spot price of copper is the price for immediate delivery. Today's spot price is £800 and people expect it to be £880 in a year's time. One option is to sell our copper at the spot at this time next year. We expect that to be £880 but we cannot be sure what the price would be next year. This is a risky business.

Alternatively, we can hedge against this risk in the forward market. Hedging is the use of forward markets to shift risk out to someone else.

Suppose we can sell a ton of copper today for delivery in a year's time at a price of £850 agreed now. We, could, of course, hedge against this risky future spot price. We know for certain what we will receive when the copper will be delivered in a year's time. But we have sold our copper only for £850, even though we expect copper to be sold at £880 on the spot market next year. We regard this as an insurance premium to get out of the risk associated with the future spot market price.

To whom do we sell our copper in the foward market? We sell it to a trader whom we know as speculator. A speculator temporarily holds an asset in the hope of making capital gain.

A speculator has no interest in a ton of copper per se. But the speculator, having promised us £850 for a ton of our copper to be delivered in a year's time, currently expects to resell that immediately it is delivered. The speculator expects to get £880 for that copper in the spot market next year. He expects to make £30 as compensation for taking this risk. If the spot market price turns out to be less than £850 next year, the speculator will lose money. £30 is the risk premum for the speculator in the foward market to take up the risky propositions that hedgers wish to avoid.

Someone buying copper at the spot market today at £800 for resale next year at £880 must compare the expected capital gain of 10% with returns and interest rates on offer in other assets. Copper must cover the opportunity cost of the returns that could have been earned by using this money elsewhere. The speculator in the forward market needs not make this comparison. No money is currently tied up in the foward market. Although the price has been agreed today at £850, the money is handed over next year only after the copper is delivered. Thus, no money is actually tied up. All the speculators have to think about is the likely spot price in a year's time and how much it could vary. The riskier the forward market price, the larger premium the speculator will need and the more the current forward price will lie below the expected future spot price.

The speculator has an open option, having taken a foward delivery without yet finding a purchaser to resell. However, other firms use copper as an input to production, may wish to buy copper for delivery within a year's time at a price agreed today. They too wish to hedge against the risky future spot price. A speculator who can make two forward contracts—one to take delivery of copper, and the other to sell copper to a copper-user—does not have an open position. The speculator's book is balanced, without any residual risk. The risky future spot price is irrelevant.

In forward markets with roughly equal numbers of people wishing to hedge by buying and selling, the speculator's book is roughly balanced and residual risk is small. Speculators need only a little compensation to cover this residual risk and the administrative costs. The current price of forward copper price is close to the expected future spot price.

However, speculation is a risky business if buyers and sellers cannot be matched up in the forward market. In practice, the spot prices that subsequently transpire can very by a large amount on either side of the estimate implicity contained in the current forward price.

Forward markets do not exist for most goods because it is not possible to write legally binding and enforceable contracts. It exists where they are very standardised commodites—22 carat gold, Japanese yen—that are easily defined. Forward markets are an important way by which individuals can reduce the risks they face, but there are limited risks that can be hedged this way.

QUESTIONS

1. A fair coin is tossed. You win £1 if tail comes. Person A does not mind whether or not she takes the bet. Person B will pay £1 to play the game. Person C demands £0.5 before being willing to play. Characterise the three persons' attitude to risk which is likely to take out insurance for car?
2. You see an advert for life insurance for anyone over 45 years old. No medical exam is required. Do you expect the premium rates to be high or low or average? Why?
3. In which of the following are risk being pooled: (a) Life insurance? (b) Insurance against flood? (c) Insurance for a pop-star's voice?
4. You set up a business to advice the unemployed on the best way to use their time to earn money. Your firm issues shares on the stock market. In equilibrium, do you expect your shares are expected to earn a higher or lower return than the stock market average? Why?
5. Why are stock market regulated to permit inside dealing where a firm's managers use inside information about the firm to buy and sell its shares?

ANSWERS

1. A is risk-neutral, B is risk-loving, and C is risk-averase.
2. People with high adverse selection and low risk are happy to be screened.
3. (a) Yes; (b) No; and (c) Yes.
4. Negative beta: You do well in a slump, where the other share are doing less well. Your shares have high price and low expected return.
5. Fear of moral hazard being exploited by people with better information and this will prevent others from dealing in shares.

CHAPTER 6

PRODUCTION AND COSTS

KEY TERMS

Marginal (physical) Product of Labour $(\Delta q / \Delta l)$: The change in total product (Δq) that occurs when an additional unit of labour is added (Δl) and all other inputs are held constant.

Diminishing Marginal (physical) Product of Labour: The extra output produced by the extra unit of labour is less than the output produced by the previous unit of labour.

Isoquant: Is a curve that shows all the possible combinations of inputs (l and k) that yield the same level of output (q).

Isocost Line: Shows all the combinations of l and k that can be purchased for a given monetary outlay (TC).

Minimum Efficient Scale (MES): The minimum point of the long-run average cost curve.

A business is a decision-making production unit. It purchases various inputs and transforms them into outputs which are ultimately bought by consumers, other businesses and government. Plant is the production unit in the industry where the business is the unit of ownership and control. The oldest form of economic activity was the production by a household for its own consumption. But gradually we came to realise the advantages of specialisation and the division of labour and few goods are now produced by a person for his or her own consumption. Today almost all goods are produced indirectly to be sold in the market. The business is an agency that carries out the production process.

The activities of the business in a modern economy are complementary to those of the household. In a simple circular flow model, businesses buy inputs owned by the household and pay wages and salaries, rent etc. in return. The household then uses the income thus received from business to purchase goods and services produced by businesses. In traditional theory, business is assumed to have one objective—to maximise profit. However, in modern theory, the businesses may have other objectives as well, such as sales-revenue maximisation or the maximisation of managerial utility and so on. We use the term industry to refer to the whole group of producers of any commodity.

Businesses decide to maximise their objectives—whatever may be their objectives. A business has to decide the level of output to produce to maximise this objective or objectives. This decision will, in turn, determine the business's purchase of factor inputs and may also influence the price at which its output could be sold.

As the society develops from feudalism to capitalism, so the form of business organisation gradually evolved.

• Types of Business Units

We now consider the legal status of the different types of businesses. The earlier forms were the sole traders and the partnership. The joint-stock company did not become common until the 19th century.

The majority of the production in a market economy is in the hands of businesses. These can be organised in the following ways. A single person's business or sole traders, has one owner-manager, who is personally responsible for everything done in the name of the business. This is the most common type of business. This is the business run by a single individual who is fully responsible for the entire profit or loss of the business. As this business is small, it can provide personal service to its customers and can respond to the requirement of the market. Decisions can be taken quickly as the owner is not required to consult anyone else.

Disadvantages with this type of business are that the owner cannot specialise in particular functions but must be a jack-of-all-trades, and the finance of the business is limited to what the owner can raise. Another disadvantage is that there is no distinction between the owner and his business. The owner has unlimited liability for any debts incurred by the business, so that, in the event of bankruptcy, all the assets are liable to seizure. These types of businesses are to be found mainly in retailing, farming, personal services, etc.

• Partnership

The logical progression from one-man business is partnership. A partnership contains two to twenty partners who jointly own a business, sharing profit and being jointly responsible for any loss. The main advantages of this type of business are that more finance is likely to be available and each partner may specialise to some extent. The major disadvantage is that of unlimited liability. In order to get more ownership capital such businesses may admit more members and thus destroy the homogeneity of the owners. Again, whenever a partner dies or resigns, a new partner has to be found. Another disadvantage is that a partnership can be dissolved whenever any party finds the existing arrangement unsatisfactory and wishes to withdraw. The law of partnership also makes it impossible for any partner to sell his share to a new party without the consent of his partners; if agreement cannot be found, the partnership may have to be wound up.

Joint-Stock Company: A joint-stock company (called a corporation in the USA) is a business regarded in law as having an identity of its own; its owners are not personally responsible for anything that is done in the name of the company by its directors. It is developed with limited liability during the second half of the 19th century. The liability of the shareholders is limited to the amount they have subscribed to the business's capital through the shares they buy. If the company should find itself in difficulties and fail to meet the demand of its creditors, the shareholders may lose their share value and nothing more. To make information available to potential shareholders, the company is required to submit details of profit, turnover, assets, etc. to the Registrar of Companies.

A joint-stock company can be either a private limited company or public limited company. The shares of a private limited company cannot be offered for sale on the stock exchange. Private limited companies require a minimum of 2 and a maximum of 50 shareholders.

The shares in a public company can be offered for sale to the public through stock market. A public company requires a minimum of 7 shareholders, but there is no upper limit. Shares can be resold in the stock market to anyone who is prepared to pay the going price. Trading in the stock market is primarily the sale and resale of existing shares of the public companies.

Joint-stock companies that have operations in more than one country are often called multinational enterprises (MNE) or transnational corporations (TNC). Their number has been increasing steadily over the years. In 2001 there were about 60,000 TNCs in the world and they controlled about 820,000 foreign affiliates, 90% of whose headquarters are in developed countries, the three major bases being the EU, Japan and the US. Together they owned stock of about $6 trillion worth of direct foreign investments; about 20% are in developing countries.

The major advantage of the joint-stock company is that it is an almost perfect device for raising a large sum of capital. In fact, by almost any measure, viz., output, employment, capital stock or contribution to the Exchequer the corporation has become a dominant form of business organisation in a modern mixed economy. Secondly, the corporation may have perpetual existence, despite shares' change of hands. Thirdly, no group of shareholders can force any other group to sell or retain their holdings, and only a majority vote is needed to reach business decisions. India's Companies Act (1956) has been passed to give almost everyone the privilege of forming a corporation for any purpose. However, the major advantage of corporation is that its income is subject to corporation tax. This is in addition to personal income-tax paid by owners on the dividend they get. This double taxation erodes the capital stock of the company.

Public corporation is a form of business organisation that has developed in the UK for running the nationalised industries. For example, the formation of public corporation for running the port of London Authority (1909) and the British Broadcasting Corporation (1927), although most were formed in the period of the post-war Labour Government of 1945-51. These public corporations are run by the Board of Directors appointed by the government.

Companies are run by a Board of Directors. The Board of Directors makes decisions about how the business is run but must submit an annual report to the shareholders. At the annual general meeting, the shareholders can vote to sack the directors, each of the shareholders having as many votes as the number of shares owned.

Companies are the main form of organisation of big business. Majority of the companies are public limited companies.

• Financing of Businesses

The money a business raises for carrying on its business is called the finance capital or real capital. The finance is provided in two basic ways: through funds provided by owners or equity, and debt; funds borrowed from outside the business. For a sole trader or a partnership, the owners provide the equity. A joint-stock company acquires funds from its owners in exchange for stocks, shares or equities. These are basically ownership certificates. The money goes to the owners of the business because they take the risk. The profits of the business paid out to shareholders are called dividends.

Another easy way to raise money is to retain current profit rather than paying out dividends to shareholders. Financing from undistributed profit has become an important source of financing in recent years. Reinvested profits add to the value of the businesses and also raise the market value of existing shares.

The following are the most popular methods of financing a company:

Bonds: A bond is a security promising to pay to certain sum of money in interest every year for a number of years until it matures at some specific date. The time at which the principal (the original amount of the debt) is repaid is called redemption date.

Henceforth, we refer to a debt instrument as bond.

Equity: This differs from bonds in that its holders share in profit or losses and remains in control of business decisions. A shareholder is paid dividends on the basis of profit made by a company after meeting its other obligations. In that sense, equities are assets of the company.

Preferred stock or preference share: Such stocks pay a stated dividends—say, a 10%, on the face value of the share purchased, irrespective of profit and loss.

In India, controls are imposed on issues of capital through shares and debentures up to rupees 50 lakhs or so. If the amount does not exceed this amount, no consent of the controller of capital issues would be necessary.

• Production, Costs and Profit

Production may be defined as a process by which resources are transformed into goods and services.

In order to produce goods and services, each business needs inputs. Many inputs enter into the production of any output. These inputs can be grouped as:

1. Inputs of some businesses may be outputs of other businesses; they are called intermediate goods.
2. Inputs produced directly by nature, such as soil, are called land, and physical and mental efforts provided by people, called labour.
3. The services of factories, machines, and other man-made aids of production, called capital.

These are called factors of production. The production function relates inputs to outputs. It describes the technological relationship between inputs and outputs. It is also an efficiency relation showing the maximum amount of output that can be produced by the business using fixed quantity of resources.

The business's production function is expressed as:

$$q = f(l, k, etc.)$$

where q is output and l and k are labour and capital inputs, respectively. We can think about other inputs as well, such as land and raw material, and so on. And 'f' tells us that q is a function of inputs.

For the sake of simplicity we assume here that the business employs only two factors of production, viz., l and k. We must also remember that it relates flows of inputs to flows of outputs. For example, if it is said that production rises from 10 to 11 units, it means that the rate of production has risen from 10 to 11 units each month. This increase in output can be achieved by increasing inputs. It is relatively easy to increase labour input somewhat quickly. On the other hand, a fairly long period of time is required to vary the quantity of capital.

The speed at which different factor inputs can be varied largely depends on the time period under consideration. We assume that the business can make decisions in two time periods, i.e. the short-run and the long-run. In the short-run some factors are fixed, and others are variable. However, in the long-run all factors are variable. In the short-run we study the returns to a variable factor (such as labour) and in the long-run we study the return to scale.

• Costs and Profit

Profit is the difference between revenues and costs, including depreciation and the opportunity costs of the owner's capital. When all costs have been correctly deducted from the sales revenue, the resulting profit is the return to owner's capital.

In economics the concept of costs and profit differ from those used by businesses because the economists take into accout, amongst other things, the opportunity cost of owner's capital as part of the cost. The opportunity cost is the alternative that is foregone when the capital is used in the owners's business. When all costs including the opportunity costs are deducted from revenues, any positive remainder is called pure, abnormal, economic or supernormal profit.

Economic profit =

total revenue (TR) – total opportunity cost of all inputs used (TC), or,

Economic profit =

total revenue – (explicit + implicit costs).

In the theory of the business and production, profit maximization is the underlying hypothesis of our predictive theory. The goal of business is the maximization of economic profit, and the business is expected to try to make the positive difference between total revenue and total cost as large as possible.

For example, the profit and loss account will help us to understand the concept:

What businesses call profit is the return to the owner's capital. In economics, we deduct from this profit figure the imputed opportunity cost of the owner's capital to obtain pure economic profit.

Profit is defined in different ways for different purposes. Businesses are interested in the return to the owner's profit and seek to maximize this. The maximization of this profit is the objective of the business. They must also conform to tax laws and accounting practices. In economics, we are interested in how profit affects resource allocation, and the definition we use is the best for our purpose.

- **Returns to a Variable Factor in the Short-Run**

In the short-run we study the behaviour of output when 'n' more units (labour hours) of a variable factor (l) are applied to a given

Profit and Loss Account for a Company for the Year ending 31 December 2007

Expenditure		**Income**	
Variable Costs:		Revenue from sales	**£900,000**
Wages, materials etc. £500,000			
Total Variable costs	£500,000		
Fixed costs:			
Managerial, interest on loans			
Depreciation allowance, etc.			
Total Fixed cost	£240,000		
Total costs	**£740,000**		
Profit (£900,000 less £740,000)			**£160,000**
Calculation of pure profit			
Profit as reported by the company		£160,000	
Opportunity cost of capital	–£100,000		
Risk premium	–£40,000		
Pure or economic profit	£20,000		

quantity of fixed factor (capital, k). Then, in the short-run, output becomes a function of labour alone. Thus, the short-run production function may be expressed as:

$$q = q(l):$$

In the short-run, the output of a business (q) varies with the input of labour (l).

- **The Production Function**

Shows the relationship between inputs and maximum physical output. A production function is a technological, not an economic, relationship. It follows that an improvement in technology that allows the business to produce more output with the same amount of inputs results in a new production function.

Table 6.1 shows production function relating total output in column (2) to the quantity of labour in column (1). The data in table 6.1 is plotted in Figs. 6.1 and 6.2.

When there is zero unit of labour (l) input, there is no output. When there are 3 units of labour input, there is a total output of 60 units and so on. Fig. 6.1 shows a total physical product curve (TP), or the maximum amount of physical output (q) that is possible when we add successive equal-sized units of labour, a labour hour (l), whilst holding all other inputs constant. The production function is not a straight line. In fact, it peaks at 7.5 labour hours and then starts to go down. To understand why it starts to go down with an individual business in the short-run, we have to analyse in detail the law of diminishing (marginal) returns (diminishing marginal product {ivity}).

But before that let us examine the meaning of columns (3) and (4), that is average (AP_l) and marginal physical products (MP_l) of labour.

The definition of the average physical product of labour (AP_l) is straight forward: It is the total product (q) divided by the variable input(l). We can see in column (3) of Table 6.1 that the average physical product of labour ($AP_l = q/l$) first rises and then falls steadily after 3.5 labour hours are hired.

Table 6.1: Relation between Output (q) and the Quantity of a Variable Factor (Labour ({l}) when a Fixed Factor (Capital {k}) is given

Variable Input Labour Hours (l)	Output			Stages of Production
(1)	(2)	(3)	(4)	
	$TP_l = q$	$AP_l = q/l$	$MP_l = \Delta q/\Delta l$	
0	0	—	—	
1	10	10	10	Increasing return to l
2	30	15	20	
3	60	20	30	
4	80	20	20	Diminishing return to l
5	95	19	15	
6	108	18	13	
7	112	16	4	
8	112	14	0	
9	108	12	–4	Negative return
10	100	10	–8	

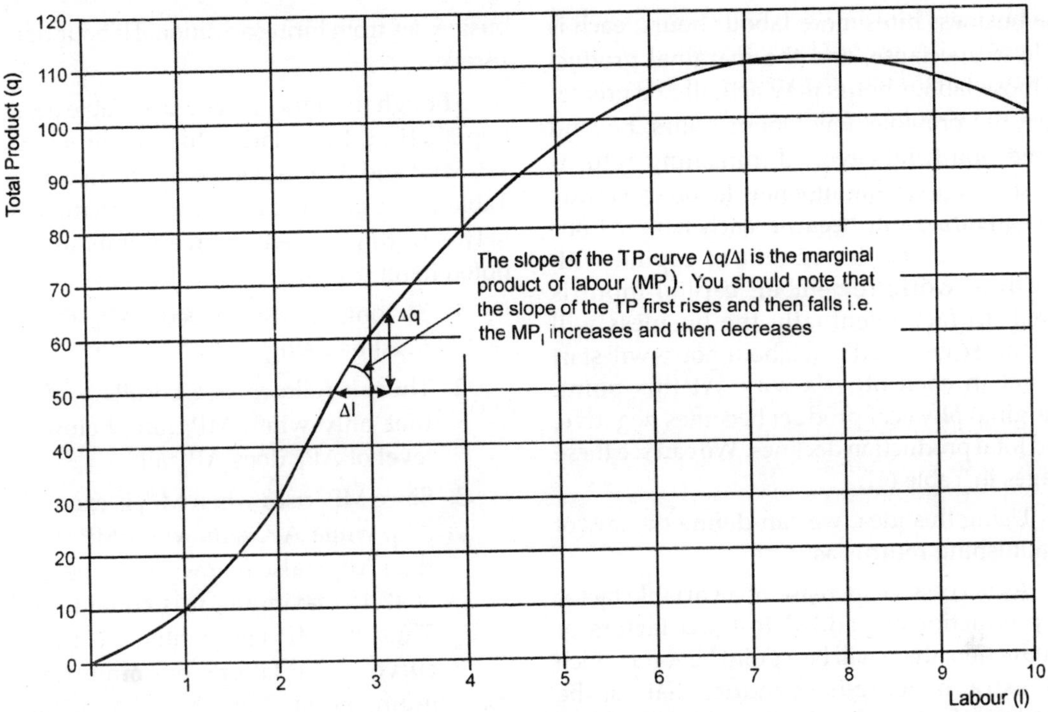

Fig. 6.1: The Total Product (TP) Curve

Marginal means 'additional'. Hence the Marginal Physical Product of labour (MP_l) is the change in total product (Δq) that occurs when an additional labour hour (Δl) contributes to an existing production process (keeping the other factors of production constant). The marginal physical product of labour (MP_l), therefore, refers to the change in output caused by a one-unit change in the labour input, (Δq/Δl).

At any point on the TP curve, the gradient (slope) of the TP measures the *marginal productivity* of labour.

• Diminishing Marginal Returns

The concept of diminishing marginal returns—also known as diminishing marginal product—applies in many situtations, namely, businesses in their use of productive inputs. When the returns from hiring more labour hours are diminishing (keeping the other factors of production constant), it does not necessarily mean that more labour hours would not be hired. In fact, labour hours will be hired until the returns, in terms of the value of the extra output produced, are equal to the additional wages that are to be paid to those labour hours that produce the extra output. Before we get into the decision making process, let us demonstrate that diminishing returns can be represented graphically and can be used in our analysis of the business.

• Measuring Diminishing Returns

How do we measure diminishing returns? First, we limit the analysis to only one variable factor of production, say l, as we can see in Table 6.1. Other factor of production, such as capital, must be held constant. Only then we can calculate the marginal returns from using more labour hours and know, as in Table 6.1, when we reach the point of diminishing marginal returns.

Initially, the marginal productivity of labour increase rapidly. Suppose the business starts with only capital and no labour. The business then hires one labour hour, who finds it difficult to get the work started. But when the business hires more labour hours, each is able to specialise, and the marginal product of those labour hours may actually be greater than the previous few labour hours. Beyond some point, however, diminishing returns must set in—not because new labour hours are less qualified but because each labour hour has, on average, fewer unit of capital with which to work; remember, capital input is fixed. In fact, eventually the business will become so crowded that labour hours will start to get in each other's way. At this point, marginal physical product becomes negative, and total production declines. We can see these stages in Table 6.1.

Using this idea, we can define the law of diminishing returns as:

As successive increase of a variable factor of production are added to fixed factors of production, there will be a point beyond which the extra, or marginal product that can be attributed to each additional unit of the variable factor of production will decline. Table 6.1 and Figs. 6.1 and 6.2 depicts this relationship.

Note that the law of diminishing returns is a statement about the physical relationships between inputs and outputs that we have observed in many businesses. If the law of diminishing returns was not a fairly accurate statement about the world, what would stop businesses from hiring additional labour hours forever.

Though the data presented in Table 6.1 are hypothetical, the relationship shown among TP, MPP and APP is widely applicable. From Table 6.1 we may also discover the relationship between MP_l and AP_l. Three points may be noted here:

1. So long as MP_l exceeds AP_l, the AP_l must be rising.
2. Thus, it follows as a corollary of this that only when MP_l falls below the level of AP_l, does AP_l fall.
3. Since MP_l rises when MP_l is exceeding AP_l, while AP_l falls when MP_l is less than AP_l, it also follows that where AP_l is at its maximum, it is equal to MP_l. Thus, the MP_l curve intersects the AP_l curve at the latter's optimum (maximum) point. You should remember that all marginal curves cut average curves at the latter's optimum points.
4. We assume that the MP_l first increase (up to 3 units of labour) and then starts to decline.

It may be pointed out here that MP_l can be zero or even negative, but AP_l can never be so. AP_l is always positive so long as TP is positive. Such a situation does not carry any

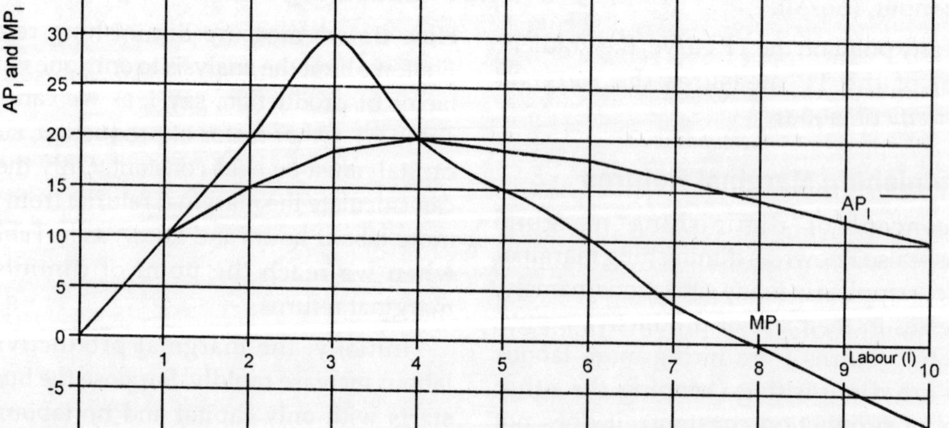

Fig. 6.2: The Average (AP_l) and Marginal (MP_l) Product of Labour

significance. For example, when 9 labour hours are employed, TP falls. Thus, no profit-maximizing producer would consider employing so many labour hours.

• An Example of the Law of Diminishing Returns

Agriculture provides an example of the law of diminishing returns. With a fixed amount of land and capital, the addition of more and more labour eventually ills diminishing marginal output. After a while, additional labour will have to start farming manually. They obviously would not be as productive as the first labour hours who manned the machines or tractors. The MPP of an additional farm labour hour, given a specific amount of capital, must eventually be less than that for the previous ones.

A hypothetical set of numbers illustrating the law of diminishing marginal returns is presented in Table 6.1. The numbers are presented graphically in Figs. 6.1 and 6.2. As Fig. 6.2 shows, marginal productivity first increases, then decreases, and finally becomes negative.

When 1 unit of labour is hired, TP goes up from 0 to 10. The marginal physical product is 10. When the second labour hour is hired, TP goes up from 10 to 30. Marginal physical product thus increases to 20. When the third labour hour is employed, total product again increases, from 30 to 60. This represents a marginal physical product of 30. When another labour hour is added, total product again increases from 60 to 80. This represents a MPP of 20. Thus, the point of diminishing marginal returns occurs after 3 labour hours are hired.

Note that after 7.5 labour hours are employed, marginal physical product becomes negative. That means that the hiring of a 10th labour hour would create a situation that reduces total product. This is sometimes called the point of saturation, indicating that given the amount of fixed inputs, there is no further positive use of the variable input. We have entered the region of negative marginal return.

• The Long-Run and Factor Inputs

In the long-run all factors are variable. Businesses wishing to maximise their profit will attempt to produce their chosen output by employing combinations of k and l which minimise their production costs. Ths cost-minimising effort can be shown graphically with the use of isoquants and isocost lines. These also enable us to trace out the path along which a business can expand output in the long-run.

Isoquants: Consider the production of a good, q, and suppose that only two factors of production, l and k, are employed. Suppose also that it is always possible to substitute k for l, and l for k, continuously in the production process. On the basis of these assumptions it follows that a given quantity of good q can be produced using many different combination of these inputs. This is shown in Fig. 6.3, where horizontal axis measures units of capital services per period (k) and the vertical axis measures units of labour per period (l).

For example, point A, on the isoquant q_0, represents just one possible combination of l and k (l_0, k_0) which can be used to produce q_0 units of output. This q_0 units of output can be produced by any number of different combinations of l and k represented by this isoquant q_0 (such as {l_1, k_1} – point B).

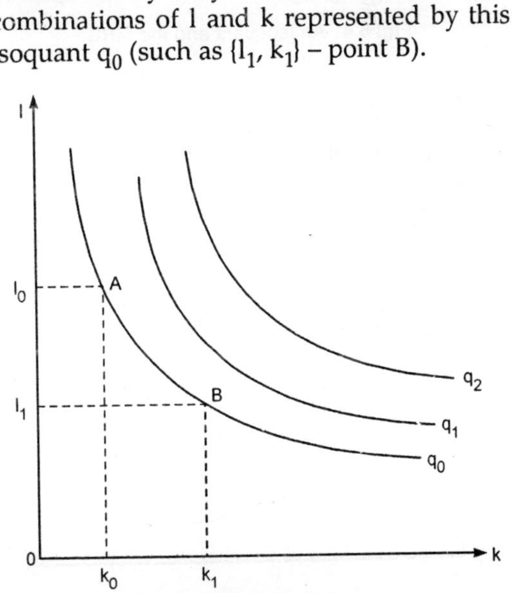

Fig. 6.3: Isoquants

Similarly, output increases as one moves from q_0 to q_1 and to isoquant q_2 (more capital and/or labour is employed and more output is produced).

An isoquant is a curve that shows all the possible combinations of inputs that yield the same level of output.

The slope of an isoquant is equal to $\Delta l/\Delta k$ = the marginal rate of substitution (MRS) of k for l.

The convex slope of the isoquant indicates the assumption of diminishing marginal rate of substitution (rate of technical substitution)

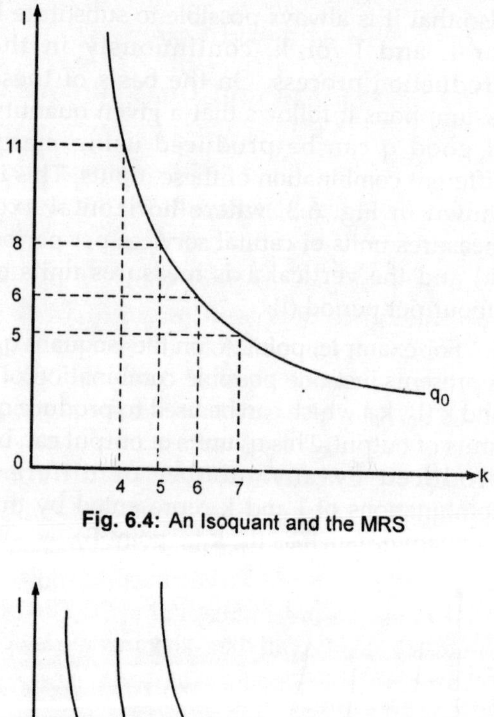

Fig. 6.4: An Isoquant and the MRS

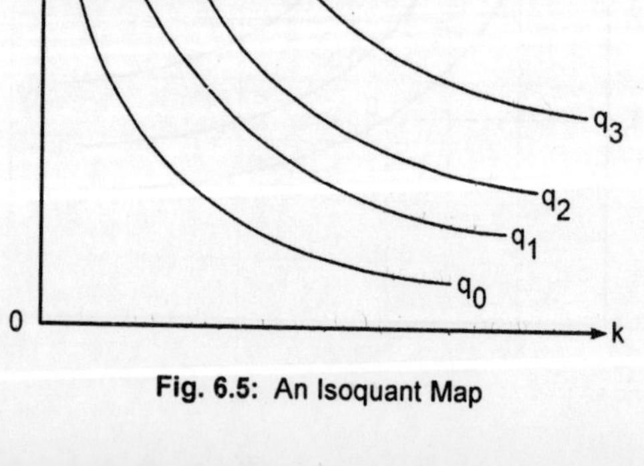

Fig. 6.5: An Isoquant Map

of labour for capital (or capital for labour). As we move along the isoquant we have to substitute less labour as we employ one more unit of capital.

Employing 5 units of capital rather than 4 units of capital we require 3 less units of labour to maintain output at level q_0. Employing 6 units of capital rather than 5 units of capital we require only 2 less units of labour to maintain output at level q_0. Employing 7 units of capital rather than 6 units of capital we require 1 less unit of labour to maintain output at level q_0. We have to give up less labour for the same quantity of capital employed.

Isoquants are similar to the indifference curves that we used to study consumer theory, where indifference curves order levels of satisfaction from low to high, isoquants order levels of output. However, unlike indifference curves, each isoquant is associated with a specific level of output.

An isoquant map is a family of isoquants which shows the production function for a good (Fig. 6.5). The isoquants, like indifference curve, have three important properties: first, no two isoquants can intersect; secondly, isoquants normally slope dowanwards from left to right; thirdly, they are convex to the origin.

• Production with Two Variable Inputs

Now let us consider the business's production technology in the long-run, where both k and l inputs are varaible. We can examine the alternative ways of producing by looking at the shape of a series of isoquants. As we know, an isoquant describes all combinations of inputs that yield the same level of output. The isoquants slope downward because both k and l have positive marginal products. More of either input increases output; so if output is to be kept constant as more of one input is used, less of other input must be used. The shape of the isoquant is shown in Figs. 6.3, 6.4 and 6.5.

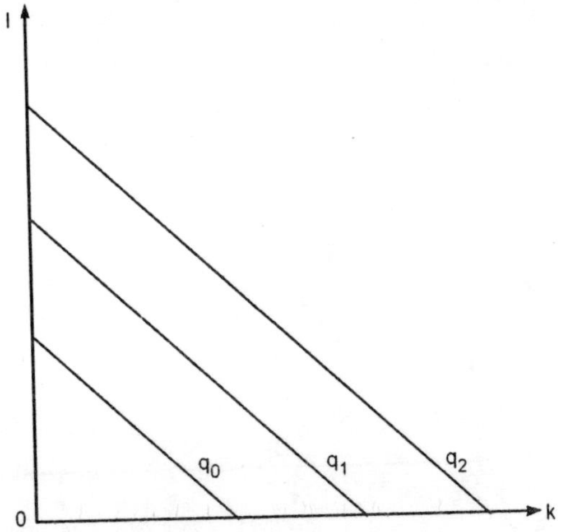

Fig. 6.6: Perfect Substitutes

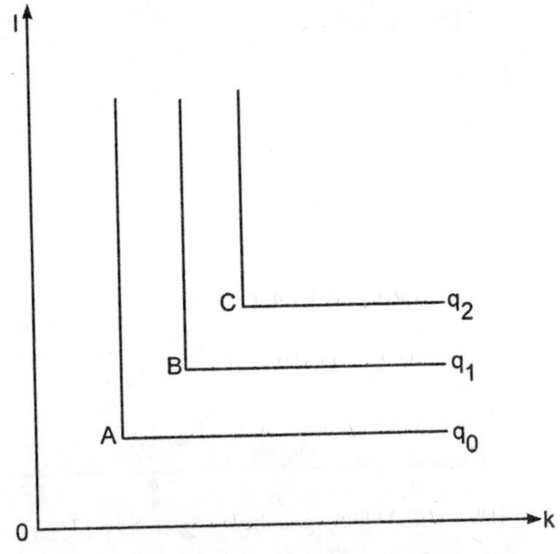

Fig. 6.7: Perfect Complements

• Isoquants

Two special cases:

1. **Perfect Substitutes:** When the production isoquants are straight lines, the MRTS is constant. This means that the rate at which k and l can be substituted for each other is the same whatever level of inputs being used as Fig. 6.6 shows.
2. **Fixed-Proportions Isoquants:** When the production isoquants are L-shaped, only one combination of l and k can be used to produce a given output. The addition of more k alone would not increase output, as the points A, B, and C in Fig. 6.7 show.

• Isocost Lines and Cost Minimizing Output

An isocost line shows all the combinations of k and l that can be purchased for a given monetary outlay.

Suppose that the price of l is £2 per unit and the price of K is £1 per unit. Table 6.2 shows the 3 combinations of the two factors that can be bought for an outlay of £10, £20 and £40. These 3 combinations are plotted in Fig. 6.8 and give the 3 isocost lines A_1B_1, A_2B_2 and A_3B_3, respectively.

In particular, the line A_3B_3 shows combinations of labour and capital that can be purchased for £30 when the price of labour is £2 and the price of capital is £1. The point A_3 indicates that all the £30 of income is being

Table 6.2: Combination of l and k for

a £10 Outlay (TC_1)		a £20 Outlay (TC_2)		a £30 Outlay (TC_3)	
Labout (£2)	Capital (£1)	Labour (£2)	Capital (£1)	Labour (£2)	Capital (£1)
5	0	10	0	15	0
4	2	8	4	12	6
3	4	6	8	9	12
2	6	4	12	6	18
1	8	2	16	3	24
0	10	0	20	0	30

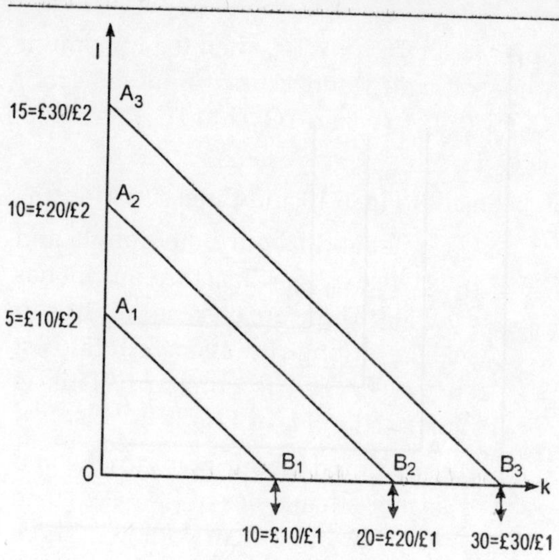

Fig. 6.8: Isocost Lines

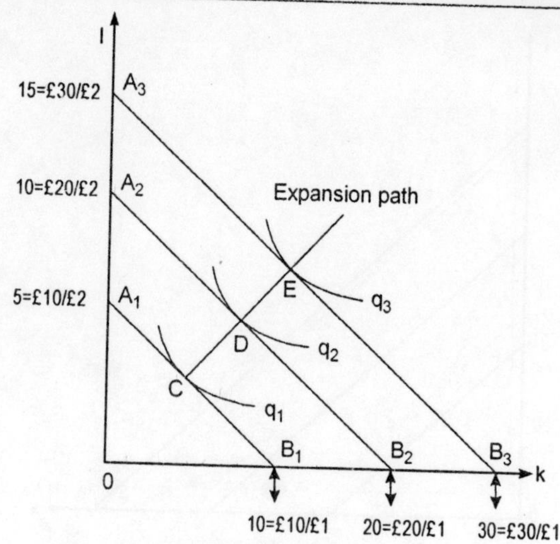

Fig. 6.9: Isocost Map

spent on labour and no income is being spent on capital and the point B_3 indicates that all the £30 of income is being spent on capital and no income is being spent on labour (of course, these are extreme points, and in practice the firm will never be at one of these points).

The slope (0.5) of the isocost lines represent the relative factor price ratio (£1/£2). A change in the relative factor price ratio will change the slope of the isocost line (not shown here).

If we draw the isoquant and isocost map together, this will give us cost-minimizing and profit-maximizing output level as shown in Fig. 6.9.

To produce a given output of good q, say q_1, at minimum cost, a business will produce at the point where isoquant q_1 is just touching, or is tangent to an isocost line A_1B_1 at point C in Fig. 6.9 which represents the point of cost-minimisation and all other combinations of k and l along q_1 would involve the business in a larger monetary outlay. If, in the long-run, the business expands it will continue to attempt to minimize its costs. Thus, the cost minimizing output q_2, would be at point D and production of output q_3 would be at point E and so on. The locus of points CDE is referred to as the business's long-run expansion path.

- **Return to Scale**

Understanding the nature of the business's long-run operation is important. The most useful place to bring a long-run analysis is with the scale of the businesses operation. The measure of increased output associated with increases in all inputs is fundamental to the long-run nature of the business's production process. How does the output of the business change (q_1 to q_2) as all its inputs (labour, capital and land) are proportionately increased? If output more than doubles ($q_2 > 2q_1$) when all inputs are doubled, there are increasing returns to scale. The automobile assembly line is a famous example of increasing returns. It is an important issue from a public policy perspective. If there are increasing returns, then it is economically advantageous to have one business rather than to have many small businesses. For example, increasing returns in the provision of electricity is one reason why we have large, but regulated, power companies.

A second possibility with respect to the scale of production is that output may double ($q_2 = 2q_1$) when all inputs are doubled. This is the case of constant returns to scale. With constant returns to scale, the size of the business's operation does not affect the productivity of its factors. Finally, when *all*

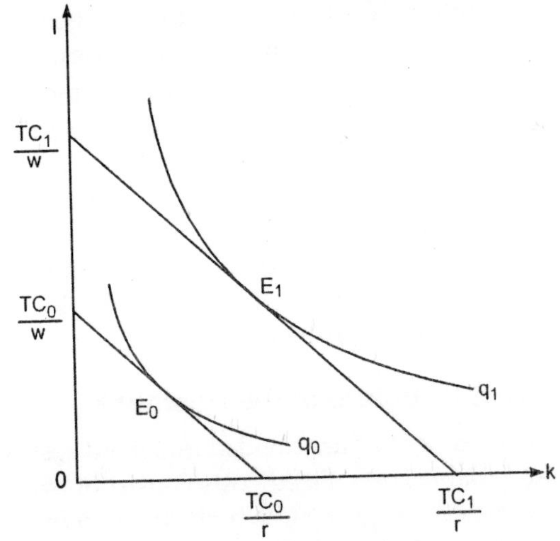

Fig. 6.10: Returns to Scale

If we let $TC_1 = 2.TC_0$ then the maximum inputs of both l and k have doubled from TC_0/w to TC_1/w and TC_0/r to TC_1/r, respectively.

Consider Fig. 6.10 and three situations:

1. If capital and labour both double and q_1 is twice q_0 ($q_1 = 2q_0$) then output has doubled. There are constant returns to scale and long-run average total cost curve (LATC) is constant. This is illustrated in Fig. 6.11(a).
2. If capital and labour both double and q_1 is **more** than twice q_0 ($q_1 > 2q_0$) then output has more than doubled. There are increasing returns to scale and the

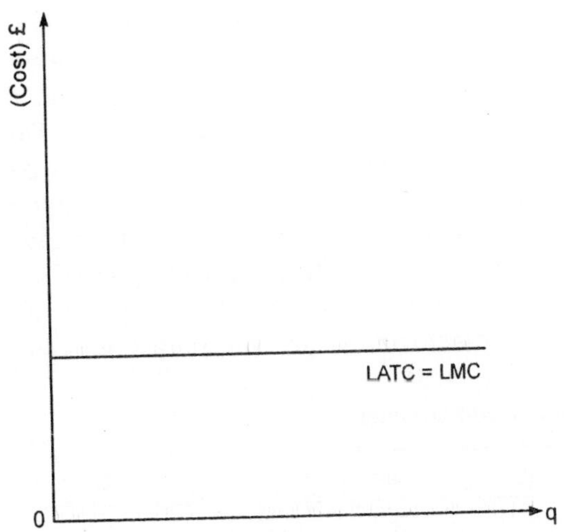

Fig. 6.11(a): Constant Returns to Scale

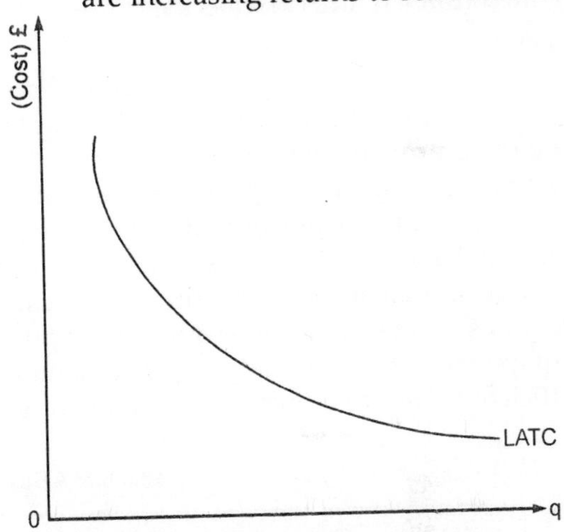

Fig. 6.11(b): Increasing Returns to Scale

inputs double the increase in output may be less than double the previous level of output ($q_2 < 2q_1$). This is a case of decreasing returns to scale and is likely to apply to any business with large-scale operations. It may result because of the problem of communication between managers and labour or becuase individuals cannot exhibit their entrepreneurial abilities in a large-scale operation. The presence or absence of returns to scale is seen in Fig. 6.10. Start at an initial equilibrium position E_0, with an original budget of TC_0, an output of q_0 and the prices of labour and capital and w and r, respectively.

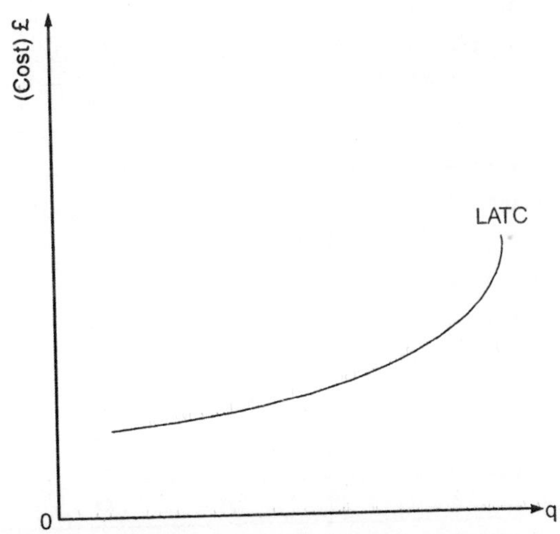

Fig. 6.11(c): Decreasing Returns to Scale

long-run average total cost curve (LATC) is decreasing. This is illustrated in Fig. 6.11(b).

3. If capital and labour both double and q_1 is **less** than twice q_0 ($q_1 < 2q_0$) then output has not even doubled. There are decreasing returns to scale and long-run average total cost curve (LATC) is increasing. This is illustrated in Fig. 6.11(c).

With increasing returns to scale, isoquants become closer and closer to one another as all inputs increase proportionally. Similarly, with decreasing returns to scale, isoquants move further and further away from each other. With constant returns to scale, they are equally spaced.

Returns to scale vary substantially from industry to industry. Other things being equal, the more prominent the returns to scale, the larger the businesses in an industry are likely to be. Manufacturing industries are more likely to have increasing returns to scale than service industries because manufacturing requires a substantial investment in capital equipment before business can operate most efficiently. Service industries are by and large labour-intensive and can usually be efficient even when producing in small quantities.

We will see that costs are the extension of the production ideas just presented. Let us consider the costs the business faces in the short-run. To make the analysis simple, we assume that there are only two factors of production, capital and labour. Our definition of the short-run will be the time during which K is fixed and labour is variable.

• Cost Structure of the Business

A business's costs are divided into fixed costs and variable costs. Fixed costs consist of pre-committed outgoings, which are payable regardless of the level of output. Variable costs represent outgoings, such as materials, distribution and energy costs, labour costs and so on, which rise or fall in accordance with the volume of output. Fixed costs can be subdivided into sunk costs and other fixed costs. Sunk costs may be defined as past expenditure on fixed assets which have no alternative use and the costs of which can be recouped only by trading. Examples of sunk costs include the cost of a nuclear plant, large steel plants and so on. By contrast, the cost of

Table 6.3: A Business's Short-Run Costs

(1)	(2)	(3)	(4)	(5)	(6)	(7)	(8)
			(2)+(3)	(2)÷(1)	(3)÷(1)	(4)÷(1)	
TP(q)	TFC	TVC	TC=TFC+TVC	$AFC = \frac{TFC}{q}$	$AVC = \frac{TVC}{q}$	$ATC = \frac{TC}{q}$	$MC = \frac{\Delta TC}{\Delta q}$
0	10	0	10	—	—	—	—
1	10	5	15	10	5	15	5
2	10	8	18	5	4	9	3
3	10	10	20	3.33	3.33	6.67	2
4	10	11	21	2.50	2.75	5.25	1
5	10	13	23	2.00	2.60	4.60	2
6	10	16	26	1.67	2.67	4.33	3
7	10	20	30	1.43	2.86	4.28	4
8	10	25	35	1.25	3.13	4.38	5
9	10	31	41	1.11	3.44	4.56	6
10	10	38	48	1.00	3.88	4.80	7

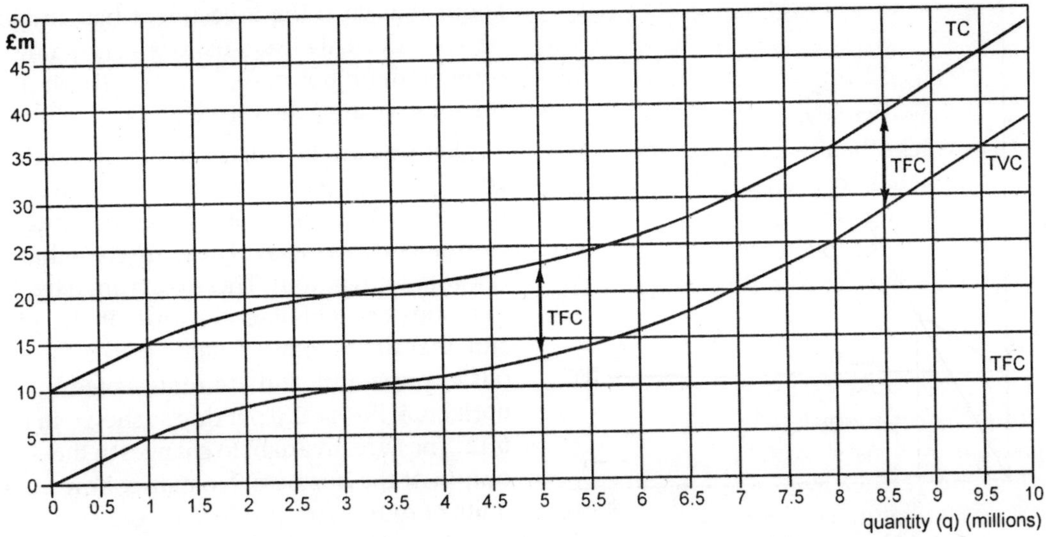

Fig. 6.12: Total Fixed Costs (TFC), Total Variable Costs (TVC) and Total Costs (TC)

the lease of an office building is a fixed cost, but not a sunk cost, since the building could be sublet. Sunk costs play an important role in determining the business's output and price strategy. Over time, all costs except sunk costs become variable. In economics, the long-run is defined as that period of time over which fixed cost can be converted into variable costs.

The cost structure of a business is shown in Table 6.3 and plotted in Fig. 6.12. Costs (£'s) are measured in the vertical axis and level of the business's output (q) on the horizontal axis. Fixed costs have to be paid regardless of the level of output and they are depicted by a horizontal line. Total variable costs are shown as an upward-sloping line, reflecting the fact that variable costs are a positive function of output. For example, a rise in output from 6m to 6.5m units raises total costs from £26 million to £28 million. The variable costs incurred in adding 0.5m units of output amounts to £2 million.

In the Table 6.3, the derivation of columns (4) through (8) is given in each columns heading. For example, column (6), AVC, is derived by dividing column (3) by column (1). MC is the change in total cost column (4) divided by change in output.

• Short-Run Cost Curves

The cost schedules in Table 6.3 are presented graphically in Fig. 6.12. This shows the total fixed costs as a horizontal straight line at a line at a value of £10. The curves TC and TVC are parallel. The vertical distance between them is £10, which is TFC.

• The Break-Even Point

In calculating the contribution of a new product to profit, variable costs are sometimes assumed to be linearly related to output. To find the break-even point we also require information on revenue as well as costs—this is also assumed to be linear. The break-even level of output (q_n) depicts a situation where certain minimum level of sales is required for the business to break-even. This is shown in Fig. 6.13 where TR = TC. The business is earning normal profit. After this point (q_n), the business enters an economic (super-normal) profit zone. Break-even points are used to estimate the effects on profit of variations in sales volumes around the break-even point. However, with a linear demand cruve, the TR schedule will be non-linear (quadratic) and the cost structure suggests a more complex picture than a linear relationship. The main point is that variable costs per unit of output are not constant as output increases. In the short-run,

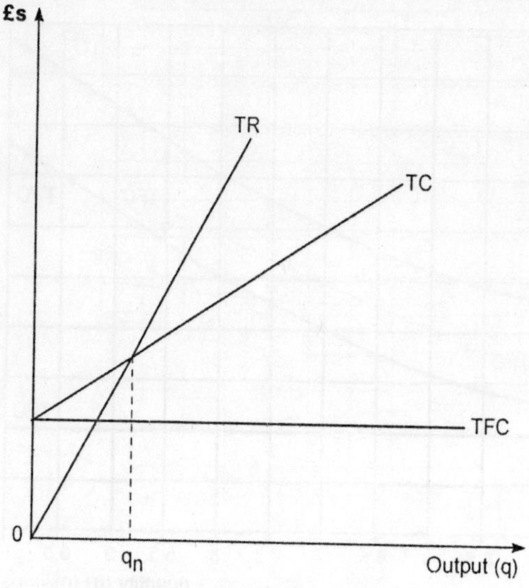

Fig. 6.13: The Break-Even Point

they tend to fall. Then, beyond a certain output level, they began to rise. A detailed discussion of the short-run cost curve will be given below.

• Short-Run Cost Curve

We know already that in the short-run, some of the business's inputs are fixed, and others can be varied to change the rate of output. The various measures of the cost of production can be distinguished.

In the short-run, a business incurs certain types of costs. We label all costs incurred total costs. Then we break total costs down into total fixed costs including sink cost and total variable cots, which will be explained below.

Thus, Total costs (TC) = total fixed costs (TFC) + total variable costs (TVC):

TC = TFC + TVC

After we discuss the elements of total costs, we will find out how to compute average and marginal costs.

• Total Fixed Costs (TFC)

We are here dealing in the short-run, during which capital is fixed. If investors in a business have already put £100 million into a new factory addition, the opportunity cost of that capital invested is now, in essence, a fixed cost. Becuase in the short-run, nothing can be done about that cost; the investment has already been made. This leads us to a very straightforward definition of fixed costs. All costs that do not vary are called fixed costs.

Let us now take an example of the fixed cost. The business's total fixed costs will equal the cost of the rent on its equipment and the insurance it has to pay. These are costs that do not vary with output. These costs are fixed for a certain period of time. However, in the long-run, they are variable. Total fixed costs are, in our example £10, and are represented by the horizontal line at £10 per day as shown in Fig. 6.12. They are invariant to changes in the daily output of the business. No matter how many units of output are produced fixed costs will remain at £10 per day.

• Total Variable Costs (TVC)

Variable costs are costs magnitude varies with the rate of production. The more the business produces, the more labour and raw materials it has to employ and hence the greater is the wages bill and the bill for raw materials. Total variable costs are to be paid as shown in column (3) Table 6.3. These are translated into total variable cost curve in Fig. 6.12. Note that the total variable cost curve (TVC) lies below the total cost curve (TC) by the vertical distance of £10. This vertical distance represents total fixed costs (TFC).

In Fig. 6.12, we see TC, TVC, and TFC.

Now we wish to consider average costs. The average cost is one in which we are measuring cost per unit of output. It is a matter of simple arithmetic to figure the averages of these cost concepts. We can define them as:

ATC = TC divided by output (TC/q).

AFC = TFC divided by output (TFC/q).

AVC = TVC divided by output (TVC/q).

Since TC = TFC + TVC

then TC/q = TFC/q + TVC/q.

Therefore, ATC = AFC + AVC

The arithmetic is done in the Table 6.3 and the numerical results are translated into a graphical form in Fig. 6.14. Becuase

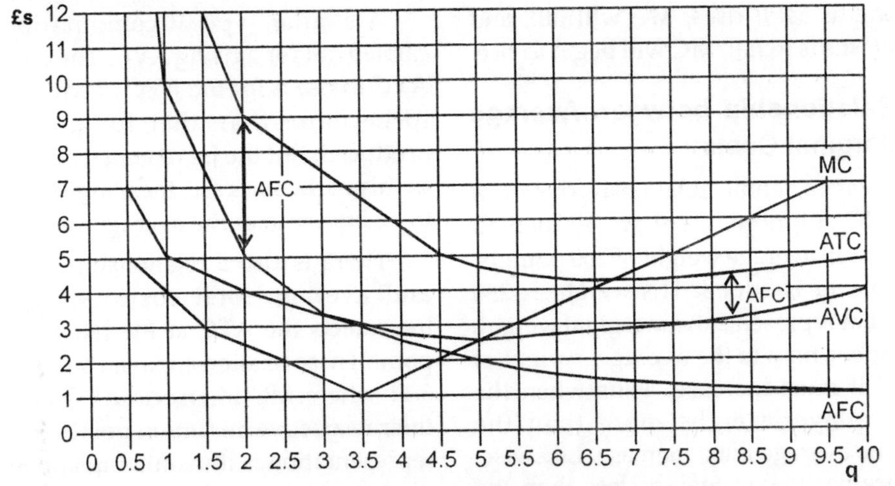

Fig. 6.14: The ATC, AVC, AFC and MC

TC = TVC + TFC, the difference between ATC and AVC will always be identical to AFC. That means that ATC and AVC more together as output expands.

Now we want to see what can be observed about the three average cost curves in Fig. 6.14.

AFC: Average fixed costs continue to fall throughout the output range. In fact, if we continue further to the right in Fig. 6.14, we would see that AFC would get closer and closer to the horizontal axis (it is asymptotic to the horizontal axis). That is because TFC remains constant. As we divide this fixed number by a larger and larger number of units of output, the resulting AFC has to become smaller and smaller. This is called "spreading the overhead".

AVC: The average variable cost is U-shaped. It is possible for the AVC curve to take other shapes in the long-run.

ATC: The average total costs curve has a similar shape to that of the AVC curve. However, it falls even more dramatically in the beginning and rises more slowly after it has reached a minimum point. It falls and then rises because ATC are the summation of the AFC and AVC curves. Thus, when AFC and AVC both falling, ATC must fall too. At some point, however, AVC starts to increase while AFC continues to fall. Once the increase in the AVC outweigh the decrease in the AFC, the ATC curve will start to increase and will develop its familiar U shape.

- **Marginal Cost**

We have already mentioned that the basis of decisions is on the margin-movement in economics is always determined at the margin. This is also true within the business. Businesses are very much interested in their MC because it refers to costs that result from a one unit change in production rate. For example, if the production of 10 calculators costs a business £48 and the production of 11 costs it £56, the MC of producing 11 units rather than 10 is £8. Thus, MC can be measured by using the formula: MC = Change in TC divided by change in output ($\Delta TC/\Delta q$). The MC of production is shown in Table 6.3 column (8).

The MC schedule is shown graphically in Fig. 6.14. Just like AVC and ATC, MC first fall and then rise. The U shape of the MC curve is a result of increasing and then diminishing marginal returns. A lower levels of output, MC declines. The reasoning is that as MPP increases with each addition of output, the MC of this last unit of output must fall. Conversely, when diminishing marginal returns set in, MPP decreases; it follows that the MC must rise when the MP begins its decline. These relationships are reflected in the Fig. 6.14.

As long as MPP rises, MC will fall, and when MPP starts to fall, MC will begin to rise.

• The Relationship between Average and Marginal Costs

There is always a definite relationship between AC and MC. Suppose, there are 10 football players with an average weight of 200 pounds. An 11th player is added. His weight is 230 pounds. That represents the marginal weight. What happens now to the average weight of the team? It must increase. Thus when the marginal player weighs more than the average, the average must increase. Likewise, if the marginal player weighs less than the average, the average weight will decrease.

There is a similar relationship between AVC and MC. When marginal costs are less than average costs, the average cost must fall. Conversely, when marginal costs are greater than average costs, the latter must rise. These relationship make sense. The only way for AVC to fall is for the extra cost of the marginal unit produced to be less than the AVC of all the preceding units. For example, if the AVC for 2 units of production is £4.00 a unit, the only way for the AVC of 3 units to be less than that of 2 units is for the variable costs of the last unit, the MC, to be less than the average of the past units. In this particular case, if AVC falls to £3.33 a unit, TVC for the three units would be 3 × £3.33, or almost exactly £10. Total VC for 2 units is 2 × £4, or £8. The MC is, therefore, £10 minus £8 = £2, which is less than the AVC of £3.33.

A similar type of computation can be carried out for a rising AVC. The only way for AVC to rise is for the AVC of additional units to be more than that for units already produced. But the incremental cost is the MC. In this particular case, the marginal costs have to be higher than the average variable costs.

There is also a relationship between MC and average total costs. Marginal cost interesects the ATC at the latter's optimum point. These relationships can be seen in figure 6.14 where MC intersects AVC and ATC at their respective minimum points. A graphical representation is illustrated in appendix II.

• Relationship between Output and Costs

In Fig. 6.15(a) MPP first rises and then falls. APP follows. The mirror image of (a) is shown in (b), in which MC and AVC first fall and then rise.

• Long-Run Cost Curves

The long-run is defined as a time period during which full adjustment can be made to any change in the economic environment. Thus, in the long-run, all factors of production are variable. We start our analysis of long-run cost curves by considering a single business contemplating the construction of a single plant (factory). The business has three alternative plant sizes from which to choose on the planning horizon. Each plant size generates its own short-run ATC curve. Now that we are talking about the difference between long-run

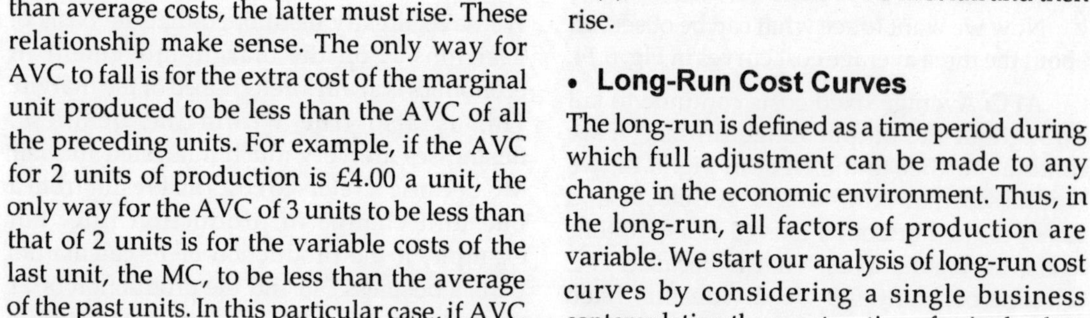

Fig. 6.15: The Relationship between Output and Costs

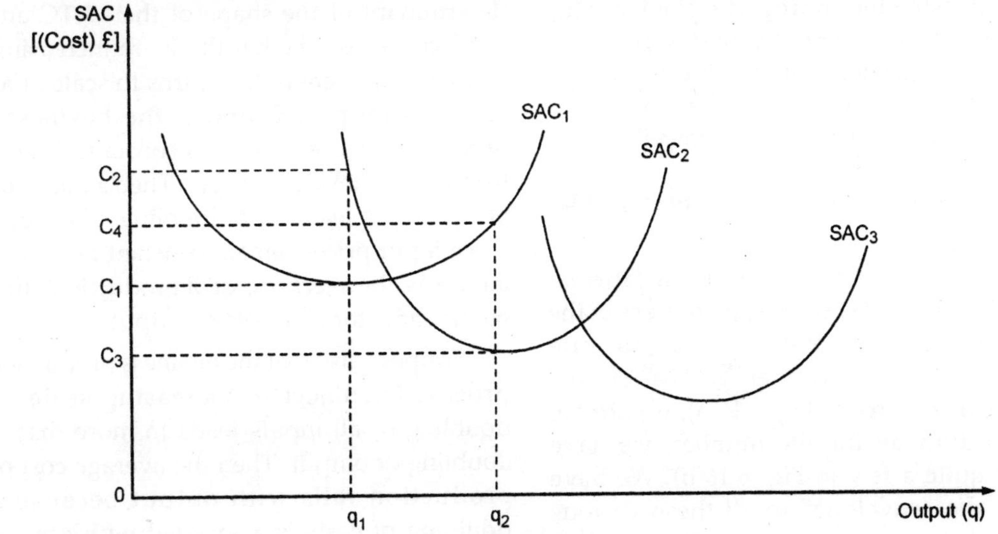

Fig. 6.16(a)

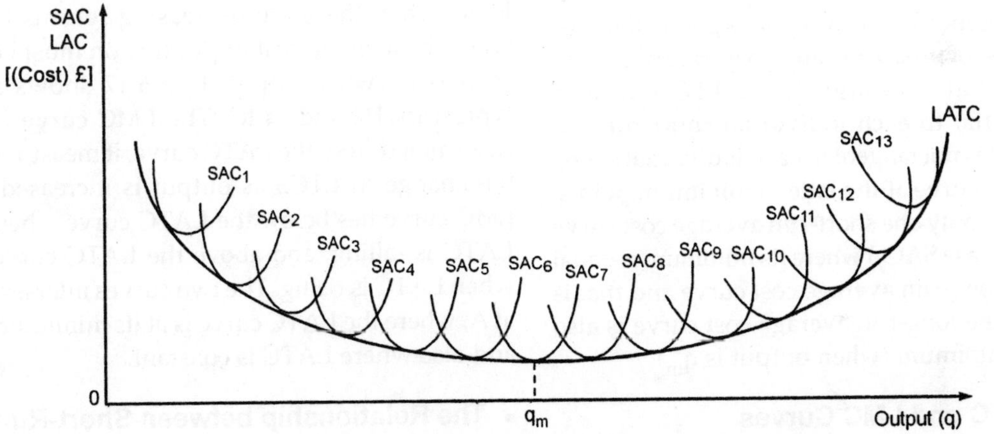

Fig. 6.16(b): Long-Run and Short-Run Average Cost Curves

and short-run curves, we label all short-run curves as S and long-run curves with an L; SAC = short-run average costs and LATC = long-run average total cost curves.

In Fig. 6.16(a), we can see short-run average cost curves for three successively large plants. Which is the optimal size to build? That depends on the anticipated normal, permanent rate of output per time period. Assume for a moment that the anticipated normal, sustained rate of output is q_1. If a plant of size 1 is built, the short-run average cost curve will be SAC_1 and the short-run cost will be C_1. If the plant size is 2, we see that, on SAC_2, the average costs will be C_2, which is greater than C_1. Thus, if the anticipated rate of output is q_1, the appropriate plant size is the one from which SAC_1 was derived.

However, if the anticipated permanent rate of output per time period goes from q_1 and q_2 and a plant of size 1 had been decided on, average costs would be C_4. If a plant of size 2 had been decided on, average costs would be C_3, which is less than C_4.

In choosing the appropriate plant size for a single-plant business during the planning horizon, the business will pick the size whose short-run AC curve generates an AC that is the lowest for the expected rate of output.

In choosing the appropriate plant size for a single-plant business during the planning horizon, the business will pick the size whose short-run AC curve generates an AC that is lowest for the expected rate of output.

• Long-Run Average Cost (LATC) Curves

If we assume that the entrepreneur faces an infinite number of choices of plant sizes in the long-run, we can conceive of an infinite number of short-run average cost curves similar to the three in Fig. 6.16(a), we are not able to draw an infinite number; we have drawn quite a few in Fig. 6.16(b). We have drawn the "envelope" to all these various short-run average cost curves. The resulting envelope is the long-run average cost curve. It represents the locus of points giving the least unit cost of producing any given rate of output. Note that although the LATC curve is tangential to each individual short-run AC curve it is not tangent to each individual short-run AC curve at the latter's minimum points. There is only one short-run average cost curve (in this case SAC_7) where its minimum is equal to the long-run average cost curve and that is when the long-run average cost curve is also at its minimum (when output is q_m).

• LATC and LMC Curves

In the long-run, the ability to change capital and labour allow the business to reduce costs along its expansion path as we can see the LATC and LMC curves. The most important determinant of the shape of the LATC and LMC curves is whether there are increasing, constant, or decreasing returns to scale at all levels of output. Suppose, the business's production process exhibits constant returns to scale at all levels of output. Then a doubling of all inputs leads to a doubling of output. Since input prices remain constant as output increases, the average cost of production must be the same for all levels of output.

Suppose also that the business production process is subject to increasing scale. A doubling of all inputs leads to more than a doubling of output. Then the average cost of production falls with output because a doubling of costs is associated with a more than twofold increase in output. By the same logic, when there are decreasing returns to scale, the average cost of production must be increasing with output. Fig. 6.17 shows a typical LATC and LMC. The LMC curve is determined from the LATC curve; it measures the change in LTCS as output is increased. LMC curve lies below the LATC curve when LATC is falling, and above the LATC curve when LATC is rising. The two curves intersect at A, where the LATC curve is at its minimum and also where LATC is constant.

• The Relationship between Short-Run and Long-Run Average Cost Curves

We know that in the long-run all inputs can be varied. As the size of the business gets larger, it will experience increasing returns to

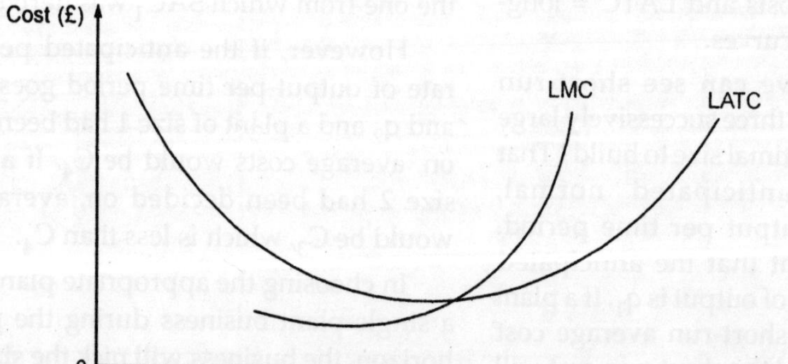

Fig. 6.17: The LATC and the LMC

scale up to a point, largely because of greater specialisation and use of more efficient technology. This implies that the LATC per unit of output will decline. For example, assume that a business produces 100 units of output with an input cost of £100, giving a long-run average total cost of £1 per unit of output. Now suppose that the business doubles its inputs and thus must spend £200 for inputs. But let us also suppose that, because of increasing returns to scale, output increases to 400 units. LATC would now be only £0.50 per unit of output. We assume that the prices of the inputs remained constant and that the long-run production function does not vary during our analysis.

As long as the business enjoys increasing returns to scale, LATC will decline. Eventually, the benefits of growing size will give way to the costly problems of coordinating a large enterprise, and LATC will rise. Although management, along with all other inputs, must, by definition, be variable in the long-run, it is not possible simply to enlarge the manage-ment as the business grows while maintaining the same degree of management efficiency. Just as the suitable technology for the business usually changes with size, so the relationship of the management to the business changes with size and hence become less efficient and the decision-making process becomes more time-consuming.

- **Long-Run Costs with Constant returns to Scale**

In the long-run a business, with constant returns to scale, can change the size of its plant, without increasing its average costs. The LATC curve = LMC curve is the envelope of the SAC curves. With constant returns to scale, LATC curve consists of the minimum points of the SAC curves as shown in Fig. 6.18(b). With constant returns to scale, the LATC curve equals the minimum points of the SAC curves not otherwise as well will see below. Now let us assume that there are many choices of plant size, each of which has an SAC curve that has its minimum at £10 level. As Fig. 6.18(b) shows, LATC curve is a straight line. Whatever the business wants to produce, it can choose the plant size that allows it to produce that output at the minimum average cost of £10.

Fig. 6.19 shows the increasing, decreasing and constant returns to scale, the analysis is essentially the same, but the LATC curve is no longer a horizontal line. Of the three plants the minimum average total cost is the lowest for a medium-size plant (SAC_3). The LATC curve exhibits initially increasing returns to scale, but at higher output levels it exhibits decreasing returns. We can see the envelope associated with five plants. If the business wants to produce q_1 output, as in Fig. 6.19,

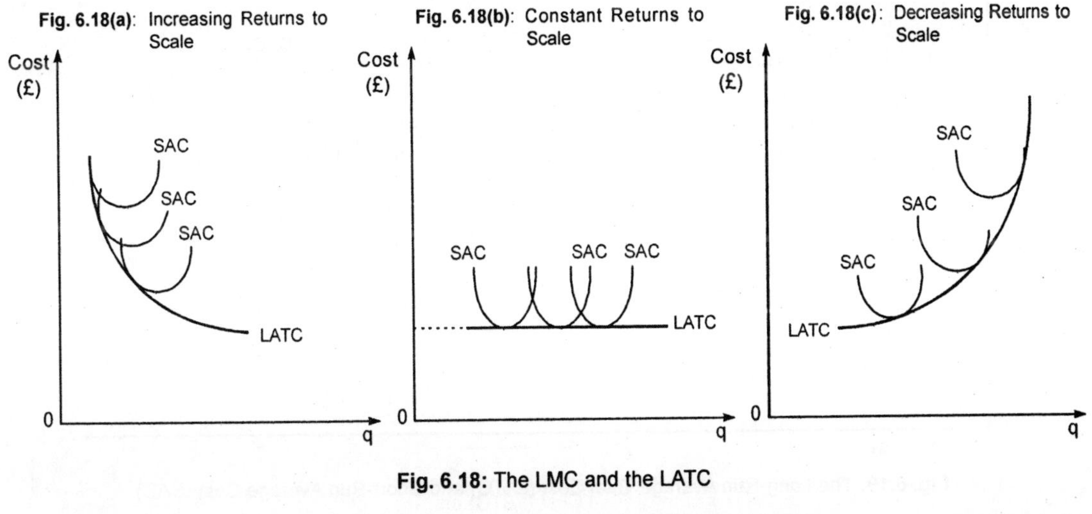

Fig. 6.18: The LMC and the LATC

building a small plant is desirable (SAC_1), so that SAC_1 is at B = £8. A small plant is a better choice than a medium-sized plant of SAC_2 at A = £10. If plant of other sizes could be built, and one size allowed the business to produce q1, at less than SAC_1, then B would no longer be on the LATC curve. In Fig. 6.19, the envelope that would arise if plants of any size could be built is given by the LATC curve, which is U-shaped. Note that the LATC curve never lies above any of the SAC curves. Also note that the points of minimum average total costs of the smallest and the largest plants do not lie on the LATC curve because there are increasing and decreasing returns to scale in the long-run. For example, a small plant operating at minimum average total cost (except SAC_3) is not efficient because the large plant can take advantage of increasing returns to scale to produce at a lower average total cost.

Finally, note that the LMC is not the envelope of the short-run MC curves. Short-run marginal costs apply to a particular plant; LMC apply to all possible plant sizes. Each point on the LMC curve is the short-run MC associated with the most cost-efficient plant.

- **Why the LATC Curve is U-shaped**

We can see that the LATC curve in Fig. 6.19 is U-shaped, similar to the U-shaped of the SAC curve developed above. The reason behind the U-shape of the two curves is not the same. The SAC curve is U-shaped because of the law of diminishing marginal returns. But the law cannot be applied in the long-run, because in the long-run, all factors of production are variable; there is no point of diminishing marginal returns because there is no fixed factor of production.

Why do we, then, see the U-shape in the LATC curve? The reasoning has to do with the economies of scale, constant returns to scale, and diseconomies of scale. When the business is experiencing economies of scale, the LATC curve slopes downward—an increase in the scale of production leads to a fall in unit costs. When the business is experiencing constant returns to scale, the LATC curve is at its minium point, in such a way that an increase in the scale of production does not change unit costs. When the business is experiencing dis-economies of scale, the LATC curve slopes upward—an increase in the scale of production increases unit costs. These three

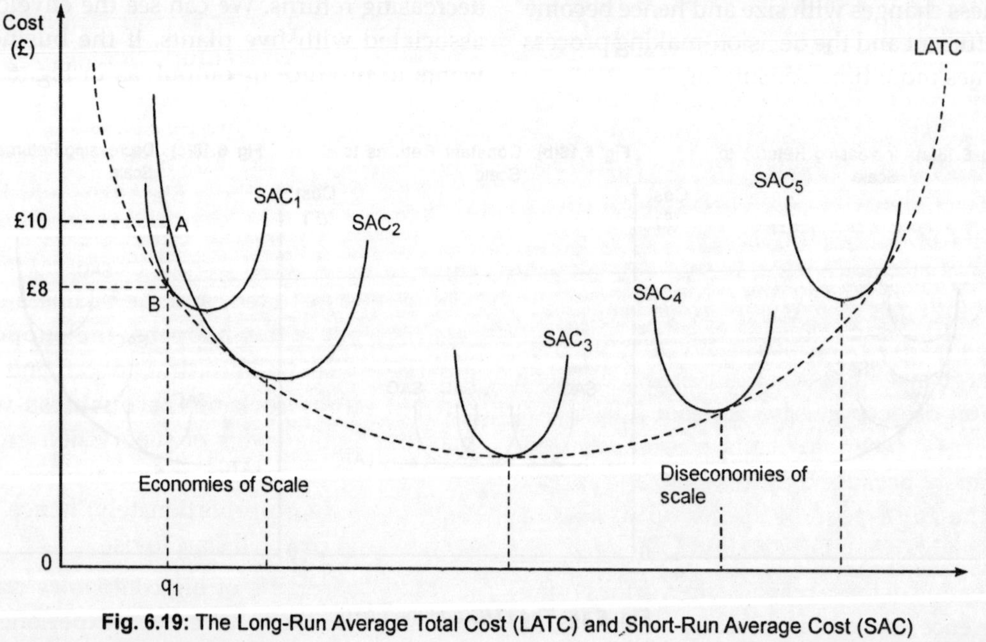

Fig. 6.19: The Long-Run Average Total Cost (LATC) and Short-Run Average Cost (SAC)

sections of the LATC curves are shown in Figs. 6.18(a), (b) and (c).

• Reasons for Economies and Diseconomies of Scale

We shall examine first some reasons why a business might be expected to experience economies of scale:

Specialisation, the dimensional factor, and improved productive equipment.

As a business' scale of operation increases, the opportunities for specialization in the use of resources also increases. This is sometimes called increased division of tasks or operations. Gains from such division of labour or increased specialisation comes as the average cost per unit of production fall. There are two types of economies of scale: internal and external economies of scale.

• Internal Economies of Scale

These economies arise from within the business itself as a result of its own decision to become big. As a result of business becoming bigger, it experiences internal economies of scale where the average cost per unit of production are falling as output is rising. Thus, the business is becoming cost efficient. There are six main categories of internal economies: technical economies, financial economies, marketing economies, managerial economies, risk-bearing economies, and welfare economies. These arise due to internal efficiency and are enjoyed especially by big businesses within the industry. The larger the scale of operation, the bigger the types of machinery it can use. Small-scale operations may not be able profitably to use large machines that can be more efficient per unit of output. Also, smaller businesses cannot use technologically more advanced machinery because they are unable to spread out the high cost of such sophisticated equipment over a large output.

For any of these reasons, the business may experience economies of scale, which means equal percentage increases in output result in a decrease in average cost. Thus output can double, but total costs will less than double; hence average cost falls.

• External Economies of Scale

These are the economies which accrue to the industry as a whole and each particular business can enjoy these economies as the industry as a whole expands. These external economies can be observed where the industry has concentrated in a particular area. Since external economies of scale are associated with industrial concentration in particular areas, they are often called the economies of concentration.

External economies can provide the following advantages: Regional specialisation of labour, education, specialised services, development of ancillary businesses, transport and information.

• Why a Business Might Experience Diseconomies of Scale

One of the basic reasons that a business can expect to run into diseconomies of scale is that there are limits to the efficient functioning of management. Moreover, as more labour hours are hired, a more than proportionate increase in managers and other staff may be needed, and this could cause increased costs per unit. This is also because larger levels of output imply successively larger plant size, which in turn implies successively larger business size. Thus, as the level of output increases, more people must be hired, and the business size gets bigger. As this happens, the support, supervisory, and administrative staff and the general paperwork of the business will increase. As the layers of supervision grow, the costs of information and communication grow more than proportionately; hence the average unit cost will start to rise.

Many observers of big companies claim that many of them have been experiencing some diseconomies of scale. Witness the problems that Ford and IBM had in the early 1990s. Analysts are of the opinion that the financial problems they faced were at least partly a function of their size relative to their smaller competitors, who could make decisions more quickly and then take advantage of the changing market conditions more rapidly. This was particularly true for IBM who initially adapted very slowly to the fact that the large mainframe computer business was declining as micro-computers became more powerful. Eventually, by the end of 1990s, IBM had adjusted to a more appropriate scale.

- **Minimum Efficient Scale**

Economists and statisticians have gathered data on the relationship between changes in all inputs and changes in average cost. It turns out that for many industries, the LATC curve is not U-shaped. Rather, it is saucer shaped. It reaches a minimum point at A as in Fig. 6.20. Prior to this point, there is a small section of declining LATC (economies of scale) and then it becomes horizontal (constant returns to scale). It then increases (diseconomies of scale) at some later rate of output (point B). At the output rate where economies of scale end and constant economies of scale start, the minimum efficient scale (MES) for the business is encountered. It occurs at point A. The MES will always be the lowest rate of output at which long-run average costs are minimized. In any industry with a LATC curve similar to the one in Fig. 6.20, larger businesses have no cost-saving advantage over smaller businesses as long as smaller businesses have at least obtained the minimum efficient scale at point A.

The MES gives us a rough guide of the degree of the competition in the industry. If the MES is small relative to the industry demand, the degree of competition in that industry is likely to be high because there is room for many efficiently sized businesses. Conversely, when the MES is large relative to the industry demand, the degree of competition is likely to be small because there is room for a relatively small number of efficiently sized businesses. Looked at another way, if it takes a very large scale of plant to obtain minimum LATC, the output of just a few of these very large businesses will fully satisfy total market demand. This means that there is no room for a large number of small plants if MES is to be obtained in that indusry.

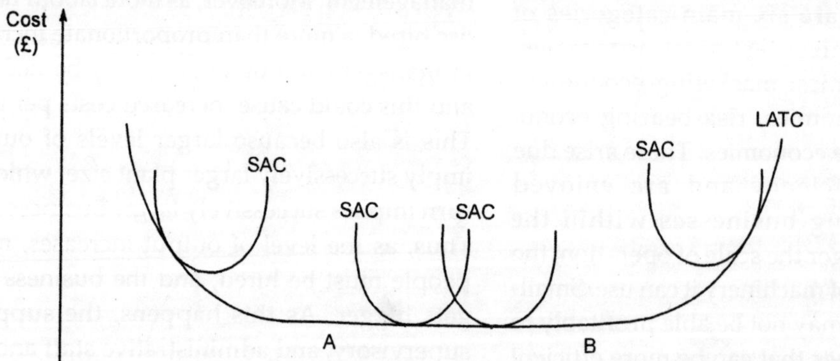

Fig. 6.20: A Saucer-shaped LATC

APPENDIX 6A.1

The Relationship between TP, APL and MPL

In the short-run one factor of production is held constant (k). Labour (l) is the variable input. The total product curve (TP) shows the relationship between the number of labour hours employed (measured in labour hours) and the output produced (q). It is ***assumed*** to be S-shaped.

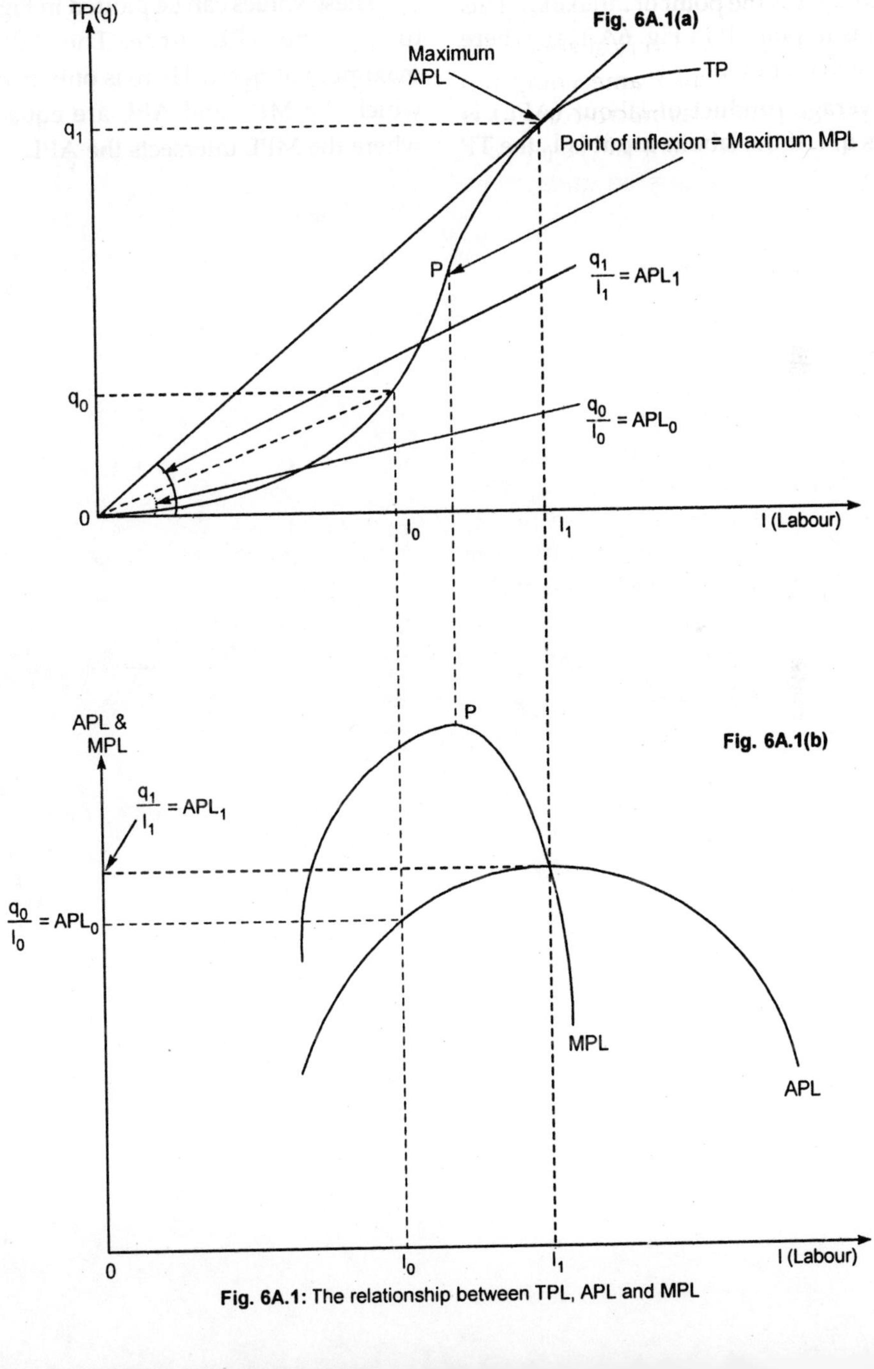

Fig. 6A.1: The relationship between TPL, APL and MPL

The slope of the TP curve is $\Delta q/\Delta l$, is the marginal product of labour (MPL). With an S shaped TP curve the slope first increases (MPL increases) and then declines (MPL declines). This is shown in Fig. 6A.1(b). These values are then plotted in Fig. 6A.1(b) creating the curve MPL. The slope of the TP is at a maximum at point P, the point where the slope of TP changes (known as the point of inflexion). This corresponds to point P in Fig. 6A.1(a), where MPL is at a maximum.

The average product of labour (APL) is defined as q/l. If the labour input is l_0 the TP curve tells us that the output produced is q_0 and the APL is q_0/l_0. The values of APL can be represented in diagram 6A.1(a) by the slope of a ray from the origin to the point on the TP curve above a particular value of q. By looking at the various rays we can see that q/l will increase up to q_1/l_1 and then decline.

These values can be plotted in Fig. 6A.1(b) to give the APL curve. The APL is at a maximum at q_1/l_1. There is only one point at which the MPL and APL are equal—this is where the MPL intersects the APL.

APPENDIX 6A.2

If we consider the TP curve in Fig. 6A.1(a) and assume only one variable input, labour. If the price of labor is w then the short-run cost of producing q is w.l. If the vertical axis of Fig. 6A.1 becomes the horizontal axis of 6A.2(a) and we measure short-run costs on the vertical axis we find that the relatonship between cost and output is TVC. Since the total fixed cost curve is constant the total cost curve is equal to the TVC curve plus a constant we can find the TC curve

TC = TVC + TFC.

Using the ideas discussed in Appendix 6A.1 we can see that a slope of a ray from the

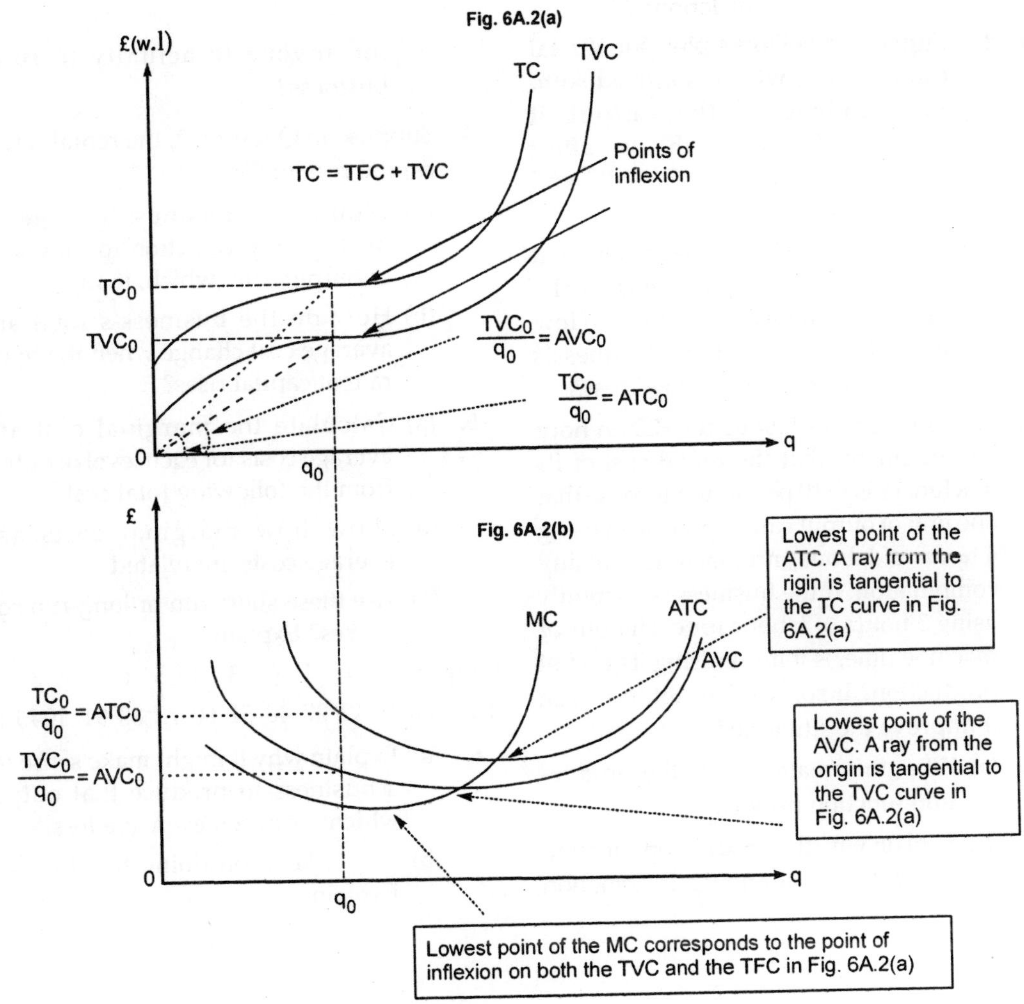

Fig. 6A.2: The relationship between TC, ATC, AVC and MC

origin to the total cost curve (TC) will give us the average total cost (ATC) and the slope of a ray from the origin to the total variable cost (TVC) will give us the average variable cost (AVC); the slope of the TC (and TVC) will give us the marginal cost (MC).

Since the rays to the origin (the AVC and ATC) fall and then rise, this will generate the 'U'-shaped ATC and AVC curves shown in Fig. 6A.2(b). Similarly the slope of the TC (or TVC) first increases and then decreases—generating the U-shaped MC curve.

QUESTIONS

1. (a) Suppose a business pays an annual franchise fee, which is a fixed sum, independent of the output it produces. How does this tax affect the business's fixed cost, MC and average cost?
   (b) Now suppose the business is charged a tax that is proportional to the number of items it produces. How does this tax affect the business's fixed cost, MC and average cost?
2. A business hires labour for £22 an hour and calculates that the rental cost of its machinery is £110 per hour. Suppose that one unit of output can be produced using 4 hours of labour and machinery in any combination. If the business is currently using 3 hours of labour for each hour of machine time, is it minimising its cost of production? If so, why? If not, how can it improve the situation?
3. (a) What information does the production function provide?
   (b) Explain why the production function does not provide enough information for anyone to actually to run a business?
4. Suppose in Question 2, the rental rate of capital rose to £3:
   (a) Would the business change its method of production for any level of output? Say which, if any.
   (b) How do the business's total and average cost change when the rental rate of capital rises?
5. (a) Calculate the marginal cost and average costs for each level of output from the following total cost.
   (b) Show how marginal costs and average costs are related.
   (c) Are these short-run or long-run cost curves? Explain.

Output:	0	1	2	3	4	5	6	7	8	9
Total cost:	12	27	40	51	60	70	80	91	104	120

6. (a) Explain why it might make sense for a business to produce that output which it can sell even at a loss.
   (b) Can it keep on doing this forever? Explain.

ANSWERS

1. (a) TC = TFC + TVC. Since franchise fee is a fixed sum, the business's fixed costs increase by the fee. Then ATC = (TFC + TVC)/q, and AFC = TFC/q, increase by the average franchise fee (FF/q). AVC is unaffected by the fee. Because MC is the change in total cost with the production of an additional unit and since the fee is constant, MC is unaffected.

   (b) When a tax is imposed on each unit produced (tax= tq), VC increases by tq. AVC increases by t, and because fixed cost is constant, ATC also increased by t. Because TC increases by t with each additional unit, MC also increases by t.

2. If the business can produce one unit of output with either 4 hours of labour or 4 hours of machinery or any combination of labour and machine, then the isoquant is a straight line with a slope of –1 and intercepts at K = 4 and L = 4. The isocost is TC = 22L + 110K, has a slope of –1/5 and intercept at K = TC/110 and L = TC/22. The cost-minimisation point is a corner solution, where L = 4 and K = 0 and TC = 88.

3. (a) Maximum output that can be obtained from specific bundles of inputs,

   (b) Also need to know prices of input and output.

4. (a) At output 4 the business would switch from column 1 to 2.

   (b) Both TC and average total cost must rise.

5. (a) MC: 15 13 11 9 10 10 11 13 16

   ATC: 27 20 17 15 14 13.3 13 13 13.3

   (b) At Q = 8, ATC is minimum = MC.

   (c) Short-run cost curves. Because, in the long-run, the cost of a zero output is zero.

6. (a) If it can over SVC.

   (b) No, only in the short-run.

CHAPTER 7

PERFECT COMPETITION AND COMPETITIVE EQUILIBRIUM

KEY TERMS

Total Revenue (TR): Is the real price per unit multiplied by the number of units sold.

Total Cost (TC): Is the sum of total fixed cost plus total variable cost.

Profit (π): Total revenue less total cost.

Marginal Revenue (MR = ΔTR/Δq): The extra revenue received (earned) from the sale of an extra unit.

Marginal Cost (MC = ΔTC/Δq): The cost of producing an extra unit.

A Pareto Optimality: Is said to exist when resources cannot be reallocated so as to make one person better off without making someone else worse off.

We have discussed, in the earlier chapter, why a demand curve is downward-sloping. The reasons for a supply curve being upward-sloping are less straight forward. In one scenario the upward-sloping supply curve can be easily explained. A rise in price will induce businesses to supply more. As output increases, so too does unit cost, and hence supply curve slopes upwards. By adding together the supply curve of the individual businesses we derive the market supply curve, and it too slopes upwards.

Complexities arise if increases in output lead to a fall in unit cost. This happens quite often because of economies of scale, and it is likely in the long-run. As markets expand, the scope for economies of scale increases. To be able to exploit scale economies and to have vigorous competition at the same time requires even larger markets. Scale economies have implications for the competitiveness of national industries and for the viability of national markets, as well as for the scope of the supply curve.

The competitive model assumes that all businesses are profit-maximizers; that they all produce the same product and each business accounts for a small fraction of the total market. Thus, the individual business has no market power. Exposure to global competition means that they have to supply at world market price or else lose sales. By assuming zero market power initially, we are able to explore important features of the market system.

• Profit Maximisation

Firms seek to maximize profit (π). Like the assumption of utility maximization, this assumption has to be interpreted as a general tendency rather than a statement that all businesses are guided by only this consideration. In the short-term, the acquisition of market share may often necessitate taking price and quantity decisions which conflict with profitability and may even involve short-term losses. Also, opportunistic behaviour is rarely the best foundation for long-term profit.

When originally conceived, the idea of profit maximization applied to owner-manager of small businesses. Provided the owner-manager did not have too strong a preference for leisure and the good life, the assumption that she/he would try to maximize profit seemed reasonable. Difficulties arose with the growth of the public limited company, and the replacement of owners by professional management. Owners (the shareholders) might still safely want to maximize profit. But managers might want the maximize something different—such as their salaries or their executive power. Since, in a limited liability business, shareholders are unable to monitor and judge performance as closely as the executives. With the possibility of conflicting objectives between owners and managers, the business might not always behave in the way one would expect on the basis of the profit-maximization assumption. In the words of Herbert Simon: Most producers are employees, not owners of businesses. Viewed from the vantage point of classical (economic) theory, they have no reason to maximize the profit of the businesses, except to the extent that they can be controlled by owners.

The divorce in objectives between owners and managers gives rise to a principal-agent problem. A business' profit is assumed to be related to managerial effort, but owners are unable to monitor and measure this effort. Hence they must think of ways of motivating the executives to maximize profit rather then their own utility. There are ways of tackling the problem. First, owners (the principal), through the Board of Directors, can devise price incentives which will motivate executives (their agent) to pursue the principal's objectives of profit maximization. Second, if they are unable to do this, owners can sell their shares to other owners who will find ways of utilising the business's assets more profitably. The threat of takeover and the consequent prospect of a new management team can be a powerful spur to performance by executives.

• Management Incentives

Owners pay executives a base salary, but they also tie remuneration to profit by payment of various forms of profit-related incentives. Examples include profit bonuses, fixed-term contracts which are renewable if a profit target is reached, and share options. Another possibility is for shareholders to apply the stick of critical review of management performance at general meetings. Profit-related incentives are only a partial answer to the problem of divergent objectives. First, the link between executive pay and management effort is difficult to quantify. Second, a more difficult problem is that the relationship between a business's profitability and managerial effort can be erratic. Profit can rise and fall because of macroeconomic development or because of a run of good or bad luck. The 1990s was a prosperous decade for business: recovery from recession, low inflation, and falling unemployment. Profit boomed as did corporate pay, but it would be difficult to argue that the high remuneration caused the economic boom. Proof of the pudding in this instance may well be executives' reluctance to rely too much on profit or share-price-related remuneration. Not surprisingly, empirical studies indicate that the correlation between executive pay and company performance is weak.

Despite these qualifications, shareholders continue to pay high levels of remuneration to their executives. Compensation to the highest paid executive shop floor pay has widened. In the 1970s typical chief executive of a large American company earned about 40 times more than the average factory worker. During the 1990s, the same executive earned over 400 times more. Executive share option schemes have soared in the US over the past decade. In 1998 alone, 92 of the America's 200 leading chief executives were given options with an average minimum value of $31m. Of course, high executive pay may prove a good bargain for the owner-shareholders if they achieve even a mild motivation effect. Shareholders may also acquiesce in high pay for their executives because, being dispersed and numerous, they have little economic incentive to monitor management directly. An individual shareholder will bear heavy costs for organising such monitoring, but the benefit will accrue to all other shareholders. Hence each individual shareholder has very little incentive to take the initiative. This is an instance of a pervasive problem in economics life called the free-rider problem.

• Threat of Takeover

Even if all the above measures fail, the threat of takeover acts as one further discipline on management. If management continuously underutilises the company's resources, the threat of takeover by another management team will be accentuated, with potentially adverse consequences for incumbent executives. While even the best-run companies can become a takeover target, the probability of this unpleasant outcome can be minimised by earning high profit. This raises the share price and makes the business too expensive for predators.

The takeover threat is particularly relevant to countries with a highly developed capital market, such as the UK and the USA. Of course, management has devised many ingenious ways of reducing this threat. Among the more familiar ones are greenmail (where the incumbent management buys off with company money), white knights (where the assistance of a friendly outsider is enlisted to ward off hostile bidders) and poison pills (which refer to provisions whereby the existing shareholders can acquire shares in the surviving business at a substantial discount from market price). This acts as a disincentive to such takeovers by making them more expensive.

Market forces, thus, in the form of both carrot of incentive and the stick of the takeover threat, impose a discipline on management and penalise the neglect of profit maximisation. At the limit, there is the threat of bankruptcy, a real danger for an under-performing business. Even the public sector businesses can be given an incentive to act like a profit maximizing business through the imposition of 'hard budget constraints' linked to a targeted return to capital.

Alternatives to the assumption of profit maximization have been explored. For example, the executives try to maximise sales, subject to a minimum level of profit to keep the shareholders happy. Besides, profit maximisation does not necessarily conflict with the objective of keeping or expanding market share. The business making the largest sustained profit will be best equipped to survive in the long term.

• Rules for Profit-Maximisation

The profit-maximization assumption is important, because it has strong implication for how businesses behave. These implications apply both to the pricing decision and to output decison. When competition is intense, businesses take price as given. The key decision becomes how much to produce: how much labour and capital to use. In making these decisions, a profit-maximizing business will be guided by certain rules.

The first rule is that the business must produce up to the point where MC = MR. At any lower output, MR > MC. At any higher output, MC > MR. This rule is derived more formally in Appendix 7A1.

Second, the business minimises the cost of producing any given level of output. It minimises costs by applying the rule: purchase each input up to the point where the net value of the output produced by that input equals the cost to the business of purchasing it. The MC of the input to the business is the price paid. The value of the extra output produced by each input equals the extra output multiplied by price (the value of its MP). Suppose this were not the case. Say the value of the MPL is £100 per day, whilst the cost of hiring extra labour is £60 per day. At the same time, the MPK is £60, but the cost of using it is £100 per day. Then, assuming no other costs, the business is making £40 profit per day from the marginal labour and losing £40 per day from the capital. The profit-maximising business should hire more labour and less capital.

The third rule is that a technically inefficient production technique should not be used. If 100 units of output could be produced by using (a) 80 units of labour and 100 units of capital, or (b) 60 units of labour and 90 units of capital, technique (b) will always be chosen by the profit-maximizer. The logic is MR = MC = P. We will see the business's demand curve is a horizontal straight line. Here the demand curve = marginal revenue curve. Profits are maximized when MC intersects the business's marginal revenue curve from below and MR = P as well.

A perfectly competitive industry is one where entry and exit are free. If businesses in an industry make profit, this attracts new businesses into the industry. Although no individual business can affect the market price, collectively their entry does have an impact. Eventually, expansion of supply by the new entrants will cause price to fall and, also raise costs in the industry as the price of inputs may also rise. In the long run, equilibrium will occur with normal or bare minimum profit. Supernormal profit are bid away by new entrants where MC = MR = ATC = P. Businesses are not in a position to make excess or supernormal profit. There will be no incentive for businesses either to enter or to leave the industry. We have reached the equilibrium price and quantity for the industry.

We will discuss here how a perfectly competitive market structure makes decisions about how much to produce. In a situtation of perfect competition each business is very small to affect the price of the product. Thus, a business, in a perfectly competitive industry, is a price-taker—the business takes the price as given, determined in the market. The business has to accept the price set by the forces of demand and supply in the market. If the price they charge is higher than the market price, nobody will buy from them. Or if the price is lower than the market price, every consumer will come to them.

Let us now examine the reasons why a business under perfectly competitive industry ends up being a price-taker.

- **Characteristics of Perfect Competition**

1. A large number of businesses in the industry. An individual business's output is very small in relation to the industry's (market) output.
2. They each produce a homogeneous product.
3. There are a large number of buyers. There is perfect consumer information about the quality of the product.
4. There is unrestricted entry and exit into the industry—

(a) If profits are greater than normal then businesses will enter the industry.
(b) If losses are being made businesses will, in the long-run, exit the business.
(c) If profits are normal there will be no entry or exit.

• Demand Curves and Perfect Competition

We know already that the more substitutes are there, the greater is the price elasticity of demand. We assumed, for the perfectly competitive business, that it is producing a homogeneous product that has perfect substitutes. That means that, if the individual business raises its price by a penny, it will lose all its customers. This is how we characterize the demand schedule for the perfectly competitive business. It is the going market price as determined by the forces of demand and supply—that is, where the market demand and supply intersects (at P_0). The demand curve of an indvidual business in a perfectly competitive industry is perfectly elastic at the going market price (P_0). In a perfectly elastic demand curve, any increase in price leads to a zero increase in the quantity demanded.

Fig. 7.1(a) shows the market demand and supply curve for the industry. Their intersection occurs at the price, say, £5. Suppose the commodity is wheat. At the going market price of £5, individual demand curve is shown in Fig. 7.1(a). At the market price, this business can sell as much output as it wishes. At the market price consumer demand is perfectly elastic. The demand curve for the individual producer shows that if the business raises its price by even a small amount, nobody will buy from it, and the producer in question will have no sales at all. The demand curve for the producer is perfectly elastic. The demand curve is shown as d in Fig. 7.1(a), whereas the market demand curve is marked as D in Fig. 7.1(b).

• How Much Should the Perfectly Competitive Producer Produce?

As we have already seen, a perfect competitor has to accept the price of the product as given. If the business raises the price, it sells nothing; if it lowers the price, it earns lower revenues per unit sold than it otherwise could. The business has one decision left: How much should it produce? We will apply our model to answer this question. We will use the profit

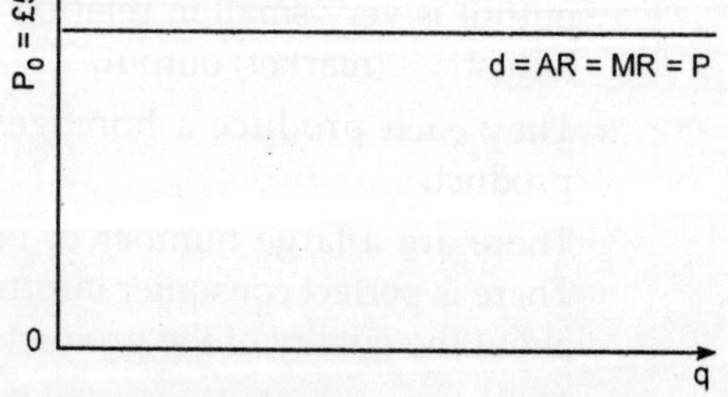

Fig. 7.1(a): Demand Curve for a Business

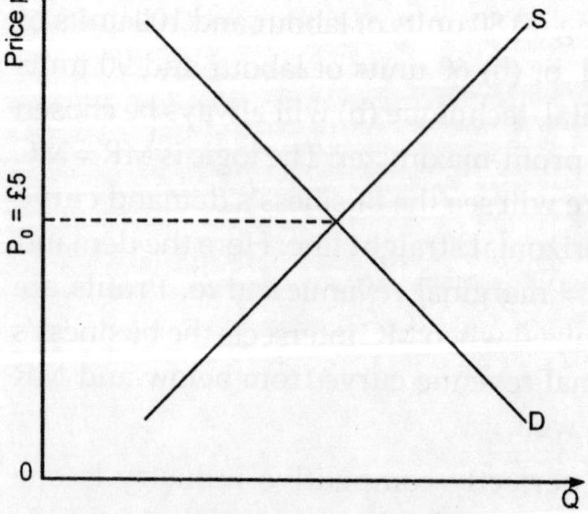

Fig. 7.1(b): Industry Demand Curve

maximization model, which assume that business's attempt to maximize their total profit (π)—the difference between total revenues and total costs. That also means that businesses wish to minimize any losses.

• Total Revenues

Total revenues are defined as the quantity sold multiplied by the price (P.q). The perfect competitor must take the market price as given. Market price is P = £5 per unit, and the total revenues (TR) = P × q, where q = total quantity sold. For the perfect competitor, P = AR since AR = TR/q = Pq/q = P, where q stands for the quantity sold by the individual business.

If we assume that all units are sold at the same price, and price is equivalent to average revenue it is also the average revenue curve = demand curve.

We are assuming that the market demand and supply schedules intersect at a price of £5 and that this price holds for all the business's production. The total revenue curve is straight line. For every unit of sales TR is increased by £5.

Profit maximization occurs where TR > TC by the largest amount {Fig. 7.2(a)} or where MR = MC [Fig. 7.2(b)]. $\Pi(q)$ is the profit function which is maximized at $q\Pi_{max}$. Appendix-1 shows in more detail way the profit maximizing level of output is where MR = MC.

• Using Marginal Analysis to Determine the Profit-Maximizing Rate of Output

It is possible to use marginal analysis to determine the profit-maximising rate of output. The result is the same as in the previous analysis as Fig. 6.2(b) shows.

When MR = MC, profit is maximized. Now that is MR. It is a change in TR resulting from a change in output be one unit. Or MR = change in total revenues/change in output ($\Delta TR/\Delta q$). In a perfectly competitive market, the marginal revenue curve is exactly equivalent to price line or the individual business's demand curve. Each time the

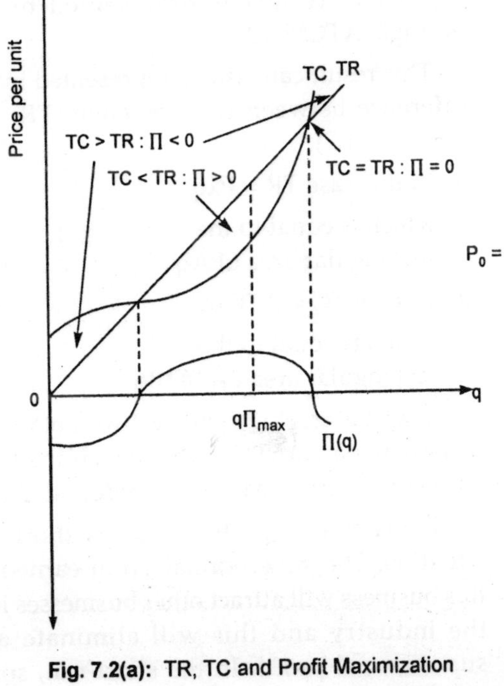

Fig. 7.2(a): TR, TC and Profit Maximization

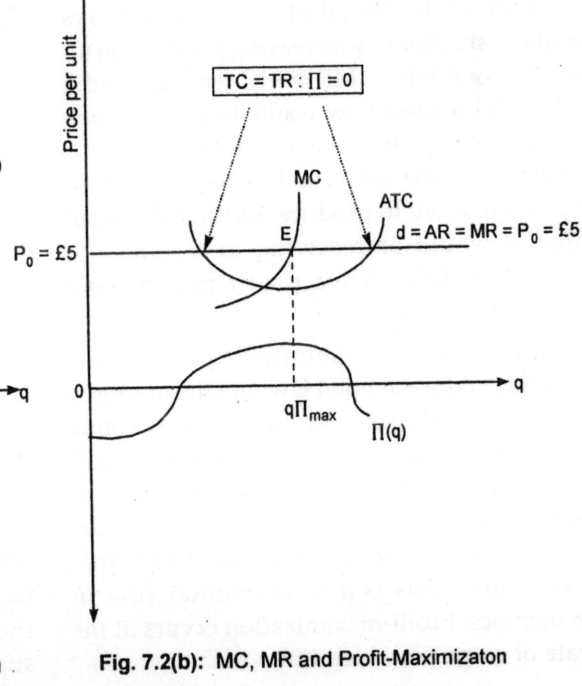

Fig. 7.2(b): MC, MR and Profit-Maximizaton

business produces and sells one more unit, TR rise by an amount equal to the market price of the good. Thus, in Fig. 7.2(b), the demand curve, d, for the individual producer is at a price of £5, the price line is coincident with the demand curve. So is the marginal revenue curve, for MR = £5 in this case. Thus, marginal revenue curve = P line = demand curve = AR.

• When are Profit Maximized?

Now we add the marginal cost curve, MC in this figure. Marginal cost (MC) is defined as the cost of producing an extra unit ($\Delta TC/\Delta q$). As shown in Fig. 7.2(b), the marginal cost curve first falls, then starts to rise because of the law of diminishing returns; eventually it intersects the marginal revenue curve from below and then rises above it.

In Fig. 7.2(b), the marginal cost curve intersects the marginal revenue curve at the same unit of output, which we have found before. The business has an incentive to produce and sell until the amount of the additional revenue received from selling one more unit equals the additional costs incurred for producing and selling the output. This is where the business maximizes profit. Whenever MR > MC, the business will always make more profit by increasing production up to the point where MR = MC (see Appendix 7A.1). If business now wants to produce one more unit of output the MC at that output is higher than the MR. The business would be spending more to produce additional output than it would be receiving in revenues; it would be foolish for profit-maximizing business to do so.

But how much should it produce? It should produce at point E where the marginal cost curve intersects the marginal revenue curve from below. The business should continue producing unit where the cost of increasing output by one more unit is just equal to the revenues obtainable from that extra unit. This is a fundamental rule in economics: Profit-maximization occurs at the rate of output at which MR = MC.

For a perfectly competitive business, this is at the intersection of d(= MR = AR) and MC. When MR > MC, each additional unit of output adds more to total revenues than to total costs, causing profit to increase. When MR < MC, each unit produced adds more to the total cost than to total revenues, causing profit to decrease. Thus, profit-maximization occurs when MC = MR.

• Short-Run Profit

To find out what our competitive producer is making in terms of profit in the short-run, without constructing the profit function. Fig. 7.3 is similar to Fig. 7.2(b) with the addition of an ATC curve (and an average variable cost {AVC} curve) but without the profit function.

Assuming the business is maximizing profit the output produced will be q*, the price charged will be P and the average total cost at output q* will be ATC*. Profit *per unit* is represented by the vertical difference between ATC and Price (ATC* and P), where P = AR.

The total (supernormal) profit this business is earning is the profit per unit (P to ATC*) multiplied by the number of units sold (q*). This product is represented by the rectangle ATC*PAB.

This result can also be represented by the difference between total revenue (TR) and total cost (TC).

In this case TR = Pxq*
which is equal to the
rectangular area 0PAq* ... (1)

In this case TC = ATCxq*
which is equal to the
rectangular area 0ATC*Bq* ... (2)

If we subtract (2) from (1) we obtain the rectangular area ATC*PAB which is the same value of supernormal profit we found above.

We should note that this is a short-run situation. The supernormal profit earned by this business will attract other businesses into the industry and this will eliminate any supernormal profit. In the short-run, some

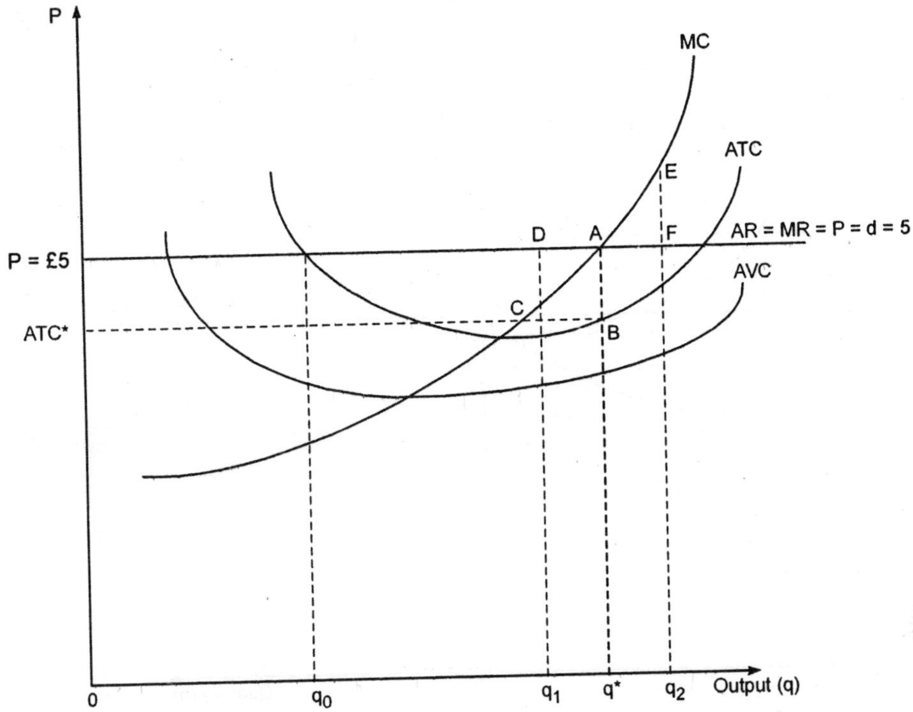

Fig. 7.3: Short-Run Profit Maximising Output of a Competitive Business

inputs are fixed and some are variable. In such a situation, Fig. 7.3 shows the output decision of the competitive business. The AR = MR are drawn as horizontal line at a price of £5. We have also drawn the ATC, the AVC and the MC curves, so that the business's profit area can be seen clearly (ATC*PAB).

Profit is maximized at point A where output is q* at a price of £5, as MR = MC at this point. At a lower output, say q_1, MR > MC, so profit could be increased by increasing output from q_1 to q* by ACD. The extra total revenue area is q_1DAq* and the extra total cost area is q_1CAq*. The difference between the two is ACD (see Appendix 7A.2).

At a higher output, say q_2, MC > MR, thus reducing output will increase profit. The area AEF of lost profit between q* and q2 is saved. This is because the extra TC between q* and q_2 is q*AEq_2 and the extra total revenue is q*AFq_2. So moving from q_2 to q* will save more in costs than is lost in revenue and so profit will increase until MR = MC.

- **A Competitive Business Minimizes its Short-Run Losses**

In cases in which ATC exceed the AR or price, profit maximization is equivalent to loss minimization. This occurs where MC = MR. Losses are shown in the area ABCD in Fig. 7.4.

This is because D to C is the loss per unit of output (ATC at q* is greater than AR at q*). So the total loss is DC × q* which is equal to the rectangular area DCBA.

If the business is sustaining losses, will it go out of business? In the long run it will, but in the short-run the business will not necessarily go out of business. As long as the loss from staying in business is less than the loss from shutting down, the business will stay in business.The business will continue production as long as it is able to cover the AVC of production, the business then able to cover at least the part of the opportunity cost—that is, part of the fixed cost.

The business has two options in the short-run. It can go on producing, or shut down. It

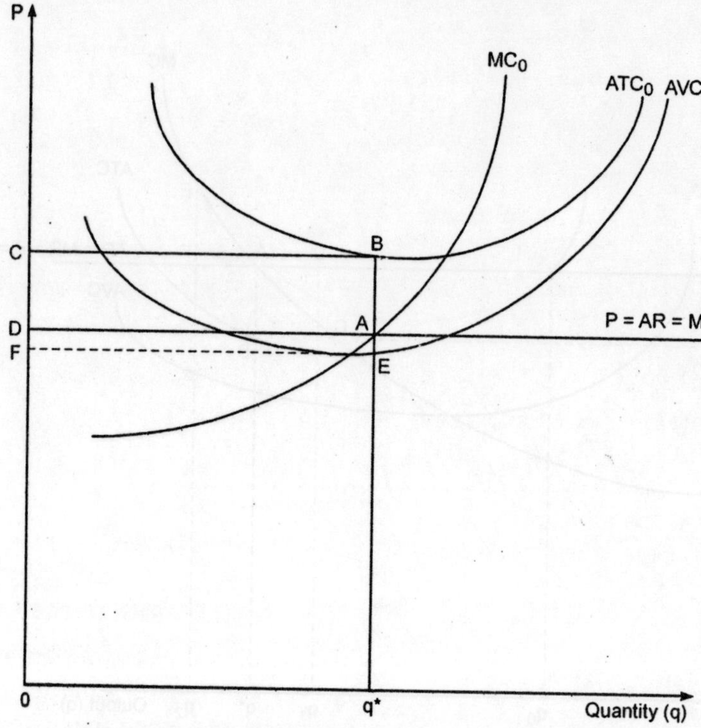

Fig. 7.4: A Competitive Business Incurring Losses in the Short-Run

will choose the most profitable alternative. In particular, a business will find it profitable to shut down when P is less than the minimum point of the AVC. In such a situation, revenues from production will not cover even the total variable cost. To continue production it is necessary that it should cover the variable cost which means P = minimum point on the AVC. The price at which a business's TR = TC, business will break-even. At this price, the business is making normal profit.

• Competitive Business Short-Run Supply Curve

A supply curve shows the relationship between price and output. We have already seen that competitive businesses will produce output up to the point where P = MC, but they will shut down when P is less than the minimum value of the short-run average variable cost (AVC) curve.

Thus, for positive output, the business's supply curve is that part of the marginal cost curve that lies above the average variable cost curve. Since the marginal cost curve cuts the average variable cost curve at its minimum point, the business's supply curve is its marginal cost curve above the minimum point of the average variable cost curve. For any price above the minimum point of the average variable cost curve, the profit-maximizing output can be read from the graph. In Fig. 7.5, at price P_1 the quantity supplied is q_1 and price P_2, the quantity supplied is q_2. For price less than minimum point of AVC, the profit-maximizing output is zero. Fig. 7.5 shows that the supply curve is that part of the marginal cost curve which is above the minimum point of average variable cost curve (point A).

The short-run supply curve for competitive business slope upwards for the same reason that the MC increases—the presence of diminishing returns. As a result, an increase in the market price will induce those businesses already in the market to increase

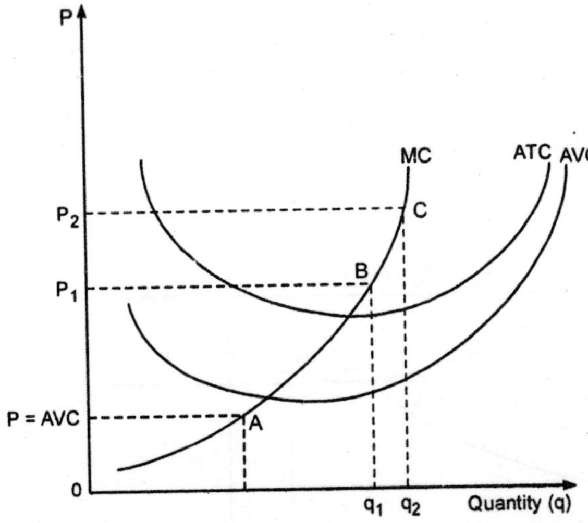

Fig. 7.5: The Short-Run Supply Curve of a Competitive Firm

the quantities they supply. The higher price makes the additional production profitable and also increases the business' total profit because it applies to all units that the business produces.

• The Short-Run Market Supply Curve

Consider Fig. 7.6 The outputs of the respective businesses at price P_a are q_{a1}, q_{a2} and q_{a3}. The output for the industry at P_a is $Q_a = q_{a1} + q_{a2} + q_{a3}$. For other prices we would obtain different quantities and points. Joining them together we would derive the industry supply curve S in the extreme right hand diagram. This is the supply curve we have been using in the earlier chapter.

• Choosing Output in the Long-Run

In the long-run all factors are variable. The business can decide to enter or leave the industry as and when they like since we are here concerned with competitive markets where there is freedom of entry and exit.

Fig. 7.7 shows how a competitive business makes its long-run profit-maximizing output decision. It faces a horizontal demand curve and a long-run average cost (LATC) curve which follow an increasing returns to scale up to q_1 output and decreasing returns to scale at higher levels of output. The long-run marginal cost (LMC) curve cuts the LATC curve from below at q_1, the minimum point of LATC.

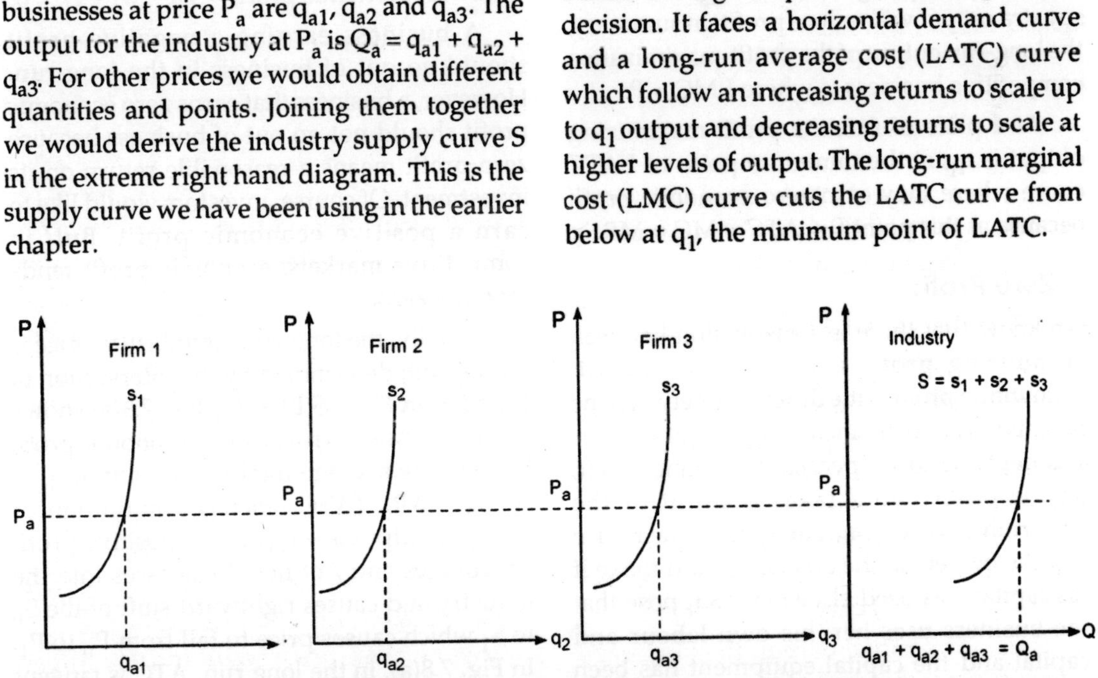

Fig. 7.6: A Short-Run Supply Curve for a Perfectly Competitive Industry

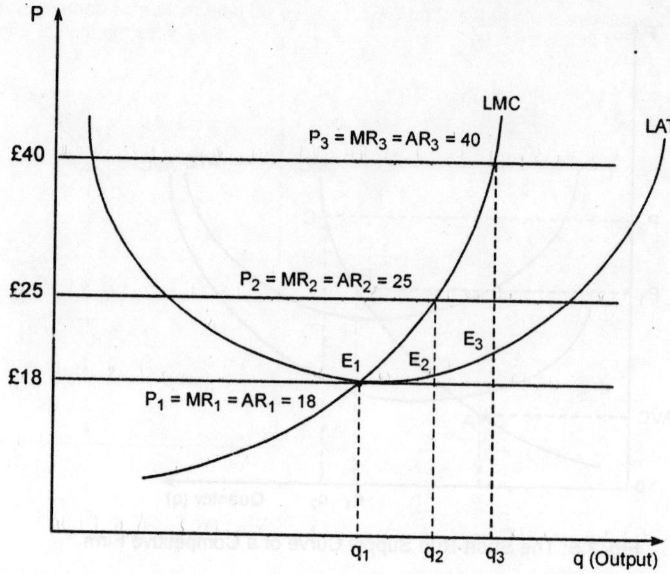

Fig. 7.7: Output Choice in the Long-Run

In the long-run the business will equate LMC to MR. If the price is £25 the long-run profit maximizing output will q_2 and the LATC will be E_2. If the price is £40 the long-run profit maximizing output will q_3 and the LATC will be E_3.

At any output greater than q_3, MC > MR, so extra output will reduce profit. In summary, the long-run output of the profit-maximization competitive business is where LMC = P.

At a price of £18, the profit-maximizing output is q_1, at the minimum point of LATC curve where they earn zero economic profit because at this point P = ATC = MC = MR.

- **Zero Profit**

We know that there is a distinction between accounting profit and economic profit. Accounting profit is the difference between the revenue and costs, including actual outlays and depreciation expenses. Economic profit, on the other hand, takes account of the opportunity costs. One such cost is the return that the owners of the business could make if his capital was used elsewhere. Suppose that the business uses her/his own labour and capital and the capital equipment has been purchased (but depreciated). The business's accounting profit is equal to TR = wl, which is positive. However, the economists' economic profit is TR less wl less the opportunity cost of capital (rk), where r is the cost per unit of capital and k is the number of units of capital employed.

Thus, economic profit = TR – wl – rk = 0.

A business earning a negative profit should go out of business in the long-run. However, a business that earns zero economic profit should not go out of business because zero profit means a reasonable return on its investment. Of course, investors would like to earn a positive economic profit. But, in competitive markets, economic profit tends towards zero.

Initially, the long-run equilibrium price is P_0 per unit, determined by the intersection of D and S_0 in Fig. 7.8(b) at E_0. Fig. 7.8(a) shows that businesses earn a positive economic profit because the average total cost at output q_0 is $ATC_0 < AR_0$. (ATC reaches a minimum of ATC_1 at output level q_1). This positive profit encourages entry of new businesses into the industry and causes rightward shift of the S_0 to S_1 which causes price to fall from P_0 to P_1. In Fig. 7.8(a), in the long run, ATC is tangent to the price line (P_1) at q_1. At that point a

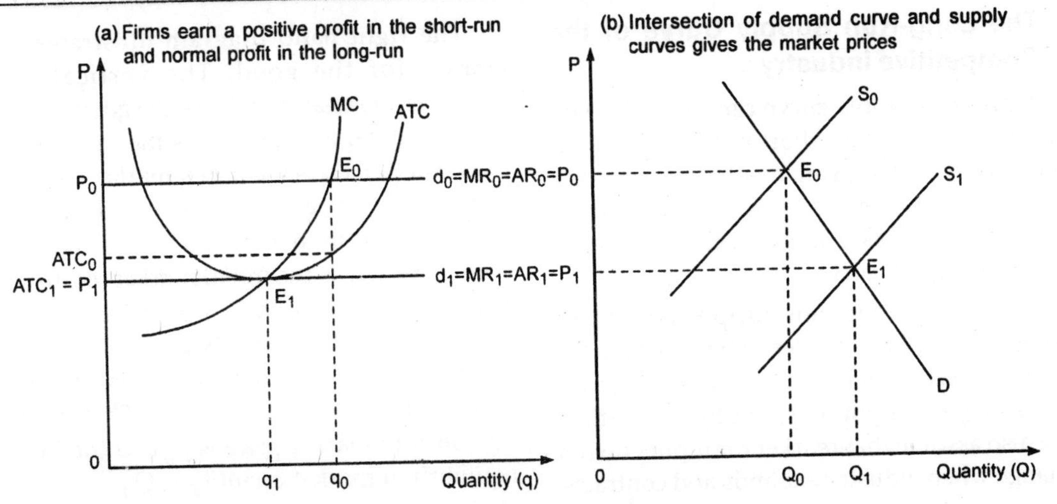

Fig. 7.8: The Adjustment Towards Equilibrium

business earns zero economic profit there is no incentive to exit from or enter into the industry. A long-run equilibrium occurs when the following conditions hold:

First, all businesses in the industry are maximizing profit.

Second, no business has an incentive to enter into or exit from the industry because all businesses are earning zero economic profit.

Third, the price of the product is such that the quantity supplied = demanded:

P = ATC = MC = MR = AR.

The dynamic process that leads the long-run equilibrium is that businesses enter the market because of the opportunity of earning positive economic profit, and leave when they are likely to lose. Yet, in the long-run equilibrium, businesses earn zero economic profit. Why do businesses enter or exit if they know that eventually they will be no better off or worse off? The answer is simple, it can take a long time to reach a long-run equilibrium and a substantial economic profit or loss can be earned in the meantime. The first business that enters a profitable industry can earn much more profit in the short-run than the businesses that enter later on. Similarly, the first to exit an unprofitable industry can save a lot of money. The long-run equilibrium tells us the direction that businesses' behaviour that is likely to take in the long-run. Thus, the idea of an eventual zero economic profit in the long-run should not discourage a manager whose reward depends on the profit in the short-run.

The long-run equilibrium condition holds on the assumption that all businesses have identical costs, and consider what would happen if too many businesses enter into the industry in response to a positive economic profit. Then the supply curve in Fig. 7.8(b) will shift further and further to the right and price will fall below P_2. At that price, businesses will lose money. As a result, some business will leave the industry. Firms will continue to leave the industry until the market supply curve shifts back to S_1. Only at this stage there is no incentive for businesses to leave or enter the industry, and the market can be in long-run equilibrium again.

If all businesses do not have identical cost curves, the businesses to leave or enter the industry, and the market, can be in long-run equilibrium again.

If all businesses do not have identical cost curves, the businesses with a lower ATC can earn economic profit even in the long-run equilibrium. If all businesses are equal, the economic profit of the business falls to zero. Thus, the condition that economic profit be zero is essential for the market to be in a long-run equilibrium.

• The Long-Run Supply Curve of the Competitive Industry

The long-run supply curve cannot be derived in the same way as the short-run supply curve; because, in the long-run, businesses can enter and leave the industry as market price changes. This makes it impossible to sum up long-run supply curve.

To derive long-run supply curve, we assume that all businesses have access to the available technology. Output can be increased by using more input only, not by innovation. We also assume that market for inputs do not change when industry expands and contracts. For example, increased demand for labour does not increase the union's ability to negotiate a better wage contract for its members.

The shape of the long-run supply curve depends on the extent to which increases and decreases of output affect the prices of inputs. It is, thus, useful to distinguish among three types of industries: constant-cost, increasing-cost and decreasing-cost.

• The Long-Run Supply Curve of a Constant-Cost Industry

Consider Fig. 7.9 and the effect of an increase in demand on a business operating in a perfectly competitive industry. Fig. 7.9 below represents a perfectly competetive market.

The right hand diagram illustrates the market for the good. The vertical axis measures the relative price of the good (P) and the horizontal axis measures the quantity of the good (Q). D_0 is the initial market demand curve which is negatively sloped and indicates that the quantity demanded varies inversely with price. 'S_0' is the initial market (industry) supply curve which is positively sloped indicating that the quantity demanded varies directly with price. E_0 is the initial point of intersection of D_0 and S_0. The initial equilibrium market price is P_0 and the initial equilibrium market quantity is Q_0.

The left-hand diagram illustrates the representative business (say, one of 40). The vertical axis measures costs, revenues and price (£'s) and the horizontal axis measures the business's output (q). The average total cost curve (ATC) measures the average total cost corresponding to each level of output and the marginal cost curve (MC) measures the marginal cost corresponding to each level of output.

Since the business is a *price taker* (the price $\{P_0\}$ being determined in the market) the business's demand curve for output (d_0) is perfectly elastic. This also means that price (P_0) is equal to marginal revenue (MR_0) and is equal to average revenue (AR_0). $P_0 = MR_0 = AR_0$.

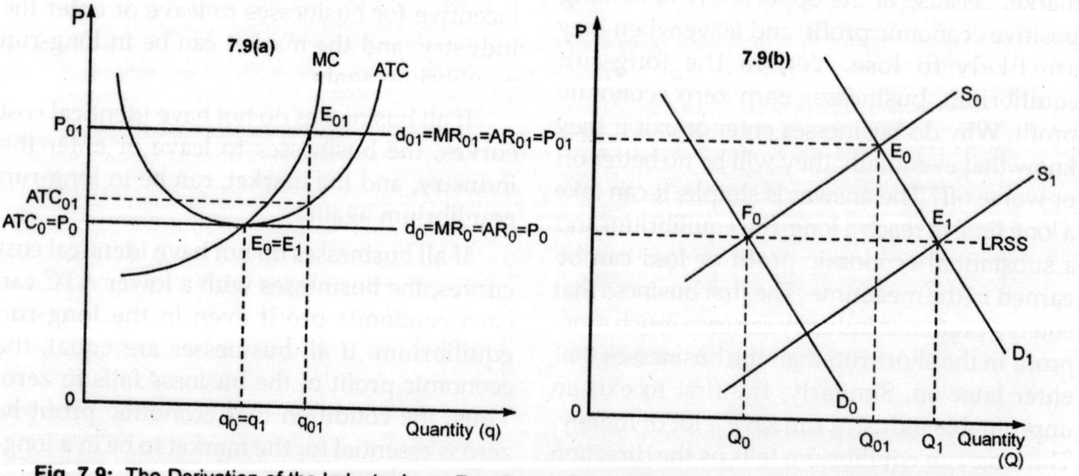

Fig. 7.9: The Derivation of the Industry Long-Run Supply Curve (all Businesses have Similar Cost Curves)

1. Start at an initial short-run equilibrium profit-maximizing position (the initial profit-maximizing position is where MC = MR). D_0, S_0, E_0, P_0, Q_0 in the market and q_0, $ATC_0 = MC = MR_0 = P_0 = AR_0$ for the representative business. The business is making a normal profit since total revenue ($P_0 \times q_0$) is equal to total cost ($ATC_0 \times q_0$). ($\Pi = 0$).

   Note: $Q_0 = 40 \times q_0$. or $q_0 = Q_0/40$.

2. Assume that there is an increase the demand for the good. (Brought about by an increase in income, a decrease in the price of a complementary good, an increase in the price of a substitute good or a change in taste). In the market 'D_0' shifts to the right to 'D_1'.

   At P_0 there is now an excess demand for the good (E_0 to E_1).

   Assume that the price rises.

   As the price increases the quantity demanded decreases along the demand curve from E_1 towards E_{0_1} and the quantity supplied increases along the supply curve from 'E_0' towards 'E_{01}'. This will continue until a new short run equilibrium position is reached at 'E_{01}', P_{01}, Q_{01}.

   On the left hand diagram $P_0 = MR_0 = AR_0 = d_0$ increases to $P_{01} = MR_{01} = AR_{01} = d_{01}$.

   Since the business is a profit-maximiser the new profit maximising level of output is where the marginal cost curve 'MC' intersects with MR_{01} (= AR_{01} = d_{01}). This is at output q_{01}.

   Note: $Q_{01} = 40 \times q_{01}$ or $q_{01} = Q_{01}/40$. At output q_{01} average total cost is ATC_{01} and price is P_{01}. Profit (Π) is positive (supernormal) since total cost ($ATC_{01} \times q_{01}$) is less than total revenue ($P_{01} \times q_{01}$). Firms are making supernormal profit.

3. In the long-run the supernormal profit will attract businesses into the industry and the amount supplied to the market will increase. The market supply curve S_{01} will shift to the right. This will reduce the price. As long as the price is above P_0, businesses in the industry will be making supernormal profit and other businesses will be entering the industry. This will shift the supply curve further to the right.

   Assuming that all the businesses in the industry have similar cost curves then this will continue until a new supply curve 'S_1' intersects 'D_1' at 'E_1' and the price is back to P_0 and output is Q_1. The increased number of businesses (more than 40) will be earning normal profit. The industry will be back in long run equilibrium.

   The long-run supply curve in an industry whose businesses have similar cost curves is a horizontal line LRSS in Fig. 7.9(b), at price P_0, which, in long-run equilibrium, is equal to the minimum point of the ATC curve and equal to marginal cost.

• The Long-Run Supply Curve of an Increasing-Cost Industry

Since input prices increase as a result of increased output, the new long-run equili-

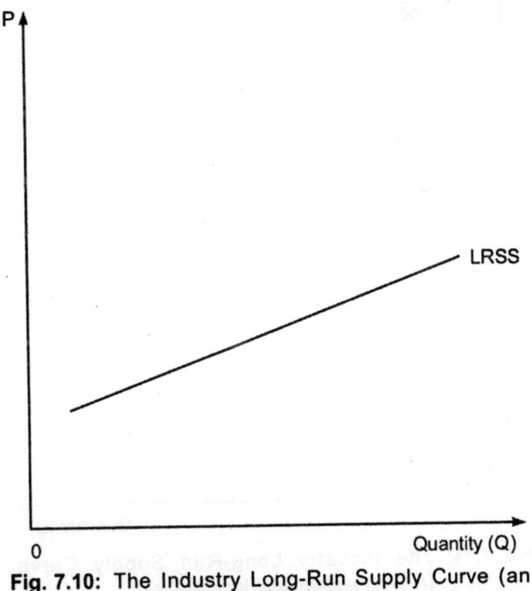

Fig. 7.10: The Industry Long-Run Supply Curve (an Increasing Cost Industry)

brium occurs at the higher price than the initial equilibrium. In an increasing cost industry, the long-run industry supply curve is upward-sloping as in Fig. 7.10. The industry produces more output, but only at a higher price, needed to compensate for the increase in input prices.

- **The Long-Run Supply Curve of a Decreasing-Cost Industry**

The industry supply curve would be downdard-sloping. In this case, the unexpected increase in demand causes industry to increase output as before. If the industry becomes larger, it can take advantage of its scale of operation to obtain some of its inputs cheaply. For example, a large industry may allow for an improved transportation system or for a better and less expensive financial network. In such a situation the business's ATC curve shift downward, and the market price of the product falls. The lower price and lower ATC of production induce a new long-run equilibrium with more businesses, more output and lower price. Thus, in a decreasing cost industry, the long-run supply curve is downward-sloping as in Fig. 7.11.

The long-run, downward-sloping supply curve also arises when expansion itself, lowers input prices or when businesses can use scale economics to produce at lower cost.

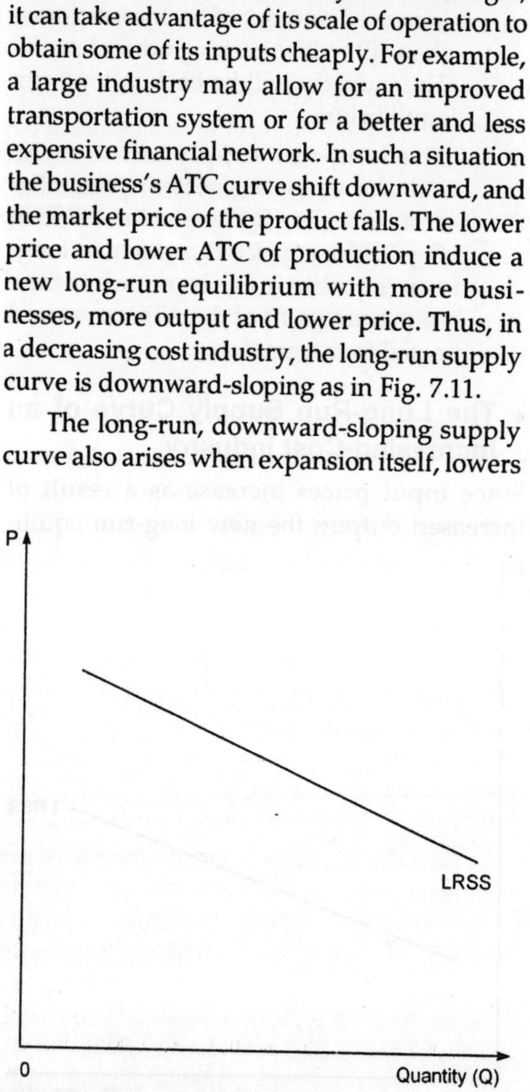

Fig. 7.11: The Industry Long-Run Supply Curve (A Decreasing-Cost Industry)

- **Production and Allocative Efficiency in a Perfectly Competitive Market**

It should be noted that, in the short-run, a business in a perfectly competitive market does not usually produce at the point where average total costs are minimized, i.e. at the lowest point on the average total cost curve. In the long-run, however, the cost minimizing output is achieved and businesses operate at the optimal scale of production as in Fig. 7.9(a) above.

Also, in perfect competition there can be no X-inefficiency in the long-run, because the businesses which are not minimizing their costs of production for any given output will be unable to compete at the market price. It is because businesses in perfect competition in the long-run produce at optimal scale and minimum production costs that we equate competition with productive efficiency.

Productive efficiency occurs when a business minimize the production cost of any level of output, given existing technology. This is point E_0 in Fig. 7.9(a) above.

Here the business is producing at optimal scale, q_0, and at the same time there is no X-inefficiency because the business is producing on its efficient ATC curve.

Production efficiency is the result of two forces:

(a) Technical efficiency—this occurs when inputs of the factors of production are combined in the business in the best possible way to produce the maximum output.

(b) Price efficiency—this occurs when inputs of the factors of production are optimally employed given their prices, so as to minimize production costs.

Economists also equate perfect competition with allocative efficiency:

Allocative efficiency denotes the optimal allocation of scarce resources so as to produce the combination of outputs which best accords with consumer demands. In other words, no other allocation of resources would produce a higher level of economic welfare, given the existing consumer demand.

Allocative efficiency is achieved when the price equals the MC of producing it. This is because price in a competitive economy reflects the marginal social benefit (MSB) to the consumer of the last unit consumed. Since consumers voluntarily buy a particular good the price of that good must measure the marginal private benefit (MPB) to the consumer of buying the last unit of the good and assuming that marginal private benefit is equal to marginal social benefit (no externalities) then, in equilibrium, P = MSB.

If the MSB > price, the consumer would buy more.

If the MSB < price, the consumer would buy less.

Marginal cost (MC) is the cost to society of producing the last unit, in terms of economic resources used up. Thus, if P > MC, economic welfare could be improved by producing and consuming more units until P = MC. The (benefit) utility gained exceeds the cost to society of providing that unit. Therefore, economic welfare is increased by contracting the supply and transferring the productive resources to other uses. Strictly, P = MC is Pareto Optimal only under a number of strict conditions; for example, there should be no externalities in production or consumption. But assuming these other conditions hold, when output in an economy are allocated so that their P = MC then Pareto Optimality is said to exist.

A Pareto Optimality is said to exist when resources cannot be reallocated so as to make one person better off without making someone else worse off.

There are three main conditions that must hold in order for a Pareto Optimum to be achieved:

1. Goods must be optimally distributed between consumers so that no reallocation increases economic welfare.
2. Inputs are allocated in such a away that no reallocation would increase the physical output.
3. Optimum amount of each output are produced so that no change in output would lead to higher economic welfare.

In perfectly competitive markets, these three conditions are met in the long-run. With P = MC (condition 1) and production cost minimised (conditions 2, 3), these help to explain why the perfectly competitive model, while abstract, is used by economists as a benchmark against which to judge actual production and the effects of actual consumption.

As final comments define economic efficiency as the product of both production and allocative efficiency. In other words, in the market an economically efficient output is one where both maximum allocation and production efficiency are achieved.

• Short-Run and Long-Run Effects of Tax

Here we consider how a business responds to a tax on its product. If a business is a polluter, an output tax can be useful way to reduce its effluent, but tax might be imposed just to raise revenue for the government.

First, suppose the output tax is imposed only on a single business, and thus does not affect the market price of the product. We will see that the tax on output encourages the business to reduce its output. Fig. 7.13 shows the relevant short-run cost curves for a business enjoying positive economic profit by producing an output of q_1 and selling the product at the market price P_1.

Because the tax is assessed for every unit of output, it raises the business's marginal cost curve from MC_1 to $MC_2 = MC_1 + t$, where t is the tax per unit of the business's output. The tax also raises the average variable cost curve by the amount t. The business will reduce its output to the point at which the MC + t = P = AR of the product at q_2, and the implicit effect of the tax is to shift the business's short-run supply curve upward.

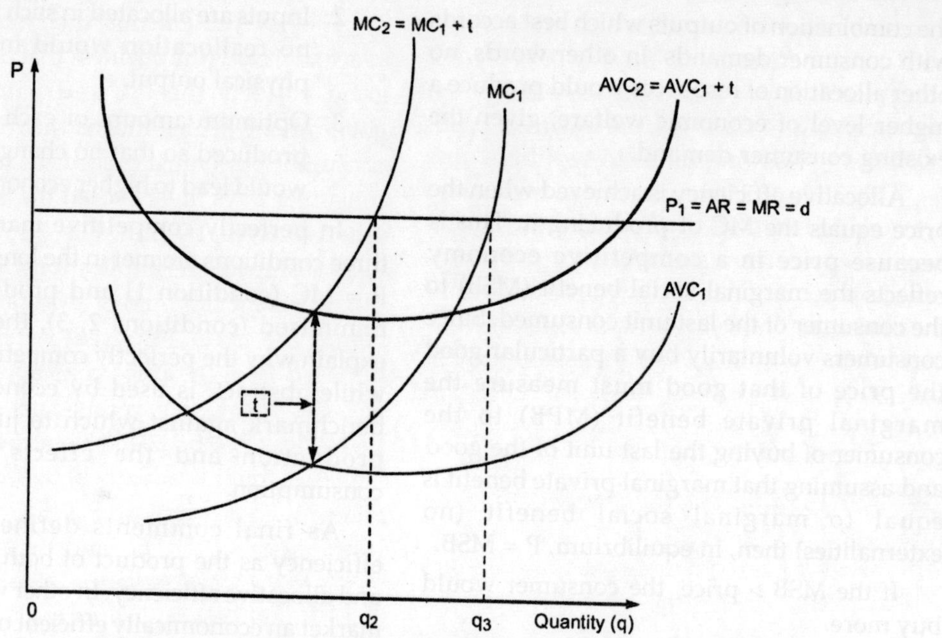

Fig. 7.12: The Effect of a Specific Tax on a Competitive Firm

If, however, the tax is greater than the business' profit margin, then the average variable cost curve will rise, and the minimum of the AVC curve will be greater than the market price of the product. The business will choose to shut down in the short-run.

Now suppose an output (specific) tax placed on all businesses in a competitive market which will shift both the ATC curve upwards by the amount of the tax and short-run supply curve for the industry upward by the amount of the tax. Fig. 7.13 illustrates this, where the upward shift in the ATC curve is from ATC_0 to ATC_1 in Fig. 7.13(a) and the upward shift in the supply curve is from S_0 to $S_{01} = S_0 + t$ in Fig. 7.13(b).

Businesses would like to sell Q_0 at a price of P_1 to cover the tax that has to be paid to the government. However, at P_1, there is an excess supply of output (E_1 to A) in fig. 7.13(b).

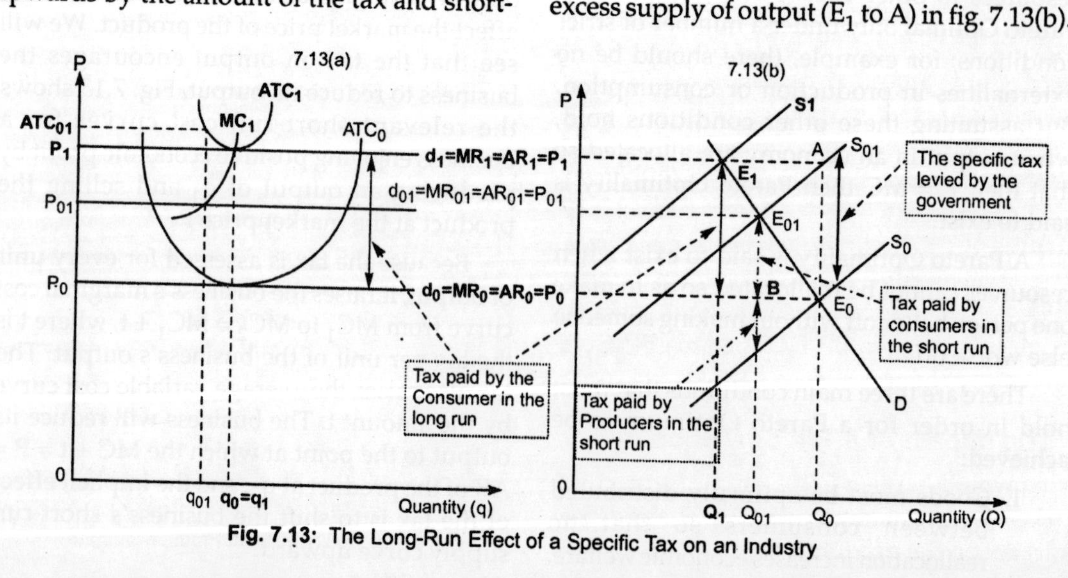

Fig. 7.13: The Long-Run Effect of a Specific Tax on an Industry

The new, short-run, equilibrium price would be P_{01}. In the short-run the tax paid by the consumer is E_{01} to B and the tax paid by the producer is B to C. at P_{01} the business profit maximising (loss minimising) output is now q_{01} [Fig. 7.13(a)]. However, at q_{01}, businesses are making loss ($ATC_{01}>P_{01}$). In the long-run businesses will leave the industry and the supply of output will fall. This will continue until the businesses in the industry are making normal profit ($S - S_1$ and $P = P_1$). The output of a business would be $q_1(=q_0)$. However there are fewer businesses in the industry to produce output Q_1.

Fig. 7.13 shows the long-run effect of the imposition of the specific tax. The output tax will raise the average total cost curve, in Fig. 7.13(a), from ATC_0 to ATC_1 and the price from P_0 to P_1. In the long-run, in a perfectly competitive industry, all the tax is paid by the consumer.

• Consumer and Producer Surplus

Consider Fig. 7.14. Because the demand curve (D) represents the price that consumers pay, it is equal to their marginal private benefit (MPB) and, with no externalities, it is equal to society's marginal social benefit (MSB). The demand curve is also the MPB and the MSB curve. The area under the MSB measures the total benefit to society (the total social benefit {TSB}). Hence if output is Q_0, the TSB is the area $0AE_0Q_0$. Since it only costs consumers the area $0P_0E_0Q_0$ to purchase Q_0 units and they receive the area $0AE_0Q_0$ then they are obtaining the area P_0AE_0 more than they are paying. The area P_0AE_0 is known as consumer surplus (CS). Businesses receive the area $0P_0E_0Q_0$ in revenue. It costs businesses the area $0BE_0Q_0$ to produce Q_0 so that the gain to business is the area BP_0E_0. The area BP_0E_0 is known as producer surplus (PS).

• The Impact of a Tax or a Subsidy

What would happen to the price of a product if the government imposed an 80p specific (per unit) tax on the product?

The government must then receive £0.8 for every unit sold (the business that produces the good collects the tax and pays it to the government) which means that the price the consumer pays must exceed the net price the consumer pays must exceed the net price the seller receives, by £0.8. Fig. 7.15 shows this relationship and its implications. Here, P_0 and Q_0, represent the market price and quantity before the tax is imposed. After the tax is imposed P_c is the price consumers pay, and P_s is the price sellers receive, net of tax. Note that P_c less $P_s = t = £0.8$. The burden of the tax is shared roughly equally between the buyers and sellers. Buyers lose $P_0P_cE_1E_0$ and sellers lose the area $P_0D_0DP_s$ and the government earns $P_sP_cE_1D$ in revenue ($80p \times Q_d$). The deadweight loss is the area E_0E_1D.

Fig. 7.15 shows that four conditions must be satisfied after the tax is in place.

First, the quantity sold and the buyer's price must lie on the demand curve.

Second, the quantity sold and the seller's price must lie on the supply curve.

Third, the quantity demanded must equal quantity supplied. And lastly, the difference between the price the buyer and the price seller receives must equal the tax £0.8. These conditions are summarized:

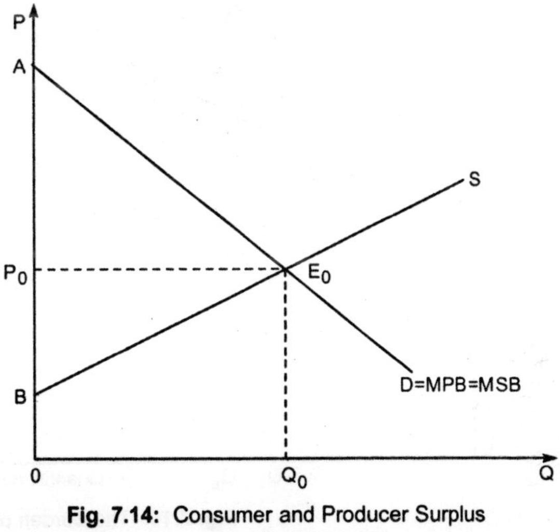

Fig. 7.14: Consumer and Producer Surplus

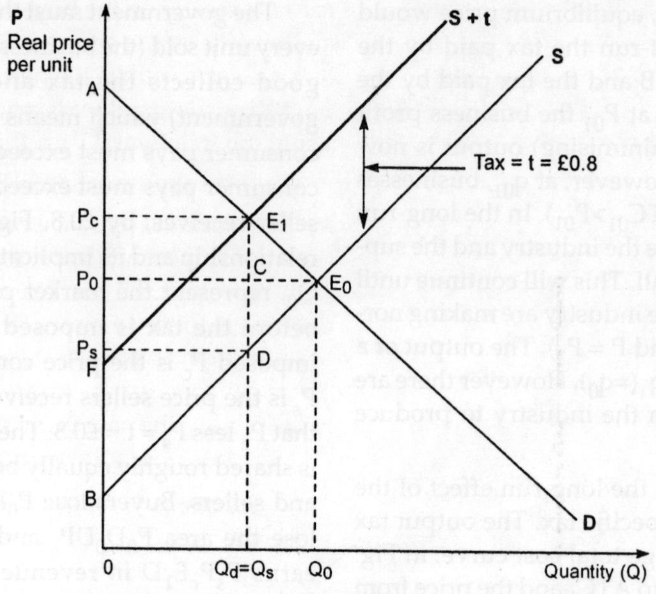

Fig. 7.15: The Impact of a Specific Tax – (t {=80p} per unit)

1. $Q_d = Q_d(P_c)$
2. $Q_s = Q_s(P_s)$
3. $Q_d = Q_s$
4. $P_c - P_s = £0.8$

If we know the supply curve $Q_s(P_s)$, the demand curve $Q_d(P_c)$, and the size of the tax 't', we can solve these equations for Pc, Ps and the total quantity demanded and supplied. The figure illustrates that a tax results in a deadweight loss. Becuase buyers pay a higher price, there is a loss of consumer surplus (CS) of the area $P_0P_cE_1E_0$.

And, because sellers now receive a lower price, there is reduction in producer surplus (PS) of the area $P_0E_0DP_s$.

Government tax revenue is t times Q_d, the sum of A + C. The total change is welfare is, change in CS plus the change in PS + the revenue received by the government. The deadweight losses are the triangles B + D. Here

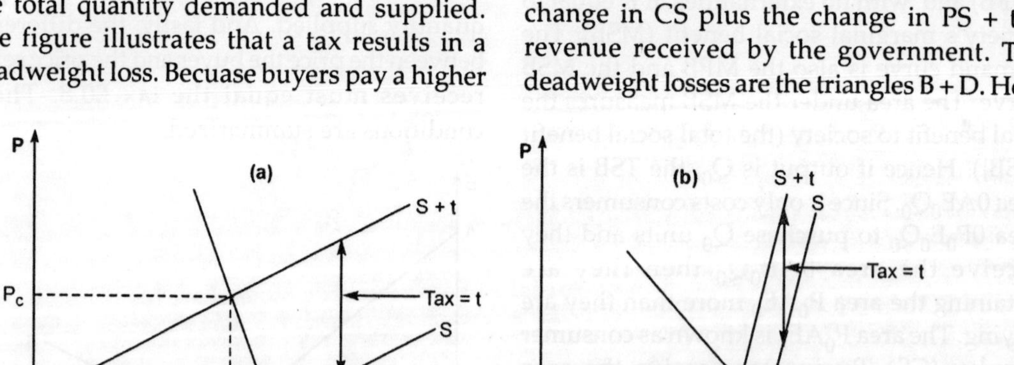

Fig. 7.16: The Burden of a Specific Tax (t per unit)

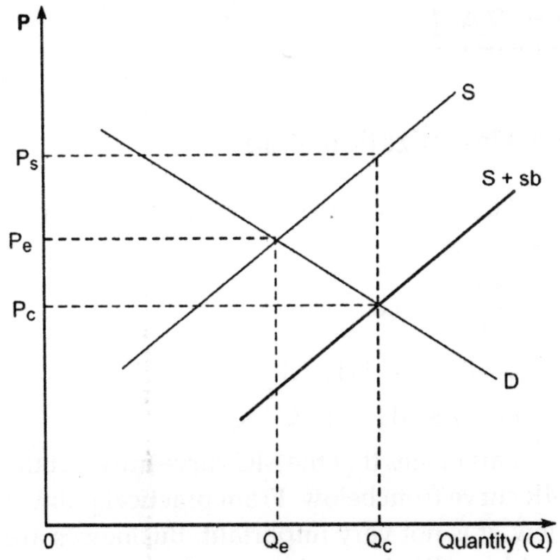

Fig. 7.17: The Effects of a Subsidy

the burden of the tax is shared almost evenly by consumers and producers, but this may not always be the case. If the demand is relatively inelastic and supply is relatively elastic, the burden of the tax will fall mostly on consumers. This is shown in Fig. 7.16(a) (P_c to P_e). On the other hand, if demand is relatively elastic and supply is relatively inelastic, the burden of the tax will fall mostly on producers as Fig. 7.16(b) shows (P_e to P_s). In general, a tax falls mostly on the buyer if E_d/E_s is small, and mostly on the sellers if E_d/E_s is large. In fact, we can calculate the percentage of the tax borne by the producers and consumers by using the following "Pass-through" formula.

Pass-through fraction = $E_s/(E_s - E_d)$.

This formula tells us which fraction of the tax is passed through to consumers in the form of higher prices. For example, when the demand is totally inelastic, so that $E_d = 0$, the pass-through fraction is 1, and all the tax is borne by consumers. And when demand is totally elastic, the pass-through fraction is zero, and producers bear the entire tax burden.

A subsidy (sb) can be analysed much the same way as a tax—it is a negative tax.

With a subsidy (Fig. 7.17), the sellers' price exceeds the buyers' price, and the difference between the two is the amount of subsidy. Like the tax, the benefit of a subsidy is split between buyers and sellers, depending on the relative elasticities of supply and demand. As with a tax, this is not always the case.

In general, the benefit of a subsidy accrues mostly to consumers if E_d/E_s is small, and mostly to producers, if E_d/E_s is large.

APPENDIX 7A.1

The Derivation of the Profit-Maximization Rule

The Profit-maximization rule can be derived as:

By definition, $\pi = TR - TC$, where π = profit, TR = total revenue, TC = total cost.

The first order condition for profit-maximization is:

$d\pi / dq = dTR/dq - dTC/dq = 0$, where q = unit of output i.e., $dTR/dq = dTC/dq$

MR = MC. This is the rule that MR must equal MC.

The second-order condition for a maximum is:

$\frac{d^2\pi}{dq^2} < 0$, i.e..

$dMR/dq - dMC/dq < 0$

or $dMR/dq < dMC/dq$.

This means that the MC curve must cut the MR curve from below. From practical point of view, it is not very important. Businesses are highly unlikely to choose minimum profit points.

APPENDIX 7A.2

Profit-Maximization Occurs When MR = MC

Marginal revenue (MR) is defined as the extra revenue received (earned) from the sale of an extra unit ($\Delta TR/\Delta q$). For example: If the business is selling 97 units the marginal revenue is the revenue received from the sale of the 98th unit. The MR curve shows the revenue received for the production of the *next* unit.

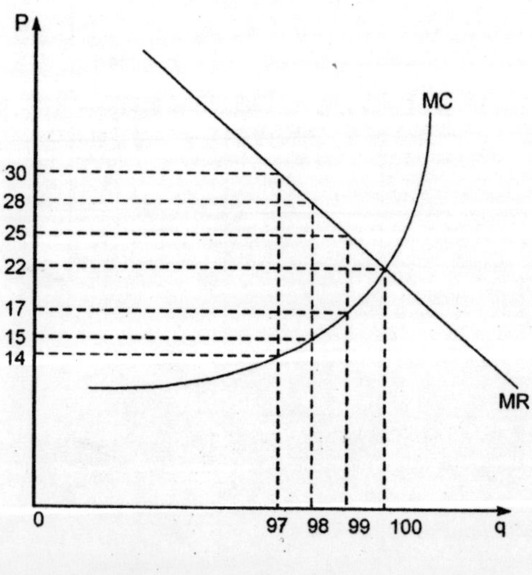

Marginal cost (MC) is defined as the cost of producing an extra unit ($\Delta Tc/\Delta q$). For example: If the business is producing 97 units the marginal cost is the cost of producing the 98th unit. The MC curve shows the cost of producing the *next* unit.

If we start q = 97, and assuming that the profit earned so far is 80, then the revenue from the sale of the 98th unit (MR) is 30 and the cost of producing the 98th unit (MC) is 14. Since the extra revenue is greater than the extra cost it is profitable to produce the 98th unit. The business would make (30–14)=16 in extra profit. 80 + 16 = 96 is total profit. It is worth producing the 98th unit.

If we produce the 98th unit is it profitable to produce the 99th unit? The revenue from the sale of the 99th unit (MR) is 28 and the cost of producing the 99th unit (MC) is 15. Since the extra revenue is greater than the extra cost it is profitable to produce the 99th unit. The business would make (28–15)=13 in extra profit. 96 +13 = 109 is total. It is worth producing the 99th unit.

If we produce the 99th unit is it profitable to produce the 100th unit? The revenue from the sale of the 100th unit (MR) is 25 and the cost of producing the 100th (MC) is 17. Since the extra revenue is greater than the extra cost it is profitable to produce the 100th unit. The business would make (25 – 17) = 8 in extra profit (109 + 8) =117 in total profit. It is worth producing the 100th unit.

If we produce the 100th unit is it profitable to produce the 101st unit? the revenue from the sale of revenue is the same as the extra cost of producing the 101st unit (MC) is 22. Since the extra revenue is the same as the extra cost it is not profitable to produce the 101st unit. The business would make zero in extra profit. 117 in total. It is NOT worth producing the 101st unit.

Since the *extra* profit of producing the 98th, 99th, and 100th units are 16 + 13 + 8 = 37, the maximum amount of profit (80 + 37 = 117) occurs when output is 100 units.

This is when MC = MR = 22.

APPENDIX 7A.3

The area under a Marginal Cost and Marginal Revenue Curve

What one has to remember is that the total area under any marginal curve is a total value.

The area under a marginal cost curve is total cost.

The area under a marginal revenue curve is total revenue.

Consider Fig. 7A.3. The profit maximizing output is when Q = 24 and the price (P_0) is 29.

Therefore, when Q = 24,

TR = 29 × 24 = **696**.

The area under the MR curve when Q_0 = 24 is $0ADQ_0$ which is the triangle 5AD (= 576) + the rectangle $05DQ_0$ (= 120) = **696**.

The area under the MR curve is equal to the value of the corresponding total revenue.

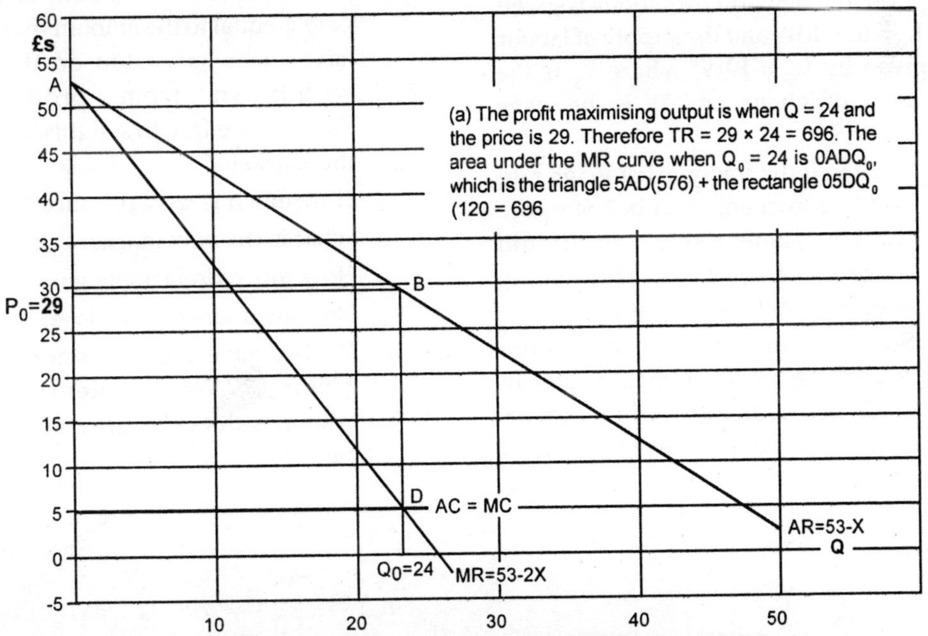

Fig. 7A.3: The Area under a Marginal Revenue Curve

QUESTIONS

1. A manager of a competitive business has a cost curve of $TC = 100 + Q^2$, where Q is the level of output and TC is total cost. ($MC = 2Q$ and $FC = £100$).
   (a) If the price of the product is £60, how much output would be produced to maximize profit?
   (b) What will the profit level be?
   (c) At what minimum price will the business be in business?
2. A tax of £1 per unit of output is introduced on one business whose product sells for £5 in a competitive market environment:
   (a) How will this tax affect the cost curves of the business?
   (b) What will happen to the business's output, price and profit in the short-run and in the long-run?
3. UK has suggested the introduction of minimum wage, with a government subsidy to employers to help finance the high wage. Examine the economics of a minimum wage and wage subsidies. Suppose the demand for labour is given by $L_d = 60 - 10W$ and the supply of labour is given by $L_s = 10W$, where L_s is the quantity of labour, and W is the wage rate:
   (a) What will the free-market wage rate and employment level be? Suppose the government sets a minimum wage of £4 per hour. How many people would then be employed?
   (b) Suppose, instead of a minimum wage, the government paid a subsidy of £1 per hour for each employee. What will the level of employment be now? What will the equilibrium wage rate be?
4. The government introduced in 1983 a new agricultural programme known as the Payment-in-Kind. Let us consider the wheat market to examine the working of the programme:
   (a) Suppose the supply function is $Q_s = 4 + 4p$ and the demand function is $Q_d = 28 - 2p$, where p = price and Q = quantity. Find the free-market equilibrium price and quantity.
   (b) Now, suppose the government wants to lower the subsidy of wheat by 25% from the free-market equilibrium by paying farmers to withdraw land from production. However, the payment is made in kind rather than in was named that way—hence programme cash.

   The wheat comes from the government's vast reserves that resulted from previous price support programmes. The amount of wheat paid is equal to the amount that could have been harvested on the land withdrawn from production. Farmers are free to sell this wheat in the market:

   How much is now produced?

   What is the new market price?

   How much do farmers gain?

   Do consumers gain or lose?
   (c) Do tax payers gain from the programme? What potential programmes does the programme create?

ANSWERS

1. (a) A profit is maximized where MC = MR. Here MR = £60. MC = 2Q. Thus, MC = MR becomes 60 = 2Q and Q = 30.

   (b) Profit = TR – TC,
   so, $(60 \times 30) - (100 + 30)^2$
   = 1800 – 1000 = 800.

   (c) The business produces in the short-run if its revenue is greater than its AVC. The farm's short-run supply curve is its MC curve above the minimum point of AVC. Here AVC = Q. And MC = 2Q. So MC > AVC for any quantity greater than zero. This means that businesses do produce in the short-run as long as P is positive.

2. (a) With the imposition of a £1 tax on a single business, all its cost curves shift up by £1, i.e. for every quantity, MC, AVC and ATC are £1 higher.

   (b) Because the business is a price-taker in a competitive market, the imposition of the tax on one business only does not change the market price.

   Given that the business's SMC curve is its supply curve above AVC curve, and that the MC curve has shifed up, the business supplies less to the market at every price. Profit is now lower at every quantity.

   (c) If the tax is imposed on a single business, in the long-run that business will go out of business unless it was earning a positive economic profit before the tax.

3. (a) In free-market equilibrium $L_s = L_d$. So, W = £3 and L_s = 30m (m denotes millions). If the minimum wage is £4, then $L_s = 40$ and $L_d = 20$, $L_s > L_d$ and employment will fall to 20m.

   (b) With the subsidy, for a wage rate W, employer will only pay W–1. The L_d = 60 – 10(W–1). So, W = £3.50 and L_d = 35m.

4. (a) Equating D = S, $Q_d = Q_s$; 28–2p = 4 + 4p, which means p* = 4 and Q* = 20.

   (b) The 25% reduction required by the Payment-in-Kind Programme would imply that farmers are required to produce 15 billion bushels. To encourage farmers to withdraw their land from cultivation, the government must give them 5 billion bushels that they, in turn, sell in the market. Since the total supply is still 20 billion bushels, the market price is still £4 per bushel. The farmers gain £20 billion from PIK programme. Consumers are not affected by PIK programme, since they pay the same price and buy the same quantity as they did in the market scenario.

   (c) Taxpayers gain because the government does not have to pay to store the wheat for a year and then ship it to other countries. The PIK programme can last only as long as wheat reserves held by the government exist. But PIK programme assumes that the land removed from production can be brought back to production at such time as stock piles are exhausted. If this cannot be done, consumers may eventually pay more for wheat-based products. Finally, since producing wheat must have cost something, the programme offers farmers a substantial windfall profit.

CHAPTER 8

MARKET POWER OF MONOPOLY, ITS SOCIAL COST AND SOME SOLUTIONS

KEY TERMS

Monopolist: A sole producer of a good for which there is no close substitute.

Monopoly Power: $= \frac{P - MC}{P}$ = Lerner's index of Monopoly Power.

Price Discrimination: Charging different prices to different customers.

Natural Monopolies: In industry with a continually falling LRAC as output increases.

Naturalized Industries: Whose ownership and management are controlled by the Government.

Privatization: Transferring government owned companies to the private sector.

In a perfectly competitive market, there are enough sellers and buyers of a product so that no single buyer or seller can affect its price. Price is determined by market forces of demand and supply. Individual businesses take the market price as given—they are price-takers—in deciding how much to produce and sell, and consumers take it as given—in deciding how much to buy.

Monopoly is the polar opposties of perfect competition. A monopoly is a market that has only one seller, but many buyers.

We first discuss the behaviour of a monopolist who is a sole producer of a product. The market demand curve relates the price that the monopolist receives to the quantity he offers for sale. We will see how a monopolist takes advantage of his control over price and how the profit-maximizing price and quantity differ from the perfectly competitive market. In general, the monopolist's quantity will be lower and its price higher than the competitive market. This imposes a cost on society because fewer consumers buy the product, and those who do pay higher price. For these reasons, economists are against monopoly. When economies of scale make monopoly desirable, we will see how the government can increase efficiency either by regulating the price or bringing the ownership of such monopoly under its control.

Pure monopoly is rare, but in many markets only a few businesses compete with each other. In any case, the businesses may be able to affect price and may find it profitable to charge a price greater than MC. These businesses have monopoly power which will be discussed later. Monopoly is a form of market power. Market power refers to the ability to affect the price of a good.

• Monopoly

A monopolist is a sole producer of a product. If the monopolist decides to raise the price of the product, he needs not worry about competitors. The monopolist has complete control over the amount of output offered for sale. But this does not mean that the monopolist can charge whatever price he wants, at least if the aim is to maximize profit. To maximize profit, he must first determine the market demand and its cost which is crucial for a business's decision-making. Given this knowledge, he must then decide how much to produce and sell. The price the monopolist charges then follows directly from the market demand curve.

• Marginal Revenue and Average Revenue

The monopolist needs to know the marginal revenue (MR) in order to choose his profit-maximising output level. The average revenue curve of the monopolist is just the market demand curve. To get the relationship among total, average and marginal revenues, consider a business facing the following demand curve: $P = 6 - Q$.

Table 8.1 shows the relation of total, average and marginal revenues. Note that total revenues is zero when the price is £6, because at this price nothing is produced and sold. However, at price £5 one unit is sold, and the total revenue is £5. As quantity increases from 1 to 2, total revenue increases from £5 to £8 and the MR is £3 and so on as the table shows. When MR is positive, total revenue is increasing with quantity, but when MR is negative, revenue is decreasing with quantity.

When the demand curve is downward-sloping, the price (AR) > MR because all units must be sold at the same price. To increase sales, the price must fall. Table 8.1 shows TR, MR and AR.

Fig. 8.1 plots AR and MR curves for the data in Table 8.1. The demand curve is a straight line; in this case MR curve has twice the slope of the demand curve.

• Price and Output Determination under Monopoly

The monopoly firm is assumed to maximize profit in a stable, known environment, with given technology and market conditions. We assume MP and, in the presence of fixed inputs, the firm's AC and MC will at some point begin to rise with the rate of output per unit of time.

However, we no longer assume that diminishing returns to and scale set in at some point. We leave the question open, and permit any one of increasing, constant and diminishing returns to scale to exist over the range of output we are concerned with. The essential difference from the competitive model is the assumption that the firm faces a downward sloping demand curve. We write it demand function in the inverse form:

$$P = D(Q), \frac{dP}{dQ} < 0 \qquad ...(1)$$

where P = price and q = quantity per unit time, and D = the demand function. We do not place

Table 8.1: P, Q and TR, MR and AR

P (Price) £s	Q (Quantity)	TR £s	MR £s	AR £s
6	0	0	—	—
5	1	5	5	5
4	2	8	3	4
3	3	9	1	3
2	4	8	–1	2
1	5	5	–3	1

restrictions on the 2nd derivative of the function, but do require its first derivative to be negative.

The firm's TC functon is

$$TC = C(Q),\ TC'(Q) > 0 \qquad ... (2)$$

where TC = total cost per unit of time. MC = positive, but do not place restrictions on the second derivative, the slope of the MC curve.

The profit function of the firm is

$$\pi(Q) = TR - TC = 0 \qquad ... (3)$$

where π = Profit per unit time. We assume that the profit maximizing output Q* is positive

Hence Q* satisfies the conditions

$$\pi'(Q) = P + \frac{QdP}{dQ} - TC'(Q) = 0 \qquad ... (4)$$

$$\pi''(Q) = \frac{2dP}{dQ} + \frac{Qd^2P}{dQ^2} - TC''(Q) < 0 \qquad ...(5)$$

where (4) is the first order and (5) the second-order condition. The term $\left(P + \frac{QdP}{dQ}\right)$ is the derivative of the TR = PQ with respect to A is MR. Thus, (4) expresses the condition of equality of MC = MR. The term $\left(\frac{2dQ}{dQ} + \frac{Qd_2P}{dQ^2}\right)$ is the derivative of MR. with respect to output and so equation(5) is the condition that the slope of the MC curve must

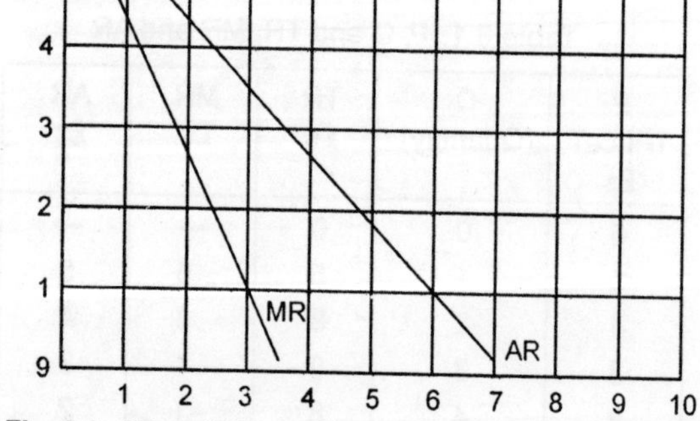

Fig. 8.1: AR and MR curves are shown when the demand curve is P = 6-Q

exceed that of the MR curve at the optimal point. If MCs are increasing with output while, by assumption, MR is diminishing with output (5) will necessarily be satisfied, since in this case

$$TC''(Q) > 0 > \frac{2dP}{dQ} + \frac{Qd^2P}{dQ^2} \qquad ... (6)$$

However, unlike the competitive case, the 2nd order condition may also be satisfied if $TC''(Q) < 0$.

More insight into this solution can be gained if we write MR as

$$MR = P\left[1 + \frac{Q}{P} \cdot \frac{dP}{dQ}\right] \qquad ... (7)$$

Given the definition of the elasticity as

$$e = -\frac{\frac{dQ}{Q}}{\frac{dP}{P}} \qquad ... (8)$$

we can write the relationship between demand elasticity and MR

$$MR = P\left(1 - \frac{1}{e}\right) \qquad ... (9)$$

Clearly, $e < 1 \Rightarrow MR < 0$

while $e = 1 \Rightarrow MR = 0$ and

$e > 1 = MR > 0$.

Combining (9) with (4), we can write the condition for optimal output as

$$P\left(1 - \frac{1}{e}\right) = TC'(Q) = MC \qquad ... (10)$$

This equation then establishes immediately the two propositions:

(a) The monopolist's chosen price > MC since its price elasticity is finite;

(b) Optimal output is always at a point on the demand curve at which e > 1. Under condition of competition each firm equates MC = MR = P but extent of the divergence of P from MC under monopoly is often regarded as a measure of the degree of monopoly power enjoyed by seller from (10)

We get $P - MC = \frac{1}{e} \propto < e < 1 \qquad ...(11)$

The left-hand side of (10) is the Lerner's index of monopoly power see more on later.

Thus, as $e \rightarrow \infty$ (the competitive case) monopoly power tends to be zero. The equilibrium condition of the firm implied by its choice of output Q* satisfying in the Fig. 8.2: In Fig. 8.2(a), the demand curve is D(Q) and the corresponding MRC = MR. Given the MC = FC(Q) and ACC, Profit – maximized output.

Since this must be sold at a market clearing price, choice of Q* requires the P* = D(Q*). We could thus regard the equilibrium position as a choice either of profit-max. Price P* or of output Q*, since each implies the other. At output Q*, profit is the difference between TR = P*q* and TC = AC.Q* as is shown by the area P*abc in Fig. (a). In(b) of the figure, the same equation position is shown in terms of TR and TC. One TR = PQ, and its slope at any point measures MR at that output. If concave shape reflects the assumption of DMR. The TC(Q) and its concave shape reflects the assumption of increasing MC. The total profit function is the vertical difference between the two curves, as is shown in the curve Π (q) in the Fig.(b). The maximization on this curve occurs at the output q*, which is also the point at which the tangents to the TR and TC curves respectively are parallel, i.e. MR = MC. The supernormal profit, i.e., profit in excess of all opportunity cost is given by the area Q*(P* – C). It can be imputed as a rent to whether property right confers on the monopoly power and prevents the non entry which will compete the profits away. It may be that this right is owned by an individual who leases it to the firm. If the supplier is rational and well-informed, he/she will lead up the price of the lease so as just to absorb the supernormal profit, and so the rent is transformed into an opportunity cost for the monopolist. This would be true for example, if the monopolist rented a particularly favourable location. If the monopolist owns the property right, then he can impute the profits as the return on this property right. Note that the identity of the owner of the right does not affect the price and output which will be set by the monopolist but simply determines the division of the spoils.

• Social Cost of Monopoly

Monopoly is a form of market failure in which it is Pareto inefficient: it would be possible to change the allocation of resources to make amount of income he would be prepared to pay in exchange of the reduction in price. The area between the market demand and price lines is the sum of the corresponding areas under the individual consumer's demand curves.

This area measures benefit to the society regardless of which consumer it accrues to. Since changes in price also change the

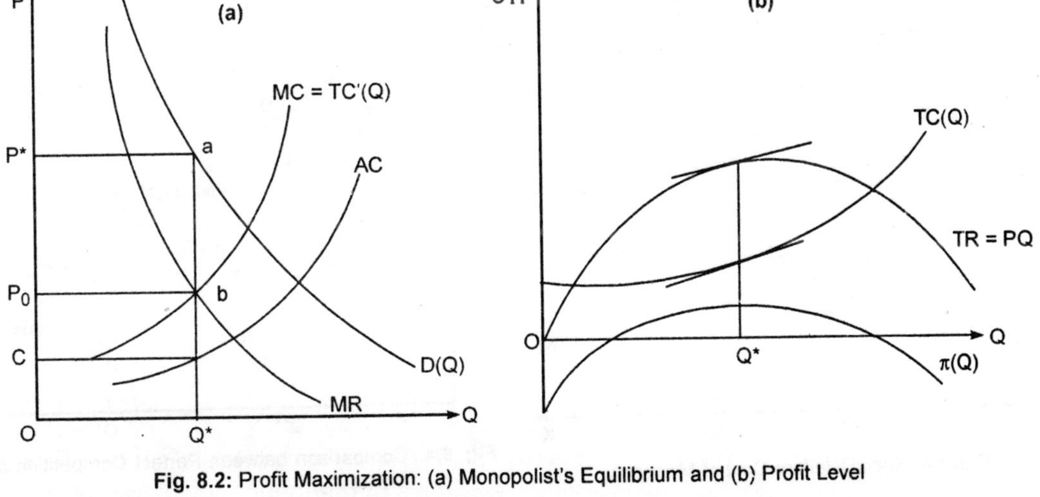

Fig. 8.2: Profit Maximization: (a) Monopolist's Equilibrium and (b) Profit Level

monopolist's Profit, we must take this into consideration of the social value of profits. The simplest assumption is that, it has the same value or consumer surplus.

Notice that this assumption implies that the distribution of income is optimal: it would not be possible to increase welfare by redistributing income among individuals. If we are prepared to make these distributional value judgements and to make the positive assumption that income effects are zero, then the measure of the welfare loss due to monopoly is the area abc in the Fig.8.3. If P is reduced from P* to P_0, so that output expands from X* to X_0, then consumers benefit by the area P^*adP_0. The firm's cost also increases by cbX_0X^* which is the area under the MC curve between Xo and X*. The sum of the gains to consumers and the change in the firm's profit is $PabP_0 + (dbX_0X^* - P^*adP_0) - (cbX_0X^*) = abc$.

We can write the monopoly welfare loss as

$$\int_{X^*}^{X_0} [D(X) - C'(X)]dx$$

$$\Rightarrow \frac{1}{2}[(P^* - P_0) + (P_0 - (cm)](X_0 - X^*) \quad ...(1)$$

where D(X) = demand function and C′(X) = MC function. Knowledge of these functions is sufficient to estimate the welfare loss due to monopoly, provided normative and positive assumptions are satisfied.

Another assumption for abc as the welfare loss can be given by remembering that the price measures the amount of money that consumers are willing to pay for an additional unit of the good. Hence the area abX_0X^* underneath the dc between X_0 and X* measures their willingness to pay for the additional output. Hence the difference between the area under the demand curve and the MC curve measures the net social loss due to monopoly restricting output to X* where MR = MC, compared with welfare maximizing output X_0 where P = MC.

Monopoly and Resource Allocation: The presence of monopoly distorts the allocation of resources because the monopoly produces a level of output for which MC = MR < P, the market price of its goods no longer conveys accurate information about production costs. Hence, consumer decision will no longer reflect true Opportunity Costs of production, and resources will be misallocated.

Basis of Comparison: To evaluate the allocational effect of a monopoly, we need a precisely defined basis of comparison. A useful comparison is provided by the perfectly competitive, constant cost industry. In this case, the industry's long-run supply curve (LRSC) will be infinitely elastic with P =

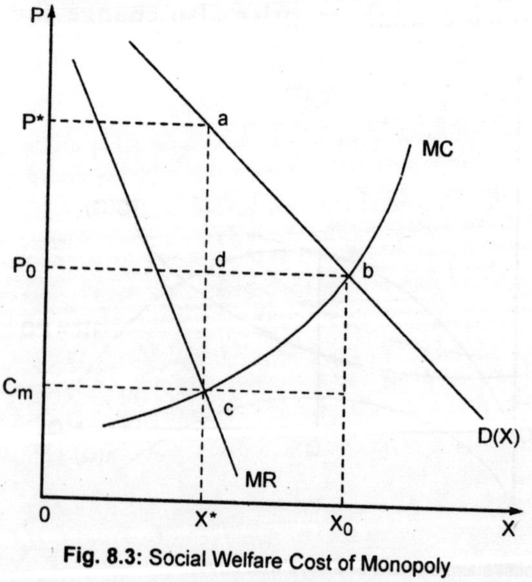

Fig. 8.3: Social Welfare Cost of Monopoly

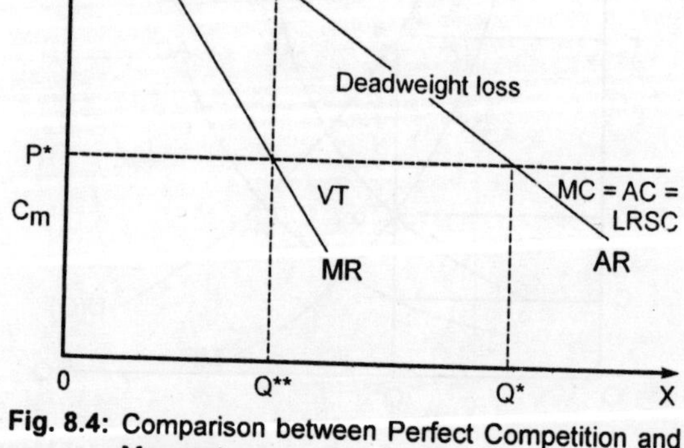

Fig. 8.4: Comparison between Perfect Competition and Monopoly

MC = AC. It is convenient to think of a monopoly as arising from a competitive industry which has now become a single plant in monopolist's empire. For example, a case of J.D. Rock- efeller's purchase of most of the US refineries in the late 19th century and his decision to operate them as part of the standard oil trust. We now compare the performance of this monopoly to the performance of the previously competitive industry to arrive at the welfare consequence of monopoly.

The quantity Q* is, likewise, not profit-maximizing. At output Q*, MC is greater than MR. Thus, if the monopolist produces a little less than Q*, this would increase total profit. The monopolist could increase profit even more by reducing output to Q**.

A profit maximizing algebraic solution is shown in Appendix 8A.1.

- **A Rule of Thumb for Pricing**

We know that price and output should be chosen so that MR = MC, but how does the manager of a business find the correct price and output level, in practice? Managers may have only limited knowledge of the AR and MR that their businesses face. Similarly, they might have little knowledge about the business's MC curve. Thus, we want to translate the condition that MR should equal MC into a rule of thumb than can be more easily applied in practice. This is done in Appendix 8A.2, where we find that

$$\frac{P-MC}{P}=\frac{1}{Ed} \quad \text{... (1) and}$$

$$P=\frac{MC}{1-(1/Ed)} \quad \text{... (2)}$$

How does the price fixed by a monopolist compare with the price under competition? In a perfectly competitive market, as we know, P = MC. A monopolist charges a price that exceeds MC, by an amount that depends inversely on the elasticity of demand is the mark up equation (1) shows, if the demand is extremely elastic, Ed is a large negative number, and P will be very close to MC, so the monopolized market looks much like a competitive one. In fact, when demand is very elastic, there is very little benefit to being a monopolist.

- **Shifts in Demand**

In a competitive market, there is a relationship between price and the quantity supplied. That relationship is the supply curve which tells us how much business will be produced at every price.

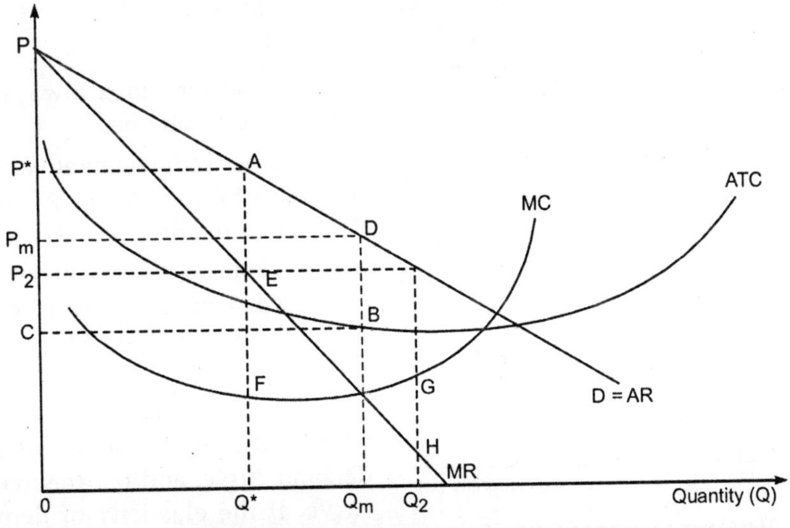

Fig. 8.5: Profit is Maximised when MC = MR

A monopolist has no supply curve. There is no one-to-one relationship between price and the quantity supplied. The reason is that the monopolist's output decision depends not only on the MC, but also on the shape of the demand curve. As a result, shifts in demand do not trace out a series of prices and quantities, as happens in a competitive market. Instead, shift in demand may lead to changes in price with no change in output, changes in output with no change in price, or changes in both.

Figs. 8.6(a) and 8.6(b) illustrate this. In Fig. 8.6(a), the demand curve is initially D_0, the corresponding MR curve is MR_0, and the monopolist's initial price and quantity are P_0 and Q_0.

In Fig. 8.6(a) the demand curve is shifted downwards and the new demand and MR curves are shown as D_1 and MR_1. MR_1 intersects the MC curve at the same point as MR_0 does. As a result, the quantity produced remains unchanged but the price falls to P_1.

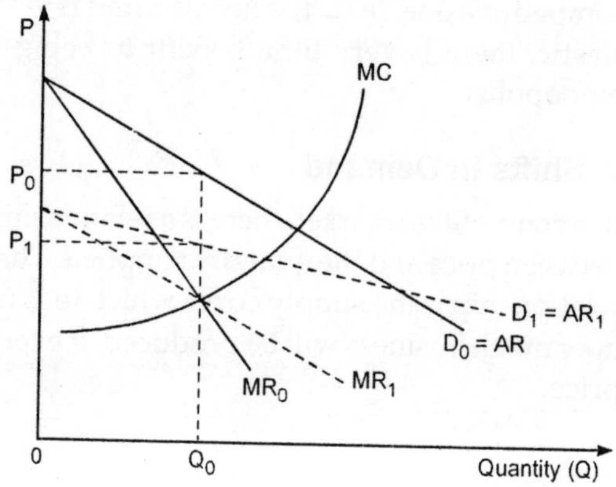

Fig. 8.6(a): The Monopolist has no Supply Curve

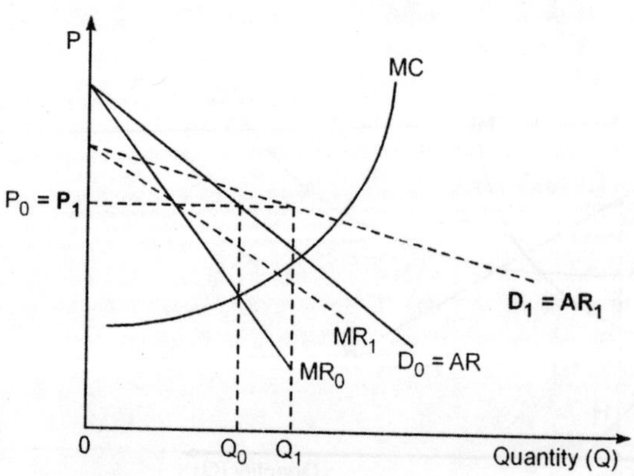

Fig. 8.6(b): The Monopolist has no Supply Curve

In Fig. 8.6(b) the demand curve is shifted upwards. The new MR curve, MR_1, intersects the MC curve at a large quantity Q_1. But the shift in the demand curve is such that the price charged is the same.

Shifts in demand usually cause changes in both quantity and price. But the case shown in Fig. 8.5 illustrates an important distinction between competitive supply and monopoly. In the case of a competitive industry, a specific quantity is supplied at each price. No such relationship exists for a monopolist.

• Measuring Monopoly Power

The distinction between a perfectly competitive business and a monopoly is that, for the competitive business, P = MC, while for the business with monopoly power, P > MC. Thus, a natural way to measure monopoly power is to examine the extent to which the profit maximizing P > MC. We can, in fact, use the mark-up ratio of $\frac{P-MC}{P}$ that was introduced as a rule-of-thumb pricing.

This measure introduced by Lerner is called Lerner's Degree of Monopoly Power:

$$L = \frac{(P-MC)}{P}.$$

This Lerner Index always has a value between zero and one.

For a perfectly competitive business, L = 0, so that P = MC. The larger is L, the greater the degree of monopoly power.

This index of monopoly power can also be expressed in terms of the elasticity of demand facing the business. We know that

$$L = \frac{P-MC}{P} = \frac{1}{Ed}$$

where Ed is the elasticity of the business demand curve, and not the market demand curve. If the elasticity of demand for the business is 6, the degree of monopoly power is 1/6. It may be noted that considerable monopoly power, does not necessarily imply high profits. Profit depends on ATC relative to price.

- **Rule-of-Thumb of Pricing and Elasticity of Demand**

We have already seen how the relationship between price, MC, and the elasticity of demand can be used as a rule-of-thumb for pricing by a monopolist. Equation given below allows us to compute price as simple mark-up over MC:

$$\frac{P-MC}{P}=\frac{1}{Ed} \quad ...(1)$$

This provides a rule-of-thumb for any business with monopoly power, if we remember that Ed is the elasticity of demand for the business and not the industry. If the demand is elastic (Ed is large) as in Fig. 8.7(a), the mark-up (MCa to Pa) is small (1/Ed is small), and the business has little monopoly power.

If the business's elasticity of demand is small, the mark-up (MC_b to P_b) will be large. Figs. 8.7(a) and 8.7(b) illustrate these two cases.

Some businesses have considerable monopoly power, and other businesses have little or none and it is the monopoly power which determines business's ability to set price > MC, and the amount by which P > MC depends inversely on the business's elasticity of demand. The less elastic its demand curve, the more monopoly power a business has. The ultimate determinant of monopoly power is, therefore, the business' elasticity of demand.

Three factors determine a business's elasticity of demand. First, the elasticity of market demand. Second, the number of businesses in the market. Third, the interaction among businesses.

Let us examine each of these three determinants of monopoly power.

- **Elasticity of Market Demand**

The demand curve of a pure monopolist is the market demand curve. In this case, the business's degree of monopoly power depends on the elasticity of market demand. More often, several businesses compete with one another, and then the elasticity of market demand sets a lower limit on the elasticity of demand for each business.

The demand for oil is fairly inelastic, at least in the short-run; that is why **OPEC** could raise oil prices far above the MC during the 1970s and even in 2008-09. The demand for other commodities— such as tea, cocoa, coffee and copper—are much more elastic, this is the

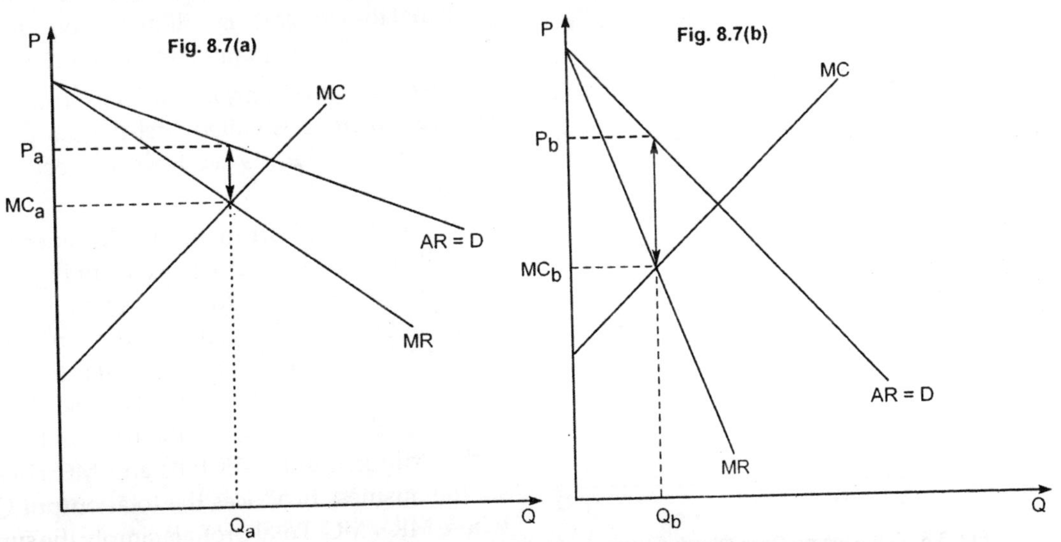

Fig. 8.7: Sources of Monopoly Power

reason why attempts by producers to cartel those markets and raise prices have, largely, failed. In each case, the elasticity of market demand limits the potential monopoly power of individual producers.

• Number of Firms

The number of businesses in the market also limits the monopoly power of a business. Other things being equal, the monopoly power of each business will fall as the number of businesses increases. As more businesses compete with each other, each business will find it difficult to raise prices and avoid losing sales to other businesses.

What matters is not mainly the number of businesses, but the number of "major players". For example, if only two or three businesses account for 85 to 90% of sales in a market, with another 30 businesses accounting for the remaining 10 to 15%, the two or three large businesses might have considerable monopoly power because the market is highly concentrated.

• The Interaction amongst Businesses

The greatest fear of some business is competition. This is mainly true, because if there are only a few businesses in a market,

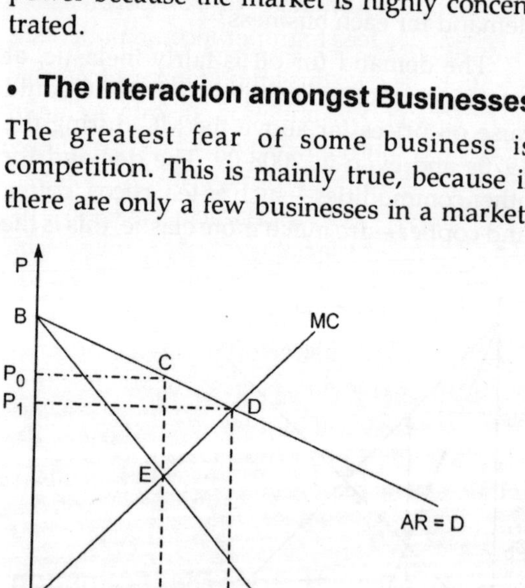

Fig. 8.8: First-Degree Price Discrimination

their managers would prefer that no new businesses should enter the market. An increase in the number of businesses can reduce the monopoly power of each incumbent business and, so, their competitive strategy is to create barriers to entry.

Sometimes there are natural barriers to entry, because of the patent on the technology needed to produce a particular product. Other legally created barriers to entry is a copyright granted to a particular business, and the need for a government license can prevent new businesses from entering the market and so on.

Finally, economies of scale may make it costly for more than a few businesses to supply the entire market. In some cases the economies of scale could be so large that it is efficient for a single—a natural monopoly to supply the whole market, which will be discussed later in this chapter.

• Price Discrimination (PD)

Price discrimination can take three different forms which are called first, second and third-degree PD. We will examine them in turn.

• First-Degree Price Discrimination

A business would wish to charge a different price to different customers. If it could, it would charge each customer the maximum price that the customer is willing to pay, which is known as the customer's reservation price.

The practice of charging each customer his reservation price is called first-degree price discrimination. Let us see how it affects the businesses profit.

We know the profit the business earns when it charges the single price P_0 in Fig. 8.8. To find out, we can add the profit on each incremental unit produced and sold, up to the quantity Q_0. This incremental profit is the MR less MC for each unit. In Fig. 8.8 this MR is highest and MC lowest for the first unit. For each additional unit, MR falls and MC rises, so, the business produces the total output Q, where MR = MC. Total profit is simply the sum of the profits each incremental unit produced, and it is given by the area in Fig. 8.8 between the MR and MC curves (the area ABE = area $OBEQ_0$ less the area $0AEQ_1$). Consumer surplus, which is the area between the AR curve and the price (P_0) that consumers pay, is shown by the area of the triangle P_0BC.

What happens if the business can perfectly discriminate price? Since each consumer is charged exactly what he is willing to pay, the MR curve is no longer relevant to the business' output decision. In fact, the incremental revenue earned from each additional unit sold is simply the price paid for that unit, and is, thus, given by the demand curve.

Since price discrimination does not affect the business's cost structure, the cost of additional unit is given by the business's MC curve. Thus, the profit from producing and selling each incremental unit is the difference between demand = AR and MC. The business charges each consumer his reservation price, so, it is profitable to expand output to Q_1.

When a single price P_0 is charged, the business' variable profit is the area between the MR and MC curves (ABE). With perfect price discrimination, this profit expands to the area between the demand curve and MC curve. From Fig. 8.8 we can see that total profit is now much larger (ABD). Since every customer is being charged the maximum amount he is willing to pay, all consumer's surplus has been captured by the business. The extra profit is the area BDE.

In practice, perfect first-degree price discrimination is impossible. First, it is not practical to charge each customer a different price. Second, a business does not know the reservation price of each customer. Even if the business could ask each customer how much he would be willing to pay, it would not receive honest answers. After all, it is in the customers' interest not to give the correct answer !

Sometimes, it can discriminate by charging a few different prices based on estimates of customers' reservation prices. This often happens when professionals, such as doctors,

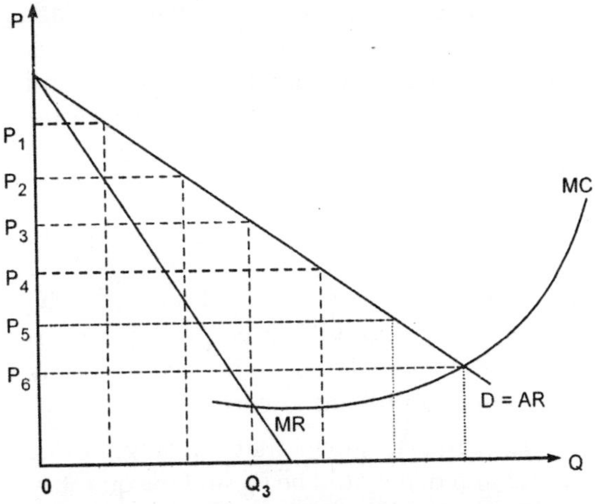

Fig. 8.9: Imperfect First-Degree Price Discrimination

lawyers, accountants etc., who know their clients reasonably well conduct business. Then, it may be possible to assess the client's willingness and ability to pay and charge fees accordingly. For example, a doctor may charge a reduced fee to a low-income patient whose ability cum willingness to pay is low, but charge higher fees to upper income patients.

Fig. 8.9 shows this kind of imperfect first-degree price discrimination. If only a single price were charged, it would be P_3 where MR = MC; the output sold will be Q_3. Instead, six different prices are charged, the lowest of which, P_6, is just the point where MC intersects the demand curve. Those customers who would not have been willing to pay a price of P_3 or greater, are better-off in this situation—they are now enjoying, at least, some consumer surplus. If price discrimination brings enough new customers into the market, consumer welfare can increase, and both consumers and producers are better-off.

• Second-Degree Price Discrimination

In some markets, each consumer purchases many units of the good over a given period, and consumer's demand declines with the number of units purchased. For example, water, gas and electricity. Consumers may each purcahse a few hundred kilowatt-hours of electricity a month, but their willingness to pay declines with increased consumption.

In this case, a business can discriminate according to the quantity consumed. This is called second-degree price discrimination, and it operates by charging different prices for different quantities or 'blocks' of the same good.

In Fig. 8.10, there are three blocks (q_1, q_2, q_3), with corresponding prices P_1, P_2, P_3. There are also economies of scale, and ATC and MC are declining. Second-degree price discrimination can then make consumers better-off by expanding output and lowering cost.

Fig. 8.10 also shows that if a single price were charged, it would be P_0, and the quantity produced would be Q_0. Instead, three different prices are charged, based on the quantities purchased. The blocks are sold at P_1, P_2, and P_3.

• Third-Degree Price Discrimination

A liquor company is prasticing third-degree price discrimination, and it does so because the practice is profitable. This form of price discrimination divides consumers into two or more groups with separate demand curve for each group (D_1 and D_2). This is most prevalent form of price discrimination. In each case, some characteristic is used to divide consumers into distinct groups. For example, for many goods, students and senior citizens are normally willing to pay less on average than the rest of the population and identity can be readily established. Their aggregate demand curve (D_1) is more elastic than D_2 as in Fig. 8.11.

If third-degree price discrimination is feasible, how should the business decide what price to charge each group? Let us think about this in two steps. First, we know that total output should be divided between the groups of customers, so that the MRs for all groups are equal; otherwise the business would not be maximizing profit. For example, if there are two groups of customers and the MR for the first group, MR_1, exceeds the MR for the second group, MR_2, the business could do better by shifting output from the second group to the first. It would be by lowering the price to the first group and raising the price to the second group. So whatever the two prices are, they must be such that the MRs for the different groups are equal.

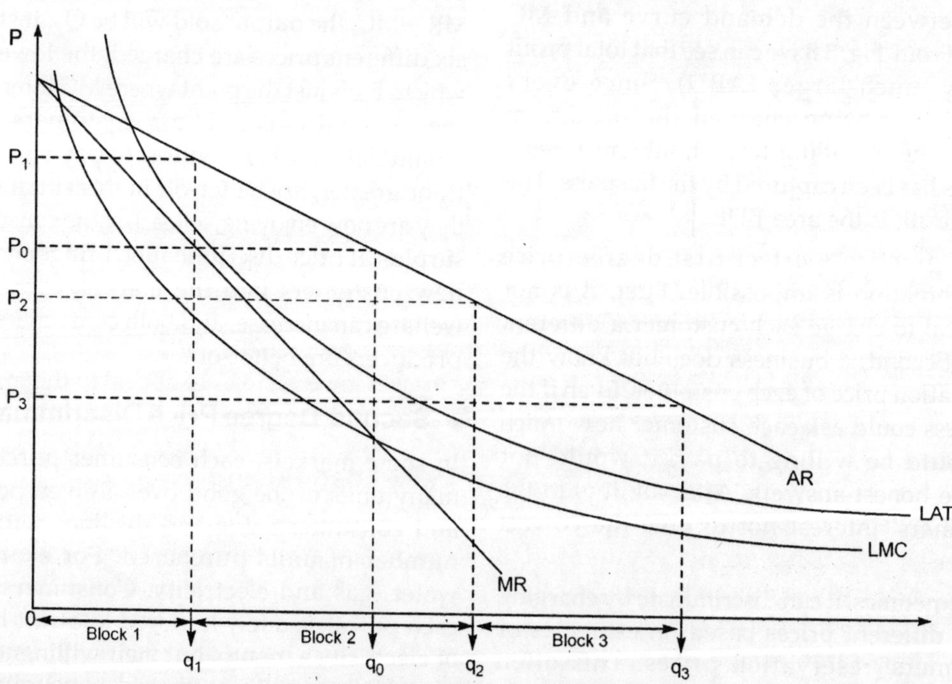

Fig. 8.10: Second-Degree Price Discrimination

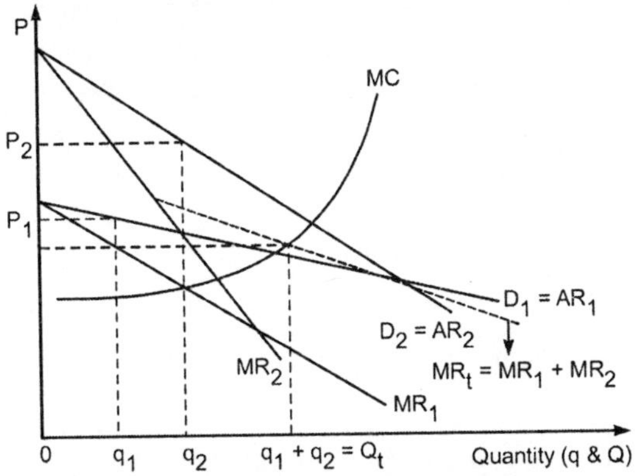

Fig. 8.11: Third-Degree Price Discrimination

Second, we know that total output must be such that the MR for each group of consumers is equal to the MC of production (MR = MC). If this was not the case, the business could increase its profit by raising or lowering total output. For example, suppose the MRs were the same for each group of consumers, but MR > MC of production. The business could increase its profit by expanding the output. It would lower its prices to both groups of customers: so that the MR for each group falls and equals MC.

In Fig. 8.11 consumers are divided into two groups, with separate demand curves for each group. The optimal prices and quantities are such that the $MR_1 = MR_2$ and equal to MC. Here, group 1, with demand curve D_1, is charged P_1 and group 2, with more inelastic demand curve D_2, is charging the higher price P_2. The total quantity Q_t is produced where MC = MR and profit is maximized.

To determine the profit-maximizing output we first have to horizontally sum the MR curves. This will give us MR_t (= MR_1 + MR_2). Setting MR_t equal to MC determines the total output Q_t and the profit-maximizing marginal cost (MC_π). To determine the output of the two different markets we set $MR_1 = MC_\pi$ and $MR_2 = MC_\pi$. This gives the output of market 1 as q_1 and the output of market 2 as q_2. The total output will be $Q_t = q_1 + q_2$. The respective prices are P_1 and P_2. The price P_1 is lower than P_2. This corresponds to the idea that the greater the elasticity, the lower the price. It may be noted here that q_1 and q_2 are chosen so that $MR_1 = MR_2 = MC$.

- **Intertemporal Price Discrimination and Peak-Load Pricing**

Intertemporal price discrimination is an important pricing strategy closely related to third-degree price discrimination. Here consumers are separated into different groups with different demand elasticities by charging different price at different points in time. Intertemporal price discrimination can be seen in Fig. 8.12. Initially, D_0 is the (inelastic) demand curve for a small group of consumers who value the product highly and do not want to wait to buy it. D_1 is the demand curve for the broader group of consumers who are willing to forgo the product if the price is too high. The strategy is to initially offer the product at a high price P_0, selling to consumers represented by the demand curve D_0. Later, after this first

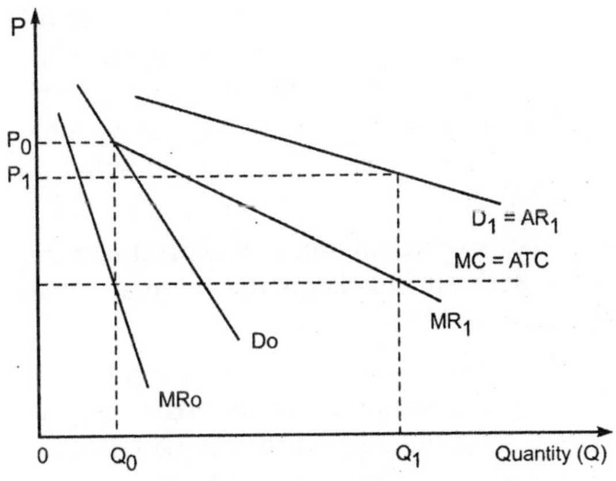

Fig. 8.12: Intertemporal Price Discrimination

group of consumers has bought the product, the price is lowered to P_1 to appeal to the mass market with demand curve D_1.

- **Peak-Load Pricing**

It is a form of inter-temporal price discrimination based on efficiency. For goods and services, demand peaks at particular times—for roads and public transport during commuter rush hours, for electricity during late afternoon, and so on. MC is also high

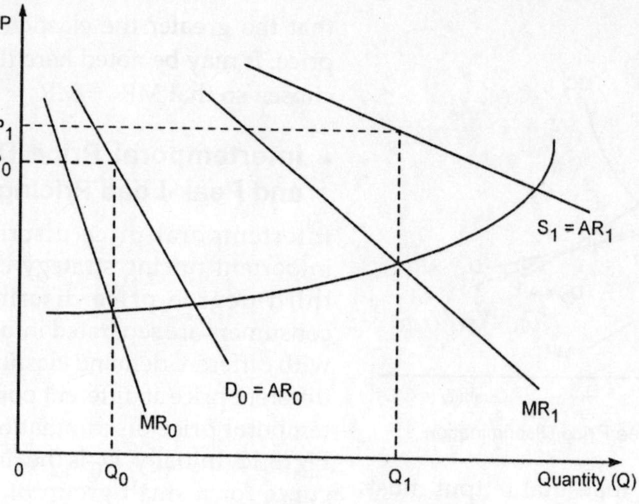

Fig. 8.13: Peak-Load Pricing

during these peak periods because of capacity constraints. Prices should, thus, be higher during peak periods as Fig. 8.13 shows, where D_1 is the demand curve for the peak period, and D_0 is the demand curve for non-peak period. The firm sets MC = MR for each period, such that price P_1 is high for the peak period, and the price P_0 is lower for the off-peak period, with corresponding quantities Q_0 and Q_1. This increases the firm's profit above what it would be if it charged one price for all periods.

It is also efficient; the sum of producer and consumer's surplus is greater because prices are closer to MC.

Peak-load pricing is different from third-degree price discrimination. With third-degree price discrimination, MR has to be equal for each group of consumers and equal to MC because the cost of serving the different groups are not independent. However, price and sales in peak and off-peak period can be determined independently by setting MC = MR for each period as Fig. 8.13 shows.

For example, a movie theatre, which charges more for the evening show than for the matinee show because, for theatres, the MC of serving customers during the matinee show is independent of the MC during the evening. The owner of a movie theatre can determine the optimal prices for the evening and matinee shows independently, using estimates of demand in each period and of the MC.

- **Imposition of Tax**

We will examine the effects on the equilibrium of the monopolist of: (a) a lump-sum tax, (b) a profit tax, and (c) a specific sales tax.

- **Imposition of a Lump-Sum Tax**

In this case we need not distinguish between the short-run and the long-run because, in general, the monopolist always realises some excess profits—both in the short-run and in the long-run. Under these conditions, the imposition of a lump-sum tax will reduce the excess profits of the monopolist because it will increase his total fixed cost. However, the MC curve of the monopolist will not be affected, and, hence, the equilibrium in the monopoly market will remain the same even in the long-run, if the long-run tax does not exceed the supernormal profits of the monopolist.

- **Imposition of the Profit Tax**

The effects of taxes on the monopoly profits are the same as in the case of a lump-sum tax. The profits tax reduces the monopoly profits, but the equilibrium of the market is not affected, so long as the tax does not exceed the normal profits of the monopolist, since, in this case, the monopolist will not cover his total costs and will close down.

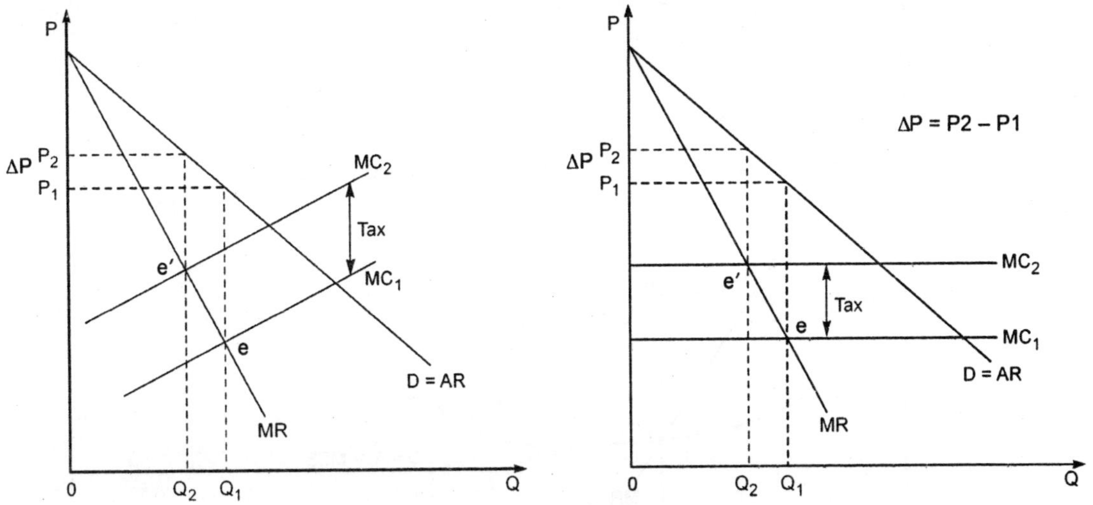

Fig. 8.14: The Imposition of Specific Taxes

• Imposition of a Specific Tax

The effects of a specific tax on the output of the monopolist are broadly the same as those in a purely competitive market. The imposition of the specific tax will shift the MC curve of the monopolist upwards, which will change the equilibrium; in the new equilibrium position (e′), the price will be higher and the quantity smaller as compared with the initial equilibrium. This is the same prediction as with the model of perfect competition.

The change in the price of the monopolist may be smaller, equal or greater than the specific tax, as in the case of pure competition as Fig. 8.14 shows.

First, if the MC of the monopolist has a positive slope, the increase in price will be smaller than the specific tax, as in the case of pure competition. The monopolist will pass to the consumer part of the specific tax.

Second, if the MC is horizontal, the monopolist will raise the price, but not by the full amount of the tax. Even when his MC curve is initially elastic, the monopolist will bear some amount of the specific tax.

Third, the examination of the conditions under which the monopolist can pass the whole tax to the consumer by charging a suitably higher price will not be discussed here.

• Natural Monopoly

Fig. 8.15 shows an industry with a continuously falling long-run average cost as output increases. Only one or very few private firm can survive in such an industry. Any firm that expands output can cut costs and thus undercut its rivals. Facing a demand curve, D and marginal revenue curve, MR, the monopolist produces output, Q_m, and earns profits equal to the area P_mCBE.

A natural monopolist's average cost keeps falling as its output increases. It undercuts all small competitors. At this output the social marginal benefit is greater than price, P_m, and also the social marginal cost at A. The monopolist produces too little. At output Q_1 marginal social benefit (MSB) is equal to marginal social cost (MSC) and this is the efficient point for society. The private monopoly creates a deadweight loss of the area AEE′.

If the firm produces at the efficient output at E′, we will get the desired output Q_1, but the price P_c(= AR) would be less than LATC at Q_1. The business is making a loss. Since marginal cost is less than average cost when LATC is falling, forcing the firm to price at MC, it is always loss making. You cannot force a private firm to make losses. Its only option will then be to shut-down.

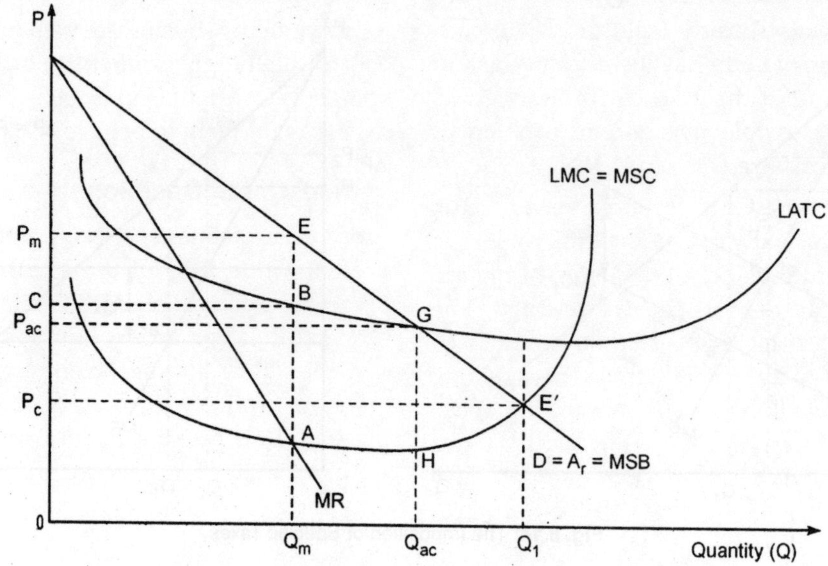

Fig. 8.15: Pricing Policy of Natural Monopoly

One solution is for the regulatory body to get close to the efficient point at E′ while letting the monopolist to break-even after allowing a proper deduction for all economic costs. By making the monopolist to produce at Q_{ac} where the price is P_{ac} at this output, the deadweight burden is cut from AEE′ to GHE′.

An even better solution would be to allow the monopolist to charge a two-part-tariff which means charging a fixed sum for access to the service and then a price per unit that will be equal to the MC of production.

The efficient point E′ = LMC is also equal to social marginal benefit (SMB). A private monopolist sets MR = MC, produces Q_m and earns profits equal to the area P_mEBC. The deadweight loss under private monopoly is AEE′. If the monopolist was forced to charge P_c the monopolist faces a horizontal demand curve P_cE′ up to output Q_1. Since P_c = MR, the monopolist would produce at E′ where MR = MC. Although efficient, the monopolist cannot be forced to produce at E′ in the long-run. Since E′ lies below LATC the monopolist is making losses and would rather go out of business.

A two-part tariff may allow it to stay in business which would be profitable and producer may continue to produce. In Fig. 8.15 the monopolist may be asked to charge price, P_c. Consumers demand the socially efficient output Q_1. Since the monopolist is now a price taker at $P_{c'}$, it is loss-minimizing for the monopolist to produce Q_1, at which P = MR = MC. The regulator may in such a situtation allow the monopolist to levy the minimum fixed charge necessary to ensure that it breaks even.

The third solution to the natural monopoly problem is to ask the monopolist to produce at the efficient point E′ at a price P_c but to provide a government subsidy to cover the losses. It is socially desirable to produce the efficient output Q_1 in the cost minimizing way. If the subsidy solution is adopted, it would be necessary for the government to get involved in the entire running of the industry so that the entire operation can be carefully monitored.

Three problems recur with all these solutions to the problem of natural monopoly. First, information is costly to acquire. It is hard to ensure the industry does minimize costs. Unnecessarily, high costs may be passed on under AC-pricing (solution 1), can result in a higher fixed charge to ensure break-even under a two-part-tariff (solution 2), or can require a large subsidy (solution 3). In each case regulatory body has the difficult task of trying to make the natural monopoly as efficient as possible. The second problem is regulatory caputre.

Regulatory Capture implies that the regulator gradually comes to identify with the interests of the business it regulates, becoming its champion—not its watchdog. The regulated devotes time, effort, and money to lobby the regulator. More subtly, the regulated business has all the inside information about its own activities, information that the regulator needs to acquire. The regulator can build up contacts with the regulated. Eventually, the regulator may sympathise with the problem of the regulated.

Third, regulators find it hard to make credible commitments about their future behaviour. For example, the regulator may encourage the monopolist to invest by promising to soften the regulation in the future. Once the investment is made and a cost sunk, the regulator can then change the ground rules, toughen the requirements. Foreseeing all this, the monopolist may never invest in the first place. There is under-investment if the regulator faces a commitment problems.

During 1945-80, many European governments concluded that least bad solution to the monopoly problems was to nationalize the monopoly industries.

Nationalized industries are state-owned businesses making private goods and services for sales in a market. In post War period many businesses were nationalized by the Labour Government during 1945-51 and the Conservative Government that came after the Labour Government in the 1950s and 1960s never de-nationalized them all. Some industries were privatized by the Conservatives which were then renationalized by the following Labour Government. However, the Conservative Government that ruled Britain during 1980s and 1990s privatized almost all of them. Even today some UK businesses remain under the control of the government (e.g. Post Office known as Consignia, NHS, etc.). How should society want them to behave?

• Investment Decisions

A private investment project is profitable if the present value (PV) of the stream of future operating profits exceeds the initial cost of the new capital. For an explanation of PV see Appendix 8A.3. Private businesses undertake the most profitable projects first. Investment proceeds until the marginal project is reached. At this point the PV of future profits = the cost of capital. We can also make the same statement using flows instead of stock. Investment proceeds as long as the rate of return exceeds the interest rate that is the opportunity cost of the funds tied up. The same principles carry over into social investment decisions provided we use social instead of private measures of costs, benefits and the discount rates.

• Initial Cost of Capital Good

Without other distortions, this is simply the private cost of the capital project. However, local unemployment may reduce the social cost of construction workers below the market wage. Without the project, the workers make no other goods. Production externalities may also lead to a divergence of private and social values. Where building capital goods fosters production externalities (e.g. skill development), this reduces the social price of the capital good.

• Evaluating the Stream of Future Costs and Benefits

Externalities cause a divergence between private and social costs and benefits.

An underground that reduces road congestion has social benefits beyond the revenue raised from fares. Society may use social—not private values—of costs and benefits.

• Choosing the Discount Rate

The discount rate is the interest rate used to calculate present values of costs and benefits. There are two reasons why society may use a lower interest rate than the private sector.

First, the public sector handles risk better. The risk is spread more thinly: the public sector has more shareholders. Second, resources used for public sector investment displace not just private investment but private consumption as well. For private businesses, the discount rate is the interest rate. For households, who shift resources between current and future consumption by saving, the after tax interest rate shows the terms on which current and future can be exchanged. The most efficient compromise involves a public sector discount rate below the interest rate used in private investment decisions, but above the post-tax interest rate used in household saving and consumption decision. To sum up, investment decisions in state-owned businesses should use social valuations of costs and benefits, and discount at the social rate of discount and not the private rate of interest.

• Pricing Decisions

But for distortion elsewhere in the economy, public sector businesses should set P = SMC. SMC (social marginal cost) should be adjusted for any production and consumption externalities that arise, ensuring that society equally values the MC and MB from the last unit of output.

• Short-Run or Long-Run MC Pricing

The one-off cost of building a plant is a stock concept. The cost is incurred at the point the plant is built. But the LMC is a flow concept, relating to the cost per period of producing output. At the discount rate r the PV (a stock concept) of a permanent flow of Ck per period is given by the perpetuity formula PV = Ck/r.

Conversely, the per-period cost Ck of an initial outlay PV can be expressed as Ck = r × PV.

Assume that SMC is constant at 'c' up to full capacity and then vertical. SMC_0 corresponds to the capacity output Q_0 and SMC_1 to capacity output Q_2. Suppose SMC_0-is relevant to demand D_1. In the short-run the efficient output is Q_1 and price is c. If the demand is D_2, the price given SMC_0 is P_2 on the vertical part of SMC_0. LMC includes the capital charge Ck. Beginning from the plant size Q_0, in the long-run society can gain the area ABE by expanding capacity until LMC=MSB at E. At plant size of Q_2 the price P_1 still lies on the SMCC which is now SMC_1. SMC pricing equates immediate MC and MB. In the LR it is by efficient investment decisions that capacity is adjusted to ensure that this is P = LMC.

Fig. 8.16 shows the SRMC = SMC_0. For simplicity, we assume existing plant has a maximum capacity of Q_0 and SMC_0 is constant at c up to full capacity, but then becomes vertical. No matter how much is spent, output cannot be increased beyond Q_0, given the existing level of capacity.

• Privatization

Privatization has become an integral part of pro-competition programme and has now become a familiar feature of new consensus economic policy. It is defined as the transfer of state owned resources to private control. This can be achieved through direct sale of the assets to the private sector.

The move to privatize began in the UK and New Zealand in the 1980s; it spread to the Continent in the 1990s and is now taking a front seat in large number of less developed countires. The US was a significant absentee from this trend, mainly because it had very few nationalized industries to privatize. Worldwide revenue from privatization amounted to $600 billion between 1990 and 1999.

Privatization can be accomplished in two ways: (1) the government can sell assets it owns to private buyers. (2) The government can stop providing service directly and rely

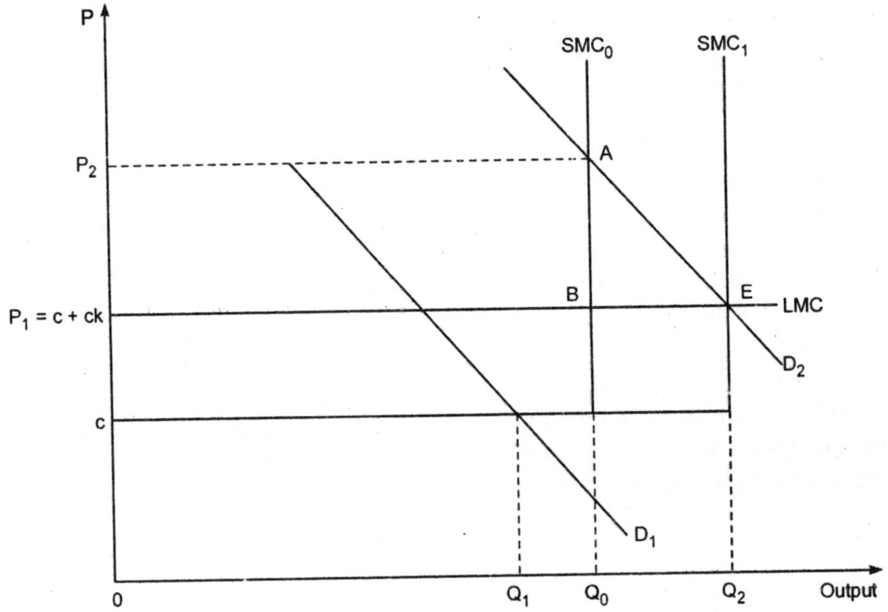

Fig. 8.16: Marginal Cost Pricing

on the private sector to deliver the services. The public enterprises relevant here are revenue-generating entities orginally owned or controlled by the state. (An example of a revenue-generating entity is a municipal corporation that gets property taxes).

• Reasons for Privatization

Over time, in many countries, the performance of the Public Sector Enterprises (PSEs) turned out to be, by and large, unsatisfactory. They incurred losses, or did not make as much profit as they should have, given that they have privileged access to capital, various subsidies, and protection from domestic and foreign competition. Governments have begun to think of privatization of PSEs as a solution to these problems.

We examine next the possible impacts of privatization to determine whether it can transform *PSEs*.

There are many reasons for privatization. The most important of them has been a disillusionment with the capacity of the nationalized industries to deliver effective and efficient services to the public and to achieve social goals they were set up to attain. In nationalized industries the principal-agent problem was particularly acute. The objectives of the politicians who owned the companies were often conflicting; the government department in charge of the company added another layer of complexity, with the result that managements had no clear objectives and no sustained incentive to perform. One major objective of privatization was to make the company more efficient.

Secondly, closely related to the above, governments wished to introduce competition into the sectors hitherto dominated by the state ownership. If this was done while the companies remained in the state ownership, their chances of successfully coping with competition would be increased by being run by the private sector rather than public sector.

Third, many nationalized industries were notorious losers. The liberalization of trade threatened even further losses. Selling them was seen as a way of reducing or eliminating budget deficit. Fiscal benefits could also accrue on the state's capital account from the sale of the assets. Obviously the proceeds from the sale of profitable state companies or from those with potential to earn more under private sector management such as telecom and energy utilities promise to be especially large. The proceeds from privatization yielded £65 billion in 1997 to the UK exchequer. During the 5 years, 1995-99, Italy's privatization proceeds came to $80 billion. According to OECD estimates, revenues from privatization between 1990 and 1998 amounted to 24% of Hungary's GDP in 1998, 20% of Portugal's GDP and 15% of New Zealand's. Many less developing countries saw privatization as a golden one-off opportunity to reduce public sector debt and to set motion a lower tax environment without damaging increases in budget deficits.

Fourth, politicians came to the conclusion that the balance of the mixed economy has shifted towards the public sector. This belief was fortified by the abuse of power by many public sector trade unions with frequent use of the strike weapon.

Former communist countries have been profoundly affected by the privatization of their economies.

However, the origin of these privatization programmes, and the context in which these are being implemented, are obviously very different to those of the west. For one thing, these countries were being transformed from a situation in which almost the entire economy was state-owned. For example, East Germany had privatized some 12,000 businesses, about 85% of all businesses in the previous regime operating under state-ownership. In many of these countries, governments had large budget deficits and a limited capacity to raise revenue through higher taxes. Thus, privatization, to them, was a way of disposing of all loss-making companies and providing desperately needed revenues to the state.

There is something paradoxical about privatization of state-owned companies in Western countries. After all these companies were originally set up to resolve economic problems and not to cause them. Many were established to deal with the problems created by private monopolies and to create competition among them so that monopoly profit and social cost of monopoly can be done away with. Nationalization was designed to encourage exploitation of scale economies and to ensure that monopoly profits, if any, would accrue to the state which they would be able to distribute in socially optimum way. In retrospect these expected advantages fail to materialise. Too often nationalized industries abused their monopoly power. They provided bad services at higher prices. They suffered extensive X-inefficiencies. Their industrial relations were surprisingly very bad. Against this background, it is easy to believe a European Commission estimate that complete liberalization of the European airline would bring about a 10% decline in costs and prices which will bring benefits of some $1 billion per year, obtained through lower pay costs, more efficient deployment of the workforces and lower overheads.

• Efficiency Gains

Proponents of privatization have argued that it can have an important effect on efficiency. Two types of efficiency gains are possible: gains in allocative efficiency, and gains in production efficiency.

(a) *Allocative efficiency*: Proper allocation of resources of the economy depends on the prices reflecting correctly the relative scarcity of resources. A resource that is more scarce should have a higher price and this would lead to it being used more sparingly. In PSEs, price sometimes do not reflect scarcity properly. For example, if the government gives a subsidy for an input used by a PSE, the PSE would tend to overuse that resource. Or, if PSE is a monopoly, then it can set its own price. Thus, kerosene may be sold at a very low price, which would encourage adulteration of diesel with kerosene (i.e. overuse of kerosene).

It is clear that for PSEs operating in competitive markets, prices would better reflect scarcities and, therefore, allocative efficiency would be high. Then the gains from privatization would be less; on the other hand, transforming a public sector monopoly into a private sector monopoly would also not lead to increases in allocative efficiency. We can expect large increases in allocative efficiency to be achieved when a public sector monopoly is privatized and the market opens up to other players.

(b) *Productive efficiency*: It relates to the optimum use of inputs in the production process. It has been argued that PSEs are likely to exhibit greater internal inefficiency than private firms for various reasons. Public managers are given numerous and inconsistent objectives. Instead of control by shareholders who are interested in profit-maximization, there is bureaucratic control which puts more emphasis on 'playing it safe'. Suppose productive efficiency requires use of an input that is not available in a competitive market. The manager in a PSE is required to obtain competitive quotations for almost everything, and hence may have no way of using that paricular input because there is only one seller in the market.

• Fiscal Impact and Distribution

Critics argue that it is likely to affect adversely the weaker sections of the community. First, it might lead to layoffs by the new owners. Or the firm may go bankrupt after privatization and the government will not be there to protect jobs. Secondly, the goods and services made available by the PSE to the poor may become less accessible. For example, a privatised railway may choose to close unprofitable routes.

A counter-argument is that the PSEs have not had a very successful record of reaching the poor and the disadvantaged sections. For example, in India, it has been repeatedly shown that the public distribution system does not do a good job of reaching essential commodities to the poorest sections, rather it is more useful to the richer sections.

When a PSE is sold off to the private sector, the government gets the sales proceeds. Further, if the PSE had been making losses and was being subsidised, then subsidies will come to an end, which further helps the government Thus, the immediate generation of revenues is supplemented by a reduction in recurrent expenditures. But does the government really gain? In the simplest case, government will be willing to pay only so much as the PSE is expected to bring in the future. The PSE is expected to generate a future stream of returns. The sum of the discounted returns is what a buyer will pay. The government would have got the same revenue had it not sold the PSE. Therefore, it would seem that privatization does not have any real impact on the government's finance.

There are two reasons why privatization might still make a difference. First, a private firm might be expected to be more efficient than PSE. Hence, the sum of the discounted returns will be higher than that under government ownership. Secondly, the government, when it privatizes, is getting fund immediately. This added liquidity might be desirable for a number of reasons, for example; the government might want to spend the amount on education or infrastructure.

It is interesting to note that in theory, for a loss-making PSE, the price might be negative. This is not very far-fetched. Government have sometimes given so many concessions to the buyer to induce them to buy loss-making concerns, that in effect the price has turned out to be negative.

• Techniques of Privatization

Divestiture: The most well known technique of privatization is the sale of equity to the general public. This is called divestiture or disinvestment, and may be complete or partial. The government may sell all its stake or only a certain part of it. This can be done through direct sale and equity offerings. However, the inadequacy of national stock markets and the lack of domestic capital have sometimes led to a shortage of local buyers, while foreign investors, unable to obtain sound information on the enterprises offered, often lacked sufficient interest. Furthermore, direct sales approach may be costly and slow, owing to the complexity of preparing for sales of each assets individually and then ensuring that buyers observed all contract provisions.

Restitution: This refers to the return of state assets to their former owners where the government's original acquisition is seen as unjust and uncompensated seizure. Thus, restitution is essential on moral grounds. For example, only limited transitional countries used restitution, such as, Estonia, and to a certain extent Czech Republic.

Management-Employee Buyouts: Under this approach, shares of an enterprise are sold or given to some managers and employees. The powerful positions of employees and managers may give this approach the twin advantages of feasibility and political popularity. It is readily and easily implemented. Well structured management-employee buyouts can sometimes lead to efficient results, since the people who know best about the enterprise become the owners.

Nevertheless, these types of buyouts suffer serious disadvantages. Yielding to insider interests often entails large costs in inefficiency and poor management. The new owners may give excessive wage increases maintaining excessively high employment, and undertake insufficient investment. Insiders may also lack many of the skills necessary to function in a market oriented economy. Further, the process is seen to be inadequate, handing employees, rather than population at large, most of the benefits.

Mass Privatization: In mass or equal access, voucher privatization, the government generally gives away or sells for a nominal fee, vouchers that can be used to purchase shares in enterprises. This technique has been used in Central and Eastern Europe, but it has proved to be popular particularly in Czech Republic.

Voucher privatization helps to overcome the shortage of domestic capital. These schemes can be particularly popular because they address the perceived unfairness of other approaches and avoid the charges of a sellout of national assets to foreigners. The difficulties associated with valuing enterprises before privatization are also avoided.

Early proponents argued that the fast pace of voucher privatization would add to the credibility of reform programmes and improve their chance of success. At times, speed could prevent employees or other interests from mobilizing opposition to privatization. Furthermore, the widespread participation of a country's citizens fosters a great understanding of reform and creates a new owner class with a stake in the process.

Mass privatization has the main risk of dispersed ownership structure which lack the focus and power to direct effective corporate management. This, in turn, may scare off potential new sources of capital.

Contracting out or leasing out of government services can be another technique of privatization. For example, a municipal corporation can contract out the task of garbage collection to a private company. Associated with the privatization are the process of liberalization and deregulation. Liberalization refers to the promotion of competition in a traditionally monopolized industry. Deregulation refers to the abolition of statutory barriers to the operation of market forces. For example, the Government of India controls the prices of many commodities through the administration.

Pricing Mechanism: If some commodity or service are taken out of the purview of this pricing mechanism, then this deregulatory measure, will be determined by market forces.

Obstacles to Privatizations: Two kinds of obstacles to privatization can be identified: implementation issue and political constraints. We take them up in turn.

Implementation issues: Technical constraints to privatization are related to both managerial deficiencies and weaknesses within the economy.

Firstly privatization requires a high level of administrative capacity. In some developing economies, there is a lack of well established, competent, management consulting groups, accounting firms, and investment bankers. These are needed to provide technical advice and valuation of PSE. As a result, in some instances, foreign experts have to be brought in.

Secondly a valuation of the PSE has to be carried out before it can be offered for sale, and the valuation excercise has faced severe problems. Valuation is a sensitive subject, politically; because government wants to get a high sales price and at the same time the valuation process might raise questions about past public management and investment decisions. There have been inordinate delays in valuation. The problem is aggravated when poor records are maintained by PSE.

Thirdly, once the valuation has taken place, administrative capacity is needed to assess buyers' bids, arrange finance and insurance, and deal with a host of complex legal issues. Sometimes, a comprehensive rehabilitation plan for the PSE has to be designed, evaluated, and financed before privatization is possible. Moreover, appropriate regulatory structures may not exist and have to be set up, particularly when privatization leads to the creation of monopoly.

Fourthly, Capital markets in many developing economies are weak and poorly regulated. Large investments in equity are quite unusal. PSEs are some of the largest firms in the country and the private sector may also be suspicious about the government's intentions, given the record of nationalization in the past. On the other hand, the government may not be willing to sell assets to foreign investors.

• Political Constraints

Generally, the costs of privatization are borne by a small group of people, e.g. the workers of the enterprise who may lose their jobs or the suppliers who may lose favourable contracts. The benefits are spread out over a large number of people sometimes a very large section of the population. Public choice theory suggests that in such situations, it will be easier to organize opposition to privatization programme than to support. Experience tells us that in many countries, privatization programmes fail to mobilize popular support, and in fact give rise to strong opposition. Trade Union tend to react strongly against privatization. Trade Union power is often concentrated in the public sector and the public sector provides a base for such power. Unions oppose Privatization, not only because of the direct effect on employment, but also because of a fear that the trade union power will be reduced in the private sector.

• Some Critical Issues

Government considering privatization of PSE must first decide on a number of critical issues:

Should restructuring occur before or after sales of the unit?

Most PSEs will not fetch a good price if they are sold in their current condition. For historical reasons, many have excess workers, and are burdened with obsolete machinery and technology, and often are run bureaucratically. Such unrestructured enterprises will fetch lower prices. One option before the government is to restructure these enterprises before placing them in the market, e.g. by laying off excess workers, by inducting new workers with appropriate skills, by selling off non-strategic parts of the business, computerization of operations, etc. These enterprises will then become attractive to private investors who would be willing to pay higher prices for them. On the other hand, proponents of speedy privatization argue that the attempt to privati-zation restructure these before privatisation will inevitably lead to delays and the entire momentum for privatization will be lost. Further, it is doubtful whether the governments are at all adept at restructuring.

How to deal with the laid-off workers?

The overstaffing in PSEs means that the restructuring process would generally involve laying-off of the workforce. Usually, forced dismissals are politically infeasible and only generate more opposition to privatization. Government may try to adopt some kind of voluntary approach including monetary compensation, retraining and redeployment.

Sometimes the government agrees to accept a lower price for the enterprise in return of an assurance from the new owner that employees will be trained even after privatization. In the previous East German privatization programme, there is an instance where an enterprise was sold for one Deutsche Mark, because the bidder promised to retain all the workers.

Retraining means giving training in skills that would help them to become productive members of the PSE itself. Or the aim may be to enable them to find alternative jobs in the private sector. Redeployment can be from one PSE to another, or it can be to private sector.

The process of laying-off poses a number of difficulties:

1. The total cost of laid-off workers can be quite high and may pose a problem to cash-strapped governments. The problem has been eased to a certain extent because multilateral agencies are now prepared to lend for severance pay packages.
2. It is not easy to estimate the right package. Usually some rules of thumb are employed to arrive at the compensation package. Generally, no attempt is made to find out whether the compensation offered is adequate or not. But to properly calculate the present value of the change in earnings resulting from dismissal, one must take into account not only the salaries, but also bonuses and other cash benefits. Moreover, it might take a long time for a laid-off worker to find an alternative job, and earnings might be close to zero in the intervening period. Further, in most developing countries, the public sector provide health coverage as well as old age pension. The greater job security in the public sector also makes employment in this sector more attractive. If all these factors are to be taken into account, then the compensation required is to be sizeable.
3. There is also another subtle problem involved here. Once a severance package has been formulated, only the highly-productive or skilled workers may accept the package and leave, because they are sure to get jobs elsewhere. The PSE would be left with low-productive or inefficient workers. This is called the adverse selection problem: since the package offered is not tailored to individual needs any employee can take the same package. But only the highly productive workers may find the package attractive and accept it.

Should the assets be given away or sold?

As we know, one way of privatization is to give vouchers to a group of people who can use these vouchers to get stakes in enterprises of their choice. The free distribution of vouchers, to all citizens, is seen to satisfy the goal of equality and to create stakes in the privatization process for everybody. this would overcome the opposition to the privatization process. However, this method is difficult to implement in large economies. Moreover, dispersed ownership can lead to corporate governance problems. Thus, many countries have opted for selling off the PSEs rather than giving them away. Those who have money or access to it are usually foreigners or people who have enriched themselves under the old system, and political opposition to the sales to these two groups of people can be very strong. One way of giving away an enterprise is to give stakes to the insiders. But this is considered to be inherently unfair to the populance at large, since it is their tax payments which helped in the setting of these enterprises. Further, since the valuation of the PSEs is a tricky business, there have been allegations that insiders often manage to grab hold of PSEs at low prices by deliberately presenting a sick picture of the PSEs to the outside world and undervaluing the assets. This is particularly important in transition economies with no experience in putting market values of the assets.

• Effects of Privatization

Privatization came in diverse form and many are of very recent vintage to determine their success or failure. Studies of the UK experience suggest a mixed bag of results. Some privatized companies have achieved a successful turnaround, notably British Telecom (BT) and British Airways (BA); but the verdict on the privatization of British Rail and Water industry is far from success. The economists described the Railway privatization as a disaster. Experience also differs between countries. In a highly generalised way one can say that privatization has been more or less successful in the UK while unsuccessful in Russia. The effect of privatization can be evaluated under many headings: effects on efficiency, on government revenue and income distribution.

A key consideration is the effect on efficiency, i.e. on total factor productivity. The resultant fall in unit costs can be passed on to the consumer in terms of lower prices and better quality. In the UK, it was estimated that telephone charges fell by 35% in real term. Electricity charges also declined in real terms. As a general rule, experience shows that the more the competition in the privatized companies, the greater the likelihood of positive outcome. This is just what the economic theory would predict. A policy environment that encourages long-run investment in the privatized industries is also important.

The effect on government revenue is more complex than it might appear. In the case of an outright sale, the gain to the state cannot be equated with the sale price. The state has replaced on asset (the state-owned company) with another (cash). To calculate the net financial gain to the state, we must compare the PV (Present Value) of the stream of revenue expected from the business had it remained in state ownership with the proceeds from the sale. The price paid for the company is thus a crucial variable. If underpaid, the privatization programme could end up worsening instead of improving government finance in the long run. Also there must be some assessment of how this extra cash accruing to the government is being used, if it is being spent on building up military power or on consumer handouts or on long-term investment for the future. The last one must have an income distribution effect. There are at least four parties to be considered: the state, employees of the privatized businesses, the consumers, and the new owners. The mode of privatization has an important bearing on the outcome. Share floating is one way, often associated with a certain predetermined allocation to the existing employees (BT-1984, British Gas (BG) 1986 and so on). Direct sale to private sector has also been used (NOB 1994, Rover cars to British Aerospace). Management buy-outs are another possibility (NF Corporation 1992 and several Bus Companies in Britain). In each case, a careful analysis is needed in order to assess the resultant income distribution effect. It is obviously for the state that is strapped for cash to be included into selling too cheap (Russia and other East European countries). Also share can be sold too cheaply to the public in order to carry popular favour or to ensure that the flotation will be a success as happened in several west European countries.

There is still some doubt that in most of the instances privatization has brought benefits to the consumer, not just in terms of lower price but also in terms of improved quality of services and efficiency. There are areas of the economy to which the ethos of a state company is particularly unsuitable and where privatization might have yielded some benefits. For example, state-owned hotel and restaurant and some manufacturing companies, where prompt decisions are needed and also some industries created on the ground of economies of scale, have never become very successful enterprises. The number and scope of privatization programme around the world shows that finance ministers are convinced that the potential benefits exceed any potential losses. But it will take time before the dynamic efficiency effects of privatization can be fully evaluated.

- **Regulation: Regulatory Reform and Natural Monopolies**

Regulatory reform is designed to promote competition, regardless of whether the industry is in state ownership or private ownership. It is a separate issue from privatization. Yet, in practice, reform of government regulation of industries, particularly state-owned utilities such as electricity, gas, water etc. has been associated with the issue of privatization.

Suppose a state-owned company exists where competition is not possible. Economics of scale are so great that is not possible for more than one company to operate in the industry. This is the case of natural monopoly. The state may still want to privatize in the hope of securing a change in the management culture of the organisation, or to add to government revenues, even though the privatized business will continue to retain monopoly power. How the costs and benefits back up in this instance? Clearly there are benefits from privatization, but these will be achieved only if there is also some state regulation here. How should the privatized monopoly be regulated? The economies of regulation now enter in the picture.

Natural monopolies were, until recently regarded as dominant in the energy, transport and telecommunication, and so on. In addition, private sector competitors were excluded by law from trying to compete with the state monopoly in these sectors. But banning competitors would be redundant if the economies of scale were really powerful; so the existence of legal restriction suggests that the monopoly was not so natural after all. When such is the case, one solution is to remove the restrictions on entry, subject to the new entrants satisfying some basic minimum operating criteria such as prudential reserve ratios, safety provisions, and so on. Privatization can then proceed, and irrespective of the fact whether deregulation comes before or succeeds, privatisation can have an important bearing on how much revenue is obtained from the sale. Deregulation has been applied to many industries in addition to those controlled by the state monopolies. Major changes have been made in the rules governing banks, stock broking, and so on.

These initiatives were inspired by belief in the merits of the free market. No less important was technological change. In some industries, it has made restrictions on new entrants unenforceable, in others it has made small production units more efficient. For example, technical advance has made even a very small electricity generating plant more efficient than it was previously. The combined effects of deregulation and technological advance opened up many hitherto restricted markets. The resultant increase in contestability has brought about huge improvements in efficiency.

However, there remain some sectors where the monopoly proves to be genuinely natural and where the degree of competition is limited. There are two major steps in dealing with the situation. The first step is to break down or unbundle the services provided by the monopoly into component parts so as to isolate the core natural monopoly element in the industry. In electricity, for example, the real monopoly is not on power generation or power distribution but the transportation of electricity through a network. By unbundling the industry into its different potentially competitive and natural monopoly components, efficiencies can be secured through the market system. The potentially competitive parts can be sold to the private sector.

The second step is how to deal with the natural monopoly element. This involves three interrelated stands pricing access and quality of service. We briefly review each of these.

Pricing: Incentive regulation refers to the design of incentives to ensure that producers keep prices and costs as low as possible. The underlying assumption is that costs are not given but are influenced by the incentives set by the regulatory authorities. If there was no regulation, the privatized monopoly might well slip into the same bad habits as the state company it replaced. Whether the new regulation achieves a superior outcome to direct provision of the goods or services by the state company, depends on the effectiveness of the regulatory system.

In the UK, following the privatization of state-owned companies (BT, BG, Water etc.) regulatory bodies were set up for each industry. Their task was to prevent the abuse of monopoly power and find ways of promoting competion. This sounds easy but the regulators frequently get into hot water in trying to achieve this objective.

There are several ways of regulating a privatized industry with strong monopoly elements:

(a) **MC pricing:** One simple way would be to oblige the monopoly business to charge a P = MC, and provide a subsidy for any ensuing loss. The drawback is the cost of the subsidy and the difficulty of determining MC.

(b) **Break-even or Average return to capital:** Alternatively, the regulator can insist on a price that allows the business to just break-even. This eliminates the monopoly profits but leaves wide open the opportunity to reap the benefits of monopoly in other guises. Some regulators use a formula related to rate of return on capital which the monopoly would not be permitted to exceed. This avoids the problem of direct price control, but has the disadvantage of reducing the incentive to businesses to minimise costs, once the permitted profit rate has been attained. Rate of return controls have been applied extensively in the US. Not surprisingly, there has been frequent disputes over the definition and measurement of rates of return in these cases.

(c) **RPI minus X:** Another possibility is to set maximum prices. The UK authorities have taken this approach. And various types of price-capping formulas have been used, known as 'RPI–X', whereby the regulator permits the business's price to rise by no more than X% points below the retail price index (RPI). In a multi-product monopoly, such as telecommunications, the regulator may opt for a tariff-basket method, whereby the authorities decide which products are placed in the basket and how the various prices are to be weighed. This means permitting lower prices for price-elastic services and relatively higher prices on price-inelastic services. While providing flexibility, regulation could be highly controversial. The public will often perceive such pricing structures as unfair, even if based on sound economic principles. Where the output is homogeneous, such as gas and electricity, the regulator may use an average revenue target, whereby the predicted rise in average revenue in the business is not permitted to exceed RPI–X.

A key problem of incentive regulation is to determine the efficiency factor X. If X is set too low, the business will make excessively high profit and regulator will lose face. If it is set too high, the business will become unviable. In deciding on the right value of X, the regulator may have to be guided by the expert with the inside knowledge of the business. Relations between the regulated and the regulator may become too close and cordial.

Another problem is that the formula could act as disincentive to efficiency if more efficient performance were to lead to subsequent upward revision of X. In practice, rate of return considerations are implicit in setting the value of X.

APPENDIX 8A.1

The Algebraic and Numerical Solution to Profit Maximizing

Algebraically also, we can see the Q_m maximizes profit. Profit is the difference between TR and TC, both of which depend on Q.

$$\Pi(Q) = TR(Q) - TC(Q)$$

As Q is increased from zero, profit will increase until it reaches a maximum, and then begin to decrease. Thus, profit-maximizing output is such that the incremental profit resulting from a small increase in Q is zero [i.e., $d\pi(Q)/dQ = 0$].

Then,

$$d\pi/dQ = dTR/dQ - dTC/dQ = 0;$$

where,

$$dTR/dQ = MR \text{ and}$$

$$dTC/dQ = MC.$$

So the profit-maximizing condition is that

$$MR - MC = 0,$$

$$\text{or } MR = MC.$$

A Numerical Example: To understand this result clearly, let us look at an example. Suppose the cost of production is

$$TC(Q) = 50 + Q^2,$$

where 50 is a fixed cost and Q^2 is the variable cost. And suppose, demand is given by $P(Q) = 40 - Q$.

By equating MR and MC, we can verify that profit is maximized when Q = 10, which corresponds to a price of £30.

ATC is TC(Q)/Q

$$= (50 + Q^2)/Q$$

$$= 50/Q + Q \text{ and}$$

MC is $dC/dQ = 2Q$.

$$TR(Q) = P(Q) \times Q$$

$$= 40Q - Q^2, \text{ so, } MR = 40 - 2Q.$$

Equating MR = MC gives

$40 - 2Q = 2Q$ or $Q = 10$.

Substituting Q in the demand equation:

$P(Q) = 40 - 10$ gives $P = 30$.

TC, TR and π are plotted in Fig. 8A.1(a). When the business produces no output or little output, profit is negative because of the fixed cost. Profit increases with output, until it reaches a maximum of £150 at Q = 10, and then decreases as Q is increased further.

At the point of maximum profit, the slopes of the TR and TC curves are the same. The slope of the TR curve is dTR/dQ, or MR, and the slope of the total cost curve is dTC/dQ or MC. Profit is maximized when MR = MC, so the slopes are equal when MR = MC.

Fig. 8A.1(b) shows the corresponding AR and MR curves, and ATC and MC curves, MR = MC at output level Q = 10, At this quantity, ATC is £15 per unit, and P(= AR) is £30 per unit, so average profit (profit per unit of output) is £30 – £15 = £15 per unit. Since 10 units are sold, profit is

$$(10 \times 15) = £150.$$

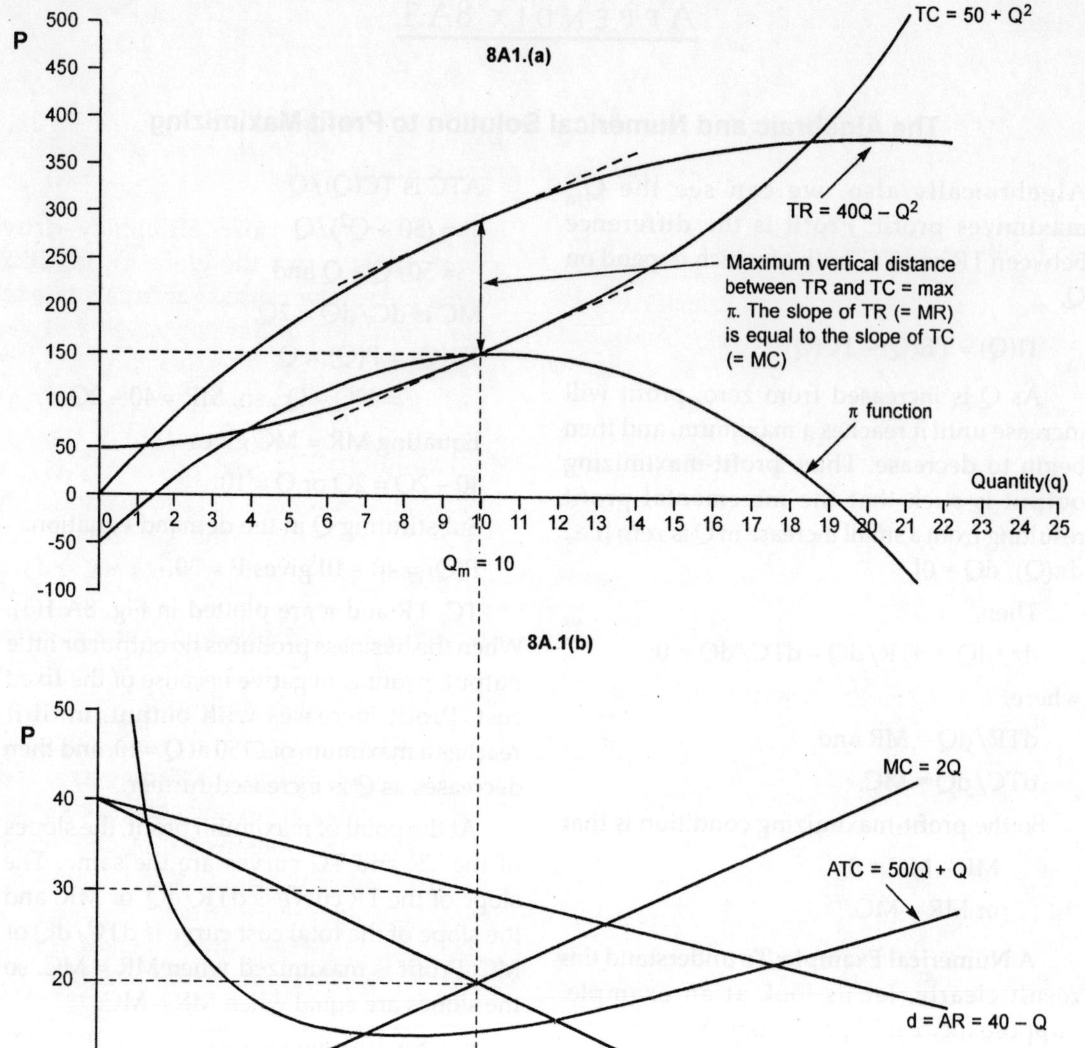

Fig. 8A.1: Profit Maximization

APPENDIX 8A.2

International privatization

The former UK Prime Minister, Mrs Thatcher, is remembered for privatizing telecommunications, gas, electricity, water, British Airways, British Aerospace, Rolls Royce, and much more. In total, US$100 billion of industrial assets were transferred from the state to the private sector under the Conservative Government of Margaret Thatcher and her successor John Major.

More recently, privatization activity in the UK has slowed down. In part this is because of the election of a Labour Government in 1997, and in part because there is relatively little state enterprise left to sell. In spite of Labour's traditional hostility to privatization, private capital has been introduced into the London Underground railway system.

As the first pie chart shows, telecoms dominated international privatization, accounting for around 36% of all sell-offs in the 1990s. Both the costs of financing modern telecommunications and the opportunity to make telecommunications markets more competitive and raise efficiency drove governments across the globe to privatize. Similar forces have caused governments to sell state enterprises in the power, oil and gas, financial and transport sectors.

In that decade over one-half of all privatizations by value occurred in Western Europe (see the second pie chart). But as privatization continues to grow in popularity, it is to be expected that the balance will shift in favour of the other regions. So far privatization has made very little impact on the economies of the Middle East andAfrica, in spite of the need for considerable industrial restructuring in these countries.

Outside the UK, privatization activity continues to grow. The year 2000 may have seen the largest value of privatization sales so far, breaking the previous record of US$160 billion worth of asset disposals. In Europe there have been major share sales in telecommunications (e.g. in Telia of Sweden and Deutsche Telekom). In Portugal, a very active market

Privatisation proceeds by sector* (1990-2000)

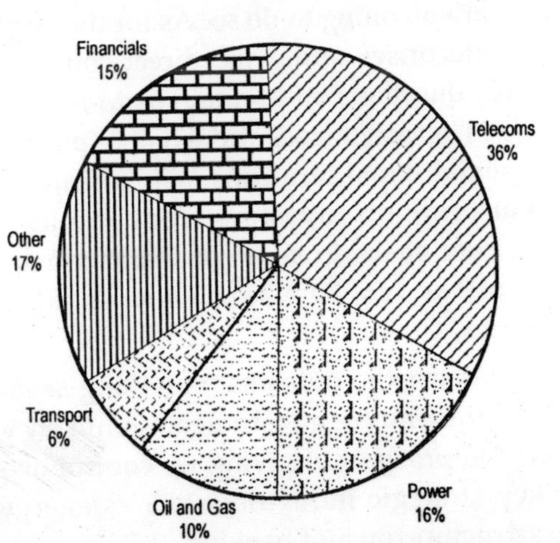

Privatisation proceeds by region* (1990-2000)

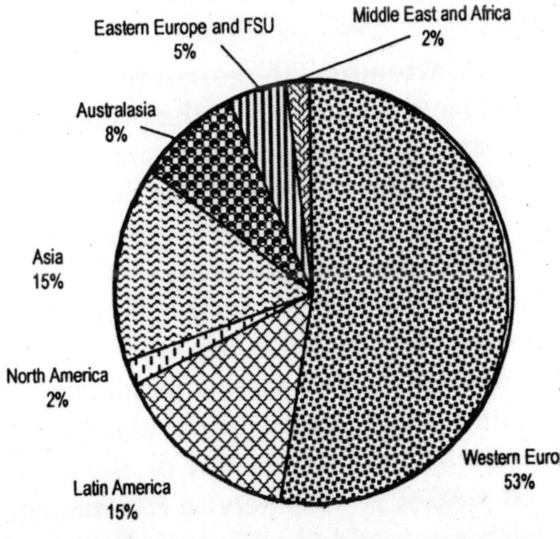

exists for 'public private partnerships' (PPPs) in the financing, operation and maintenance of roads, rail and water services. Other countries are also experimenting with PPPs, particularly the UK, to finance roads, schools, hospitals and other public infrastructure.

Activity

Assess the likely impact of international privatization on:

(a) the competitive environment for firms; and
(b) industrial policy.

APPENDIX 8A.3

Privatization in China

Privatization is a process that has swept the globe, engulfing market-based and planned economies alike. How the process is handled in a particular country, however, depends to a large degree on the historical, political, social, cultural and economic environment in which any change is occurring.

To illustrate this, consider developments in China. Historically, the Chinese economy has been dominated by state owned enterprises (SOEs) which have traditionally fulfilled a social as well as an economic role in Chinese society. As a result of the increasingly poor performance of these enterprises, various attempts at reform have been undertaken in recent years, culminating in the sale, contracting out or closure of nearly 100,000 small and medium sized SOEs in the late 1990s and the conversion of many larger public sector enterprises into multi-shareholder entities.

These attempts at restructuring the economy have continued into the twenty-first century and have gained added importance following China's accession to the World Trade Organisation (WTO) – a development which will increasingly expose Chinese businesses to fierce foreign competition in their domestic markets. In 2003, the Chinese government established a public sector body – the State-owned Assets supervision and Administration Commission of the State Council (SASAC) – to Supervise and manage the state's assets and to act as shareholder on its behalf. This body has the power to appoint, remove, reward and fine top executives and has been given responsibility for the assets of around 200 major state enterprises, with the local authorities making decisions regarding state enterprises that have been set up at city and provincial levels. The aim of these arrangements is separate government administration and ownership of the various enterprises from their day-to-day management and to provide opportunities for the development of a strong private sector.

Under the current provisions, the expectation is that the economy will experience a new round of privatization as new business opportunities are opened up to domestic and foreign investors. Indeed, a number of local authorities have already sold off locally-owned assets to Chinese and overseas buyers and others are planning to do so. As for the larger state enterprises under the direct control of SASAC, questions still remain as to how far they will be 'privatized' and whether political and social considerations will ultimately prevent foreign investors from gaining a significant share in some of China's major enterprises, as has happened in other countries.

Whatever the outcome, one thing seems certain, the Chinese government is unlikely to relish the prospect of giving up control over its key strategic industries such as energy, infrastructure, oil and banking.

APPENDIX 8A.4

Rule of Thumb Pricing

To do this, we write the expression

$$MR = \frac{d(TR)}{dQ} = \frac{d(P.Q)}{dQ}$$

It may be noted that the extra revenue from an incremental unit of quantity, d(P×Q)/dQ, has two components:

$$\frac{d(P.Q)}{dQ} = \frac{P.dQ}{dQ} + \frac{Q.dP}{dQ} = P + \frac{Q.dP}{dQ}$$

Producing one extra unit of output and selling at price P brings in extra revenue of P. Since the business faces a downward-sloping demand curve, producing and selling an extra unit also results in a small drop in price dP/dQ, which reduces the revenue from all units sold.

$$\text{Thus, } MR = P + \frac{Q.dP}{dQ}$$

Multiplying the right hand side by P/P = 1 does not change its value.

This gives

$$MR = \frac{P}{P}\left(P + \frac{Q.dP}{dQ}\right) = P + P.\left(\frac{Q}{P}\cdot\frac{dP}{dQ}\right)$$

The elasticity of demand is defined as Ed = –(P/Q) (dQ/dP). Hence, (dP/dQ) is reciprocal of the elasticity of demand, 1/Ed, measured at the profit-maximizing output, and

$$MR = P - P(1/Ed).$$

Now, since the objective of the business is to maximize profit, we can equate MR = MC, Therefore P – P(1/Ed) = MC, which can be rearranged to give us

$$\frac{P - MC}{P} = \frac{1}{Ed} \qquad \dots (1)$$

This provides a rule of thumb for pricing.

The term $\frac{P - MC}{P}$

is the mark-up over MC as a percentage of price which states that this markup should, equal minus the inverse of the elasticity of demand. Equivalently, we can rearrange this as:

$$P = \frac{MC}{1 - (1/Ed)} \qquad \dots (2)$$

For example, if the elasticity of demand is 4 and MC = £9 unit,

$$P = \frac{£9}{(1 - 1/4)} = \frac{£9 \times 4}{3} = £12 \text{ per unit.}$$

APPENDIX 8A.5

Price Discrimination

Algebraically, let us suppose that the price P_1 is charged to the first group of consumers, P_2 the price charged to the second group, and $TC(Q_t)$ the total cost of producing output $Q_t = q_1 + q_2$. Then, total profit is given by

$$P_1q_1 + P_2q_2 - TC(Q_t).$$

The business should increase its sales to each group of consumers, q_1 and q_2, until the incremental profit from the last unit is zero, as given below.

The incremental sales to group one

$$d\pi/dq_1 = d(P_1.q_1) - dTC/dq_1 = 0$$

Here $d(P_1.q_1)/dq_1$ is the incremental revenue from an extra unit of sales to the first group (i.e. MR_1). The next term dTC/dq_1 is the incremental cost of producing this output, i.e. MC.

Thus, we have $MR_1 = MC$.

Similarly, for the second group, we have:

$MR_2 = MC$.

Bringing them together we get:

$$MR_1 = MR_2 = MC \qquad \text{... (1)}$$

The relative prices to each group of consumers must be related to their elasticities of demand. We can write MR in terms of the elasticity of demand:

$$MR = P(1 - 1/Ed) \text{ and}$$

so, $MR_1 = P_1(1 - 1/E_1)$ and

$MR_2 = P_2(1 - 1/E_2)$,

where E_1 and E_2 are the elasticities of demand in the first and second markets, respectively. Now equating MR_1 to MR_2 ($MR_1 = MR_2$), we obtain the following relationship between the two prices:

$$\frac{P_1}{P_2} = \frac{\left(1-\frac{1}{E_2}\right)}{\left(1-\frac{1}{E_1}\right)} \qquad \text{... (2)}$$

As it is expected a higher price will be charged to consumers with lower elasticity. If the elasticity of demand for consumers in group 1 is 2, and the elasticity of demand for consumers in group 2 is 4, we will have

$$\frac{P_1}{P_2} = \frac{\left(1-\frac{1}{E_2}\right)}{\left(1-\frac{1}{E_1}\right)} = \frac{(1-\frac{1}{4})}{(1-\frac{1}{2})} = \frac{\frac{3}{4}}{\frac{1}{2}} = 1.5$$

In other words, the price charged to the first group of consumers should be 1.5 times as high as the price charged to the second group.

QUESTIONS

1. A business faces the following AR (Demand) curve: $P = 100 - 0.01Q$, where P is price, measured in pence and Q is weekly production. The business's cost function is given by: $TC = 50Q + 30,000$. Assuming the business maximizes profits
   (a) What is the level of production, price and total profit per week?
   (b) The government decides to levy a tax of 10 pence per unit on this product. What will the new level of production, price, and profit be, as a result?
2. Price discrimination requires the ability to sort customers and the ability to prevent arbitrage. Explain how the following can function as price discrimination schemes and discuss both sorting and arbitrage:
   (a) Requiring airline travellers to spend at least one Saturday night away from home to qualify for a low fare.
   (b) Insisting on delivering cement to buyers, and basing prices on buyers' locations.
   (c) Selling food-processors along with coupons that can be sent to manufacturer to obtain a £10 rebate.
   (d) Offering temporary price cuts on bathroom tissue.
   (e) Charging high-income patients more than low-income patients for plastic surgery.
3. Sal's satellite company broadcasts TV to subscribers in London and Cambridge. The demand functions for each of these two groups are given:
   $Q_L = 50 - 1/3.P_L$
   $Qc = 80 - 2/3Pc$
   where Q is in thousands of subscribers per year, and P is the price per year. The cost of providing Q units of service is given by:
   $TC = 1,000 + 30Q$ where $Q = Q_L + Q_c$.
   (a) What are the profit-maximizing prices and quantities for London and Cambridge markets?
   (b) As a consequence of a new satellite deployed recently, people in Cambridge receive Sal's London broadcasts, and people in London receive Sal's Cambridge broadcasts. As a result, anyone in Cambridge or London can receive Sal's broadcasts by subscribing in either city. Hence, Sal can only charge a single price. What price should he charge, what quantities will he sell in London and Cambridge?
   (c) In which of the above situations, (a) or (b), is Sal better-off?
   In terms of consumer's surplus, which situation do people in London prefer and which do people in Cambridge prefer?
   And, why?
4. Why do sports clubs have both an initital membership fee and an annual subscription for people who are already members?
5. It has been suggested that since BT is regulated by OFTEL it would make sense to establish OFAIR to regulate BA. Do you think it is a sensible suggestion?
6. Cheap season tickets keep commuters off congested rush-hour roads. Commuters should pay extra since most trains lie idle the rest of the day. Adjudicate between these two views. Does the answer depend on how cars and parking are being priced?
7. 'The Channel Tunnel, built with private money, was then unable to keep up the interest payments on its debts. It should never have been built'. Discuss.
8. When the ministry of defence ordered the design and manufacture of new fighter aircraft, it could issue a fixed price contract or a cost-plus contract. Explain how incentive differ in the two contracts. When would cost-plus be socially desirable?

ANSWERS

1. (a) The optimal production is where MR = MC

If the demand function is linear:

$P = 100 - 0.01Q$, then

$MR = 100 - 2(0.01)\,Q$ because,

$TR = 100Q - 0.01Q^2$

Total cost, $TC = 30{,}000 + 50Q$,

so $MC = 50$.

Thus, setting MR = MC

we get $100 - 0.02Q = 50$,

so $Q = 2.500$.

Substituting the profit-maximizing quantity into the demand function,

$P = 100 - 0.01 \times 2{,}500 = 75$.

Total profit is:

TR – TC

$= [(100 \times 2500) - 0.01(2500)^2] - [30{,}000 + (50\times 2500)]$

$= [250000 - 62500] - [155000]$

$= 187500 - 155000 = 32500$ per week

(b) Suppose, initially, the consumer must pay the tax. Since the total price (including the tax) remains unchanged, the demand function can be written as

$P + t = 100 - 0.01Q$.

$P = 100 - 0.01Q - t$.

Because the tax increases the price of each unit, TR, for the monopolist decreases by tQ, and MR decreased by t: $MR = 100 - 0.02Q - t$ where $t = 10$ pence.

To determine the profit-maximizing level of output with the tax, we have

$MR = MC : 100 - 0.02Q - 10 = 50$

$Q = 2{,}000$ units.

From the demand function,

$P = 100 - 0.01 \times 2{,}000 - 10 = 70$.

Total profit is $-30{,}000 + 50 \times 2{,}000 - 0.01 \times 2000^2 = £300$ per week.

Note: Total price paid by the consumer is 80p, while the monopolist only receives 70p. Thus, both the consumer and the monopolist each pay 5p of the tax.

The same answer would be obtained if the monopolist had to pay the tax. The cost function of the monopolist would then be

$TC = 50Q + 3{,}000 + tQ$

$= (50 + t)Q + 3{,}000$.

The slope of the cost function is: $(50 + t)$, so $MC = 50 + t$.

We set MC = MR.

$100 - 0.02Q = 50 + t$

Gives, $Q = 2{,}000$.

Thus, the burden of the tax is reflected in the price of the good, whoever may send the tax to the government.

2. (a) The Saturday-night requirement separates business travellers—who prefer to return home for the weekend, from tourists—who travel on the weekend.

(b) By basing prices on the buyer's location, sorting is done by geography. Then prices can reflect transportation charges, which can vary from customer to customer. The customer pays for these transportation charges —whether delivery is received at the buyer's location or at the cement plant.

(c) Rebate coupons with food-processors separate consumers into two groups:

1. customers who are less price-sensitive (those who have a lower elasticity of demand) do not request the rebate and
2. customers who are more price-sensitive (those who have a higher demand elasticity) request the rebate.

(d) A temporary price cut on bathroom tissue is a form of inter-temporal price discrimination. Price-senstitive customers buy more tissue than they would otherwise during the price cut. Non-price sensitive customers buy the same amount that they buy without the price cut.

(e) The plastic surgeon may not know who is a high-income patient and who is a low-income patient, but can guess. One strategy could be to initially quote a high price, observe the patient's reaction, and then negotiate the final price. Arbitrage is no problem because plastic surgery cannot be transferred from low-income patients to high-income patients.

3. (a) A monopolist with two markets should sell quantities in each market so that (MRL = MRc), in both markets are equal and equal to MC, MC is slope of the TC curve, 30. Total revenue in the two markets are TRL—(P × Q)L and TR_0 = (P × Q)c.

To determine MR in each market, we solve for price as a function of quantity.

Then TRs are:

$TR_L = Q_L.P_L$ = QL $(1503Q_L)$ and

$TR_c = Q_cP_C = Q_c\{120(3.2)Q_c\}$.

The MR curves:

$MR_L = 150 - 6Q_L$ and

$MR_c = 120 - 3Q_c$.

We, then, set each MR = MC(30),

$Q_L = 20, Q_c = 30$.

With these quantities, we solve for price in each market

$P_L = 150 - 20 \times 3 = 90$ and

$P_c = 120 - (3/2) \times 30 = 75$.

(b) With the new satellite, Sal can no longer separate the two markets. The total demand function is the horizontal summation of the two markets. Above a price of 120, the total demand is just the London demand function. Below a price of 120, we add the two demands:

$Q_T = 50 - (1/3)P + 80 - (2/3)P$

$= 130 - P$

Sal maximizes profit by choosing a quantity so that MR = MC.

TR = PQ = Q(130 – Q)

$= 130Q - Q^2$, so MR = 130 – 2Q.

Setting MR = MC, a profit-maximising quantity of 50 with a price of 80 is obtained.

Although a price of 80 is charged in both markets, different quantities are purchased.

In the London market, quantity is

50 – (1/3)80 = 23.1/3...and, in the Cambridge market, quantity is

8 – (2/3)80 = 26.2/3.

Total quantity of 50 units are purcahsed at a price of 80.

(c) Sal would be better-off with the highest profit. Under the market conditions in (3a), profit is equal to the sum of TR from each market—The TC of production in both markets

$P_L.Q_L + P_c Q_c - 1{,}000 - 30(Q_L + Q_c)$

= 20.90 + 30.75 – 1,000 + 30(20 + 30)

= 1,500.

Under the market conditions in (b) profit is = TR – TC of production in both markets:

Qp – (1,000 + 30Q)

= 50.80 – (1,000 + 30 × 50) 1,500.

Thus, Sal makes more money when the two markets are separated. Under the market condition in (a), in the London market, consumer's surplus is (150 – 90) 20 (1/2) = 600, in the Cambridge market consumer's surplus is (120 – 75) (30 × 1/2) = 675 under the market condition in (b), in the London market, consumer's surplus is = 816, and in the Cambridge market, consumer's surplus is = 533. The Londoners prefer (b) because the equilibrium price is 80 instead of 90; so their consumer's surplus is higher. The customers in Cambridge prefer (a), because the equilibrium price is 75 and not 80.

4. This is an example of two-part tariff which yields more revenue. It cannot discriminate between existing members, can do so only between old and new members.
5. BA faces stiff international competition and hence there is no need for regulator, OFAIR.
6. Commuters travel when the MC is very high and ideally should pay more, but big congestion externalities on rush-hour road could easily justify cheap rail tickets. First best is to tax the externalities appropriately.
7. Big externalities; it helps other industries that even do not use the Channel tunnel rail. Could be socially desirable even if it is privately unprofitable.
8. Fixed-price makes companies bear all risk (thus raising the tender price they charge) but gives them bigger incentive to keep cost down (since they get all the benefits). Cost-plus gives less incentive to keep the cost down but prevents companies terrified by all the risk they bear (for which they have to charge). It is better if little prospect of cost escalation, easy to monitor management but large exogenous uncertainties.

CHAPTER 9

MARKET STRUCTURE AND IMPERFECT COMPETITION

KEY TERMS

Monopolistic Competition: has many sellers producing products that are close substitutes for one another—limited ability to affect its output price.

Oligopoly: Is an industry with few producers each recognising that its own price depends not merely on its own output but also on the actions of its important competitors in the industry.

Monopoly: Is a single business industry. It can choose the output that it wishes to produce (usually a profit maximizing output).

Contestable Market: A market that businesses can freely enter or exit without incurring sunk costs.

Sunk Cost: An expenditure that has already been made and cannot be recovered.

THE STRUCTURE OF MARKETS (INDUSTRY)—PERFECT AND IMPERFECT COMPETITION

We have seen that the perfectly competitive business faces a perfectly elastic demand curve and the perfectly competitive industry's demand curve is negatively sloped. The imperfectly competitive business or industry (a monopolistically competitive industry, an oligopoly or a monopoly) faces a downward (negative) sloping demand curve.

Monopolistic competition has many sellers producing products that are close substitutes for one another—limited ability to affect its output price. e.g. corner grocer shop.

Oligopoly—is an industry with few producers each recognising that its own price depends not merely on its own output but also on the actions of its important competitors in the industry, e.g. the motor car industry.

Monopoly—is a single business industry. It can choose the output that it wishes to produce (usually a profit maximizing output), e.g. a gas or electricity producer.

What we are trying to do in this chapter is to try and explain the structure of particular industries. Why are some industries perfectly competitive, monopolistically competitive, oligopolies or monopolies?

• Why Market Structures May Differ

Consider Fig. 9.1. If all businesses face LAC_1—each business produces q_1. The total output of the industry will be $q_1 \times n_1 = Q_1$, where n_1 is the number of businesses in the industry. In perfect competition and mono-polistic competition n_1 is large. There is room for a large number of businesses in this type of industry.

If businesses in a particular industry face LAC_2 (there are more economies of scale than LAC_1) the industry can support at least two businesses. Each of the (n) businesses can produce output q_2. The output of the industry is then $n \times q_2$. If the business tried to increase output beyond q_2, costs would rise and this would prevent it from expanding output and driving out its competitors.

If the LAC of the industry is similar to LAC_3 then there are large economies of scale relative to the size of the market. There will only be room for one business. The lowest point on LAC_3 occurs at an output that is large relative to the market demand curve D. This is a natural monopoly.

Consider LAC_3 and suppose four businesses produce output q_3: $Q_3 = 4 \times q_3$. If the price is P_3 the businesses will break-even. If one business expands its output it will make a profit. It can now reduce the price it charges and drive the other businesses out of business. The business that expands will take the whole market. It will become a monopoly—a 'natural' monopoly.

The one business that takes over the market will *wish* to produce a level of output where long run marginal cost curve is equal to marginal revenue. (LMC = MR; say output Q_4 and price P_4). There is no room for a new entrant. They need a large output to obtain economies of scale.

The lowest point on the long-run average cost curve is known as the **Minimum Efficient Scale (MES)**. It is the output at which the long-run average cost curve (LAC) stops falling.

Generally, the MES relative to the size of the total market, as represented by the demand curve, is the crucial determinant of market structure. Later in this chapter we will discuss the effect of potential competition from new entrants to an industry on the behaviour of existing or incumbent businesses.

• Oligopoly and Monopolistic Competition

The essence of oligopoly is the interdependence of businesses. With significant economies of scale, there are only a few

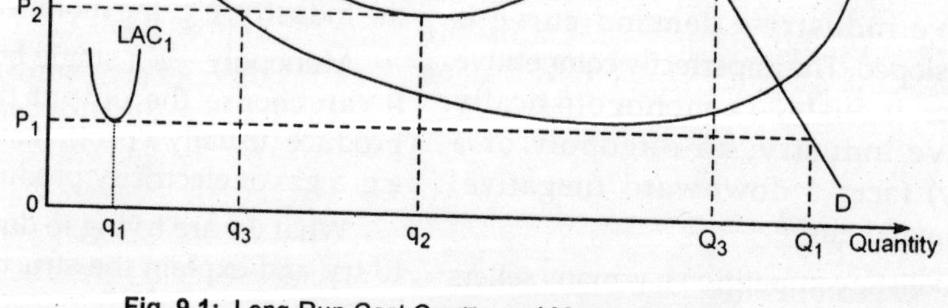

Fig. 9.1: Long-Run Cost Curves and Market Structure

businesses or a few potential entrants. Each business's demand curve is senstitive to how its rival reacts. Since each business must estimate the position of its own demand curve, it must think carefully about how it believes rival business will behave.

In contrast, the theory of monopolistic competition envisages a large number of small businesses, so that each business can neglect the possibility that its own decisions provoke any adjustment in other businesses' behaviour. We also assume free entry and exit from the industry in the long-run. In this respect, the framework resembles our earlier discussion of perfect competition. What distinguishes monopolistic competition from perfect competition is that each business faces a downward-sloping demand curve because the business's product is differentiated.

Monopolistic competition describes an industry in which each business can influence its market share by changing its price relative to its competitors. Its demand curve is downward-sloping because different businesses' products are not homogeneous. These industries exhibit product differentiation. For the corner grocer, this differentiation is based on location, and also on brand loyalty. The special features of a restaurant and a hairdresser may allow these businesses to charge a slightly different price from other producers in the same industry wihout losing all its customers or completely taking over the entire market.

Brand loyalty and product differentiation may be important in many industries without being monopolistically competitive. Brand loyalty limits the substitution between Ford and Volkswagen in the car industry but the key feature of the industry remains the oligopolistic interdependence of the decisions of different businesses because there are so few producers in the industry.

• Monopolistic Competition

Monopolistic competition requires not merely product differentiation, but also limited opportunity for economies of scales so that there are a great many producers who can neglect their interdependence on any particular rival. Hence, many of the best examples of monopolistic competition are service industries where economics of scale are limited.

The industry demand curve is the horizontal sum of the demand curves of the individual businesses in the industry. The market share of each business depends on the number of businesses and on the price it charges. For a given number of businesses, a shift in the industry demand curve will shift the demand curve of each individual business. For a given industry demand curve, an increase (decrease) in the number of businesses in the industry will shift the demand curve of each business to the left (right) as its market share falls (rises). For a given industry demand curve, number of businesses, and price charged by all other businesses, a particular business can increase its market share to some extent by charging a lower price and inducing some consumers to switch over to its particular product.

Fig. 9.2 illustrates the supply decision of a monopolistically competitive business. Given its own demand curve, d_0, and MR curve, the business produces q_0 at a price P_0 making a short-run profits = $q_0 \times (P_0–ATC_0)$.

In the long-run, these businesses attract new entrants, who dilute the market share of each business in the industry, shifting their demand curve to the left. Entry stops when each business's demand curve has shifted so far left that P = AC, and businesses are just breaking-even ($P_1 = ATC_1$) which occurs when demand has shifted to d_1 and the business produces q_1 at a price P_1 to reach the tangency equilibrium at point E.

In monopolistic competition, the long-run tangency equilibrium occurs where each business's demand curve is tangent to its ATC at the output level at which MC = MR. Each business is maximizing its profits but just breaking-even. There is no further entry or exit at this point.

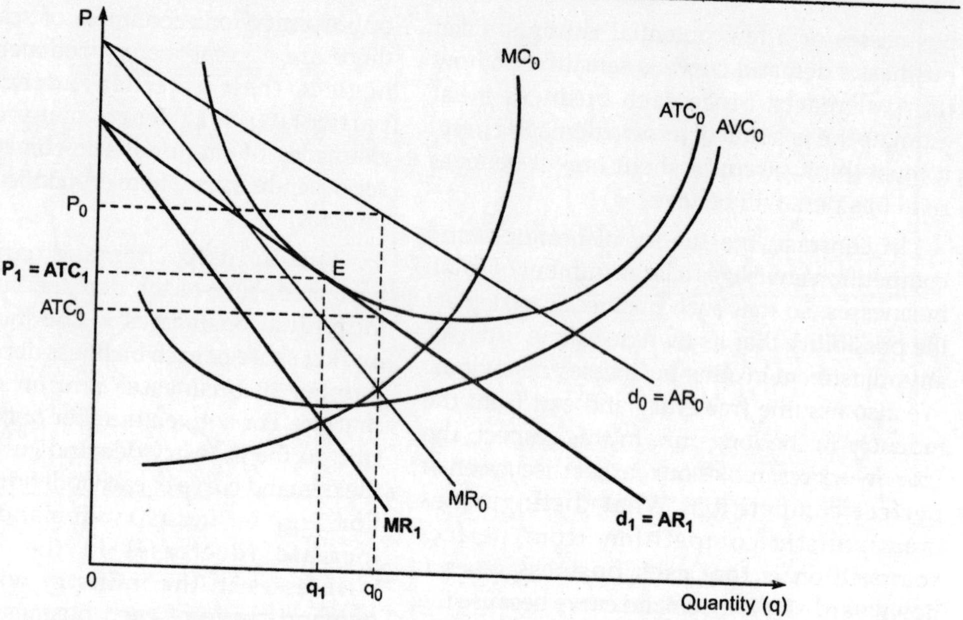

Fig. 9.2: Monopolistic Competition: Long-Run Equilibrium for the Business

Two things are worth noting about the long-run equilibrium. First, the business is not producing at minimum point on the ATC. It has excess capacity and, hence, it could reduce ATC by expanding output but its MR would be too low to be profitable. Second, the business retains some monopoly power, as price exceeds MC, because of the special feature of its particular brand or location. This helps to explain why businesses are eager to attract new customers at the existing price. But, under perfect competition, the business does not care whether other customers are buying at the existing price with P = MC; the business is already selling as much as it wants.

The theory of monopolistic competition provides interesting insights when there are many goods, each of which is a close but not perfect substitute for each other. For example, it explains why Britain exports cars (Jaguars) to Europe and at the same time imports other variety of cars (BMW) from the Continent. In the absence of trade, the domestic car market would have room for only a few varieties. Producing a large number of brands at low output would increase ATC. International trade allows each country to specialize in a few types of car and produce a much larger output of that brand than the home market can support. By swapping these cars between countries, it is possible to give customers a wide range of choice while allowing each individual producer to enjoy economies of scale and hold the price down.

- **Monopolistic Competition and Economic Efficiency**

Perfectly competitive markets are preferred because they are economically efficient—so long there are no externalities and nothing impedes the workings of the market, the total consumer's and producer's surplus is as large as possible. Monopolistic competition is similar to perfect competition in some respect, but is it an efficient market structure? Comparison between the long-run equilibrium of a monopolistically competitive industry and the long-run equilibrium of a perfectly competitive industry will be able to answer this question. Under perfect competition, as in Fig. 9.3(a), P = MC, but under monopolistic competition, P > MC, so there is a deadweight loss as shown by the area ABC in Fig. 9.3(b). In both types of markets,

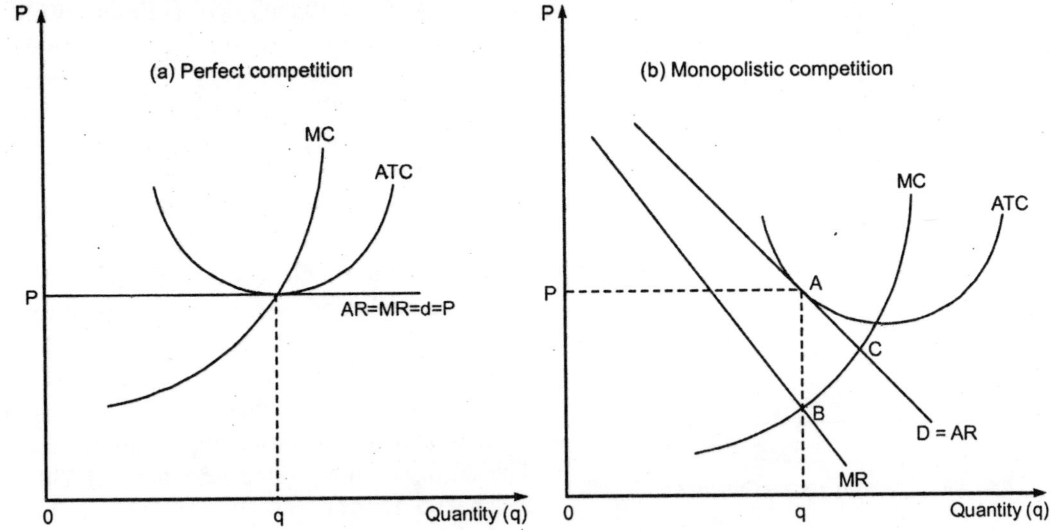

Fig. 9.3: Equilibrium in Competitive Markets

entry occurs until profits are driven to zero. Under perfect competition, the demand curve facing the business is horizontal, so the zero-profit point occurs at the point of minimum ATC. Under monopolistic competi-tion, the demand curve is downward sloping, so zero-profit point here is to the left of the minimum point of ATC at point A.

In evaluating monopolistic competition, these inefficiencies must be balanced against the gains to consumers from product diversity.

• Oligopolistic Industries

The key to an oligopoly industry, unlike perfect competition and monopolistic competition, is that each business will have to consider how its own action affects the decision of its competitors, who are few in numbers. Each business has to guess how its rival will react. Before discussing smart guesses, we introduce the tension between competition and collusion when businesses know that they are interdependent.

Collusion is an explicit or implicit agreement to avoid competition. Let us neglect the possibility of entry of new businesses and focus on existing businesses to keep the analysis simple.

• The Profit from Collusion

As sole decision-makers in the industry, a monopolist will choose industry output to maximize total profits. Hence, the few producers in an industry can maximize their total profit by setting their total output as if they were monopolist. Fig. 9.4 shows an industry where each business, and the whole industry, has a constant long-run average cost (LRAC) curve and a constant long-run marginal cost (LRMC) curve at the level of price P_c. A competitive industry produces Q_c at a price P_c but a multiplant monopolist maximizes profits by making output Q_m at a price P_m. If the oligopolists collude to produce Q_m they act as a collusive monopolist. Having decided industry output, the businesses agree how to share the total output and profits among themselves.

However, it is not easy to stop businesses from cheating on the collective agreement. In Fig. 9.4 joint profit is maximized at a total output Q_m and price P_m. Yet each business can expand output up to Q_c. Firms can expand output, selling below agreed price P_m, and making extra profit since the MR is greaer than MC for a short period. This business gains at the expense of its collusive partners. Industry

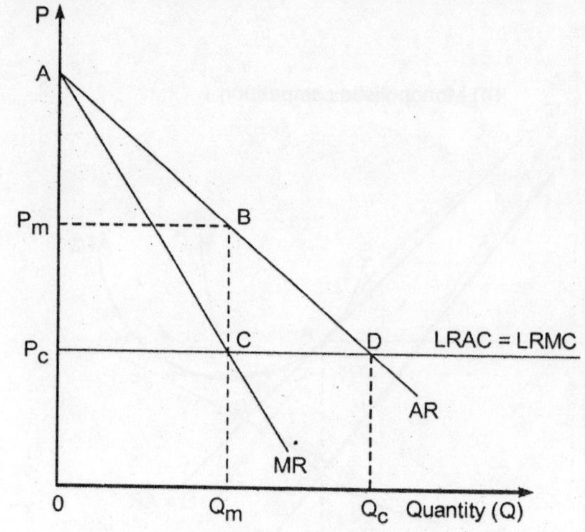

Fig. 9.4: Collusion Versus Competition

output is higher than Q_m, total price falls and other businesses suffer.

Oligopoly businesses can collude to restrict output to Q_m, and increase price to P_m and also to increase joint profit equal to what multiplant monopolist would get. But for each business, price > MC, has an incentive to cheat on the collusive agreement and expand its output.

Oligopolists are torn between collusion and competition, the former to maximize profit and the later to raise market share and individual profits at the expense of rival. Yet if all businesses compete, joint profits will come down to a very low level.

Therein lies the dilemma.

Cartels: Collusion could be easier if formal agreement between the businesses can be made legally binding. Such agreements, called cartels, were common in the late 19th century, agreeing market shares and prices in many industries. Cartels are now outlawed in many western industrialized countries. There are big penalties if anybody violates the law. But informal agreements and secret deals are sometimes discovered even today.

Cartels across countries are not easy to outlaw. The most known such cartel is OPEC. Its members meet regularly to fix prices and output. Initially, OPEC succeeded in reducing quantity to force up the price of oil. As a result, OPEC revenue in real term rose by 500% between 1973 and 1980. Yet some economists predicted that OPEC, like many cartels before it, would quickly collapse. Usually, the incentive to cheat is too strong to resist, and once somebody breaks ranks others follow suit. One reason why OPEC was successful for so long was the willingness of Saudi Arabia, the largest oil producer, to restrict its output further when small members wished to expand theirs. By 1986, Saudi Arabia was no longer willing to be guided by this rule, and refused to keep the price higher any longer. The oil price, thus, collapsed from just $30 to $9 a barrel. During 1987-98, apart from a short period during the Gulf war, oil price fluctuated between $8 and $20 a barrel. After 1998 OPEC recovered its earlier arrangements again.

• The Kinked Demand Curve

Where there are more than a few businesses in the industry with a non-standardised product and where demand and cost conditions are changing rapidly each business's demand curve will depend upon how its competitors react.

Suppose, starting from market price P_0, each business beleives that

(a) the other businesses in the industry will match any price cut, but

(b) that an increase in price will not be matched.

The business would then face the following inverse demand curve: d = AR(ABd). Because the demand curve is kinked the marginal revenue curve (ACDMR) will be discontinous at the actual output produced.

Price increases lead to a large loss of market shares but price cut increase quantity q only by increasing industry's sales. MR is discontinuous at q_0. The oligopolistic business will produce q_0 output at the point where MC_0 = MR.

The following figure shows the demand curve, 'd_0' that each business would then face.

The price is P_0 and the business is producing Q_0. Since competitors do not follow suit, a price increase will lead to a large loss of market share to the other businesses in the industry. The business's demand curve is elastic above B, at prices above the current price P_0. Conversely, a price cut is matched by other businesses and market share remain unchanged. Sales increase only because the industry, as a whole, moves down the market demand curve as price falls. The demand curve d_0 is much less elastic when the price is reduced below P_0.

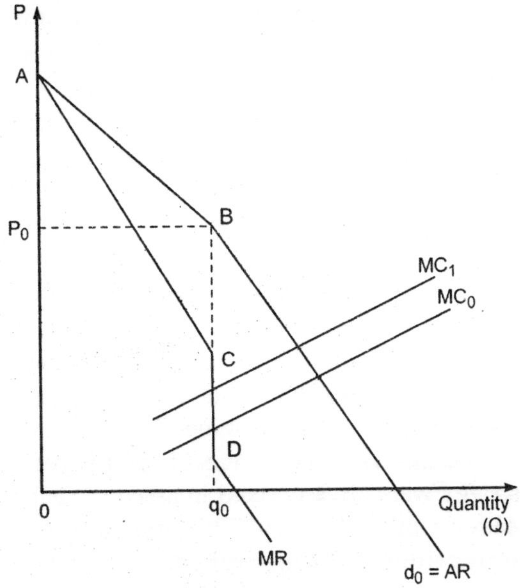

Fig. 9.5: The Kinked Demand Curve

The important point to note is that the MR curve is discontinuous at the output q_0. Below q_0, the elastic part of the demand curve is relevant, but at the output q_0, the business suddenly encounters the inelastic portion of its kinked demand curve and MR suddenly falls. q_0 is the profit-maximizing output for the business, given its belief about how competitors will respond. An important implication of the model is that even if the MC curve of a single business shifts up or down by a small amount, it will not change price, P_0, or output, q_0. In contrast, a monopolist facing a continuously downward-sloping MR curve would adjust quantity and price when the MC curve shifted. The kinked demand curve model may explain the empirical finding that businesses do not always adjust prices when they face a change in costs.

The model, however, does not explain what determines the initial price P_0. One possible interpretation is that it is the collusive monopoly price. Each business believes that an attempt to undercut its rival will provoke them to cooperate among themselves and retaliate in full. However, its rival will be happy for it to charge a higher price and see its market share destroyed.

One advantage of interpreting P_0 as a collusive monopoly price is that it contrasts the effect of a cost change for a single business and a cost change for all businesses. The latter will shift the MC curve up for the industry as a whole and increase the collusive monoply price. Each business's kinked demand curve will shift upwards since the monopoly price, P_0, has increased. Thus, we can reconcile the stickiness of a single business's prices with entire industry mark-up prices when all business's costs are increased by higher taxes or inflationary wage settlements in the whole industry.

• Game Theory and Independent Decision-Making

Game theory is a study of strategic interaction between players. These occur frequently in economics, and in the rest of the world. Oligopolies present one of the most common areas where game theory is used in economics and it is also used in financial markets.

Like poker players, oligopolists try to anticipate their rival's moves to determine their own best action. To study interdependent decision-making, we use game theory. The players in the game try to maximize their own payoffs. In an oligopoly; the businesses are the players and their payoffs are their profits in the long-run. Each player must choose a strategy.

A strategy is a game plan describing how a player acts, or moves, in each possible situation.

As usual, we are interested in equilibrium. In most games, each player's best strategy depends on the strategies chosen by other players. It is silly to pickpocket when the police have CCTV cameras, or to go for four centre backs in soccer when the opponent has no proven goal scorer.

In Nash equilibrium, each player chooses the best strategy, given the strategies being followed by other players. Nobody then wants to change strategy, since other player's strategy were already fixed in assessing each player's best strategy. This definition of equilibrium, and its application to game theory was invented by John Nash.

- **The Prisoners' Dilemma**

Consider that two people have been imprisoned and kept in separate cells, but with little evidence to convict them. The prison authority tells each person that the other one has confessed the crime, and she should do the same to make the best of a sticky situation.

If both people confess they get six years in jail. If only one confesses, he gets one year and the other gets nine years. If neither confesses, they each get two years.

Now each person has to decide whether or not to confess. If the other person has confessed, then by not confessing they get nine years, whereas, by confessing they get six years. If the other person has not confessed, then by not confessing they get two years, whereas, by confessing they get one year. It is clear that it is the best, in either case, to confess. Thus, the outcome will be that they both get six years, since they both make the same decision.

In this explicit format the problem is not easily recognized as the prisoners' dilemma, and so a format called payoff matrix has been developed. In the scenario described here, the prisoners make their choices simultaneously. They each decide whether or not to confess.

In this case, we can see that if prisoner 2 is going to confess, then it is ideal for prisoner 1 to confess. If prisoner 2 is not going to confess, it is still the best choice for prisoner 1 to confess. Thus, it is ideal for prisoner 1 to confess regardless of what prisoner 2 does and this confession is his dominant strategy. The situation is exactly the same for prisoner 2.

The dominant strategy is defined as one that is optimal for a player, no matter what an opponent does.

Table 9.2 illustrates a game between only two members of the cartel. Each business can select a high output or low output strategy. In each box of table 9.2 the left number shows business A's profits and the right number, business B's profits for the output combination.

The left and right numbers in each box indicate profits to business A and B respectively. Whether B pursues high or low output, A makes more profits going high, so does B, whichever A adopts. In equilibrium both go high. Yet both would make greater profits.

When both have high output, industry output is high, the price is low, and each business makes a small profit of 1 unit. When

Table 9.1: The Prisoner's Dilemma

		Prisoner 2	
		Confess	Do not confess
	Confess	6 6	1 9
Prisoner 1			
	Do not confess	9 1	2 2

Table 9.2: Economic Example of the Prisoner's Dilemma

		Firm B's output	
		High	Low
Firm A's	High	1 1	3 0
output:			
	Low	0 3	2 2

each has low output, the output is like collusive monopoly. Prices are high and each business does better, making a profit of 2 units. Each business can do better (a profit of 3 units) when it alone has high output; the other business's low output keeps the industry output down and the price up. In this situation we assume the low-output business to make a zero profit.

Now we can show how the game will unfold. Consider business A's decision when business B has a high output strategy. Firm A will be one of the two left-hand boxes. Firm A obtains a profit of 1 unit by choosing high but a profit of zero by choosing low. If business A thinks business B will choose high output, business A prefers high output itself. But business A must also think what to do if business B chooses low-output strategy. This puts business A in one of the tworight boxes. Firm A still prefers high output for itself, which yields a profit of only 2. Firm A has a dominant strategy, whatever strategy B has adopted; A does better to choose a high-output strategy.

Firm B also has a dominant strategy to choose high output. If business B anticipates that business A will go high, facing a choice of the two boxes in the bottom now, but B still wants to go high. B does better to go high whatever strategy A adopts. Both A and B have a dominant strategy to go high. Equilibrium is the top left-hand box. Each business gets a profit of 1 unit. Yet both businesses would do better, getting a profit of 2, if they collude to form a cartel and both produce low-bottom right-hand box. But neither can risk going low. Suppose A goes low. B, comparing the two boxes in the bottom row, will then go high, preferring a profit of 3 to a profit of 2. And in this situtation A will be earning a profit of zero. A can figure all this out in advance, which is why its dominant strategy is to go high.

This shows the tension between competition and collusion. In this example, it appears that the output restricting cartel will never get formed, since each player can already foresee the overwhelming incentive for the other to cheat on such an arrangement. How can then cartels ever be sustained? If there is binding commitments only then it can survive.

A commitment is an arrangement, entered voluntarily, that restrict future actions. If both businesses could simultaneously sign an enforceable contract to produce low output they could achieve the cooperative outcome in the bottom right-hand box, each earning a profit of 2. This beats the Nash equilibrium of the game (top left-hand box) when collusion cannot be enforced. Without a binding commitment, neither business can go low because then the other business can go high. Binding commitments, by removing this temptation, let both businesses go low. Both businesses then gain. The idea of commitment is importation, and we shall encounter it many times. Just think of all the human activities that are the subject of legal contract, a simple commitment simulteneously undertaken by two businesses or parties.

Although this insight is powerful, its application to oligopoly requires care. Cartels within a country are usually illegal, and OPEC is not held together by a contract enforceable in international law. Is there a less formal way in which oligopoly bisunesses can avoid cheating on the collusive low-output solution to the game? If the game is played only once, this is difficult.

- **Repeated Games**

In the real world, game is repeated many times: businesses choose output levels day after day. Suppose two players try to collude on low output: business B says it will subsequently react by raising its output. Firm A make similar promise.

Assume that the agreement has been in force for some time and both businesses have stuck to their low output deal. Firm A thinks that business B will go low as usual. Firm A can make a temporary gain now if it cheats and go high. Instead of staying in the bottom right-hand box with a profit of 2, it can move to the top right-hand box and make a profit of 3. However, from now onwards, business B also will go high and then A can do no better than continue to go high too, making a profit of 1 forever. But refusing to cheat today it can continue to stay in the bottom right-hand box and make 2 forever. In cheating, A swaps a temporary gain for a permanent reduction in future profits. Thus, punishment strategies can sustain an explicit cartel or implicit collusion even if no formal commitment exists.

It is all very well to promise to punish the other player's behaviour only if your threat is credible.

A credible threat is one that, after the fact, is still optimal to carry out.

In the preceding example, once A has cheated and gone high, it is then in B's interest to go high. Hence a threat to go high if A ever cheated is a credible threat.

These insights shed light on the actual behaviour of OPEC in 1986, when Saudi Arabia decided to raise its output, leading to a collapse of oil prices. In the 1980s, other members of OPEC had gradually cheated on the low-output agreement. Trusting that Saudi would still restrict its oil output to sustain a high price and the cartel's prestige. They hoped Saudi's threat to adopt punishment strategy was empty threat. They were wrong. As Fig. 9.6 shows, once the other oil producing countries increased their outputs, Saudi Arabia felt that they had to increase their output.

Suppose an oligopoly industry has a dominant business and a competitive fringe of businesses selling as much as they wish at the going price. The dominant business (df) is

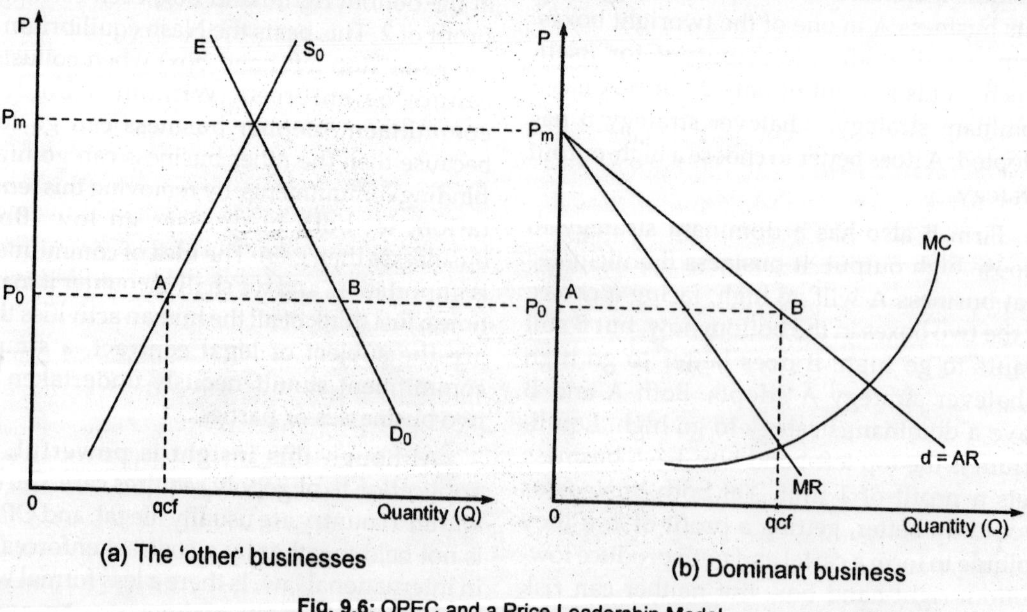

Fig. 9.6: OPEC and a Price Leadership Model

large enough to influence price and output through its own actions. Fig. 9.6(a) shows the demand curve, D_0, for the industry and the supply curve, 'S_0', for the competitive fringe (cf) as a whole. In oil industry, the competitive fringe has a rising long-run supply curve since different oil fields have very different extraction costs. It takes high prices to make it profitable to exploit higher cost fields in OPEC and non-OPEC countries. At each price, the fringe businesses produce as much as they want and are on their supply curve. At price P_m the competitive fringe produces all of the output and the dominant business will produce nil.

The dominant business meets excess demand at each price. Thus, Fig. 9.6(b) shows that dominant business's demand curve as d = AR, the difference between D_0 and S_0 at each price such as P_0 where AB must be the same in both figures. Facing a demand curve d_0, the dominant business produces output qcf where MC = MR. The price is P_0, the competitive fringe is happy to produce qcf and the market clears.

Total demand is P_0 to B made up of P_0 to A supplied by the fringe businesses and A to B supplied by the dominant business.

Saudi Arabia's willingness to maintain the cartel has kept OPEC together. Since other countries can produce as much as they wish at the agreed price, there is little incentive for OPEC members to cheat. Saudi Arabia would accept the residual demand ED implied. In return, Saudi Arabia was allowed to fix the price and choose at which point on D_0 it wishes to produce. It sets the price P_0 to achieve an output at which MC = MR. This bargain partly explains the inherent tension at OPEC meetings. The supply curve of fringe slopes upward because it requires a higher price to make it profitable to exploit high-cost wells. However, higher prices yield larger profits to those with low-cost wells. Hence, the competitive fringe tended to want a higher price than Saudi Arabia wished.

Saudi Arabia was able to counter this pressure by threatening not to accept ED as the residual demand curve. By producing at a price-quantity combination ED, Saudi can reduce the quantity available to other members. Generally, other members preferred Saudi to take dominant role and set the price provided; it then produces at the appropriate point on d_0.

After 1980, new oil discoveries and a resumption of production in Iran and Iraq shifted the supply curve of the competitive fringe to the right. At the same time, the world recession shifted the supply curve of the competitive fringe to the right. At the same time, the world recession shifted the demand curve for oil to the left and thus, Saudi's demand curve ED shifted far to the left. Its output fell sharply and so did the oil prices. Thus, its ability to impose discipline on other OPEC members began to weaken and the cartel began to show signs of breaking up.

- **Implicity Agreement: Price-Leader**

When explicit price agreements are illegal, businesses often find ways to cooperate implicity. Such agreements require two things: a method of communicating the agreed price to all businesses in the industry, and secondly, a way of checking that businesses are not cheating by undercutting implicity price agreement. One way to communicate the implicity price is one business to take the leadership role.

A price-leader is a business whose price changes are the signals for other businesses to follow suit. The leader judges when to change the price and the other businesses follow the leader and all prices change together without any explicit agreement.

This model is a good example of price behaviour in the cigarette industry and in petrol-filling stations. In both cases, a large number of brands or outlets are controlled by a few companies. Sometimes we find an initial move by the leader which is not followed by the rest of the industry and the movements are reversed. Sometimes other members follow suit and the new price sticks.

• Conditions Favourable to Cooperation

collusion between businesses is the easiest when it is legally permitted and when profits are not threatened by the entry of new businesses to the industry. Licensing arrangements are one way to control entry. For example, if professional bodies of doctors, lawyers, etc. can control examination requirements, standards and licences, they would be able to regulate the flow of new entrants into the industry. Then by arguing that it is unethical to compete over price, they can increase the price without fearing a flood of new entrants.

Implicit agreement may succeed when it is easy to communicate the agreed price and to detect cheating. Thus, collusion is easier the fewer the number of businesses in the industry, and the more standardized the product is.

• Non-cooperative Oligopoly

Collusion is difficult if there are many businesses in the industry and the product is not standardized. It is also difficult if demand and cost conditions are changing fast. It would be even more difficult when businesses cannot discover the price charged by their competitors. Each business has an incentive to cheat its rivals.

In the absence of collusion, the business's decision is strategic. Its demand curve depends on how competitors react. We have already seen that a collusive monopoly solution will prevail when each business believes that any price cut will be completely matched by other businesses.

There is a complete spectrum of beliefs about competitor's reactions, ranging from no price response to complete response. For each belief, the individual oligopolist will behave as if it faces a different demand curve and will make different price and output decisions.

• Reaction Function

In a one-off game each player had a dominant strategy, to produce high output whatever its rival did. This led to a poor outcome for both, because they were not cooperating despite interdependence. When the game is repeated, commitments and punishment strategies helps players to cooperate and find an outcome that is better for both of them. In punishing a rival, a player's actions change in response to bad behaviour by the rival. Dominant strategies are rare. Moreover, each player's best action depends on the actual or expected actions of other players. How a player reacts depends on what it assumes about its rivals' behaviour.

For simplicity we analyze duopoly model in which there are only two players. We start our analysis with the simple Cournot model which considers the output of the other firm as given.

• The Cournot Model

Our starting point here is a simple duopoly model introduced by Cournot the French economist, in 1838. Suppose the firms produce a homogeneous product and know the market demand curve. Each firm decides how much to produce and the two firms make their decisions at the same time. When a firm makes its decision to produce, it takes its competitor into consideration. It knows that its competitor is also deciding to produce, and the price it receives will depend on the total output of both the firms.

The essence of the Cournot model is that each firm treats the output level of its competitor as fixed, and then decides how much to produce. Let us consider that firm 1's profit-maximizing output decision depends on how much it thinks firm 2 will produce. Suppose firm 1 thinks that firm 2 will produce nothing, its demand curve is the market demand curve. In Fig. 9.7 this is shown as $D_1(0)$, which is the market demand curve since firm 2 produces zero output. The corresponding MR curve is $MR_1(0)$, and it intersects its MC curve, MC_1, at an output of 50 units. Thus, if firm 2 produces nothing, firm 1 produces the entire output 50 units. On the other hand, if firm 1 thinks firm 2 will produce 50 units, its demand curve will shift to the left by 50 units. The corresponding MR curve is

$MR_1(50)$. Firm 1's profit-maximizing output is now 25 units, the point where $MR_1(50) = MC_1$. Now, if firm 1 thinks firm 2 will produce 75 units, then firm 1's demand curve and MR

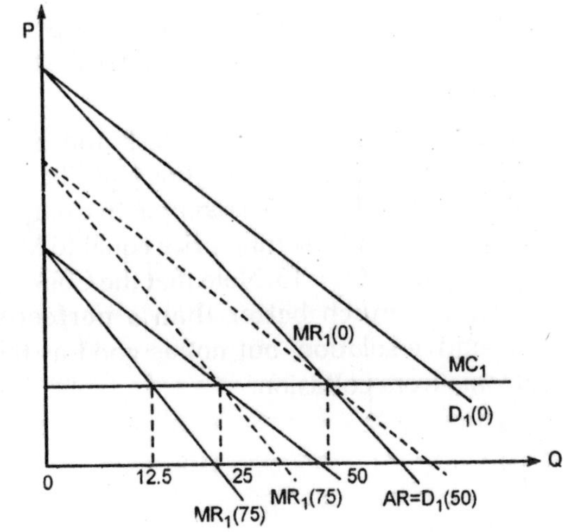

Fig. 9.7: Firm 1's Output Decision

curve would be $D_1(75)$ and $MR_1(75)$. Then, firm 1's profit-maximizing output would be 12.5 units, the point where $MR_1(75) = MC_1$. Finally, suppose firm 1 thinks firm 2 will produce 100 units. Then firm 1's demand and MR curves would intersect the MC on the vertical axis and it should produce nothing.

To sum up the analysis: If the firm 1 thinks that firm 2 will produce nothing, it will produce 50 units; if it thinks firm 2 will produce 50 units, it will produce 25 units; if it thinks firm 2 will produce 75 units, it will produce 12.5 units; and if it thinks firm 2 will produce 100 units, then it will produce nothing. Firm 1's profit-maximizing output is, thus, a decreasing function of how much it thinks firm 2 will produce. This schedule is firm 1's reaction function and it is denoted by $Q_{1*}(Q_2)$. Fig. 9.8 shows firm 1's reaction curve.

Similar analysis will generate firm 2's reaction curve on the basis of what it thinks firm 1 will produce. Firm 2's reaction curve is denoted by $Q_{2*}(Q_1)$ which relates its output to the output it thinks firm 1 will produce. Firm 2's reaction curve is also given in Fig. 9.8

How much will each firm produce? Each firm's reaction curve tells it how much to produce, given the output of its competitors. In Cournot equilibrium, each firm correctly assumes how much its competitors will produce, and, thereby, maximizes its own output. Thus, the equilibrium output would be found at the intersection of the two reaction curves known as Cournot equilibrium. In this equilibrium, each firm assumes correctly how much its competitor will produce, and, thus, it maximizes its profit accordingly. Suppose the firms are producing an output level that is different from Cournot equilibrium. Will they adjust their outputs until the Cournot equilibrium is reached? Unfortunately, the model does not reflect anything about the dynamics of the adjustment process. We need different model to understand the dynamics of adjustment. It is rational to assume that its competitor's output is fixed, if the two firms are making their production decisions only once because, then, their output cannot change. It may also be rational once they are in the Cournot equilibrium because, then, they would have no incentive to change their output.

Example: A'Linear Demand Curve:

Let us assume two identical firms are facing a linear market demand curve. This will enable us to show clearly the meaning of a Cournot equilibrium. We compare it as the competitive equilibrium and collusive equilibrium.

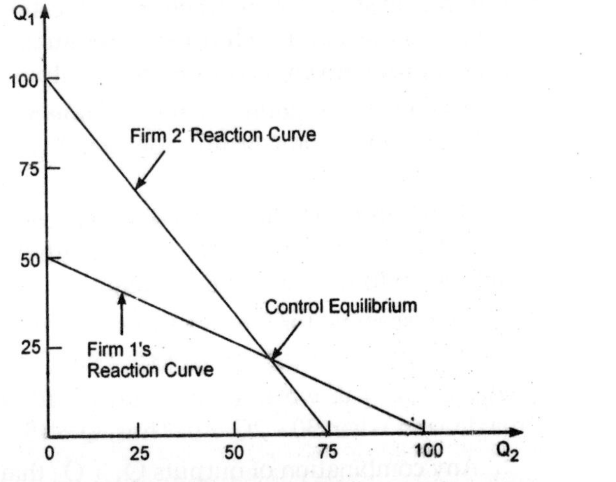

Fig. 9.8: Reaction Curve and Cournot Equilibrium

Suppose, the duopolists face the following market demand curve: P=30 – Q, where Q is the total product of both firms (i.e. $Q=Q_1+Q_2$). Also assume that both firms have zero MC : $MC_1 = MC_2=0$.

Now, we can determine the reaction curve for firm 1. To maximize profit, the firm equates MC = MR. Firm 1's total revenue. $TR_1=PQ_1=(30-Q)Q_1 = 30Q_1-(Q_1+Q_2)Q_1$. The firm's $MR_1=dTR_1/dQ_1 = 30-2Q_1-Q_2$. Now, setting MR = MC = 0, and solving for Q_1, we find:

Firm 1's reaction curve:

$Q_1 = 15 - \frac{1}{2}Q_2$ .... (1). Similarly, we find firm 2's reaction curve: $Q_2 = 15 - \frac{1}{2}Q_1$ ...(2).

The equilibrium output levels are the values of Q_1 and Q_2 that are at the intersection of the two reaction curves, i.e., those are the solutions of equations (1) and (2). By replacing Q_2 in equational (1), we get :

$Q_1 = 15 - \frac{1}{2}(15 - \frac{1}{2}Q_1) = 15 - 7.5 + \frac{1}{4}Q_1$; $Q_1 = 10$ and $Q_2 = 10$. Cournot Equilibrium = $Q_1 = Q_2 - 10$. Thus, the total quantity is Q = 10 + 10 = 20, so the equilibrium price is P = 30 – Q = 10.

Fig. 9.9 shows the Cournot reaction curves and Cournot equilibrium. Firm 1's reaction curve shows its output Q_1 in terms of firm 2's output Q_2. Similarly, firm 2's reaction curve shows Q_2 in terms of Q_1. The Cournot equilibrium is at the interaction of the two curves. At this point each firm is maximizing its own profit, given its competitor's output.

Instead of competing, if they collide and try to maximize joint profit, how much will they produce?

Total profit is maximized when total output Q is produced at a point where MR=MC, which is zero at this example.

Total revenue for the two firms is:

TR = PQ = (30 – Q) Q, so MR = 30 – 2Q. Setting MR = 0, we find the total profit is maximized when 30 – 2Q = 0. Thus, Q = 15.

Any combination of outputs $Q_1 + Q_2$ that add up to 15 maximizes total profit. The curve $Q_1 + Q_2 = 15$, called contract curve, is, therefore, all pairs of outputs Q_1 and Q_2 that maximize total profit.

This curve is also shown in Fig. 9.9.

If the firms agree to share the profit equally, they will each produce half of the total output: $Q_1 = Q_2 = 7.5$.

Both the firms produce less and earn higher profits than in Cournot equilibrium which is shown below. The competitive output levels are found by setting price equal to MC, so we get $Q_1 = Q_2 = 15$. Note that the Cournot solution is much better than a perfectly competitive solution, but not as good as the outcome from collusion.

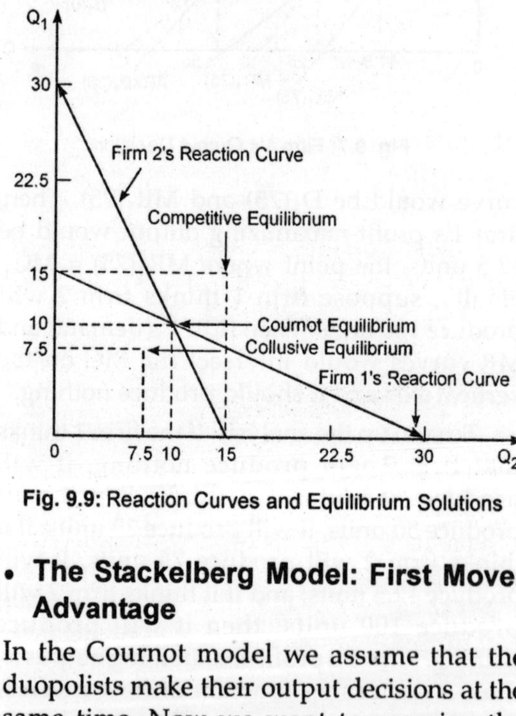

Fig. 9.9: Reaction Curves and Equilibrium Solutions

• The Stackelberg Model: First Mover Advantage

In the Cournot model we assume that the duopolists make their output decisions at the same time. Now we want to examine the advantage of the first mover. There are two questions of interest in this situation. First, is it advantageous to go first? Second, what is the resulting equilibrium?

Again we assume that the market demand curve is given by P = 30 – Q, where Q is the total output and the MC of both firms is zero. Suppose, firm 1 sets its output first and then firm 2 makes its output decision. In setting output, firm 1 must, therefore, consider the reaction of firm 2. This is different from the Cournot model in which neither firm has the opportunity to react.

Let us start with firm 2; because it makes its output decision after firm 1, and takes firm 1's output as given. Thus, firm 2's profit-maximizing output is given by the Cournot reaction curve, as we have found before.

Firm 2's reaction curve:

$$Q_2 = 15 - \frac{1}{2}Q_1 \quad .... (2)$$

Firm 1 chooses Q_1, its profit-maximizing output, where its MC=MR=0.

Recall that firm's total revenue is:

$$TR_1 = PQ_1$$
$$= 30Q_1 - Q_1^2 - Q_2Q_1 \quad .... (3)$$

Since TR_1 depends on Q_2, firm 1 anticipates how much firm 2 will produce. Firm 1 knows that firm 2 will choose Q_2 according to its reaction curve given in equation (2).

Substituting equation (2) for Q_2 into equation (3), we find firm 1's TR_1 as:

$$TR_1 = 30Q_1 - Q_1^2 - (15 - \frac{1}{2}Q_1)Q_1$$
$$= 30Q_1 - Q_1^2 - 15Q_1 + \frac{1}{2}Q_1^2 = 15Q_1 - \frac{1}{2}Q_1^2$$

So, its MR_1 = $15 - Q_1$. Then setting $MR_1 = MC_1 = 0$, we get $Q_1 = 15$. And from 2's reaction function (2), we find $Q_2 = 7.5$ units and, thus, firm 1 will make twice as much profit. Going first gives firm 1 an advantage. It seems advantageous to announce output first. Why, then, going first is a strategic advantage?

The reason is that announcing first creates a fait accompli, and no matter what your competitor does, your output will remain unchanged and large. To maximize profit, your competitor must take your large output as given and set a low level of output for itself. This kind of 'first mover advantage' occurs in many strategic situations, as we will see later.

The Cournot and Stackelberg models are alternative representations of oligopolistic behaviour. Which model would be more appropriate depends on the industry. For an industry composed of roughly equal strength of competitors, none of whom have a strong operational advantage or leadership position, the Cournot model may be more appropriate, whereas, some industries are often dominated by a large firm that normally takes the lead of setting prices and new production levels. The Sport shoe industry is an example in point, with Nike as the leader. In such a situation, the Stackelberg model may be more appropriate.

• Price Competition with Homogeneous Products–The Bertrand Model

Our assumption so far was that oligopolistic firms compete by setting quantities; but, we find many oligopolistic industries with competition in mind. Here we can use the Nash Equilibrium concept to study price competition, first in an industry with homogeneous product, and then in an industry with product differentiation.

Again, another French economist Joseph Bertrand developed this model where, like Cournot model, firms produce a homogeneous product. Now they chose prices rather than quantity, which can dramatically affect the outcome.

We will return to duopoly example of the previous section, discussed above, in which market demand curve is $P = 30 - Q$ where $Q = Q_1 + Q_2$ is a homogeneous product. This time we assume that both the firms have a marginal cost of £3. $MC_1 = MC_2 =$ £3.

We know Cournot equilibrium for this duopoly, which results when both firms choose output simultaneously, is $Q_1 = Q_2 = 8$. We also know that the equilibrium market price is £14, so that each firm can make a profit of £88.

Now suppose these two firms compete by simultaneously choosing a price instead of a quantity. What price will each choose, and how much profit will each earn? The answer is that, because the good is homogeneous, consumer will buy only from the lowest price-seller. Thus, if the two firms charge different prices, the lowest-price seller will supply the entire market, and the higher price firm will sell nothing. If both firms charge the same price, consumers would be indifferent as to which firm they buy from; we can, thus, assume that each firm would then supply half a market.

The Nash Equilibrium in this situation is the competitive outcome, i.e., both firms set price equal to MC : $P_1 = P_2 = MC = £3$. Then industry output is 27 units, of which each firm produces 13.5 units.

Since P = MC, both firms have zero economic profit. This is a Nash Equilibrium because neither firm would have any incentive to change its price. Suppose firm1 raised its price. It would, then, lose all its sales to firm 2, and would, thus, be worse-off. Instead, if it lowered its price, it would capture the entire market, but it would still be worse-off because it would lose money on every unit it produced. Hence, firm 1 has no incentive to deviate, it is doing the best it can, given what its competitor is doing.

A Nash Equilibrium cannot be at a price higher than the competitive price, because, in this situation, if either firm lowered its price a bit, it could capture the entire market and make substantial profit. Thus,each firm would wish to undercut its competitor until the price dropped to £3.

By changing the strategic choice variable from output to price, we have achieved a dramatically different result. In the Cournot model, each firm produces 8 units of output and charges price of £14. In Bertrand model, the market price is £3.

The Bertrand model has been criticized on the following grounds: First, when firms produce a homogeneous product, it is natural to assume that the firms will compete by setting quantity, rather than price. Second, even if the firms do set same price as the model predicts, there is no reason to believe that sales would be divided equally between the firms. But despite this criticisms the Bertrand model is useful because it shows how the equilibrium outcome in an oligopoly can depend on the firms' choice of crucial variables.

- **Price Competition with differentiated Product**

Oligopolistic markets can have some degree of product differentiation. Market shares are determined not just by prices, but also by durability and differentiation and design and performance of each firm's product. It is quite natural for firms to compete by choosing prices rather than quantities. To see how price competition can work with differentiated products, we will go through the following example.

Suppose, each duopolist has a fixed cost of £20 but zero variable cost and that they face the same demand curves.

Firm 1's Demand curve:

$$Q_1 = 12 - 2P_1 + P_2 \quad \text{.... (4)}$$

Firm 2's Demand Curve:

$$Q_2 = 12 - 2P_2 + P_1 \quad \text{.... (5)}$$

When P_1 and P_2 are the prices charged by firm 1 and firm 2 respectively, and Q_1 and Q_2 are the quantities they sell. It may be noted that the quantities each firm can increase sell when its competitor charges higher price and decrease sell when the firm raises its own price.

If both firms set their prices at the same time, we can use the Cournot model to determine equilibrium. Each firm will choose its own price, taking competitor's price as fixed.

We consider the case of firm 1. Its profit is: profit = P_1Q_1 minus the fixed cost of £20.

Substituting Q_1 from the demand curve of equation (4), we get $\pi = P_1Q_1 - 20$

$$= 12P_1 - 2P_1^2 + P_1P_2 - 20$$

At price P_1, is the profit maximized? To answer this question, we need to know P_2, which firm 1 assumes as fixed. However, whatever price firm 2 charges, firm 1's profit is maximized when $\frac{d\pi}{dP_1} = 0$.

Taking P_2 as fixed, firm 1's profit-maximizing price is given by

$$\frac{d\pi}{dP_1} = 12 - 4P_1 + P_2 = 0.$$

From this equation, we can find the reaction curve of firm 1: Reaction curve of firm 1: $P_1 = 3 + \frac{1}{4}P_2$.

This indicates to firm 1 what price to set, given that firm 2 has set its price P_2.

Similarly, we can find the firm 2's reaction curve as follows:

Reaction curve firm 2: $P_2 = -12 + 4P_1$

These reaction curves are drawn in Fig. 9.10. The Nash Equilibrium is at the point where the reaction curves intersect, where each firm charges a price of £4, and earns a profit of £12. At this point, since each firm is doing the best it can, given the price of its competitor, neither firm has an incentive to change its price. Also shown in the diagram is the collusive equilibrium which they can set, if they cooperate. In this case price is £6.

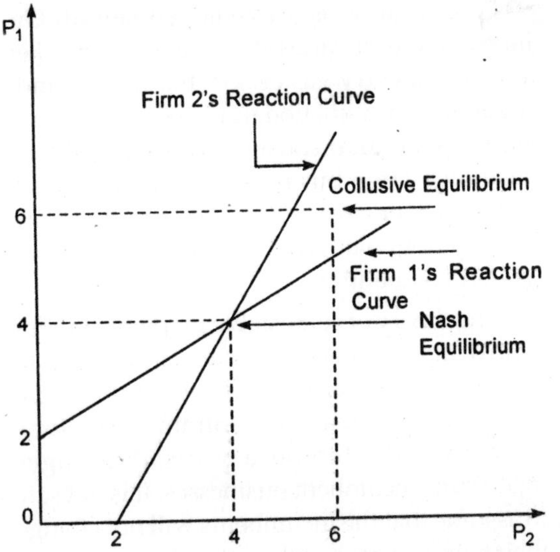

Fig. 9.10: Reaction Curves and Equilibrium Solutions

• Entry and Potential Competition

So far our analysis concentrated on imperfect competition between existing businesses. We now discuss the effect of potential competition from new entrants to the industry on the behaviour of existing or incumbent businesses. Three cases must be distinguished: where entry is easy, where it is difficult by accident, and where it is difficult by design.

Contestable Market: Free entry into and exit from, the industry is a key feature of perfect competition, a market structure in which each business is tiny relative to the industry. Suppose we observe an industry with few incumbent businesses and we assume that it is an oligopolistic industry making large profits. If the industry faces free entry and exit of new firms because the industry is a contestable market then the few incumbent firms cannot make excessive profit.

By free entry, we mean that all businesses have access to the same technology and hence have the same cost curves. By free entry, we also mean that there are no sunk or irrecoverable costs.

A contestable market allows hit-and-run entry. If the incumbent businesses do not behave as if they were a perfectly competitive industry (where P = MC = minimum point of LAC), an entrant can step in, undercut them and make temporary profit before quitting again.

As globalization proceeds, we should remember that foreign business could be potential entrants. This can take two forms: First, if monopoly profits are too high in the domestic market, competition from imports may increase supply, bidding down prices and profits in the domestic market. In the extreme case we are back in the competitive world.

Globalization also raises the likelihood that foreign businesses will establish production facilities in the home market, a tangible form of entry. By raising potential entrants, it increases the relevance of contestable markets. Moreover, we may think of an entrant as having to start from scratch. When a foreign business enters the domestic market, its developed production and marketing expertise will help the home market.

Globalization is a two-edged sword. On the one hand, it raises the size of the market and makes entry easier. On the other hand, by allowing multinationals to operate in many countries simultaneously, globalization may encourage large businesses with substantial market power to operate. Coke and Pepsi are globally dominant, and Cola provides only a limited competition.

The theory of contestable markets remains controversial. There are many industries in which sunk costs are hard to recover or where initial expertise may take entrants some time to remove the temporary disadvantages against the incumbent businesses. It is not safe to assume that the incumbents will not change their behaviour when threatened by entry. But the theory does say that market structure and incumbent behaviour cannot be deduced simply by counting the number of businesses in the industry.

• Innocent Entry Barriers

An innocent entry barrier is one not deliberately erected by incumbent businesses. There are three types of entry barriers: product differentiation, absolute cost advantages, and scale economics. The first of these may not be an innocent entry barrier. The second ones, where incumbent businesses have lower cost curves than those of new entrants, may be innocent. If it takes time to learn the business, incumbents will face lower costs, at least in the short-run. In contrast, if the incumbents have undertaken investment or R & D specially with a view to deterring entrants, this is not an innocent barrier.

• The Role of Scale Economics as an Innocent Entry barrier

If minimum efficient scale is large relative to the industry's demand curve, an entrant cannot get into the industry without considerably depressing the price and it may prove simply impossible to break in and earn a profit. The greater are such innocent entry barriers, the more appropriate it is to neglect potential competition from entrants. The oligopoly game then reduces to competition between incumbent businesses. Where innocent entry barriers are low, one of the two things may happen. Either incumbent businesses from exercising much market power or else incumbent businesses will try to design some entry barriers of their own.

• Strategic Entry Deterrence

A strategy is a game plan where decision-making is interdependence.

A strategic move is one that influences the other person's choice, in a manner favourable to one's self, by affecting the other person's expectations of how one's self will behave.

A single incumbent business plays a game against a potential entrant. The entrant can come in or stay out. If the entrant comes in, the incumbent can opt for easy life, accept the new rival, and agree to share the market—or it can fight. Fighting entry means producing at least as much as before, or more, so that industry price collapses. In the price war, or predatory pricing by the incumbent, both businesses do badly and make losses as shown in each of the possible three outcomes.

Table 9.3: Strategic Entry Deterrence

	Entrant		
	In		Stays out
	Accept		Fight
	Share	War	No war
Profits without the entrant	1 1	−1 −1	5 0
Profits with the entrant	−2 1	−1 −1	2 0

If the incumbent is unchallenged, it does very well, making profits of 5. The entrant makes nothing. If they share the market, both make small profits of 1. In a price war, both make losses. How should they go?

Suppose the entrant comes in. Comparing the left two boxes of the top row, the incumbent does better to fight. The entrants can fight this out. Any threat by the incumbent to resist entry is not a credible threat, when it comes to crunch, it will be better to cave in. If the incumbent succeeds in keeping the entrant out, he can make a profit of 5, the equilibrium of the game is that the entrant will come in and the incumbent will not resist. Both make profits of 1, the top left-hand box.

The incumbent may have got its act together before the potential entrant appears on the scene. It may be able to invent a binding pre-commitment, forcing itself to resist entry and thereby scare off a further challenge. The incumbent would be ecstatic if the entrant guaranteed to shoot the incumbent if they ever allowed an entry to be unchallenged. Entrants would expect a fight, would anticipate a loss of 1, and would stay out, leaving the incumbent to earn a permanent profit of 5.

Without entrant, the incumbent can achieve the same result by economic means. Suppose the incumbent invested in expensive excess capacity that is unused at low output. The incumbent has low output in the absence of entry, or if an entrant is accommodated without a fight. Suppose in this situation the incumbent loses 3 because of excess capacity. The second row in the figure reduces the incumbent profit by 3. In a price war, the incumbent's output is high and the spare capacity is no longer wasted; hence we do not need to reduce incumbent's profit in the middle column of boxes in the figure. Now consider the game again. If the entrant comes in, the incumbent loses 2 by caving in but only 1 by fighting. Hence entry is resisted. Knowing this, the entrant does not enter, as he is likely to lose in a price war. Hence the equilibrium of the game is the bottom right-hand box and no entry takes place. Strategic entry deterrence has been successful. It has also been profitable. Even allowing for the cost of 3 of carrying the excess capacity, the incumbent still makes a profit of 2, which is better than the profit of 1 when no deterrence was attempted and the entrance is allowed to come in.

Strategic entry deterrence is behaviour by incumbent busineses to allow entry difficult.

Does deterrence always work? No. Suppose in, table 9.3, we change the right-hand column. In the top row, the incumbent gets a profit of 3 if no entry occurs. Without the pre-commitment, the equilibrium is the top left-hand box as before. But if the incumbent has to spend 3 on a spare capacity pre-commitment, it now makes a profit of zero in the bottom right-hand box when entry is deterred. The entrant is deterred, but the incumbent would have done better not to invest in spare capacity but to let the entrant in.

This model suggests that price wars should never happen. If the incumbent is really going to fight, then the entrant should not have entered. This requires that the entrant knows accurately the profits of the incumbent and thus correctly predict its behaviour. In the real world, entrants can get it wrong. Moreover, if the entrant has much better financial backing than the incumbent, a price war may be a good investment for the entrant. The incumbent will exit first, and the entrant will be able to cash up and get its losses back with interest.

The spare capacity must be available to incumbent so that output can be increased by a reduction in price; thus reducing overall profit and deterring potential entrants. Otherwise they are an empty threat; and they must increase the chances that the incumbent will fight. e.g. the Stagecoach bus company. They cut fares, sometimes to zero ! Ran buses a minute before their rival's timetables.

Anything with the character of fixed and sunk costs may be a deterrent to entry. Fixed costs will increase scale economics. This will make it necessary for any entrant to have to produce high output in order for profitable production to be possible. As sunk cost cannot be recouped; this is also a deterrent to potential entrants.

Advertising in order to build up goodwill and/or brand loyalty can also be entry barrier. For example soap or washing powder producers.

Another deterrent is product proliferation. If the incumbent has only one brand, an entrant may come in with a different brand. But if the incumbent has a complete range of brands or come in with a different brand. But if the incumbent has a complete range of brands or models, an incumbent will have to compete across the whole product range. This means more expenditure on development, investment and advertising. For example the cosmetics industry.

High research and development expenditure that is required to develop new products can also be a disincentive to new entrants. For example the drug industry.

However, if entry is easy because of low start up costs or very low 'sunk costs' (costs that cannot be recouped after entering an industry) then the single incumbent or apparent monopolist may find it unprofitable to depart significantly from perfectly competitive output and price.

To sum up: Most industries are imperfectly competitive. Here we study different types of imperfect competition. Game theory in general allows economists to analyze many of the practical concerns of big business.

We have learned first, market structure and the behaviour of incumbent businesses simultaneously. Economists used to start with a market structure, determined by the extent of the scale economics relative to the industry demand curve, then deduce how the incumbent businesses would behave (monopoly, oligopoly, perfect competition, etc), then check out these predictions, such as the extent to which P > MC. We realize that strategic behaviour by incumbent businesses can affect entry, and hence market structure, except where entry is very easy. Second, we have learned the importance of potential competition, which may come from domestic businesses considering entry or from imports from abroad.

Finally, we have seen how many business practices of the real world can be understood as strategic competition in which, to be effective, threats must be made credible by prior commitment.

APPENDIX 9A.1

Game Theory—Some Specific Examples

Two-Person, Zero-Sum Games: Having seen the basic tools of Game theory, we now analyses some more specific examples. The first case that we want to look at is that of two-person zero-sum games. As the name suggests, the game involves two players. The zero-sum means the sum of the pay-offs of the 2 players is zero that means, whatever one player get, the other player gets the reverse.

For example, the game of matching pennies is a two-player zero-sum game. In this game, two pennies are flipped. If the two pennies are both heads or both tails, then player 1 wins the other player's penny. If the two pennies land as opposites, then player 2 wins. Thus, the pay off matrix for matching pennies is as follows:

		Player 2 Heads	Player 2 Tails
Player 1	Heads	1, –1	–1, 1
	Tails	–1, 1	1, –1

Often, two player zero-sum games can be written as a simple matrix, since player 2's pay-offs are simply the negative of player 1's pay-offs. Thus, the above game could be written as:

		Player 2 Heads	Player 2 Tails
Player 1	Heads	1	–1
	Tails	–1	1

By looking for a Nash Equilibrium in this game (or any other non-constant[1]game two player zero-sum game) we will not find one in pure strategies. This is because whatever player 1 plays, player 2 loses. Thus, in all cases, either player 1 has the incentive to deviate to win more (or lose less), or player 2 has an incentive to deviate, to lose less (or win more).

We have seen that for zero-sum games, there does not exist a Nash Equilibrium in pure strategies. However, the game still may have a value or an equilibrium.

Sequential Games: We begin by looking at zero-sum sequential games. Consider the following game:

We analyse the game using Zermelo's algorithm (backward induction). The algorithm tells us that we should take a given sequential game and analyse it backwards. Thus, we take each of the final decision nodes and choose the option that the player would choose at best for himself if he was to find himself at the that node. For example, at player 2's final decision node, he can choose between a pay-off of –4 or –6. He will choose –4 since this is the best for him. We show this decision by a darkened line. Once all the final nodes are analysed, we move back one stage and analyse these decision nodes. Here (at player 2's only other decision nodes) he has the choice between -3 and –4. He will choose –3. Finally, we can see that player 1 will play in such a manner that he gets 3, since this is greater than zero. Thus, by following their optimum strategies, the players will get 3 and –3 respectively. Thus, we call 3 the "value" of the game, since this is its equilibrium outcome.

A Nash Equilibrium can also be calculated using Zermelo's algorithm. In the above example, the Nash Equilibrium is the strategy that gives the pay-off 3, but also includes the optimum choices at nodes that are not on the optimal path. In other words, if all the choices

1 By non-constant we mean that the pay-off should not be same for all outcomes.

at the nodes are left or right, the Nash Equilibrium is (left, left, right, left). This shows the optimal choice at each of the decision nodes, even if they are not reached by the optimal pay-off. Thus, backward inclusion can give us the Nash Equilibrium.

Solution of 2-Persons Game

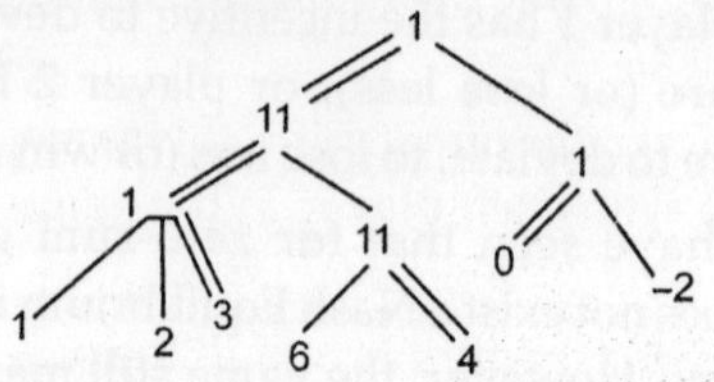

Constant Sum Games: A constant sum game is one where the sum of the pay-offs is the same for all strategy pairs.

		Player 2 Left	Right
Player 1	Top	1, 5	6, 0
	Bottom	4, 2	3, 3

The above game is one with a constant sum of 6. This is because the sum of the pay-offs under each outcome is 6. Such a game can easily be converted into a zero sum game without changing the analysis of the game. The conversion can either be by removing 6 from player 1's pay-off or by removing 6 from player 2's pay off. Thus the game becomes:

		Player 2 Left	Right
Player 1	Top	1, –1	6, –6
	Bottom	4, –4	3, –3

Thus, the result, for zero-sum games hold true for constant sum games. However, we must remember to add to player 2's pay-off when stating pay-offs to our analysis.

Minimax and Maximin: Since, simultaneous move zero sum and constant sum games do exist in real life, we need to develop some tools to give us an insight into what the outcome will be. For this reason, the minimax and maximin ideas have been developed.

We consider the following games:

Player 1	Player 2 C_1	C_2	C_3	Row min-
Y_1	1	6	0	0
Y_2	2	0	3	0
Y_3	3	2	4	2
Column Max	3	6	4	

To workout the minimax value for player 1, we take the maximum values from the columns and we, then, select the minimum value from the column maxima.

Minimax = min (Column maxima)

Similarly, to work out the maximin values we work out the row minima and we, then, take the maximum of these values.

Maximin = max (row minima)

The minimax value will always be greater than or equal to the maximin value. If the minimax equal the maximin, the game is said to have a saddle point at this strategy pair.

Dominant Strategy: Often in a game, a player has many strategies to choose from and this can be quite a complex task. However, we know from real life that when faced with certain situations, there are often some options which are definitely inferior to other options, regardless of what else happens. For example, it is obviously bad to drive with our eyes closed, irrespective of what other drivers choose to do. For this reason, we will always choose to drive with our eyes open.

Looking at driver 1's options we can see that it is always better for him to drive with

		Driver 2 No Sunglasses	Sunglasses	Eye closed
Driver 1	No Sunglasses	3, 3	2, 4	4, –6
	Sunglasses	4, 2	4, 4	3,–5
	Eyes closed	–6, 4	–5, 3	–8, –8

sunglasses rather than to drive with his eyes closed, since the pay-offs are higher, regardless of what driver 2 does[2]. Thus, we can say, the strategy of driving while wearing sunglasses dominates the strategy of driving with our eyes closed. The same can be said for driver 2. After eliminating the dominant strategies the game becomes:

		Driver 2: No Sunglasses	Driver 2: Sunglasses
Driver 1	No Sunglasses	3, 3	2, 4
	Sunglasses	4, 2	4, 4

The game can now be analysed to show that a Nash Equilibrium exists at the strategy pair.

N-player Games: Until now we have only analysed games in which there are two players. However, there are many instances when there are games with many players. For example, most graces have more than two competitors, oligopolies have more than two firms, a league with many teams, etc.

To continue analysing these situations with the models we have seen so far would mean that we would need to work in 3-D, 4-D and N-D matrices. Since this is a very abstract and complex way of proceeding, we simplify our analysis by making a simple assumption we assume that all players in the game, except one, act as a single player would act. Thus in an oligopoly situation, we take firm 1 to be player 1 and all the other firms in the industry to be player 2. Thus, we can analyse from firm 1's point of view what its the best course of action would be.

Example. Consider an oligopolistic industry with 5 firms which produce textbooks, where price is the strategic variable and price decisions are taken simultaneously. If all the firms charge a low price, then each firm in the industry makes a profit of 2 lakhs. If all the firms charge a high price, then each firm makes a profit of 4 lakhs. If one firm were to charge a low price while others charged a high price, they would make a profit of 5 lakhs, while everyone else made profits of 1 lakh. If one firm charged a high price while others charged a low price, the high price firm would make loss of 1 lakh, while everyone else made profits of 4 lakhs.

Write down the bimatrix for this game, stating clearly who each player in the game represents.

Find the Nash Equilibrium in the one shot game. Find the Nash Equilibrium in the infinitely repeated game, with no discounting.

Solution

		Player 2: Low Price	Player 2: High price
Player 1	Low price	2, 2	5, 1
	High price	–1, 4	4, 4

In this game, player 1 represents firm 1. Player 2 represents firms 2, 3, 4 and 5. The payoffs given are for firm 1 and for the other firms. For example, the pay-off –1, 4 means that firm 1 makes a loss of 1 lakh, while each of the other 4 firms makes a profit of 4 lakhs.

The Nash Equilibrium in one shot game is low price. The Nash Equilibrium in the infinitely repeated game could either be (Low price, Low price) n-times or (High price, High price) n-times. This is because there is no incentive to deviate from either policy (see oligopoly case).

Nash Equilibrium: To determine the likely outcome of a game, we have been seeking a "stable equilibrium". Dominant strategies are stable, but in many games, dominant strategies do not exist, so, we need to be able to analyse games without dominant strategies. We need a more general equilibrium concept. Thus, we introduce a Nash Equilibrium as a set of strategies in such a way that each player is doing the best it can, given the action of its opponents. Since each player has no incentive

---

2 4 > –6 if driver 2 does not wear sunglasses, 4 > –5 if driver 2 does wear sunglasses and 3 > –8, if driver 2 drivers with his eyes closed.

to deviate from a Nash Equilibrium, the outcome is stable. We consider the game below:

Player 1 \ Player 2	Left	Right
Top	4, 2	0, 0
Bottom	0, 0	2, 4

The best the player 1 can do, given that player 2 has played left, is to play top. We call this pair of strategies a Nash Equilibrium. Similarly, bottom right is also a Nash Equilibrium (NE). The concept was formalised since dominant strategies are often difficult to find or may not exist. However, the NE of a game depends what both players do.

We can say that a pair of strategies can be called a Nash Equilibrium if A's choice is optimal given B's choice and B's choice is optimal given A's choice. The NE of the prisoners' dilemma is (confess, confess) as we have seen above.

The NE of a game is the generalisation of the Cournot equilibrium for oligopolies, seen above, where each first maximizes its own payoff, given the other firm's.

Actions. It is helpful to compare the concept of a NE with that of an equilibrium in dominant strategies. Dominant strategies: I am doing the best I can, no matter what you do, you are doing the best you can, no matter what I do.

Nash Equilibrium: I am doing the best I can, given what you are doing. You are doing the best you can, given what I am doing.

Note that a dominant strategy equilibrium is a special case of a NE.

QUESTIONS

1. An industry demand curve is as follows:

A	1	2	3	5	6	7	8	9	10	11
P	10	9	8	7	6	5	4	3	2	1

   (a) Suppose it is monopolist whose MC = 3: What price and output are chosen?

   (b) If there are two businesses whose MC = AC = 3: What price and output will maximize joint profits if they collude?

   (c) Why might each business wish to cheat if it can avoid retaliation by the other?

2. The above industry demand curve applies for two businesses, A and Z, who begin with half the market each when charging the monopoly price. Z wishes to cheat believing that A will stick to its old output level: (a) show the demand curve Z believes it faces. (b) What output would Z then chooses?

3. Vehicle repairs suggest that mechanics should be licensed so that repairs should be done only by qualified people. We can argue that customers can always ask whether a mechanics is trained in a reputable institute without requiring to see license. (a) Evaluate the arguments for and against licensing car mechanics. (b) Are the arguments the same for licensing the doctors?

4. Think of five adverts on TV. Is their function primarily informative or the erection of entry barriers to the industry?

5. Parents know that children sometimes need to be punished, but also know that, when come to the crunch, the child will be let off with a warning. Can the parents undertake any pre-commitment to make the threat of punishment credible?

6. A monopolist can produce at a constant AC = MC = 5. The business faces a market demand curve given by Q = 53 – P.

   (a) Calculate the profit-maximizing price and output and profits for the monopolist.

   (b) Suppose the second business enters the market. Let Q_1 and Q_2 be the outputs of the first and second business, respectively. Market demand is $Q = Q_1 + Q_2 = 53 - P$. Assuming that the second business has the same cost condition as the first, write the profits of each business as functions of Q_1 and Q_2.

ANSWERS

1. (a) Output 4 and price 7. (b) Again the answer is the same. (c) Since each business that MC = 3, and MR > 3, if it alone expands; price will not fall if other businesses do not expand their output.
2. (a) the demand curve for monopolist Z: output = 1, 2, 3, 4, 5, 6, 7 and the price = 8, 7, 6, 5, 4, 3, 2 and total revenue will be: 8, 14, 18, 20, 20, 18, 14 and MR as follows: 8, 6, 4, 2, 0, –2 and –4.
   (b) Monopolist will choose output = 3.
3. If motor mechanics were trained from a reputable institute, this will save customers cost of checking themselves. For mechanics, after a bad experience, we can go elsewhere. Reputation helps solve the information problem. For doctor, you might be dead after the bad experience.
4. A few convey new information and many erect entry barriers.
5. Agreeing policy with parents may have good effect, if you depart from the agreement you would look silly.
6. (a) The monopolist wants to choose quantity to maximize his profit = PQ - TC (Q). To find the profit-maximizing quantity, we find differentiation with respect to a dQ = 48 – 2Q = 0, thus, Q = 24 and P = 29 and Profit = 976.

   (b) When the second business enters, price can be a function of the output of two businesses: $P = 53 - Q_1 - Q_2$. Profit function of two businesses can be written as: $p_1 = PQ_1 - TC(Q_1)$ and $p_2 = PQ_2 - TC(Q_2)$.

CHAPTER 10

THE THEORY OF DISTRIBUTION

KEY TERMS

Marginal Physical Product of Labour (MPP = mpl): The additional output produced as the input of labour is increased by one unit, e.g. $\Delta q/\Delta l$=mpl.

Marginal Revenue Product of Labour: The change in total revenue resulting from the employment of one more or one less unit of labour. It is equal to the marginal product of labour (mpl) multiplied by MR.

The Marginal Value Product (MVP) [also known as the value of Marginal Product (VMP)] of a Variable Factor: Is the market value of the MPP of the variable factor.

Marginal Factor Cost (MFC): Is the change in total cost resulting from the employment of one more or less unit of a variable factor.

Marginal Disutility of Work (mdw): When employment is an amount 'l_0' (mdw l_0) is the extra disutility of work produced when an extra unit of labour (a labour hour) is supplied. ('l_0' labour increases to 'l_{0+1}')

So far we have been discussing the output market—the market for goods and service (q or Q). Now we will trun our attention to the factor markets for factor inputs (labour, capital and land). Much of our material will be familiar because the same factors that shape the demand and supply in the output markets also affect factor markets. Factor markets, like output markets, can have similar structure. We will examine three different factor market structures: (1) Perfectly competitive factor markets, (2) markets where buyers of factors have monopsony power, and (3) markets where sellers have monopoly power (the four relationships between perfectly competitive and monopsonistic factor markets and perfectly competitive and imperfectly competitive goods and services markets are shown in appendix 10A.1).

We will discuss various equilibrium conditions in the factor market. This involves the study of the functional distribution of income. There are three major divisions of income which the factors of production receive: Labour receives wages. Land receives rent. Capital receives interest and profit.

According to traditional distribution theory, the distribution of income is simply a special case of price theory.

This can be summarised in three major points:

1. The income of any factor of production (and, hence, the amount of the national product that it receives) depends on the price that is paid for the factor.
2. Factor prices and quantities are determined by demand and supply in the factor markets in exactly the same way that price and quantities of goods and services are determined in commodity markets.
3. To explain distribution of income through price theory it is necessary to identify the main determinants of demand for and supply of factors of production. It is also necessary to allow for any intervention into free market by governments, trade unions or similar institutions.

• The Determination of Wages in a Perfectly Competitive Labour Market

We are here concerned with the distribution of income among the members of a society. We analyse the factors determining how the output of an economy is divided up, and shared out among the members of the society.

In a capitalist economy or market economy there are two basic factors influencing the distribution of income to the owners of the factors of production. One is the pattern of ownership of the factors of production; the second is the prices at which the services of the factors of production sell in the factor market.

The ownership of the factors can be regarded as given, so that we concentrate on the determination of factor prices. In a market economy, the factor prices are determined by the demand and supply condition of the factors. Here we concentrate on labour input (measured in terms of labour hours) and examine the variables which influence the determination of wages. These influences can also be adapted to the determination of other factor prices. The marginal productivity theory of the demand for a factor of production is a general theory of the demand for any variable factor.

• The Demand for a Factor of Production

The demand for a factor of production is a derived demand; it is necessarily derived from the consumer's demand for the goods and services (q) for which the factor is used. We start this section by considering a single business' demand for labour (l), assuming that the labour is a variable factor of production and that all other factors are fixed. This will enable us to determine the total demand for labour of an entire industry.

It is the flow of the services of labour (the number of labour hours per unit of time) from the stock of labour that are purchased. The firm cannot own units of labour; slavery is outlawed !

• The Individiual Business' Demand for Labour

Our assumption here is that businesses maximize profit. We know that businesses maximize profit by producing up to the point where marginal revenue = marginal costs. An implication of this is that a business will hire units of variable factors of production until the last unit hired adds as much to revenue as to costs. This result brings us to the important concepts of Marginal Revenue Product (MRP), the Value of the Marginal Product (VMP), and Marginal Factor Cost (MFC).

Definition: The Marginal Revenue Product (MRP) of a labour is the change in total revenue resulting from the the employment of one more or one less unit of labour factor. It is equal to the marginal physical product of labour (MPP {also known as the marginal product of labour [mp_l]}) of the variable factor multiplied by MR:

Definition: The marginal value product (MVP) {also known as the value of the marginal product (VMP)} of labour factor is the market value of the marginal physical product of labour. Thus, the MVP = MPP times Price.

Definition: Marginal factor cost (MFC) is the change in total cost resulting from the

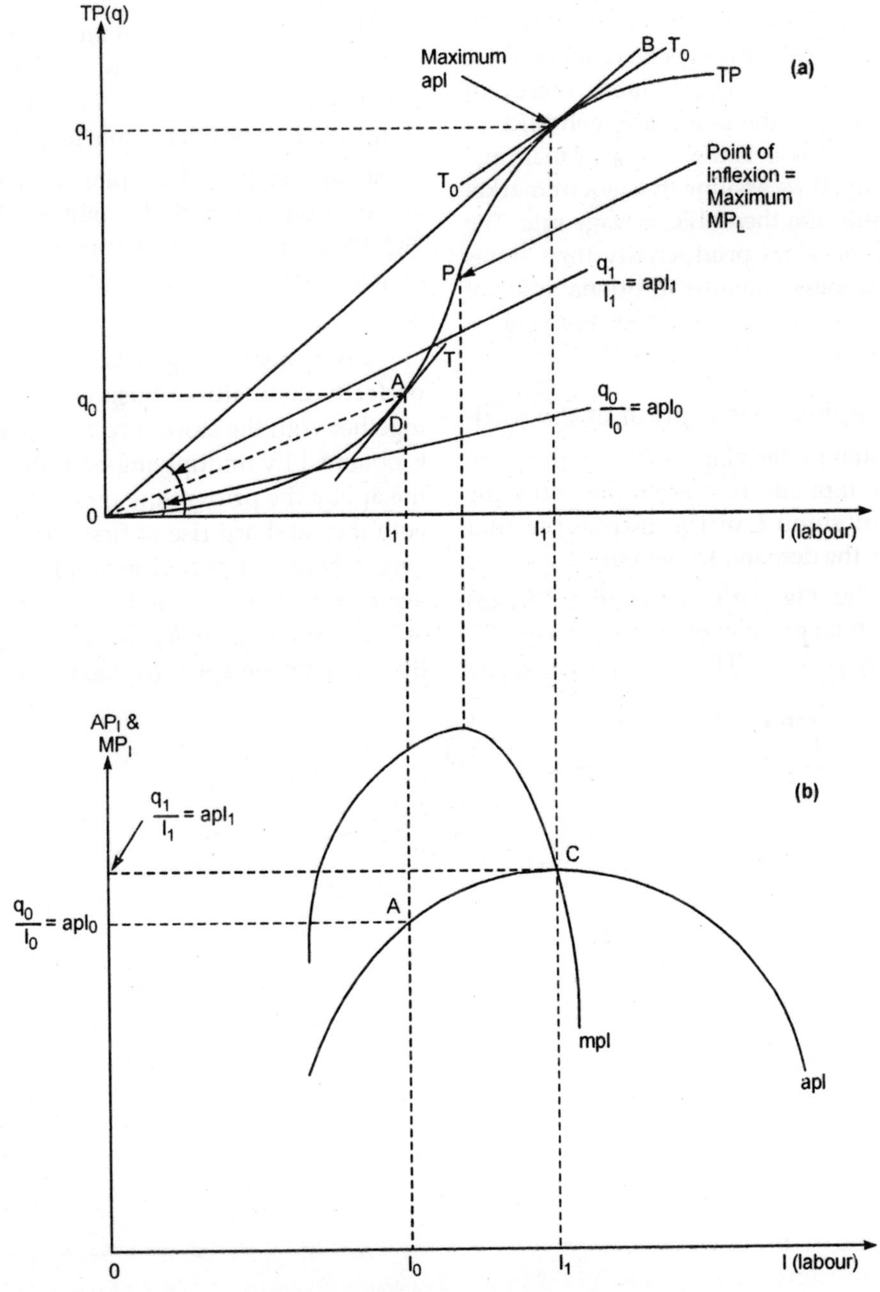

Fig. 10.1: The Derivation of mpl and apl

employment of one more or less unit of the variable factor.

Note that if the business is selling its product in a perfectly competitive market, so that P = MR, then it must also be true that MRP= MVP = MFC.

It should be clear from the above definiton that a profit maximizing business selling its product in a perfectly competitive market will hire extra unit of the variable factor of production up to the point at which MRP (= MVP) = MFC. This is the theory of marginal productivity. If we assume that labour market in its equilibrium then MFC = wage rate. The theory of marginal productivity then states that the business will hire additional units of labour up to the point at which the wage = MVP of labour.

• The Graphical Derivation of the MRP

The first step in deriving the mrp curve is to derive the mpl curve. It is, in fact, only the downward sloping of the mrp curve that represents the demand for labour.

Consider Fig. 10.1 above. Fig. 10.1(a) shows the total product of labour curve (TP). Since the *slope* of the TP curve (measured by the slope of a tangent to points on the TP such as tangent TT at point D, T_0T_0 at point E or slope (tangent) OB at point C) is the marginal product of labour ($\Delta TP/\Delta l \approx dTP/dl$) then TP exhibts increasing and then, diminishing marginal productivity of labour. In Fig. 10.1(b) mpl is a plot of these values.

The slope of a ray from the origin (such as OA or OB) is a measure of the average product of labour (apl). The slope 0A is equal to q_0/l_0 (= apl_0), the slope OB is equal to q_1/l_1(= apl_1).

In Fig. 10.1(b) apl is a plot of the slopes of all rays from the origin to points on TP. From Fig. 10.1(a) we can see that there is only one pont where apl is equal to mpl—that is at point C.

Now consider Fig. 10.2 which shows a perfectly competitive business's mrp curve together with the associated arp curve which is obtained by multiplying both the mpl and the apl by the price of the product. Note that both mrp and arp rise at first but eventually decline because both apl and mpl increase and decrease as shown in Fig. 10.1(b), mrp cuts arp at its maximum point for the same reasons that the mpl cuts the apl at its maximum point.

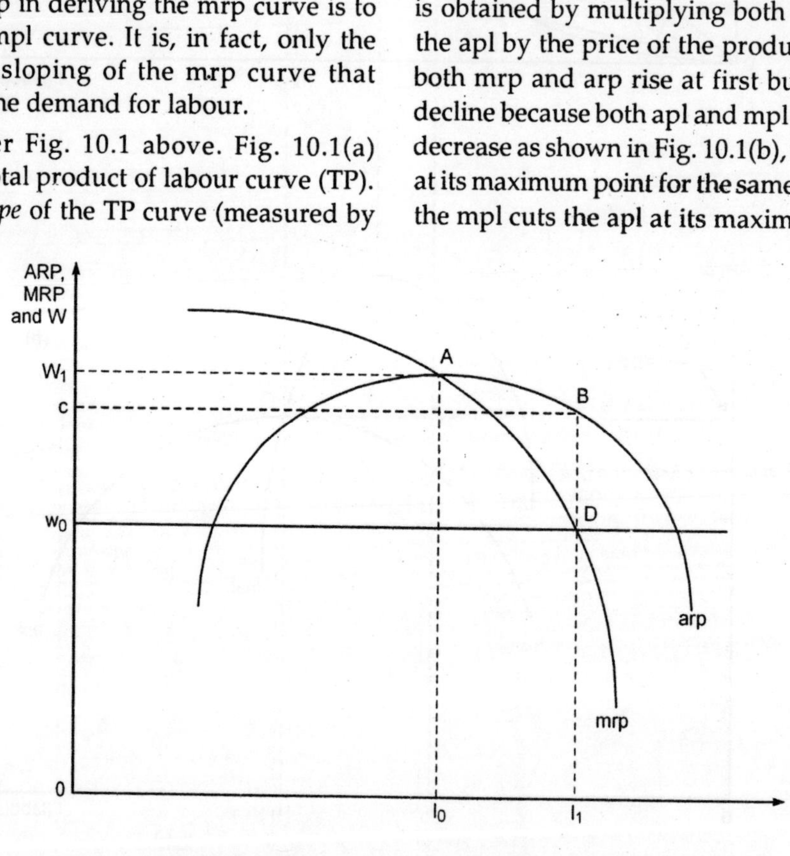

Fig. 10.2: The Business' Demand Curve for Labour

If the wage rate is W_0 (see Fi.g 10.2) the business will hire l_0 units of labour, and the arp of labour = l_0B = 0C, so the business benefits from a monetary surplus of BD (= CW_0) per unit of labour employed. This will cover the other costs of production including fixed costs. The business will not pay a wage rate more than W_1; if it does, the wage would be greater than the arp of labour; the business would then be unable to cover its variable costs and would close down. Thus, it is only the section of the mrp below its intersection with the arp that represents the individual business's demand curve for labour would be steeper but downward-sloping. We derive the industry demand curve for labour in appendix 10A.2.

Let us consider the numerical example set out in the Table 10.1. The example is that of a wheat farmer who is operating in a perfectly competitive product (q) market and perfectly competitive factor markets (K and l and L_n) and whose only variable factor of production is labour. Table 10.1 illustrates the 'law of diminishing returns' because as more and more workers are employed, the MPP of labour (mpl) eventually declines. Now suppose that the price of wheat is given as £2 per tonne: this enables us to calculate the mrp (= MVP). Ths is shown in column (3) of Table 10.1 and, since the price of wheat (q) is constant, it follows that this must eventually decline as more and more workers are hired.

We can state the following general rule for profit-maximizaton: profit-maximizing businesses will hire additional units of the variable factors up to the point at which the last unit hired adds just as much to revenue as to costs; that is until the factor's mrp = MFC. The equilibrium condition for a profit-maximizing business is mrp = MFC. This condition must be satisfied for all variable factors employed if the business is to maximize its profit.

If the business purchases its variable factor in a perfect factor market, so that it can purcahse any quantity without influencing its price, the MFC = price of factor. In this case the equilibrium condition becomes mrp = price of the factor of production (labour, capital or land).

Thus, a business's mrp curve is its demand curve for a variable factor on the assumption that all other factors of production are held constant.

Now suppose that labour is the only variable factor and is sold in a perfect market. A profit-maxmizing business will employ additional workers up to the point at which the wage rate is equal to the mrp of labour.

Consider Table 10.1 again. If the weekly wage is £24, the farmer will maximize profit

Table 10.1: The Derivation of mrp

Number of units of labour(l) (1)	mppl (Tonnes wheat per week) (2)	Price of Wheat (£2) (3)	mrpl = mvpl = P × mpp = £2×mpp (4)	Money Wage (W) (5)
1	4	2	8	24
2	10	2	20	24
3	11.5	2	23	24
4	14.5	2	29	24
5	20	2	40	24
6	12	2	**24**	**24**
7	5	2	10	24
8	3	2	6	24
9	1	2	2	24
10	0.6	2	1.2	24

by employing 6 units of labour, as the mrp of the 6th unit of labour is equal to £24. The farmer would not hire a 7th unit of labour, as it would add only £10 to revenue, but £24 to costs, thus reducing profit by £14. If the weekly wage falls to £6, the farmer would employ 8 units of labour, once again mrp is equal to the wage rate.

Fig. 10.3 shows the demand curve for labour (MVP {= MVP}) of a profit-maximizng business that sells its good or service (q) in a perfect market. Assume that labour is the variable factor and that the business purchases labour in a perfectly competitive labour market (see Fig. 10.8) and so is able to hire any number of workers at the market wage (W_0). This means that it faces a perfecly elastic supply curve of labour (sl_0) at the market wage (W_0).

Note: If the mrp = MVP then a business sells its good or service (q) in a perfectly competitve market.

When the supply of labour facing the business is sl_0, and the demand for labour is dl, the business hires l_0 units of labour at wage W_0 since this will maximize profit.

This equates mrp and wage {MRP(l_0) = W_0 where mrp(l_0) is the value of the marginal revenue product when l_0 labour hours are employed}. If the business hired fewer than l_0 units of labour, it could increase profit by hiring additional workers, for the mrp would be greater than the wage.

Conversely, if the business hired more units of labour than l_0, it could increase its profit by hiring less labour, for mrp would be less than the wage. Profits are only maximised if the mrp labour = wage rate which is the same as profit maximizing conditions in the output market where MR = MC.

In the short-run one factor of production is held constant (k). Labour (l) is the variable input.

Now consider the quantity of labour the business will hire if the wage increase to W_1 so that the supply curve shifts upwards to sl_1. The business maximizes its profit by moving along the labour demand curve until the new wage rate W_1 = mrp(l_1) and l_1 units of labour are hired. This is because, if W_0 increases to W_1, then W_1 will now be greater than mrp(l_0). When W_1 > mrp(l_0) it is profitable for the business to employ less labour. As *less* labour is employed the mrp will *increase* (since we assume diminishing marginal productivity of labour). Eventually the mrp will increase until

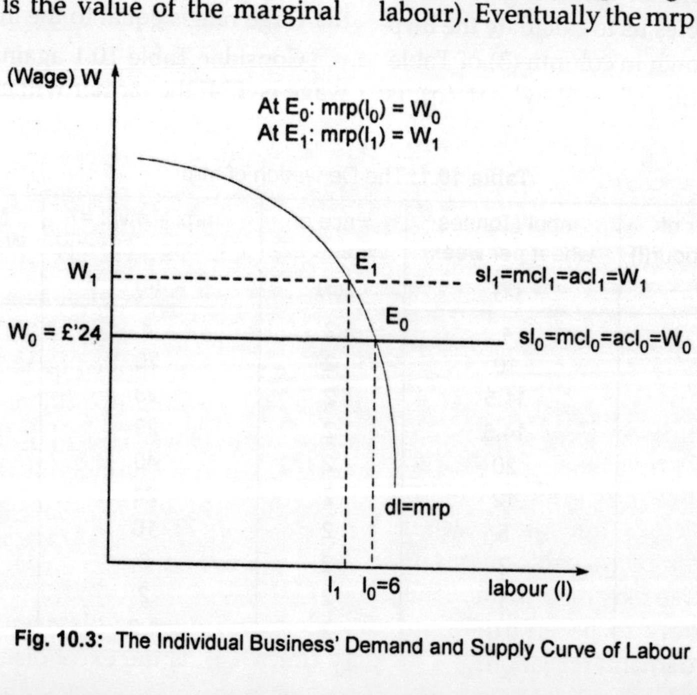

Fig. 10.3: The Individual Business' Demand and Supply Curve of Labour

it is equal to W_1. $W_1 = mrp(l_1)$ is the new profit maximizing position and there will be no movement from this point. Any reduction of labour input from l_1 will profit. If $l_0 < l_1$ when $W=W_1$ then the business is no longer maximizing profit.

If mrp = MVP (MR = P) then a business sells its product (q) in a perfectly competitive market for a constant price (P).

If, however, the business is selling its product (q or Q) in an imperfect market, she/he will face a downward sloping demand curve (d or D). In order to sell an extra unit the business has to accept a lower price for its product. Thus, in this case there is a decrease in revenue from selling an extra unit of output, MR < AR (=P), as the producer has to reduce the price on all other units sold.

In the case of business selling an extra unit of output (q or Q) in an imperfect market both the marginal productivity of labour and MR delcine. *Ceteris paribus*, mrp will be steeper than MVP.

• The Limitation of the Marginal Product Theory

The analysis presented above is known as the marginal productivity theory of the demand for a variable factor. Since this theory ignores the supply side, it cannot be regarded as a complete theory of factor pricing. Moreover, we assume that labour is a homogeneous factor which sells for a single price in a perfectly competitive labour market. In reality, of course, labour is not a homogeneous factor because of different innate characteristics and skills; and labour markets are by no means perfectly competitive.

It was also mentioned earlier that the theory is based on the assumption that business attempt to maximize profit. We know that private businesses may have other objectives; for example, public corporations do not normally attempt to maximize profit. Thus the theory is unlikely to be an adequate explanation for the demand for labour.

The theory also assumes that wage level and labour productivity are independent. This may not be true. Increased wages may call forth extra effort from the labour force, so that productivity increases. It is also possible that higher wage bills induce managers to exercise their supervisory function more effectively, which could result in extra output. Finally, it is possible that higher wages, which lead to improved nutritional standards, may result in more productive workers in the long-run. Such changes in productivity increase MPP(mpl) of labour, and thus shift a business' mrp curve to the right.

The marginal productivity theory is often criticised on the ground that businesses do not know a factor's mrp, because of insufficient information about the productivity of marginal workers. That does not matter. If the business maximizes profit, then the business must be paying factors their mrp, regardless of whether the business calculates the mrp or not.

• The Supply of Labour

The Individual's Supply of Labour (l)

When we consider an individual's supply of labour, we have to take into account possibility of backward-bending supply curve. Consider Fig. 10.4, which shows an individual's indifference map between work and play (leisure {Ls}). The horizontal axis measures hours of leisure per day (the number of hours worked per day is 24 less the number of hours of leisure) and the vertical axis measures the daily earnings (this is equal to the number of hours worked multiplied by the hourly wage rate). The maximum numbers of hours of leisure the individual is willing to take is given by 0Ls (24) hours. The individual regards work as 'bad' (there is increasing marginal disutility of work {mdw}) and his wage as 'good'.

Definition: The marginal disutility of work (mdw) when employment is an amount 'l_0' (mdw{l_0}), is the extra disutility of work produced when an extra unit of labour (a labour hour) is supplied. ('l_0' labour increase to 'l_{0+1}').

We also assume that a worker can choose how many hours to work.

The wage rate is the price that the worker places on leisure time because the wage is the income that worker gives up to enjoy leisure. As wage rate increases, the price of leisure also increases. The opportunity cost of leisure will increase.

Each indifference curve joins together those combinations of the daily wage and hours worked per day which yields the same amount of utility to the individual. Clearly, for the individual to stay at the same level of utility, as he works more hours he must receive a higher daily wage. Why is this the case?

We assume (unrealistically?) that people do not like working; and that there is increasing marginal disutility of work (mdw). The mdw is the value of the leisure being sacrificed in order to work another labour hour. If $P.mdw(l_0) < W$ then people wish to work longer (supply more) labour hours. If $P.mdw(l_0) > W$ then people wish to work (supply) fewer labour hours. The equilibrium situation is when $P.mdw\ (l_0) = W_0$. People are willing to work exactly (l_0) labour hours when the wage is W_0. W_0 exactly compensates them for working the extra hour. Hence people need a higher wage than W_0 to supply more labour hours. This means that the indifference curves must slope upward. It also follows that the higher the indifference curve, the greater the level of utility.

Consider the rays, RQ and PQ, whose slopes represent different wage rates. The slope of PQ represents wage equal to £10 per hour (point P is then £240 {=24 hours multiplied by £10}). At this wage rate, the indivdual maximizes his utility by choosing point A and by enjoying 16 hours of leisure and earning £80. This puts him at point A on the highest attainable indifference curve IC_0.

If the wage rate increases to £20 per hour, the budget line rotates to RQ (point R is now £480). Now the worker will maximize his/her utility at B by choosing 9 hours of leisure per day, whilst earning £300. More labour will be supplied (point 'S_0' to point M in Fig. 10.5). As we already know that price change brings in both a substitution effect (A to C) and income effect (C to B).

If we now plot the individual's supply of labour against the different wage rates, we obtain the backward-bending supply curve, point M to point S, shown in Fig. 10.5. Fig. 10.4 shows that as the wage rate increases from PQ

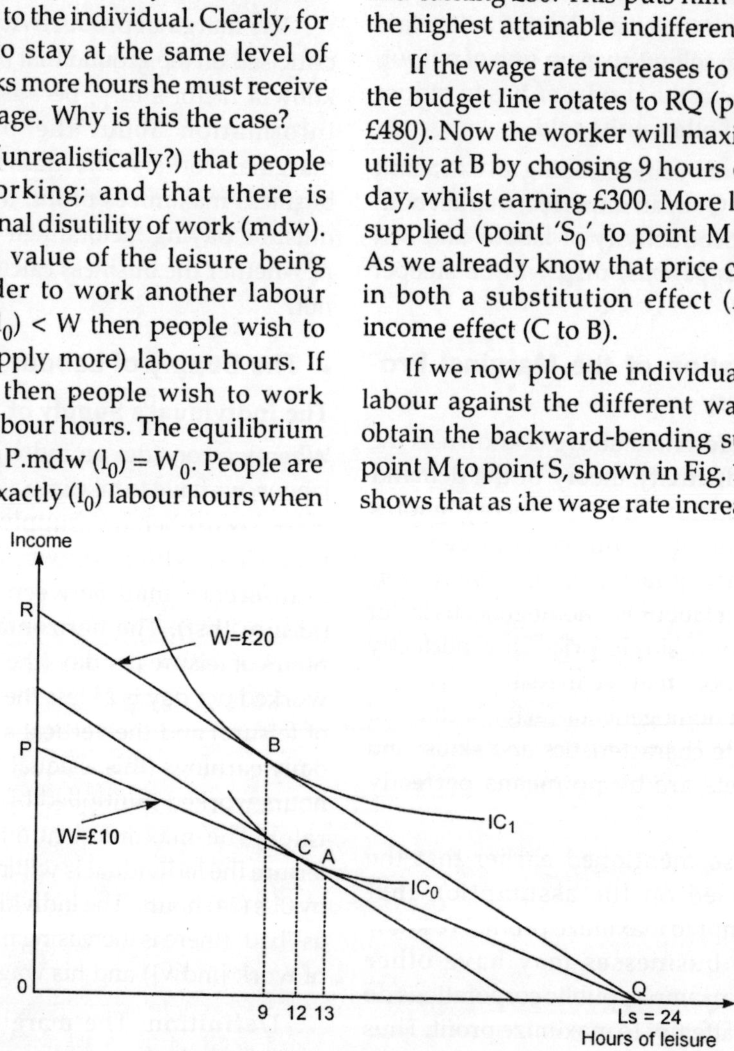

Fig. 10.4: The Work-Leisure Decision

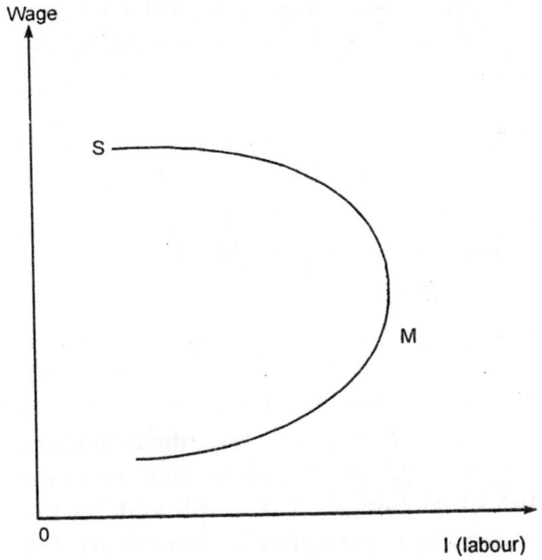

Fig. 10.5: The Individual's Supply of Labour

(£10) to RQ(£20), the individual offers to work more hours. As the price of labour rises, leisure is becoming more expensive relative to working. The workers substitute extra hours of work for leisure; this is called the substitution effect.

But as the wage rate rises, the individual's real income also increases, which also increases his demand for normal goods, including leisure; this is called income effect. When the wage rate rises above RQ the income effect predominates over the substitution effect, so that increases in the wage rate reduce the number of hours the individual offers to work. The supply curve becomes backward-bending.

For example, in real life, a backward-bending labour supply curve might apply to a college student working during the summer to earn living expenses for the school year. As soon as a target level of earnings is reached, the student stops working and allocates more hours to leisure. An increase in the wage rate will then lead to fewer hours worked because it enables them to reach the target level of income faster.

When the wage rate increases, the hours of work supplied increase initially but eventually decrease as individuals choose to enjoy more leisure. The backward-bending portion of the labour supply curve arises when the income effect associate with higher wage (E to D) is greater than the substitution effect (B to E).

When the wage rate increases from £20 to £25 per hour, the worker's budget line shifts from RQ to SQ. In response, the workers move from B to D, while decreasing work hours from 15 to 12. This reduction in hours worked arises because the income effect outweights the substitution effect. Then, the supply of labour curve becomes backward bending (point M to point S in Fig. 10.5).

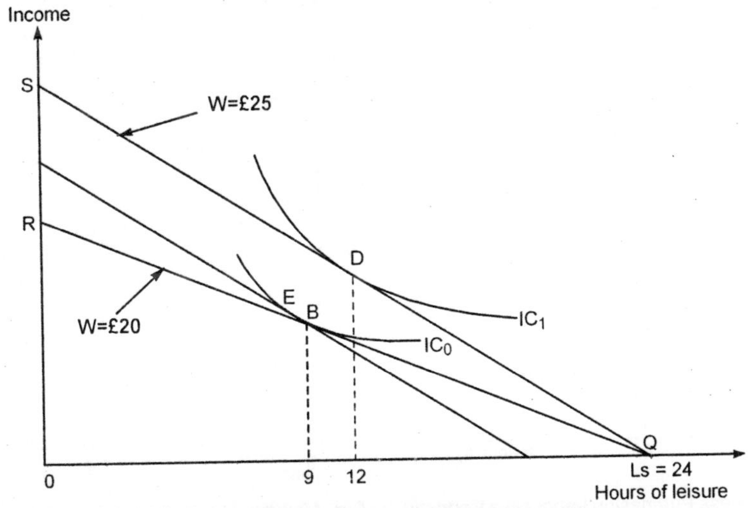

Fig. 10.6: The Work-Lesiure Decision

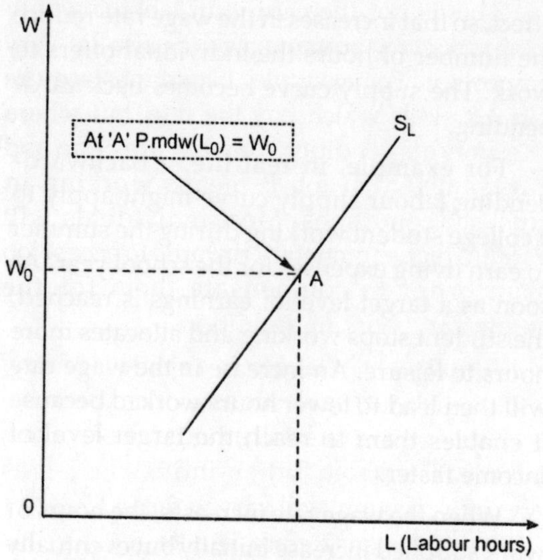

Fig. 10.7: The Supply of Labour to an Industry

However, in macro and microeconomics we usually draw the individual supply curve of labour as a positively sloped relationship between labour and the wage rate.

• The Supply of labour to an Industry

If we sum up the individual supply curves of labour and can obtain a supply curve of labour that an industry would face. This is positively sloped and is shown in Fig. 10.7.

Labour will be employed until the money wage rate is equal to the price multiplied by the marginal disutility of work.

• The Supply of Labour to a Business and the Determination of the Amount of Labour Employed: (a Perfectly Competitive Labour Market)

In Fig. 10.8(b) we put together the (upward) industry's market supply (average cost) of labour (S_L) and the industry's demand for labour (D_L). The intersection of the two determines the wage rate (W_0) the businesses in the industry have to pay for labour and the amount of labour (L_0) employed by the industry. L_0 is measured in *labour hours.* Fig. 10.8(a) shows the wage (W_0) that the businesses in this particular industry have to pay for labour which is determined by supply (S_L) and demand (D_L) in Fig. 10.8(a). The business is a price taker. Since the business can purchase as much labour as it wishes at W_0 the supply of labour (sl_0) to the business is perfectly elastic (horizontal).

The amount of labour employed will be l_0, which is determined by the intersecion of sl_0 and dl(W_0 = MVP) in Fig. 10.8(a).

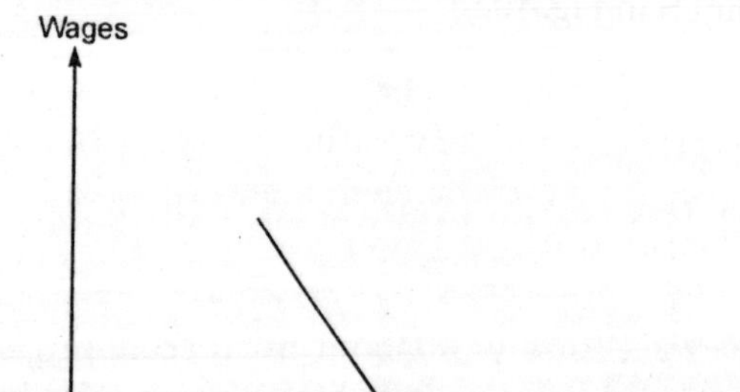

Fig. 10.8(a): A Business Purchasing Labour in a Perfectly Competitive Market

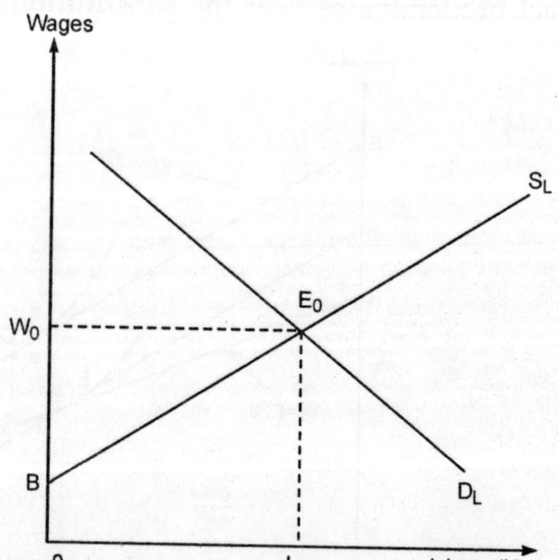

Fig. 10.8(b): The Determination of the in Price of Labour in a Perfectly Competitive Labour Market

• Economic Rent

We can use Fig. 10.8(b) to illustrate the concept of economic rent as applied to a perfectly competitive labour market. The equilibrium price of labour is W_0, and the quantity of labour (measured in *labour hours*) supplied to the market (industry) at this wage rate is L_0. The supply of labour (S_L) is upward sloping and is the average cost of labour. The market demand curve for labour is downward sloping reflecting the individual business' negatively sloped marginal revenue product or marginal value product curves. Since the market supply curve of labour tells us how much labour will be supplied at each wage rate, the minimum expenditure needed to employ to L_0 units of labour is given by the area $0BE_0L_0$ the area below the supply curve to the left of the equilibrium supply of labour L_0. This is because the area under the S_L curve is the total value of the marginal disutility of work. (The individual supply curves of labour are equal to the value of the marginal disutility of work and so the S_L curve represents the aggregate value of the marginal disutility of work, and the area under it is the total value of the marginal disutility of work).

In a perfectly competitive market all workers are paid the wage W_0. This wage is required to get the marginal worker to supply its labour, but all other workers earn rents becuase their wage is greater than what would be needed to get them to work. Since total wage payments are equal to the area $OW_0E_0L_0$, the economic rent earned by the worker is given by the area BW_0E_0. From the worker's point of view, economic rent is similar to consumer surplus.

If we ask what induces the owners of factors of production to allocate them to particular uses, the hypothesis of equal net advantage is relevant. This states that the owners of factors of production will move them between different uses until there is no further advantage, in another move. For the owners of non-human factors of production, monetary advantage will be really important.

This is not the case with labour, where non-monetary advantages will also be very important. For example, if two jobs require similar skills which pay the rate, but where the working condition for job A are clean and pleasant whilst job B means working in unclean conditions. Most individuals will require higher monetary rewards to accept job B in order to compensate them for the unpleasant working conditions.

The supply of labour to a single industry, then, is likely to be elastic as an increase in the industry's wage rate will induce some workers to transfer from other industries. This elasticity, though, will vary with the length of time period considered. The longer the time period, the greater will be the elasticity of supply because there are barriers to the mobility of labour.

The total supply of labour in an economy depends on the size of the population, the age composition of the population and many institutional and social factors. For example, the school leaving age and retirement age are institutional factors. These influence the supply of labour.

Other institutional factors, such as the length of the average working week and of holidays, are also significant. The participation rate is influenced by many factors, such as the level of unemployment benefits relative to wage level and social attitude towards the participation of women in the work force.

• The Elasticity of the Supply of Labour

The total supply of labour in an economy is not perfectly inelastic as higher wage rates in particular industries are likely to draw extra workers into the labour force and will induce some workers to work longer hours.

LABOUR MARKETS THAT ARE NOT PERFECTLY COMPETITIVE

Labour markets are sometimes imperfect. On the demand side, there are product monopolies and monopsonies (that is, monopoly buyers of labour). On the supply side, there are trade union monopolies which have developed the well known institution of collective bargaining.

In considering such imperfect markets, the essential point to note is that traditional analysis is merely an extension of the principles of the marginal productivity theory. By comparing the wage rates and the levels of employment that would prevail in perfect and imperfect labour markets, we can draw conclusions about the welfare implications of different market structures.

In the following sections, we examine the case of product monopolist and that of a monopolistic buyer of labour. On the supply side, we consider the influence of trade unions and collective bargaining.

• The Hiring Policy of a Profit-Maximising Product Monopolist

A product monopolist faces a downward-sloping demand curve for the good he is producing. This means that if he employs additional workers, he must lower the product price to sell the additional output. As shown in Fig. 10.9, the MRP curve lies below the MVP curve for the same reasons as the monopolist's MR curve lies below the AR curve.

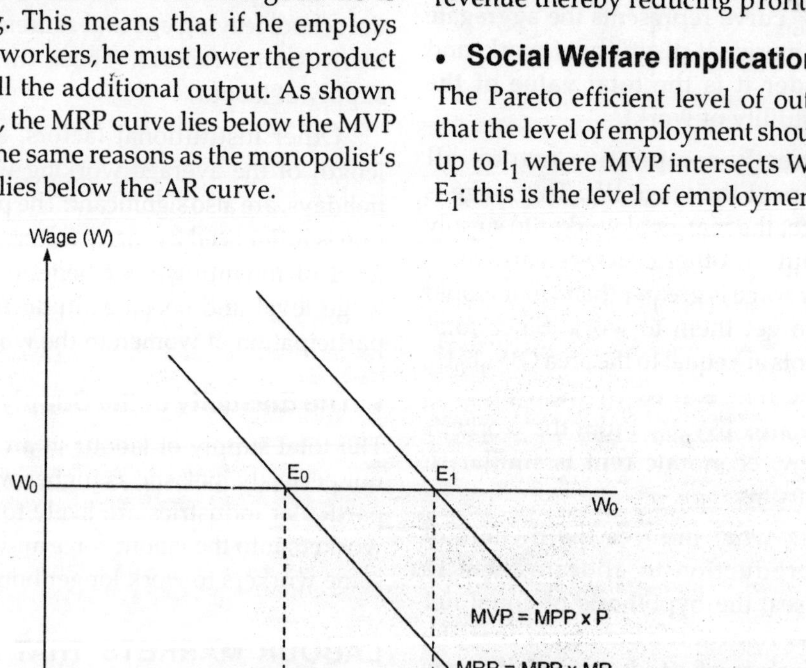

Fig. 10.9: The Hiring Policy of a Profit Maximizing Monopolist

Fig. 10.9 shows that the monopolist is operating in a perfectly competitive labour market and faces an infinitely elastic supply curve of labour, W_0W_0, paying a market wage rate W_0 per hour where a monopolist faces a downward-sloping demand curve represented by the MRP < MVP because monopolist's MR < AR. Thus a monopolist will employ l_0 units of labour as indicated by the intersection of mrp with W_0 at point E_0. Whereas a perfecly competitive business will employ l_0 units represented by the intersection of MVP (=MPP × P) with W_0W_0 at E_1.

Assume that the monopolist is operating in a perfectly competitive labour market and so faces an infinitely elastic supply curve of labour, W_0W_0, paying a fixed wage rate W_0 per hour as in Fig. 10.9. Then, such a monopolist will employ l_0 unit of labour where the MRP intersects with W_0 curve at point E_0. Employment of extra units of labour beyond l_0 would mean that the wage bill would increase by more than the increase in total revenue thereby reducing profit.

• Social Welfare Implication

The Pareto efficient level of output requires that the level of employment should be pushed up to l_1 where MVP intersects W_0W_0 at point E_1: this is the level of employment that would be achieved under conditions of perfect competition in all markets. Thus, monopolist employs less labour than a perfect competition, because the monopolist also restricts output to a level below that is required for Pareto efficiency.

• Monopsonistic Buyer of Labour

Now we consider the case of a monopsonist who sells his product (q) in a perfectly competitive market. By definition, a monopsonist is the only buyer of labour in a particular market and is in a position to influence the prevailing wage rate and the level of employment. The equilibrium level of employment of the monopsonist will be influenced by the marginal cost of labour (MC_L—also known as marginal expenditure {ME}) and the position where MRP = MVP_L. The MC_L has two components. First, the employer can hire additional workers only by offering a higher wage rate. Second, assuming that all workers are paid the same wage, any higher wage paid to attract additional workers will have to be offered also to the existing work force. Thus the MC_L exceeds the average cost of labour (AC_L). In Fig. 10.10 the upward-sloping supply curve of labour S_L is in fact the AC_L: it shows the wage rate that has to be offered to attract a given supply of labour.

Given that the monopsonist is a profit maximizer, the number of worker he is willing to employ will be determined by the intersection of the MC_L curve with the MRP = MVP curve, and he will employ L_0 units of labour. The wage rate W_0 is given by the intersection of the line E_0L_0 with S_L at point F.

In a perfectly competitive case, however, wage rate would be higher at W_c and level of employment L_c.

Social welfare implication is that the employer will pay lower wage than the value of the mpl and employ a smaller work force than that required by Pareto efficiency.

When the buyer of labour has monopsony power, the MC_L or ME curve lies above the AC_L or AE (average expenditure) curve because the business raises the wage rate as more labour is hired. The number of labour purchased is given by L_0, at the intersection of the MC or ME curve and $MRP_L = D_L$ curve. The corresponding wage rate W_0 is lower than the competitive wage W_c.

• Factor Market with Monopoly Power

Just as buyer of labour can have monopsony power, a seller of labour can have monopoly power. There are relatively few pure monpolies in factor markets, but in many

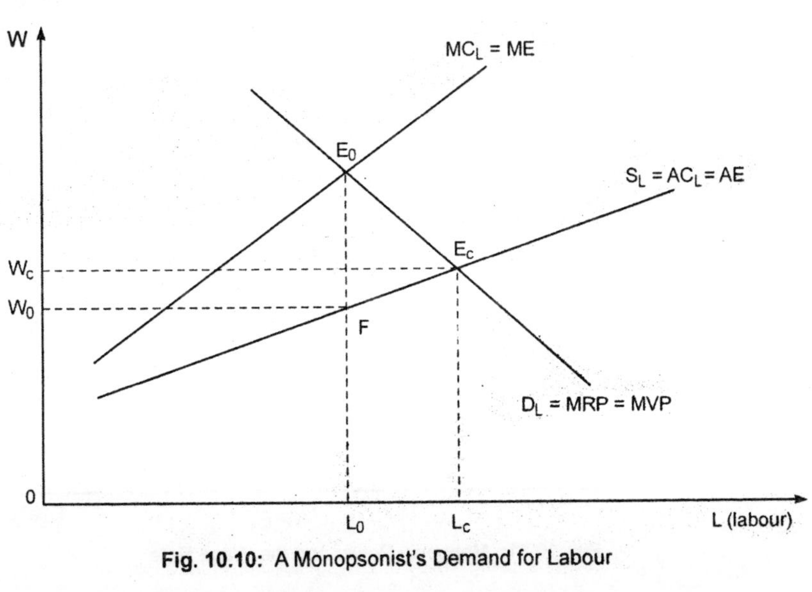

Fig. 10.10: A Monopsonist's Demand for Labour

industries businesses have some monopoly power in the sale of products that other businesses will use as factors of production. The most important example of monopoly power in factor markets involves labour unions, we will concentrate our attention there. We will briefly describe how a monopoly labour union might increase the well-being of its members and affect no unionised workers.

- **Monopoly Power Over the Wage Rate**

Fig. 10.11 shows a demand for labour curve in a market with no monopsony power—it aggregates the MRP of the businesses that compete to buy labour.

The labour supply curve (S_L) describes how union members would supply labour if the union exerted no monopoly power. Then the labour market would be competitive, and L_c workers would be hired for a wage of W_c at point C.

Because of its monopoly power the union can choose any wage rate and the corresponding quantity of labour supplied. If the union wanted to maximize the number of workers hired, it would choose the competitive outcome at C.

Suppose the union wished to obtain a higher than competitive wage. Then, it could restrict its membership to L_1 workers. As a result, businesses would pay a wage rate of W_1. Those union members who work, are better off, while those people who do not work, are worse off.

Is this policy worthwhile? Yes, if the union wishes to maximize the economic rent that its workers receive. By restricting membership, the union would be acting like a business that restricts output to maximize profit. Profit to a business is the revenue it receives less its opportunity costs. Rent to a union represents the wages its members earn in excess of their opportunity cost. To maximize rent, the union must choose the number of workers hired, so that the MR to the union is equal to the extra cost of inducing the worker to work. In Fig. 10.11 this involves choosing the quantity of labour at which the MR crosses the supply curve. We have chosen the wage-employment combination of W_1 and L_1 with this in mind. The area below the labour demand curve, and above the labour supply curve and to the left of L_1, represents the economic rent that workers receive. A rent maximizing policy can benefit non-union workers if they can find

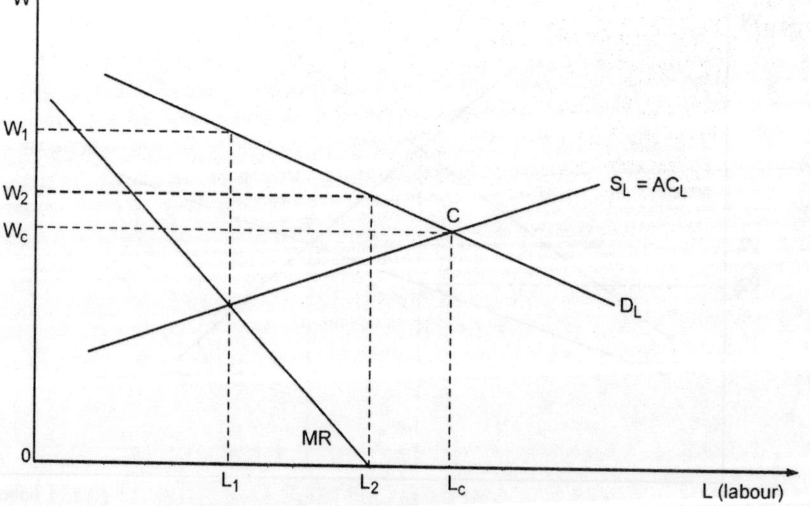

Fig. 10.11: Monopoly Power and the Wage Rate

non-union jobs. However, if these jobs are not available, rent maximization may create too sharp a distinction between winners and losers. An alternative objective is to maximize the aggregate wages that all workers receive. To achieve this goal the number workers hired is increased from L_1 until the MR to the union is equal to zero. As any further employment decreases total wage payments, aggregate wages are maximized when the wage is equal to W_2 and the number of workers is equal to L_2.

When the the seller of labour is a monopolist, it chooses among the points on the buyers demand curve D_L. The seller can maximize the number of workers hired, at L_c, by agreeing that workers will work at wage W_0. The quantity of labour L_1 that maximizes the rent that workers will work at wage W_0. The quantity of labour L_1 that maximizes the rent that employees earn is determined by the intersection of the MR and supply of labour curves; union members will receive a wage rate W_1. Finally, if the union wishes to maximize total wages paid to workers, it should L_2 union members to be employed at wage rate W_2 because the MR to the union will then be zero.

• A Two-Sector Model of Labour Employment

When the union uses its monopoly power to increase its members wages, fewer unionised workers will be hired. It is important to understand what will happen to the non-unionized part of the work force.

Assuming that the total supply of unionised and non-unionised workers is fixed at L_c. Fig. 10.12 shows that the total market supply of labour (union and non-union) is given by S_L(= L_c at W_c).

The demand for labour by businesses in the unionised sector is given by D_u, and the demand in the non-unionized sector by D_{nu}. The total market wage (W_c) the demand for unionized labour is L_{u0} and the demand for non-unionized labour is L_{nu0}, and the total demand for labour is $0L_c$ ($=0L_{u0} + 0L_{n0}$).

Now suppose the union chooses to increase the wage of its members above the competitive wage W_c, to W_u. At this wage, the number of workers hired in the non-unionized sectors, the wage rate in the non-unionized sector adjust until equilibrium is reached. The new wage rate in the non-unionized sector adjust until equilibrium is reached. The new

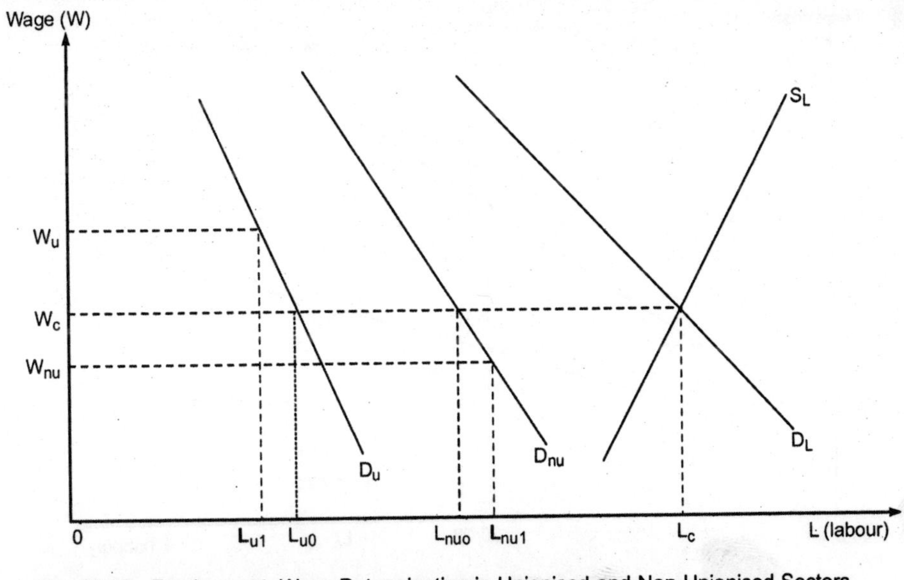

Fig. 10.12: Employment, Wage Determination in Unionised and Non-Unionised Sectors

wage rate in the non-unionized sector needs to fall to W_{nu} to employ those who have joined the non-unionized sector. Once the wage has reached W_{nu} then the jobs lost in the unionized sector ($L_{u1} - L_{u0}$) have been fully replaced by jobs in the non-unionized sector ($L_{no1} - L_{nu0}$). Hence L_c now equals ($0L_{u1} + 0L_{nu1}$).

This shows an adverse effect of union strategy of raising wages; non-unionized wages fall. Unless the demand for labour is perfectly inelastic, union workers are helped at the expense of non-union workers.

When the monopolistic union raises the wage in the unionized sector of the economy from W_0 to W_u, employment in that sector falls, as shown in the diagram (from L_{u0} to L_{u1}). Since the total supply of labour is given by S_L, the wage in the non-unionized sector must fall from W_0 to W_{nu}, as given by the demand curve D_{nu}.

- **Bilateral Monopoly in the Labour Market**

Bilateral monopoly is a market in which a monopolist sells to a monopsonist. In a labour market, bilateral monopoly arises when representatives from a union and companies that hire a type of worker meet to negotiate wages. Fig. 10.13 shows a bilateral bargaining situation. The S_L curve represents the supply curve for skilled worker, and the business's demand curve for labour is given by D_L(=MRP).

If the union had no monopoly power, the monopsonist would make its hiring decision on the basis of its marginal expenditure curve ME(=MC_L), choosing to hire 20 workers and paying them £10 per hour, where the MRP_L = ME of the business.

The seller of labour faces a demand curve D_L that describes the business's hiring plans as the wage rate varies. The union chooses a point on the demand curve that maximizes its members' wages. As the wage paid to all workers falls when the number hired increases, the MR curve describes the additional wages that the union gets for its members when the number hired increases.

The supply curve of labour (S_L) tells the union the minimum payment necessary to encourage workers to offer their labour. Suppose the union wishes to maximize the economic rent of its members and the union in this case views the supply curve as the marginal cost of labour. To maximize the rent that is earned, the union chooses a wage £19 which makes MR = MC. At £19, the business would hire 22 workers. This result depends

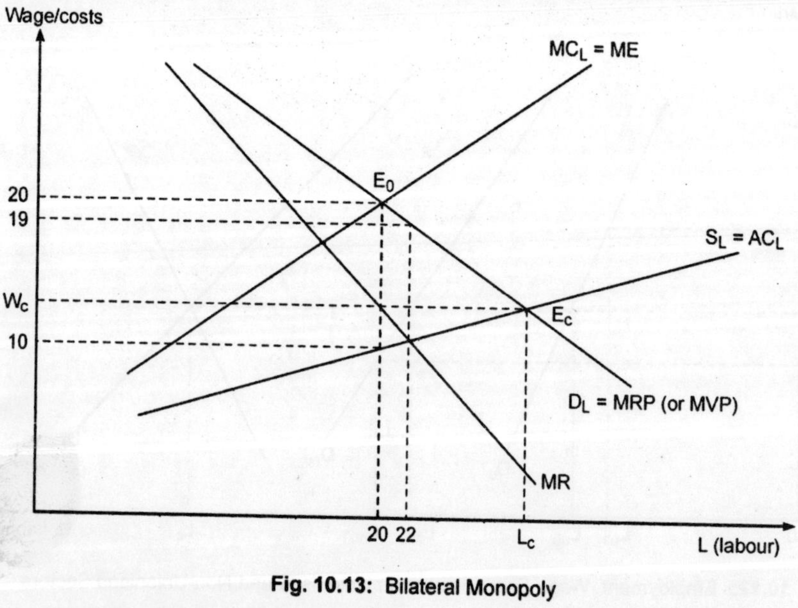

Fig. 10.13: Bilateral Monopoly

on the bargaining strategies of the two parties. If the union can make a credible threat to hire non-union labour, they might secure a wage closer to £10. If both parties can make credible threats, the resulting agreement might be close to the competitive outcome of about £15 as the figure shows.

Bilateral Monopoly: When the labour market is a Monopolist-Monopsonist situation, the wage rate that is negotiated will be between a high of £19, determined by the MR and S_L curves, and a low of £10, determined by the intersection of D_L and MC_L as the figure shows.

• Do Labour Markets Clear?

So far we have assumed that wages are flexible. The equilibrium wage equates demand and supply of labour. Now we consider other issues:

• Minimum Wage Agreements

Fig. 10.14 shows the market demand curve for labour D_L and the supply curve for labour S_L for a particular perfectly competitive industry. Free market equilibrium is at C where the wage is W_c and employment is L_c. For skilled workers, the equilibrium wage is W_2 which is greater than the minimum wage at W_1. The minimum wage at W_1 is irrelevant to skilled workers. Suppose the minimum wage is W_1, above the free-market equilibrium wage W_0. At W_1 there is excess supply of labour L_2–L_1.

Since the the business cannot be forced to hire workers they do not need, employment is L_1 and the number of workers L_1 to L_2 who would like to work are involuntarily unemployed. Workers are defined as being involuntarily unemployed if they are willing to work at the going wage but cannot find jobs.

A national minimum wage may exceed the free market equilibrium wage for low skilled occupations. If so, those workers lucky enough to find jobs get higher wages than before but the total amount of employment is lower than the free market equilibrium. Minimum wage may explain involuntary unemployment among low skilled workers.

Free market equilirbium occurs at the wage W_c and quantity of employment L_c. A minimum wage of W_1 is irrelevant. However, a minimum wage of W_1 is greater than W_c and will restrict the actual quantity of employment to L_1, leaving a quantity L_1 to L_2 of workers involuntarily unemployed. They would like to work at this wage rate but cannot find jobs.

• Trade Unions

A strong trade union may act in a similar way, as Fig. 10.14 shows. if a union in an industry

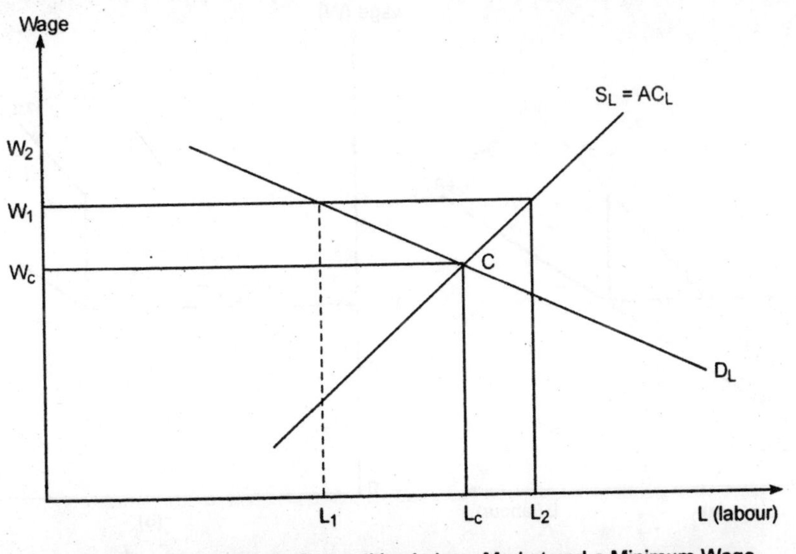

Fig. 10.14: A Perfectly Competitive Labour Market and a Minimum Wage

forces businesses to pay a wage W_1, above the free market equilibrium wage W_c, the result is fewer jobs in the industry. By raising the wage from W_c to W_1, the union reduces employment from L_c to L_1. How unions trade off higher wages for lower employment would be discussed later on. The effect is already clear here. If the union chooses a wage W_1, the resulting unemployment is collectively voluntary but may be individually involuntary for the unlucky union members who lose their jobs.

- **Trade Unions and a Monopsonistic Industry**

The introduction of collective bargaining (or a minimum wage) into a monopsonistic labour market will change the supply curve of labour. Consider Fig. 10.15(a) and assume that the wage rate is set at W_u either through the introduction of collective bargaining or through the introduction of a minimum wage. Then:

Up to point 'x' the wage = the average cost of labour = MC_L.

Below point 'x' (W_u) both the average cost and the MC_L no longer exists.

The new average cost curve is W_u-x-S_L

The new MC_L is W_u-x-y-MC_L

The 'new' MC_L and AC_L are shown in Fig. 10.15(b).

Now consider Fig. 10.16. Without the introduction of collective bargaining or a minimum wage the profit maximizing level of employment would be L_0 and the wage paid would be W_0.

If now, collective bargaining or a minimum wage (W_u) is introduced, the MC_L and the AC_L are W_u-x-y-MC_L and W_u-x-S_L respectively. The new, profit maximizing, level of employment wage (W_0) and employment is higher than it was previously (L_0) at L_u. Unlike the competitive case both the wage and employment are higher.

To say more we need to discuss how decisions are made within unions.

- **Scale Economics**

Involuntary unemployment may reflect scale economics and imperfect competition. These create entry barriers and prevent new businesses from joining an industry.

- **Insiders and Outsiders**

The previous explanation emphasizes entry barriers for new business. Insiders-outsiders

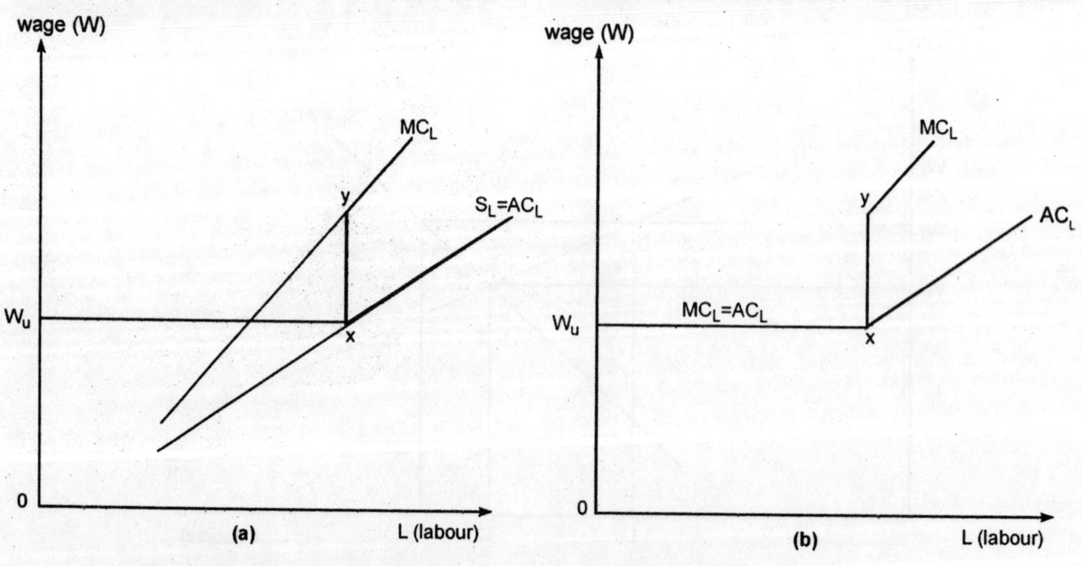

Fig. 10.15: A Monopsonistic Labour Market and Collective Bargaining

theories emphasize barriers to entering employment in existing businesses. Insiders have jobs and are represented in wage bargaining. Outsiders do not have jobs and are unrepresented in wage bargaining.

Entry barriers may have many forms. It is costly to advertise for workers, interview them, evaluate what sorts of jobs they should be offered, train them to activities specific to the business, build up teamwork and allow new employees to master their new jobs. They are innocent entry barriers.

But existing workers (insiders) may also erect strategic barriers to entry by outsiders, even without the pressure of the formal trade unions. For example, insiders may threaten to create industrial disruption if too many outsiders are taken too quickly or if outsiders offer to work at a lower wage than that being paid to insiders.

When such entry barriers confront outsiders, the insiders can raise their own wage above that for which outsiders would be willing to work without inducing a spate of hiring of outsiders.

- **Efficiency Wage**

So far, we have assumed that information is cheap to come by. In fact, businesses face two problems: it is hard to tell whether a job application will be from a productive worker, and hard to monitor whether workers shirk after being employed. Given the cost of evaluating new workers, and after monitoring their performance on the job, what is the policy for a business? The efficient wage theory argues that it is profitable for businesses to pay existing workers a wage above their transfer earnings. Efficiency wages are higher wages that raise productivity through their incentive effect. First, suppose workers quit their job if they get better wage elsewhere. If businesses pay a wage that is the average of that faced by productive and unproductive workers, it is the productive workers who are likely to get better offers elsewhere and quit. Eventually, the business will be left only with the unproductive workers. Paying a wage premium helps retain best quality workers.

Second, when workers shirk on the job they may get caught. Once caught, they are sacked. How big is the penalty for being caught? It is the difference between the current wage and what the worker gets in unemployment benefit or in subsequent jobs. The higher the wage paid by the existing employer, the larger the penalty of being caught shirking. To increase the penalty and to reduce the incentive to shirk, businesses pay existing workers a higher wage than on average is necessary to get them to supply their labour.

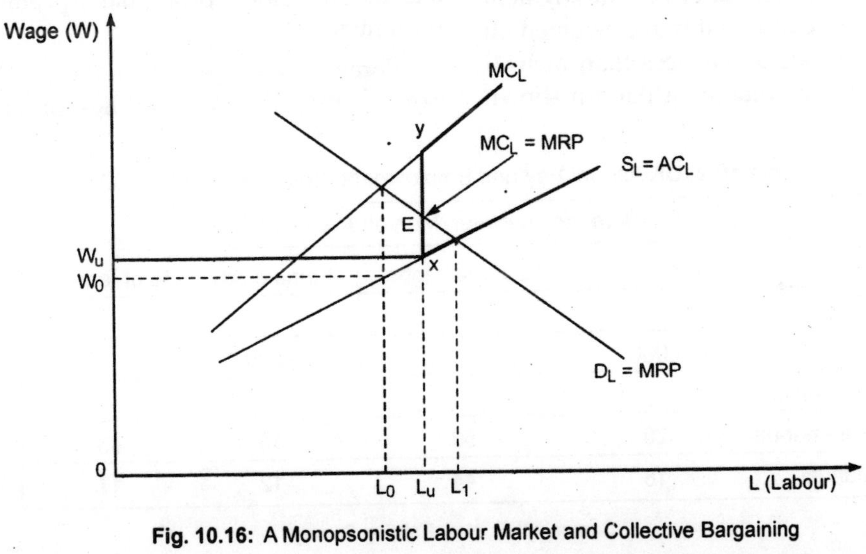

Fig. 10.16: A Monopsonistic Labour Market and Collective Bargaining

Again, the implication is that some workers may be involuntarily unemployed. They may be willing to work for wages at or below those paid to existing workers, but have little chance of getting a job at such wages.

Minimium wage agreements, trade union power, scale economics, insider-outsider distinctions, and efficiency wages are possible explanations for insufficient wage flexibility in the short-run to keep the labour market in continuous equilibrium. Whether the labour market is always in equilibrium, and the length of time for which disequilibria persist, are questions that require answers.

• Discrimination between Different Types of Labour

It is well-known that women and ethnic minority labour are discriminated against in the labour market.

Some jobs pay more than others. Differences in average earning of different groups can arise for two distinct reasons. Different groups may get different shares of the high-paying jobs, or may get paid different amounts for doing the same job.

Table 10.2 shows full time weekly earnings in 2000 in different occupations, and the pattern of male and female employment. Few women do manual jobs, most do secretarial or selling jobs. Yet the pattern of employment is not the major cause that makes women on average earn £7000 a year less than men. If women had the employment pattern shown for men in table, the average earnings for women would hardly change. Women earn roughly two-third less than men whatever job they do.

Table 10.2 deals only in broad job categories. Within each, there will be many levels. Table 10.2 either implies that women get paid less than men for the same job, however narrowly the job is defined, or that men get promoted and trained faster within these broad job categories. The percentage of women in professional and managerial occupation is comparable with that of men; but few women are on the boards of major companies.

Why do businesses promote and train women more slowly? Suppose a business bears some of the cost of training. The business makes a hard-nosed investment decision. Assuming men and women are of inherently equal ability and educational attainment, it costs the business same to train either sex.

Suppose businesses believe that women are more likely than men to interrupt, or even terminate, their careers at a young age. As a matter of fact, women are likely to have babies and discontinue their careers. Businesses may conclude that the present value of the extra productivity benefits in the future is lower from women than men simply because many women might work fewer years in the future. It is therefore, more profitable to promote and train men.

Some women plan to have a full-time career, either remaining childless or returning

Table 10.2: UK Annual Pay and Employment (Full-time adults) 2000

Differences between Men and Women				
	Male pay	% of male jobs	Female pay	% of female
Jobs				
	£000		£000	
Occupation:				
Non-manual	28	56	19	83
Manual	18	44	12	17

Source: ONS, New Earning Survey.

to work almost immediately after children are born. It would make sense for businesses to invest in such people. How is it possible for a business to know whether young women are planning to stay? Asking such a question is pointless because young women have no incentive to tell the truth.

Suppose businesses offer young workers the choice between a relatively flat wage-earning profile and a steep profile that begins at a lower wage but pays a much higher wage later in worker's career. In this way, businesses can make the two profiles of equal value to someone planning a lifetime career. The sacrifice (low wages) is recouped with interest later (high wages). Someone planning to quit the labour force, say at the age of 30, will never opt for the steeper profile.

Wage earning profiles may induce recruits to reveal their true career plans. If women or any other group with a high risk of quitting at a young age, accept the steeper profile, the business can embark on training with some confidence that its investment will not be wasted. Some businesses may still try to pay female workers less than male workers who are identical in every respect, including the risk of quitting. This is overt discrimination.

Discrimination is the different treatment of people whose relevant characteristics are identical. Society may discriminate against women in more subtle ways. Our analysis suggests that paternity leave for fathers, the provision of creches for working parents, or a greater acceptance of part-time working by both sexes, would reduce incentive for hard-nosed businesses to decide to favour the training of men.

Whether or not society wishes to organize its work and home life, no such principle is justified on matter of economics alone.

• Access to Education

Some businesses may treat both sexes equally, but still pay men more than women because men have more educational qualification than women. The case of pay differentiation by sex then lies not in the labour market but in education.

Table 10.3 shows full-time and part-time students in 3 types of educational institutions: further education, university undergraduates, and postgraduates. In 1971 male students substantially outnumbered female students in all forms of further and higher education. By 1998 the gender gap had subsided.

Table 10.3: UK Students 1971-98 (thousands)

	Male		Female	
	1971	1998	1971	1998
Further education:				
Full-time	116	532	95	533
Part-time	891	1257	630	1721
Undergraduate:				
Full-time	241	528	173	599
Part-time	127	229	19	305
Postgraduate:				
Full-time	33	87	10	80
Part-time	15	130	3	124

Source: ONS: Social Trend

Nevertheless, current data on earning patterns reflect that past inequalities in education cast a long shadow over today's job market.

Racial Discrimination: The same general principles apply to racial discrimination and earning differences between white and non-white. Many studies confirm the data that, on an average, non-whites earn less than whites.

Wage earning profiles for non-white men are much flatter than those for white men. White men are much more likely to achieve steady promotion and rising earnings. In turn, this provides an incentive for whites to do more difficult jobs where training and experience are important. Part of the problem for non-white men lies in the type of the education they receive. The pay-off to education is often low for non-whites who attend a typical inner city school; whether this reflects lack of resources or the disadvantageous background of many people, businesses may believe that these potential workers will have lower productivity and will be harder to train. Hence, they get less training. A large proportion of non-white workers are restricted to unskilled and low-paid jobs.

Table 10.4 shows that Muslim women from Pakistan and Bangladesh have low participation rates in the labour force. This reflects a different willingness to supply their labour. However, most of the minority groups have unemployment rates well above those of majority groups.

Again, it is hard to draw a line between discrimination in the labour market and elsewhere in society. Businesses have to act in the interest of their shareholders. So long as businesses perceive that different groups of workers already have different characteristics, or will behave differently during their working life, businesses will wish to treat different groups differently. Unless society removes these differences in characteristics, opportunities and behaviour of different groups of workers, the eradication of blatant racism or sexism will be difficult and it will be nearly impossible to remove the pay differences as well.

Table 10.4: Ethnic Groups, UK 2001

	Participation rate (%)		Unemployment rate (%)	
	Men	Women	Men	Women
White	85	75	6	4
Blacks	76	65	17	13
Indian	83	66	8	8
Pakistan/Bangladesh	69	31	16	19

Source: ONS, Labour Market Trends

QUESTIONS

1. (a) Why can a top golfer earn more in a weekend than a university professor in a year?
   (b) Why can students of economics expect to earn more than equally smart students studying philosophy?
2. A worker can earn £20,000 a year for the next 33 years. Alternatively, the worker can take 3 years off to go on a course where fees are £10,000 per year. If the interest rate is zero, what future income must the worker then have, to make the investment in education profitable?
3. If the EU membership raises competition between European businesses, what is likely to happen to wages of European workers? Why? Would it be appropriate for European unions then to amalgamate?
4. Consider the effects on the overall level of income inequality of each of the following:
   (a) an increasing participation of women in the labour force as many women work in the full-time jobs in the workplace,
   (b) increasing use by employers of guest workers from low-income countries,
   (c) increasing number of minority groups studying law and medicine,
   (d) cuts in the standard rate of income tax, together with elimination of personal income tax deduction.
5. A recent Wall Street Journal asks, 'why do football players earn millions of pounds for their negligible contribution to society while major contributors—such as teachers, policemen, firemen and so—earn barely enough to survive? Answer this question in detail.

ANSWERS

1. (a) Top golfers are in scarce supply, but in big demand.
   (b) Economics students have more human capital relevant to high paying jobs.
2. Lose £30,000 while taking training. Future salary of £23,000 for 30 years repays this investment of human capital.
3. Wages fall if less monopoly profit for unions to chase after. Larger unions would help restore workers' bargaining power but might prevent gains from competition being realized.
4. (a) It depends on the sort of households from which women workers are coming If they are primarily coming from low-income households then it would be likely to reduce inequality, as it would boost incomes in the lower part of the income distribution. However, if the income increase is coming from partners who are already earning a reasonable income then it will tend to extend the existing inequality. In practice, in the UK, at present, there does seem to be a trend towards greater inequality, with families dividing into two: no-one working family or two or more working family.
   (b) This is likely to increase inequality in the host country: it will add new individuals and households at the bottom of the income scale, which will increase the variance of income.

(c) This can be argued either way. If we assume that minority groups tend to have lower income, the answer depends on whether those individuals who become doctors and lawyers end up moving above the middle income range; then this will reduce income inequality. The answer also depends on whether they displace members of the majority groups from these two well paid professions; if so, then what the latter will end up with? Alternatively, they may increase the overall number of lawyers and doctors, which will tend to reduce salaries in these professions and reduce inequality. Finally, the implicit assumption, that the minority groups have lower income to start with, may not be true in all cases, at least for some ethnic groups in the UK, in which case inequality is likely to increase with more of them entering law and medicine.

(d) The cut in the standard rate of income tax will tend to increase inequality, as the tax system is progressive. Personal income tax deduction is mainly for work-related purposes (membership of the professional bodies, buying books by academics and so on) and is likely to benefit high income groups more. Thus, the two effects are likely to offset each other, and which one, of them dominates will be an empirical matter.

5. The main reason for the high salaries of football players is their high marginal revenue product; they are worth a lot to their employers, who know very well that their fans will pay well to see the players. Very few people have their particular talent, so employers are in a relatively weak position; the players have monopoly power, and the clubs' monopsonist power is reduced. This is opposite to the case of the teachers and the other occupations in the question, where there is a single employer and a large number of employees-union; bargaining may improve their position. Finally, it is worth noting that the major contributors are in fact making collective contribution: high value is placed on teachers or ambulance service as a whole, rather than on the contribution of a single teacher or ambulance personnel.

APPENDIX 10A.1

The Relationship between the Product (goods and services) Markets and the Factor (labour) Markets.

1. The Relationship between a Perfectly Competitive Labour Market and a Perfectly Competitively Product Market.

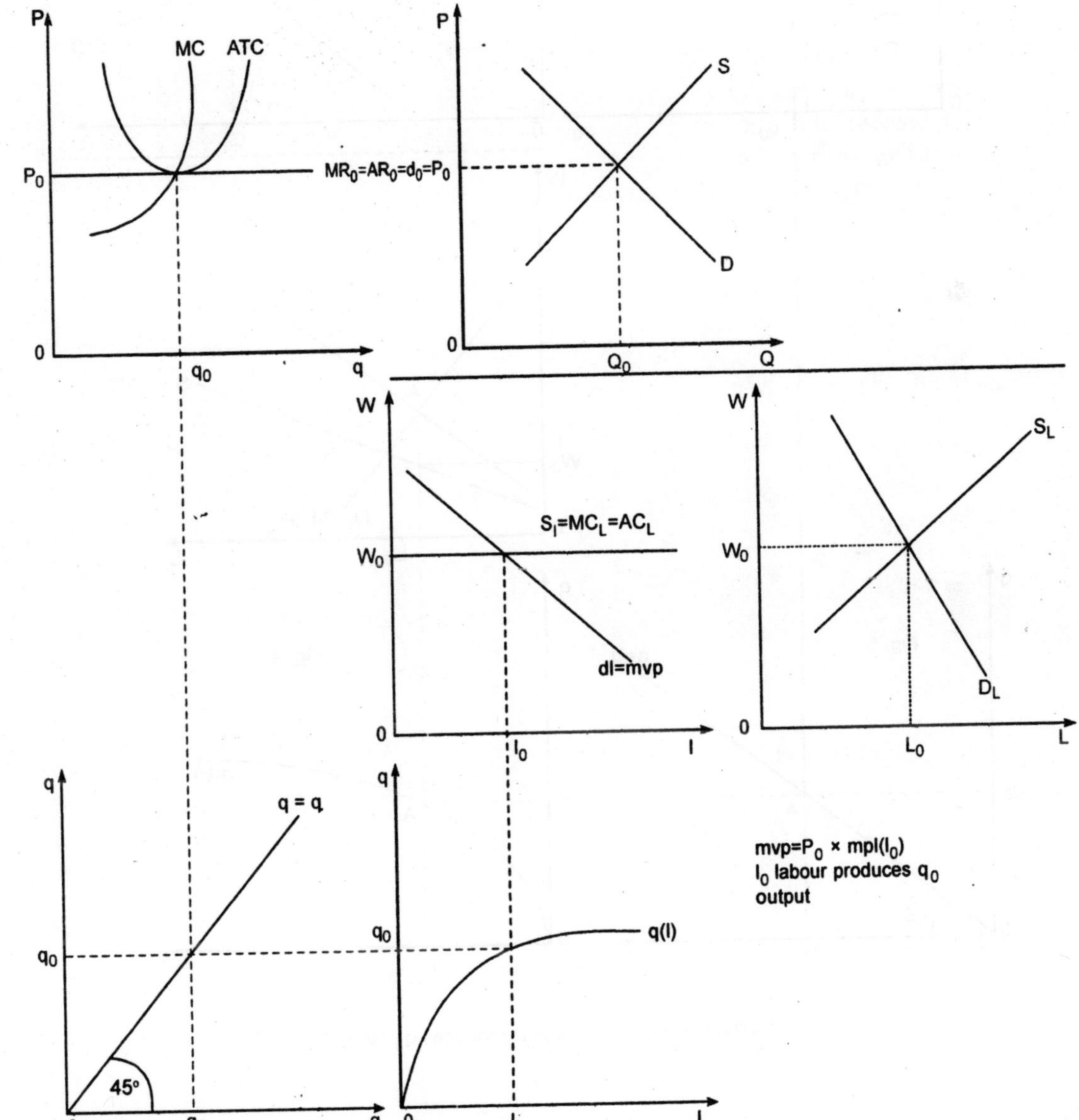

2. The Relationship between a Perfectly Competitive Product Market and a Monopsonistically Competitive Labour Market.

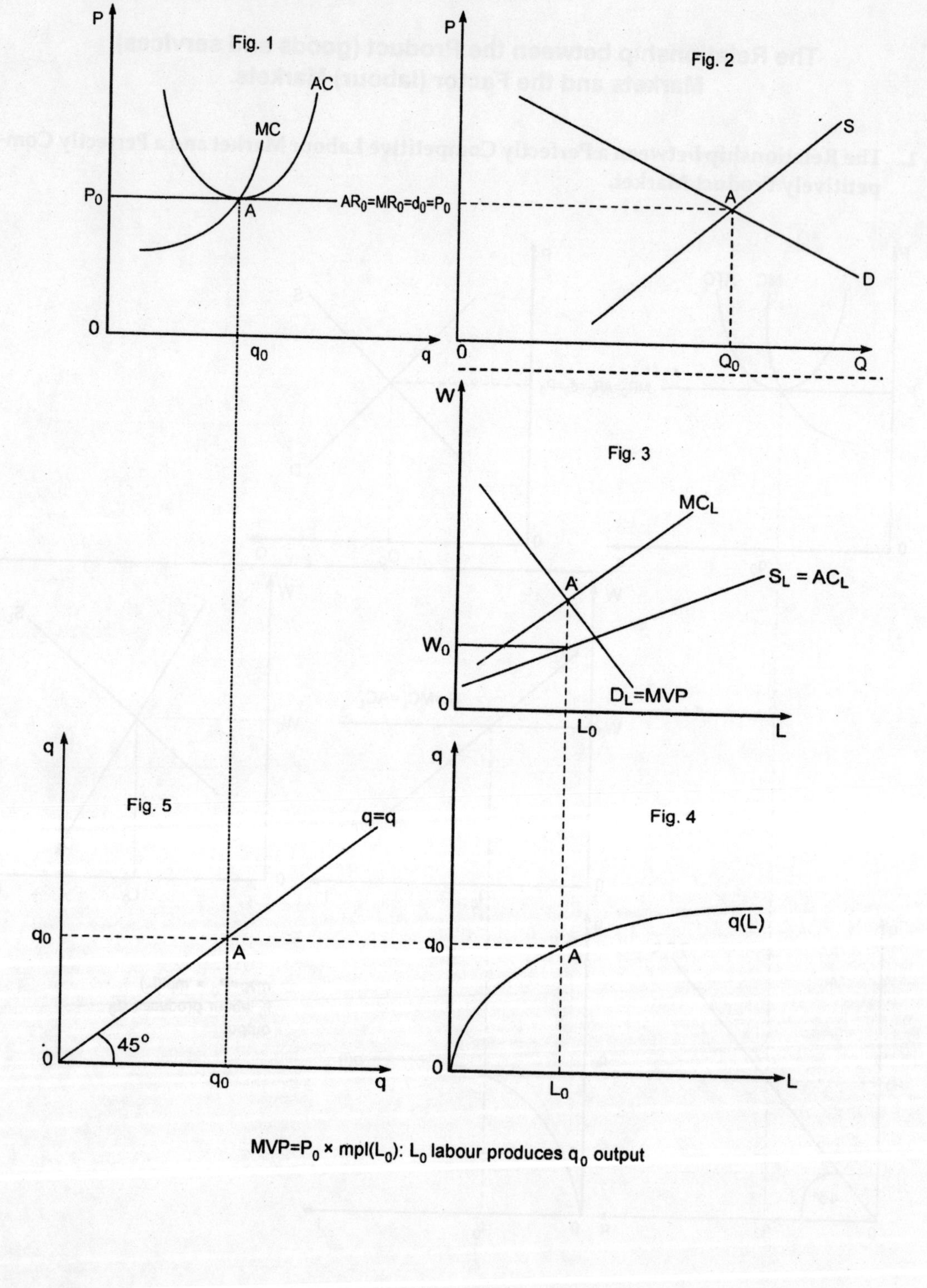

$MVP=P_0 \times mpl(L_0)$: L_0 labour produces q_0 output

3. The Relationship between a Perfectly Competitive Labour Market and a Non-Competitive Product Market.

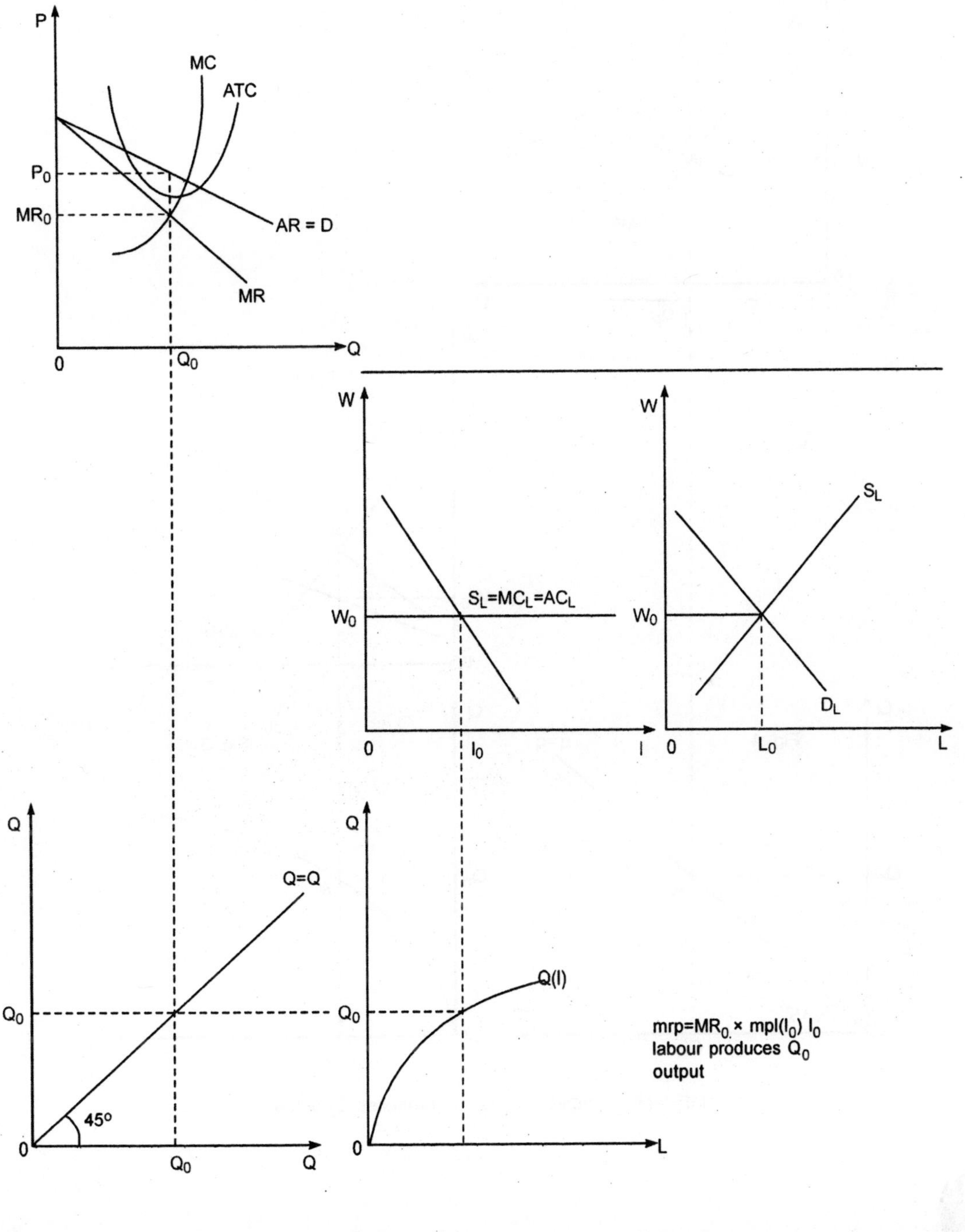

4. The Relationship between a Monopoly Product Market and a Monopsonistically Competitive Labour Market.

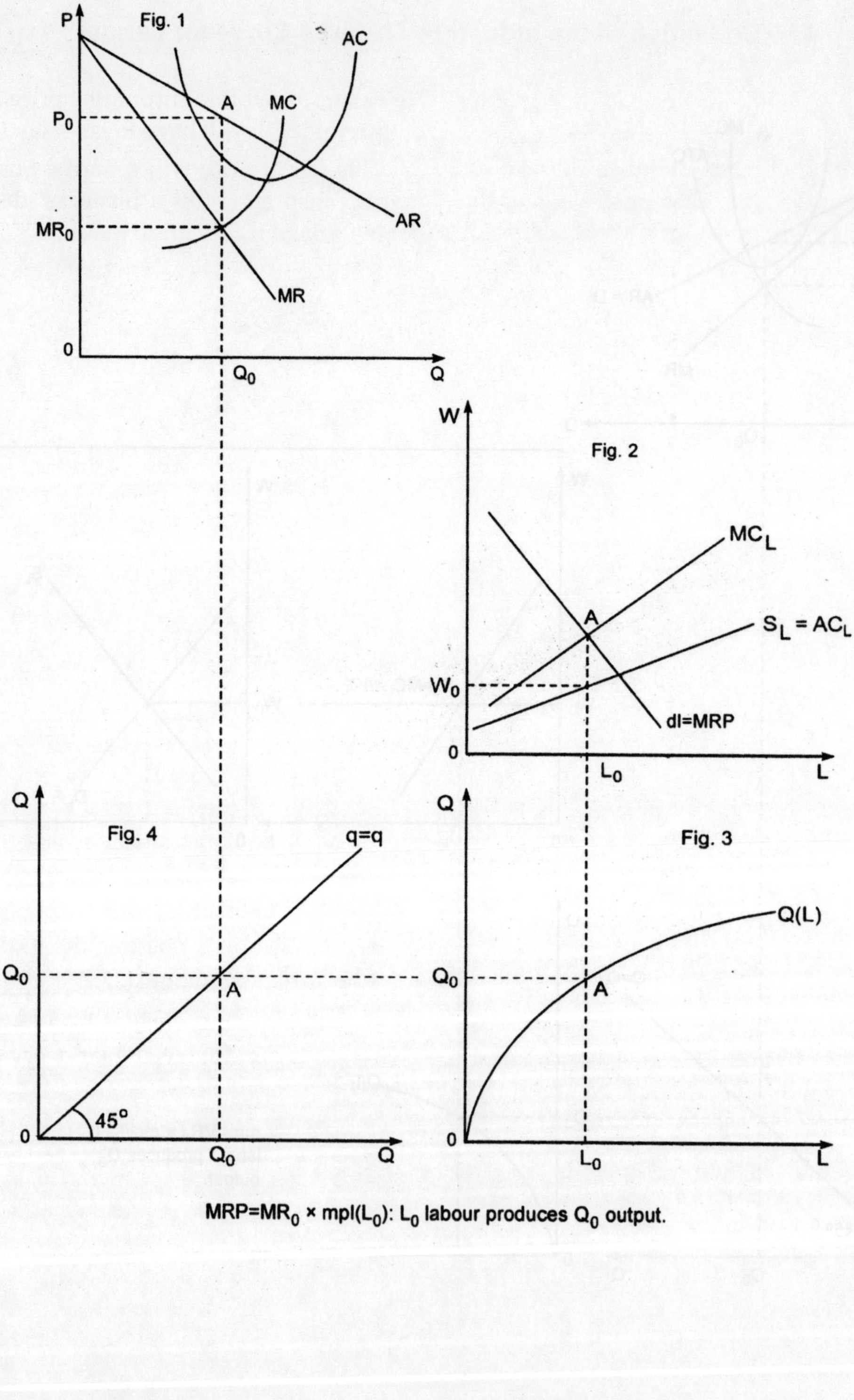

$MRP = MR_0 \times mpl(L_0)$: L_0 labour produces Q_0 output.

APPENDIX 10A.2

The Derivation of the Industry's Demand Curve for Labour

$MVP_0(P_0)$ is the horizontal sum of each business' mvp of labour (or mrp of labour) schedule {$dl(P_0)$} when the price charged for output (q or Q) is P_0. Each business, and the industry as a whole, set the mvp of labour (or mrp of labour) equal to W_0. Hence E_0 is a point on the industry's demand curve for labour (LD). If there are 40 firms in the industry then $L_0 = 40 \times l_0$.

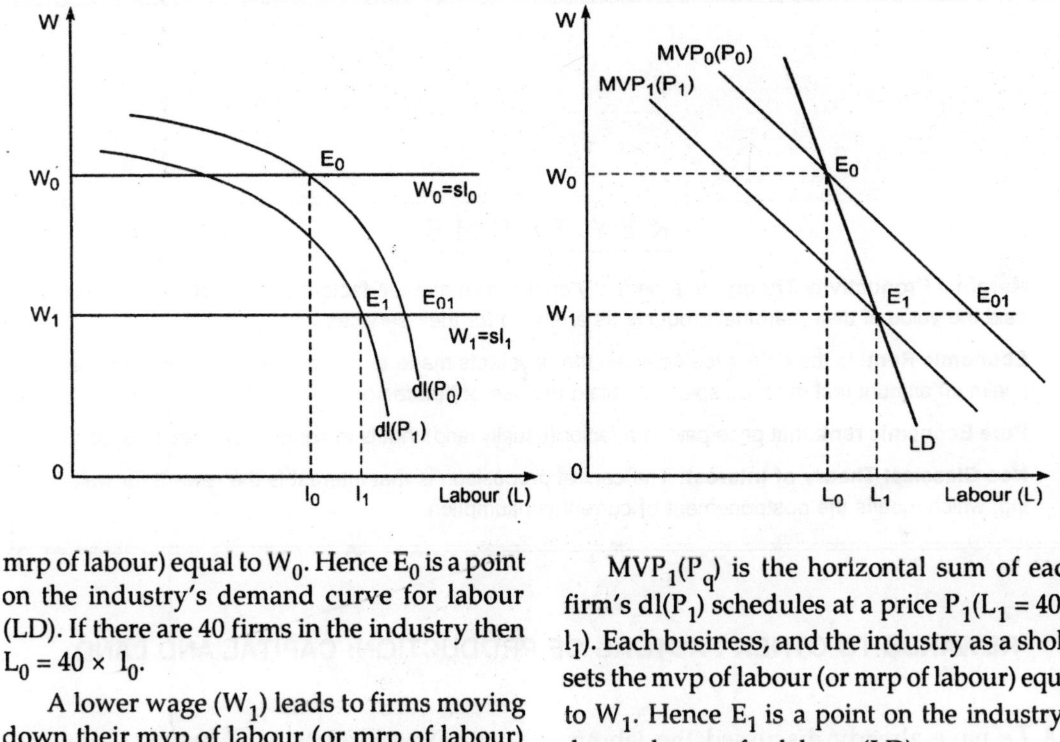

A lower wage (W_1) leads to firms moving down their mvp of labour (or mrp of labour) schedules to E_{01}. (At W_1 each firm will wish to employ more labour and produce more output (q[or Q]) shifting the industry's supply curve for goods and services to the right). However, to sell this output, the price of the output (q[or Q]) will have to fall—say to P_1.

This fall in price will reduce a business' mvp or mrp and shift a business' demand curve for labour {$dl(P_0)$} to the left.

$MVP_1(P_q)$ is the horizontal sum of each firm's $dl(P_1)$ schedules at a price $P_1(L_1 = 40 \times l_1)$. Each business, and the industry as a shole, sets the mvp of labour (or mrp of labour) equal to W_1. Hence E_1 is a point on the industry's demand curve for labour (LD).

Joining all points such as E_0 and E_1 will give LD, the industry demand curve for labour.

CHAPTER 11

THE THEORY OF DISTRIBUTION—OTHER FACTORS

KEY TERMS

Marginal Productivity Theory: In a perfectly competitive market, factors of production would be paid the value of their marginal products as a reward for their services.

Economic Rent: Is the difference between the payments made to a factor of production and the minimum amount that must be spent to obtain the use of that factor.

Pure Economic rent: that price paid to a factor (usually land) that is in completely inelastic supply.

Neo-Classical Theory of Interest: The central proposition is that interest is the reward for waiting, which means the postponement of current consumption.

REWARDS TO OTHER FACTORS OF PRODUCTION: CAPITAL AND LAND

We have already discussed the labour market in isolation and considered how wages are determined in a modern market economy. We now wish to discuss in greater detail the determination of the relative shares of the total national income going to the respective owners of the three factors of production: labour, capital and land (the factor of production that nature supplies). Economists are interested in these distributive shares because they represent the most important measure of the welfare of the owners of factors.

First, we wish to develop a general theoretical approach to distribution. Then, with its help consider the particular rewards going to land and capital. The general theoretical approach focuses attention on: (a) Ricardo's theory of distribution; (b) the marginal productivity theory of distribution; (c) the relation between distributive shares and technical progress; (d) we then investigate theories of rent, interest and profit and also consider briefly the controversy between the two Cambridges over the reward to capital, and finally examine the Ricardian and Marxian views of the falling tendency of the rate of profit.

However, the most important point to remember that there is no universally accepted view of why different factors of production get what they receive in payment. This is so because the total value of goods and services produced is a result of the cooperation and collaboration between productive resources. The rewards to factors, thus, are explicitly or implicitly mingled with property rights which, in turn, are institutionally determined. As a result, a Pareto efficient distribution of income based on given property rights may not be the income distribution pattern which maximizes society's welfare. As we have already noted that a Pereto efficient allocation of resources can co-exist with large scale poverty which, from the standpoint of social welfare maximization, may be considered to be undesirable.

Economists have developed two main approaches to distribution:

1. a functional distribution approach and
2. a personal distribution approach.

According to the former, the forces of demand and supply determine the price of a factor of production just like they determine the price of a commodity. The marginal productivity theory has sprung up from this approach.

In the later approach, empshasis is placed on the actual size of the income accruing to individuals and families and so is concerned with measuring the inequalities of income and wealth.

• Ricardo's Theory of Distribution

David Ricardo identified three classes in society—Landlords, labourers and capitalists who receive rents, wages and profit respectively. Rents and wages, according to Ricardo, are part of the costs which capitalist must meet so as to be able to carry on production; whatever is left over is the capitalists' profit. Thus, profit is a residual.

The main idea of Ricardo's theory is that the demand for investment in the production of commodities comes from the capitalist which is stimulated by the desire to earn profit. Any increase in investment, increases the demand for labour and, through competition, pushes up the wage rate above what Ricardo called its 'subsistence level'. This subsistence wage level was defined by Ricardo as the wage that finances a family's customary standard of living. An increases the supply of labour thus decreases wages back to the subsistence level. So, in Ricardo's model, the share of wages in the total national income can, in the long-run, be no higher than that required for mere subsistence.

It also follows that with a rising population the demand for land will increase and so tend to raise rents. Payment of these rising rents by capitalists will reduce their profit. Since, in the long-run, wages are kept equal to the subsistence level, it follows that capitalists will experience a falling rate of profit because of ever-rising rents.

• The Marginal Productivity Theory Again

We know that in perfectly competitive markets factors of production would be paid the value of their marginal products as a reward for their services by profit-maximizing businesses. The neo-classical school argued that all factors made some contribution to production and that it was just that they should receive payment equal to their marginal contributions. This was quite different from the view of Marx who believed that labour was the source of production and so should receive the total value of output as payment; anything less he regarded as capitalist exploitation of labour.

• Technical Progress and Income Distribution

Economists argue that when technical changes occur, these changes can bring about alteration in the relative shares of land, labour and

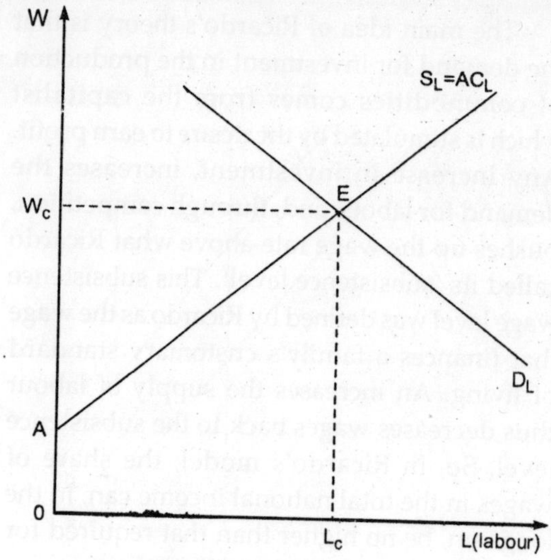

Fig. 11.1: Economic Rent

capital. Marx was one of the first economists to argue that labour-saving technology would lead to rising unemployment, a decline in the share of wages and conflict between labour and capital.

Broadly speaking, technical progress can be either neutral or non-neutral. Neutral technical progress is that which leaves the ratio, in which labour and capital are employed, unchanged and so does not alter the wage-profit ratio. Non-neutral technical progress could be either labour-saving or capital-saving. It is often argued that labour-saving technical progress tends to lower the share of labour in the national income, whilst capital saving technical progress tends to lower the share of capital. It is important to remember that a labour-saving technical progress may actually depress the share of profit and raise the share of wages through the law of diminishing returns. It may also be possible that as industries become more capital intensive, larger units of capital per head of the labour force are employed. This implies greater labour productivity and a decline in the marginal productivity of capital (the extra output produced by an extra unit of capital $\{\Delta q/\Delta k\}$), where k is capital. As a result, we should expect a rise in wages and a fall in profit.

• Economic Rent—The Reward to Land

The concept of economic rent helps to explain how factor markets work. Economic rent is the difference between the payments made to a factor of production and the minimum amount that must be spent to obtain the use of that factor. Fig. 11.1 explains the concept of economic rent as applied to a competitive labour market. The equilibrium price of labour is W_c, and the quantity of labour supplied is L_c. The labour supply curve is the upward-sloping function S_L, and the demand for labour is the downward-sloping schedule D_L. The labour supply curve tells us how much labour will be supplied at each wage rate, the minimum expenditure needed to employ L_c units of labour is given by the area $0AEL_c$.

In perfectly competitive markets, all workers are paid the wage W_c. This wage is required to get the marginal worker to supply her/his labour, but all other intra-marginal workers earn rents because their wage is greater than the wage that would be needed to get them to work. Since total wage payments are equal to the aea $0W_cEL_c$, the economic rent earned by labour is given by the area AW_cE. From the worker's point of view, economic rent is similar to consumer surplus. In the labour market the economic rent is the excess of wages paid above the minimum amount needed to be paid to hire workers. The equilibrium wage is given by E, at the intersection of the labour supply and demand curves. Because the supply curve (S_L) is upward sloping, some workers would have accepted jobs for a wage less then W_c and the area AW_cE is the economic rent received by all workers.

• Rent and Land

Rent arises from the inelasticity of supply. When the supply is perfectly elastic, economic rent would be zero. The supply of land is inelastic. Thus, the supply curve of land is vertical as in Fig. 11.2. That is to say, no matter what the prevailing market price for land, the quantity supplied will remain the same. The term rent has been associated with the payment for the use of land.

When the supply of land (SLn) is perfectly inelastic, the price of land is determined at the point of intersection of the demand curve and the supply curve, and the entire value is economic rent. When demand is D_0, the economic rent per acre is given by R_0 and when demand increases to D_1, the rent increases to R_1.

Thus, no matter what the price is, the quantity and quality of resource will remain at its current levels, and there is pure economic rent only. We defined pure economic rent as the price paid to land that is in completely inelastic supply. It is also a term used for any payment in excess of that needed to keep a particular factor in its current use. This is different from common use of the rent which includes a payment for the use of land as we pay wages for the use of labour.

Ricardo used rent as a payment for the "original and indestructible quantities of soil" on the assumption that land has only one use—that of growing foodstuff. Thus, he pointed out that the supply of land is fixed—its supply price is zero. It is the community's demand for food that determines the demand for land. In other words, the demand for land is a derived demand. Fig. 11.2 shows the perfect inelasticity of the supply of land, SLn intersecting with the community's demand for land, D_0. The equilibrium price of land is R_0. Now, suppose, that the demand for land increases to D_1. This will raise the equilibrium rent from R_0 to R_1. Thus, rent is demand determined.

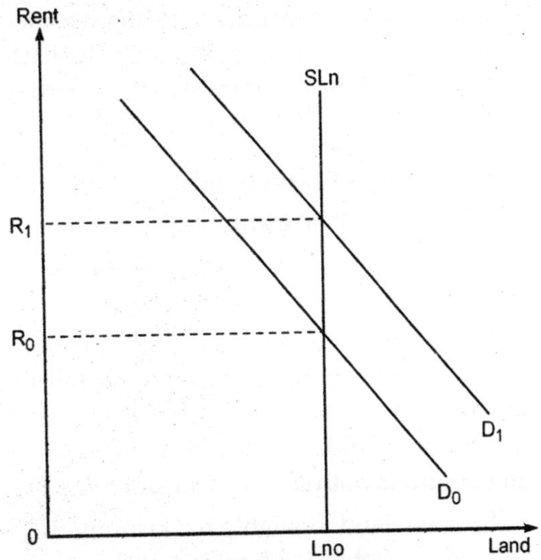

Fig. 11.2: The Rent of Land

• Assessing Ricardo's Theory of Rent

It may be objected that land does not have original and indestructible powers so that rent cannot be regarded as purely demand-determined. Good quality land, after constant cultivation, can lose its fertility considerably. Furthermore, it is unrealistic to assume that land has only one use. Instead, it has many alternative uses so that the supply of land to a particular use cannot be regarded as perfectly inelastic.

The theory is helpful in understanding the reasons for the rapid rise in rents in less developed countries. Most of these countries suffer from over-population which leads to rising food prices and rising rents. Also, because of lack of alternative investment and employment opportunities land has become a major source of investment and employment with a resultant steep rise in land prices and land rents. Many irrigation and housing projects have provided a great stimulus to large-scale speculative activity in land transactions, pushing up rent even further.

• Economic Rent and Transfer Earning

Ricardo's theory of rent assumes a fixed supply of land so that all rent is a surplus over and above the cost of keeping land in its present use. Such surplus has become known as economic rent and it has been pointed out that it can be expanded to other factors as well. We now define economic rent as transfer earnings. Transfer earnings are the payment required to keep a factor in its present use. Economic rent is any payment in excess of transfer earnings.

- **Allocating a Fixed Supply of land (L_n) Between Competing Uses**

Suppose that there are two uses for land: Housing and farming.

If there is a different rental rate for farming and housing then land will be transferred between the two to obtain the higher return. Hence, in equilibrium, there would be the same return in both sectors. Consider Fig. 11.3.

L_F is the land available for farming, L_H is the land available for housing and L_n is the total amount of land available. R_0 is the initial rental rate. Then, in equilibrium,

At R_0: $L_F + L_H = L_n$ $(0L_F + 0L_H = 0L_n)$.

The land available for farming (L_F) plus is the land available for housing (L_H) is equal to the total amount of land available (L_n).

- **The Allocation of Land and The Abolition of a Government Subsidy for Housing**

Consider Fig. 11.4 and assume that there are only two uses for land, private housing (H) and other (O).

1. Start at an initial equilibrium position DH_0, F_0, LH_0, L_0, R_0, E_0. $(0LH_0 + 0L_0 = OL_n)$. The rental rate is R_0.

(2) Abolish the subsidy paid to private homeowners. The demand for land for housing will fall. DH_0 will fall to DH_1. The rental rate will fall to R_{01}.

Since the rental rate for other uses of land is still R_0 then there is now a financial incentive to transfer land from housing (earning R_{01}) to other uses (still earning R_0).

Land will be transferred from housing to other uses. Less will be use for housing and more for other uses.

The transfer will continue until the rate of return is the same in both sectors. i.e. until the rental equals R_1 and $0LH_1 + 0L_{01} = 0L_n$. Points E_1.

(*N.B.:* The distance LH_1 to LH_0 is equal to the distance L_0 to L_{01}).

- **The Value of land**

The value of land is equal to the present value (PV) of its earnings (rent). We assume the rent is constant in real terms (at R_n).

$$PV = \frac{R_n}{(1+r)} + \frac{R_n}{(1+r)^2} + \ldots + \frac{R_n}{(1+r)^n} + \ldots = \frac{R_n}{r}$$

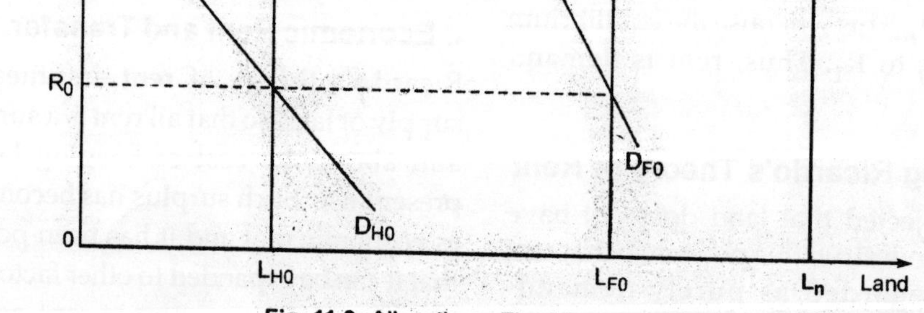

Fig. 11.3: Allocating a Fixed Supply of Land

If rentals (R_n) increase then the present value of the rent from the land will increase. The land is more valuable and it will increase in price.

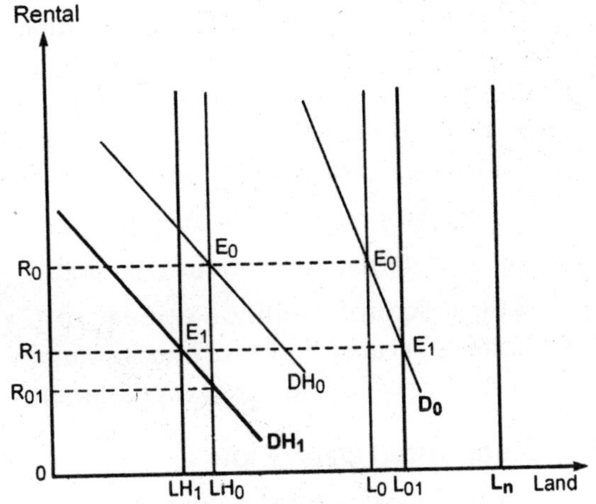

Fig. 11.4: Removing a Housing Subsidy

If interest rates fall, the present value of the rent from the land will increase. The land is now more valuable and will increase in price.

• Interest—the Reward to Capital

Just as wages represent the price of labour and rent is the price of land, so interest is the price of capital. Interest represents the cost or price of capital—if the finance has to be borrowed, interest has to be paid on it; if one uses her/his own finance to bankroll investment, the interest that could have been earned by lending the finance is an opportunity cost. In the neo-classical model with perfect competition, the cost of capital is equal to the value of the MP of capital or the Marginal Efficiency of Capital (MEC). Just as the MRP is the demand curve for labour, thus the MEC curve could be described as the demand curve for capital.

Now, we outline the neo-classical theory of interest and then, set out the main ciriticisms levelled against it by the Cambridge economists.

• The Neo-Classical Theory of Interest

The central proposition is that interest is the reward for waiting, which means the postponement of current consumption. The longer the period of waiting, the higher the rate of return on capital. According to the neo-classical theory of interest, the price of capital is determined by the total demand for and the supply of capital. As illustrated in Fig. 11.5 below, using more resources to produce capital goods in the present period (A to B) means giving up some quantity of consumer

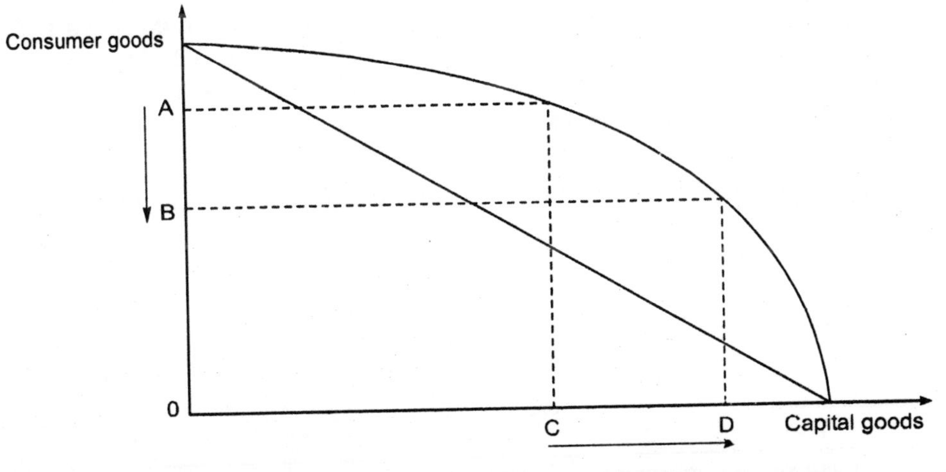

Fig. 11.5: The Choice between Consumer Goods and Capital Goods

goods in the present period (C to D). In other words, capital accumulation (or investment) necessitates some saving. In the neo-classical model, saving means providing the supply of loanable funds and releasing some resources from the production of consumption goods into the production of capital goods. Investment, on the other hand, is seen as providing the demand for loanable funds.

The higher the rate of interest, the more willing households and individuals will be to save and so sacrifice some of the present consumption for future consumption. This implies that the supply of loanable funds plotted against the rate of interest will yield a curve which slopes upwards from left to right as shown in Fig. 11.6.

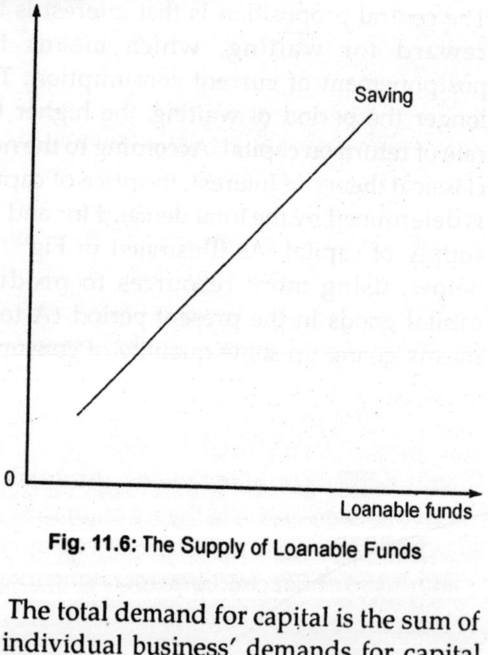

Fig. 11.6: The Supply of Loanable Funds

The total demand for capital is the sum of all individual business' demands for capital at different interest rates. It is here that the marginal productivity of capital (MPC) or (MEC) comes into the analysis. Given perfect competition, the interest rate facing a single business can be taken as given. To determine how much investment to undertake, a business must estimate the MPC or (MEC) of a project and compare it with the project's real cost. There are various methods to estimate the investment appraisal and the traditional methods of doing this: (a) the pay-back method; and (b) the average rate of return method. The more modern methods use discounted cash flow analysis. These methods are:

(a) the net present value method; and

(b) the internal rate of return method.

The discount methods appeal to the economists because they take into account the opportunity cost of the use of capital funds.

• Discounted Cash Flow

Discounted cash flow is the method of appraising the value of an asset based upon the idea that the value depends upon when the income from it is to be received. It is always better to receive income now rather than in the future. For example, £100 received now would produce £110 in a year's time if invested at 10%, £121 in two years' time, and so on. Conversely we could discount the present value of income by asking what amount of income today would be necessary to produce £100 in 1 year's time, 2 years' time and so on. To do this we discount income by the rate of interest. Thus, for example, if £90.91 were invested at 10% this would be worth £100 in 1 year's time, whereas £82.64 invested would be worth £100 in 2 years' and so.

• Present Value

It is possible, therefore, to discount the future earning of a project. If, for example, an investment produces an income of £2000 per year for 5 years and we assume an interest rate of 10%, then we could discover its present discounted value (PDV) as follows:

Year:	1		2		3		4		5
PDV=	£1,818.18	+	£1,652.89	+	£1,502.63	+	£1,366.03	+	£1,241.84 =£7,581.57

This compares with the undiscounted earnings of: £2,000 × 5 = £10,000.

The discounted values can be found from the table. However, this can also be calculated from the formula: PV = $A/(A + r)^n$, where A = amount of earnings per year, r = the constant rate of interest and n = number of years of the project.

Thus, in our example above we would obtain the calculation:

$$PDV = £2{,}000/(1+0.1) + £2{,}000/(1+0.1)^2 + £2{,}000/(1+0.1)^3 + £2{,}000/(1+0.1)^4 + £2{,}000/(1+0.1)^5 = £7{,}581.57.$$

• Net Present Value Method

Having obtained the present discounted value we can arrive at the net present value by subtracting from it the initial cost of investment. Suppose the project we have considered above had an original cost of £5,000, then: NPV = £7,581.57 – £5,000 = £2,581.57.

The result is positive which indicates that it is an acceptable project.

• The Internal Rate of Return Method

This method seeks to find the rate of interest that will discount the proceeds from the project to the original cost.

If the internal rate of return is greater than the rate of interest paid for borrowing the finances, then the project is worth undertaking. If, in our example, the capital cost were £2,000 a year over 5 years, a rate of 28.5% would discount this flow of proceeds to £5,012. If we subtract this total from the initial cost of £5,000 we obtain an answer of almost zero. Thus, 28.5% is the internal rate of retun. If the market rate of interest is higher than the rate of interest then the project is profitable.

Since a business will undertake the most profitable capital project first, the expected rate of return will decline as more and more units of capital are employed (because of diminishing marginal productivity). This is presented in Fig. 11.7 sometimes called the MEC curve and can be interpreted as the business's demand for capital.

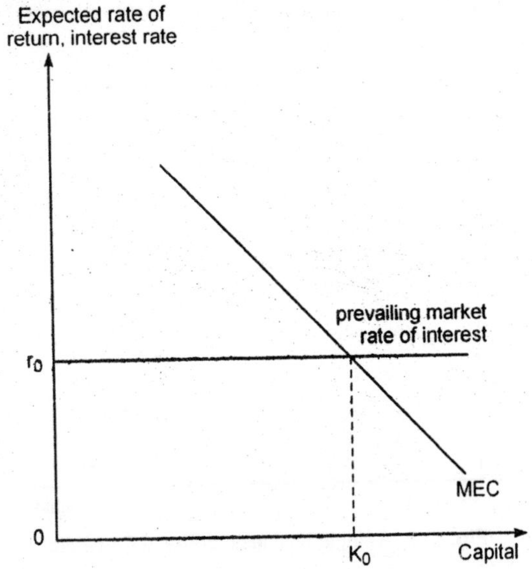

Fig. 11.7: A Single Business' Demand for Capital

Aggregating all business' demands for capital and drawing the total demand curve against the shown in Fig. 11.8 below. The equilibrium rate of interest (or equilibrium price of capital) is determined at the point (E) where the two curves intersect as shown in the graph.

Fig. 11.8 suggests that if, for some reasons, there was an autonomous increase in savings, this would depress interest rates and so reduce the cost of additional investment. Since additional investment yields diminishing return, the neo-classical theory of interest also suggests that such investment will only be undertaken under conditions of falling interest rates.

• The Price of Capital Assets

As we have seen above the price of capital assets will depend upon the discounted expected returns ($E\pi_i$) from the capital asset. i.e., the present value of the capital assets' expected stream of earnings:

$$PV = \frac{E\pi_1}{1+r} + \frac{E\pi_2}{(1+r)^2} + \dots + \frac{E\pi_n}{(1+r)^n}$$

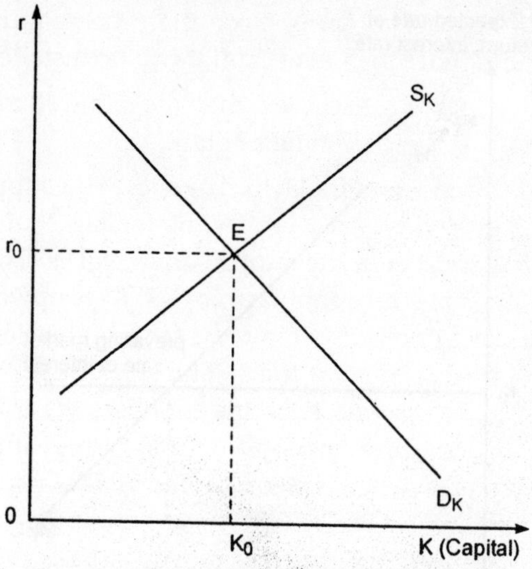

Fig. 11.8: A single business' demand for capital

If the present value (PV) is greater than the cost of the capital asset then it is worth purchasing. If the present value (PV) is less than the cost of the capital asset then it is not worth purchasing.

Up to now we have been considering the demand and supply of the stock of capital. A stock variable is the quantity of an asset at a point in time, e.g. the size of the housing stock or the amount of money in an economy at a particular point in time.

We are now going to consider the flow of service that the stock of capital will provide during a given period of time, e.g. the rental income from a stock of houses per annum: or 40 labour hours per week.

The cost of capital services is the rental that has to be paid for the service e.g. car hire or the rental of office space.

• The Business' Demand for the Use of the Services of Capital

The marginal value product (mvp = P.Δq/Δk) of capital is the increase in the value of a business output when one more unit of capital service is employed. The marginal revenue product (mrp = MR.Δq/Δk) of capital is the increase in the revenue earned by a business when one more unit of capital service is employed. We also assume that the marginal productivity of capital declines as output increases and this will give us the negatively sloped demand for capital service as in Fig. 11.9. Assuming that the business is purchasing its capital service in a perfectly competitive market it will face a perfectly elastic supply curve (sk) for capital service (the business can purchase as much capital as it wishes at r_0). Similarly as we have seen in the previous chapter, equilibrium occurs where mvp of capital or mrp of capital is equal to the cost of capital (r_0).

The mvp (=P.Δq/Δk), (or the mrp [=MR.Δq/Δk]), of capital curve is the business' demand curve for capital services (dk); it is influenced by:

1. The price of output. If the price of output (P) increases (decreases) then marginal revenue (MR) will increase (decrease) and the mvp (=P.Δq/Δk), (or the mrp[=MR.Δq/Δk]) will increase (decrease) and the demand for capital curve (dk) will shift to the right (left).
2. The amount of labour available. An increase in the amount of labour will increase the productivity of capital (Δq/Δk). The mvp (P.Δq/Δk) (or the mrp [MR.Δq/Δk]) will increase and the

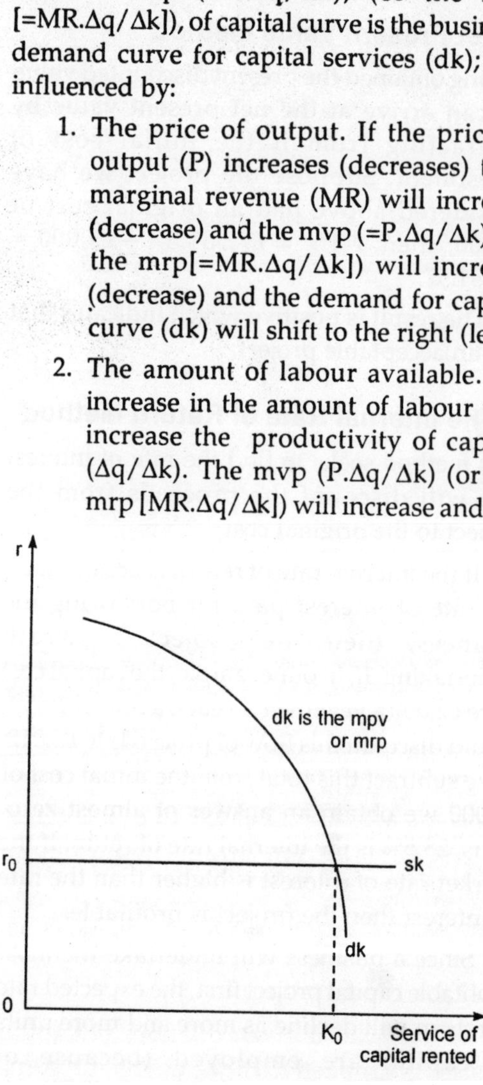

Fig. 11.9: The Demand for Capital Services

demand for capital curve (dk) will shift to the right.

3. Technical advance. This is an increase in the productivity of capital. The mpk ($\Delta q/\Delta k$) will increase. The mvp of capital curve will shift to the right.

   The industry's demand curve for capital is the sum of the business's demand curves.

• The Supply of Capital Services to a Business

In the short-run the stock of capital is FIXED.

In the long-run the change in the stock of capital depends upon net investment. Net investment is equal to gross investment less depreciation (capital consumption).

The required rental rate on capital is the rental rate that just allows the owners of capital to cover the opportunity cost of owning the capital.

For example: Suppose the cost of a machine is £100,000 financed by borrowing from a bank at a real rate of interest of 5%.

How much must the machine earn to at least break even?

i. Interest costs are £5,000 per annum.

ii. Assume that the machine depreciates by 10% p.a. (£10,000).

The minimum required real rate of return (the real rental) is £5,000 + £10,000 = £15,000.

The return is £15,000/£100,000 = 0.15 = 15%.

So, the annual cost = asset price × (interest costs + depreciation rate). The minimum return required is 15%.

• The Long-Run Supply Curve of Capital for the Economy

In the long-run a given quantity of capital services is supplied to the economy if it earns the required rental.

If capital earns more than the required rental rate then new capital will be installed.

If capital earns less than the required rate, then depreciation takes place.

Consider Fig. 11.10. The short-run supply of capital is vertical reflecting the fact that, in the short-run, the supply of capital is fixed. The long-run supply curve (LRSK) is upward sloping reflecting the need for a higher level of depreciation as the capital stock increases. We are assuming that the suppliers of capital need a higher price to supply more capital goods and, hence, depreciation increases with an increasing price. The owners of capital then require a higher rental rate to supply more capital goods to offset the higher price of the capital goods (the greater value of the depreciation). Thus, the higher long-run flow of capital services will only be supplied if the rental rate increases.

The supply curve will shift upwards ($LRSK_0$ to $LRSK_1$) if the real interest rate increases. The suppliers of capital need a higher return (a higher rental rate) to offset the higher opportunity cost of the finance tied up in purchasing capital goods.

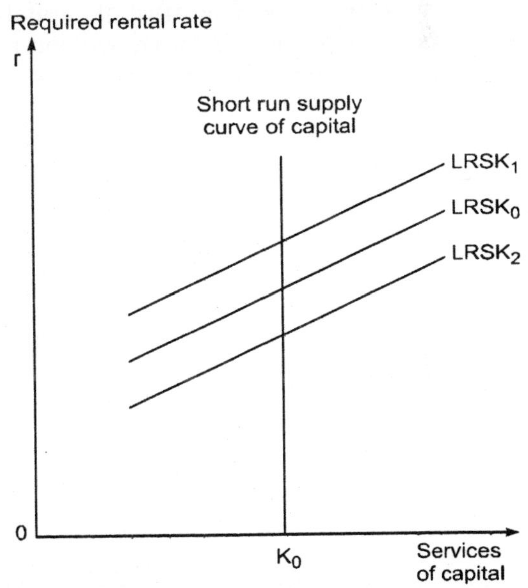

Fig. 11.10: The Long-Run Supply of Capital

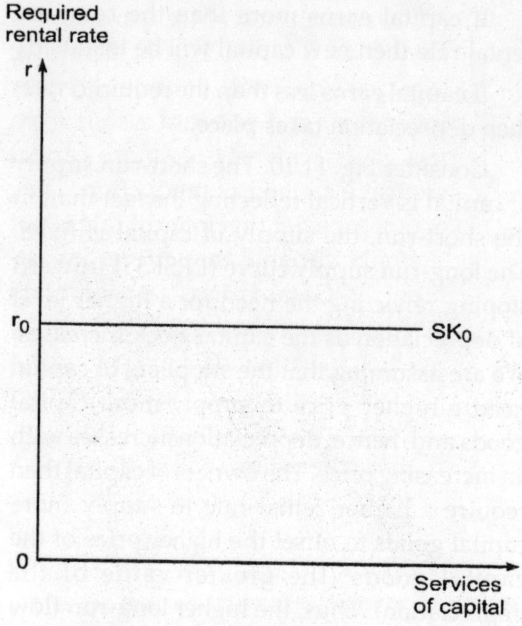

Fig. 11.11: The Long-Run Supply of Capital

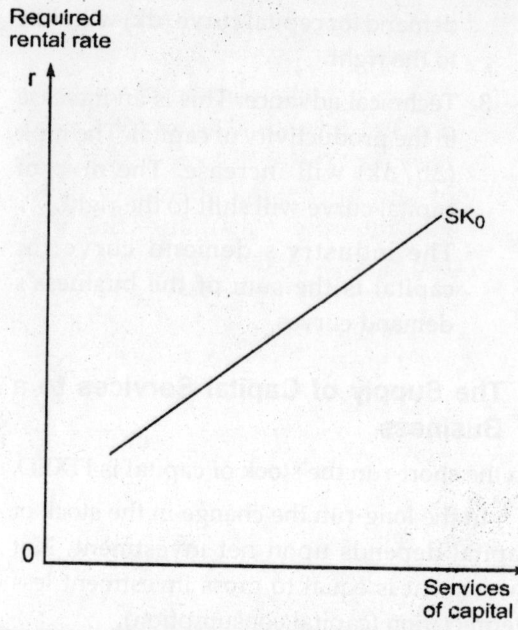

Fig. 11.12: The Long-Run Supply of Capital to a Large Industry

The Long-Run Supply Curve to an Industry

1. **Small industry:** We assume that the industry can obtain as much capital as it wishes at the going rental rate (r_0) as in Fig. 11.11. The supply of capital to the industry is perfectly elastic.
2. **Large industry:** The price of capital increases as more is purchased and a large rate of return is required.

• The Short-Run and Long-Run Adjustment of the Capital Stock (a Small Industry)

(a) Start, in Fig. 11.13, at the initial equilibrium position E_0, where the short-run supply curve of capital services is SS_0, the long-run supply curve of capital services is SK_0 at the rental rate, r_0. DK_0 is the initial demand for capital services and is the mvp or

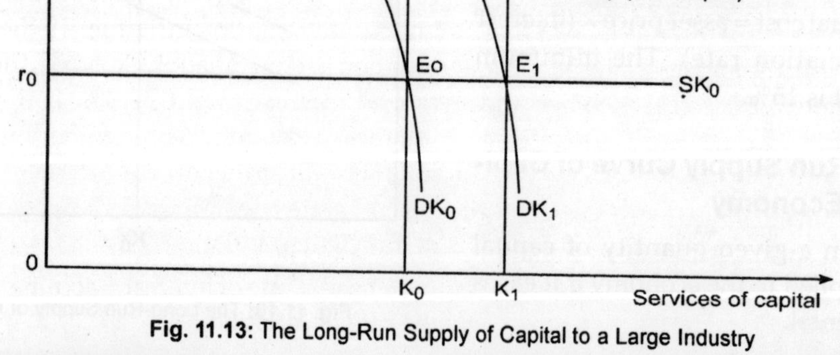

Fig. 11.13: The Long-Run Supply of Capital to a Large Industry

mrp. K_0 is the initial amount of capital services employed in the industry.

(b) Assume that there is an increase in the demand for output (q or Q) for this business. This will increase the price of output (P), the business' marginal revenue (MR) and the mvp $(=P.\Delta q/\Delta k)$, (or the mrp$[=MR.\Delta q/\Delta k]$). It is profitable for this industry to employ more capital. DK_0 shifts to the right to DK_1.

In the short-run the return on capital in this industry rises to E_{01}.

(c) In the long-run the higher return on capital in this industry will encourage more investment in the industry and the supply of capital will increase. As long as the return on capital is above r_0, more capital will be installed.

(d) As more capital is employed, the return on capital will fall below r_{01}. As long as the return on capital is above r_0, more capital will be installed. Positive net investment (the addition to the stock of capital) will continue until the return on capital is back to the point which is equal to r_0. This happens when K_0 has increased to K_1 and the new equilibrium is set at E_1.

Criticisms of the Marginal Productivity Theory

Following criticisms will be considered:

(a) It ignores the possibility that savers may have a given purpose for which they are saving—to buy a car or children's education and so on. In such a case, a higher interest rate may reduce savers' willingness to save because rising interest raise real incomes and so reduce the amount of saving necessary.

(b) A substantial amount of saving in industrial societies is done as a matter of habit and custom, independent of interest rate.

(c) A basic conclusion of the neo-classical theory of interest is that a falling interest rate will induce greater investment and so cause a shift from less capital intensive to more capital intensive method of production. They do not consider that interest rate is not the only variable that affects investment. Cambridge economists (England) said that this conclusion may not hold in particular, they pointed out the possibility of re-switching. According to the neo-classical theory, a falling interest rate will cause a switch from less capital intensive to more capital intensive methods of production and this is the view supported by Cambridge economists at the US, led by Solow and Samuelson. They maintained that the MEC (or marginal productivity of capital) will decline as the capital stock expands, yielding the downward sloping demand curve for capital.

English economists at Cambridge led by Joan Robinson and Kaldor, though, maintain that the marginal productivity of capital may increase over part of its range, yielding a backward bending demand curve for capital.

• Real versus Nominal Interest Rates

So far, we have assumed that there is no inflation. In a world of inflation, nominal interest rates will be higher than they would be in an inflation free world. Basically, market rates of interest rise to take account of anticipated rate of inflation. If there is no inflation and no inflation expected, the market rate of interest might be 5%. If the rate of inflation, goes to 10%, then the anticipated inflation will be higher. The market or nominal rate of interest will rise to 15% to take account of anticipated inflation. Thus:

The real rate of interest = nominal rate less the rate of inflation.

We can expect to see high nominal rate of interest in periods of high and rising inflation, though the real rate of interest may not necessarily be high.

• The Allocative Role of Interest

The interest rate allocates funds to consumers and to investors. Within the business, interest allocates funds to different investment projects. Those investment projects whose rates of return are higher than the market rate of interest will be undertaken, given an unrestricted market for loanable funds.

It is important to remember that the interest rate performs the function of allocating capital but what that ultimately does is to allocate real physical capital to various investment projects.

• Furture and Present Consumption, Saving, Investment, and the Real Interest Rate

Fig. 11.14 shows the production possibility frontier, FP, feasible combination of current and future consumption of goods that the economy can produce. At point P the economy only produce for current consumption, and at point F only for future consumption.

The production possibility frontier FP shows the different amounts of investment in the capital stock. At point P no investment is undertaken, the existing capital is sold off. Future consumption is zero. At point F all current resources are going in investment to raise the capacity of the economy to make consumption goods in the future. Current consumption is zero. Moving down FP, more and more resources are transferred from future to current consumption. As the curvature of the production possibility frontier reflects diminishing returns in this trade off.

The slope of the frontier demonstrates the extra future consumption from sacrificing a unit of current consumption. The slope has magnitude $-(1+i)$ where i is the rate of return on investment. The negative sign means

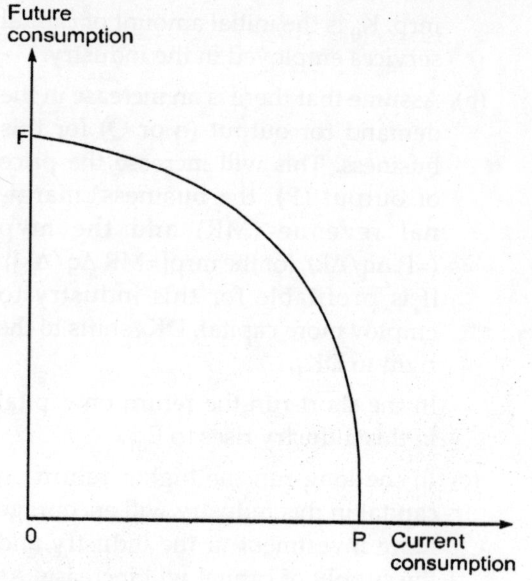

Fig. 11.14: The Choice beteen Current and Future Consumption

sacrificing current consumption to add to future consumption.

What about consumer tastes? Both current and future consumption are desriable, so we can imagine a standard indifference map. The more impatient are consumers for current consumption, the steeper the indifference curve. Impatient people will give up lots of future consumption to get a bit more today. Thirsty people have flatter indifference curves. In Fig. 11.15, U_0 is the highest indifference curve that can be reached, and E is the best allocation of current resources between consumption and investment.

The real interest rate may adjust to accomplish this outcome, even though decisions to add to the capital stock are taken by businesses, and decisions about savings are taken by households. Saving is defined as the difference between current income and current consumption.

Businesses will invest until the real rate of return i is equal to r real rate of interest at which they can borrow. Households face a budget line of slope $-(1+r)$, since by saving and lending they can exchange £1 of consumption today for £$(1+r)$ of consumption in the

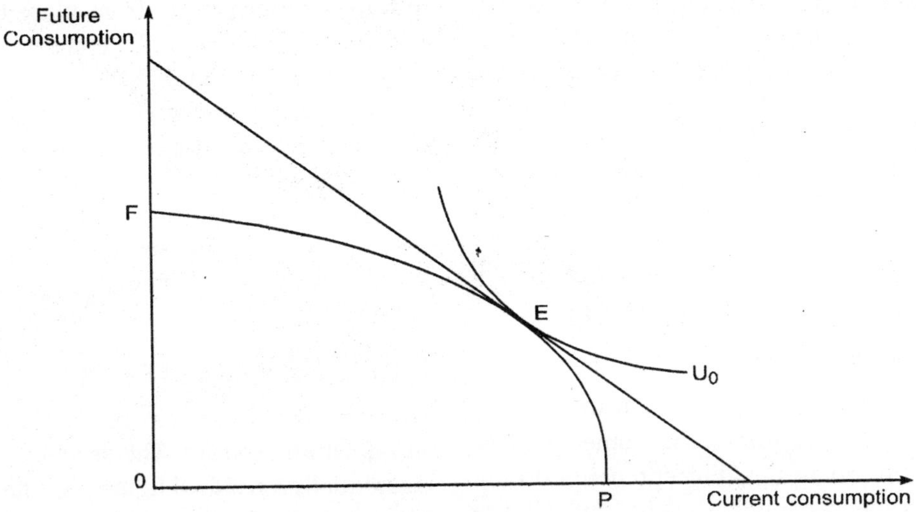

Fig. 11.15: Present and Future Consumption

future. Households save up to the point where their indifference curve is tangent to the budget line with a slope of $-(1 + r)$. Equilibrium occurs where S – I. Households and businesses are happy with the same transfer of resources from the present to the future. Fig. 11.16 shows the equilibrium real interest rate is r. Businesses wish to be at E where i = r. Households want to be at the same point E, where their indifference curve U_0 is tangent to the line $-(1 + r)$.

By devoting more current resources to investment, society can trade off current for future consumption, moving up (from P) the frontier FP. The frontier has a slope of $-(1 + i)$, where i is the rate of return on investment. Facing a real interest rate r, producers will choose E and so will consumers. The equilibrium real interest rate balances the productivity of investment and thriftiness of consumers.

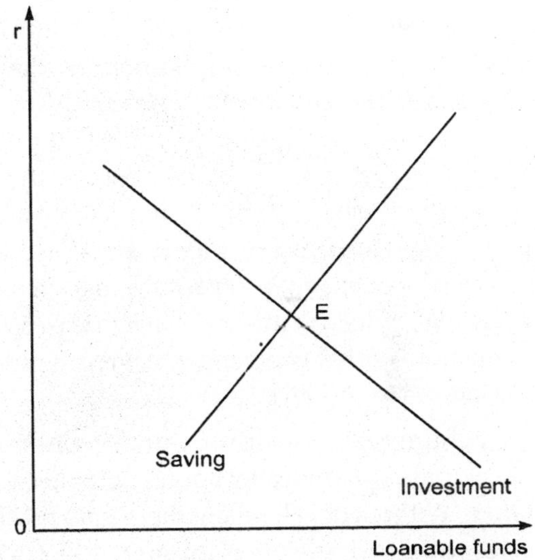

Fig. 11.16: The Equilibrium Real Rate of Interest

• Enterprise and Profit

Labour, natural resources and capital do not naturally form themselves into a wealth—making combination. Someone must make the decisions. The people who take this task are providing a special service because they must, in so doing, take a risk. Economists term this decision-taking and organizational factor as enterprise and the person who supplies it as the entrepreneur. Profit is the reward for entrepreneurial talent.

The entrepreneur's function is to organise the business. In order to produce goods and services it is necessary for someone to take a risk by producing in anticipation of demand. Entrepreneurs differ from other people involved in the business in that the amount of income they earn is uncertain. The workers, the capitalists and the landlord—all have to be paid an agreed contractual amount for the business not to go into liquidation. There is no way in which one can contract to make a profit, and if the entrepreneur is unlucky he or she will be left with no profit at all. We assume that the entrepreneurs will always try to maximize the profit of the business and will act in a rational and sensible manner.

• The Role of Profit

Since goods must be produced in anticipation of demand, it is essential that someone takes the risk of doing this. Entrepreneurs do not act from a sense of public duty but out of desire to make profit. Adam Smith argued that the 'invisible hand' of self-interest guided the economy to the best possible use of its resources. This was because, to produce profitably, the business would not only have to produce the goods which people wanted but also would have to produce them at minimum cost in order to compete with its rivals. Profit acts not only as an incentive to encourage businesses but it also acts as indicator. For example, if profit is high in one particular industry; this indicates that people want more of that good and encourages more businesses to produce it.

Schumpeter saw profit and economic development inextricably bound up with each other: 'Without development there is no profit, without profit no development. For the capitalist system it must be added that without profit there would be no accumulation of wealth.'

Thus, profit acts as an incentive to businesses and encourage them to take risks, as a measure of efficiency and as a spur to the introduction of new products and processes. It is the job of the entrepreneur to achieve the optimum combination of factors of production at the least possible cost to satisfy the demand for the commodity. It is an economic problem because the supply, and hence the prices, of resources differ greatly from place to place. Thus in every situation the entrepreneur has to work out the combination of resources which is economically correct. If they do it successfully, they will be rewarded with profit, if unsuccessful, they will end up making a loss. Since they are responsible for production decisions we can see that entrepreneurs are one of the most vital cogs in the economic system.

• Different Views of Profit

We know the distinction between economic and accounting profit. The accounting profit is essentially a residual figure, i.e., the income which is left over after all the expenses have been met. Even so, one might talk of profit before tax and after tax, distributed or undistributed and so on. It is also possible that a business owns some of the resources it uses: for example, it may have the freehold premises. It must be taken into consideration before profit is calculated.

It may be possible for a business to make an accounting profit but an economic loss. This can be best explained by taking a simple example. Suppose a self-employed solicitor works in premises which he or she owns. At the end of the year he or she finds they have made £4,000 per annum and the interest he or she could have earned by not investing the capital on buying the house. Under the circumstances, the economists would have taken all these into consideration. Economists also have a view of the normal profit which is needed to keep the resources in business. Any profit in excess of normal profit is abnormal or supernormal profit. So people can take a different view about some of which we will consider below.

• Profit and Returns to Other Factors

As we saw in our example of the solicitor, much of what is commonly called profit is in fact the implicit cost of other factor of production. Thus, for example, the owner of a corner shop might say he or she has made

£16,000 profit but in fact £6,000 should be payment for his own labour, £3,000 is rent for the shop which is his or her own, and so on. This principle can apply to any organization.

• The Return to Innovation

Schumpeter's view was that profit is the reward for bringing new product and processes to the market, which is called innovation. Innovation is the application of invention to industry. If someone is enterprising enought to bring in new product or process and it is successful, then they will for some time make a large or economic profit. This will disappear after a while when competitors copy the process.

• Risk, Uncertainty and Profit

F. H. Knight said that profit is the reward for risk taking. Profit arises because the future is uncertain. This would certainly include the innovator's profit because this can be viewed as the reward for the risk of bringing in a new product.

To a certain extent all the factors of production may earn a profit for uncertainty. For example, when a young person decides to be trained as a lawyer, she/he is taking a risk in the sense that it is uncertain whether society will hire their services in the future. It holds true for other occupations. If the risk is successfully taken then the person receives a reward, if unsuccessful a loss may be incurred.

• Monopoly Profit

When a company has reached a dominant position in the market, it may reap a rich reward without taking high risk. However, it is not entrepreneurs who might benefit form monopoly power. A trade union might also use its monopoly power to obtain a great reward for its members. Similarly, any factor which is earning an economic rent could be regarded as making a monopoly profit. Economists condemn monopoly profit because they cause a distortion in the allocation of resources. Schumpeter is an exception who maintained that monopolies, with their economies of scale and ability to innovate, are the engine of economic growth. Monopoly profit is possible when there are barriers to entry. Monopoly profit due to entry restrictions are often called monopoly rents. Basically, monopoly profit are capitalized into the value of the business that owns the particular right to have the monopoly.

• Falling Tendency of the Rate of Profit

We have already seen how Ricardo perceived the falling tendency of the rate of profit in his theory of distribution. Marx also made a major contribution to the ideas of Ricardo and to those of other economists of his time.

Practically, falling tendency of the rate of profit is associated with the process of industrialization. When total production expands, the total amount of profit increases, but the rate of profit per unit falls. Ricardo's theory of distribution demonstrated this tendency. The smaller the rate of profit, the weaker the incentive for capitalists to invest more in plant and equipment. Eventually, investment may cease completely so that the expansion of output comes to an end. Then, the economy is said to have reached a 'stationary state'.

Marx's argument, however, is that labour is the sole producer of value, but the workers are paid no more than subsistence wage which is less than the full value of their produce. The surplus over and above the workers' subsistence wage is the profit expropriated by the capitalists. By the phrase 'subsistence wage', Marx, like other economists of his time, meant wage which is just enough to maintain a customary standard of living. The capitalists' desire to earn profit and accumulate leaves the workers with no independent means of livelihood—they have no other alternative but to a accept employment from the capitalists at the subsistence wage. Yet capital itself is not productive without the aid of labour.

Marx further points out that because of competition capitalists are required to improve their methods of production by installing new and better machines and equipments. This means an increase in depreciation costs which will in turn adversely affect the rate of profit.

Capitalists can increase profit by increasing work-hours or by wage cuts, either of which might be resisted by the working class. Alternatively, capitalists may reduce the cost of capital and of raw materials by introducing technical progress, or by finding newer and cheaper sources of raw material and estalishing markets overseas for finished products.

Marx maintains that even if these counteracting tendencies succeed at first, they will not prevent the inevitability of falling profit. Such low profit rates will then lead to frequent crises.

QUESTIONS

1. (a) Consumer durables such as washing machines are part of capital stock, but do not generate any financial income for their owners. Why do we include consumer durables in the capital stock?

   (b) To wash our clothes we can take them to launderette and spend £2 per week indefinitely or buy a washing machine for £400. It costs £1 per week to run a washing machine, and the interest rate is 10% per annum. Do you think buying washing machine is profitable? Does this help you to answer (a)?

2. (a) A bank offers £1.10 to be paid next year for every £0.90 paid in this year. What is the implicit rate of interest?

3. A business buys a machine today for £10,000 earns a rental of £3,600 for each of the next 2 years (payable at the end of the years), and sells it for a scrap value for £9,000 at the end of the second year. Use the data below to determine if the machine is worth buying when the interest rate is 10% per annum.

   At 10% interest rate the value of £1 lent today is:

Year	0	1	2
	£1	£1.10	£1.21

   PV of £1 earned in:

Year	0	1	2
	£1	£0.91	£0.83

4. The interest rate falls from 10% to 5%. Discuss in detail how this affects the rental on capital services and the level of the capital stock in an industry in the short and long-run.

5. Suppose a plot of land is suitable only for agriculture. Can the farming industry experience financial distress if there is an increase in the price of land? Is your answer likely to be affected if land can also be used for housing?

6. Why are these statements wrong?

   (a) Inflation leads to high nominal interest rates. This reduces the PV of future income. (b) If the economy continues to become more capital intensive, eventually there will be no jobs left for workers to do. (c) Since the economy's supply of land is fixed, it would be supplied even at zero rental, which should thus be the equilibrium rental in the long-run.

ANSWERS

1. (a) Some flows of consumption services are provided most efficiently by buying consumer durable.
   (b) The launderette costs £104 a year. Buying a washing machine costs £52 a year and £40 interest forgone. Better to buy.
2. You make 20 on every 90 you put in, about 22% a year.
3. (3600 × 0.91) = (£3276) + (£12,600 × 0.83 = £10,458) = £13,734. It is worth buying.
4. It raises the PV of existing stream of rentals, raising the incentive to build more capital assets. This slowly reduces the equilibrium rental on capital until long-run equilibrium is restored.
5. The demand for land is a derived demand. If supply is fixed, a rise in demand for land can bid up land prices. Tenant farmers face higher rentals but extra income from their crops is what started the process. Farmers lose in land prices and rentals bid up by higher demand for housing.
6. (a) It makes future nominal income rise.
   (b) Higher labour productivity and wage income also raise the demand for goods.
   (c) True if only one possible user is there. Competition between users is what bids up price.

APPENDIX 11 A.1

Compound Interest and Present Value

Start with **compound** interest.

£100 today when the rate of interest prevailing in the economy is 10% is worth £110 in one year's time which is equal to the original £100 + £10 in interest.

Future value of £100 in one year's time when the rate of interest is equal to £100 × (1 + 0.1) = £110.

£100 today, when the rate of interest prevailing in the economy is 10%, is worth £121 in two years' time. This is equal to the original £100 + £10 + £11 in interest. In the first year, the interest earned is £10. In the second year 10% interest is not only earned on the £100 but also on the £10 earned in the first year—an extra £1.

The future (compound) value of £100 in two years' time when the rate of interest is equal to £100 × $(1 + 0.1)^2$ = £121.

In general the future (compound) value of an amount 'A' earning interest of 100r% for 'n' years is equal to

$A(1 + r)^n$

Example: How much is £1,500 worth if it earns 8% compound interest for 4 years?

A = £1,500, r = 0.08 (8%), n = 4.

Then $A(1 + r)^n$ = £1,500 × $(1.08)^4$
= £2,040.73.

Present Value

We can argue the opposite way. If the rate of interest is 10% then £121 receivable in two years' time is worth £121 in one year's time and £100 now. It is the reverse process of compounding.

In general, the PV (present value) of an amount 'Πn' receivable in 'n' years time when the rate of interest is 100r% is equal to

$$\frac{\Pi n}{(1+r)^n}$$

e.g. **1.** Find the present value of £1,100 receivable in one year's time and £1,210 receivable in two years' time when the rate of interest is 10%.

$$P.V. = \frac{£1,100}{(1+0.1)} + \frac{£1,210}{(1+0.1)^2}$$

$$= £1,000 + £1,000 = \mathbf{£2,000}$$

e.g. **2.** A $2\frac{1}{2}$% consol pays a fixed amount of £2.50 p.a. **for ever.** If the market rate of interest is 100r% then the market price is equal to

$$\frac{£2.50}{(1+r)} + \frac{£2.50}{(1+r)^2} + \ldots + \frac{£2.50}{(1+r)^n} + \frac{£2.50}{(1+r)^{n+1}} + \ldots$$

The sum of this infinite series is equal to £2.50/r.

If the rate of interest is equal to 0.1 (10%), then the price of the bond is:

$$£2.50/0.1 = £25$$

If r = 0.125 (12.5%) then the price of the bond = **£20** (= £2.50/0.125)

CHAPTER 12

GOVERNMENT EXPENDITURE AND REVENUE

KEY TERMS

Government Expenditure (GE): GE rose steadily in many countries until 1970s; since then it is going down to allow private sector to increase its activity. Government must balance its budget cyclically.

Tax Revenue (TR): TR has mainly come from two types of taxes—direct tax and indirect tax. Direct tax is generally more progressive than indirect taxes.

Transfer Payment: is the payment by the government against which no payment is required. It is primarily concerned with equity and income distribution. Public goods are goods which are provided by the government to avoid the free rider problem.

Government Macroeconomic Policies: Fiscal policy helps government to raise huge amount of money to achieve government objectives which may not be satisfied by the private sector.

The scale of government rose steadily until the 1970s. Many people then felt it had become too large. The private sector would be better able to allocate these resources. High taxes were stifling private enterprise.

Now the pendulum is swinging back.

Table 12.1: Government Spending as a Percentage of GDP

	1880	1929	1960	2002
Japan	11	19	18	37
USA	8	10	28	29
Germany	10	31	32	44
UK	10	24	32	39
France	15	19	35	50
Sweden	6	8	31	53

Source: World Bank, World Development Report, OECD Economic Outlook

Table 12.2: Breakdown of UK Government Spending (% of GDP)

	1956	1976	2001
Total spending	33.9	46.9	40.4
Goods and services	20.7	25.9	22.2

Source: ONS, UK National Accounts; HM Treasury, Budget 2001.

Table 12.3: Government Activity in 2002 (% of GDP)

	UK	US	Germany	France
Expenditure	40	30	50	44
Tax Revenue	41	31	49	42
Budget Surplus/Deficit	1	1	–1	–2

Source: OECD Economic Outlook

Table 12.4: UK Income Tax Tates, 1978-2000

Taxable Income	Marginal tax rate (%)	
	1978-79	2001-02
1,880	34	10
5,000	34	22
10,000	34	22
20,000	45	22
30,000	50	40
40,000	70	40
70,000	83	40

Source: HMSO, Financial statement Budget Report: ONS, Budget 2001
Note: Taxable Income is after deducting allowances. In 2001-02, a single person's allowance was £4615

Governments in developed capitalist countries are promising higher spending on health, education, transport, and so on. Table 12.1 shows how government in some industrial countries grew in the last century.

Table 12.2 confirms that the UK government expenditure fell after 1970s, and decomposes total government spending into government purchases of goods and services—national health service, schools, defence—and transfer payments, such as social security, state pensions, debt interest.

Transfer Payment requires no goods and services in return during that time period.

Much of government expenditure is financed by tax revenue. The government need not balance its budget every year. Government must balance its budget over the cycles. Table 12.3 shows that by 2002 the UK, US, France and Germany were expected to have budgets close to balance. The budget surplus (deficit) is the excess (shortfall) of its spending over its revenue.

Now we examine some microeconomic issues. First, we distinguish between marginal and average tax rates. The marginal tax rate (MTR) is the fraction of last amount of income paid in taxes. The average tax rate (ATR) is the fraction of total income paid in taxes.

In a progressive tax structure, the average tax rate rises with an individual's income. The government takes proportionately more from the rich than from the poor. In a regressive tax structure, the average tax rate falls as income rises, taking proportionally from the rich.

Table 12.4 shows that the UK, like most other countries, has a progressive income tax structure. In Fig. 12.1 we explain the situtation. We plot pre-tax income on the horizontal axis and post-tax income on the vertical axis. The line OG, with a slope of 45 degree, implies no taxes (pre-tax income). A pre-tax income OA on the horizontal axis = the post-tax income OA on the vertical axis (same units on both axis). Now suppose there is an income tax, but the first OA income is tax-free. If the MTR on taxable income is constant, individuals face a schedule OBCD, keeping a constant fraction of each income of pre-tax income above OA. The higher the MTR the flatter is BC. To calculate the ATR at point D, we join up OD. The flatter the slope of this line the higher is the ATR. Even with a constant MRT, and a constant slope of BC, the initial tax allowance makes the tax structure progressive. The higher is the individual's gross income, the smaller is the tax allowance as a percentage of gross income, so higher is the fraction of total income on which tax is paid.

But Table 12.4 demonstrates that the MRT may also rise with income. As individuals move into higher tax bands, they pay higher

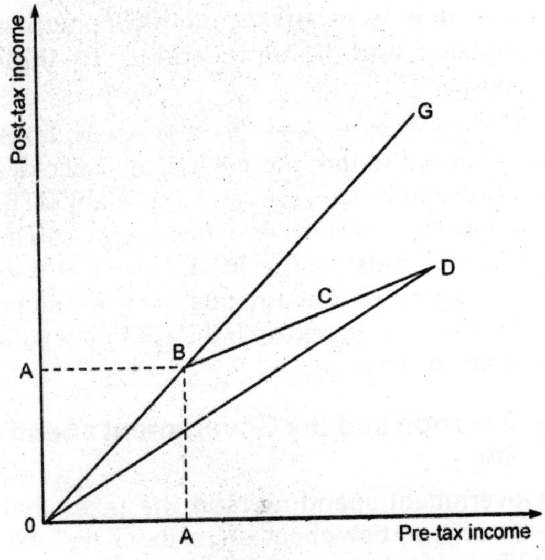

Fig. 12.1: A Progressive Income Tax

marginal tax rates, moving on to even flatter portions of the schedule. The average will then rise sharply with income.

It can also be seen that the UK MTR fell a lot in the last two decades, especially for the very rich. For example, a millionaire paying an 83% tax rate for all taxable income above £70,000 in 1978 paid only 40% in 2001. The UK was not alone in cutting the tax rates. There was worldwide move to cut tax rates. This reflects increasing competition between

Table 12.5: Expenditure and Revenue of the UK Central and Local Government in 2000-01

Expenditure	billion (£)	Revenue	billion (£)
Current spending on goods and services	191	Direct Taxes	152
Transfer payments: social security	122	Indirect taxes	138
Debt interest	23	Other taxes	20
Others	31	Social security contributions	63
Depreciation	15	Other Revenue	26
Total current spending	382	Total current Revenue	398
Capital Spending	20		
Less depression	–15		
Capital Transfers	6		
Net capital spending	11		
Budget surplus and net debt repayment	5		

Source: ONS, UK National Accounts

governments to attract mobile resources (physical and human capital) to their countries.

The 45-degree line OG shows zero taxes or transfers so that pre-tax income coincides with an allowance of OA and a constant MTR, t, the post-tax income schedule is OBCD. The slope depends on the MRT (on BCD it is ({1 – t}). The ATR at any point D is the slope OD. A tax is progressive if the ART rises with pre-tax income.

• Taxation and the Government spending

Government spending, and the taxes that finance it, are now about 40% of the GDP. Table 12.5 shows the composition of Government spending and tax revenue in 2001.

Nearly half of total government spending, went on transfer payments such as pensions, debt interest, and so on. Of the remaining half that went directly to goods and services, the most important spending categories are health, defence, education and so on. Table 12.5 also shows the different categories of taxes that finance the government spending.

Direct taxes are taxes on income and wealth. Indirect taxes are taxes on spending and output. The most important direct taxes are income tax, and corporation tax on company profits. The most important indirect taxes are VAT, excise duties and customs duties. Note that since state provision of retirement pensions is included on the expenditure side as transfer payments, pension contributions under the NIC are included in the revenue side.

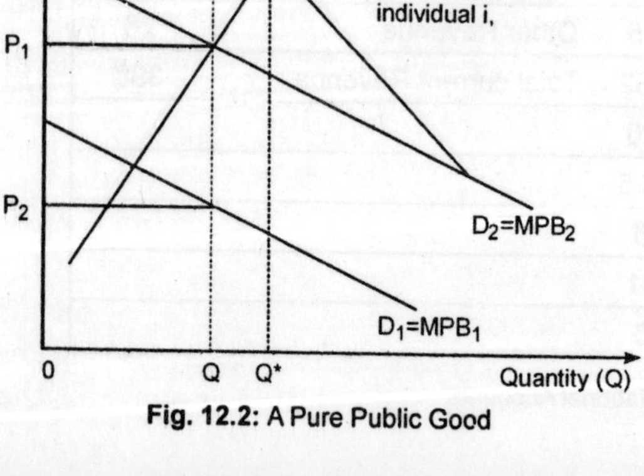

Fig. 12.2: A Pure Public Good

A private good is excludable, which means that if you consume it nobody else can use it. Most goods are private goods.

A public good is non-excludable, which means that if you consume it everybody else can also consume it in exactly the same quantity. For example, clean water and air and national defence. If air is pollution free, your consumption of its does not reduce my consumption of it. Similarly, national defence; we all consume the same quantity of it. We may get different amounts of utility if our tastes differ, but we all consume the same quantity.

The key aspects of public goods are: (1) that it is possible for one person to consume it without reducing the consumption for others, and (2) the impossibility of excluding anyone from consumption except at a prohibitive cost. For example, many people can watch a football match, especially if it is on TV, without reducing the quantity consumed by other viewers; but exclusion is possible.

Free-Rider: Public goods are wide open to free-rider problem if they are supplied by the private sector. Since you get the same quantity of national defence as everyone else, whether or not you pay for it, you never buy national defence in a free-market; nor does anyone else. No defence is demanded even though we all want it.

Public goods have a strong externality. If you buy defence everyone else also gets the benefits. Since marginal private and social benefits diverge, private market will not produce the socially desirable quantity. Government intervention is needed.

• The Marginal Social Benefit (MSB)

Suppose the public good is pure water supply. The more infected the water, the more people are liekly to get cholera. Fig. 12.2 supposes there are two people in a community. The first person's demand curve for pure water, D_1, shows his marginal benefit. D_2 is the marginal benefit of pure water to the second person. Demand curve D is the marginal social benefit of pure water. At each level of public good, we vertically sum the marginal benefit of each individual to get the marginal social benefit. At the output Q the marginal social benefit is $P = P_1 + P_2$. We sum vertically at the given quantity Q because everyone consumes the same quantity of a public good. Fig. 12.2 also shows the marginal cost of the public good. If there are no production externalities then the marginal private cost is equal to marginal social cost (MSC). The socially efficient output of the public good is Q*, where MSB = MSC.

What happens if the good is privately produced and marketed? Person one might pay P_1 to have a quantity Q produced by a competitive supplier where P = MC. At the output Q the price P_1 = MPB (marginal private benefit) that person 1 gets from the last unit of the public good. Person 2 will not pay to have the output increased beyond Q. Person 2 cannot be excluded from consuming the output Q that person 1 has commissioned. At the output Q, person 2's MPB = P_2 which is less than P_1. Person 2 will not pay the higher price needed to induce a competitive supplier to expand output beyond Q. This quantity privately produced and consumed in a competitive market is below the efficient quantity Q*.

$D_1 + D_2$ are the demand curves of the two individuals and show the MPB of the last unit of the public good to each individual. What is the MSB of the last unit to the group as a whole? Since both individuals consume whatever quantity of the good is produced, we must add up vertically the price each is prepared to pay for the last unit. At the output Q the MSB = $P_1 + P_2$. The demand curve D showed the MSB and is obtained by vertically adding the demand curves of the two individuals. If MC is the private and the SMC of producing the public good the socially efficient output is Q* at which SMC = SMB.

• Revelation of Preferences

If it knows that the MSB curve is the demand curve D, the government can decide the efficient output of the public good. How does the government discover the individual demand curves that must be vertically added to get D? If the people's payments for the good are related to their demand curves, everyone will lie. People will understate how much they value the good in order to reduce their own payments, just as in a private market. Conversely, we are all for safer streets if we do not have to contribute to the cost. In practice, democracies try to resolve this problem through elections of governments. Politics lets society get closer to the efficient answers than the market can. Different parties offer different quantities of public good together with a statement of how it will be financed by taxes.

• Government Production

The output of the public goods must be decided by the government, not the market. This need not mean that government must produce the goods itself. Public goods may not be produced by the public sector. National defence is a public good largely provided by the public sector though may not be produced by the public sector. Street-sweeping, though a public good, can be subcontracted to private producers, even if government must determine its quantity and pay for it. Conversely, state hospitals involve public sector production of private goods. One person's hip replacement operation prevents the busy surgeon from operating on someone else's.

• Transfer-Payments and Income Distribution

Government spending on transfer payments is primarliy concerned with equity and income distribution. By spending money on the unemployed, the old and the poor, the government alter the distribution of income and welfare that a free market economy would otherwise have produced, there is a minimum standard of living below which no citizen should be allowed to go. The specification of this standard is a pure value judgement.

To finance this expenditure, the government taxes those who can afford to pay. Then as a whole, the tax and transfer system takes money from the rich and gives to the poor, who get cash transfers to enjoy the consumption of public goods paid for by income taxes raised from the rich. The desirable amount of redistribution is a value judgement on which people and parties will disagree. There is trade-off between efficiency and equity.

• Merit Goods

Merit goods are goods that society thinks everyone should have regardless of whether an individual wants them. Merit goods are education and health. Merit bads are cigarettes and heroin. Since society places a value on these goods from the value placed on them by the individual, individual choice in a free market leads to a different allocation from the one that society wishes.

There are two aspects of merit goods. The first is externalities. The second aspect is that society believes that individuals no longer act in their own best interests. For example, addiction to gambling and drugs are socially bad. Economists rarely subscribe to paternalism. The function of government intervention is less to tell people what they ought to like than to allow them better to achieve what they already like. However, the government sometimes has more information and is in a better position to take a decision.Many people may hate going to school, but later are glad that they did.

• The Principles of Taxation

In this section we will consider three things. First, we consider different types of taxes through which government can raise revenue. Then we consider the equity implication of taxation. Finally, we examine efficiency implications of taxation.

Types of Taxes: Income tax in peace time was introduced only in 1840s, and Value Added Tax (VAT) not until the 1970s.

How does the UK tax structure compare with that in other countries? Table 12.6 presents data for several countries. The most notable features of the UK tax system are its low reliance of social security contributions, but high reliance on indirect taxes on spending. For example, although the UK rate of VAT is not high by world standards, the UK has very heavy specific taxes on tobacoo, alcohol and fuel.

• Fair Tax Policy

Progressive taxes reflect the principle of ability to pay. This reflects a concern about vertical equity. The benefit principle is that people getting most benefit from public spending should pay most for it.

Table 12.6: Sources of Revenue (as a Percentage of Total Taxes)

Taxes	UK	USA	France	Germany	Sweden	Japan
Direct	38	45	22	30	42	34
Indirect	43	29	34	30	32	28
Social security contribution	18	25	43	40	26	36
Capital	1	1	1	0	0	2

Source: ONS, Economic Trends, March 1999.

Two factors make the entire tax and benefit structure more progressive than an examination of income tax alone would suggest. First, transfer payments actually give money to the poor. The old get pensions, the unemployed get unemployment benefit, and as a final safety net, anyone whose income falls below a certain minimum stand is entitled to supplementary benefit. Second, the state provides public goods that can be consumed by both rich and poor equally, even if the poor may not have paid any taxes to finance these goods.

However, the system of tax, transfer, and spending have some regressive elements that take proportionately more from the poor. Beer and tobacco taxes are huge earners for the government. And the poor spend a much higher proportion of their income on these goods than do the rich. Regressive taxes inhibit redistribution from the rich to the poor.

• Tax Incidence

Incidence of tax is the final burden once we allow for all induce effects of a tax. The ultimate effect of a tax can be very different from its initial effect. Fig. 12.3 shows the market for labour. D_0 is the demand curve and S_0 is the supply curve. Without income tax labour market equilibrium is at E_0.

Now the tax is imposed. If we measure the gross wage on the vertical axis, the demand curve is unaltered. Firm's demand for labour depends on the gross wage that they pay. Worker's preferences are unchanged, but it is wage net-of-tax that workers compare with the marginal value of their labour in deciding how much labour to supply. 'S_0' is labour supply in terms of the net-of-tax wages, but we must draw S_1 to show the supply of labour in terms of the gross or tax inclusive wage. The vertical distance between S_0 and S_1 is the tax on earnings from the last hour's work D_0 and S_1 show the behaviour of firms and workers at any gross wage. At the new equilibrium E_1, the gross wage is W_1 and firms demand L_1 labour. The vertical distance between W_1 and W_1-tx. It has raised the wage that firms pay but lowered the take-home pay for workers. The incidence of the tax falls on both firms and workers. It falls partly on firms, who pay a higher gross wage W_1, and partly on workers, who receive the lower net wage W_1-tx. The area of pure waste is the area AE_1E_0 which is a deadweight loss.

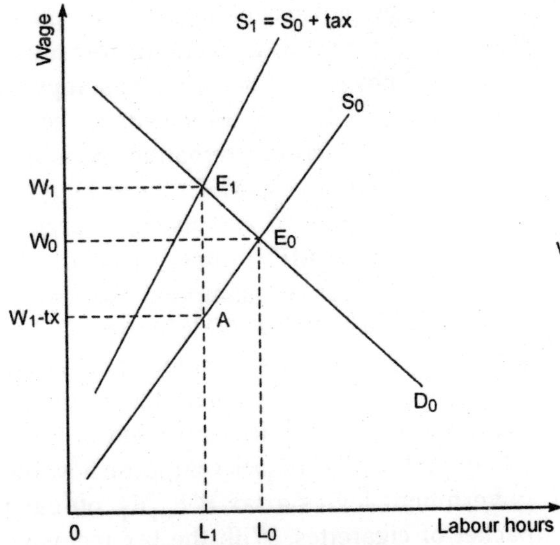

Fig. 12.3: A Tax on Wages

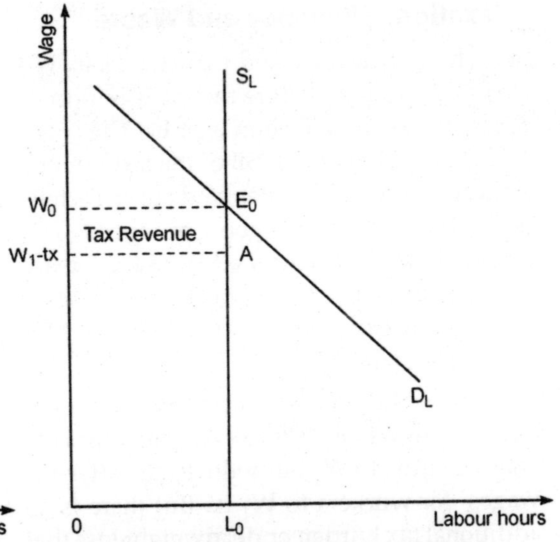

Fig. 12.4: Taxing an Inelastic Factor Supply

- **The Tax Wedge**

The tax wedge is the gap between the price paid by the buyer and the price received by the seller. The incidence of burden of a tax cannot be established by looking at who hands over the tax to the government. Taxes alter equilibrium price and quantities and these induced effects must be taken into account. However, the general conclusion is that the more inelastic the supply curve and more elastic the demand curve, the more the final incidence will fall on the seller rather than the purchaser.

Fig. 12.4 shows he extreme case in which supply is completely inelastic. With tax on, equilibrium is at E_0 and the wage is W_0. Since the vertical supply curve S_0 means that a fixed quantity of L_0 is supplied whatever the after tax wage, a tax on wages leads to a new equilibrium. Only if the gross wage is unchanged will firms demand the same quantity of L_0 that is supplied.

If the supply curve is S_L, a tax AE_0 per unit leaves the quantity L_0 unaffected. Since the demand curve is D_L is unaltered, the tax has no effect on the pre-tax wage rate. The full incidence of tax falls on workers whose after tax wage is reduced by the full amount of the tax.

- **Taxation, Efficiency and Waste**

Taxes have efficiency and equity effects. We use Fig. 12.3 again. Before the tax is imposed, labour market equilibrium is at E_0. The wage W_0 measures both the MSB of the last hour of work and its MSC. The demand curve D_0 tells us the MB of the extra good produced. The supply curve S_0 tells us the MV of the leisure being sacrificed in order to work another hour, the MSC of extra work. At E_0 MSC = MB, which is socially efficient.

When the tax is imposed, the new equilibrium is at E_1. The tax AE_1 increases the wage to firms to W_1 but reduces the after-tax wages for workers to W_1-tx. But there is an additional tax burden or deadweight loss that is pure waste. It is the triangle AE_1E_0. By reducing the quantity of hours from L_0 to L_1, the tax drives a wedge between MB and MSC. This distortion makes free market equilibrium inefficient.

- **Must Taxes Distort?**

Government needs tax revenue to provide goods and transfer payments. Fig. 12.4 shows what happens when a tax is levied on goods and services whose supply is completely inelastic. There is no change in equilibrium quantity. Hence there is no distortion. The equilibrium quantity is the efficient quantity.

Thus, a general principle of taxation is that when either the supply or demand curves for a good or service is very inelastic, a tax leads to small change in equilibrium quantity. Hence, the deadweight burden is small. Given that government would have to raise some tax revenue, waste would be small if the tax is imposed on goods whose supply or demand is most inelastic.

In the UK tax system, the heavily taxed commodities are alcohol and tobacco, which are the most inelastic in demand. So far we have discussed the taxes that do least harm in efficiency terms. Sometimes taxes improve efficiency and reduce waste. The most important example is when externalities exist.

Cigarette smokers pollute the air for other people but ignore this in deciding how much to smoke. They cause a negative consumption externality. Fig. 12.5 shows the supply curve S_0, with no production externalities. S_0 is also the marginal social cost (MSC) curve. D_0 is the private demand curve, and also the marginal private benefit (MPB) curve to smokers. Because of harmful consumption externality, the marginal social benefit (MSB) curve D_1 lies below D_0. With no tax, equilibrium is at E_0, but there are too many cigarettes produced and consumed. The efficient quantity is Q_1 where MSB = MSC (D_1=S_0). Suppose now the government levies a tax = $E_{01}E_1$, on each packet of cigarettes. With the tax inclusive price on the vertical axis, the demand curve

D_0 is unchanged, but the supply curve shifts up to S_1. Each point on S_1 allows producers to receive the corresponding net of tax price on S_0. The tax shifts equilibrium to E_1. The efficient quantity Q_1 is produced and consumed. Consumers pay P_1 and producers receive P_{01} after tax is paid at the rate of $E_{01}E_1$ per packet.

The tax rate $E_{01}E_1$ guides the free-market to the efficient allocation. This is the right tax rate. A tax rate $E_{01}E_1$ leads to the efficient quantity being produced because this is the size of the marginal externality when Q_1 is produced. A tax at this rate makes consumers behave as if they took account of the externality, though they think about the tax-inclusive price only.

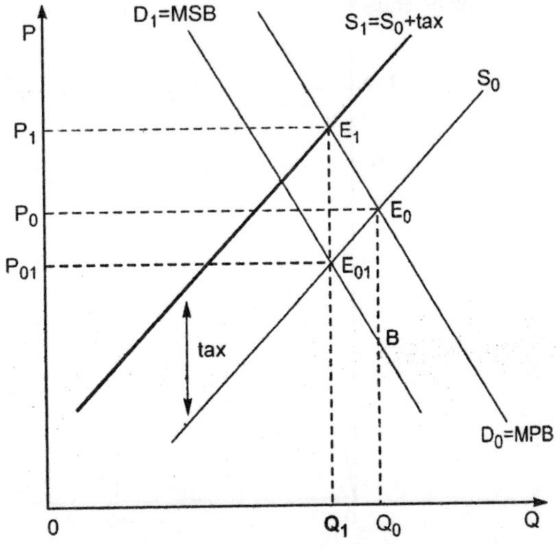

Fig. 12.5: Taxes to Offset Externalities

When externalities create distortions, the government can improve efficiency by levying taxes. The fact that alcohol and tobacco have harmful externalities, it is proper to impose tax heavily on them.

Given market demand D_0 and supply S_0 equilibrium is at E_0 with quantity Q_0. With a negative consumption externality, the MSB=D_1 lying below D_0. E_{01} is socially efficient equilibrium with output Q_1. At this output the ME=E*F. A tax rate of $E_{01}E_1$ per unit has shifted the private supply curve from S_0 to S_1 leading to a new equilibrium at E_1 at which the socially efficient quantity Q_1 is produced and the deadweight burden of externality $E_{01}E_0$ B is eliminated.

TAXATION AND SUPPLY—SIDE ECONOMICS

Supply-side economics analyses how taxes and other incentives affect national output when the economics is at full capacity. Suppose the government cuts spending and tax rates. First, by spending less on goods and services, the government frees resources for use by the private sector. If the private sector is more productive than the public sector, the transfer of resources may increase output. Whether the private sector actually uses resources more productively than the public sector is unclear.

What about the effects of lower tax rates? Fig. 12.3 suggests that tax distortions cause inefficiency. Lower taxes mean lower deadweight burden. The size of this gain depends on supply and demand elasticity. If either elasticity is small, the social gain is also low.

We have already seen that labour supply is fairly inelastic for those already in employment, but a bit more elastic for those thinking of joining the labour force. Cutting income tax rates may increase labour supply, but perhaps by less than many advocates of tax cuts believe.

• The Laffer Curve

The Laffer curve shows how much tax revenue is raised at each possible tax rate. Consider Fig. 12.6. The tax revenue (tax take) of the government is measured on the vertical axis and the rate of taxation is measured on the horizontal axis.

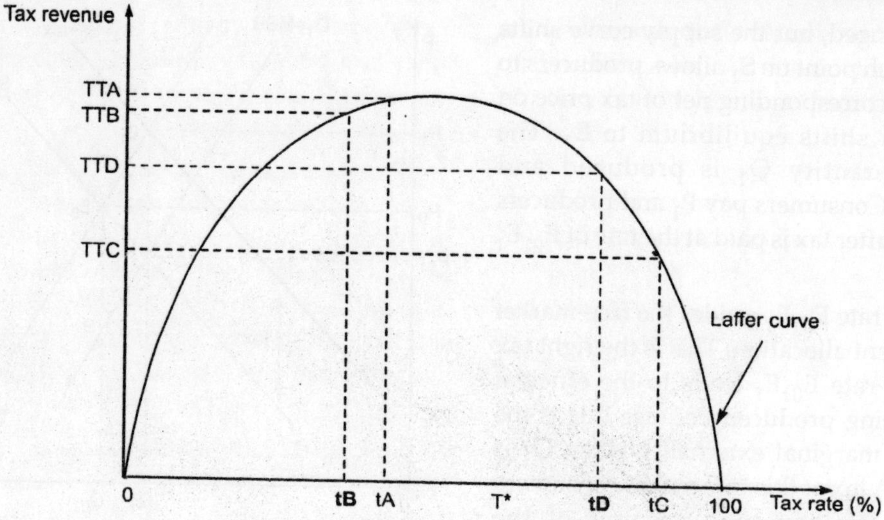

Fig. 12.6: The Laffer Curve

Fig. 12.6 demonstrates that with a zero rate the government collects zero revenue. At the opposite extreme, with 100% tax rate, tax revenue will also be zero, people will not find it useful to work. Beginning from a zero rate, a small increase in tax rate yields some tax revenue. Initially tax revenue rises with rising tax rate, beyond the tax rate T* higher taxes have major disincentive effects on work effort and revenue start falling.

If there is big government we need big taxes and such countries may have tax rate above T*. In such a situation tax cuts will have a miraculous effect. Professor Laffer pointed out that government would get more revenue by cutting taxes. By reducing the tax distortion and increasing the amount of work, lower tax rates would be more than offset by higher incomes to tax.

The shape of the Laffer curve is not in dispute. However, many economists disputed the view that in fact tax rates were above T*. Thus cutting tax rates may eliminate some of the deadweight loss, but government should expect their tax revenue to fall if tax rates were cut. Governments wishing to avoid borrowing need to cut their spending if they want to cut tax rate.

The Laffer curve shows the relationship between tax rates and tax revenue. Moderate tax rate raises some revenue. Beyond T*, higher tax rates reduce revenue because of a disincentive effect. At 100% tax rate, revenue will be zero again.

If the tax rate is tC then the tax take is **TTC**. Cutting the tax rate to **tD** will **increase** the tax revenue to **TTD**.

Supply-siders believe that a tax cut would lead to a large increase in both labour supply and investment, and hence to a large expansion in income/output. More income means more tax revenue for the government.

However, if the tax rate is **tA** then the tax take is **TTA**. Cutting the tax rate to **tB** will **decrease** the tax revenue to **TTB**. Proponents of income tax cuts argue that the tax rate is tC rather than **tA**.

• Economic Sovereignty

Economic sovereignty is the power of national government to make decisions independently of those made by other governments.

Even in an isolated economy, government cannot do anything they like. With market economies they have to work within the forces of demand and supply. It is generally more efficient to have high tax rates on things for which the demand and supply was inelastic; high tax rates on things with elastic demand and supply induces large distortions since equilibrium quantity is very sensitive to the price. We apply this insight to economies open to interactions with the rest of the world.

International capital is now highly mobile across the countries. Suppose the UK government tries to levy a large tax on capital in Britain. Lots of capital will quickly move elsewhere to escape the taxes. The tax base quickly shrinks. So the high tax rates may raise little tax revenue. In contrast, since people are much less mobile than capital across national boundaries, the tax base for taxing worker's income in Britain is much less sensitive to tax rates than the tax base for capital taxes.

Even today people are comparatively more mobile across national boundaries than they were a few decades ago. Today communication is easier, transport costs are lower, and satellites pay no attention to national frontiers on a map. Migration affects not just taxation but government spending as well. Suppose a country wishes to implement a generous welfare state. As a close economy, all it has to worry about is how much of its tax base disappears from work into leisure. If welfare is too generous, people may not work enough. As an open economy, it also has to worry whether more generous welfare provision will lead to more migration into the country as foreigners take advantage of the generous welfare provision.

Closer economic integration with other countries or what is known as globalisation effectively undermines the sovereignty of nation states. As modern technology undermines even barriers between countries, the same process is in work. The economic sovereignty of the nation states, their economic freedom, is steadily being constrained by competition from abroad.

National sovereignty is undermined not just by competiton between countries for tax bases but also by two other factors. The first is other cross-country spillovers such as acid rain, greenhouse gases, or threat of pollution from a nuclear accident.

The second is the scope of redistribution. Economics is about equity as well as efficiency. In an important sense, the right jurisdiction for government is the area within which citizens feel sufficient identity with one another that the rich are prepared to pay for the poor, and the fortunate are prepared to sacrifice for the unlucky.

European nation states have long history of strong national identities. But these are not always set in stone. Countries such as Germany, Belgium, France, Italy, Spain and the UK have faced strong internal pressures to allow part of their country's national sovereignty to secede. In the opposite direction, some Europeans now feel as much a citizen of Europe rather than their own particular nation.

Nation states are not yet obsolete. But they are coming under increasing pressure. Further developments in technology will increase the transactional scope of economic interactions and cultural identity. The proliferation of internet and e-commerce will only accelerate this process.

Political economy is the study of how governments make decisions. Government is the most important single economic agent in the economy. It is important to develop theories of how governments behave. We are not going to analyse the consequence of a policy, which no government will implement.

Voters elect governments to set expenditure and taxation policy, to pass new laws, and establish new regulations. The electorate chooses government according to alternative policy packages offered by the competing political parties, but hardly allows a referendum on each issue. Government may also have its own agenda, which may be to promote what it thinks is good for the society or may simply try to get re-elected.

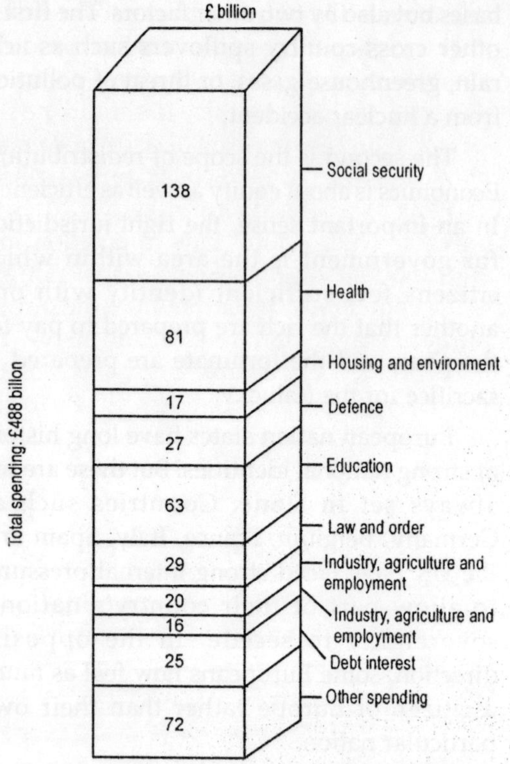

Fig. 12.7: The Allocation of UK Government Spending, 2004-05

• Government of the Macroeconomy: Policies

Government macroeconomic objectives represent the goals and ends which government pursue within the framework of a market-based economy. Since there is no gurantee that the free market will automatically deliver the objective to the satisfaction of a country's political decision makers, all governments at times intervene in the working of the economy to push it in a direction consistent with their stated aims. In broad terms this intervention usually takes three main forms, described as fiscal policy.

• Fiscal Policy

Each year, governments raise and spend huge amounts of money. UK government estimates for 2004-05 suggest that government spending will be about £488 billion and is to be allocated in the manner illustrated in Fig. 12.7. This spending will be funded mainly from taxation (direct and indirect) and national insurance contributions (see Fig. 12.8). The PSNB is estimated at £33 billion.

Fiscal policy involves the use of changes in government spending and taxation to influence the level and composition of aggregate demand in the economy and, given the amounts involved, this clearly has important implications for business. Elementary circular flow analysis suggests, for instance, that reductions in taxation and/or increases in government spending will inject additional income into the economy and will, via the multiplier effect, increase the demand for goods and services, with favourable consequences for business. Reductions in government spending and/or increases in taxation will have the opposite effect, depressing business prospects and probably

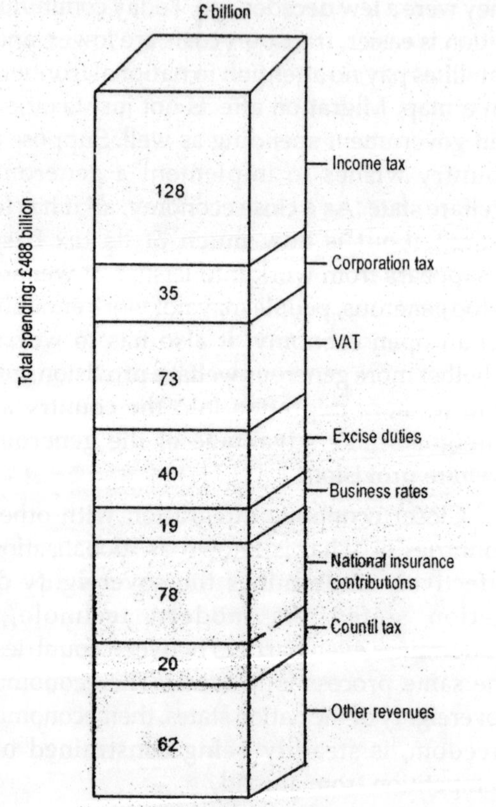

Fig. 12.8: Sources of Government Revenue, 2004-05

discouraging investment and causing a rise in unemployment.

Apart from their overall impact on aggreagate demand, fiscal changes can be used to achieve specific objectives, some of which will be of direct or indirect benefit to the business community. Reductions in taxes on company profits and/or increases in tax allowances for investment in capital equipment can be used to encourage business to increase investment spending, hence boosting the income of firms producing industrial products and causing some additional spending on consumption. Similarly, increased government spending targeted at firms involved in exporting, or at the creation of new business, will encourage increased business activity and, additionally, may lead to more output and employment in the economy.

In considering the use of fiscal policy to achieve their objectives, governments tend to be fated with a large number of practical problems that generally limit their room to manoeuvre. Boosting the economy through increase in spending or reduction in taxation could cause inflationary pressures, as well as encouraging an inflow of imports and increasing the public sector deficit, none of which would be welcomed by entrepreneurs or by the financial markets. Thus, the fiscal attempts to restrain demand in order to reduce inflation will generally depress the economy, causing a fall in output and employment and encouraging firms to abandon or defer investment projects until business prospects improve. Added to this, it should not be forgotten that government decision makers are politicians who need to consider the political as well as economy implication of their policies. Thus, white cuts in taxation may receive public approval, increase may not; and if implemented, the latter may encourage higher wage demands. Similarly, the redistribution of government spending from one programme area to another is likely to give rise to widespread protests from those on the receiving end of any cuts: so much so that governments tend to be restricted for the most part to changes at the margin rather than undertake a redical reallocation of resources and may be tempted to fix budgetary allocations for a number of years ahead (e.g. the comprehensive spending review in the UK).

Other factors too—including changes in economic thinking, external constraints on borrowing and international agreements—can also play their part in restraining the use of fiscal policy as an instrument of demand management, whatever a government's preferred course of action may be. Simple prescriptions to boost the economy through large-scale cuts in taxation or increase in government spending often fail to take into account the political situation faced by most of the governments.

QUESTION

1. Which of the following are public goods?
   (a) The fire brigade;
   (b) Clean street;
   (c) Refuge collection;
   (d) Cable TV;
   (e) Social toleration;
   (f) The postal services.
2. Why does society try to ensure that every child receives and education? Discuss the different ways this could be done and give reasons for preferring one method of providing such an education.
3. How would you apply the principles of horizontal and vertical equity in deciding how much to tax two people, each capable of doing the same work, but one of whom chooses to devote more time to sun bathing and thus has a low income?

4. Classify the following taxes as progressive or regressive:
   (a) 10% tax on all luxury goods;
   (b) taxes in proportion to the value of owner-occupied houses;
   (c) taxes on beer;
   (d) taxes on champagne.
5. There is a flat-rate 30% income tax on all income over £2000. Calculate the average tax rate at income level of £5000, £10000 and £50000. Is the tax progressive? Is it more or less progressive if the exemption limit is raised from £2000 to £5000?
6. Suppose the labour supply is completely inelastic.
   (a) Show why there is no deadweight loss if wages are taxed. Who bears the incidence of the tax?
   (b) Now suppose the labour supply is quite elastic. Show the area that is the dead-weight burden of the tax. How much of the tax is ultimately borne by firms and how much by workers?
   (c) For any given supply elasticity show that firms bear more of the tax the more inelastic is the demand for labour.
7. Why are these statements wrong?
   (a) taxes always distort;
   (b) If government spends all its revenue, taxes are not a burden on society as a whole.

ANSWERS

1. All except (d)
2. Education is a merit good (all people may not know what is good for them). So government may have to provide at least some of it; externalities (we like educated people to interact with); equity (help promote equality of opportunities).
3. Vertical equity says that taking some from the rich and giving it to the poor: ideally wants to redistribute from the person getting more of all goods. Horizontal equity means that all are treated in a similar way.
4. All taxes are progressive except beer, which is a larger share of poor people's income.
5. 18%, 24%, 28.8%. It is progressive, and more so the higher the exemption level.
6. (a) No change in labour supplied, so there is no distortion and no distortion triangle.
   (b) Distortion triangle will be bigger, and firms now bear most of the tax.
   (c) If the supply elasticity is zero entire tax burden will be borne by the workers and if it is perfectly elastic tax burden will be borne by the firm.
7. (a) What about financing of the public goods, offsetting externalities, provision of social insurance, and redistribution?
   (b) Marginal taxes usually create distortions.

CHAPTER 13

INDUSTRIAL AND COMPETITION POLICY

KEY TERMS

Competition Policy: enhances efficiency of the economy by promoting and safeguarding competition and avoid monopolization of the economy.

Industrial Policy: it aims to offset externalities affecting production decisions by private firms.

Sunrise Industries: are the emerging new industries of the future. For example, complex and genetic industries.

Sunset Industries: are those of the past, now in long-term decline. For example, are old heavy industries, such as steel and ship-building.

Merger: is the voluntary union of two or more firms.

Competition policy enhances efficiency by promoting or safeguarding competition. Competition policy entails rules about conduct of firms or the structure of industries. The former aims to prevent abuse by a monopoly and the latter seeks to prevent monopolies.

Some industries are natural monopolies. Scale economies are so large that breaking them up makes no sense, and competition from other firms provides no discipline. They are natural monopolies and have been nationalized in many European countries to use them for the interest of the society. After 1980s, the UK government pioneered the privatization of those industries. Other countries have followed suit. Since scale economies do not vanish with privatization, continuous regulation has been necessary. First, we deal with cases where scale economies are less significant. Competition policy has become an important form of government intervention.

Other motives for intervention are to increase production efficiency. If inefficiency arises not from scale economics and market power, but from the environmental externalities, what other kind of market failure can we think about? Essentially all the other externalities associated with production.

Industrial policy aims to offset externalities affecting production decisions by firms.We discuss four such production externalities or market failures: privacy of intervention and knowledge creation; spillovers across borders that lead to policy competition between governments; capital market failures that explain why new businesses are so difficult to start; and locational externalities.

Industrial Policy: Inventions and the patent system—Information is a very special economic commodity. It is very hard to trade information: the buyers need to see it but, having seen it has no incentive to pay for it. One example is invention. The problem is that the inventor finds it difficult to privately appropriate profit from an investment during this period.

A patent is a temporary legal status awarded to an inventor who registers the invention.

Research and Development (R & D): Research is the process of invention. Development makes research commercially viable.

Most of the countries subsidise R & D, which account for about 2% of GDP in advanced countries. Why are the market failures in R & D that patent system cannot offset? This is because the large projects are risky for an individual company. For example, Boeing describes a project as betting the company: failure of one new project could threat its existence as company. Private individuals and business executives are normally more risk-averse.

Private firms may undertake less R & D than socially desirable becuase the social return exceeds the private return to those making the decisions. Society needs a lower rate of return, or use a lower discount rate to evaluate the future benefits of the project, for two reasons: first, the government can pool the risk across many projects in its portfolio; second, even if a project goes wrong, the government can spread burden across the entire population. Thus, society needs a smaller risk premium than that required by private individual. This is one reason to subsidise R & D. Thus the private benefit to the investor becomes a social benefit. This is the second reason to subsidise R & D.

- **Strategic International Competition Policy**

We consider the commercial airline industry again. Effectively there are two large firms left in the world market. Boeing and McDonnell-Douglas have merged in 1996 and become one company. The other major player is the European consortium Airbus industry.

Suppose Airbus asks the governments of its member producers (Germany, France, the UK and Spain) for launch aid, a grant or loan on favourable terms to help with R & D on new aircraft in addition to the standard arguments for R & D support, what extra issues does international competition raise?

First, Airbus may survive and succeed even without government support. If so, public subsidies are simply a transfer payments to Airbus shareholders, a poor idea. Second, launch aid may be necessary for the success of the Airbus company. If Airbus pulls out, Boeing-McDonnell-Douglas will be the sole producer without fear of competition. In that it would be surely easy for Boeing to raise the price of commercial aircraft. Consumers of air-travellers would be losers because they will have to pay higher prices, and Boeing would be the sole beneficiary, as they will earn monopoly profits. It may be worth preventing this.

Financial support is a commitment by European governments not to let Airbus to be bullied out of the industry. Boeing may conclude that there is no point attempting a price war to force Airbus to exit. A European commitment may prevent a price war that would otherwise occur. Strategic international competition can provide a rationale for strategic industrial policy.

- **Sunrise and Sunset Industries**

The next aspect of industrial policy concerns dynamic change, the rise and fall of industries and firms companies them.

Sunrise industries are the emerging new industries of the future. Sunset industries are those of the past, now in long-term decline. For example, Sunrise industries are computer and genetic. Sunset industries in development economies of the West are old heavy industries, such as steel and ship-building, now suffering from huge excess capacity, undercut by more efficient producers in the pacific basin.

Why not leave such changes to market forces? What market failures might justify government intervention through industrial policy? We begin with Sunrise industries.

In these industries, two types of market failure are normally put foward to justify the case for government intervention. First, there may be imperfection in the market for lending to new companies and new industries. Banks and other traditional lenders may be too risk-averse, or too unfamiliar with the new business, to lend money needed through the early loss-making years. Second, the market may be too slow to provide the relevant training and skills: catch 22 situation. These arguments may justify industrial policy to subsidise Sunrise industries. But two questions need answering. First, why are markets short sighted and uninformed? Second, even if markets get it worng, can the government do better? The strategy of trying to outguess the market by 'picking winners' is highly discredited. Civil servants and politicians are unlikely beat analysts in industry and finance. If industrial policy is to be pursued, it is better to diagnose the cause of market failure and provide incentive to those market decision-makers than to take into account when undertaking their professional analysis.

Sunset industries present different probelms. It may be desirable to spend what could otherwise be dole money on temporarily subsidising the lame ducks to ease the transition. Sometimes, a sharp shock is needed to signal the extent of adjustment eventually required and the government's commitment to seeing the adjustment take place. Strategic considerations are important here too.

• Economic Geography

Economic geography popularized by Paul Krugman means that firm's location affects its production costs. A beneficial locational externality occurs if a firm's costs are reduced by locating near similar firms.

A firm's costs of production depend on its proximity to other firms because of three reasons: the interaction of scale economics and risk, transport and transactions costs, and technological spillovers.

Suppose a worker invests in very special skills, such as designing racing cars. With only one firm in the local market, the worker is dependent on one employer. Having this specific skill is really risky. With a cluster of similar employers, risks to workers fall. They no longer require such a large 'risk premium' or 'compensating differential' in their wage. Labour is cheaper for firms. Where did scale economics come into argument? Without them, each locality could have a thinly smattering of every firm. It is the presence of scale economics that forces firms into all or nothing choices between different locations.

A second reason is transport cost. Shops may cluster because of transport costs for consumers but large producers cluster because of features of production. Closeness to raw material is an obvious example. Discovering a coal seam or iron ore leads to a profusion of heavy industrial business in the locality.

Most significant of all is the spillover in technology itself. Important example is silicon valley in California, clusters of computer-based producers who find it advantageous to be in proximity. Although in competiton with one another, they also feed off each other's ideas just as the most competent Professors attend each other's seminars. The same hold good in businesses from software design to satellite technology. In such examples, we can see that one firm's cost curve depends on how many other similar firms are situated nearby. This idea of a locational externality clarifies a concept that politicians have discussed for years but

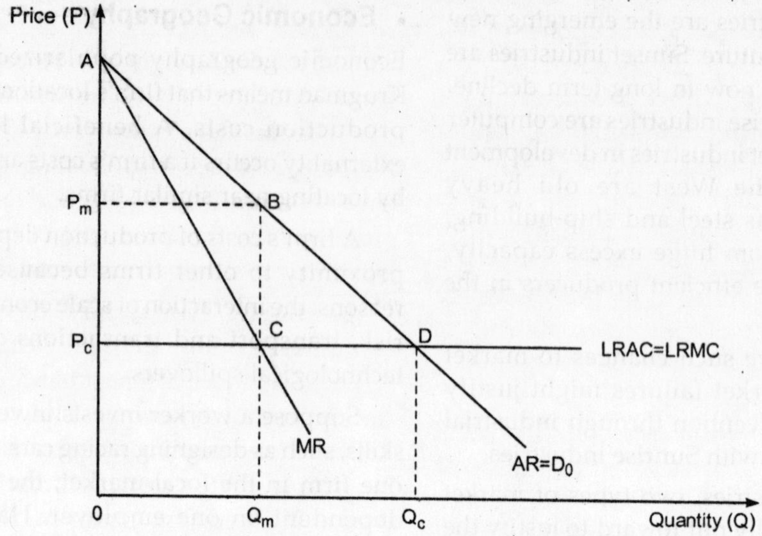

Fig. 13.1: The Social Cost of Monopoly

whiich previously economists have had trouble providing with a coherent interpretation.

The industrial base of a country or region is a measure of the stock of existing producers available to provide such locational externalities.

This emphasis on industrial base carries the presumption that the externalities are more significant for producers than for consumers, because of the specificity of investment required and minimum size that scale economies imposed.

In contrast, if the minmum efficient scale of specific investment is large, countries or regions may find that there are two equilibria—one in which nobody enters and one in which many firms enter, each benefit from the presence of the other. Yet achieving the second outcome efficiently requires coordination of the entry decision of different producers to internalise the externality facing each firm: it neglects the benefits that its own entry creates for other firms.

• The Social Cost of Monopoly

Competitive equilibrium is efficient in the absence of market failure. Each industry expands output to the point at which P = MC = MSB = MSC. Resource reallocation cannot make everyone better off.

When an industry is imperfectly competitive, each firm has some monopoly power. Since demand curve slope downward, Price is > MR = MC. The excess price over MC is a firm's monopoly power. The price MSB of the last unit of output then exceed the Marginal Private Cost (MPC) and Marginal Social Cost (MSC) of producing that last unit. From society's point of view, industry output is too small. Expanding output adds more to social benefit than to social cost. How do we measure the social cost of monopoly power and inefficient resource allocation?

Imperfect competition needs some scale economics to limit the number of firms an industry can support. Nonetheless, to introduce the idea of the social cost of monopoly power, it is convenient to ignore the economies scale altogether.

What happens if a competitive industry is taken over by a single firm that then operates as a multiplant monopolist? In Fig. 13.1, under perfect competition LMC is the industry supply curve. With constant return to scale, LRMC = LRAC of the industry. Given the demand curve D_0, the competitive industry produces an output Q_c at a price P_c. If the industry now becomes a monopolist it will maximize profit by producing output Q_m at a price P_m (where MC = MR). The area P_mP_cCB is the monopoly profit from selling Q_m output at a price greater than LRMC = LRAC. The area BDC is the social cost of monopoly power. At Q_m the marginal social benefit (MSB) of another unit of output is P_m but the LRMC = marginal social and private cost (MSC). Society would try to raise output up to point D at which MSB = MSC. The area BDC is the social gain of extending output.

The demand curve measures the MPB (marginal private benefit) to consumers of each unit of output and the LRMC curve measures the extra resources used to make each unit of output.

Hence the area between D_0 and LRMC up to the output produced measures the total surplus (in this case the area P_cABC) to be divided between consumers and producers. Producers' surplus (the area $0P_cABC$) is the excess of revenue (the area $0P_mBQ_m$) over total cost (the area $0P_cCQ_m$). Total costs are the area under the LRMC curve up to this output (the area $0P_cCQ_m$).

Consumers' surpluses are maximized at Q_c at which the area between the demand curve and the LMC is maximized.

The social cost of monopoly is the failure to maximize social surplus. This is found by adding together the deadweight burden such as the area BCD for all industries in which MC and MR are less than P and MSB.

At an output below the efficient level, the deadweight burden area shows the loss of social surplus. Is the social cost of monopoly really large? Some economists, such as Stigler believe it is small. Other economists, such as professor F.M. Scherer, argued that it is as large as 7% of US GDP.

Why such disagreement? First, the area of the deadweight burden in Fig. 13.1 depends on the elasticity of demand curve. In calculating the deadweight burden under monopoly, different economists use different estimates of the demand elasticity.

Second, the welfare cost of monopoly is not just the deadweight loss. Since monopoly may yield high profits to the firm, firms spend a lot to secure and acquire monopoly positions. We have also seen that existing oligopolists have an incentive to advertise too much in order to raise the fixed cost of being in the industry, an entry barrier to new firms.

Similarly, firms may devote large quantities of resources trying to influence the government in ways that enhance or preserve the monopoly power. They may also deliberately maintain extra production capacity to create a credible threat to flood the market if an entrant comes in. Society may have to devote a large quantity of resources to lobbying the government or maintaining overcapacity which are really waste.

Modern economic analysis also stressed the role of information. Those running a monopoly have inside information about the firm's true cost opportunities. They know more than shareholders or a regulator. Perhaps the monopolist could have lower costs if its managers put in extra efforts.

Economists call this 'managerial slack' or X-inefficiency. Lack of competition gives the firm an 'information monopoly' on its own cost possibilities. Outsiders cannot find out.

If a competitive firm gets lazy, it loses market share and goes out of market. If a monopolist gets lazy, it simply makes a bit of less profit. From the social point of view, its costs curves are unnecessarily high and spend extra resources to make this output.

- **Price Discrimination Monopoly**

The social cost of monopoly arises because the monopolist cannot always price discriminate. Perfect price discrimination makes the demand curve and the MR curve coincide. Then P = MR = MC. The monopolist produces the socially efficient output.

Price discrimination is possible only in special circumstances. Consumers must not be able to set-up a second-hand market; and producer is able to establish separate sub-markets. Price discrimination in services is easier since resale is impossible. For example, a doctor operating a patient cannot resale it to anybody else. Price discrimination by large monopolists is precluded when an universal service requirement is legally forcing the monopolist to supply to all parts of the country at a uniform price, even though the price of rural delivery are much higher.

• The Distribution of Monopoly Profits

Society does not care just about the inefficiency of imperfect competition. It may also care about two other aspects of monopoly power: the political power that large companies exert, and the distributional issue of the fairness of the large profits, a monopolist can earn.

Monopoly profits are a private tax. The ultimate recipients of monopoly profits are the monopolist's shareholders. Much of the stock market is held by the pension funds and insurance companies that eventually make payments to workers. Some monopoly profits go to the less well off. But most do not.

Suppose the government imposes a profit tax, how does this affect the monopolist's output decision? It does not. For a given tax rate, higher pre-tax profits must raise post-tax profits. Hence, the monopolist produces exactly the same output as in the absence of a profit tax and, facing the same demand curve, and will charge the same price as before.

A monopolist cannot shift the tax on to anybody else. Society can tax as much of the monopolist's profits as it wants, without affecting the monopolist's behaviour, at least in the short-run.

An occasional windfall tax may remove monopoly profits without adversely affecting the incentive on efficiency. However, the expectation of regular resort to such taxes will undermine incentives to invest. Costs would then become higher than they might have been.

• Must Liberalization Help

We know that more competition is always better. Beginning from a distorted position, elimination of all market failures would always increase efficiency. But partial elimination or reduction can make things worse rather than better, sometimes two distortions may offset each other. Removing just one makes the other worse.

Suppose there are large economies of scale and a falling ATC costs. A monopolist is bad for the reason outlined above, but it does at least produce on a large scale and lets society benefit from scale economics. Suppose the government insists on more competition, say entry of a second firm. Dividing the market would make both firms unable to reap scale economics. More competition may reduce profit and drive price close to MC; it may also reduce information monopolies, forcing more expenditure on cost reduction to shift cost curve down. But if the scale economics are big enough, both producers have large costs than the original monopolist. Society may be worse off because it would have to spend more resources on production. With this brief discussion of market power, we can understand the role of competition policy.

• Competition Policy

Society would definitely gain more from greater competition, if only it could be secured, than it would not lose from giving up economies of large scale by allowing fresh entry. Promotion of competition in certain industries is likely to be beneficial. This can be achieved by setting rules for conduct or by taking steps to ensure a market structure in which competition can prevail.

In the USA, competition policy has been based on breaking up big companies to achieve a market structure favourable to competition. UK competition policy is, on the other hand, more pragmatic, a case-by-case assessment without a prior presumption that the existence of the monopoly power is bad.

• UK Competition Law

Monopoly policy has been reassessed in the 1973 Fair Trading Act and amended in the

Competition Act of 1980 and 1998. The 1973 Act introduced a Director-General of Fair Trading to supervise many aspects of competition and consumer law, including regulation of quantity and standards. The Director-General is responsible for monitoring company behaviour and, subject to a ministerial veto, can refer individual cases to the competition commission for a through investigation.

A company can be referred to, if it supplies more than 25% of the total market. The commission can also be given cases where two or more distinct firms by implicit collusion operate to restrict competition. The commission investigates whether a monopoly, or potential monopoly, acts against the public interest.

There is no presumption that monopoly is bad. The commission is charged to investigate whether or not monopoly acts against the interest of the public, a wide brief that in recent years has stressed 'maintenance and promotion of effective competition'.

The Restrictive Practices Court examines agreements between UK firms, such as collusive pricing behaviour. All agreements must be notified to the Director-General of Fair Trading, who refers them to the court unless they are voluntarily abandoned or judged of trivial significance. The court will find against these agreements unless they satisfy one of eight 'gateways' or justifications, for example, their removal would cause serious unemployment in the area. For restrictive practices, the burden of proff lies on companies to show that they are acting in public interest. In contrast, the legislation of monopolies is more open-minded. The commission has to show companies are acting against the public interest.

The UK is also subject to the monopoly legislation of the European Union. Article 85 of the Treaty of Rome is similar to UK legislation on restrictive practices. Agreements have to be notified and are likely to be outlawed. Article 86 bans the abuse of a 'dominant position' as a monopolist.

The 1998 Competition Act brought UK policy more in line with European Law. The terms of reference of the competition commission were supplemented by two new prohibitions. Essentially, there is a ban on agreements that prevent, restrict or distort competition in the UK, and a ban on conduct that amounts to abuse of a dominant position within the UK.

• UK Competition Policy in Practice

The competition commission has wide power to make recommendations, and the minister normally act on its recommendations. Yet only a few companies have so far been penalized as a result of investigations. More frequently, the commission has relied on informal assurances that criticized behaviour will be suspended.

It has investigated a wide range of cases, from beer to breakfast cereals, from contraception to cross-channel ferries. Since it has looked at each case with an open mind, its judgements have stressed different aspects of behaviour in different cases. A large market share has not always attracted an unfavourable judgement. For example, the ice cream wars by Birds Eye Walls was a case in point. The commission ruled that there was no evidence that BEW had refused to supply other wholesalers. It concluded that BEW had restricted and distorted competition, found no offsetting benefits to the public interest, and recommended that BEW be required to supply wholesalers on the same terms as it did to others.

It also has the power to investigate regulated industries such as utilities. In 1999, it reported on claims that charges by Vodafone, BT, etc. for calls from fixed phones to mobile phones were too high. It concluded that emerging competition in telecommunication was not yet sufficient to discipline these monopoly suppliers, and that at the end of 1998 charges made by Cellnet and Vodafone were 22% higher than the public interest benchmark—calculated from a hypothetical suppliers, with the scale economies corresponding to a 25% above a public interest benchmark. Therefore, the commission recommended that the licenses of Cellnet, Vodafone and BT be modified to impose price ceilings on the charges.

• Restrictive Trade Practices (RP)

Since restricted practices legislation was first introduced in 1956, over 5000 agreements have been registered. Most were abandoned before they went to the court. The result looks impressive as most explicit price fixing has gone.

First, they may simply have forced collusive agreement underground. Recent legislation and policy has tightened up 'information agreements' that could be the basis of secret collusion. Second, the various 'gateways' have let some doubtful agreements be ratified. Finally, tighter control of restrictive practices agreements between firms has been an incentive for merger. By formally merging, companies can continue old practices within the merged company.

• Mergers

Merger means two firms can unite in two different ways form one company.

A firm makes a take over bid for another firm by offering to buy out the shareholders of the second firm. Managers of the victim firm will try to resist since they are likely to lose jobs, but the shareholders may accept the offer if it is attractive.

A merger is the voluntary union of two firms that they think will do better together.

Are mergers in the public interest, or do they just create private monopoly?

The production process has several stages. The first stage might be iron ore extraction, the second stage is to manufacture steel from ore, and the third stage is the production of cars from steel.

A horizontal merger is the union of two firms at the same production stage in the same industry. A vertical merger is the union of two firms at different production stages in the same industry. In a conglomerate merger, the production activities of the two unrelated firms are joined together.

A horizontal merger may allow more economies of scale. One big car company may be better than two small ones if each firm was previously producing below minimum efficient scale. In vertical merger, there may be gains in co ordination and planning. It may be easier to make long-term decisions about the best size and type of steel mill if a simultaneous decision is taken on the level of car production to which steel output forms an important input. The conglomerate mergers have very little opportunity for a direct reduction of production costs.

• Two Other Benefit of Mergers

First, if the company has an inspired management team, it may be more productive

Table 13.1: Mergers and Take over in the UK (1972-2000): (Annual Average)

	Number	Value (1998 £billion)
1972-78	640	1
1979-85	490	4
1986-89	1300	43
1990-94	590	10
1995-98	580	31
1999-2000	540	61

Source: British Business 1989, Business Trend 1997, ONS.

to allow this team to manage both businesses. Second, by pooling their financial resources, the merged firms may enjoy access to cheaper borrowing, letting them take more risks and undertake larger research projects. There may also be economies of scale in marketing. These gains could explain why merger make sense even for companies producing completely different product.

If companies achieve any of these benefits, they will be in a position to increase productivity and lower costs. These private gains are also social gains. If these were the only considerations, private and social calculations would coincide. However, in some situations private and social assessment may diverge. First, the merger of two big firms gives the merged company a monopoly power from a large market share, which would enable them to restrict output and increase prices, a bigger deadweight loss for the society especially apparent in conglomerate mergers. A tobacco producer and a food manufacturer can easily use their joint financial power to start price war in one of these industries. With large financial resources, they are not the first to go bust. By forcing out increase in their market share, they deter entry, and charge higher prices.

Merger policy must thus compare the social gain with social costs.

Table 13.1 shows annual average of take overs and mergers involving only UK firms. It shows merger booms in the late 1980s and again after 1995. What were the reasons?

The two merger booms coincided with high values of the stock market, which raised the value of both firms involved in the merger. Table also shows the key aspect of the merger booms was the value of the mergers, more than the number of them.

Second, mergers are often associated with opportunities to rationalise industrial structure.

Two major developments in European markets were the periods preceding the creation of the single European market in 1992 and the launch of the Euro (single currency) in 1999. A large market raises scope for scale economies and increase competition.

Third, the combination of new technology and deregulation has been changing market structure both in the UK and in its main trading partners. Segmentation of national markets has been breaking down in many industries including telecommunication, financial services and so on. Cross-border mergers have allowed leading players to respond to larger markets.

The increase in market size in the last 15 years has also influenced the type of mergers taking place. Conglomerate mergers had grown steadily in 1960s and 1970s, and also in 1980s. However, financial deregulation has made it easier to raise finance.

• Merger Policy

There had been no anti-merger policy to reduce the development of large companies. There are currently two reasons for referring a proposed merger to an investigation by the competition commission: (1) that the merger will promote a new monopoly as defined by 25% market share used in deciding references for existing monopoly positions, or (2) that the merger involves the transfer of at least £70 million worth of company assets.

The merger legislation was introduced in 1965, only 4% of all merger proposals have been referred to the competition commission. For much of the period government policy has been to consent to, or actively encourage mergers.

Merger Policy in the UK reflected two assumptions: (1) the cost savings from economies of scale and more intensive use of scarce management talent could be quite large; and (2) the UK was part of an increasingly competitive world market so that the monopoly power of the merged firms, and the corresponding social cost of the deadweight burden, would be quite small. Large as they were, the merged firms were small in relation to European or world markets, and would face relatively elastic demand curves, giving little scope to raise price above MC.

Nevertheless, nearly half of the proposed mergers actually referred to the competition commission were found to be against the public interest. However, investigation was a lengthy process, a delay during which company share prices could change, upsetting the original negotiations about the terms on which the relative shares of the companies should be valued. In practice, even the threat that a merger might be referred was often sufficient for the companies to abandon the merger.

QUESTIONS

1. With constant AC = MC = £5, a competitive firm produces 1 million units of output. Industry was taken over by a monopolist, and output falls to 800,000 units and the price rises to £8. AC and MC are unchanged. What is the social cost of monopoly?
2. Suppose when the monopolist takes over, AC and MC increases to £6 and output falls to 600,000 units at a P = £11. What is the social cost of monopoly now?
3. Explain the difference between the US and the UK policy towards monopolies and mergers.
4. Most of the footballs are produced in a small village in India. Why do markets of footballs cluster together? Why not in Sweden?
5. Why are these statements wrong? (a) Monopolies make profits and should therefore, be well-run companies, (b) Monopolies create social waste. Thus, we should ban firms producing over 20% of the market. (c) Mergers are definitely beneficial; otherwise companies should not merge.

ANSWERS

1. Triangle has height of £3, and length of 200,000. Thus the cost is £300,000.
2. The area now has height of £6 and length of 200,000, and the cost of 1200,000. In addition, 600,000 units are now produced at £1 more than it is really necessary. Total social cost is £1800,000.
3. In short, US presumes large size is always bad, and tries to break up big firms, or regulate them if they can not be split up. UK policy is on a case-by-case basis, as large firms achieve scale economies as well.
4. It is because of local externalities. But the entire production cluster in a sensible place. High-wage Sweden is not a good place for labour-intensive business.
5. (a) Profit reflects monopoly power, but may not be well-run companies.

   (b) Benefits of scale economies and incentive to innovate may outweigh the other costs of monopoly.

   (c) Private benefits of merger are nothing but monopoly profits, which may be social cost.

CHAPTER 14

WELFARE ECONOMICS

KEY TERMS

Pareto-Efficiency: For a given set of resource, consumer tastes, and technology, an allocation is, Pareto-efficient if there is no other allocation that makes some people better off and nobody worse off.

Theory of the Second Best: If there must be a distortion, it would not be correct to keep the distortion in one market. It would be more efficient to spread the distortion more thinly over a wide range of markets.

Externalities: Arise when the action of producers or consumers affects the consumption and production of others, other than through the normal working of the price mechanism.

Welfare economics deals with both positive and normative issues. It does not describe how the economy works but assesses how best in works.

There are two views about the working of the market economy. First view is that the market fosters choice, incentive and efficiency. The second view is that market often fails which require government's intervention. What lies behind the disagreement? Two themes recur in our discussion of welfare economics. The first is allocative efficiency. Is the economy getting the most of its scarce resources? The second is equity. How fair is the distribution of income and wealth between the members of the society?

• Equity and Efficiency

Equity may be horizontal which means identical treatment of identical people, or vertical, that is, the different treatment of different people in order to reduce the conseqences of their innate differences.

Whether or not either concept of equity is desirable, is a pure value judgement.

Horizontal equity rules out discrimination between people of equal economic circumstances. Vertical equity is the Robin Hood principle of taking from the rich to give it to the poor.

There is hardly any disagreement about horizontal equity. Although people often disagree to the extent to which resources should be distributed from the 'haves' to the 'have nots' to increase vertical equity.

• Efficiency in Resource Allocation

A resource allocation is a description of who does what and who gets what?

Suppose a dictator makes the allocation. Feasible allocations depend on the technology and resources available to the economy. The ultimate worth of any allocation depends on consumer tastes, which determine how people value what they are given.

To try to separate the discussion of equity and efficiency, the modern welfare economics uses the idea of Pareto efficiency. For a given set of resource, consumer tastes, and technology, an allocation is Pareto-efficient, if there is no other allocation that makes some people better off and nobody worse off.

In Fig. 14.1, a move from point A to point B to point G is a Pareto gain. Sen is better off, Ray no worse off. If point B or point G is feasible, then point A is Pareto inefficient. A move from point A to point D makes Ray better off but Sen worse off. The Preto criterion has nothing to say about this change. To evaluate it, we need a judgement about the relative value of the individual's utility. The Pareto principle is of limited use in comparing allocation on efficiency grounds. It only allows us to evaluate moves to the north-west or south-west in Fig. 14.1. Yet this is the most we can say about efficiency without making value judgements about equity.

Provided people assess their own utility by the commodities they receive, point B is better than point A and point A in turn better allocation than point C. But a comparison of point A with point D, point E or point F requires us to adopt a value judgement about the relative importance to us about two consumers utility.

In Fig. 14.2, we take the argument a stage further. By reorganizing production, we can make the economy produce anywhere inside or on the frontier AB. A pareto gain can be achieved by a move from inside the frontier to the frontier. Any point inside the frontier is Pareto inefficient.

Someone can be made better off without making anyone worse off. But all points on the frontier are Pareto efficient. One person can get more only by giving another person less. Since Pareto gain is not possible, every point on the frontier is Pareto efficient. Thus we can say that the society should never choose an

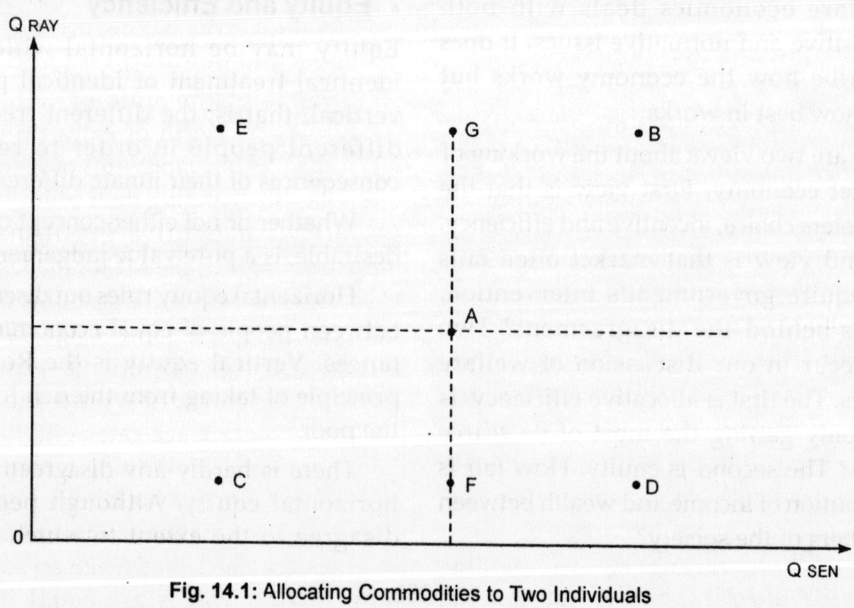

Fig. 14.1: Allocating Commodities to Two Individuals

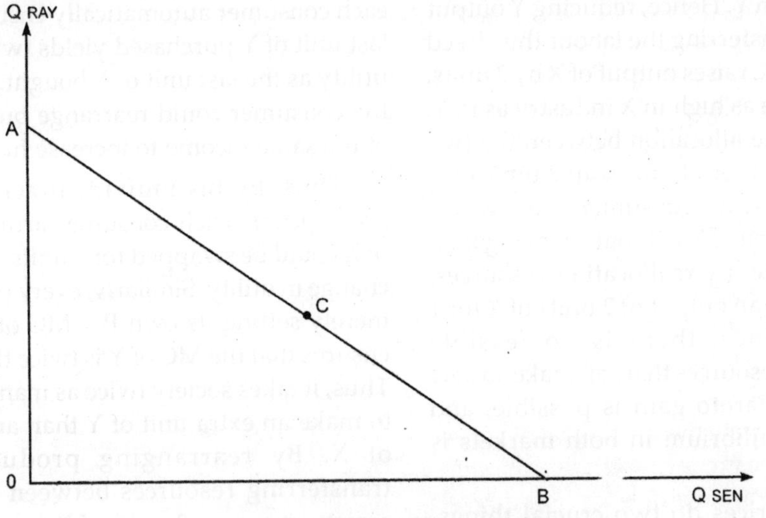

Fig. 14.2: The Efficiency Frontier

inefficient allocation inside the frontier. Now the question is, which of efficient points on the frontier the is most desirbale one will depend on the value judgement about the relative value of the two members of the community, a judgement about equity.

The frontier AB shows the maximum quantity of goods, which the economy can produce for one person given the quantity of good being produced for other the other person. We know all points on the frontier are Pareto-efficient. Ray can only be made better off by making Sen worse off, and vice versa. The distribution of goods between them is much more equal at point C than point A or point B.

- **Pareto Efficiency and Perfect Competition**

We now turn to the most important question of whether the allocation of resources as determined by a free market is Pareto-efficient. The answer is no, unless highly unrealistic assumptions are made. Nevertheless, the economic theory has shown that under these assumptions (e.g. perfect competition exists in all markets) the price mechanism would act automatically to bring a Pareto-efficient allocation of resources, i.e., under condition of competitive equilibrium, free market economy will automatically bring a Pareto optimal allocation of resources.

Suppose in such a market, there are many producers and consumers, but only two goods, X and Y. Each market is free and perfectly competitive. In equilibrium, suppose the price of X is £5 and the price of Y is £10. Labour is the variable factor of production and workers can move freely between industries. Now we can argue the following points.

The last unit of Y yields consumers £10 worth of extra utility. If it yielded less (more) utility than £10, its buying price, then the last consumer will purcahse less (more) of Y.

Similarly, the unit of X must yield consumers £5 worth of extra utility. Hence consumers can swap 2 unit of X for one unit of Y without changing their utility. Since, in a perfectly competitive profit maximizing industry, P = MC, the MC of the last unit of X is £5 and the MC of the last unit of Y is £10. Labour earns the same wage rate in both industries in competitive equilibrium. Otherwise, workers would move to the industry where wage rate is higher. In each industry, the MC = W/mpl, where mpl is the marginal productivity of labour. Higher wages raise MC, but a higher mpl means fewer extra workers are needed to make an extra unit of output. And wages are equal in the two industries X as in Y. Hence, reducing Y output by one unit, transferring the labour thus freed to the industry X, raises output of X by 2 units. The mpl is twice as high in X industry as in Y. Feasible resource allocation between the two industries allows society to swap 2 units of X for 1 unit of Y. Thus, consumers can swap 2 units of X for 1 unit of Y without changing their utility. Therefore, by reallocating resources, producers swap an output of 2 units of X for 1 unit of X. Hence, there is no feasible reallocation of resources that can make society better off. N_0 Pareto gain is possible, and competitive equilibrium in both markets is Pareto efficient.

Note that prices do two crucial things. First, they ensure that the initial position of competitive equilibrium is indeed a Pareto equilibrium. By balancing the quantities supplied and demanded, prices ensure that the final quantity of goods being consumed can be produced. They also ensure that it is a feasible allocation.

But in competitive equilibrium prices perform a second role. Each consumer and each producer is a price-taker and cannot affect market prices. Knowing nothing about the actions of other producers and consumers, each consumer automatically ensures that the last unit of Y purchased yields twice as much utility as the last unit of X bought. Otherwise, the consumer could rearrange purchases out of the same income to increase his utility.

Thus, by his individual actions facing given prices, each consumer arranges 1 unit of X could be swapped for 2 units of Y with no change in utility. Similarly, every producer, by merely setting its own P = MC of its output, ensures that the MC of Y is twice the MC of X. Thus, it takes society twice as many resources to make an extra unit of Y than an extra unit of X. By rearranging production and transferring resources between industries, society can swap 2 units of X for every 1 unit of Y, exactly the trade-off without someone else worse off. Fig. 14.3 makes the same point. D is the market demand curve for one of the goods, say Y. At a price P_0 a quantity Q_0 is demanded. The last unit of Y demanded yields consumers P_0 pounds worth of utility; otherwise a different unit would have been bought. Hence, the demand curve, D, also shows the MU of the last unit of Y bought. When Q_0 units of Y are purchased, the last unit of Y yields exactly P_0 pounds worth of utility to consumer.

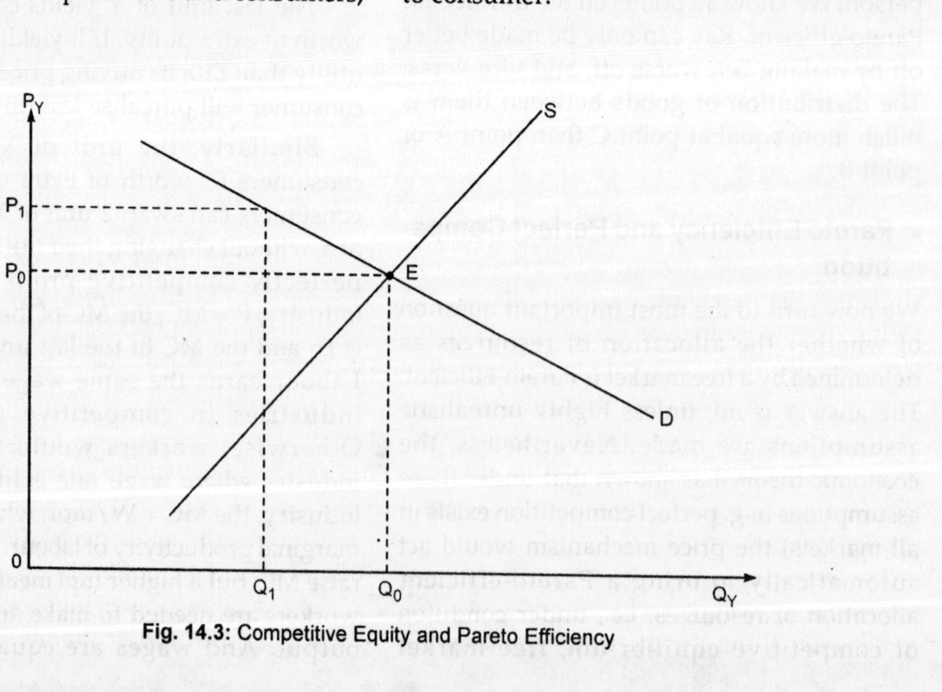

Fig. 14.3: Competitive Equity and Pareto Efficiency

In a competitive industry, the supply curve S, is also MC of Y. The variable factor, labour, is paid its MVP in each industry. Labour mobility ensures that wage rates are equal in two industries. Hence, the MC of making the last unit of Y is the value of X sacrificed by using the last worker to make Y and not X. Price ensures that both industries are in equilibrium. Fig. 14.3 shows that in equilibrium at E the MU of the last unit of Y equals its MC. But the MC of the last unit of Y is the value of the X sacrificed, P_x the unit of X forgone by using labour to make the last unit of Y. However, the industry that produces X is also in equilibrium. An equivalent diagram for X industry shows that the equilibrium P of X is also the MU of the last unit of X purchased. Hence the value of X, sacrificed to make the last unit of Y, is also the MU of the last unit of X times the number of X sacrificed.

At any output such as Q_1, the last unit of Y must yield consumer P_1 worth of extra utility; otherwise they would not demand Q_1. The supply curve, S, for the competitive Y industry is also the MC of Y. If the X industry is also in competitive equilibrium, the price of a unit of X is the value of its MU to consumer. Thus, the MC of Y is not only its opportunity cost in X, but is also the value of the MU, consumer would have derived from X.

Hence, at any Y output below Q_0 the MU of Y exceeds the MU of X sacrificed to produce an extra Y. Above Q_0 the MU of Y is less than the MU of X sacrificed. The equilibrium point E for Y and the corresponding equilirbium for X thus ensure that resources are efficiently allocated between the two industries. No reallocation would make all consumers better off.

Thus, provided the X industry is in competitive equilibrium, the MC curve for the Y industry is the extra pound worth of utility sacrified by using scarce resources to make another unit of Y rather than an extra unit of X. It is the opportunity cost in utility terms of the resource being used in Y industry. An equilibrium in the Y industry by equating the MU of Y to the MU of X sacrificed to make the last Y, guarantee that society's resources being are allocated efficiently.

At any output of Y below the equilibrium quantity Q_0, the marginal consumer benefit of another Y exceeds the marginal valuation of X that would have to be sacrificed to produce that extra Y.

At any output of Y above Q_0, the society is devoting too many resources to the Y industry. The marginal value of the last Y is less than the marginal value of X that could have been produced by transferring resources to X industry. Competitive equilibrium ensures that there is no resource transfer between industries that would make all consumers better off.

• Equity and Efficiency

We have seen above that there are many Pareto efficient allocation, each with a different distribution of utility between different members of the society. A competitive equilibrium in all markets generates a particular Pareto-efficient allocation. What, then, determines which is the best?

People have different innate abilities, different human capital, and wealth. These differences mean people earn different incomes in a market economy. They also affect the pattern of consumer demand. Different inheritances of ability, capital and wealth imply different demand curves and determine different equilibrium prices and quantities. In principle, by varying the distribution of initial income-earning potential, we could make the economy pick out each possible Pareto-efficient allocation as its competitive equilibrium.

The idea is that the government is elected to express the value judgements of the majority. If the market gets the economy to the Pareto-efficient frontier, the government can make the value judgement about which point on the frontier the economy should attain.

Different efficient allocations correspond to different initial the economy should attain. Different efficient allocations correspond to different initial distributions of income-earning potential in a competitive economy. Can the government confine itself to redistributing income and wealth through taxation and welfare benefits without having to intervene to ensure that resources are allocated efficiently?

This seems a powerful case for the free enterprise ideal. The government should allow the markets get on with the job of allocating resources efficiently. There is no need for government regulation or state-run enterprise. Nor need the free enterprise ideal be disturbed. The government can redistribute income without impairing the efficient functioning of a free market economy. The left wing and right wing case can be made by rigorous economic arguments. Of course, there are some qualifications in the above argument. Under certain conditions free markets lead to a Pareto-efficient allocation. These conditions explained the difference between the two views. The left believes that the qualifications are so serious that substantial government intervention is necessary to improve the way the economy works. The right believes that they are minor qualifications which can not seriously challenge the case for a free market economy.

- **Distortions and the Second Best**

Competitive equilibrium is efficient because the independent actions of producers setting P = MC and consumers setting P = MB, ensure that the MC of producing a good = its marginal benefit to consumers. A distortion exists if society's MC of producing a good is not equal to the marginal benefit of consuming that good.

- **Taxation is a Distortion**

To finance subsidies to the poor, Government must tax the incomes of the rich or the goods rich people consume. Suppose everybody buys meals, but only the rich people can afford to go to the cinema. A subsidy for the poor can be financed by a tax on rich people's income or on the good Y, which only rich people consume.

In Fig. 14.4 the pre-tax price of Y to consumer exceeds the post-tax price received by the producers of good Y. The difference between the two prices is the tax on good Y. Consumers equate the tax-inclusive price to the value of the marginal benefit they receive from the last unit of good Y, but the producers equate the MC of good Y to the lower net-of-tax price of good Y.

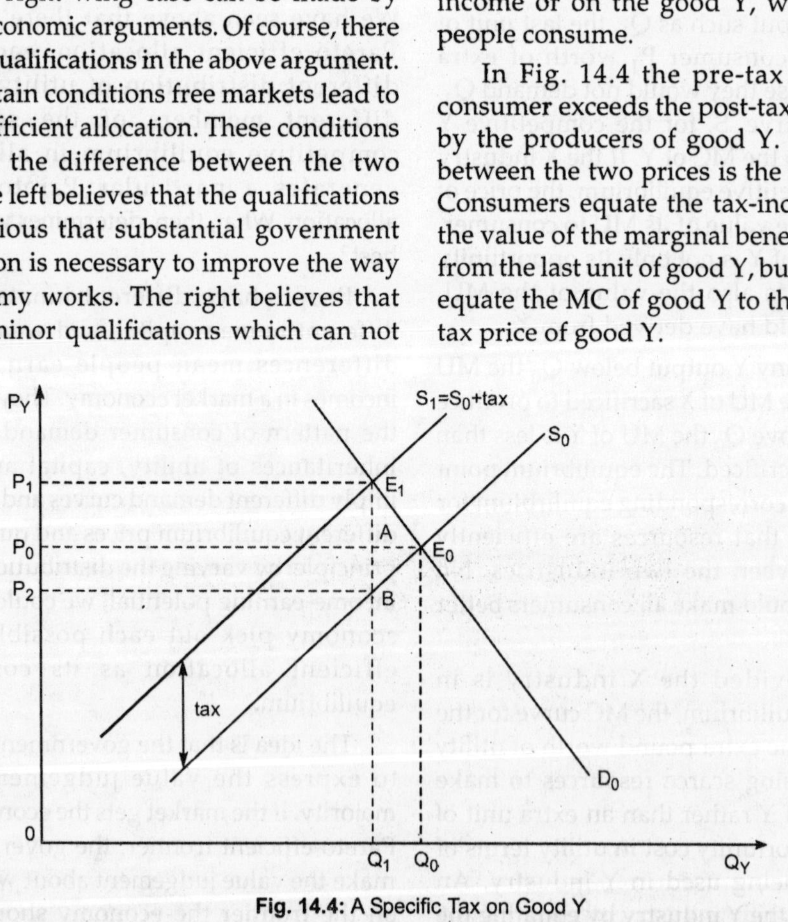

Fig. 14.4: A Specific Tax on Good Y

In a competitive equilibrium the price system no longer equates the MSC to MSB. The tax on good Y causes too few units of good Y to be produced. Making another unit of Y adds more to social benefit than to social cost.

D_0 is the demand curve for Y and the marginal benefit of the last unit of Y consumed. S_0 is the quantity of Y supplied at each price and also the MSC of producing Y.

Suppose each unit of Y bears a tax of E_1 to B. To show the tax-inclusive price required to induce producers to produce each unit of output, we must draw the new supply curve S_1 (= S_0 + tax) which is vertically above S_0 by the amount of the specific tax (E_1B). The equilibrium quantity sold of Y is Q_1.

Consumers pay a price P_1, producers receive a price P_2, and the tax per unit of Y is E_1 to B. At the equilibrium quantity Q_1 the marginal benefit is P_1 but the MSC = P_2. Society would make a net gain by producing more Y. Hence the equilibrium quantity Q_1 is socially inefficient.

We have seen above that the MC of one unit of good Y is equal to the value of the extra unit of good X that the society could have had instead. When good Y are taxed, the MSB of another unit of Y exceeds its MC, and would exceeded the MSB of the extra unit of good X that society could have had by using resources differently. By transferring labour from X to Y, society could make some people better off without making anyone worse off.

The tax, thus, causes a discrepancy between the price purchaser pays and the price supplier receives. The invisible hand no longer equates MSB of resources in different uses. The choice between equity and efficiency is probably clear. If the economy is perfectly competitive, and if the government is happy with the current income distribution, competitive free market equilibrium is efficient and the distribution of income is desirable.

If the government wants to increase taxes, whether to distribute income or to subsidize others, this will introduce distortion. The resulting equilibrium may have more desirable distribution, but it would be less efficient. Government may have to make trade-off between efficiency and equity.

• The Second Best

When there is no distortion in the market for X, a tax on Y leads to inefficient allocation. If we could abolish the tax on Y neither industry would be distorted and we then get first best allocation of resources. The first best allocation has no distortion and most efficient system.

Suppose that we cannot get rid of the tax on Y, because the government needs tax revenue to pay for national defence. Given an unavoidable tax on Y, it is necessary that the government should also tax industry X.

This view is also wrong. Suppose both industries are in equilibrium, but there is a tax on Y. Then too few Y will be produced and consumed. Given an inevitable tax on Y, a tax on X would help and not hinder.

A suitable tax on X could restore the original relative price of X and Y. With only two goods this would restore the first best. However, there is always a third good, leisure. Households reduce consumption of leisure in order to supply labour for work. Taxing X and Y get the right balance between them, but makes the price of both wrong, relative to leisure. With higher taxes, the net wage falls, changing the price of lesiure.

In contrast to the first-best allocation, when we achieve full efficiency by removing all distortions, we have now developed the principle of the second best. The first best removes all distortions. The second best cannot remove some distortions.

The theory of the second best says that, if there must be a distortion, it would not be correct to keep the distortion in one market. It would be more efficient to spread the distortion more thinly over a wide range of markets.

There are some inevitable distortions in the real world. The government can increase the overall efficiency of the whole economy by introducing new distortion to offset those that already exist. We want to know the sources of those inevitable distortions that the government could take action to offset.

- **Market Failure**

We have seen that a perfectly competitive economy can achieve Pareto-efficient allocation of resources. But most markets violate some of the assumptions of free-market model. Some deviations from the ideal free market models which generate efficient economy are called market failure. Market failures imply that the market equilibrium is inefficient. We can list the sources of distortions that generate market failure. Market failure may come from the following sources (a) Imperfect competition, (b) Externalities, (c) Public good, (d) Lack of information.

- **Imperfect Competition**

A profit maximizing firm, operating under the conditions of monopoly or any other imperfect market, produce and sell output at which MC = MR. Equilibrium will thus occur with MC being less than the market price (P_m). From the arguments given above this implies social inefficiency, i.e. welfare loss to the society. Since consumers equate price to marginal benefit (MB), MB > MC. Such industries produce too little and charge higher prices. Higher output adds more to consumer benefit than the production costs or the opportunity cost of the resources used. This is illustrated in Fig. 14.5, where the area BCD represents the welfare loss to the society, with the firm producing Q_m rather than Q_c.

- **Equity**

Taxation induces allocative distortions by driving a wedge between the price consumer pays and the price producers receive.

- **Externalities**

Externalities arise when the action of producers or consumers affects the consumption and production of others, other than through the normal working of the price mechanism. This is likely to result in social inefficiency because individuals normally consider only the price costs of their decisions. They largely ignore, or are unaware of, the social costs and benefit of their actions. External effects can be either positive or negative. For example, a chemical firm discharges waste into a lake, polluting the water. It affects the production of anglers (fewer fish) or the consumption of swimmers (dirty water). Without market for pollution,

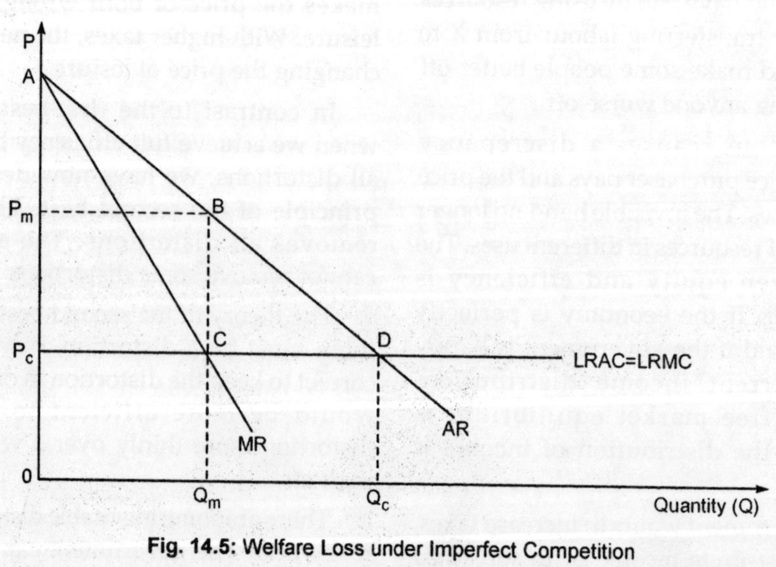

Fig. 14.5: Welfare Loss under Imperfect Competition

the firm can pollute the lake without cost. Its self-interest leads it to pollute until the marginal benefit of pollution (cheap production) = its MC, which is zero. It ignores the MC of pollution imposed on anglers and swimmers. This is a case of negative externality. We can categorize these spillover effects under the following heading:

(a) **Production on consumption:** A negative example of this would be the adverse effect of pollution on recreational areas. A positive externality could result from the warm water discharge from many industrial cooling processes making river more attractive to bathers.

(b) **Production on production:** A negative externality would result if the release of industrial waste into rivers decreases the catch of commercial fishermen. A positive externality in this category is something that is arising from the utilizing of non-patented inventions. As inventors would receive no payment for their efforts this AR suggests that under laissez-faire too little would be spent on research and development.

(c) **Consumption on production:** Negative externalities might arise from the careless discharging of packaging on farmland. Alternatively, congestion caused by private motorists will increase the transportation costs of many firms. Positive externalities in this category are in principle possible, but in practice of little significance.

(d) **Consumption on consumption:** Negative externalities of this categories include unwelcome noise from radios or aeroplane. Positive externalities include neighbours enjoying the sight of each other's beautiful gardens. So far we have discussed about non-pecuniary external effects. There can be pecuniary external effects. Pecuniary external effects are the effect of prices in one sector of the economy upon other sectors of the economy. As we know, prices are determined by the interaction of all the economic units, i.e., producers and consumers, in the economy. Hence, the act of demanding or supplying these units by one group will affect the prices faced by other groups. Although such changes can cause a redistribution of welfare among such units, they are not a cause of social inefficiency. This is because such effects work within the price mechanism; they are not external to it and are thus not ignored by profit or utility maximizing decision-makers. For example, if firms in one industry increase their demand for a particular factor input, this is likely to raise the price of this input. It is not a case of market inefficiency because it is the normal working of the price mechanism; the increased price of the factor of production merely reflects that it is scarce in relation to the demand for it. Such price increases provide an incentive for producers to economise in their use and conveys to the consumers the fact that to have more of one product they must have less of another. It is exactly this type of consideration that brought about the efficient balance between wants and efficiency. In view of the confusion between pecuniary externalities and true spillover effects, it might be better to call the former the price effects. However, in a world of imperfect information, pecuniary effects do have an importance as regards efficiency. In case of externalities, there is a divergence between the individual's comparison of MC and benefits and society's comparison of MC and benefits. Free market can not induce people to take account of indirect effects if there is no market in these indirect effects.

- **Divergence between Private and Social costs and Benefits**

Competitive equilibrium is at E_0. The market clears at price P_c which producers equate with marginal private cost. Now suppose pollution causes a production externality which makes MSC greater than MPC. The demand curve D_0 measures the marginal social benefit because consumers equate the value of the MU of the last unit to the price. By inducing an output Q_c which is greater than Q_1, the efficient output, free market equilibrium leads to social cost equal to the area E_1FE_0. This shows the excess of social cost over social benefit in moving from Q_1 to Q_c. With no production externality, MPC = MSC. Demand curve D_0 measures the MPB and the free market equilibrium is at E_0. The beneficial consumption equality make MSB > MPB. E_1 is the social efficiency point. By producing at Q_0 instead of efficient output Q_1, free market equilibrium wastes the area E_0FE_1.

- **The Efficient Quantity of an Externality**

MB is the marginal benefit to the neighbour and MC to us of a fence of size f. The efficient size is f_0 where the MC = MB. Beginning from

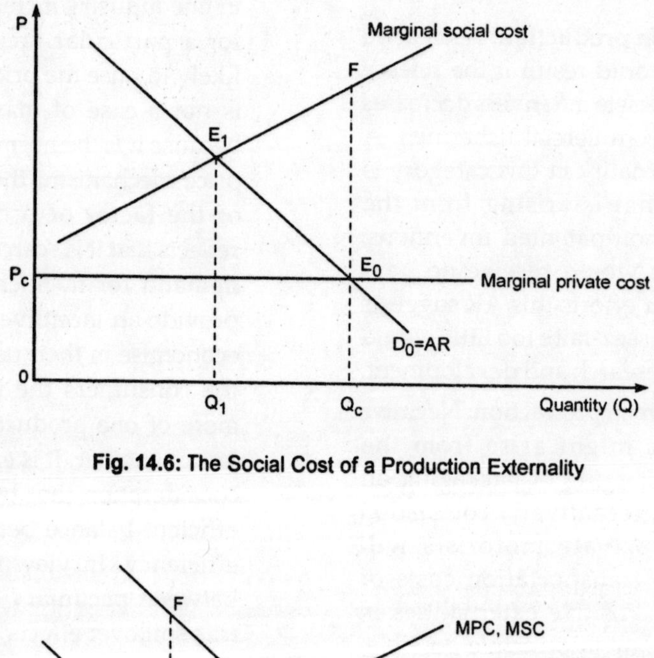

Fig. 14.6: The Social Cost of a Production Externality

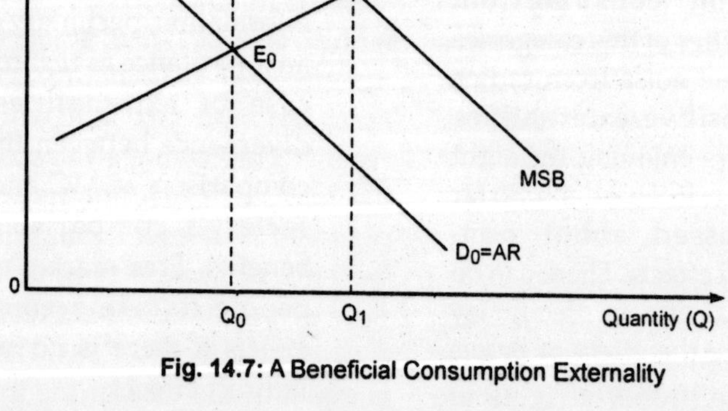

Fig. 14.7: A Beneficial Consumption Externality

f_1 we might bribe our neighbour the value $f_0E_0Cf_1$ to cut back to f_0. Below f_0 we have to pay more than it is worth to us to have the fence cut back further. Alternatively, our neighbour might pay us the value of the area OAE_0f_0 to have a size f_0. Property rights, in this case whether we are legally entitled to compensation for loss of light to our garden, determine who compensates whom, but not the outcome f_0 of bargaining.

well defined, the use of property will generally involve contracting between the owners of those properties. If we own a land, we might contract with another who wants to use our land for raising cow or sheep. The contract could be written in the form of a lease agreement.

• Voluntary Agreements

Is it possible for externalities to be internalised via voluntary agreement? For example,

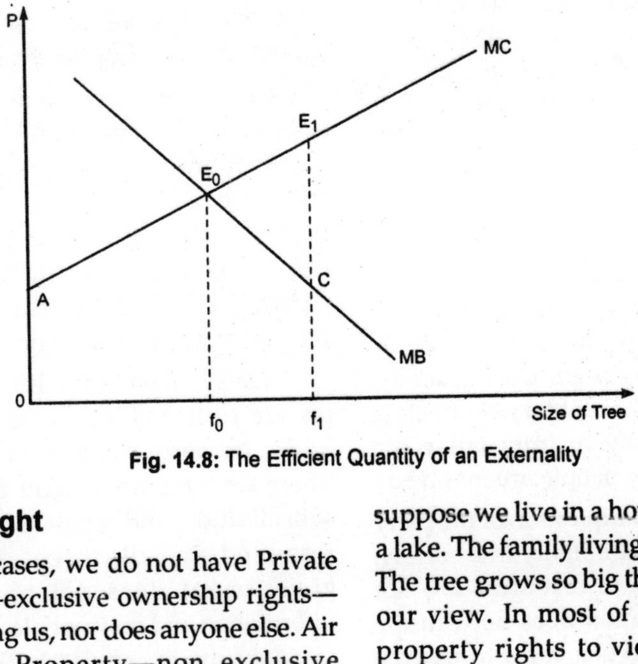

Fig. 14.8: The Efficient Quantity of an Externality

suppose we live in a house with a nice view of a lake. The family living below us plants a tree. The tree grows so big that it eventually blocks our view. In most of the cities, no one has property rights to views; thus, we cannot usually go to court to obtain relief. We do have the option of contracting with our neighbour, however.

We have the option of paying our neighbours to cut the tree. We could start out with an offer of a small amount and keep going up until our neighbours agree or until we reach our limit. Our limit will equal the value we place on having an unobstructed view of the lake. Our neighbours will agree if the payment is at least equal to the reduction in their intrinsic property value. Our offering the payment makes our neighbours aware of the social cost of their actions. The social cost here is equal to the care of the tree plus the cost

• Property Right

In most of the cases, we do not have Private Property right—exclusive ownership rights—to air surrounding us, nor does anyone else. Air is a Common Property—non exclusive resource. Therein lies the crux of the problem. When no one owns a particular resource, no one has any incentive to protect it. If one person decides not to pollute the air, there will be no significant effect on the total level of pollution.

Basically, pollution occurs where we have poorly defined private property rights, as in air and common bodies of water. We do not have visual pollution problem in our own room. That is our own property, which we choose to keep as clean as we want.

Where the private property rights exist, individuals have legal recourse to any damages sustained through the misuse of their property. When private property rights are suffered by us from an impeded view of the lake.

In essence, our offer of money to our neighbours indicates to them that there is an opportunity cost to their actions. If they don't comply, they forfeit the money that we are offering them. The point here is that opportunity cost always exists, whoever has property rights. Thus, we would expect under certain circumstances that voluntary contracting will occur to internalise externalities. This is the famous Coase theorem. The question is, when will voluntay agreements occur?

• Transaction Costs

One important condition for the outcome just outlined is that the transaction costs must be small relative to the expected benefits of reaching an agreement. If we expand our example to a much larger one, such as air pollution, the transaction costs of numerous house owners trying to reach agreements with the individuals and companies that create the pollution are relatively high. Consequently, we don't always expect voluntary contracting to be an effective way to internalise the externality when many people are involved.

We can approach the question of property rights by assuming that initially in a society, many property rights to resources are not defined. But this situation does not cause a problem so long as no one cares to use the resources for which there are no property rights or so long as enough of these resources are available that people can have as much as they want at a zero price. Only when and if an use is found for a resource or the supply of resource to be inadequate at a zero price, does a problem develop. The problem requires that something be done about deciding property rights. If not, the resources will be wasted and possibly even destroyed. Property rights can be assigned to individuals who will then assert control; or they may be assigned to government, which can maintain and preserve the resource, charge for its use, or implement some other rationing device. What we have seen with common property such as air and water is that governments have attempted to take over the control of those resources so that they cannot be wasted or destroyed.

Another way of viewing the pollution is to argue that property rights are sacred and that there are property rights in every resource that exists. But each individual may not have the right to act on anything that is not his or her property, and that they do not have the right to pollute because that amounts to using property which does not belong to him or her.

Clearly, we must fill the gap between private costs and social costs in situation in which property rights are not well defined. There are three ways to fill the gap: taxation, subsidisation, and regulation. Government is involved in all three. Unfortunately, government does not have the prefect information and may not pick the appropriate tax, subsidy, or regulation. We also have to consider cases in which taxes are hard to enforce or subsidies are difficult to be given out to worthy recipients. In such cases, outright prohibition may be the optimum solution to a particular pollution problem.

QUESTIONS

1. An economy has 10 units of goods to share out between two people. (X, Y) means that the first person gets a quantity X, and the second person a quantity Y. For each of the allocations (a) to (e), say whether they are (1) efficient and (2) equitable: (a) [10, 0], (b) [7, 2], (c) [5, 5], (d) [3, 6], (e) [0, 10].
2. The price of X is £1 and of Y is £5. There is perfect competition and no externality. What can we say about (a) the relative benefit to consumers of a marginal Y and a marginal X, (b) the relative marginal production cost of Y and X; and (c) the relative marginal product of variable factors in the Y and X industries? Why is this equilibrium efficient?
3. In deciding to drive a car in office time, you think about the cost of petrol and the time of the journey. Do you slow other people down by driving? Is this an externality? Will too many, or too few people drive car in office time? Should commuter parking in cities be restricted?
4. In 1885, 300 people died when the steam boiler exploded in the Thames boat. Four friends joined together to form a private company offering to insure any boiler that they had inspected for safety. Boiler inspections reduced the explosion rates. Would the company have been successful if it had certified boilers but not insured them at the same time? Explain.
5. (a) Why might society ban drugs that neither help nor harm the diseases they are claimed to cure?

   (b) If the regulatory bodies are blamed for bad things that happen despite regulations but not blamed for good things prevented by too much regulation, will regulatory bodies over-regulate activities under their scrutiny?

ANSWERS

1. (a) Efficient, not equitable, (b) Neither efficient nor equitable, (c) Both efficient and equitable, (d) Neither efficient nor very equitable, (e) Efficient but not equitable.
2. (a) 1 Y worth 5 X to consumer utility, (b) MC of Y 5 times that of X, (c) mpl in X industry is 5 times higher than in Y industry. Equilirbrium equates MSC and MSB.
3. Yes, to all questions.
4. No.
5. (a) Such activities waste scarce resources. (b) Yes.

GLOSSARY

Accounting Cost: Actual expenses plus depreciation charges for capital equipment. (These charges are determined by the Internal Revenue Service).

Adverse Selection: High-risk individuals are more likely to buy insurance than low-risk individuals. If insurance companies must charge a single premium because they cannot distinguish among these individuals, if may become unprofitable to sell insurance. Similarly, if a single price is to be charged for indistinguishable low and high quality products, high quality products may not be sold.

Antitrust Laws: Regulations intended to promote a competitive economy by prohibiting actions that restrain competition.

Arc Elasticity of Demand: Used when dealing with a relatively large price change, the arc eleasticity is equal to $\left(\frac{\Delta Q}{\Delta P}\right)\left(\frac{P}{Q}\right)$. Where P and Q are the averages of the prices and quantities before and after the price change.

Asymmetric Information: A situation in which a buyer and a seller have different information about a transaction.

Average Cost: Production cost per unit of output.

Average Expenditure ≡ Average Revenue: The price per unit paid by a buyer ≡ The price per unit received by a seller.

Average Product: Total output per unit of a particular input.

Average Revenue: Revenue divided by the number of units sold, i.e., price per unit.

Backward-Bending Labour Supply Curve: The portion of the labour supply curve at which the wage rate increases and the hours of work supplied decrease, giving the curve a negative slope.

Bandwagon Effect: A positive network externality in which an individual demands a good in part because many other people have the good.

Barrier to Entry: Anything that makes it prohibitive for new businesses to enter a market; it is necessary if incumbent businesses are to maintain monopoly power.

Bilateral Monopoly: A market with one buyer and one seller.

Budget Line: Represents all combinations of goods that can be purchased with an individual's income.

CAPM (Capital Asset Pricing Model): A model in which the risk premium for a capital investment depends on the correlation of the investment's return with the return on the entire stock market.

Cardinal Utility Ranking: A quantitative measure of the value of a good in terms of a basic unit of utility.

Cartel: A group of businesses that explicitly agree to set price and/or to limit output.

Ceiling Price: A maximum price that businesses are allowed by the government to charge for a good.

Clayton Act: As amended by the Robinson-Patman Act, a law that makes it illegal to discriminate by charging buyers of essentially the same product different prices.

Coase Theorem: When parties can bargain without cost and to their mutual advantage, the resulting outcome will be efficient, regardless of how the property rights are specified.

Commodity: A good or service.

Common Property Resource: A resource, such as air and water, to which anyone has free access.

Comparative Advantage: A country has a comparative advantage over another country B in producing a good if the cost of producing the good in A, relative to the cost of producing other goods in A, is lower than the cost of producing the good in B, relative to the cost of producing other goods in B.

Competitive Markets: Markets in which buyers and sellers individually have little or no ability to affect prices.

Complements: Goods that tend to be used together, so that an increase in the price of one good tends to decrease the demand for its complement.

Constant Cost Industry: An industry whose long-run supply curve is horizontal.

Constant Returns to Scale: When a doubling of inputs causes output to double.

Consumer Price Index: A measure of the aggregate price level based on a large market basket of goods; calculated by the U.S. Bureau of Labour Statistics.

Consumer Surplus: The difference between the amount consumers are willing to pay for a good and the amount they actually pay. It is represented by the area under the demand curve above the price line.

Contract Curve: A curve that includes all efficient allocations of two goods between two consumers, or two inputs between two production functions, in an Edgeworth box.

Cooperative Game: A game in which players can negotiate binding contracts that allow them to plan joint strategies.

Cost Function: A relationship between the cost of production and the level of output of a business or businesses.

Cournot Equilibrium: The Nash Equilibrium that occurs when businesses simultaneously choose the quantities they will produce.

Cournot Model: An oligopoly model in which businesses assume that their competitors' outputs are fixed and simultaneously decide how much to produce.

Cross-Price Elasticity of Demand: The percentage change in the quantity demanded of a good that results from 1 percent increase in the price of another good.

Deadweight Loss: A measure of efficiency loss, given by the sum of lost consumer and producer surplus, less revenues to the govenment.

Decreasing Cost Industry: An industry whose long-run supply curve is downward sloping.

Decreasing Returns to Scale: When a doubling of inputs causes output to increase by less than a factor of two.

Demand Curve: The amount of a good consumers are willing (and able) to purchase as a function of its price.

Discount Rate: A rate used to compare the value of the dollar received in the future to a dollar received today.

Diseconomies of Scale: When a business's costs more than double in response to a doubling of output.

Diseconomies of Scope: When one business produces less of two outputs than two separate specialized businesses could produce.

Diversifiable Risk (also Non-systematic Risk): Risk that can be eliminated by diversifying, e.g., by investing in many projects or by holding the stocks of many companies.

Dominant Strategy: A strategy that is optimal regardless of how one's competitors behave.

Duality in Consumer Theory: The optimum allocation of income between two goods may be determined by choosing the highest indifference curve that is tangent to the budget line, or by choosing the lowest budget line that touches a given indifference curve.

Durable Goods: A consumption or capital good bought to provide services for a long-time.

Economic Profit: The difference between a business's revenues and costs, including any opportunity costs.

Economic Rent: The difference between the payments made to a factor of production and the minimum amount that must be spent to obtain the use of that factor.

Economies of Scale: When a business's costs less than double in response to a doubling of output.

Edgeworth Box Diagram: A diagram that shows all possible allocations of two goods between two people, or of two inputs between two production processes.

Effective Yield: The interest rate that equates the price of a bond with the present discounted value of its expected future payments. It is also called the rate of return on the bond.

Efficiency Wage: The wage a business will pay to an employee as an incentive not to shirk.

Elastic Demand: When the precentage change in quantity demanded of a good in response to 1 percent change in price is greater than one in magnitude.

Elasticity: A measure of the percentage change in one variable resulting from a 1 percent increase in the other variable.

Emissions Standard: A legal limit on how much pollutant a business may emit.

Engle Curve: A curve that describes the relationship between the quantity of a good consumed and income.

Equal Marginal Rule: A rule for optimization when two or more options are available, i.e., to maximize utility, a consumer should equalize the marginal utility of each dollar spent on each good consumed.

Equilibrium Price (also Market Clearing Price): The price at which the quantity supplied and quantity demanded are equal.

Excess Demand: Demand that results when the quantity demanded exceeds the quantity supplied because a price ceiling keeps the price of good below its equilibrium price.

Expansion Path: A curve that describes the combinations of labour and capital a business will choose to minimize costs for every level of output.

Expected Value: The average value of a set of uncertain outcomes.

Difference between Men & Women
UK Annual Pay *Employment, 2000

Occupation	Male Pay (£000)	% of Male Jobs	Female Pay (£000)	% of Female Jobs
Manufactureing	25.6	57	18.2	82
Services	29.2	43	20.6	10

Source: ONS New Earning survey

Access to Education
UK Students 1991-2003 (thousands)

Further edudation	Male			Female		
	1991	2002	2003	1991	2002	2003
F-T	116	569		95	559	
P–T	891	1665		530	2562	
Undergraduate						
F-T	241	519		173	620	
P–T	127	263		19	412	
Post graduate						
F–T	33	94		10	93	
P–T	15	133	3	153		

Source: ONS, Social Trends

Racial Discrimination
Ethnic Group, UK, 2002

Further Edudation	Participation Rate (%)		Unemployment Rate (%)	
	M	W	M	W
White	85	75	5	4
Black	77	64	17	13
Indian	80	69	6	8
Pakistani	74	36	14	19
Bangladeshi	75	22	21	16

Source: ONS, Labour Market Frends

Pay Differentials for Uk Men

Percentage Extra pay for	Union	Non-Union
Education & Traning		
GCSEs	+5	+13
A-Levels	+16	+21
University Degree	+32	+47
Post graduate Degree	+50	+50
Other higher Education	+18	+21
Apprenticieship	+11	+9
Personal		
Ethnic Minority	–1	–5
Years Experience		
5	+13	+10
15	+30	+28
30	+35	+32
Percentage Extra wage in Britain at age 33 for		
	M	W
First degree	+15	+32
Post graduate degree	+15	+35
Extra effect by Subject		
Arts	–10	+5
Economics	+15	+24
Chemistry/Biology	–19	–11
Maths/Physics	+9	+16

Source: Blundell at al 'Return to HE in Britain' Economic Journal 2000

Explicit Cost: The actual outlays by a business, including wages, salaries, costs of materials, property rentals.

Externality: An action by either a producer or a consumer that affects other producers or consumers, yet is not accounted for in the market price.

Feedback Effect: A price or quantity adjustment in one market that is caused by price and quantity adjustment in related markets.

First-Degree Price Discrimination: Charging each person his/her reservation price for a good.

Fixed Cost: A cost that does not vary with the level of production, such as plant maintenance and insurance.

Fixed Inputs: Factors that cannot be changed in the short-run.

Fixed-Proportions Production Function: When the production isoquants are L-shaped, so that only one combination of labour and capital can be used to produce each level of output.

Free Entry (Exit): When businesses may enter (exit) an industry without incurring a sunk cost.

Free Rider: A consumer or producer that does not pay for a non-exclusive good in the expectation that others will.

General Equilibrium Analysis: A method of analysis that determines the prices and quantities in several markets.

Giffen Good: A good whose demand curve slopes upward as a result of a large income effect.

Income Consumption Curve: A curve that includes the utility-maximizing combinations of goods associated with every income level.

Income Effect: The increase in consumption brought about by an increase in income, when the prices of goods are held constant.

Income Elasticity of Demand: The percentage change in the resulting from 1 percent increase in income.

Increasing Cost Industry: An industry whose long-run supply curve is upward sloping.

Increasing Returns to Scale: When a doubling of all inputs causes output to more than double.

Indifference Curve: A graphical representation of all combinations of market baskets that provide the same level of satisfaction.

Indifference Map: A set of indifference curves that describes the consumer's preferences among various combinations of market baskets.

Inelastic Demand: When the percentage change in the quantity demanded of a good in response to 1 percent change in price is less than one in magnitude.

Inferior Good: A good for which consumption falls as an individual's income rises.

Intertemporal Price Discrimination: Separating consumers into groups with varying demand functions and charging them different prices at different points in time.

Isocost Line: A curve that shows all the possible combinations of inputs that yield the same output.

Isoquant: A curve that shows all the possible combinations of inputs that yield the same level output.

Isoquant Map: A set of isoquants, each of which shows the maximum output that can be achieved for any set of inputs.

Labour Productivity: The average product of labour as applied to an industry or to the economy as a whole.

Law of Diminishing Returns: As the use of an input increases (while other inputs remain constant), additional output produced will eventually decrease.

Learning Curve: The relationship between a business's cumulative output and the (declining) amount of inputs needed to produce a unit of output.

Marginal Cost (or Incremental Cost): The increase in cost from producing one additional unit of output.

Marginal Expenditure: The incremental cost of purchasing one additional unit of a good.

Marginal Private Benefit (MPB): MPB is the incremental benefit of an activity as viewed by the individual.

Marginal Product of Inputs: The additional output produced as the input is increased by one unit. Eg. $\Delta q/\Delta k$ = marginal product of capital.

Marginal Productivity: The measurement of the marginal product at a point. Eg. dq/dk = marginal productivity of capital.

Marginal Rate of Substitution: The amount of one good an individual will give up to gain one more unit of another good. ($\Delta q_2/\Delta q_1$).

Marginal Rate of Technical Substitution: The amount by which one input can be reduced when one extra unit of another input is used, so that output remains constant. ($\Delta k/\Delta l$).

Marginal Rate of Transformation: A measure of how much of one good must be given up to produce an additional unit of another good.

Marginal Revenue: The change in revenue resulting from one-unit increase in output.

Marginal Revenue Product: The additional revenue resulting from the sale of output in a non perfectly competitive market created by the use of one additional unit of an input. (MR. $\Delta q/\Delta l$).

Marginal Social Benefit (MSB): MSB is the incremental benefit of an activity as viewed by society. (=SMB).

Marginal Social Cost (MSC): MSC is the incremental cost of an activity as viewed by society. (=SMC).

Marginal Utility: A measure of the additional satisfaction obtained from consuming one additional unit of a good.

Marginal Value Product: The additional revenue resulting from the sale of output in a perfectly competitive market created by the use of one additional unit of an input. (P.$\Delta q/\Delta l$).

Market: A collection of buyers and sellers who interact, resulting in the possibility of exchange.

Market Demand Curve: The horizontal summation of all individual consumers' demand curves.

Market Power: The ability to profitably affect price. It refers to either monopoly or monopsony power.

Market Signalling: The process by which sellers end buyers information about a product's quality.

Mark-up Pricing: Increasing the production cost of a good by a fixed percentage to determine a sales price.

Monopolistic Competition: A market in which businesses complete by selling differentiated (heterogeneous) products that are highly substitutable for one another, and there is free entry and exit.

Monopoly: A market with only one seller.

Monopoly Power: The ability of a business to profitably charge a price higher than marginal cost.

Monopsony: A market with only one buyer.

Monopsony Power: The ability of buyer to purchase a good at a price below its marginal value.

Nash Equilibrium: A set of strategies or actions in which each player is doing the best it can, given the action of its opponents.

Natural Monopoly: An industry in which economies of scale are so great that the efficient level of production for one business satisfies the entire market demand.

Net Present Value: The present discounted value of expected future cash flows from an investment, less the cost of the investment.

Network Externality: The dependence of an individual's demand on the consumption levels of other people.

Nominal Discount Rate: A discount rate that includes the effects of inflation.

Nominal Price: The price actually quoted for a good at a given point in time; also called the current dollar price.

Non-Cooperative Game: A game in which negotiation and enforcement of a binding contract are not possible.

Non-Exclusive Good: A good that people cannot be excluded from consuming, and for the use of which it is difficult to charge them.

Non-Rival Good: A good for which consumption increases when income rises.

Oligopoly: A market with few sellers.

Oligopsony: A market with few buyers.

Opportunity Cost: The cost associated with opportunities that are foregone by not putting the business's resources to their highest value use.

Opportunity Cost of Capital: The rate of return that one could earn by investing in a different project with similar risk.

Ordinal Ranking of Utility: Values that denote relative levels of satisfaction, assigned when the particular unit of utility is unimportant.

Pareto Efficiency: An allocation of goods in which one person must be made worse off in order to make another person better off.

Partial Equilibrium Analysis: A determination of the equilibrium prices and quantities in a particular market that ignores effects from other markets.

Peak-Load Pricing: A form of intertemporal price discrimination in which peak users pay more than off-peak users because marginal cost is higher during peak periods.

Perfect Competition: A market in which all goods are homogeneous, there are no barriers to entry, and no business can affect the market price.

Positive Analysis: An explanation or prediction of an economic activity.

Predatory Pricing: A pricing policy designed to drive one or more competitors out of business and/or discourage new entrants to a market.

Present Discounted Value: The current value of an expected future cash flow.

Price-Consumption Curve: A curve derived by tracing the utility-maximizing combination of two goods as the price of one changes.

Price Discrimination: different prices to different customers.

Price Elasticity of Demand: The percentage change in the quantity demanded of a good resulting from 1 percent increase in the price of that good.

Price Leadership: A form of implicity collusion, where one business in the market sets the price and other businesses follow suit.

Price Support: A policy by which the government sets the market price of a good, usually an agricultural product, above the free market level and buys up whatever output is needed to maintain that price.

Price Taker: A business with no influence over the market price.

Principal-Agent Problem: The problem that arises when managers (agents) pursue their own goals, even if that entails lower profits for the owners of the business (the principals).

Producers' Surplus: The sum over all units of production of the difference between the market price of the good and the marginal cost of production.

Production Possibilities Frontier: A curve that includes various combinations of two goods that can be produced given fixed quantities of inputs.

Profit Maximization: The goal of a business; it is achieved when the marginal revenue of the business is equal to the marginal cost of production, at a point where the marginal cost is rising rather than falling.

Public Good: A non-exclusive and non-rival good.

Rate of Return: The discount rate that makes the net present value of an investment equal to zero.

Rate-of-Return Regulation: Setting a price that gives a monopoly a competitive return on its assets.

Real Discount Rate: The discount rate that applies when cash flows are in real terms, i.e., after netting out inflation.

Real Price: The price of a good relative to the aggregate price level; also called the "constant dollar" price.

Reservation Price: The maximum amount that a customer is willing to pay for a good.

Return: The total monetary flow an asset yeilds as a fraction of its price.

Revealed Preference: An approach to consumer theory in which preferences are determined by observing the choices consumers make.

Risk: The possibility of several different outcomes occurring when the probability of each outcome is known.

Risk-Averse Individual: A person who prefers a certain income to a risky alternative with the same expected income.

Risk-Free Return: A return which is free of risk, whether of default or interest rate fluctuations. An example is the return on U.S. Treasury bills.

Risk-Loving Individual: A person who prefers a risky alternative to a certain one even though both offer the same expected income.

Risk-Neutral Individual: A person who is indifferent between earning a certain income and earning a risky one with the same expected income.

Risk Premium: The amount of money that a risk-averse individual will pay to avoid taking a risk.

Second-Degree Price Discrimination: Charging different prices for different quantities of the same good.

Sequential Game: In this kind of game players move in simultaneously.

Snob Effect: A negative network externality in which an individual's demand for good is higher the fewer are the other people who have it.

Social Marginal Benefit: SMB is the incremental benefit of an activity as viewed by society. (=MSB).

Social Marginal Cost: SMC is the incremental cost of an activity as viewed by society. (=MSC).

Stackelberg Model: A model of oligopoly in which one business sets output before the other businesses do.

Strategic Move: An action that constrains one's own behaviour in a way that yeilds a strategic advantage.

Substitutes: Goods or services that compete in the market, so that if the price of one good increases, the quantity demanded of the substitute will also increase.

Substitution Effect: The change in consumption of a good that is associated with a change in its price, while the level of satisfaction is held constant.

Sunk Cost: An expenditure that has already been made and cannot be recovered.

Supply Curve: The amount producers are willing to sell as a function of the market price.

Technical Efficiency: When businesses combine their inputs to produce a given output as inexpensively as possible.

Third-Degree Price Discrimination: Dividing consumers into two or more groups with different demands for a product in order to charge different prices to each group.

Tit-For-Tat Strategy: In a repeated game, a strategy that responds in kind to an opponent's previous play. The strategy cooperates with cooperative opponents and retaliates against uncooperative ones.

Total Cost: The total cost of production, composed of fixed and variable costs.

Total Fixed Costs: Costs that do not vary with output (q).

Total Private Benefit: The total benefit the consumer receives from consuming a commodity (good or service). It is the area under the marginal private benefit curve (MPB).

Total Social Benefit: The total benefit society receives from consuming a commodity (good or service). It is the area under the marginal social benefit curve (MSB).

Total Social Cost: The social cost to society of a particular activity.

Total Variable Cost: Costs that vary with output (q).

Transitivity of Preferences: If a consumer prefers basket A to basket B, and also prefers basket B to basket C, then he will prefer basket A to basket C.

Two-Part Tariff: A form of pricing in which consumers are charged a second product from the same business.

Uncertainty: The possibility of several different outcomes occurring when the probability of each is unknown.

Utility: The level of satisfaction that a person gets from consuming a good or undertaking an activity.

Utility Possibilities Curve: A curve that includes all efficient allocation of resources measured in terms of an utility levels of two individuals.

Variable Cost: A cost varies with the level of output, such as expenditures, on wages and raw materials.

Welfare Effects: Gains and losses by government brought about by government policy.

PART II

MACROECONOMICS

CHAPTER 1

AN INTRODUCTION TO MACROECONOMICS

KEY TERMS

Nominal Output: Output measured at Market Prices including indirect taxes. When Indirect táxes are taken away we get measure output at factor cost.

Real Output: Output measured at Constant Price.

Unemployment: (People) work force not working and Receiving benefit. Involuntarily unemployed are workforce who are willing to work at going wages rate but cannot fixed job. Voluntarily Unemployed are those who are unwilling to work at market real wage rate.

Balance of Payment: Where a countrys financial transactions with the rest of the world are recorded.

Exchange Rate: Is the price of one currency against another.

Current Account: Records the flows of goods and Services.

Capital Account: Records flows of financial assets.

General Price Level: It finds an average price of goods and services produced in the Economy.

Interest Rates: Is the payment for the use of financial capital.

Whilst microeconomics considers the economic behaviour of individuals, firms, markets etc., macroeconomics emphasises the interactions in the economy as a whole and deals with economic aggregates. So, for example, if we speak about consumption expenditure we are referring to the total (aggregate) expenditure by all consumers.

These aggregates include:

Income/Output (both nominal and real). A common measure of income/output is Gross Domestic Product (GDP).

Definition: Gross Domestic Product (GDP) is the output produced by the factors of production located within the domestic economy (for more information see chapter 2).

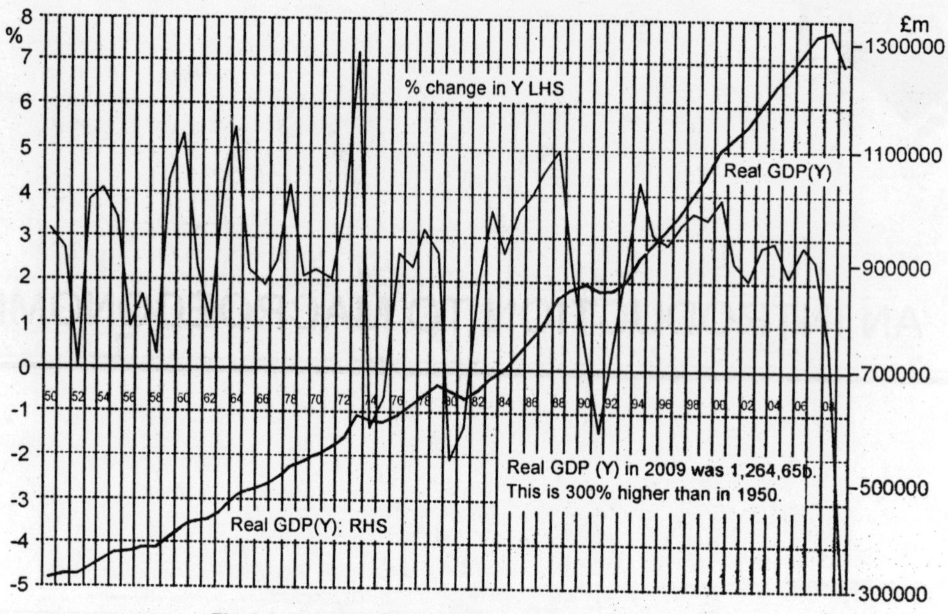

Fig.1.1: UK-Real GDP(Y) 2005 % change in real GDP

The **nominal** (current price) GDP (measured at market prices) of the UK in 2009 was £1395.87 **billion**. That is approximately £22,740 per person (per capita). The population of the UK in June 2009 was estimated to be 61,383,000.

Another measure of output is Gross National Product (GNP).

Definition: Gross National Product (GNP) is the output (of goods and services) produced by the factors of production (land, labour and capital) regardless of where these factors of production are located (Within the domestic economy or abroad).

The **real** income/output of the UK economy (GDP) in 2009 (measured in 2005 market prices [GDP at market prices are obtained when the prices of final goods and services include indirect taxes]) was over £1264.65 billion. The real income/output of an economy can be thought of as the income generated (or the quantity of goods and services produced) by an economy over a particular period of time (usually a year).

We will see, in chapter 2, that the value of income generated is equivalent to the value of output produced by an economy. If you can imagine all the food, cars, clothing, transport services, banking services etc. produced by the UK economy in one year and then, in your minds eye, add them all together this will give you an idea of the **real** income/output of the UK economy in that particular year. The terms real income and real output will be used interchangeably throughout the book.

In practice an aggregate figure for the real income/output of the UK economy is obtained by adding together the output of goods and services measured in monetary terms. If the price level is held constant from year to year then the change in the value of income/output measures the change in real output over time. Fig. 1.1 shows the UK's real GDP (2005 market prices, left-hand scale) and its percentage increases and decreases (right hand scale) for the years 1950 to 2009. However, indirect taxes only increase the value of output not the quantity of goods or services produced. For this reason, it is probably better to use changes in GDP at factor cost as the measure of the change in the output of an economy. However, the UK government generally uses changes in GDP at market prices. This can lead to a dif-

UK Real GDP (Y): Selected percentage changes (inclusive years)	1955-73	1973-79	1981-92	1992-97	1997-2007	2009
GDP	3.07	2.3	2.1	2.65	2.84	-5

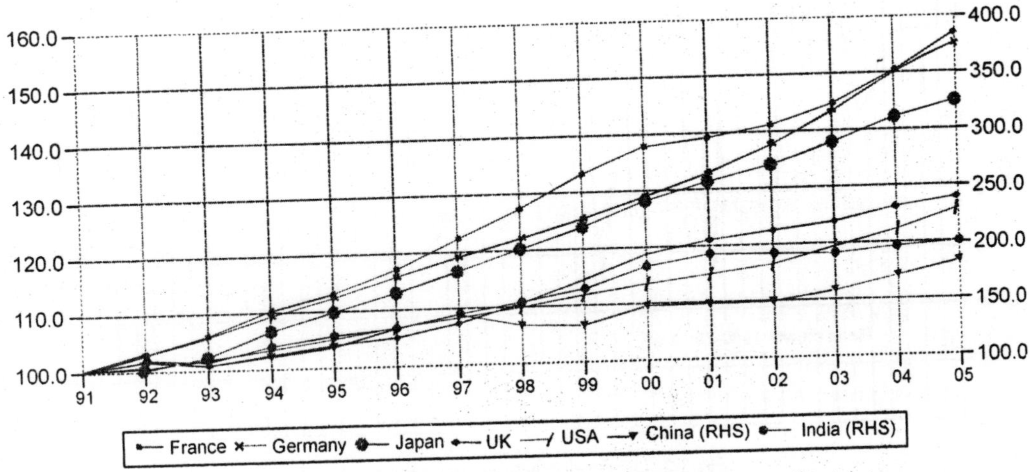

Fig.1.2: Comparative Real GDP (1991=100)

ferent rate of change of GDP at factor cost and GDP at market prices if indirect taxes increase at a higher or lower rate of growth than GDP at factor cost.

Although real GDP usually increased and, occasionally, decreased over the period 1950-2009, **overall** there was an **increase** in real income of about 300%. This averages out at just over 2.37% per year.

We can see that **changes** in real income vary from year to year. Large increases in income/output were recorded in 1960, 1964, 1973 and 1988. In several of the years (1974, 1975, 1980, 1981, 1991 and especially 1990) there was a fall in income/output – a recession. Strictly speaking a recession is defined as output falling for two successive quarters (six months).

During the 1950's and 1960's, there was high investment (brought about by a decline in the cost of capital funds), an unusually rapid rise in productivity and real wages, low inflation and low unemployment. These features of the 1950's and 1960's have caused the period to be acclaimed as a **'Golden Age'**.

Fig. 1.2 shows the **relative** growth in real GDP for China, France, Germany, India, Japan, the UK and the USA since 1991 (1991=100). All but China use the left hand scale (LHS).

As we can see real GDP grew by about 235% in China, 96% in India, 51.5% in the USA, 42.7% in the UK, 28% in France, 19.6% in Germany, and 22.6% in Japan.

Short-term increases in real income/output are not necessarily the same as the economic growth of an economy. We will define **economic growth** as an increase in the underlying productive potential of an economy (determined by an economy's factors of production and 'technological progress'). Hence, in the short-term, in an economy with a large quantity of unemployed resources (there is an output gap), it is possible to increase output without any corresponding increase in the underlying productive potential.

One good measure of growth is the growth of output per head of the economy. Fig. 1.3 shows the annual increase in output per head for the UK economy for the period 1961-2009.

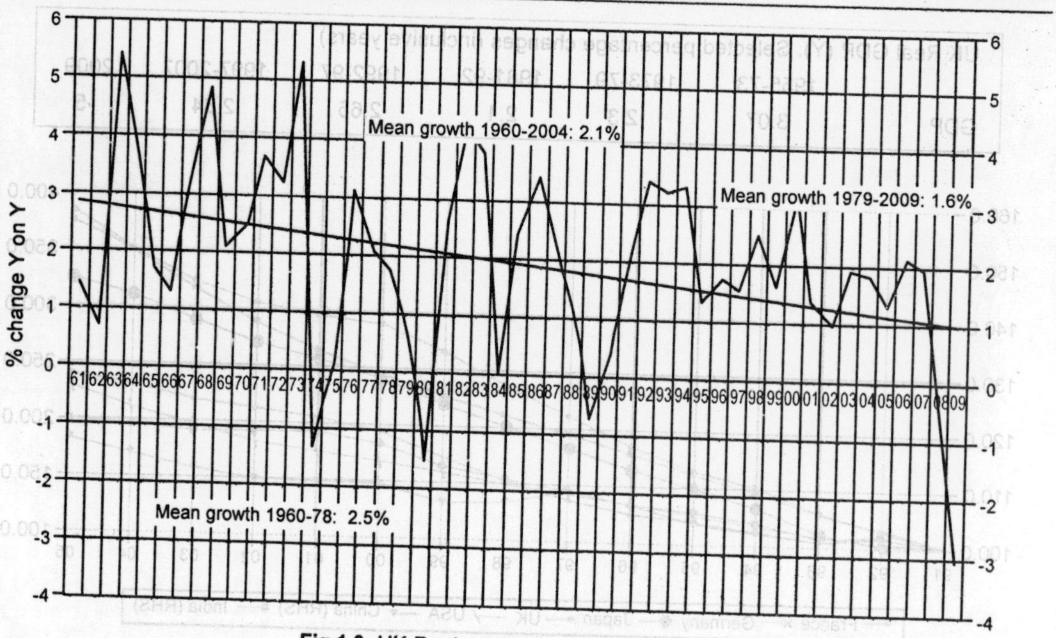

Fig.1.3: UK-Productivity (whole economy)

Fluctuations in income around a long-term trend are known as the business or **trade cycle**. Fig. 1.4 shows, for the years 1961 to 2009, that real GDP fluctuated around an average annual growth rate of 2.42%. The UK treasury estimates (in 2003) that the trend rate of growth (Yf) has increased to 2.7% per annum or above-made up of an 0.7% increase in labour supply and a 2% annual increase in GDP. The figures for the US and the EU are estimated to be 3.5% and 2% respectively.

Nominal income/output is income/output valued in terms of the current years prices (in the UK food, cars, clothing, transport services, banking services etc. will be measured in terms of pound sterling (£'s). Nominal income/output can change if either real income/output changes or the price level changes.

Unemployment (Also see page 18 and chapter 8).

Fig. 1.5 shows the UK's percentage unemployment for the period 1960 to 2009.

From less than 2% in 1974 unemployment rose to over 10% in 1986. As can be seen, unemployment continued to rise after the 1979-81 recession, then fell to below 6% in 1990 before increasing to 10.5% in 1993 and 7.6% in 2009 as the economy again went into recession. However, in recessions, new jobs are as likely to be created as in booms but more jobs are destroyed during recessions than are destroyed during in booms.

Until 1993 the **long-term trend** in unemployment had been upwards. Fig. 1.6 shows inter-country relative trends in unemployment.

From 1992 onwards (until recently) there have been falls in unemployment in the USA and the United Kingdom. (However, see the comments on UK unemployment made on page 18). Other countries have not been so successful in reducing their levels of unemployment.

Unemployment never drops to zero for various reasons:

1. There are always people changing jobs and temporarily recorded as unemployed. These are known as the **frictional** unemployed.
2. Some people are unemployed because of some long-term change in demand or technological conditions. e.g. unem-

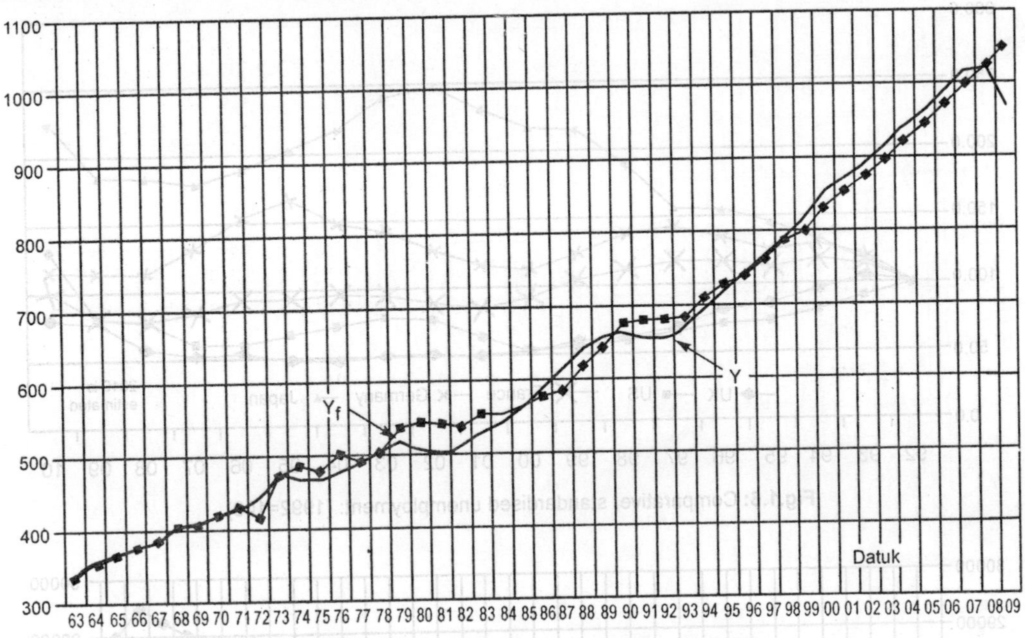

Fig.1.4: GDP (Y) and full employment GDP (Y_f)

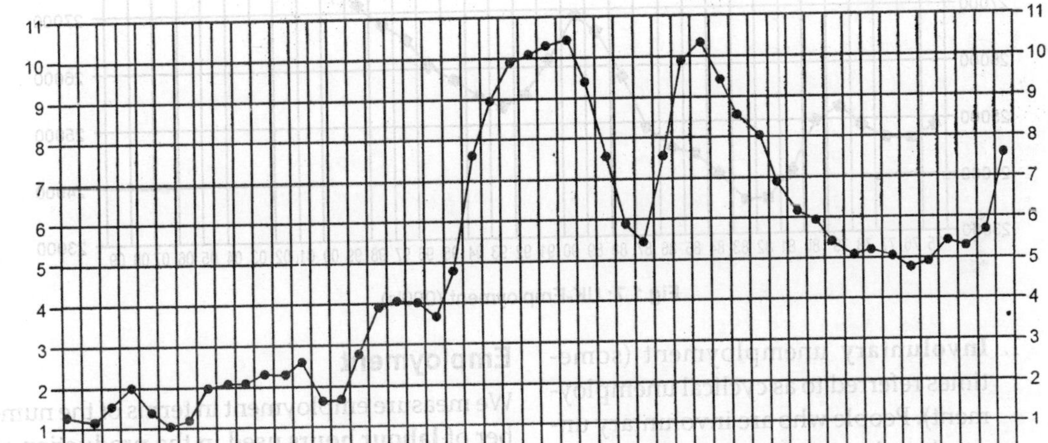

Fig.1.5: Claimant unemployment (%)

ployment of coal miners as a result of the decline in the demand for coal or the reduction in the number of people employed in the banking industry partly due to the introduction of new technology. These people are **structurally** unemployed.

3. **Seasonal** unemployment is unemployment, as its name suggests, due to seasonal variations in demand. e.g. Agriculture, construction or tourism.

4. The hard core of people are virtually unemployable are known as the **residual** unemployment.

However, for expositional purposes, we will emphasise two broad measures of unemployment:

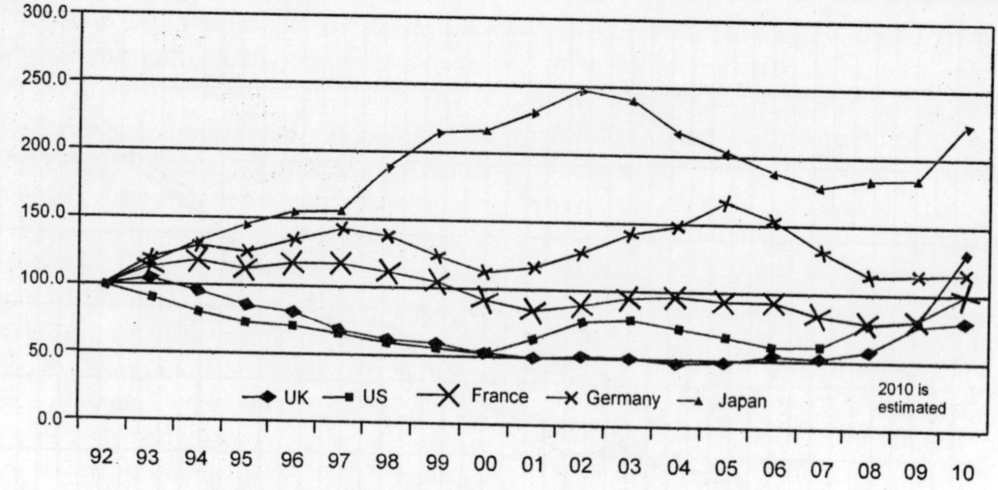

Fig.1.6: Comparative, standardised unemployment: (1992=100)

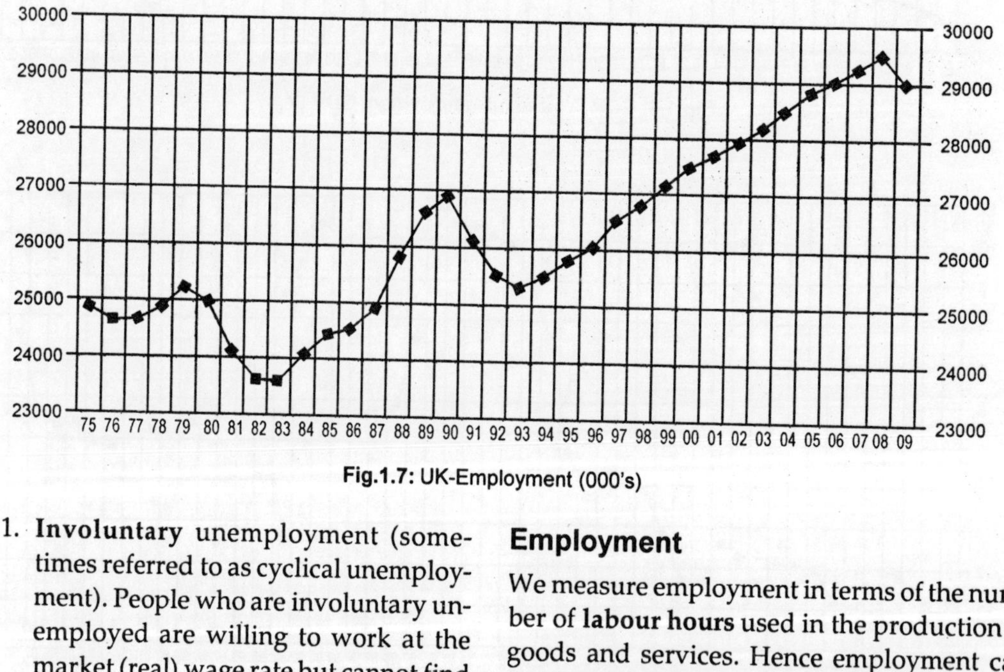

Fig.1.7: UK-Employment (000's)

1. **Involuntary** unemployment (sometimes referred to as cyclical unemployment). People who are involuntary unemployed are willing to work at the market (real) wage rate but cannot find a job.
2. **Voluntary** unemployment (sometimes referred to as structural unemployment). People who are voluntary unemployed are unwilling to work at the market (real) wage rate even if they could find employment.

Employment

We measure employment in terms of the number of **labour hours** used in the production of goods and services. Hence employment can be increased, up to full employment, by employing more labour (women or men) and/or by the existing labour force working longer hours.

We will define **full employment** as a situation of **no involuntary unemployment**. There will, however, be some **voluntary** unemployment.

The number of voluntarily unemployed, when there is no involuntary unemployment, is known as the **NAIRU (non-accelerating inflation rate of unemployment) OR the natural rate of unemployment.** The practical difficulty is measuring the natural rate of unemployment. Different economists will give different estimates of the NAIRU (natural rate). Some "new Keynesian" economists argue that there is no natural rate of unemployment in the sense of a rate to which the actual rate tends to return. Instead, when actual unemployment rises and remains high for some time, the natural rate of unemployment rises as well. The dependence of the natural rate of unemployment on actual unemployment is known as the hysteresis hypothesis. One explanation for hysteresis in a heavily unionized economy is that unions directly represent the interests only of those who are currently employed. Unionization undermines the ability of those outside the union to compete for employment. After prolonged layoffs employed workers inside the union may seek the benefits of higher wages for themselves, rather than moderating wage demands to promote the rehiring of unemployed workers. The downside to the hysteresis hypothesis is that once unemployment becomes high—as it did in Europe in the recessions of the seventies—it is relatively impervious to monetary and fiscal stimulus, even in the short-run.

Although a large number of jobs were created, in the UK, in the period 1983-89 a large proportion of them were part-time. Between 1990 and 1993 there as been a large decline in the number of jobs available and a consequent rise in unemployment. Some of this unemployment is due to heavy spending in the service sector on computers and other aspects of computer technology. This heavy spending is followed by big cuts in employment as computers replace staff. From 1993 onwards (until recently) the situation has improved somewhat. Up to September 1996 the workforce in employment has risen by 463,000 - made up of 81,000 full-time and 382,000 part-time jobs. Of the part-time jobs women took 231,000.

Fig.1.8 shows inter-country relative trends in employment. The USA has been relatively successful in creating new jobs, its employment is about nearly 100% higher in 2004 than 1962.

Aggregate consumption expenditure (C): It is defined as the aggregate flow of expenditure by consumers (you and me) on goods and services. **Goods** are such things as food, cloth-

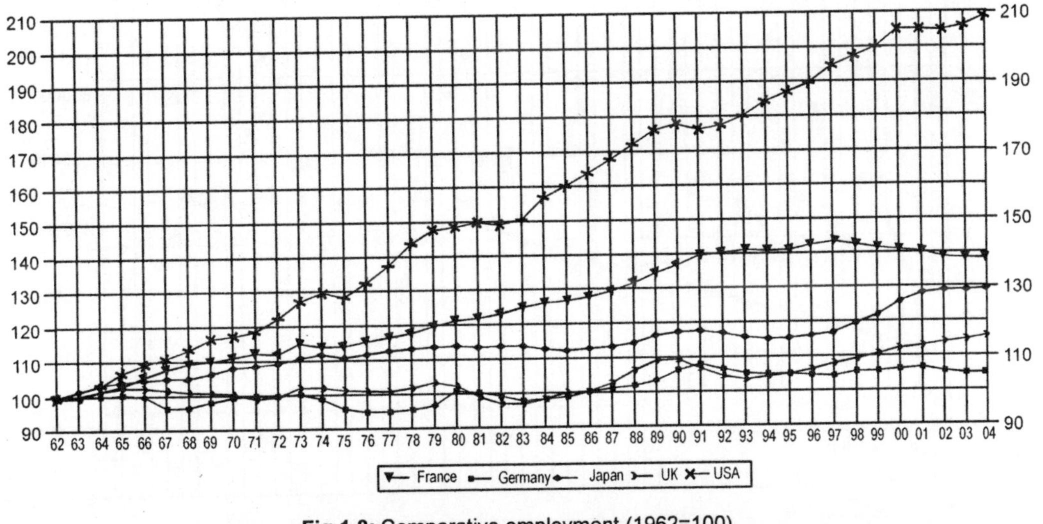

Fig.1.8: Comparative employment (1962=100)

ing, washing machines, TV's etc. **Services** are such things as transport, banking, insurance etc.

Consumption expenditure accounted for about 63% of the output of the UK economy in 2007 (up from a low point of 59% in 1977 – see Fig. 1.10). As it is such a large percentage of output it is of great interest to economist to try explain variations in consumption expenditure. Figure 1.9 shows real consumption expenditure (in 2005, £'s million (right hand scale [RHS])) and its annual percentage change (LHS). The **main** determinant of real consumption expenditure is real income. We will see later that as aggregate income increases then aggregate consumption expenditure increases. This is 'induced' consumption expenditure. Other factors that affect consumption (interest rates, wealth etc) affect what is known as autonomous consumption expenditure.

Saving (S): Is non-consumption expenditure: It is disposable income that is not consumed.

That is Disposable income less consumption expenditure. S = Yd – C. Disposable income is the income remaining after deducting direct taxes and adding on transfer payments (benefits, B).

Investment expenditure (I): The flow of expenditure by firms on new physical capital assets: Machinery, factories, roads, housing etc. It is ***not*** buying shares, depositing money in Building Societies etc.. Buying shares etc is the best thought of as financial investment.

Fig. 1.10 shows, amongst other things, investment as a proportion of GDP.

We can be observed investment expenditure varies from less than 10% of GDP in 1950 to 17.7% in 1998.

R.C.O. Matthews in a celebrated article entitled: Why has Britain had Full Employment since the War? (Economic Journal, September 1968) traced the high level of demand in the post war period to the high level of investment in the private sector. Not only did investment affect the level of aggregate demand it also had supply side implications. High levels of investment will increase the productive potential of the economy. Dick Sargent in his book, *To Full Employment: The Keynesian Experience and After (2004), argues that, in the UK in the 1950's and 1960's, it was*

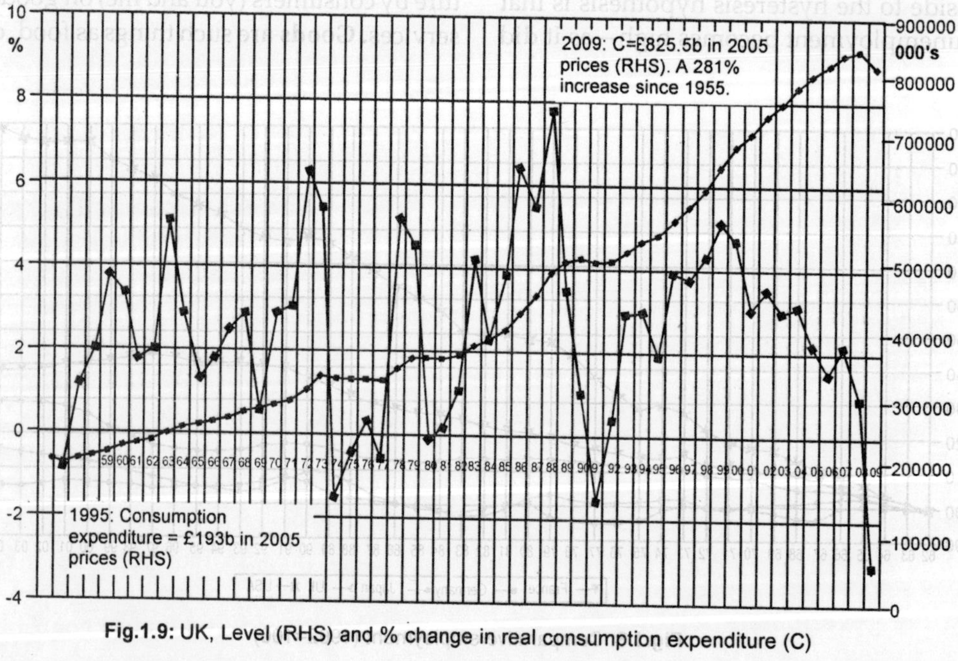

Fig.1.9: UK, Level (RHS) and % change in real consumption expenditure (C)

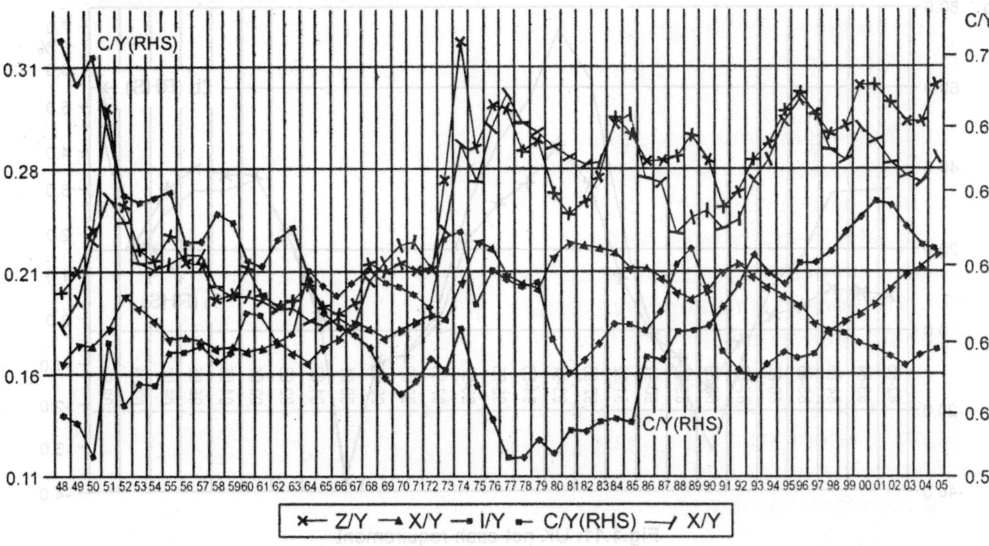

Fig.1.10: Expenditure as a proportion of GDP

the high level of investment and the growth in capital stock that enabled both aggregate demand and output to increase with a concomitant low level of inflation and not the adoption of 'Keynesian economics'.

Government expenditure (G): Is the flow of expenditure by the government on both current and capital outlays. Current expenditure includes salaries and other day to day expenditures. Capital expenditure includes the building of roads, new hospitals, schools etc..

It raises taxation (direct and indirect) to pay for its expenditures. Any expenditure not covered by taxation has to be covered by borrowing. To meet the Maastricht criterion the (PSNCR) Public Sector Net Cash Requirement (formally the PSBR [the public sector-borrowing requirement]) has to be not more than 3% of GDP.

A change in government expenditure and/or taxation is known as **FISCAL POLICY**.

Fig. 1.11 shows the net borrowing of the government of the UK.

In some years, 1987-90, the public finances were in surplus and the government was able to repay some of the national debt. Years in which the government borrows (recently 2001-02 to 2008-09 [and beyond]) to finance its expenditure are years in which there is an increase in the national debt. (The national debt more than doubled between 1992-3 and 1997-8 from £200 billion to £410.1 billion).

Balance of payments: Is a record of a country's financial transactions with the rest of the world.

Exports: Sales of goods and services overseas.

Imports: Purchase by the domestic economy of overseas goods and services

The balance of payments comprises two broad categories:

1. **The Current Account**. This records flows of goods (visibles) and services (invisibles), and other net income from abroad.

   Visible goods are, as the name suggests, such things as washing machines, food, oil etc.

   Invisible trade includes such things as shipping services, insurance, and tourism etc.

   Net income from abroad includes transfer payments between countries (foreign aid, and budget contributions

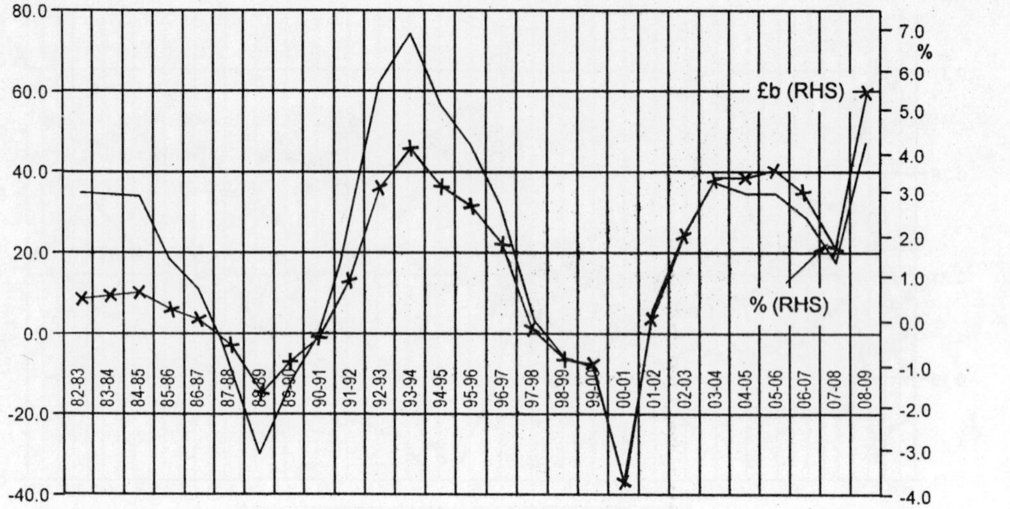

Fig.1.11: UK net cash requirement

Recent current account balances in £'s billion:

1990	1991	1992	1993	1994	1995	1996	1997	1998	1999	2000	2001	2002	2005	2006	2007
-22.3	-10.7	-12.9	-11.8	-6.6	-8.5	-7.3	-1.8	-3.2	-21.7	-24.8	-21.9	-16.5	-31	-50.7	-59.7

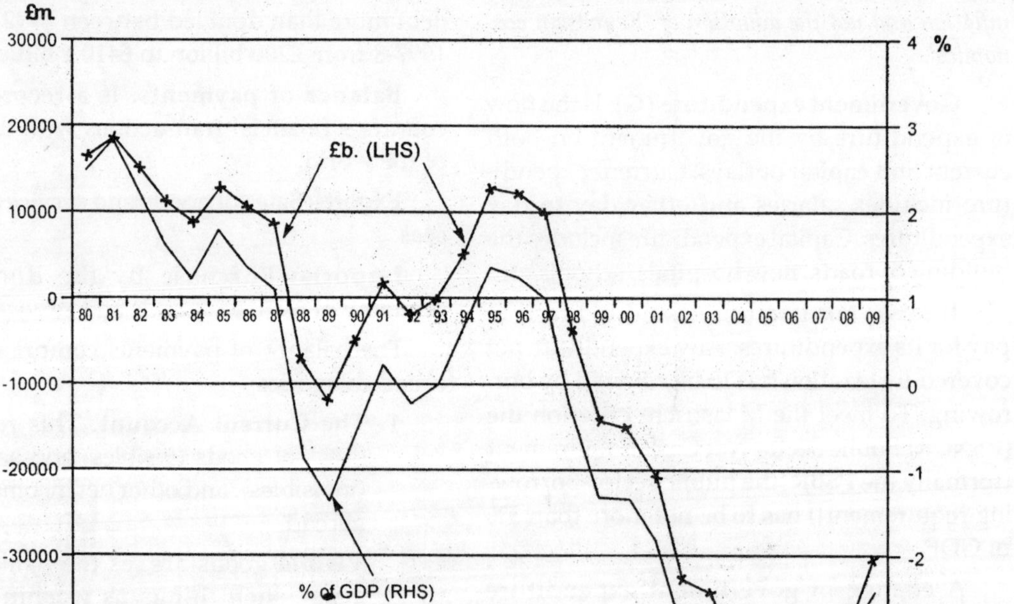

Fig.1.12: UK-current account balance

to the European Union), and property income (these arise when residents of one country own income-earning assets, such as stocks, shares or property, in another country).

Between 1981-92, exports rose by an average of 3.6% per year. Between 1981-92 imports rose by an average of 6.3% per year: This helps to account for the large current account deficits of 1988-93. However, the large deficits of 1999-2005 are a much smaller percentage of GDP. It should be also be noted that imports and exports have grown from about 20% of GDP to around 30% of GDP.

Fig. 1.12 shows the UK's current account balances from 1981 to 2009. We can see that there were surpluses in 1981-82 (when the economy was in recession) and large deficits in 1988-90 and 1999-2008 when there were increases in GDP. (As income/output rises [falls] imports increase [decrease]).

2. **The Capital Account**. This is a record of the flows of finance brought about international dealings in real and financial assets. Real assets include overseas factories or offices. Financial assets include shares in overseas companies, overseas government stocks, and other financial assets.

The Exchange rate

Is the price at which two currencies exchange. The value of the pound sterling (£) refers to the **nominal exchange rate** for the pound: That is, how many units of a foreign currency foreigners are willing to pay for a pound? For example, if the pound's exchange rate against the Euro is 0.84, then 1 Euro is worth 60p. (£1 = €190).

Fig. 1.13 shows the relationship between the pound sterling and the US dollar. The rise in the exchange rate between 1977 and 1981 meant that the pound was **appreciating** (you have to give fewer pounds to receive 1 US dollar). (The relative price of exports increased

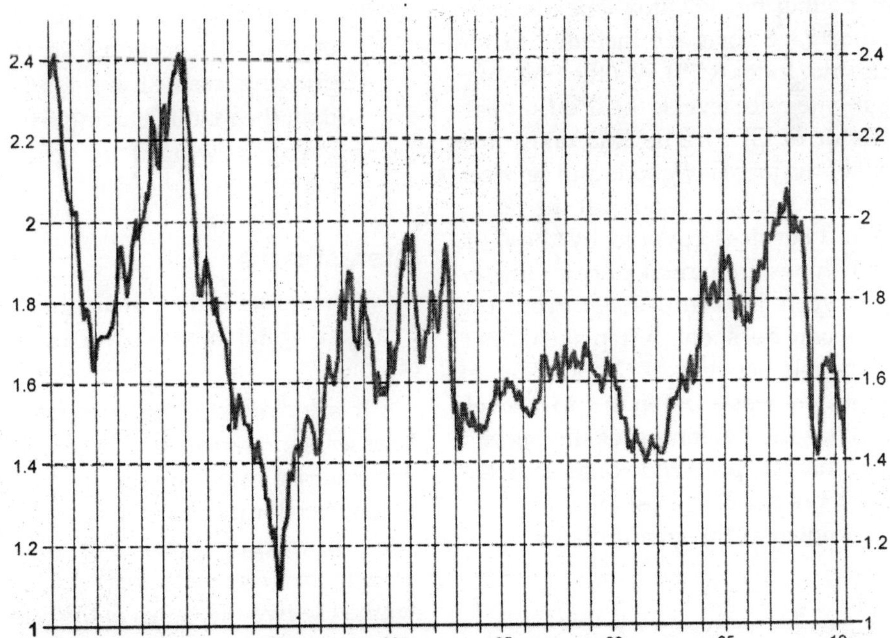

Fig.1.13: $/£ nominal exchange rate

and the relative price of imports decreased). From 1981 to 1996 the pound depreciated (you have to give more pounds to receive, for example, 1 dollar). From 1996 sterling started to appreciate again. At the end of 2003 the dollar is falling against both the Euro and the pound sterling.

Fig. 1.14 shows the relative behaviour of exchange rates against a basket of other currencies.

The DM and Yen are the currencies that have appreciated over this period.

The Indian Rupee depreciated the most. The pound sterling depreciated by 21.6%.

The general (aggregate) price level

At the macroeconomic level it is convenient to find an average of the prices of goods and services produced in the economy.

One measure, used in the UK that is now in the process of being superseded is the retail price index (RPI). The new measure is the consumer price index (CPI). This, like the RPI, is a weighted average of the prices of goods and services produced in the UK economy. However, neither house valuations nor even average mortgage costs are included in the Consumer Price Index (CPI). Another measure of the aggregate price level is the IPD (implicit price deflator of GDP). The IPD takes into account all of the prices of goods and services produced in an economy – not just the prices of goods and services covered by the CPI. Figure 1.15 shows an annual price index for the UK between 1782 and 2002. From the diagram it can be seen that prices were reasonably stable between 1782 and 1939. In many years there was a **fall** in the price level. It is only since the beginning of the Second World War that the price index has shown a substantial increase. This post-1940 increase in prices is known as the great inflation.

Inflation

We will define inflation as a **persistent rise** in the average price level not as an increase in the general price level. With this definition a 'one off' increase in the price level brought about by, say, an increase in value added tax (VAT) is not inflation. However, an increase in VAT, may 'trigger off' inflation (see chapter 9).

Fig. 1.16 shows the percentage change in the UK's retail price index for the period 1960 to 2009. We can see that prices increased by over 24% in 1975, 18% in 1980 and 9.46% in 1990. However, since 1990 the trend of price increases has been downwards.

Fig. 1.17 shows inflation rates for the France, Germany, Japan, the UK, the USA and India.

One should also note that changes in the RPI and the CPI may not give an accurate picture of the rate of inflation. We have already mentioned that neither house valuations nor even average mortgage costs are included in the CPI. Also, a general price index may,

1. Under-estimate quality and technological improvements in goods and services.

2. Not properly reflect the composition of output in an economy i.e. If prices are growing less fast in the service sector than the manufacturing sector and too great a weight is given to the manufacturing sector.

Interest rates

An interest rate is the payment for the use of financial capital (money) over a certain period of time.

It is convenient to split interest rates into 3 classes; short term (up to 5 years [the shortest term interest rate is determined by the Bank of England monetary policy committee (MPC)]), medium-term (5 to 10 years) and long-term (over 10 years). We should emphasise two measures of the interest rate:

1. The nominal rate, and,
2. The real rate.

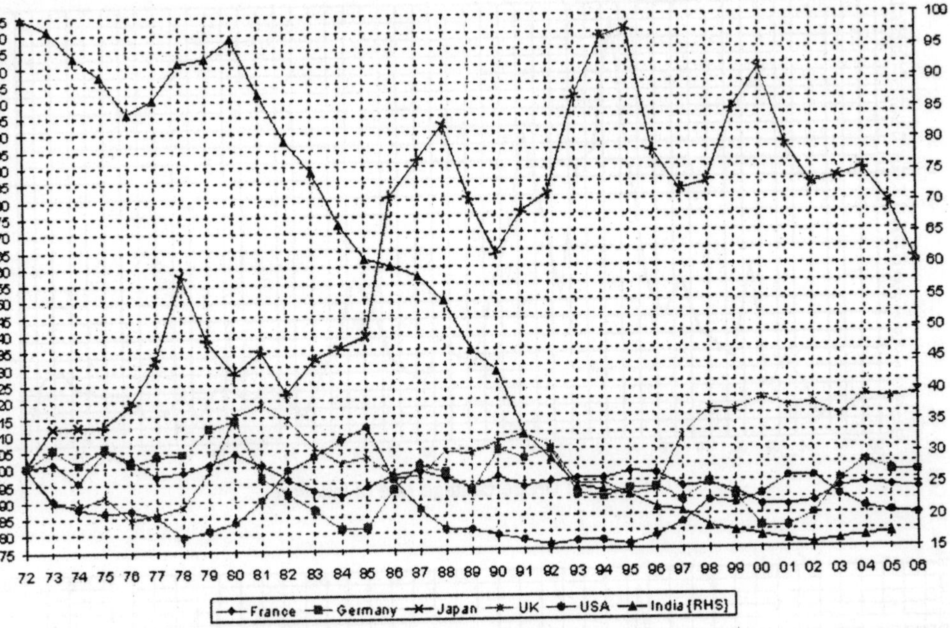

Fig.1.14: Comparative exchange rates (1972=100)

Recent percentage changes in the CPI (consumer price index)

1989	1991	1992	1993	1994	1997	2000	2001	2002	2003	2004	2009
5.1	7.5	4.2	2.5	2.03	1.8	0.76	1.23	1.31	1.29	1.37	0.6

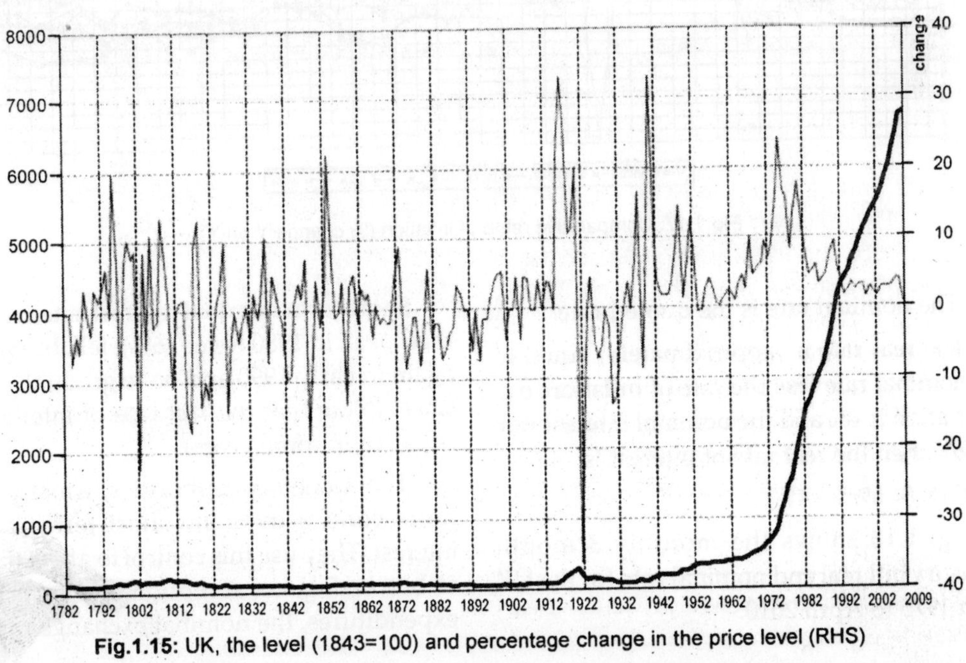

Fig.1.15: UK, the level (1843=100) and percentage change in the price level (RHS)

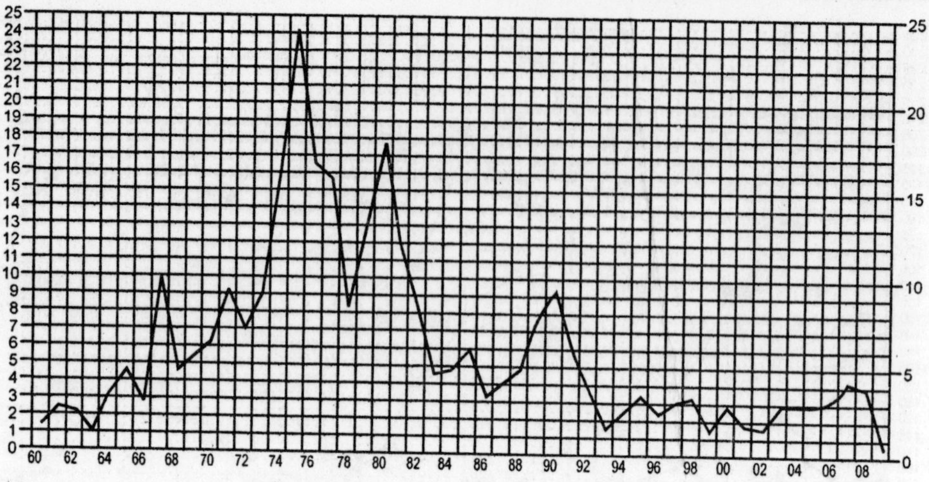

Fig.1.16: UK percentage rate of inflation

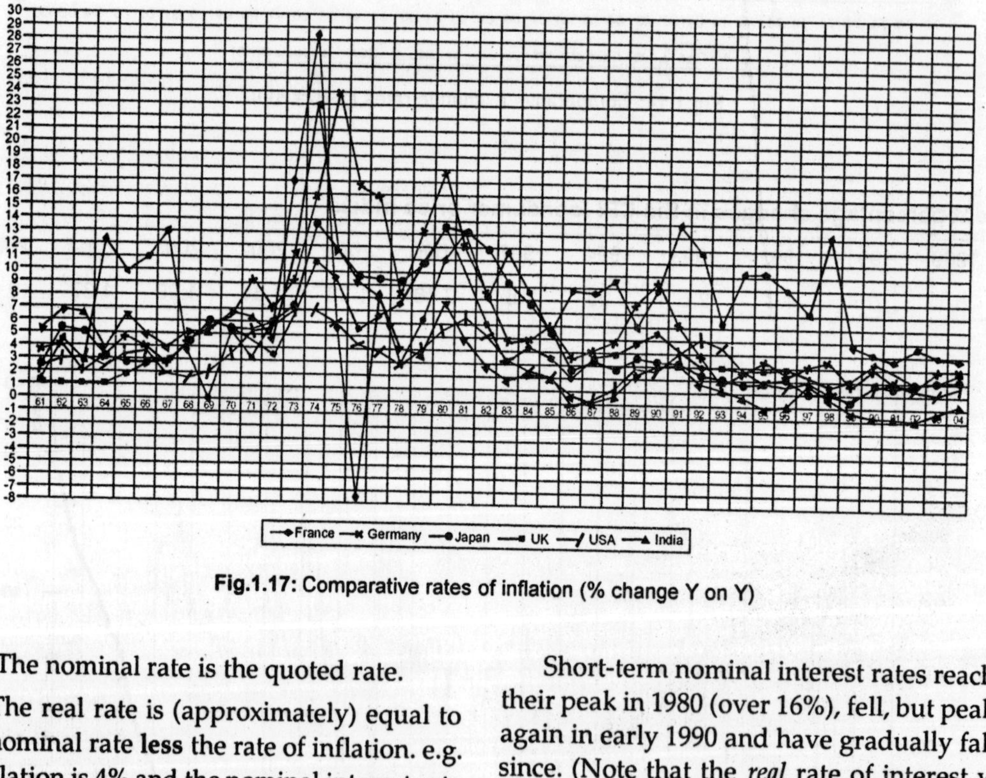

Fig.1.17: Comparative rates of inflation (% change Y on Y)

The nominal rate is the quoted rate.

The real rate is (approximately) equal to the nominal rate **less** the rate of inflation. e.g. If inflation is 4% and the nominal interest rate is 6½% then the real rate of interest is

2½% (= 6½% - 4%).

Fig. 1.18 shows the monthly 3 month Treasury bill real and nominal rate for the UK from 1975 to April 2010.

Short-term nominal interest rates reached their peak in 1980 (over 16%), fell, but peaked again in early 1990 and have gradually fallen since. (Note that the *real* rate of interest was negative in some years).

The monetary authorities, usually, have more control over the short-term rates of interest. They use this control to affect the cost of borrowing, consumption and investment expenditures, the nominal exchange rate and hence the income/output and rate of inflation of the economy.

Long term rates are more affected by factors not under the control of the government such as the rate of inflation and the world's demand and supply of finance.

Fig. 1.19 shows the nominal and real long-term interest rate in the UK economy.

'In many years the real interest rate was negative; 1971, 1972, 1974, 1975, 1979, 1989, 1997, 2008 and 2010. Between 1991 and 2007 the real rate of interest has varied between 1% and 7%.'

It is (theoretically) the real rate of interest that affects the behaviour of economic individuals.

As we will see the higher the real rate of interest the lower the level of economic activity.

The nominal stock of money (M): is the face value of the stock of money (however defined) measured at a moment in time.

A change in the money supply and/or the rate of interest is known as **MONETARY** policy.

The real stock of money (L = M/P): is the quantity of goods and services that can be exchanged for the nominal stock of money.

Fig. 1.20 plots the growth in M4 and the RPI. For many of the past 13 years the growth of M4 has been well above the percentage change in the RPI.

'This indicates that factors, other than the growth in the supply of money, affect the rate of inflation.'

The money wage (W): The nominal (current money) value of the average hourly wage rate.

The real wage (w = W/P): are the goods and services that can be exchanged for the money wage.

If the money wage were £8 per hour (W=£8) then the real wage (w = W/P) are the goods and services that can be exchanged for

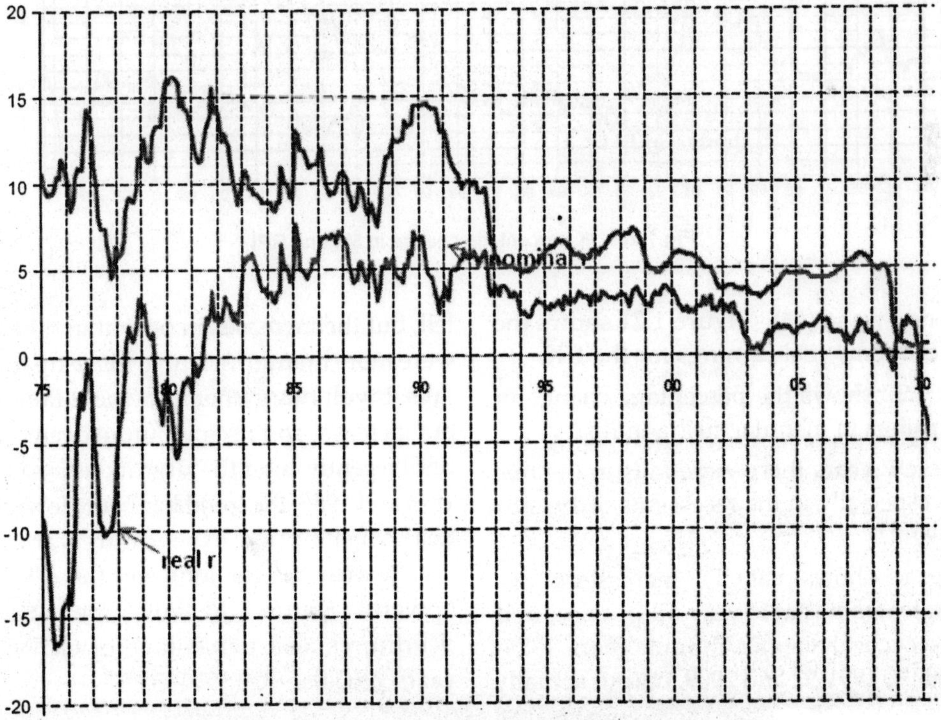

Fig.1.18: UK short-term (3 month treasury) and real interest rate

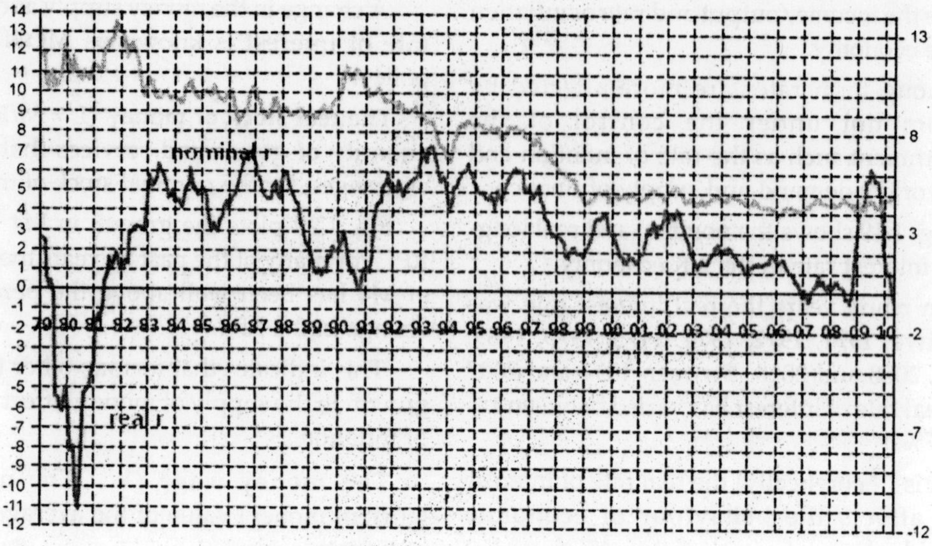

Fig.1.19: Long-term nominal and real rate of interest

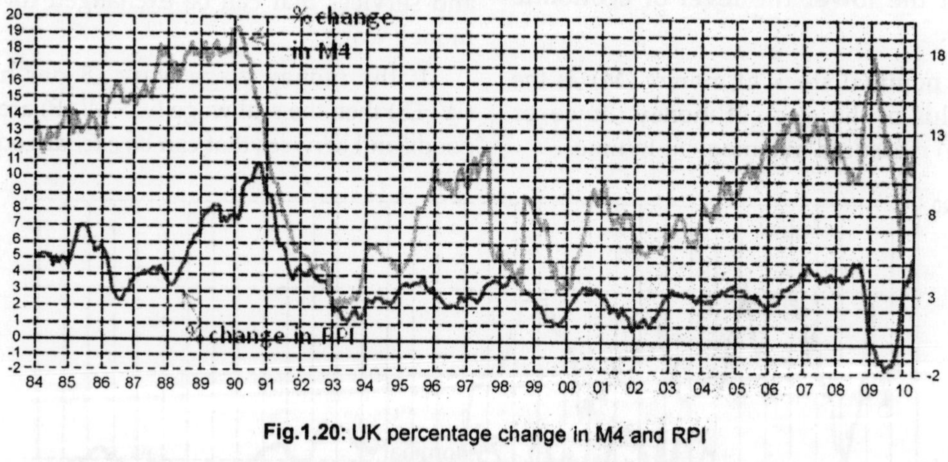

Fig.1.20: UK percentage change in M4 and RPI

the money wage (£8). Figure 1.21 shows the whole economy real earnings for the UK.

Fig. 1.22 shows the percentage change in real earnings in manufacturing industry.

In a few years there were falls in the real wage - especially in the recessions of 1980-81 and 1990-92.

Fig. 1.1 shows that GDP increases at different rates from year to year-output rises and falls in a cyclical manner. In some years, 1974-75, 1980-81, 1991-92 and 2009. output actually fell, but the increases in output in other years were more than sufficient to make up for these falls. Involuntary unemployment falls as output increases and rises as output decreases but, until recently, after the large increases between 1974 and 1986, the trend has been downwards. Real consumption expenditure varies from year to year but the long run trend has been upwards. Figure 1.10 shows the various expenditures as a percentage of GDP for the years 1960-95.

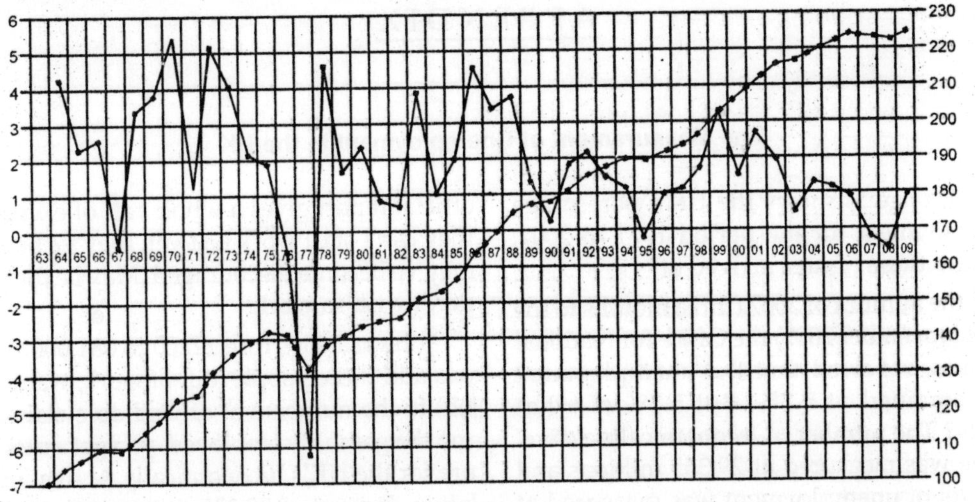

Fig.1.21: The level (1963=100) and percentage change in real earnings (whole economy)

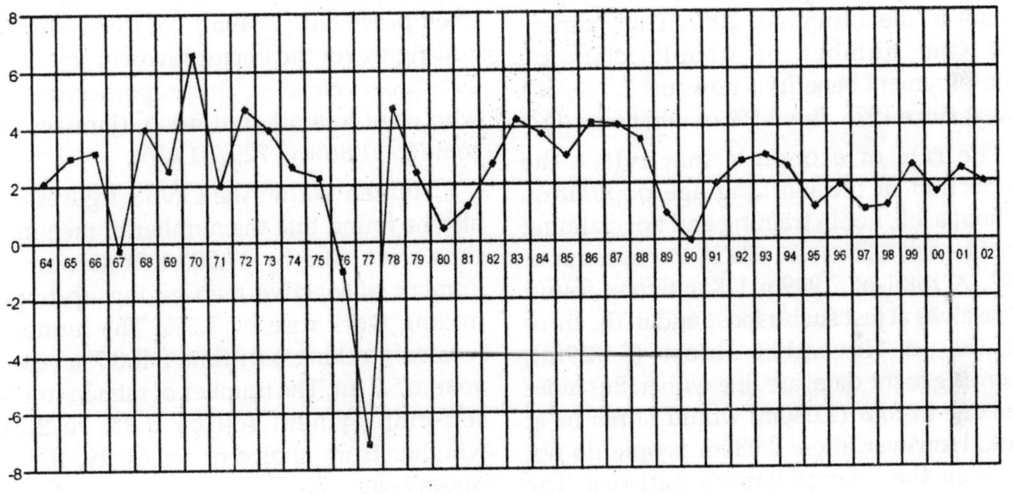

Fig.1.22: Percentage change in real manufacturing earnings

Figs. 1.2, 1.6, 1.8, 1.14 and 1.17 show the comparative performances of the UK, France, Germany, Japan and the USA for real GDP, unemployment, employment, nominal exchange rates and prices respectively.

APPENDIX

The Measurement of Unemployment in the UK

Fig. 1.5, page 5, shows the UK's percentage unemployment for the period 1971 to 2007. How are these figures arrived at?

In the autumn of 2007 (three months to the end of November 2007) the Office for National Statistics, reported that the unemployment rate remained at 5.3%. But 5.3% of what exactly? The number of 'economically active' people was measured at 29.355 millions and the level of unemployment was measured at 1.649 millions (1.6492/29.355) = 5.3%.

Some 175,000 people entered the jobs market in the autumn of 2007. The claimant rate (the number of people claiming unemployment benefit) is now just 2.5%—it's lowest since 1975. But 2.5% of what exactly?

The rate of economic inactivity—the proportion of the working age population without a job, nor in training and not claiming benefit—fell 0.2% to 21.0% in the autumn of 2007. A total of 7.909m UK citizens found themselves at just such a loose end in the three months to November. Most (5.829m), according to the data, are fine with it. But more than one-in-four (2.080m) would rather be at work. However, these 2.080m people do not figure in the unemployment statistics. The official report gives a whole raft of excuses—they can't start work just yet, they've been ill, they've become discouraged. May be they just don't wish to work.

Job vacancies rose 12200 to 681,000. But if you add these people (out of work, wanting a job) to the numbers of official dole-claimants and the gainfully employed, you get a new figure for the UK's 'Economically Active' population. Instead of 29.355, it becomes 31.435m (29.355m + 2.080m). Add the 'missing' unemployed (2.080m) to Britain's official level of unemployment (1.649m), and you also get a new figure for the unemployment *rate*. It's not 2.7% ... or even 5.3%. The proportion of people who want to work, but don't, (January 2008) come to 11.86% (3.729/31.435).

Hidden within the ONS's figures it can also be found that the number of men in full-time work rose by 47,000 this autumn. The number of inactive men giving up hope of finding work rose by 1.3%. The number of women working part-time fell 0.7% year-on-year to 5.71m. The number of men in full-time self-employment fell by 0.2% to 2.31m, whether from choice or necessity, the data doesn't say.

CHAPTER 2

THE MEASUREMENT OF NATIONAL INCOME/OUTPUT

KEY TERMS

Capital: The stock of factories, plants, equipment, stocks and other resources of production.

Final Good: A good that is produced for final use and not for the production of other goods.

Gross Domestic Product (GDP): The output (or goods and services) produced by the factors of production (land, labour organisation and capital) located within the domestic economy.

Gross National Product (GNP): The output (of goods and services) produced by the factors of production (land, labour organisation and capital) regardless of where these factors of production are located.

National income accounting

One way in which the UK government finds out how economy is doing is to measure the national output of goods and services of the economy.

In the UK there are thousands of different goods and services produced; they can be all added together if they are measured in a common currency unit (£'s).

One measure is GDP (gross domestic product), which measures the output produced by factors of production located in the domestic economy regardless of who owns these factors.

GDP can be valued in nominal terms (the prices currently prevailing) or in real terms ≈ the sum of the actual output of goods and services produced, [in practice goods and services are valued in prices prevailing at some particular calendar date. At the present time 1985 prices are used].

GROSS DOMESTIC PRODUCT can be measured in three ways.

1. **OUTPUT method:** Output can be measured in two ways:

   a. The value of the final output produced.

b. The value added at each stage in the production process; Because of the difficulty of defining final output the value-added method is used:

Definition: Value added; is the value of a business's output less the value of its purchases (raw material and semi-finished goods) from other businesses.

2. **INCOME method**; is the sum of the total incomes generated in the production of goods and services; (earned by the factors of production).

   Labour : wages, salaries

   Land : rent

   Capital : interest

   'Risk' (Entrepreneur) : profit

3. **EXPENDITURE method**; is the total expenditure (by all groups) on final goods and services.

Value of expenditure at market prices is the sum of expenditures on consumption, investment, government and exports less expenditure on imports = $C + I + G + X - Z$

The value of expenditure at factor cost is the sum of expenditures on consumption, investment, government and exports less expenditure on imports and less the value of indirect taxation = $C + I + G + X - Z - T_e$

The following example may help to clarify the above.

For simplicity we will assume that the economy has no public sector (no government expenditure, taxation or benefits ($G = T_d = T_e = B = 0$) and the cost of raw materials for the plastic and electronics producers are zero.

INC.GEN = income generated: ELECT.= Electronics: E.P.= Electronics producer:

P.P.= Plastics producer: M.P.= machine producer: M.P.P.= Mobile phone producer: CONS.= consumer.

The fifth row of the following table considers one of the transactions of the electronics producer. The electronics producer is selling electronics to the value of 2,000 to the machine producer. Since we (unrealistically) assumed that the cost of raw materials to the electronics producer was zero then the value added by this transaction is 2,000 minus zero which is equal to 2,000. Similar the seventh row gives 3,000 as the value added by the sales to the mobile phone producer. The

1	2	3	4	5	6	7
GOOD	SELLER	BUYER	TRANSACTION	VALUE	EXPENDITURE	INC.GEN.
		VALUE	ADDED			
ELECT.	E.P.	M.P.	2,000	2,000	2,000	
ELECT.	E.P.	M.P.P.	3,000	3,000	3,000	
MACHINE	M.P.	M.P.P.	6,000	4,000	6,000	4,000
PLASTIC	P.P.	M.P.P.	500	500	500	
PHONE M.	P.P.	CONS.	8,000	4,500	8,000	4,500
		total	19,500			
		TOTALS	**14,000**	**14,000**	**14,000**	

total sales of electronics of 5,000 does not show up as expenditure on **final** goods since electronics is an intermediate good which will be utilised in the later stages of the production process.

As people own (directly or indirectly) all the factors of production both the 2,000 and the 3,000 are fully paid out to people in the form of factor incomes (wages, salaries, rents, profits and dividends). Hence in the sixth column we enter 2,000 and 3,000 respectively.

The ninth row gives the transaction value of the machine producer. Since the machine producer has purchased 2,000 of electronics and sells the machine for 6,000, to the mobile phone producer, the machine producer adds value of 4,000. This is also paid out in the form of incomes.

The eleventh row shows the transaction values of the producer of plastic. The sales are 500 and the cost of raw materials are zero; hence the value added by the plastics producer is 500 - also paid out as incomes.

The thirteenth row indicates the purchases and sales of the mobile phone producer. Sales to the consumer are 8,000. **Raw material** purchases are 3,000 of electronics and 500 of plastic. Hence the value added by the mobile phone producer is 8,000 minus 3000 minus 500 which is equal to 4,500. 4,500 is also paid out in the form of incomes.

Note that the purchase of the machine is investment and is not classified as a 'raw material. Hence, its value is not included when estimating value added.

GDP measured by the value added (column 5) is 14,000.

GDP measured by the income method (column 6) is 14,000.

The purchase of the machine is investment and comes under final expenditure (column 6). Hence, investment = 6,000.

Note: Any output that is not sold goes into inventories (stocks). Inventories are classified as investment expenditure.

The sale of the mobile phone is consumption expenditure and comes under final expenditure (column 6).

GDP measured by the expenditure method is 14,000.

The three methods of measuring GDP give the same value: 14,000.

In this **simple** case the total value of incomes received by people is 14,000 and their aggregate consumption expenditure is 8,000. Income not consumed is defined as saving. So in this case saving (S) is 14,000 less 8,000, which is equal to 6,000. This level of saving is also equal to investment expenditure.

An economy with no government expenditure or taxation and no exports or imports will mean that aggregate investment is equal to aggregate saving. We will see that this rule does not carry over to an open economy with a government sector.

The Government Sector

Fiscal policy is the government's decision about the level of Government expenditure and the level of taxation: (N.T. and T_e).

The budget deficit is the excess of government outlays (G) over government receipts (N.T. + T_e). (In the UK, in the financial year 1993-94, the PSBR. was £34.5b. [the PSBR has now been replaced by the PSCR—the public sector cash requirement]).

The budget deficit has to be financed (mainly by borrowing):

1. From the non-bank public.
2. From overseas governments, businesses or individuals.
3. From the banking sector. (This can increase the domestic money supply).
4. It can also finance the deficit by printing new money.

The government borrows by selling bonds; in return it pays interest.

As a result of the borrowing the government builds up its debts to the public.

This is the NATIONAL DEBT: It is the stock of outstanding government debt.

Y_d = disposable income = $Y - T_d + B$. The income remaining after direct taxation has been taken away and benefits added.

The government raises revenue both through direct taxation (T_d) and indirect taxation (T_e).

Government expenditure (G) is on goods and services including investment programmes in roads, schools, hospitals etc.

The government also distributes transfer payments (B) pensions, unemployment benefits, subsidies to private and public firms. Benefits do not require the provision of any goods or services in return not included in the measure of GDP: They are a redistribution of income from the taxpayer to the recipient of the benefit.

We can think of benefits as negative taxes. We will define NT (net taxes) as direct taxes less benefits ($= T_d - B$).

Note that the total tax take (T) is $NT + T_e$.

Aggregate Personal Disposable Income

$(Y_d) \equiv Y - T_d + B$

$S \equiv Y_d - C$ or, rearranging

$$Y \equiv C + S + T_d - B \qquad (1)$$

The valuation of GDP

We can value **GDP** in one of two ways:

a. At market prices. These are prices inclusive of indirect taxes. The price includes any specific and/or value added tax. They are 'retail' prices.

b. At factor cost These prices exclude indirect taxes. They are factory gate prices. Prices before the imposition of any indirect taxation.

GDP (in a closed economy) at market prices $\equiv C + I + G$

Indirect taxes only increase the value of output not the quantity of goods or services produced. For this reason it is probably better to use changes in GDP at factor cost as the measure of the change in the output of an economy. However, the UK government generally uses changes in GDP at market prices. This can lead to a different rate of change of GDP at factor cost and GDP at market prices if indirect taxes increase at a higher or lower rate of growth than GDP at factor cost.

So let $Y \equiv$ **GDP** at factor cost

$$\equiv C + I + G - T_e$$

The Overseas Sector

Exports (X) are domestically produced goods and services sold abroad.

Imports (Z) are goods and services produced abroad and are purchased for use in the domestic economy. There is a flow of income from the domestic economy; Z is negative expenditure.

Domestic expenditure

$\equiv C + I + G + X - Z - T_e$ (at factor cost)

$$\text{or } Y \equiv C + I + G + X - Z - T_e \qquad (2)$$

Combining equations (1) and (2)

$$S + T_d + T_e + Z \equiv I + G + X + B \qquad (3)$$

The left hand of equation (3) are **withdrawals (W_d)** from the circular flow of income and the right-hand variables of the equation are **injections** (J) into the circular flow of income (See figure 2.1).

From GDP to GNP: Foreign residents own some factors of production in the domestic economy and domestic citizen's own overseas assets. There is a two-way flow of interest, dividends, rents and profits. This flow is known as property income.

GNP is defined as the value of income/output produced by the factors of production regardless of where the factors of production were employed.

GNP measure the income/output of a country and this is equal to GDP plus net property income.

GNP = GDP plus net property income.

NNP (net national product) = GNP less depreciation (capital consumption).

Per capita real GNP = GNP/population.

Per capita GNP is often given as a measure of a country's wealth, but it is an average value it does not take into account the distribution of income.

Also not taken into account are:

i. Externalities. These are such things as noise, pollution, congestion, climate change (global warming) etc. They do not, usually, have a market price. They are not included in the measure of national income because only goods and services that have a market price are included.

   The scientific consensus is that increases in national income/output are leading to an excess of greenhouse gases and dangerous (for humanity) climate change. This is a very large negative externality. Economics is a discipline in which the factors of production – land, labour and capital - are supposed to be harnessed to maximise production at the cheapest price. By these criteria, an economy is doing twice as well if it is growing at 4% rather than 2% and disastrously badly if consumers are not consuming from dawn till dusk. Globalisation is seen as the ultimate form of a market economy, according to the prevailing model, because a more efficient use of the factors of production (and using lower priced labour in countries such as China, India and Vietnam) leads to lower prices and therefore permits higher levels of consumption. All this consumption (involving international as well as domestic transportation) is at the forefront in the release of greenhouse gases that is leading to climate change. The atmosphere is treated as free dumping ground (just as rivers in the UK used to be) and the invisible greenhouse gases are very large externality. Currently, greenhouse gas concentrations in the atmosphere are around 380 parts per million (ppm), compared with around 220 ppm during the last ice age. Climatologists estimate that 400ppm - of thereabouts - is the tipping point and if we push concentrations much above that the process of climate change could become irreversible. This will lead to disastrous climate change and rising sea levels. Large parts of the world, including London and parts of southeast England, will be flooded.

ii. Other things that are not usually given a monetary value are such things as Household work, DIY (do it yourself), unreported employment. These are difficult to incorporate into the measure of national income.

iii. Leisure. If individuals choose to take more leisure rather than produce goods and services then the measured national income of a country may be lower but the 'prosperity' of the population may be greater.

Making allowances for (i), (ii) and (iii) can either increase or decrease GNP.

GDP and quality changes

Increases in GDP can also come about due to increases in the quality of goods and services that a country produces. A method used in the USA is the application of 'hedonic pricing'. This is a method of adjusting the increase in the price level for quality changes. It assumes that the quality of goods and services (especially computers and information technology products) increases from year to year. Consider table 2.1 for a fictional economy Keteris whose currency is the Keterian dollar (K$). In the year 2002 and 2003 there was no increase in nominal GDP.

Table 2.1: Hedonic prices and GDP

Year	Money (nominal) GDP	Real GDP
2002	K$200 billion	K$200 billion
2003	K$200 billion	K$210 billion

But, if we assume that there was an increase in the quality of goods and services of 5% between 2002 and 2003, then this is taken into account by the increase in real GDP from K$200 billions in 2002 to K$210 billions in 2003.

The Circular Flow of Income

Consider Fig. 2.1. If we start at BUSINESSES in the bottom right hand corner we see that the national income generated is 'Y'. Households earn this income, but before they receive it, part is taken, by the government in the form of direct taxes (T_d) (taxes on profits, wages and salaries). This is a withdrawal from the circular flow.

The government also adds to the income received by households by the payment of benefits (B), (income support, unemployment benefit, student grants, housing benefit etc.).

Households end up receiving disposable income (their incomes after taxation plus benefits – $Y_d = Y$ less T_d plus B).

Households either save (S) their disposable income ($S = Y_d - C$) or spend it on consumption goods (C).

Investment (I) is the purchases, by firms, of new capital assets. This is an injection into the circular flow.

The government purchases goods and services from businesses (G). This is an injection into the circular flow.

Z are imports of goods and services: This leads to a withdrawal of income from the circular flow.

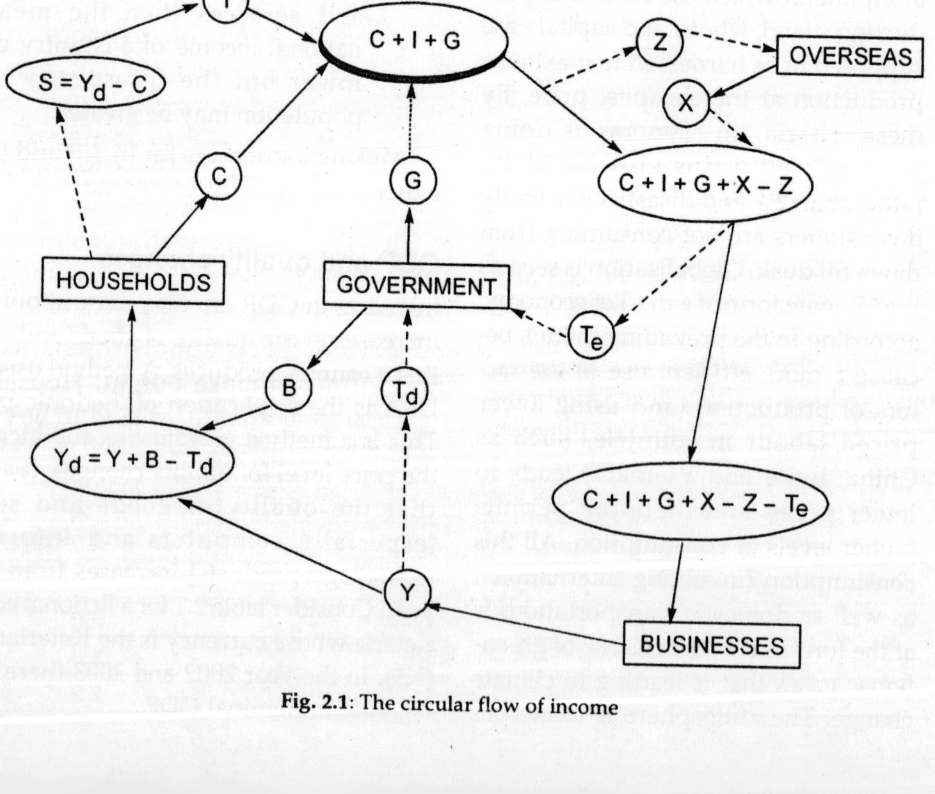

Fig. 2.1: The circular flow of income

X are exports of goods and services: This leads to an injection of income into the circular flow.

The value of output produced at factor cost $(C + I + G + X - Z - T_e)$ is what remains after the government deducts indirect taxation from the value of output produced at market prices $(C + I + G + X - Z)$.

Withdrawals are equal to injections:

$$S + T_d + T_e + Z \equiv I + G + X + B$$

International Comparison of GDP

Our purpose of GDP measures is to make an international comparison of living standard or real income. It is natural for us to want to know whether people have higher living standards in UK or USA or Germany or France. However, comparisons using measures such as GDP must be conducted with great care. There are many dimensions to living standards that are not measured by GDP or GNI. For some purposes we may want to compare the absolute size of an economic relative to another, we may be interested to know how well off is the average individual in each country.

For this purpose we want look at GDP per head. To get this figure we divide GDP by total population of the country. This tells us the share of total GDP that is available for the average citizen.

GDP in each country is measured in local currency of this country. So, to make comparison, we have to convert different countries' GDP into some common currency. To do this, we have to use an exchange rate. But the problem is that exchange rate fluctuate daily, sometimes dramatically. To solve of the problem of making comparisons using unreliable exchange rates, economists make comparisons of GDP using the exchange rate that equates the prices of a representative bundle of goods and services of two countries. This is known as purchasing power parity (PPP) rate. Some comparisons of GDP per capita in different countries (using PPP exchange rates) are given in table 2.2. Figures are expressed in US dollar's.

Several other indicators of material well-being are also included in the table. Broadly speaking they tell the same story as the GNI figures - the inhabitants of the richer countries can purchase more goods and services and tend to have longer life-expectancy. However, the rankings would be different for each possible indicator of well-being. The significance of this is that GNP per capita contains some useful information but other important indicators sometimes tell a slightly different story.

SUMMARY

1. The notion of national income accounting has been introduced and the equivalence of national income, product and expenditure demonstrated. We highlighted the problems of using national income as an indicator of economic welfare. Finally, we considered briefly the meaning of an equilibrium in macroeconomics.
2. Households supply inputs used by firms to make output. Households' income from firms used to buy firm's

Table 2.2: Annual average rate of growth of per capita income – 1970-2000 (%)

Country	Rate	Country	Rate
Canada	2.6	India	6.0 (1992-2001)
China	7.0	Japan	3.9
France	2.7	Spain	3.0
Germany	2.2	UK	2.3
Italy	2.8	USA	2.9

output. This is a circular flow between households and firms.

3. GDP, the value of output made in a country, is measured in three ways: value added in production, factor income including profits, or final expenditure.
4. Leakages from the circular flow are those parts of the payment by households that do not come back to the firms as spending by households on the output of firms. Leakages are saving, taxes net of subsidies, and imports. Injections are sources of revenue to firms that do not originate from household spending. Injections are investment by firms, government spending on goods and services, and exports. By definition total leakages = total injections.
5. GNP = GDP + net property income from abroad.
6. NNP = GNP – Depreciation.
7. Nominal GNP measures income at current prices. Real GNP measures income at current prices.
8. Per capita real GNP = real GNP divided by the total population.
9. Real GNP and per capita real GNP are crude measure of national and individual welfare. They ignore non-market activities, bads such as pollution, valuable activities such as work in the home, and production unreported by tax evaders. Nor do they measure the value of leisure. However, GNP is the most widely used measure of national performance.

In this chapter we have looked at the measurement of real income/output. We were measuring the real income/output generated in, usually, the previous year (*ex post*).

In the following chapters we will look at, amongst other things, the determination of real income/output in the following year (*ex ante*). To do this we will examine more closely three important, but different, sectors of the economy (and, implicitly, a fourth - the market for government bonds).

The important three sectors are:

1. The real sector – the sector that determines the equilibrium real income/output of the economy.
2. The financial (monetary) sector – the sector that helps to determines the equilibrium rate of interest and the demand and supply of money.
3. The labour market–the sector that determines the real wage and the level of employment and unemployment.

In chapters six and seven we will see how the real and financial (monetary) sectors link together to simultaneously determine the rate of interest, the level of real income/output and the price level.

QUESTIONS

1. Discuss which of the following are microeconomic and which are macroeconomic issues. House prices, Unemployment in East of England, food prices, pensions, the EU single currency, the CAP, high street spending, Income tax rates, mortgage interest rates.
2. The data below shows final sales and purchases of intermediate goods in car production. What is the firm's contribution to GDP?

	Sales	Intermediate goods
Purchased		
Car producer	1000	330
Windscreen producer	200	10
Tyre producer	80	30
Steel producer	50	0

3. GNP at market price is £300 billion. Depreciation is £30 billion, indirect taxes £20 billion.
   (a) What is the Nation Income?
   (b) Why does depreciation cause a discrepancy between GNP and national income?
   (c) Why do indirect taxes enter the calculation?
4. GNP = 2000, C = 1700, G = 50, and NX (Net Export {X – M}) = 40
   (a) What is the value of investment ?
   (b) If X = 350, what are imports?
   (c) If depreciation = 130, What is national income?
   (d) In this example NX are positive; could they be negative ?
5. Given the data below:
   (a) What is 2002 GNP in 2001 prices.
   (b) What is the growth rate of real GNP from 2001-2002?
   (c) What is the inflation rate?

	Nominal GDP	GNP deflator
2001	2000	100
2002	2400	110

6. Should there be comprehensive measure of GNP.
   (a) time spent by student in lecturers
   (b) the income of muggers
   (c) the wages paid to traffic wardens
   (d) dropping litter
7. Which of the following are instrument of macroeconomic policy and which are targets:

   The exchange rate; real wages; VAT rates; Government spending on road building; exports; private gross capital formation; personal consumption.
8. Using the expenditure - based definition (C+ I +G + NX), explain where each of the following expenditures appears in the national income accounts measure of GDP, if at all: state pensions, company pensions, student grants, theatre receipts, salary of civil servants, unsold cars in showrooms, receipts from beer sales in a student union bar, receipts from purchases of new copies of this book, receipts from purchases of second-hand copies of this book.
9. Discuss the strengths and weaknesses of using GDP as a measure of national well-being
10. What would it mean to be told that a country's GNI (gross national income) was greater than its GDP? Is GNI or GDP the more appropriate target for government policy.

ANSWERS

1. House prices, Unemployment in East of England, food prices, pensions and the CAP are all fundamentally microeconomic issues; the EU single currency, high street spending, income tax rates and mortgage interest rates are all principally macro issues.
2. Value Added = 670 + 190 + 50 + 50 = 960
3. (a) £250 Billion
   (b) National Income is net national product at basic prices. Depreciation is part of the cost of producing output,
   (c) They reduce the purchasing power of given gross income.
4. (a) 210, (c) 1870
   (b) 310, (d) yes, if X< M
5. (a) 2200 (b) 10% (c) 10%
6. (a) Leisure is lost but investment in human capital occurs
   (b) No - just a transfer payment,
   (c) yes
   (d) pollution should ideally be subtracted from GNP.
7. Instruments of macroeconomic policy are the variables the government can change directly, whether or not outcome is exactly as anticipated. From this list VAT rates, VAT revenue, government spending on road building, and the exchange rate are instruments of macroeconomic policy. Real wages, exports, private gross capital formation, personal consumption, and VAT revenue are targets of policy.
8. State pensions, student grants, company pensions are transfer payments and do not fall into any of the expenditure - based measure of GDP. Theatre receipts, receipts from sales of new books, and students' union bar receipts are all part of private consumption expenditure. Unsold cars in the showroom are part of firms' inventories and are classified as investment expenditure. Salaries of civil servants come under the heading of government consumption expenditure. Purchase of second- hand books are not expenditure on final goods, so do not appear into any of the categories of expenditure-based GDP.
9. Where there is a significant difference between GDP and GNI, GDP is a better indicator of the size of an economy but GNI is a better indicator of living standards. National well - being is an ill-defined concept but may include some notion of political and economic freedom as well as living standards, another poorly defined concept. International comparison may founder on exchange rate fluctuations and comparisons over time are confused by changes in the value of money. GDP per head is more useful than GDP but gives no clue to the distribution of income, another relevant factor. Apart from all the considerations above there are the problems of omission from official statistics of non-market activities, both legal and illegal, and any cost attached to pollution or other economic bad associated with economic growth.
10. A country's GNI is greater than GDP when the net effect of three adjustments from GDP to GNI is positive.The three adjustments involved net income from abroad and are
    (a) Wages and salaries paid to citizens working abroad and remitted to their home countries, flowing both into and out of an economy.
    (b) An adjustment for taxes paid on goods produced elsewhere and subsidies received.
    (c) Property and entrepreneurial income received from abroad. GDP is more appropriate target of government policy since it is more easily influenced then GNI.

CHAPTER 3

THE DETERMINATION OF THE OUTPUT OF AN ECONOMY: THE REAL SECTOR

KEY TERMS

Consumption Expenditure (C): Aggregate household spending on domestically produced consumption goods and services measured in real terms.

Marginal Propensity to Consume (mpc): The *proportion* of *extra* income spent on domestically produced consumption goods ($\Delta C/\Delta Y$).

Average Propensity to Consume (apc): Aggregate consumption expenditure as a proportion of aggregate income/output (C/Y).

Investment Expenditure: Total real investment expenditure, including unsold output put into stock (inventory).

Desired or Planned Investment (I): Total investment spending that businesses want to make. It does not include unwanted stock accumulation.

Planned Aggregate Demand (AD): Planned expenditures on consumption, investment, government and net exports. (in real terms).

Equilibrium in the Real Sector: When aggregate demand (AD) is equal to output (Y).

Saving (S): Disposable income not consumed.

This chapter presents the basic model of the **real** sector of the economy (the sector where goods and services are produced). All variables are, unless specified, **aggregates** (totals), **measured in real** terms (constant prices).

We are going to build a simple, short run, model of the real sector of the economy, a model that will determine, **Y**, a measure of the **real income/output** of an economy.

We make the following assumptions to simplify matters (Be sure to read, assumption 8).

1. The main determinant of (real) aggregate consumption expenditure is (real) aggregate income. The relationship between aggregate consumption and aggregate income is known as the consumption function. We will assume a

linear relationship between consumption and income of the form:

$C = a + bY$

'a' is known as (aggregate) **autonomous** consumption expenditure. Aggregate autonomous consumption expenditure is determined by factors **other than** changes in income. (These factors are considered in more detail in chapter 6). As autonomous consumption **increases** [decreases] consumption expenditure **increases** [decreases].

'b' is known as the '**marginal propensity to consume**' (mpc). The value of the mpc is between zero and one.

The product '**bY**' (b*Y) indicates that, as income (Y) increases by **one** unit, consumption expenditure increases by 'b' units. The **changes** in consumption expenditure (C) are *induced* (brought about) by changes in income/output (Y).

If, for example, the mpc = 0.8, then an **increase** [decrease] in aggregate income of £1,000,000 leads to consumption expenditure **increasing** [decreasing] by £800,000 (= b*Y = [0.8*£1,000,000]).

Definition: The marginal propensity to consume, mpc, is equal to the *proportion* of extra income spent on domestically produced consumption goods ($\Delta C/\Delta Y$). It is the value of the change in consumption expenditure divided by the change in income that brought about the change in consumption expenditure. In the above example the mpc = 0.8 which is equal to the change in consumption expenditure (£800,000) divided by the change in income that brought it about (£1,000,000). (800,000/1,000,000 = 0.8).

An example of a consumption function (C = 70 + 0.75Y) is shown in table 3.1. The data shows the level of consumption expenditure at different level of income. Autonomous consumption expenditure is 70 and, in this case, the marginal propensity to consume, mpc, is equal to 0.75 (A more general derivation of the mpc is given at the bottom of page 36).

Fig. 3.1 shows the relationship between consumption expenditure (C) and income (Y) using the data from Table 3.1.

As income increases disposable income and hence consumption expenditure increases **along** the consumption function.

As income decreases disposable income and hence consumption expenditure decreases **along** the consumption function.

Example: Consider figure 3.1. If income is Y_0 (= 400), then the level of consumption expenditure, C_0, is 370 (= 70+0.75*400). If income increases to Y_1 (= 800), then the level of consumption expenditure, C_1, increases to 670 (= 70+0.75*800)

Another economic term that it is useful to understand is the **average propensity to consume**.

Definition: The average propensity to consume (apc) is aggregate consumption expenditure divided by aggregate income. Note that the average propensity to consume does not

Table 3.1: The Consumption Function

Income(Y)	Consumption expenditure(C)
0	70
200	220
400	370
600	520
800	670
1000	820
1200	970

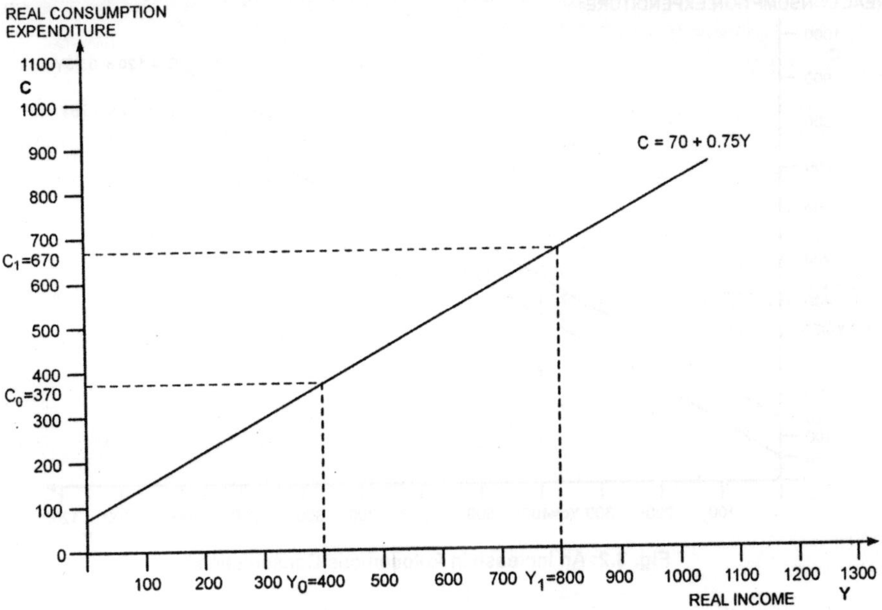

Fig. 3.1: The Consumption Function

have to equal the marginal propensity to consume.

For example, in Fig. 3.1, at an income of 400, consumption expenditure is 370 and the average propensity to consume (apc) = C/Y = 0.925 (=370/400) whilst the mpc = 0.8.

If people increase their autonomous consumption expenditure **at a given level of income** then the average propensity to consume at that income level will increase (their *average propensity to save* will *decrease*). An **increase** [decrease] in the level of autonomous consumption expenditure is equivalent to an **increase** [decrease] in the average propensity to consume.

If autonomous consumption increases [decreases] the consumption function is shifted upwards [downwards] parallel to the original consumption function. There is more [less] consumption expenditure at each level of income (See Fig. 3.2).

Example: Consider figure 3.2. If income is Yo (say 400), then, when the consumption function is C = 70 + 0.75Y, the level of consumption expenditure, C_0, is 370 (70 + 0.75*400). At an income level of 400 the average propensity to consume is C_0/Y_0 = 370/400 = 0.925.

If autonomous consumption expenditure increases by 50 then the new level of autonomous consumption expenditure is 120. The new consumption function is now C = 120 + 0.75Y. At the same income level of 400, the level of consumption expenditure, C_1, increases to 420 (120 + 0.75*400). The new level of the average propensity to consume (apc) is now C_1/Y_0 = 420/400 = 1.05. The increase in autonomous consumption from 70 to 120 has led to the apc increasing from 0.925 to 1.05.

2. There is a level of **aggregate demand** (AD) (total expenditure) in the economy (measured at market prices) that is determined by the sum of consumption expenditure, investment expenditure, government expenditure, and net exports.

AD = C + I + G + NX

(If we wish to take into account taxes on expenditure then these should be subtracted from aggregate demand).

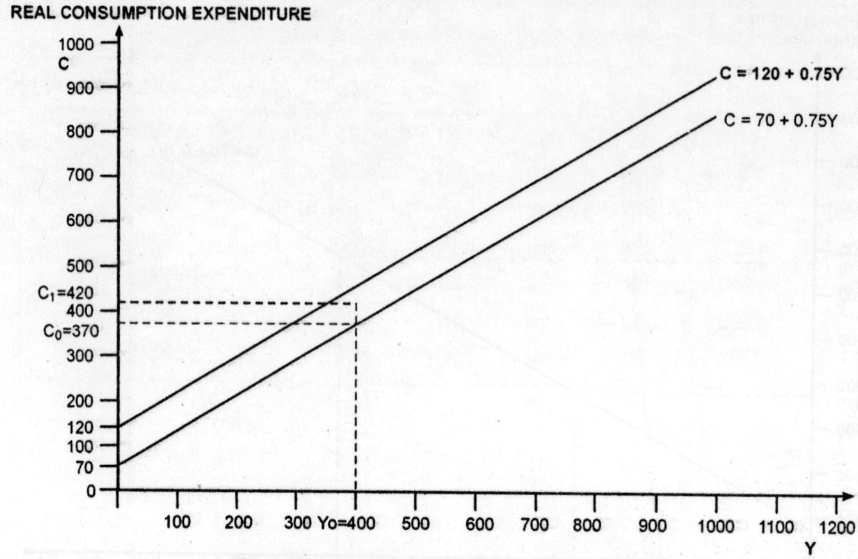

Fig. 3.2: An Increase in Autonomous Consumption

Then, aggregate demand (AD) at factor cost is equal to C + I + G + NX - Te

3. **There is a full employment** level of income/output of an economy (Y_f). This is the **maximum** income/output that an economy can produce (supply) when all resources are fully employed. This is the potential output of the economy. We will define **full unemployment** (potential output) as a situation of **no involuntary unemployment**. (There is however some **voluntary** unemployment at Y_f). For a more precise definition of both voluntary and involuntary unemployment see chapter 8.
4. There is a level of income/output **below** full employment income/output. This is the **actual** level of income/output of an economy (**Y**). **Below** full employment there exists some **involuntary** unemployment. There is an output/income gap when Y is less than Y_f.

The planned aggregate demand schedule

When we considered national income accounting we were looking at **past** transactions and have shown that the value of income is equivalent to the value of output and is also equivalent to the value of expenditure.

When considering the **future course** of the economy we are dealing with planned aggregate demand (planned expenditures) where planned aggregate demand at market prices = C + I + G + NX. (If we wish to include taxes on expenditures [also measured in real terms] these should be subtracted from aggregate demand). Then, planned real aggregate demand at factor cost, is equal to:

$$C + I + G + NX - T_e$$

If, for the moment, we keep planned investment expenditure, planned government expenditure, planned net exports and planned indirect taxation **constant** and add to, or in the case of indirect taxation subtract from, the consumption function, we can plot the resulting **planned aggregate demand schedule.**

Definition: The planned aggregate demand schedule shows the relationship between the level of real planned aggregate demand and the level of real income.

Table 3.2 presents the planned aggregate demand schedule (**AD**) when investment ex-

Table 3.2. The Composition of the Aggregate Demand Schedule

Income	C	I	G	NX	Te	$AD=C+I+G+NX-T_e$
0	70	35	40	10	25	130
200	220	35	40	10	25	280
400	370	35	40	10	25	430
600	520	35	40	10	25	580
800	670	35	40	10	25	730
1000	820	35	40	10	25	880
1200	970	35	40	10	25	1030

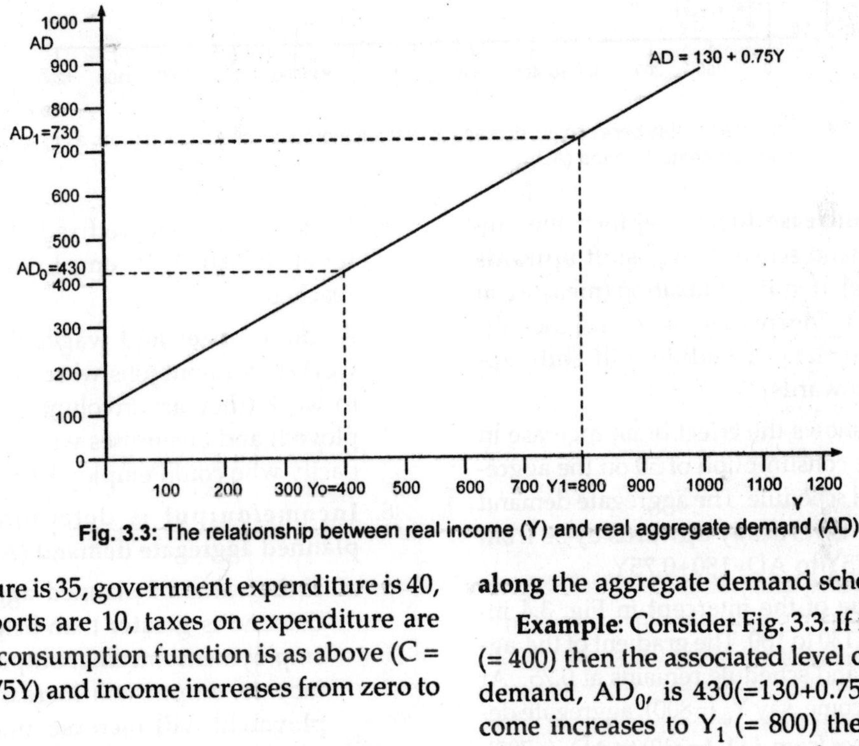

Fig. 3.3: The relationship between real income (Y) and real aggregate demand (AD)

penditure is 35, government expenditure is 40, net exports are 10, taxes on expenditure are 25, the consumption function is as above ($C = 70 + 0.75Y$) and income increases from zero to 1200.

Fig. 3.3 illustrates the data from table 3.2. Fig. 3.3 is referred to as the **aggregate demand-income/output diagram**.

As income increases [decreases], disposable income increases [decreases], consumption expenditure increases [decreases] and hence aggregate demand increases [decreases] **along** the aggregate demand schedule.

Example: Consider Fig. 3.3. If income is Y_0 (= 400) then the associated level of aggregate demand, AD_0, is 430(=130+0.75*400). If income increases to Y_1 (= 800) then the corresponding level of aggregate demand, AD_1, is 730(=130+0.75*800).

Shifting the aggregate demand schedule

If autonomous consumption '**a**' or investment '**I**' or government expenditure '**G**' or net ex-

YOU SHOULD REMEMBER

If the slope of the aggregate demand schedule is 0.75, then, an increase in income/output of 100 will lead to aggregate demand increasing by 75.

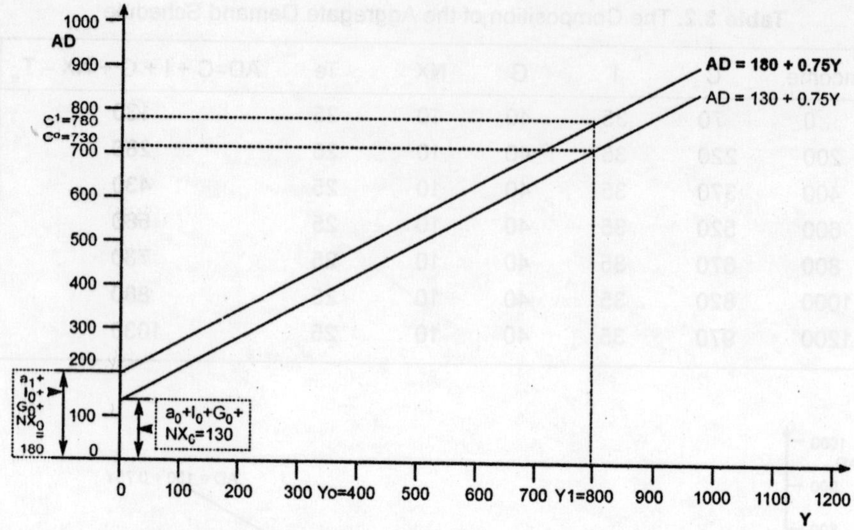

Fig. 3.4: **The relationship between an increase in real autonomous consumption (from a_0 to a_1) and real aggregate demand (AD)**

ports 'NX' **increase** [decrease] then the aggregate demand schedule will shift **upwards** [downwards]. If indirect taxation (measure in real terms) 'T_e' **decreases** [increases] then the aggregate demand schedule will shift **upwards** [downwards].

Fig. 3.4 shows the effect of an increase in autonomous consumption of 50 on the aggregate demand schedule. The aggregate demand schedule shifts vertically upwards by 50 from AD=130+0.75Y to AD=180+0.75Y.

The value of the intercept in Fig. 3.4 increases from 130 to 180. The gradient of the aggregate demand schedule remains at 0.75. At any given income, say Y_0 (=800), aggregate demand increases from AD_0 (=730) to AD_1 (=780).

5. In the short run the only variable factor is **labour**. i.e. to produce **more income/output** requires **more labour.** As income/output increases employment increases, and **involuntary** unemployment falls.
6. Prices and wages are fixed at a given level (until full employment is reached).
7. At these prices and wages there are workers without jobs who would like to work (they are involuntary unemployed) and businesses with spare capacity who could employ labour.
8. **Income/output** is determined by **planned aggregate demand** (AD)
   a. If the value of planned aggregate demand is **greater** than below full employment income/output, then income/output will **increase, employment will increase and there will be a fall in involuntary unemployment.** There will be no change in the price level.
   b. If the value of planned aggregate demand is **less** than income/output, then income/output will **decrease**, employment will decrease

YOU SHOULD REMEMBER

The aggregate demand schedule would also shift upwards by 50 if investment **or** government expenditure **or** net exports increased by 50 **or** taxes on expenditure decreased by 50.

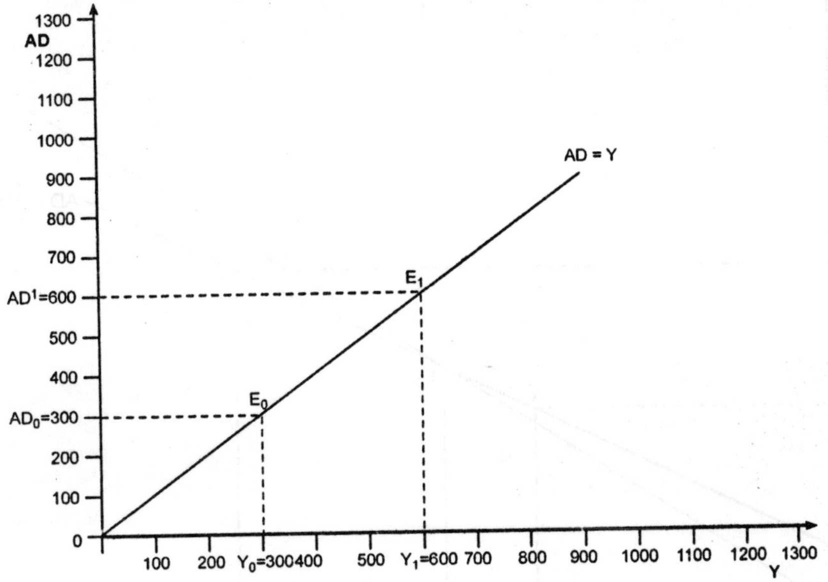

Fig. 3.5: The locus of points where real aggregate demand (AD) is equal to real output (Y)

and there will be an increase in involuntary unemployment. There will be no immediate change in the price level.

c. If the value of planned aggregate demand is **equal** to the value of income/output, then income/output, employment and unemployment will be **unchanged**. The economy will be in **equilibrium**. We will assume that if, at an equilibrium position, there is some involuntary unemployment then money wages and prices will, eventually, start to fall.

d. If the value of planned aggregate demand is **greater** than **full employment income/output**, then **income/output** and employment will be **unchanged** but there will be an **increase in the price level.**

The determination of equilibrium income/output in the real sector of the economy

In Fig. 3.5 a locus of points, where aggregate demand is **equal** to income/output, traces points of equilibrium in the economy. This is the AD = Y schedule. It is only a 45-degree line when the units are the same on both axis. (However, we will assume that this is always the case).

Point E_0 in Fig. 3.5 indicates that the level of planned aggregate demand (AD_0) (=300) is equal to income/output Y_0(=300). Similarly point E_1 indicates that the level of planned aggregate demand (AD_1)(=600) is equal to income/output Y_1(=600).

If we turn back to Fig. 3.3 we could, using a ruler and trial and error, find a point on the aggregate demand curve where planned aggregate demand is equal to income/output.

But, as in Fig. 3.6, if we first plot the aggregate demand schedule from figure 3.3 and then plot the AD=Y schedule from figure 3.5, then the **intersection** of the two schedules determines the unique level of equilibrium output/income (Y_0). This is the point where the AD=Y schedule intersects the planned aggregate demand schedule, **AD=130+0.75Y**. i.e. where $AD_0 = Y_0 = 520$ at point E_0.

Fig. 3.6 is often referred to as the *'Keynesian Cross Model'* or the *'Income-Expenditure Diagram'*.

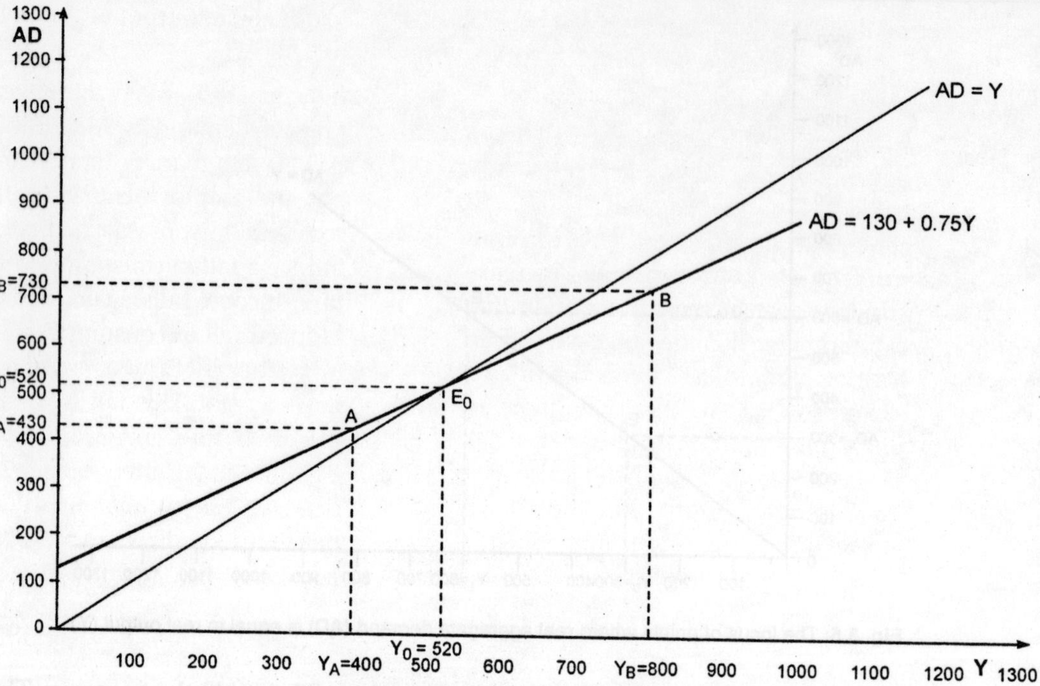

Fig. 3.6: Equilibrium in the goods market

Definition: The real sector of the economy is in short run equilibrium when planned aggregate demand, (AD) just equals the income/output that is actually produced (Y) i.e. when **AD=Y**. In the case of figure 3.6 where $AD_0 = Y_0$. i.e. point 'E_0'. In this case both aggregate demand (AD_0) and income/output (Y_0) are equal to 520.

The adjustment towards equilibrium

If income/output is Y_A (= 400) then the level of planned aggregate demand will be AD_A, (= 430) (point '**A**' on figure 3.6). Since planned aggregate demand is greater than actual output Y_A (assuming Y_A is below full employment output) then income/output will **increase** until it reaches Y_0.

If income/output is Y_B, (= 800) then planned aggregate demand will be AD_B, (= 730) (point '**B**' on figure 3.6). Since planned aggregate demand is less than actual output then income/output will **decrease** until it reaches Y_0.

When planned aggregate demand (AD_0) is **equal** to income/output (Y_0) then income/output will be **unchanged** at Y_0 - point '$\mathbf{E_0}$'. Y_0 is the equilibrium income/output of the economy.

YOU SHOULD REMEMBER

1. If planned aggregate demand is greater than below full employment income/output then income/output (and employment) will increase (involuntary unemployment will fall).
2. If the economy is at full employment then the price level will increase–there will be no change in income/output or employment.
3. If planned aggregate demand is less than actual income/output then income (and employment) will decrease (involuntary unemployment will increase).

The method of adjustment is similar in both 1. and 2.

Consider Fig. 3.6:

1. If income is $Y_A(=400)$ then planned aggregate demand is $AD_A(=430)$. Since AD_A is greater than Y_A then income/output will increase. As incomes increase disposable incomes increase and induce an increase in consumption expenditure. Income increases again leading to an induced increase in consumption - leading to another increase in income and consumption etc etc. This increase in income and consumption will not continue indefinitely - a new equilibrium will be established at Eo when both aggregate demand (AD_0) and income/output (Y_0) will be equal to 520.
2. If income is $Y_B(=900)$ then planned aggregate demand is $AD_B(=805)$. Since AD_B is less than Y_B then income/output and employment will fall. As incomes fall disposable incomes fall and induce a fall in consumption expenditure. Income falls again leading to an induced fall in consumption - leading to another fall in income and consumption etc. etc.. This fall in income, employment and consumption will not continue indefinitely - a new equilibrium will be established at E_0 when both aggregate demand (AD_0) and income/output (Y_0) will be equal to 520.

The marginal propensity to consume (mpc = $\left(\text{mpc} = \frac{\Delta C}{\Delta Y} = b\right)$ The *proportion* of *extra* income spent on domestically produced consumption goods.

Since we assume that there is a unique **linear** relationship between consumption and income,

$C = a + \mathbf{b}Y,$

we can use this relationship to derive a general form of the **mpc** (**b**).

Since

$C_1 = a + \mathbf{b}Y_1$ (1) and,

$C_0 = a + \mathbf{b}Y_0$ (2)

Then, subtracting (2) from (1) gives

$C_1 - C_0 = a - a + \mathbf{b}Y_1 - \mathbf{b}Y_0$

$= \mathbf{b}Y_1 - \mathbf{b}Y_0 = \mathbf{b}(Y_1 - Y_0)$ or

$C_1 - C_0 = \mathbf{b}(Y_1 - Y_0)$

Since $(C_1 - C_0) = \Delta C$, and $(Y_1 - Y_0) = \Delta Y$

Then,

$\Delta C = \mathbf{b}\Delta Y$ or the **mpc** is

$$\frac{\Delta C}{\Delta Y} = b$$

A numerical example when $C = 30 + 0.75Y$ (**b** $= 0.75$)

If $Y_0 = 100$ then $C_0 = 105$

If $Y_1 = 200$ then $C_1 = 180$

$$\text{Then } \frac{\Delta C}{\Delta Y} = \frac{180-105}{200-100} = \frac{75}{100} = 0.75 = b$$

CHAPTER 4

APPLYING AN AGGREGATE DEMAND/ INCOME MODEL (a Keynesian Cross Model)

KEY TERMS

Fiscal Policy: A change in the government expenditure and/or taxation is known as fiscal policy.

Budget Deficit: If government spend more than tax-revenue, there will be budget deficit.

Budget Surplus: When government spend less than tax revenue.

Balance Budget Multiplier: If the budget is kept balanced, then $\Delta G = \Delta T$, multiplier is equal to 1.

1. CHANGES IN GOVERNMENT EXPENDITURE

As well as being ablve to vary the rate of direct and indirect taxation the government can also change its spending plans. It can reduce or increase government expenditure. A change in government expenditure and/or taxation is known as **FISCAL POLICY**. Fig. 4.1 shows the effect of an increase in level of government expenditure (For simplicity we assume a closed economy and one with no taxes or benefits).

If we start at an initial equilibrium level of income/output Y_0 (=520), E_0: AD=130+0.75Y. (The level of government expenditure is 40).

Problem: If Y_1 (=920) is thought to be full employment income/output how can income/output be increased?

Solution: Increase aggregate demand by increasing government expenditure by an amount equal to $(G_1 - G_0)$ $(=\Delta G = 100)$ which is equal to the vertical distance E_0 to 'A' in Fig. 4.1.

AD=130+0.75Y is shifted upwards to AD=230+0.75Y.

The movement from one equilibrium position (E_0) to another equilibrium position (E_1).

Consider Fig. 4.1. The increase in government expenditure of 100 has, initially, increased the level of aggregate demand from point 'E_0' on AD=130+0.75Y to point 'A' on AD=230+0.75Y the level of aggregate demand (AD_A=620) is now greater than income/output Y_0(=520) and income/output increases. The increase in government expenditure of 100

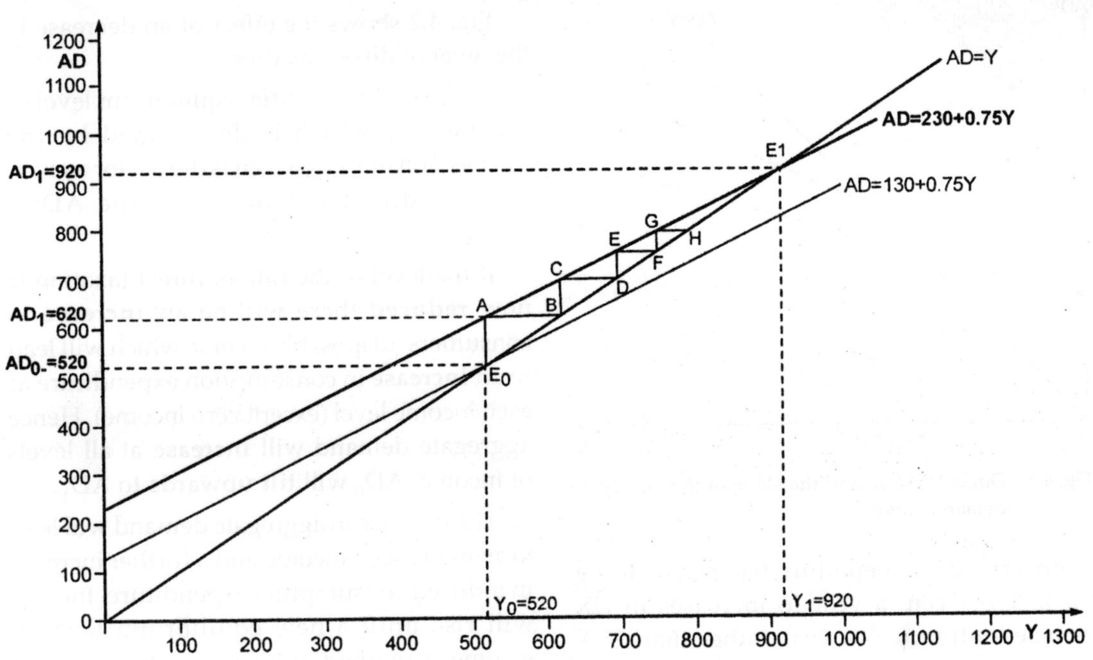

Fig. 4.1: An increase in real government expenditure

initially generates an increase of in income/ output of 100 (assuming no imports or other withdrawals from the circular flow). The economy moves from point 'A' to point 'B'. This increase in income/output will increase disposable income (=100 since we assume no imports, taxes or benefits). People receiving this extra income will spend a part of it on consumption goods (consumption expenditure will, initially, increase by 75 since the mpc is 0.75). The economy will move from point 'B' to point 'C'. This will generate 75 more in income (moving from point 'C' to 'D'), which generates (induces) more consumption expenditure (0.75x75 = 56.25 - moving from point 'D' to 'F'). Increases in consumption and income/output will continue (F to G, G to H, etc) until the economy reaches a new equilibrium at E_1. This is when $AD_1 = Y_1$ (= 920).

N.B. The increase in consumption expenditure (from 'B' to 'E_1'- 300) has been **induced** by the initial increase in **autonomous expenditure** (in this case government expenditure).

Thus an increase in government expenditure of 100 will lead to an increase in aggregate demand of 400, an increase income/ output of 400 (the 400 increase in output is made up of 100 of government expenditure and an increase in induced consumption expenditure of 300). In the UK between 2002 and 2007, it has been estimated that increase

YOU SHOULD REMEMBER

1. As government expenditure is increased the aggregate demand schedule shifts upwards, income and employment increase and there is a decrease in involuntary unemployment.
2. As government expenditure is decreased the aggregate demand schedule shifts downwards, income and employment decrease and there is an increase in involuntary unemployment.

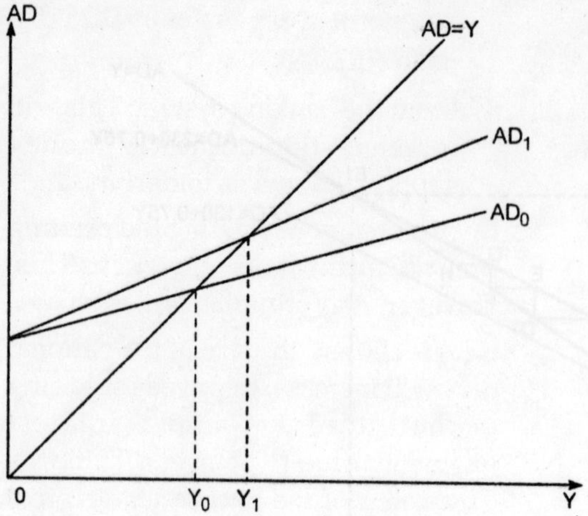

Fig. 4.2: Direct taxation and the slope of the aggregate demand curve

in government expenditure has been adding up to 1 per cent a year to increases in UK income/output (3% a year rather than 2%). N.B. The change in income, ΔY, $(=(Y_1-Y_0)=400)$ is greater than the change in government expenditure, $\Delta G,(=(G_1-G_0)$ = the vertical distance 'E_0' to 'A'= 100), that brought it about. The change in income is a multiple of government expenditure (in this case income/output increases by four times the increase in government expenditure). This is known as the **multiplier** effect. A **simple** numerical example of the multiplier effect is given using the data in table 4.3 in appendix I at the end of this chapter.

2. CHANGES IN DIRECT TAXATION

The government has the ability to increase or reduce the level of taxation, both direct and indirect.

Fig. 4.2 shows the effect of an decrease in the level of direct taxation.

If we start at an initial equilibrium level of income, Y_0, which is determined by the intersection of AD_0 (which is drawn for a given level of direct taxation) and the AD=Y schedule.

If the level of the rate of direct taxation is now **reduced** there will be an **increase** in consumers' disposable income which will lead to an **increase** in consumption expenditure at each income level (except zero income). Hence aggregate demand will **increase** at all levels of income. AD_0 will **tilt upwards** to AD_1.

The increase in aggregate demand will lead to an increase in income and a further increase in induced consumption expenditure. Income will rise until a new equilibrium level of income is reached at Y_1. (The intersection of AD=Y and AD_1). It has been estimated that a 10p increase in income tax will lead to a fall in output of £30 billion per annum.

A numerical example illustrating this effect can be found in appendix II at the end of this chapter.

We will see later that the UK government cut the rate of direct taxation not to increase national income but because it believed that cuts in income tax led to favourable supply side effects.

This analysis suggests that in a recession the government can increase the level of income/output and employment by increasing government expenditure or reducing taxation. This will increase aggregate

YOU SHOULD REMEMBER

1. As direct taxation is increased the slope of the AD schedule decreases, aggregate demand, income and employment decrease and there is an increase in involuntary unemployment.
2. As direct taxation is decreased the slope of the AD schedule increases, aggregate demand, income and employment increase and there is a decrease in involuntary unemployment.

demand, increase income/output (by a greater amount than the increase in government expenditure or cut in taxation), and increase employment and reduce involuntary unemployment.

Why don't governments cut taxation or increase government expenditure and increase aggregate demand and reduce the level of involuntary unemployment?

1. The government is uncertain of how much of the unemployment in the economy is involuntary and how much is voluntary. Hence it does not accurately know how much of the unemployment can be eliminated by increasing aggregate demand. (The position of full employment income/output (Y_f) is unclear). Some economists and governments believe that 'market forces', falls in wages and prices, will eliminate involuntary unemployment. This precludes the need for expansionary fiscal and monetary policies.
2. An increase in government expenditure or a reduction in taxation will, *ceteris paribus*, reduce the budget surplus, lead to a budget deficit, or increase the size of any budget deficit. The UK's Chancellor of the Exchequer has, what is known as, a "Golden Rule". This stipulates that the current expenditure part of the budget must be balanced over the course of the economic cycle. On the capital account the government can borrow for investment purposes.

If the deficit is increased it will need financing; either,

a. By borrowing:
   i. From the public; this may push up long-term interest rates. The US Federal Reserve has estimated that every one percentage point increase in the budget deficit will drive up long-term interest rates by 0.25 of a point (0.25%).
   ii. From the banking system: This will increase the domestic money supply, (known as underfunding).

b. By printing money: Using the printing press to print more currency. This, however, may stimulate inflation.

If (a) is chosen, the size of the national debt will increase; this needs servicing in the future. i.e. annual interest payments have to be made. The UK's Chancellor of the Exchequer attempts to keep the governments' net debt (which includes borrowing incurred for investment, but excludes the value of government assets) to 40% of GDP.

3. An increase in aggregate demand will, in the 'real world' probably bring about a rise in the price level; this may 'trigger off' an inflationary spiral. If income/output is at Yf then there will be no change in output but prices will rise by an even greater amount (see the chapter 9).
4. It takes time to recognise that aggregate demand has changed. Statistics may be out of date. An increase or decrease in government expenditure or taxation may over or under stimulate aggregate demand.
5. The government also faces uncertainty over the time taken for fiscal policy to work. It is difficult to estimate the time taken for the effects of changes in government expenditure and/or taxation to have their full effect on the economy.
6. Investment and autonomous consumption are assumed constant. If income increases then investment or autonomous consumption may increase and further increase aggregate demand. The increase in aggregate demand may become excessive. i.e greater than Y_f. This may 'trigger off' inflation.

7. Up to now we have assumed that imports are fixed at a particular level. A more realistic assumption is that imports are dependent upon the level of income that an economy generates. With this in mind we will assume that imports are positively related to domestic income.

   As income increases imports increase but by a smaller amount than the increase in income.

   Assume that Z = **m**Y, where **m** is the marginal propensity to import and is a positive fraction i.e. it is between zero and one.

   For example if **m** = 0.3 then, for every £1,000 increase in income, imports will increase by £300. i.e. Z = 0.3Y

   If income increases more imports may be sucked into the domestic economy. Also, goods that would have been exported can be more easily sold in the home market. Either way, the surplus on the balance of payments will be reduced or the balance of payments may move into deficit or the size of the deficit will increase.

8. Is an increase in aggregate demand effective in creating employment? In the U.K. during the years 1982-92 the output/income of the economy increased by 26%, but employment only increased by 7%. Between 1992 and 2005 the output/income of the economy increased by 45%, but employment only increased by 12.3%.

9. We will see later (chapter 10) that, in an economy with floating exchange rates and a free flow of financial capital, fiscal policy is not able to consistently affect the output and employment of an economy.

Because of the above considerations the use of expansionary fiscal policy to reduce involuntary unemployment has lost its attractions to some economic policy makers. We will see in, chapter

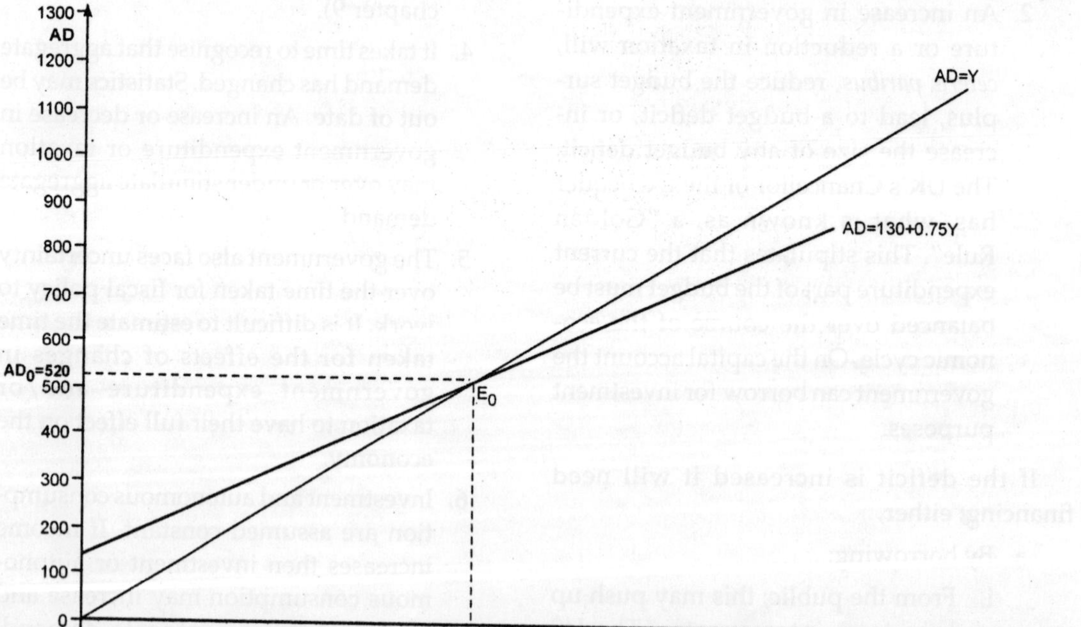

Fig. 4.3: Aggregate demand and income/output

7, that a belief (by **some** economists) in the self-regulating forces of a mixed economy precludes the need for an expansionary fiscal policy.

The Complete Model of the Goods Market (The real sector)

With the aggregate demand schedule AD = 130 + 0.75Y (derived from the numbers in second table in the previous chapter), the equilibrium level of aggregate demand/ income/output is 520 (= $AD_0 = Y_0$). In this simple case the value of the intercept is 130. This is made up of autonomous consumption (a_0) of 70, investment expenditure (I) of 35, government expenditure (G_0) of 40, net exports (NX_0) of 10 and taxes on expenditures (Te_0) of 25. ($a_0 + I_0 + G_0 + NX_0 - Te_0 = 130$).

If there is an **increase** in planned autonomous consumption expenditure (a_0), and/or planned investment expenditure (I_0), and/or planned government expenditure (G_0) and/or planned exports then this will lead to an increase in planned aggregate demand and an **upward** shift in the aggregate demand schedule.

This will lead to an increase in aggregate demand, income/output and employment and a fall in involuntary unemployment.

Since $AD = C + I + G + X - Z - T_e$

Then **reducing** imports (this increases net exports) or indirect taxation will **increase** aggregate demand, increase income/output and employment and reduce involuntary unemployment.

We will see later, that investment and autonomous consumption expenditures are affected by the rate of interest (**r**) and the stock of money (**L = M/P**)(M is the **nominal** stock of money and P is the price level).

APPENDIX I

The Simple Multiplier Effect: A Numerical Example

Table 4.1 illustrates the multiplier effect for an mpc of 0.75 (75%). We will let the initial aggregate demand schedule be 130+0.75Y. We will assume that government expenditure increases by 100 (a similar result would hold if autonomous expenditure increased by 100 or investment increased by 100, or net exports increased by 100 or taxes on expenditure decreased by 100).

The initial increase in government expenditure (100) shifts up the aggregate demand schedule parallely to 230+0.75Y. At the initial level of income/output (Y_0=520) there is a new level of aggregate demand (AD_A=620, point A). Output/income will increase by 100 to point B. People will receive this 100 in income and increase their consumption expenditure by 75 (induced

Table 4.1: The Multiplier Effect

"Round"	Received income	Spending	
1	–	100	← Initial government expenditure
2	100	75	↑
3	75	56.25	
4	56.25	41.1875	← Induced consumption expenditure (300)
–	–	–	
–	–	–	
Sum of the *remaining* rounds	168.75	127.5625	↓
Totals	400	400	

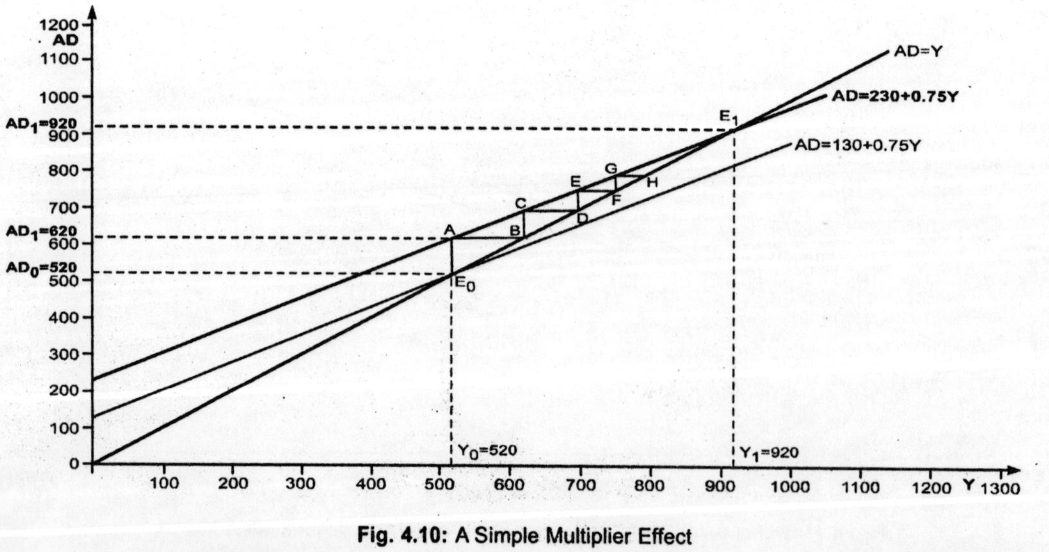

Fig. 4.10: A Simple Multiplier Effect

consumption rises by 75). Aggregate demand will now increase by 75 (point B to point C). Output/income will now rise by 75 (points C to D). Induced consumption and income will continue to increase (D to E to F etc) until, eventually, the economy reaches a new equilibrium at an income/output level of 400. This 400 increase in income/output is made up of the initial increase in government expenditure of 100 **plus** 300 in increased (induced) **consumption** expenditure. Thus, in this numerical example, most of the 400 in extra output is made up of induced consumption expenditure.

Referring to Fig. 4.10, the vertical distance between the two aggregate demand schedules is equal to 100 and the distance Y_0 to Y_1 is equal to 400. In this example the multiplier is 4, which is equal to $\Delta Y/\Delta G = 400/100$. This simple multiplier is derived on the assumption that there are no withdrawals from the circular flow of income other than saving. If there are other withdrawals from the circular flow (taxes and/or imports) then the size of the multiplier will be **much** smaller than 4. An estimate of the size of the multiplier for the UK economy is 1.2.

APPENDIX II

1. A change in the rate of taxation, the slope of the aggregate demand schedule and income/output: A simple numerical example

Government expenditure	(**G**) = 100	Direct taxation	$(\mathbf{T_d}) = 0.5\mathbf{Y}$
Investment expenditure	(**I**) = 200	Net exports	(**NX**) = 70
Consumption	$(\mathbf{C}) = 200 + 0.9\mathbf{Y_d}$	Indirect taxation	$(\mathbf{T_e}) = 20$
Disposable income	$(\mathbf{Y_d}) = \mathbf{Y} - \mathbf{T_d}$	We will assume zero benefits.	

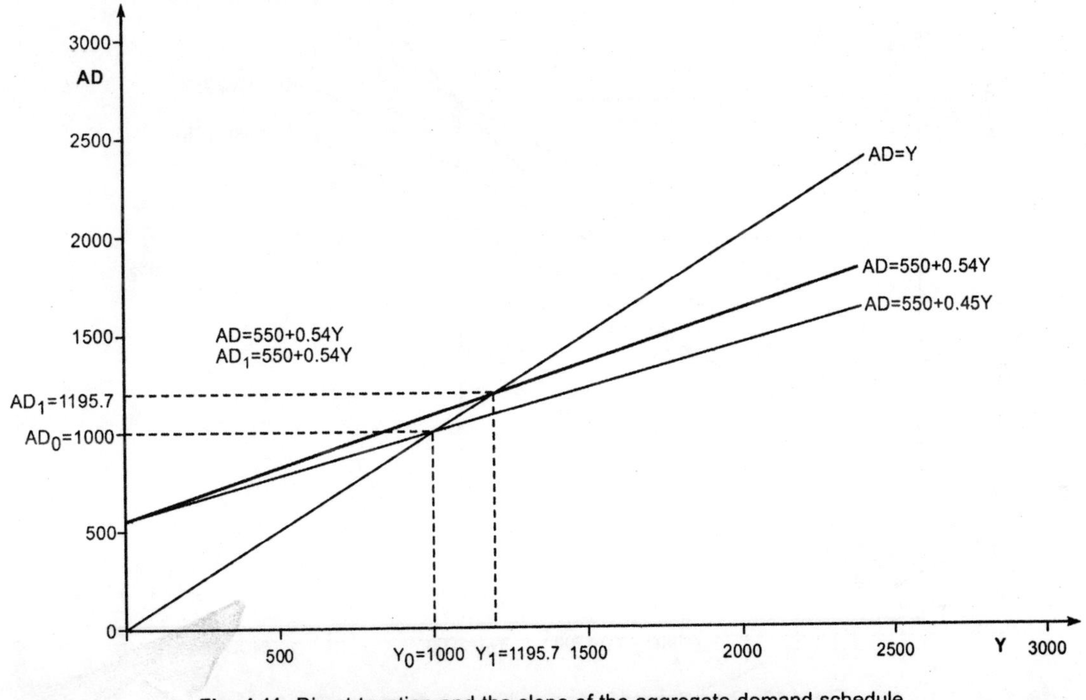

Fig. 4.11: Direct taxation and the slope of the aggregate demand schedule

Substituting the data from above into the following aggregate demand schedule and note that the average **rate** of direct taxation is 0.5.

$$AD = C + I + G + NX - T_e$$

We find that the equation of the aggregate demand schedule is equal to 550 + 0.45Y. The intercept is 550 and the slope is 0.45. Figure 4.11 shows a plot of this equation. The equilibrium level of income/output (Y_0) is 1,000.

If the rate of direct taxation is **reduced** from 0.5 to 0.4, then the new equation of the aggregate demand schedule is found to be 550 + 0.54Y. The intercept is unchanged, but the slope of the aggregate demand schedule **increases** from 0.45 to 0.54. Plotting AD=550 + 0.54Y in figure 4.11 we find that the new equilibrium level of income/output increases to 1,195.7 (=Y_1).

The Balanced Budget Multiplier

1. Consider Fig. 4.12. Start at point E_0, where $C=300+0.75Y_d$, $I_0=100$, $G_0=150$, $T_d=200$. Since $Y_d = Y - T_d$ then $Y_d = Y-200$. Substituting Y_d into C=100 + 0.75Yd gives a consumption function C=150 + 0.75Y where the intercept of the consumption function, ao, is equal to 150. Also, because, AD = C + I + G, then AD = 400 + 0.75Y.

   Since the equilibrium condition is Y = AD, then Y = 400 + 0.75Y: Solving: $Y_0 = 1600$

2. Increase both G and T_d by 100. The increase in G will shift the aggregate demand schedule up to AD = 500 + 0.75Y. *ceteris paribus* output would increase to (Y_{01} = 2000) [in this case, with an MPC of 0.75 the multiplier is 4]. But direct taxes have also increase by 100. The new consumption function would be C = 75 + 0.75Y where the new consumption intercept is a_1(=75), and the new aggregate demand schedule will be AD = 425 + 0.75Y.

3. In equilibrium Y = AD or Y = 425 + 0.75Y. Solving, Y = 1700 – point E_1.

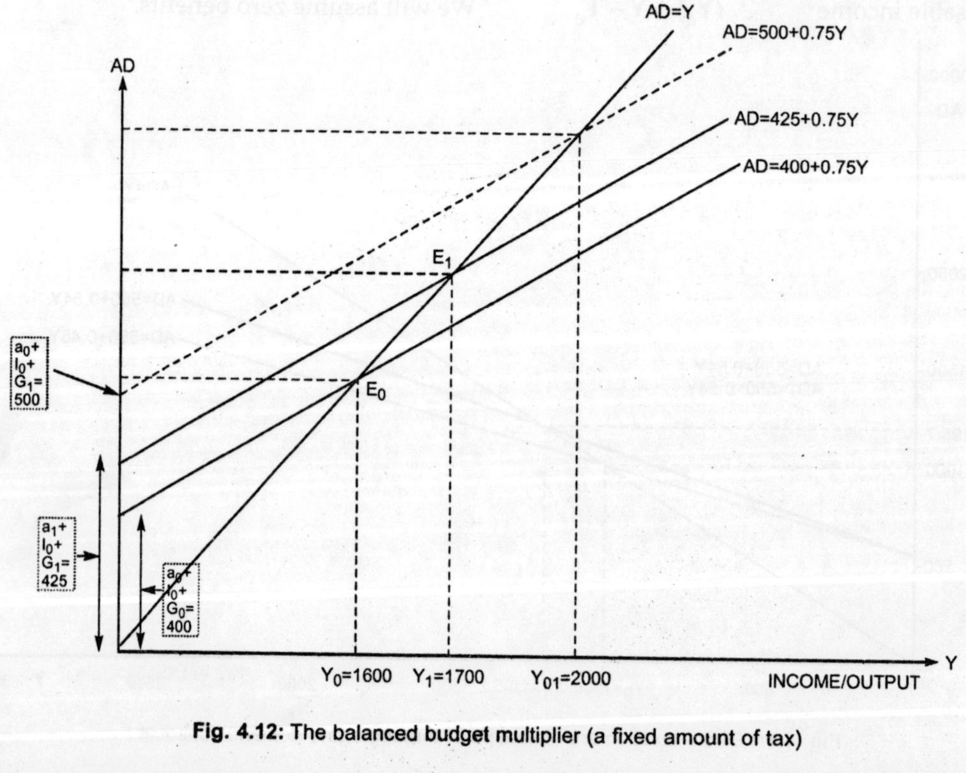

Fig. 4.12: The balanced budget multiplier (a fixed amount of tax)

4. The increase in G and T_d of 100 has led to an increase in output of 100 – the balanced budget multiplier.

At first glance it seems that an increase in G and T_d of 100 would lead to no change in income/output (withdrawals and injections the same?).

However if the extra 100 in taxes raised by the government (and spent) were left with consumers they would only spend 75% of it – in this case 75 (their MPC is 0.75). The multiplier would only act on the 75 that consumers spend (in this case they save 25).

Taking 100 from consumers the government would spend the full 100 (the government is spending the 75 that the consumers would spend plus the 25 that the consumers would save) and the multiplier would act on the full 100.

The net effect is that an extra 25 is spent (100-75).

The multiplier of 4 acts on the extra 25 to produce the extra income/output of 100.

1. Consider Fig. 4.13. Start at point E_0, where $C = 200 + 0.9Y_d$, $I_0 = 200$, $G_0 = 150$, $T_d = 0.5Y$. Since $Y_d = Y - T_d$ then $Y_d = Y - 0.5Y$. Substituting Y_d, $Y_d = Y - T_d$ and $T_d = 0.5Y$ into $C = 200 + 0.9Yd$ gives a consumption function $C = 200 + 0.45Y$ where ao = 200. Also, because, AD = C + I + G, then AD = 550 + 0.45Y. Because the equilibrium condition is Y = AD, then Y = 550 + 0.45Y

   Solving: Y_0=1000
2. Increase both G and T_d by 110. The increase in G will shift the aggregate demand schedule up to AD = 660 + 0.45Y. *ceteris paribus* output would increase to (Y_{01} = 1200) [in this case, with an MPC of 0.45 the multiplier is 1/0.55=1.82]. But the direct rate (t) has also been increased (from 0.5 to 0.55[approximately]) so that direct taxes have also increased by 110. The new consumption function would be C = 200 +0.4054Y where autonomous

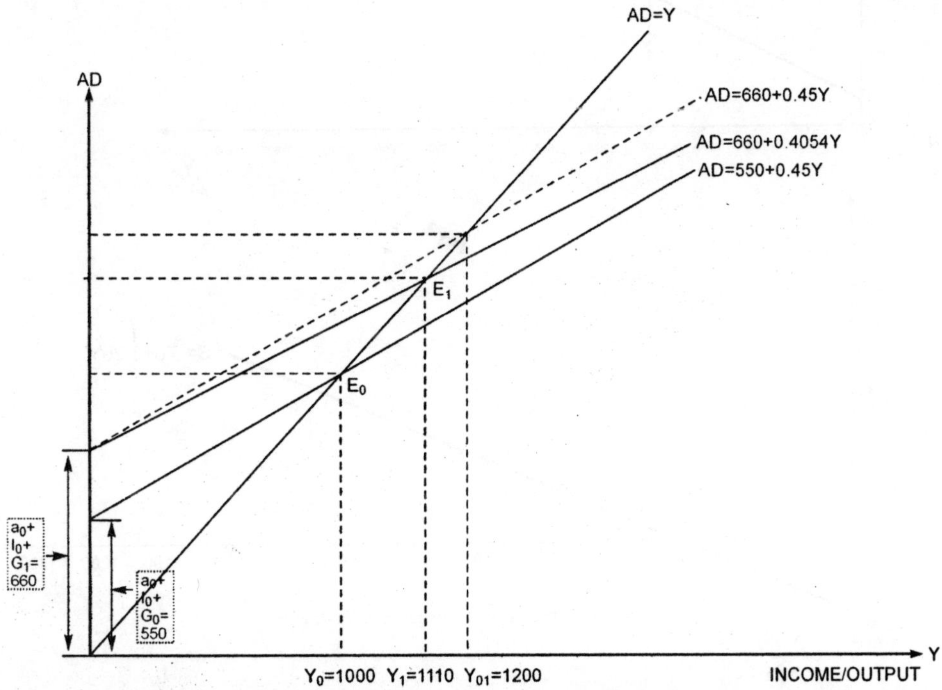

Fig. 4.13: The balanced budget multiplier (direct tax as a proportion of income)

consumption is still a_0 = 200, and the new aggregate demand schedule will be AD = 660 + 0.0.4054Y.

In equilibrium Y = AD or Y = 660 + 0.4054Y. Solving, Y = 1100 – point E_1.

The increase in G and Td of 110 has led to an increase in output of 110 – the balanced budget multiplier.

At first glance it seems that an increase in G and T_d of 110 would lead to no change in income/output (withdrawals and injections the same?).

However if the extra 110 in taxes raised by the government (and spent) were left with consumers they would only spend 90% of it – in this case 99 (the MPC out of disposable income is 0.9). The multiplier would only act on the 99 that consumers spend.

Taking 110 from consumers the government would spend the full 110 and the multiplier would act on the full 110.

The net effect is that an extra 11 is spent (110-99).

The multiplier of 10 acts on the extra 11 to produce the extra income/output of 110.

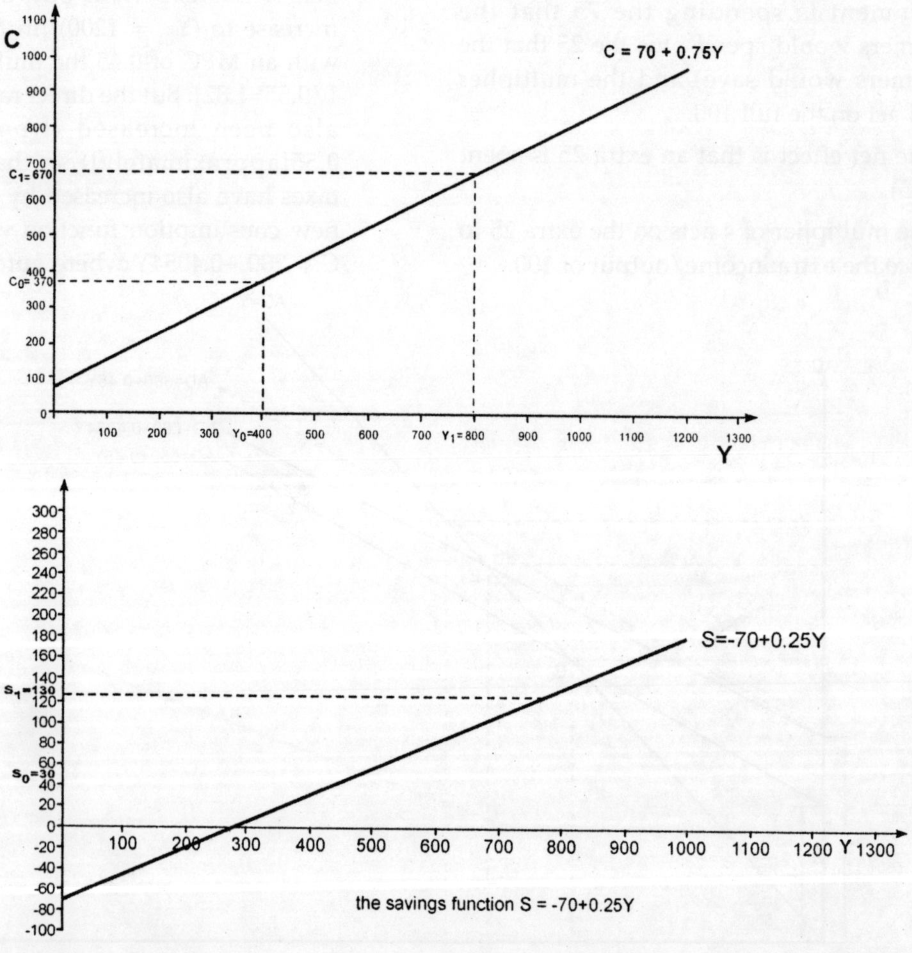

Fig. 4.14: The relationship between the consumption function and the savings function (Assume no investment, government or texes).

With the consumption function: C = 70 + 0.75Y the level of consumption (C_0) when income is 400 (Y_0) is 370. The average propensity to consume is 370/400 = 0.925.

The level of consumption (C_1) when income is 800 (Y_1) is 670. The apc is 670/800 = 0.8375.

If the çonsumption function is C = 70 + 0.75Y, then the savings function is found from S = Y – C.

Saving (S) is then equal to Y – (70 + 0.75) = **–70 + 0.25Y**.

Plotting the savings function, we find that the level of saving (S_0) is 30 when the level of income (Y_0) is 400. The average propensity to save (aps) is 30/400 = 0.075

When income increases to Y_1 (=800), then saving S_1 increases to 130. The average propensity to save is now 130/800 = 0.1625.

Note, in this **simple** model, that when income is 400 the level of consumption expenditure is 370 and the level of saving is 30. (Y = C + S or Y – C = S). When income is 800 the level of consumption expenditure is 670 and the level of saving is 130. (Y = C + S or Y – C = S).

Also, the sum of mpc and mps, at a particular level of income, is unity.

At an income of 400 the apc = 0.925 and the aps = 0.075. (apc + aps = 1).

At an income of 800 the apc = 0.8375 and the aps = 0.1625. (apc + aps = 1).

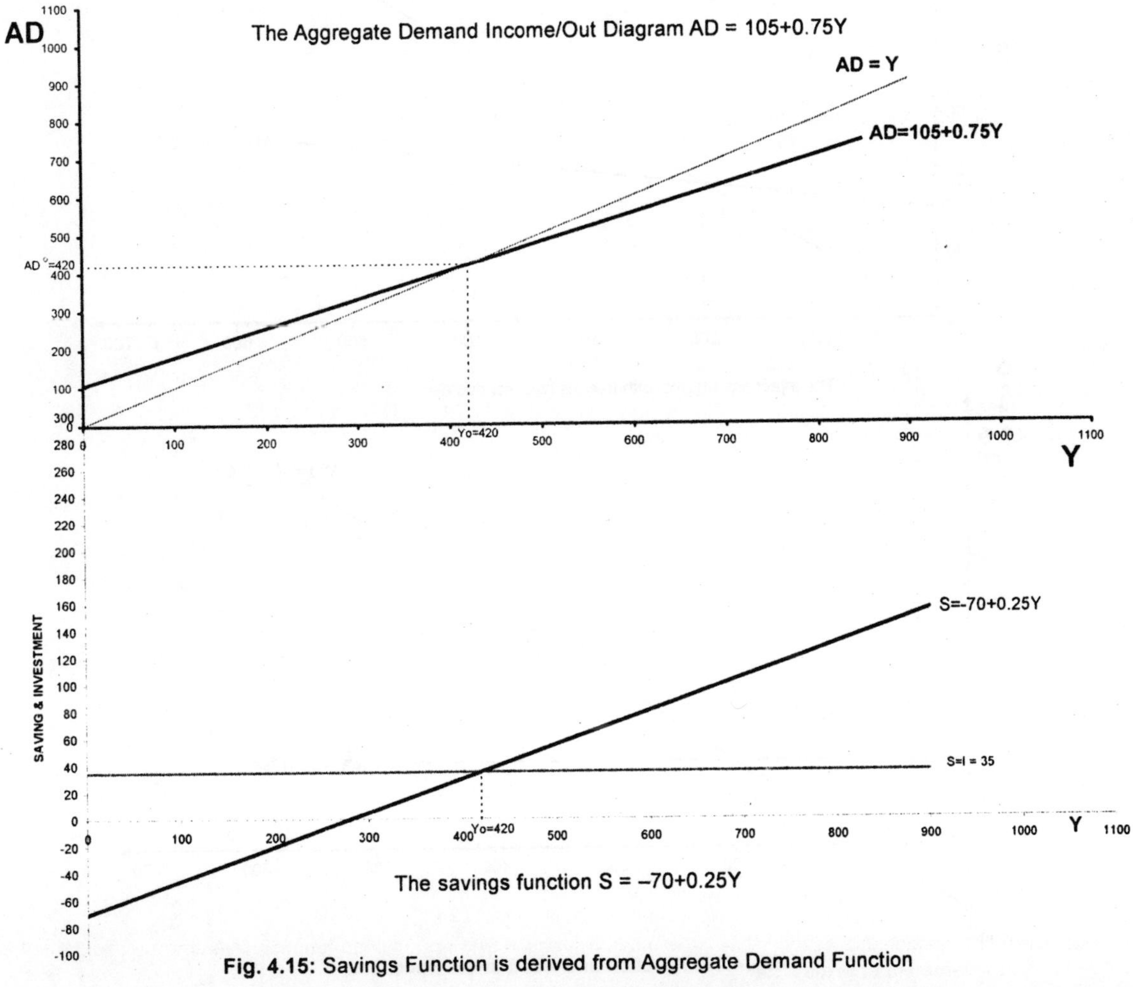

Fig. 4.15: Savings Function is derived from Aggregate Demand Function

2. Equilibrium in both the aggregate demand-income/output diagram and the savings function diagram.

Letting I = 35, G = 0, NX = 0 and $T_e = 0$, then aggregate demand is C + I.

When C = 70 + 0.75Y, then, AD = 105 + 0.75Y

The equilibrium level of income is 420. (Found from solving Y = 105+0.75Y).

The savings function (S) is (Y – [70 + 0.75Y]) = **S = –70 + 0.25Y**

With investment expenditure of 35 the equilibrium level of income is 420. (Found from solving –70+0.25Y = 35).

3. Equilibrium in both the aggregate demand-income/output diagram and the withdrawals/injections schedule diagram.

Letting I = 35, G = 40, X = 15, Z = 0.35Y and T_e= 0.2Y, then aggregate demand is

$C + I + G + X - Z - T_e$

When

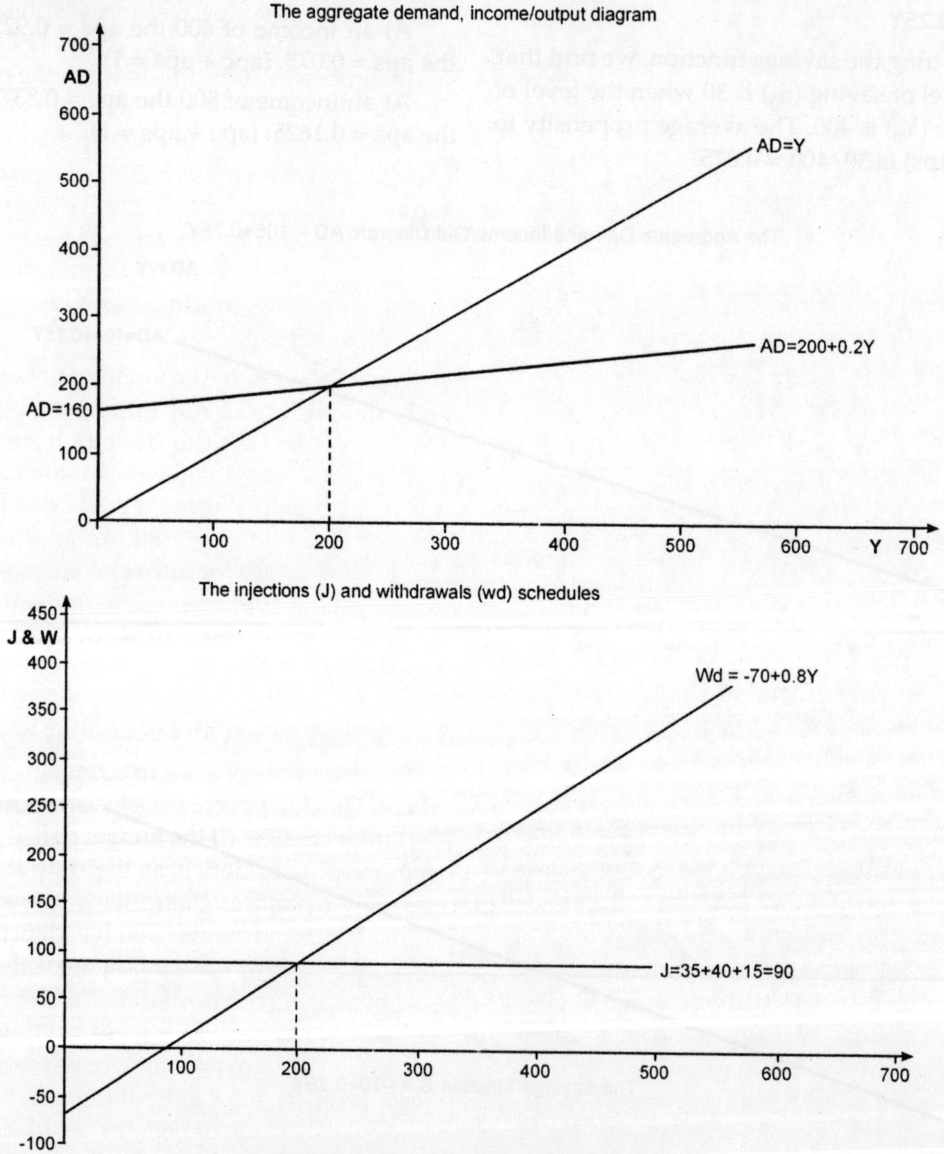

Fig. 4.16: Injection and withdrawals Functions

$C = 70 + 0.75Y$

Then,

$AD = 160 + 0.2Y$

The equilibrium level of income is 200.

The withdrawals function is

$Wd = -70 + 0.8Y$

With investment expenditure of 35, government expenditure of 40 and exports of 15 then the injections function (J) is 90.

When injections are equal to withdrawals: $J = W_d$

$90 = -70 + 0.8Y$

The equilibrium level of income is 200.

The Government Sector, Fiscal policy and Budget Deficits/Surpluses

Fiscal policy is the government's decision about the level of government expenditure, level of benefits and the level of taxation.

In the UK, and in most developed nations, the government is responsible for a large proportion of aggregate demand whether through government expenditure (G) or through the payment of benefits (B) to individuals (pensions, unemployment benefits etc). To finance this expenditure, partially or wholly, the government raises revenues by levying taxation. There are two broad categories of taxation – direct (Td) and indirect taxation (Te). Direct taxes are usually taxes on incomes; the incomes of individuals or companies. Indirect taxes comprise of specific and *ad valorem* taxes.

A specific tax is an amount per unit tax – for example so many pence per litre of petrol.

An *ad valorem* tax is a tax that increases as the price of the good increases. It is usually charged as a percentage of the price of the good or service. An example of an *ad valorem* tax in the European Union is VAT – value added tax. In the UK the highest rate of VAT is 17.5% of the value of the good or service.

The budget deficit is the excess of government outlays (G + B) over government receipts ($T_d + T_e$). Under the terms of the stability and growth pact the members of the European Union have, amongst other things, to restrict any budget deficit to 3% of their GDP and not go above a 60% public debt to GDP ratio. Any borrowing undertaken by the government will increase the size of the national debt. This is known as the Public Sector Net Cash Requirement [PSNCR] (previously known as the Public Sector Borrowing Requirement [PSBR]). Figure 4A1 shows the Public Sector Net Cash Requirement for the UK economy from 1982-83 to 2007-08. Government finances were in surplus from 1987-88 to 1990-91 and again from 1998-99 to the beginning of 2001 (this is when the output of the economy was increasing). The recessionary years of 1990-92 and 2008-2009 and the slowdown from 2001 onwards led large budget deficits and Public Sector Net Cash Requirements. The large increase in the budget deficit since 2001 has mainly been brought about by increases in public expenditure (G).

Incidentally some economists believe that budget deficits are not important because people realise that the deficits need to be financed and that the level of their taxation will increase in the future. People will reduce their consumption expenditure and increase their saving to pay for future tax increases. In the jargon this is known as the Barro-Ricardo equivalence proposition or Ricardian equivalence.

The budget deficit and economic activity

A likely outcome of a fall in economic activity (real income [Y] decreasing) is an increase in the budget deficit. (If the budget deficit moves from surplus to deficit as the output of the economy decreases then this is known as a ***cyclical*** deficit. If there is a budget deficit when the economy is at full employment then this is known as a ***structural*** deficit). The cyclical deficit comes about because, as unemployment increases, the government receives less in direct taxation and pays out more in benefits (a large percentage of benefits are likely to be spent since they are, generally, paid to the

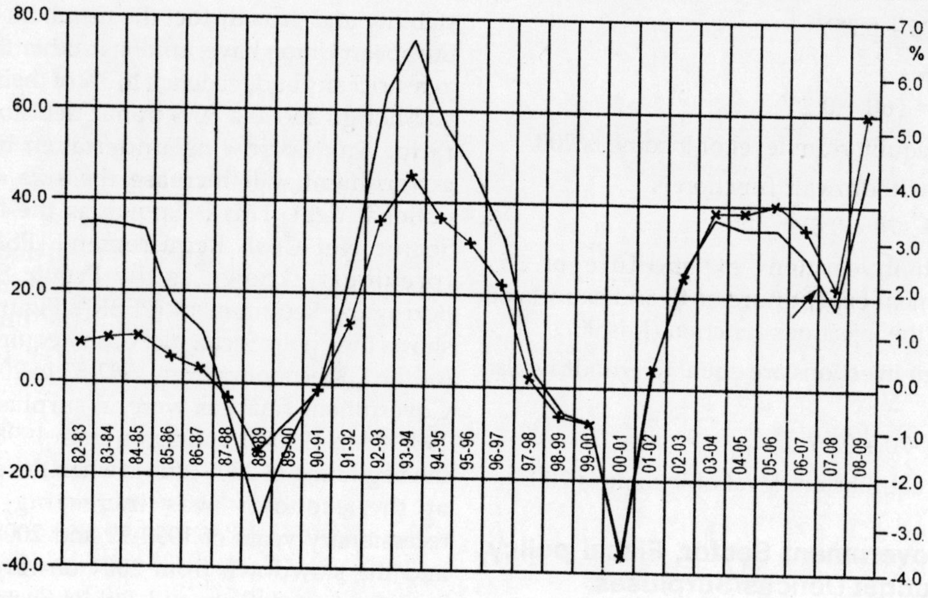

Fig. 4.A1: UK-net cash requirement

poorer sections of society. This helps to offset the fall in aggregate demand and fall in employment – it is a built in [automatic] stabiliser). Also, because economic activity falls, less indirect taxation is paid. This scenario applies to the UK, German and French economies, where the slowdown in economic activity from 2000, has led to an increase in budget deficits.

This has led to problems for Germany and France where their budget deficits are likely to rise above 3% of GDP. Interest rates, controlled by the European Central Bank, were (Sept 2003) said to be too high for the German economy. However, in the short run, the German government cannot cut taxes or increase government expenditure as this would, in the short run, increase the budget deficit and go against the terms of the 'stability and growth pact'.

The budget deficit and economic activity: A numerical example

Assume the equations for the model are:

$C = 200 + 0.9Y_d$ (1) Consumption is a function of real disposable income

$I = 200$ (2) Investment expenditure is at a level of 200

$G = 300$ (3) Government expenditure is at a level of 300

$X = 300$ (4) Export demand is at a level of 300

$Z = 100 + 0.3Y$ (5) Imports increase as income increases.

$T_e = 100 + 0.22Y$ (6) Indirect taxation increases as income increases.

$Y_d = Y - T_d + B$ (7) Real Yd is real income (Y) less direct taxation plus benefits

$T_d = 200 + 0.1Y$ (8) Direct taxation increases as income increases.

$B = 200 - 0.1Y$ (9) Benefits fall as income increases.

$$\therefore\ AD = C + I + G + X - Z - T_e$$

$$\Rightarrow AD = (200 + 0.9Y_d) + 200 + 300 + 300 - (100 + 0.37 - (100 + 0.22)$$

$$\Rightarrow AD = (200 + 200 + 300 + 300 - 200) + 0.9Y_d - 0.37 - 0.202Y)$$

$\Rightarrow AD = 800 + 0.9Y_d - 0.52Y$ (10)

Where $Y_d = Y - T_d + 3$

$\Rightarrow Y_d = Y - (200 + 0.17) + (200 - 0.1Y)$

$\Rightarrow Y_d = Y - 0.17 - 0.17$

$\Rightarrow Y_d = Y - 0.27 \Rightarrow Y_d = 0.5.7$ (11)

Substituting (11) into (10) gives

$\therefore\ AD = 800 + 0.9(0.8Y) = 0.52Y$

$\Rightarrow AD = 800 + 0.72Y - 52Y$

$\Rightarrow AD = 800 + 0.2Y$ (12)

In equilibrium,

$\therefore\ AD = Y \Rightarrow 800 + 0.2Y = Y$

$\Rightarrow 800 = 0.8Y \Rightarrow Y = 1375$ (13)

Solving (12) and (13) gives **Y = 1000**

Total taxation $= T_d + T_e$

$= 200+0.1Y + 100+0.22Y$

200+100+100+220=**620** (14)

Total expenditures by the government $= G + B$

$= 300+(200\text{-}0.1Y)$

$= 400$ (15)

There is a budget **surplus** of 620-400= **220**

Assuming that exports increase to 500. Then, reworking our figures, we will find that Y=1250, taxes increase to 720, government outlays (G+B) fall to 375 and the budget surplus increases to 325. As output increases the budget surplus increases (or any budget deficit decreases).

Assuming that exports fall to 100. Then, reworking our figures we will find that Y= 750, tax revenues falls to 540,government expenditures rise to 425 and the budget surplus falls to 95. As output decreases the budget surplus decreases (or any budget deficit increases).

QUESTIONS

1. If people, on aggregate, receive an extra £1,000,000 in extra incomes, will they increase their consumption expenditure by £1,000,000, more than £1,000,000, or less than £1,000,000?
2. When the economy is in equilibrium, how are aggregate demand and income related? Investment and savings?
3. What will happen to the average propensity to consume (apc) if autonomous consumption expenditure declines?
4. What will happen to aggregate demand if imports fall?
5. What does the AD=Y line represent? How does it help you find equilibrium?
6. What is difference between a change in autonomous consumption expenditure and an induced change in consumption expenditure?
7. Will an increase in investment expenditure of £100,000 lead to an increase in national income of £100,000?
8. Suppose the marginal propensity to consume (mpc) is 0.8. By how much must government expenditure increase for national income to go up by £50 billion?
9. Suppose people spend 80p of every new pound on consumption expenditure. If 50p is spent on domestically produced consumption goods and 30p on imported consumption goods. What is the multiplier?
10. Will an increase in aggregate demand lead to an increase in the general level of prices?

ANSWERS

1. Consumers will increase their expenditure by less than £1,000,000. This is because the mpc is between zero and one.

   On aggregate consumers will spend a fraction of their income and save the remainder.

2. When an economy is in equilibrium aggregate demand is equal to income/output. In a **very simple** model of the economy (a closed economy with no government expenditure or taxation) saving is equal to investment when the economy is in equilibrium.

3. If autonomous consumption declines this will lead to a fall in the APC.

4. If imports fall then aggregate demand (AD=C+I+G+X-Z) will increase.

5. The AD=Y line is a locus of points where aggregate demand is equal to output.

   Given the aggregate demand schedule, the intersection of the AD=Y line and the aggregate demand schedule determines the equilibrium level of income/output in an economy.

6. A change in autonomous consumption expenditure increases or decreases the level of autonomous consumption 'a' in the consumption function: C = a + bY.

   An induced change in expenditure refers to changes in consumption expenditure brought about by changes in income. i.e. bY in C = a + bY.

7. Any change in investment expenditure of £100,000 will lead to a change in national income greater than the £100,000.

   This is because the initial change in investment expenditure will, in a closed economy with no government sector, lead to income increasing by £100,000. A fraction of this will be spent on consumption goods and services, which will generate more income and more consumption expenditure etc., etc. The **aggregate** change in income will be greater than £100,000.

8. In a closed economy with no government sector and a marginal propensity to consume (mpc) of 0.8 the multiplier is 5 (= 1/[1–mpc]). For income to increase by £50 billion. then government expenditure must increase by £10 billion (=£50 billion/5).

9. The 30p spent on imports is a withdrawal from the circular flow of income (m=30/100 = 0.3). This withdrawal will reduce the size of the multiplier. Only 50p will be spent on domestically produced goods (mpc=0.5).

   The multiplier will be 1/[1–mpc+m] = 1/[1–0.8+0.3] = 1/[1–0.5] = 1/[0.5] = 2.

10. We are assuming that only if there is no **involuntary unemployment** in the economy will an increase in aggregate demand lead to an increase in the price level. I.e. the output of the economy is below Y_f.

CHAPTER 5

THE DETERMINATION OF THE OUTPUT OF AN ECONOMY: THE FINANCIAL (MONETARY) SECTOR OF THE ECONOMY

KEY TERMS

Money: Notes plus coin plus current account (sight) deposits. Wealth held in the form of money does not pay a rate of interest.

Nominal Money Balances: Face value of money.

Real Money Balances: Quantity of goods and services that can be exchanged for nominal money balances.

An Irredeemable Bond (Perpetuity): A piece of paper promising to pay the owner a constant interest payment (called the 'coupon') forever. It pays the owner a positive nominal rate of interest.

Real Wealth: Money balances plus the value of irredeemable bonds, both measured in real terms.

Demand for Money: Aggregate amount of money held by people.

Equilibrium in the Money Market: The real demand for money (LL) is equal to the real supply of money (L = M/P).

WHAT IS MONEY?

Money is an asset (a store of wealth) that can be exchanged for goods and services. Currency (such as £1 coins and £10 notes) and cheque accounts all serve as money. Money by delivery settles a contractual obligation.

Theoretically, in the UK, the supply of money is under the control of the Bank of England (see chapter 11). The nominal stock of money is said to be exogenously determined (determined outside of the economic system).

Money is the most **liquid** of asset: **Liquidity** refers to the speed and certainty with which an asset holder can convert the asset into money.

Although there are many definitions of money we will define the *nominal* supply of money (M)as **coin plus notes plus current account deposits.** The real stock of money ($L \equiv M/P$) is the quantity of goods and services that can be exchanged for the nominal stock of money. The quantity of goods and services that can be exchanged for the nominal stock of money depends upon price level (P). For as given stock of money (M) the lower is the price level the higher is the real stock of money. More goods can be obtained for a given money stock.

We will assume that **wealth held in the form of money does not earn a rate of interest**.

Most money in developed countries are current account bank deposits. Cash is a small proportion of a country's money supply. In Feb.2007, the notes and coins in circulation in the UK accounted for just 3.1% of the total money supply. The rest, £1.496 trillion are bank deposits.

The Functions of Money

1. It is a medium of exchange. Goods and services are exchanged for income using money as the medium of exchange: Labour or other services are usually exchanged for incomes via the intermediary of money. Money is a claim on resources in an economy that utilises money contracts to organise production and trading activities.
2. It is a unit of account in which prices are quoted and accounts are kept.
3. It is a store of value money can be used to transfer wealth from the present to the **future.**
4. It is a standard of deferred payment a unit of account over time. In entering contracts people agree to pay or to be paid in the future, usually in the form of money. (The alternative is to pay or be paid in goods or services).
5. It is a means of transferring income from the future to the present. **Borrowing** money is a means of transferring future income to the present.

Trade without money is **barter**. To barter, you have to find someone who

(a) has what you want, and

(b) wants what you have.

Until that person is found you do not have a double coincidence of wants, since both (a) *and* (b) have to be true for barter to occur.

With money trade can take place by having people sell what they have or buy what they want for money. Money does not require a double coincidence of wants.

Money and Income

At the microeconomic level people are usually paid their incomes in the form of money and so tend to identify money with income.

At the **macroeconomic** level, however, money **is not** the same as income.

We have seen in chapter 2 that incomes are generated in the production of goods and services over a period of time and is equal to the value of goods and services produced in that period of time. Income is a 'flow' variable. It is generated (earned) over time.

One definition of the amount of money in an economy is coin plus notes plus current

YOU SHOULD REMEMBER

1. Money is a means of exchange. Using money for trade eliminates the need for barter.
2. Money serves as a unit of account, a store of value, a means of deferred payment and a means of transferring wealth over time.
3. The definition of money (M) is notes plus coin plus current account deposits.

account deposits (M1 in the UK) and is measured at a moment in time. It is a 'stock' variable. At any moment in time the country's supply of money is held by individuals (directly or indirectly).

Other definitions of money include interest earning deposit accounts ('time deposits') of commercial banks and building society. These are generally less liquid and less useful for financing immediate transactions.

Money can and does increase over a period of time; the measure used is the **growth** in the stock of money.

DEFINITION: The Demand for Money: This is the amount of **money** (*NOT INCOME*) that people, **on aggregate**, wish to **hold** (*NOT BORROW*).

The amount of money circulating in an economy is measured in millions of pounds and is, at any given time, held by people (directly or indirectly). It is part of their stock of wealth.

Surprisingly as it may seem we have to explain why people wish to hold part of their wealth in the form of money which earns a zero rate of interest when they could hold all their wealth in the form of bonds which would pay them a positive rate of interest. Our assumption of a zero (or very small) rate of interest means that holding wealth in the form of money loses millions of pounds in interest payments.

For simplicity we are assuming that people can hold their wealth **only** in the form of money balances **or** irredeemable bonds, both measured in real terms.

$$Wh \equiv L + Bd$$

where Wh = aggregate financial wealth in an economy.

L = real amount (supply) of money (L = M/P).

Bd = real value of bonds.

Assume that the type of bond is an irredeemable bond; a perpetuity; a piece of paper issued by the government or a firm promising to pay the owner a constant interest payment **for ever**. The price of this piece of paper is equal to the present value (PV) of its expected stream of earnings. (See example 2 in the appendix to this chapter).

The PV of a bond (its market price) =

$$\frac{\textit{constant} \text{ interest payment per year (its coupon)}}{\text{market rate of interest}}$$

For example, if the constant (**fixed**) interest payment is £2.50 per year and the interest rate is 10%, then the market price of bonds is £2.50/0.1: equal to £25. The return on bonds is 10%.

If the rate of interest falls to 5% and, since bonds pay a fixed amount of £2.50 per year, then £2.50 on £25 is a return on bonds of 10%. As funds switch into bonds to earn the higher interest rates this will cause the price of bonds to increase to £50 when the return on bonds will also be 5%.

As the rate of interest falls (rises) bond prices increase (decrease).

Of course, in the real world, people can hold their wealth in many more ways than in the two assets money and perpetuities. For example, bills, redeemable bonds, shares, foreign currency and assets, gold and property.

For simplicity we have assumed that there are only **two** ways of holding wealth - money which earns **no** interest and irredeemable bonds which earn a **positive** rate of interest.

YOU SHOULD REMEMBER

1. People hold their wealth in the form of money that pays no interest or in the form of irredeemable bonds which pay a positive rate of interest.
2. As the price of bonds increases [decreases], interest rates fall [rise].

Benefits from holding (demanding) money

1. The transactions motive. In a monetary economy people receive income in the form of money in return for providing factor services (labour, land etc.) and use money to exchange income for goods and services.

   Money is acceptable as a means of payment because it is the most **liquid of assets.**

   Payments and receipts are not synchronised; money is held between receiving payments and making purchases. This is the transactions demand for money.

   Since people hold money balances in order to finance transactions, and since the number of transactions is roughly proportional to the level of real national income, the transactions demand for money (measured in real terms) is assumed to be proportional to real income (Y).

   As real income **increases** [decreases] the transactions demand for money balances **increases** [decreases] in proportion to the increase [decrease] in real income.

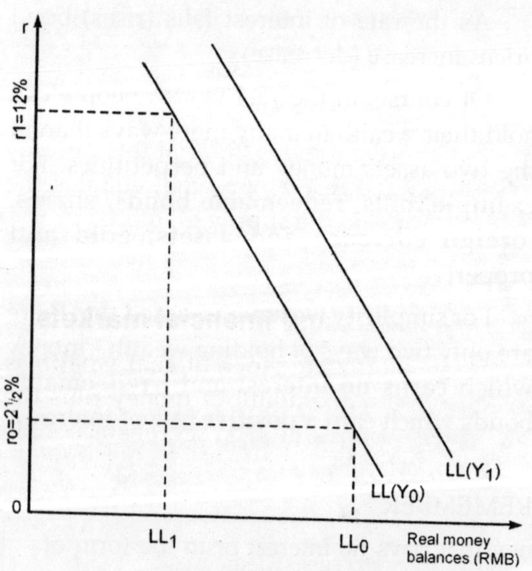

Fig. 5.1: The demand for money schedule

2. The precautionary demand for money. As we live in an uncertain world assume that some money is held to meet unforeseen expenses. For example, the expense of an unexpected car repair may be met more cheaply out of money holdings than by selling off other assets.

   We will also assume that the demand for money for precautionary purposes **increases** [decreases] in proportion to the **increase** [decrease] in real income.

3. The asset motive or the speculative demand for money.

After holding some of their wealth in the form of transactions and precautionary money balances why do some people keep their wealth in the form of money (earning **no** interest) when they could exchange the money for bonds and earn a positive rate of interest?

If the rate of interest is perceived to be low, say 2½% (Fig. 5.1), (bond prices are high) some (probably most) people *expect* interest rates to rise (bond prices to fall) and hence, to prevent a loss of wealth, these people will not purchase bonds but will hold their wealth in the form of money.

There will be a high real demand for money (LLo) at a low interest rate.

Similarly, if the price of bonds is perceived to be low then the rate of interest is perceived to be high, say 12% (Fig. 5.1).

There will be an expectation of a fall in the rate of interest and an increase in bond prices (or at least no further increase in the rate of interest and hence a safe way of earning interest).

There will be a low demand for money (LL_1) at a high interest rate.

Also, holding wealth in the form of money balances earns NO interest payments. Hence, the **opportunity cost** of holding wealth in the form of transactions, precautionary or speculative money balances is the interest that could have been earned by exchanging the money for bonds. The higher the rate of interest the greater is the incentive for people to economise on the holding of wealth in the form of money.

Assume that holdings of money for transactions, precautionary and speculative purposes also varies with variations in the price level. For example, if **prices** double, then the demand for money, in nominal terms, for transactions, precautionary and speculative purposes also doubles. Hence the demand for real money balances (**LL**) will be unchanged.

On aggregate, the demand for real money balances (**not loans or income**), is positively related to real income and is negatively related to the interest rate. (**LL = L(Y,r)**)

In Fig. 5.1, the demand for money schedule (**LL(Y_0)**) shows the relationship between the demand for real money balances (RMB) and the rate of interest (r) for a **given** level of real income (**Y_0**).

At a rate of interest of 2½% the demand for money is LL_0. At a rate of interest 12% the demand for money will be LL_1.

For a given level of income an increase [decrease] in the rate of interest will lead to a fall [rise] in the demand for money **along** a given demand for money schedule (in this case LL_0).

At any interest rate an increase in real income will lead to an increase in the demand for money for transactions and precautionary purposes (from LL_0 to LL_1) and **shift** the demand for money schedule to the right. (from LL(Y_0) to LL(Y_1).

Equilibrium in the financial (money) market

There will be equilibrium in the financial (money) market when the quantity of real money balances supplied equals the quantity of money (measured in real terms) demanded. i.e. when **the real supply of money is equal to the real demand of money (L=LL** or L=L(Y,r)).

We will assume that the supply of money is exogenously determined (determined outside the economic system by the monetary authorities [but, also, see page 186]) and is not affected by the rate of interest. Remember that all the money supplied (notes and coin and current account bank deposits) is held (demanded) by people (directly or indirectly).

The real supply of money schedule is drawn as a vertical line (L_0) as in Fig. 5.2.

The demand for money schedule is as in Fig. 5.1, drawn for a given level of real income Y_0.

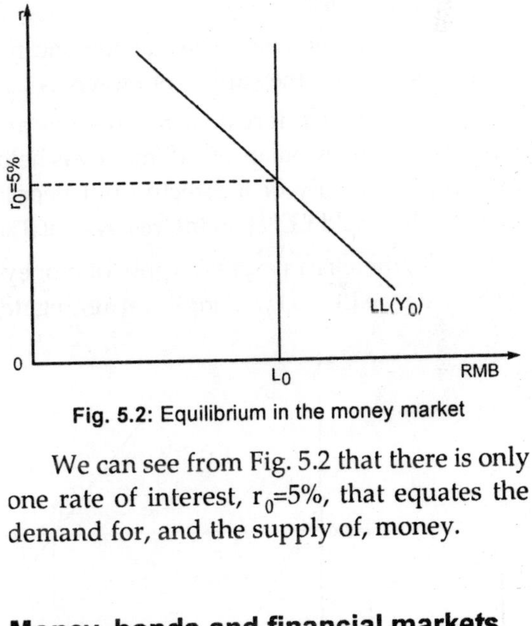

Fig. 5.2: Equilibrium in the money market

We can see from Fig. 5.2 that there is only one rate of interest, r_0=5%, that equates the demand for, and the supply of, money.

Money, bonds and financial markets

Since the aggregate stock of real wealth is equal to the real amount of money plus the real value of bonds, and, on aggregate, people

YOU SHOULD REMEMBER

1. As income **increases** [decreases], the demand for money **increases**[decreases].
2. As the rate of interest **increases** [decreases], the demand for money **decreases** [increases].

have to decide how they wish to divide up their wealth between **money** and **bonds**. Then any statement regarding what is happening in the money market is simultaneously a statement regarding what is happening in the bond market.

Together the money market and bond market make up the financial markets.

On **aggregate** any excess demand for money must be exactly matched by an excess supply of bonds.

We are assuming that people have decided upon their aggregate expenditures and that they are considering the **proportion** of their wealth they will hold in the form of money or bonds.

We can now see that 5% is an equilibrium interest rate. Consider Fig. 5.3, and let the interest rate be 8%.

At a rate of interest of 8% the demand for money is LL_1, but the supply of money is L_0.

At a rate of interest of 8% people are holding L_0 money balances (all money is held by people, directly or indirectly) but people only wish to hold LL_1 at an interest rate of 8%.

At 8% there is an excess supply of money. (The distance LL_1 to L_0). People, on aggregate, are holding too much of their wealth in the form of money (it may be better to think of wealth holders being insurance companies or pension funds and that an excess supply of money means that they are too liquid at the current rate of interest).

To try correct this situation people (insurance companies or pension funds) buy bonds. i.e. They exchange their excess money balances for **bonds**.

This leads to increase in demand for a fixed supply of bonds, an increase in the price of bonds and a fall in the rate of interest.

At all interest rates above 5% there is an excess supply of money and an excess demand for bonds. Above 5% bond prices will be increasing and the interest rate falling.

The interest rate will fall until it reaches 5% when the demand for money is equal to the supply of money. People, on aggregate, are now content with their holdings of money and their holdings of bonds.

The effect of a reduction in the real stock of money

This can be effected in one of two ways.

a. By a reduction in the nominal stock of money with prices constant (M in

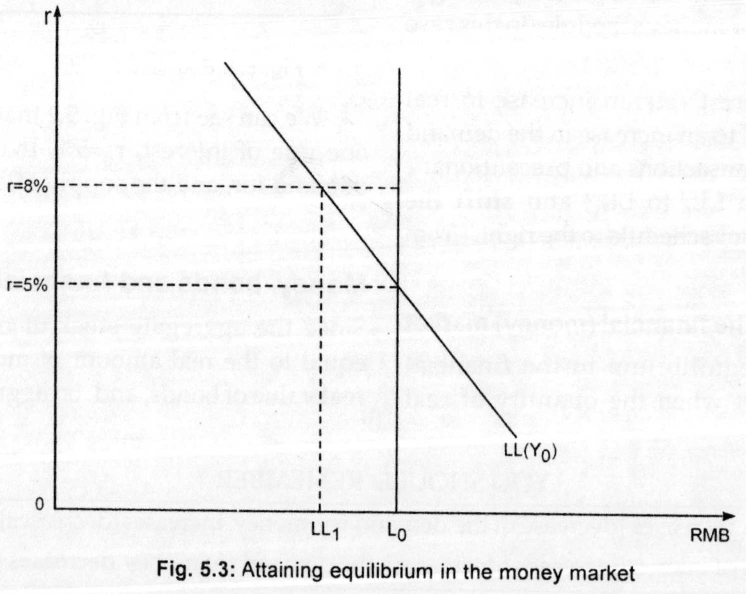

Fig. 5.3: Attaining equilibrium in the money market

M/P declines). This reduction (or increase) is known as MONETARY POLICY. **OR,**

b. By an increase in the price level with the nominal stock of money constant (P in M/P increases).

In either case the real stock of money reduced.

Consider Fig. 5.4 and start at E_0, an initial equilibrium position, where the supply of money (L_0) is equal to the demand for money ($LL(Y_0)$) and the rate of interest is 4%.

Reduce the real stock of money. The supply of money will be reduced from L_0 to L_1.

At ro there is now, on aggregate, an excess demand of money (point A to point E_0). In trying to rebuild their money balances people sell bonds. There is an excess supply of bonds. This will lead to a fall in the price of bonds and a rise in the rate of interest.

As long as there is an excess demand for money there is an excess supply of bonds, bond prices will be falling and interest rates rising.

Interest rates will continue to increase until the excess demand for money is eliminated. i.e. until the rate of interest reaches 6%, when the demand for money is once more equal to the supply of money (E_1). The markets for money and bonds are back in equilibrium. (Assume that the there is no change in the position of the demand for money schedule $LL(Y_0)$ - We will see later that the demand for money schedule [$LL(Y_0)$] usually shifts as the rate of interest rate changes).

Note. The interest rate always changes by a sufficient amount to equate the demand for, and supply of, real money balances. i.e. until people are content to hold (demand) the lower, or higher, amount of money supplied.

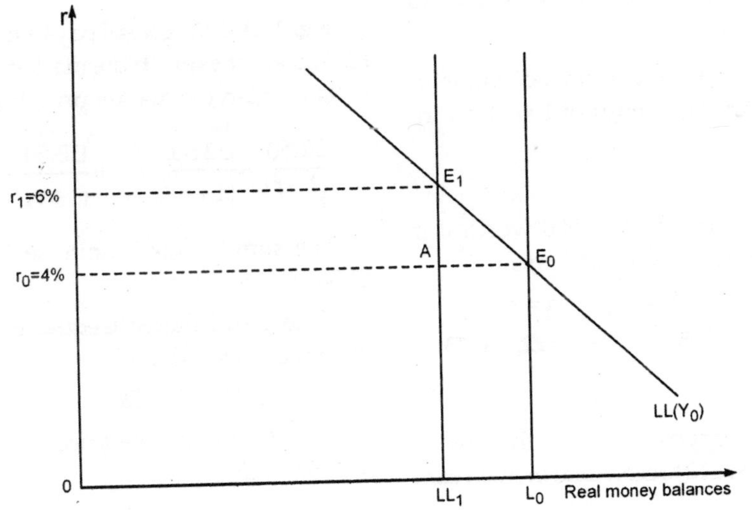

Fig. 5.4: A reduction in the real stock of money

YOU SHOULD REMEMBER

1. There is equilibrium in the financial (money) market when **the real supply of money is equal to the real demand of money** (**L=LL** or L = L(Y,r) [since **LL=L(Y,r)**]).
2. LL (the amount of money people wish to hold [demand]) depends upon real income (Y) and the rate of interest (r). LL=L(Y,r)

APPENDIX 5A.I

Compound Interest and Present Value

Start with **compound** interest.

£100 today when the rate of interest prevailing in the economy is 10% is worth £110 in one years time which is equal to the original £100 + £10 in interest.

Future value of £100 in one years time when the rate of interest is equal to £100 × (1 + 0.1) = £110.

£100 today when the rate of interest prevailing in the economy is 10% is worth £121 in two years time. This is equal to the original £100 + £10 + £11 in interest. In the first year the interest earned is £10. In the second year 10% interest is not only earned on the £100 but also on the £10 earned in the first year - an extra £1.

The future (compound) value of £100 in two years time when the rate of interest is equal to £100 × $(1 + 0.1)^2$ = £121.

In general the future (compound) value of an amount 'A' earning interest of 100r% for 'n' years is equal to

$$A(1+r)^n$$

Example: How much is £1,500 worth if it earns 8% compound interest for 4 years?

A = £1,500, r = 0.08 (8%), n = 4.

Then $A(1+r)^n$ = £1,500×$(1.08)^4$ = **£2,040.73**

Present Value

We can argue the opposite way. If the rate of interest is 10% then £121 receivable in two years time is worth £121 in one years time and £100 now. It is the reverse process of compounding.

In general the P.V. (present value) of an amount 'Πn' receivable in 'n' years time when the rate of interest is 100r% is equal to

$$\frac{\Pi n}{(1+r)^n}$$

e.g. 1 Find the present value of £1,100 receivable in one years time and £1,210 receivable in two years time when the rate of interest is 10%.

$$P.V. = \frac{£1,100}{(1+0.1)} + \frac{£1,210}{(1+0.1)^2}$$

$$= £1,000 + £1,000 = £2,000$$

e.g. 2 A 2½% consol pays a fixed amount of £2.50 p.a. **for ever.** If the market rate of interest is 100r% then the market price is equal to

$$\frac{£2.50}{(1+r)} + \frac{£2.50}{(1+r)^2} + \ldots + \frac{£2.50}{(1+r)^n} + \frac{£2.50}{(1+r)^{n+1}} + \ldots$$

The sum of this infinite series is equal to £2.50/r

If the rate of interest is equal to 0.1 (10%), then the price of the bond is:

$$£2.50/0.1 = £25$$

If r = 0.125 then the price of the bond = **£20** (=£2.5/0.125).

APPENDIX 5AII

The LM Curve

DEFINITION: The LM curve shows the relationship between the rate of interest and the level of real income/output in the financial (money) market when the financial (money) market is in equilibrium(i.e. when the real demand for money is equal to the real supply of money [LL=L]). Although the LM curve gives us no more information than the demand for money schedule combined with the supply of money schedule it will be useful in later analysis.

The Derivation of the LM Curve

Fig. 5A.1 shows the usual supply and demand for money diagram and Fig. 5A.2 the space in which the LM curve will be constructed.

If we start at L_0, $LL(Y_0)$, in Fig. 5A.1 then the initial equilibrium level of output is Y_0 and the initial rate of interest is r_0.

Since we have set the initial rate of interest to be r_0 we can mark that off on the vertical axis of Fig. 5A.2 and, by marking off Y_0 on the horizontal axis, we can obtain a point in Fig. 5A.2 at r_0, Y_0 (point A) .

If we now increase the level of real income from Y_0 to Y_1 then there will be an increase in the demand for money (for transactions and precautionary purposes) and $LL(Y_0)$ will shift to the right to $LL(Y_1)$ in Fig. 5A.1. At r_0 there will be an excess demand of money which is equivalent to an excess supply of bonds. The price of bonds will fall and the rate of interest will increase (from ro to r_1) until we are back in equilibrium in Fig. 5A.1. We now have another point on 5A.2 at r_1, Y_1(point B).

For each level of output there will be a unique rate of interest. Joining up these points will give us the LM curve, $LM(M_0/P_0)$, in Fig. 5A.2.

The LM curve will be shifted if the real stock of money (**M_0/P_0**), changes. Mathematically, a change in the nominal money supply (M) or a change in the price level (P) can bring this about.

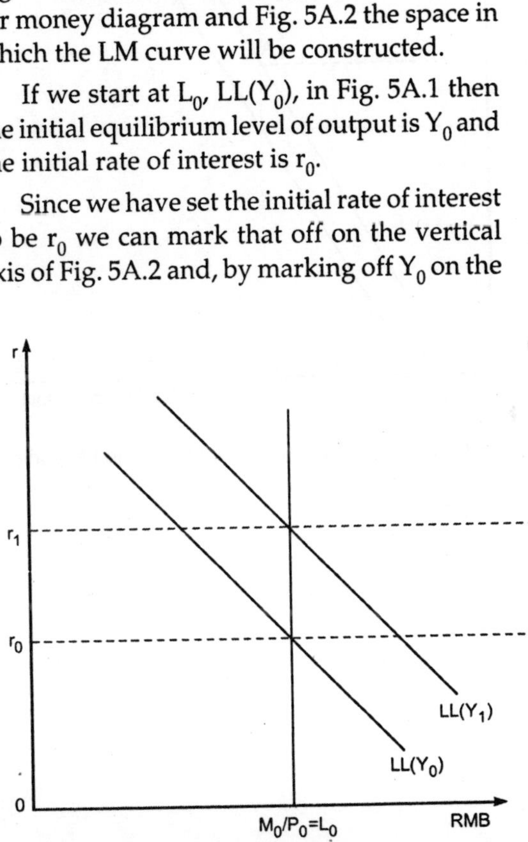

Fig. 5 A.1.: Increase in real income

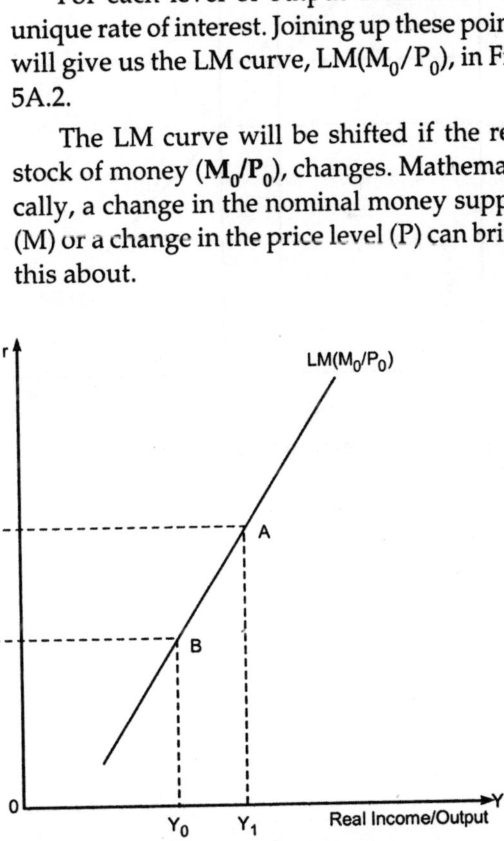

Fig. 5 A.2: The LM Curve

Figs. 5A.3 and 5A.4 show the effect of an increase (from $L_0=M_0/P_0$ to $L_1=M_1/P_0$) in the real stock of money (in this case brought about by an increase in the nominal stock of money [from M_0 to M_1]).

An Increase in the Real Stock of Money and The LM Curve

If we start at r_0, $LL(Y_0)$, $L_0=M_0/P_0$ in figure 5A.3 and r_0, Y_0 in Fig. 5A.4. Then, by changing the level of real income, we can derive, in Fig. 5A.4, the LM curve - $LM(M_0/P_0)$.

If we now increase the nominal stock of money from M_0/P_0 to M_1/P_0 the real stock of money will increase from L_0 $(=M_0/P_0)$ to L_1 $(=M_1/P_0)$. Assuming income remains at Y_0 then, in Fig. 5A.3, the rate of interest will fall to r_1 (explain why). We can now plot a new point in figure 5A.4 at r_1, Y_0.

If we again change the level of income we can trace out a new LM curve - $LM(M_1/P_0)$. The increase in the real stock of money has shifted $LM(M_0/P_0)$ downwards (to the right) to $LM(M_1/P_0)$.

The increase [decrease] in the real stock of money will shift the LM curve to the right [left].

Note : the real stock of money could also be increased [decreased] by a fall [rise] in the price level (P).

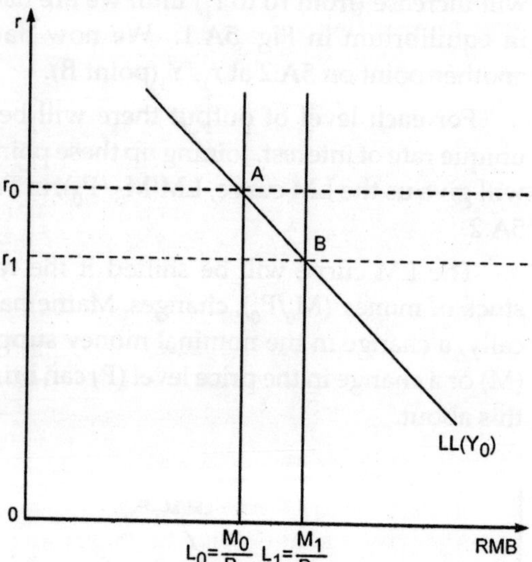

Fig. 5A.3: An increase in the real stock of money

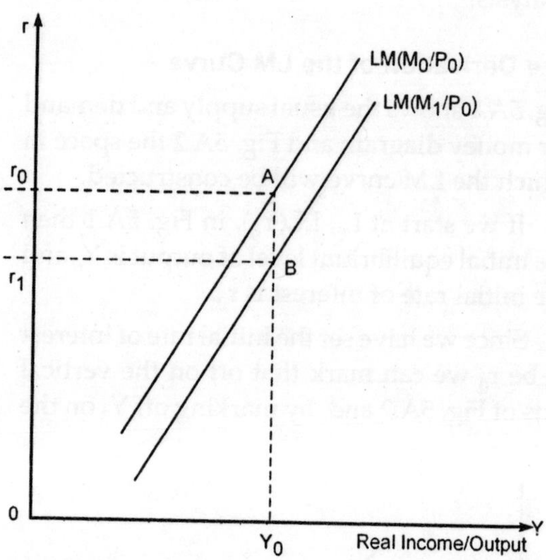

Fig. 5A.4: The corresponding shift in the LM curve

QUESTIONS

1. How does money make it easier for people to buy and sell goods and services?
2. Why is income not money at the macroeconomic level?
3. What are people borrowing when they borrow money?
4. What is meant by 'the demand for money'?
5. Why do people hold their wealth in the form of money that earns no interest?
6. What is a perpetuity (an irredeemable bond)?
7. Explain why the demand for money schedule is negatively sloped?
8. Why does a change in real income shift the demand for money schedule?
9. Why is an excess demand for money equivalent to an excess supply of bonds?
10. Explain why an increase in the price level will lead to a decrease in the real supply of money but no change in the real demand for money.

ANSWERS

1. In a monetary economy, people do not have to find someone who has the goods and/or services they want and, simultaneously, want the goods and/or services they have.
2. Income is a flow of new wealth (the value of goods and services produced) generated over a period of time. Money is coin plus notes plus current account deposits measured at a moment in time.
3. A borrower is transferring goods and services (income) from the future for consumption today. The borrower has persuaded the lender that the borrower will have sufficient **future** income to repay income consumed today (financed by the borrowing).
4. The demand for money refers to peoples decisions, on aggregate, of how much of their wealth people wish to **hold** in the form of money.
5. People demand (hold) money for transactions, precautionary and speculative purposes.
6. It is a piece of paper (an irredeemable bond) issued by the government (or a firm) promising to pay the owner of that bond a **fixed** payment per year. An example of this type of bond is a 2½% consol. Its market price can be found in any of the 'quality' newspapers. It pays a fixed amount of £2.50 per annum (its coupon). It has a **nominal** value of £100 but does not have a redemption date. Its **market price** will not be £100 until long term rates of interest fall to 2.5%.
7. There are two reasons why the demand for money is negatively sloped. Firstly, at high (low) rates of interest the opportunity cost of holding wealth in the form of money is high (low). Secondly, at 'high' ('low') rates of interest bond prices are 'low' ('high'). There is more (less) chance of bond prices rising (falling). At 'high' ('low') interest rates people hold less (more) of their wealth in the form of money.

   N.B. To say that the demand for money is low at high interest rates is **not** an answer to this question!
8. Real income is a proxy for the number of transactions taking place in an economy. The number of transactions increases if real

income increases. Hence if real income increases the demand for money for transactions and precautionary purposes increases at all rates of interest.

9. On aggregate, people hold their wealth in the form of money or bonds. To change the **composition** of a given stock of wealth requires the exchange of money for bonds. Any excess supply of (demand for) money is equivalent to an excess demand for (excess supply of) bonds.

10. The real stock of money (L) is the nominal stock of money (M) divided by the price level (P). (L=M/P). An increase in the price level will reduce the quotient M/P and hence reduce the real stock of money.

If the price level increases and the number of transactions remains the same then the value of transactions increases. To finance this increase people will carry more money. The nominal demand for money will increase. We assume that if the price level doubles then the demand for nominal money balances doubles. Hence the real demand for money remains the same.

CHAPTER 6

THE DETERMINATION OF THE OUTPUT OF THE ECONOMY: LINKING THE REAL AND FINANCIAL SECTORS

KEY TERMS

Real Autonomous Consumption: That part of real consumption expenditure that does not vary with income.

Wealth: Real money balances and bonds.

Real Balance Effect: The change in real consumption expenditure brought about by a change in the real stock of money.

Consumer Credit: Loans available, to consumers, to finance real consumption expenditure (usually durable goods).

Consumer Confidence: Consumers' expectations of future prospects.

In chapters 3 and 4 we considered the determination of the real income/output of an economy using a one-sector model of the economy (the 'real' sector). Before linking the 'real' sector of chapters 3 and 4 with the financial (monetary) sector of chapter 5 we will examine some of the economic variables, other than income, that affect real consumption expenditure as well as the factors that affect investment expenditure.

1. Real Consumption Expenditure

In chapter 3 we assumed that real consumption expenditure was determined by the following linear relationship:

$$C = a + bY$$

Where **C** is real consumption expenditure and **Y** is real income. **bY** is that part of real consumption expenditure that varies as real income varies. I.e. as real income increases, disposable income increases, and real consumption expenditure increases (real consumption expenditure is induced by a change in income). '**a**' is real autonomous consumption. Real autonomous consumption expendi-

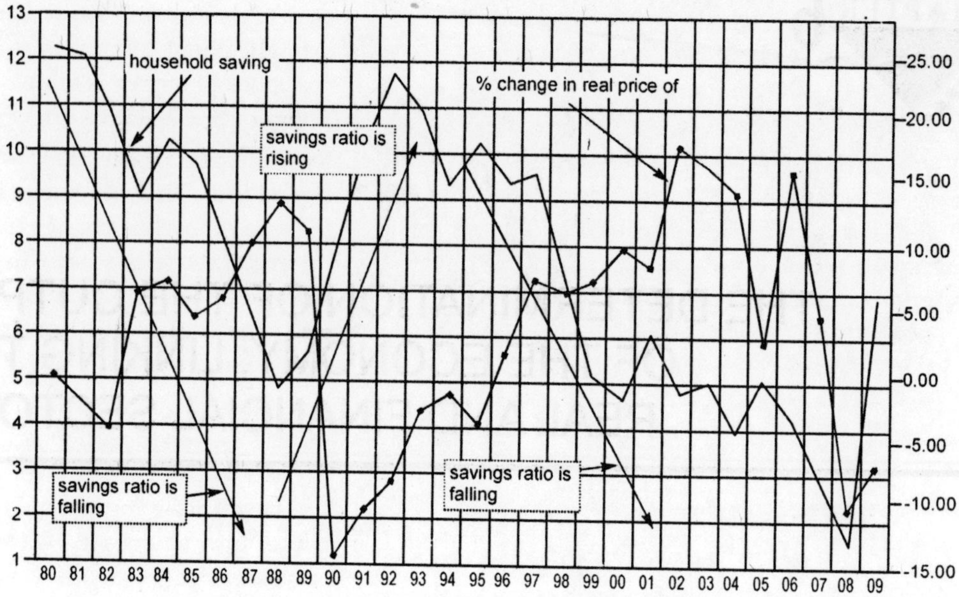

Fig. 6.1: UK-Household saving ratio (%) and percentage change in real price of housing

ture is that part of real consumption that does not vary with income. Changes in the real autonomous consumption expenditure component of aggregate demand are important determinants of changes in the income/output of the UK economy (See Fig. 6.1).

The fall in output in the UK economy in the years 1990-92 was exacerbated by the fall in the average propensity to consume (apc) (there was a rise in the savings ratio (S/Y) and a fall in real autonomous consumption expenditure.)

The increase in the UK's **real** autonomous consumption expenditure in the years 1992-94 and 2003 was one of the main contributory factors to the increase in income/output UK economy during that time. Real disposable incomes only increased by 2.6% between 1992-94, whereas real consumption expenditure increased by 11.8% (the personal savings ratio fell). If the apc had remained constant over the period 1992-94 then real autonomous consumption and aggregate demand would have been £34 billion lower (measured in 1990 prices). The Bank of England estimated that, in 2003, mortgage equity withdrawal was £53 billion (equivalent to the entire GDP of Ireland). This equates to £8 out of every £100 of consumer spending.

Fig. 6.1 shows the movement in the UK's personal savings ratio and the real price of houses (the main constituent of wealth for most people in the UK) for the years 1980-2007. During most of the eighties house prices increased and the savings ratio fell (real autonomous consumption increased). The fall in house prices and the rise in the savings ratio (fall in autonomous consumption) from 1988 to 1992 was a contributory factor to the recession of 1990-92. The fall in house prices in 2008-09 has driven the US and UK economies into recession.

THE DETERMINANTS OF REAL AUTONOMOUS CONSUMPTION

Some of the main variables that affect real autonomous consumption expenditure are:

a. **Wealth**. People can hold wealth in many ways. In the UK property (houses, flats etc) is the main source of a large number of peoples' wealth.

Other ways in which people can hold their wealth are in the form of bonds (stocks), shares, gold, or money balances.

For simplicity we will assume that wealth can be held in only **two** ways, **real money balances** and **bonds**. You can think of bonds as being an all encompassing term that includes property and shares. These tend to vary with the rate of interest. As interest rates increase, houses, shares and bonds generally fall in price. (See the appendix at the end of chapter 5).

We will assume that if people hold their wealth in the form of money they will earn **no interest** whereas holding wealth in the form of bonds is rewarded with a **positive rate of interest**.

We will emphasise two ways by which the **wealth** of people can be changed;

i. **By a change in the real stock of money**. As the real stock of money increases (decreases), real wealth increases (decreases). The change in real consumption (autonomous) brought about by a change in the real stock of money is known as the **Pigou or real balance effect**.

ii. **By a change in the real value of bonds (Bd)**. This can come about if the rate of interest changes. As the interest rate falls (rises) then the price of bonds (P_b) increases (falls) and the value of bonds (Bd) increases (decreases).

For example, if wealth increases people will reduce their additions to their stock of wealth; i.e. reduce their level of saving and/or borrow more and increase their real consumption expenditure at all levels of income. Real autonomous consumption increases (from a_0 to a_1). This will shift the consumption function and the aggregate demand schedule upwards (from AD_0 to AD_1) as in Fig. 6.2.

b. **Consumer credit**. Since consumer durables (television sets, washing machines, cars etc.), are generally rela-

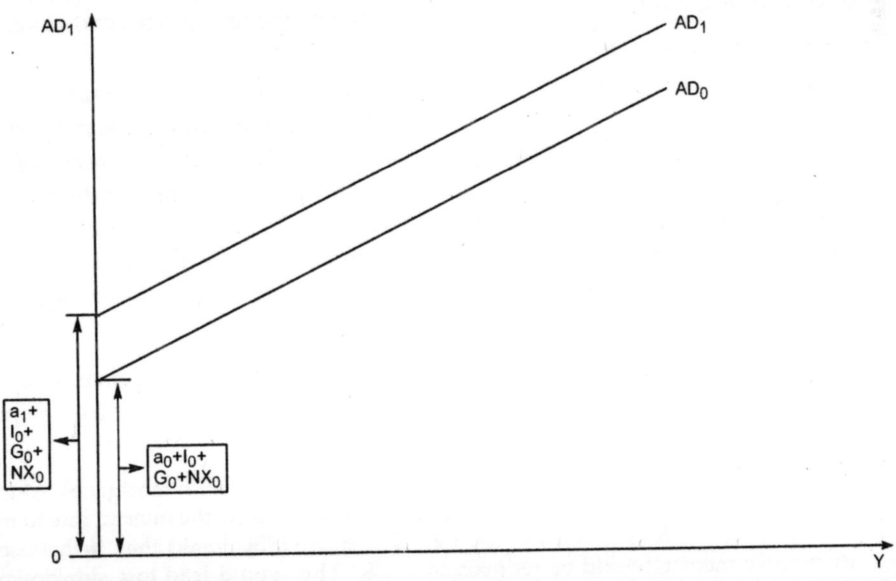

Fig. 6.2: An increase in autonomous Consumption expenditure and the aggregate demand schedule

tively expensive, a large number of people have to borrow if they wish to finance durable consumption expenditure. This is determined by:

i. **The length of the loan repayment period**: A longer repayment period usually means a smaller monthly or weekly payment and this generally leads to more borrowing and hence more real consumption expenditure. It has been reported that, in the UK, people look for small initial mortgage payments when looking to purchase property.

ii. **The size of the deposit**: A large deposit is harder to find and a deterrent to the purchase of consumer durables and houses. Lower deposits encourage borrowing.

iii. **The interest rate** (r): We can think of the interest rate the cost of linking the present to the future. As well as being the return on wealth held in the form of bonds, it is also the cost of borrowing. A fall in the rate of interest will reduce the cost of transferring income from the future to the present and reduce the cost of consuming today.

Lower interest rates will reduce:

(α) **The cost of borrowing**: The fall in the cost of borrowing will encourage consumers, on aggregate, to borrow more. At a given income real consumption expenditure will increase. There will be an increase in the level of real autonomous consumption expenditure and the apc (average propensity to consume).

(β) **Mortgage repayments**: This will leave some people with more disposable income[1] (although people with interest earning deposit accounts will earn less interest on their wealth). As people with interest earning accounts usually have a smaller average propensity to consume than people with mortgages this will, generally, lead to an overall increase in real consumption expenditure. Both real autonomous consumption expenditure and the apc will increase.

Also, changes in the rate of interest, have, especially in the UK, led to changes in property prices. Increases in property prices have enabled people to borrow money against the value of their property (the equity). This money has usually been exchanged for consumer goods. (The equity in the property has also been used to provide security against bank loans for investment purposes).

It has been estimated that, in the UK in 1988 when there was a large increase in house prices, real consumption expenditure was boosted by 2.5 per cent (by £7.46 billion in 1988 prices). Real autonomous consumption was £7.46 billion higher than 'normal' in 1988. Of course the apc increased in 1988.

Falls in property prices can have the opposite effect. Real consumption expenditure fell by 1.5 per cent below 'normal' in 1992. Real autonomous consumption and the apc both decreased in that year due, to a great extent, to a fall in property prices in that year. See Fig. 6.1.

Hence a rise [fall] in the rate of interest will lead to a decrease [increase] in borrowing and a decrease [increase] in real consumption expenditure. A rise [fall] in the rate of interest leads to a decrease[increase] in real autonomous consumption expenditure and a decrease[increase] in the average propensity to consume.

c. **Consumer confidence**. Whether or not consumers will save a given proportion

[1] Increases in interest rates will reduce the disposable income of people with mortgages. At the time of writing (October 2003) the UK base rate is 3.5%. The bond market expects the interest rate to increase to between 5 and 5.25%. It has been estimated (by John Butler of HSBC bank) that, if this occurs, then consumers' disposable income would be reduced by 1.5%. This would lead to a slowdown in retail sales and a significant increase in home repossessions.

of their incomes partly depends upon their expectations of what is going to happen in the future. If consumers are reasonably confident as to the size and reliability of their future incomes and/or the value of their wealth they will borrow more and/or save less and hence consume a larger proportion of their incomes. Average Propensity to Consume (apc) will increase. See Fig. 6.3.

Likewise, if they feel insecure about their future incomes and/or the value of their wealth they will tend to save more and/or borrow less and consume less out of a given income. Average Propensity to consume (apc) will decrease.

Factors affecting consumer confidence.

i. **Changes in the size of aggregate wealth/debt**. Consumers who benefit from increases in their wealth (due to increases in the value of their property, bonds or shares) will be more likely to either

(α) Spend a higher proportion of their incomes, and/or

(β) Borrow more to finance real consumption expenditure

In either case real autonomous consumption expenditure and the apc will increase.

Consumers with high levels of debt are likely to save more (consume less) in order to reduce debt.

In the UK, over the period 1990-93, house prices fell. Some families found that the size of their mortgage was greater than the value of their property. They suffered from what was known as 'negative equity'. The proceeds from the sale of their property would not be sufficient to redeem their mortgage. The sale of the property would still leave the mortgagee in debt to mortgager (usually the building society).

These people will be less confident about the future and tend to save more and consume less.

ii. **Interest rates.** If consumers think that an increase in the rate of interest is the start of an upward trend in interest rates they will be more cautious in taking out loans with variable interest rate charges. Real consumption expenditure will tend to fall.

iii. **Security of employment**. Consumers who are confident about their employment prospects will be more likely to consume a greater proportion of their incomes and/or borrow more and have higher apcs. Insecurity of employment will lead to a lower apc.

iv. **Changes in taxation**. An increase in taxation will, other things being equal, reduce real incomes. This as we have seen will reduce real consumption expenditure. Higher taxation will also probably affect consumer confidence and real consumption expenditure.

In the UK in April 1994 taxation was increased. In May 1994 borrowing by consumers (excluding mortgage lending) rose by £203 million, less than half the £412 million that consumers borrowed in April 1994. Also mortgage borrowing fell by £100 million from £1,500 to £1,400 million between April and May 1994.

As consumers' confidence increases real autonomous consumption increases (from a_0 to a_1) and shifts the real aggregate demand schedule upwards (the intercept increases from $a_0+I_0+G_0+NX_0$ to $a_1+I_0+G_0+NX_0$). The increase in real aggregate demand will lead to an increase in real income/output from Y_0 to Y_1.

YOU SHOULD REMEMBER

a. Real autonomous consumption and the average propensity to consume (apc) are affected by:
   i. The wealth of consumers.
   ii. The rate of interest.
   iii. Confidence.

b. Real autonomous consumption and the apc will increase [decrease] if
   i. The wealth of consumers increases [decreases].
   ii. Consumers increase [decrease] their borrowing.
   iii. Consumers are more [less] confident about the future. An increase in consumer confidence can lead to an increase in real autonomous consumption and an increase the average propensity to consume. The aggregate demand schedule will shift upwards as in figure 6.3. (Note that there is no change in government expenditure [G] or the real stock of money [L] or the rate of interest [r]).

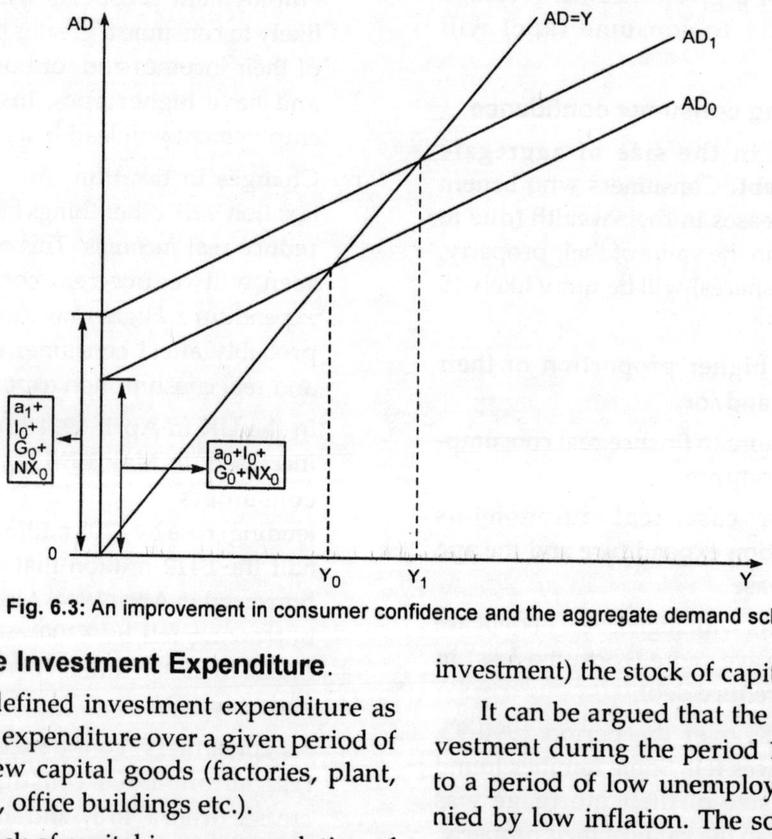

Fig. 6.3: An improvement in consumer confidence and the aggregate demand schedule

2. Private Investment Expenditure.

We have defined investment expenditure as the flow of expenditure over a given period of time on new capital goods (factories, plant, machinery, office buildings etc.).

The stock of capital is an accumulation of investment over a long period of time.

Investment is a flow variable. It is an addition to the stock of capital.

Net investment is an addition to (positive net investment) or a reduction in (negative net investment) the stock of capital.

It can be argued that the high level of investment during the period 1950 to 1970 led to a period of low unemployment accompanied by low inflation. The so called 'Golden age'. The investment affected both the demand side of the economy and, by building up the stock of capital, increased the ability of the economy to produce more goods and services. It affects the supply side of the economy. Increases in the demand for goods and services were able to be met, without a large increase in the price level (inflation), by the increased capacity of the economy brought about by investment.

We will only consider the determination of real private investment expenditure, that is, investment under the control of individuals or firms and not investment expenditure determined by the government.

Determinants of private investment expenditure.

a. **The rate of interest**: Each investment project undertaken is expected to earn more than the cost of the project. Capital goods are durable and any profits earned from them are spread over a number of years. Any calculation of yield, therefore, must allow for the fact that any profit earned in the future is worth less than the **same sum** today. See appendix I at the end of chapter 5.

The method of comparing the profitability of an investment project.

Present Value (PV): An entrepreneur can decide whether or not to invest by comparing the cost of the project (C_t) with the present value (PV) of its expected stream of net revenues (ENR's). Expected net revenues are the expected total revenue (ETR) from the sale of the extra output less the expected costs (ETC) of producing the extra output. We are interested in net revenues because the two other elements of cost, the interest rate and the cost of the project, are considered separately. The interest rate is used to discount the expected net revenues (to find the projects PV) and does not directly enter into the firm's costs of production. The PV is then compared with the cost of the project.

$$PV = \frac{ENR_1}{(1+r)} + \frac{ENR_2}{(1+r)^2} + \ldots + \frac{ENR_n}{(1+r)^n}$$

If PV is greater than the cost of the project (Ct) it is more profitable to purchase the machine and to earn the stream of net revenues than to earn a rate of interest of 100r% on the finance ($=C_t$) for 'n' years.

Example: A machine costing £215 has a life of 2 years and is expected to earn net revenues of £121 in each year. The rate of interest is assumed to be 10%.

Is it profitable to purchase the machine?

Then $C_t = £215$, $ENR_1 = £121$, $ENR_2 = £121$

We do not just add £121 to £121 (=£242) which, of course, is greater than £215 and say that the project is profitable and should be undertaken.

We have to discount expected future net revenues by the rate of interest and compare this value with the cost of the machine.

$$\text{Find the PV} = \frac{£121}{(1+0.1)} + \frac{£121}{(1+0.1)^2} = £210$$

In this case the present value is less than cost. The machine is not worth purchasing.

However, if r = 0.05 (5%), then

$$PV = \frac{£121}{(1+0.05)} + \frac{£121}{(1+0.05)^2} = £225$$

In this case the PV of £225 is greater than the cost of the machine (£215). A greater return is obtainable by purchasing the machine than earning 5% compound interest on the finance (£215) for two years. The machine is now worth purchasing.

NOTE: As the interest rate falls [from 0.1 (10%) to 0.05(5%)] the PV increases (from £210 to £225).

In general

$$PV = \frac{ENR_1}{(1+r)} + \frac{ENR_2}{(1+r)^2} + \ldots + \frac{ENR_n}{(1+r)^n}$$

i. As the rate of interest increases the present value of expected net revenues (PV) will decrease.

   At the margin, some projects that were profitable at the lower rate of interest are now not profitable. Hence investment decreases as interest rates rise.

ii. An increase in the rate of interest may also affect expected net revenue (ENR).

Since ENR's = expected total revenues (ETR) less expected total costs (ETC) an increase the rate of interest may:

(α) Reduce the expected revenues of firms if firms think that an increase in interest rates precedes a fall in economic activity and a fall in sales and revenues.

This will reduce expected total revenues (ETR) and hence reduce expected net revenue (ENR).

(β) Probably increase the cost of inputs for firms (the costs of overdrafts will increase leading firms to try increase their prices) and increase their expected total costs (ETC). This will also reduce expected net revenue (ENR).

As the rate of interest increases [decreases] the present value of an expected stream of net revenues decreases [increases]. At the margin, projects that were not [were] profitable at the higher [lower] rate of interest are now profitable [not profitable]. Hence investment increases [decreases].

The investment demand schedule II(Cto) shows how much investment firms wish to undertake at each rate of interest. Figure 6.4 shows the effect of a fall in the rate of interest.

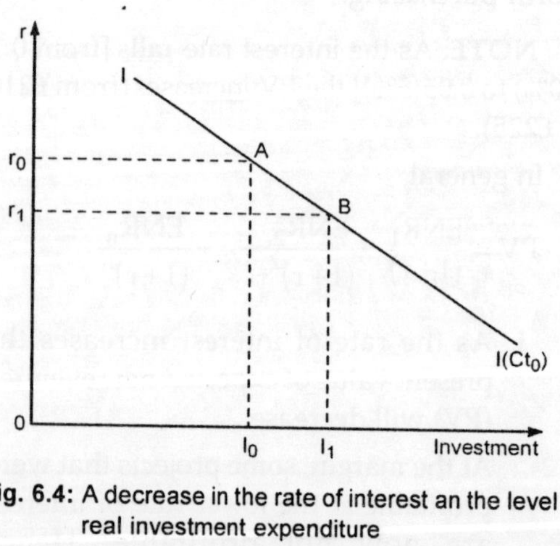

Fig. 6.4: A decrease in the rate of interest an the level of real investment expenditure

If the rate of interest is ro, the level of investment expenditure is I_0.

If the rate of interest falls to r1 investment expenditure increases to I_1.

Both r_0, I_0 (point 'A') and r_1, I_1 (point 'B') are equilibrium positions.

At r_0, when the cost of capital is Ct_0, then,

$$Ct_0 = \frac{ENR_1}{(1+r_0)} + \frac{ENR_2}{(1+r_0)^2} + ... + \frac{ENR_n}{(1+r_0)^n}$$

point 'A'

At r_1, when the cost of capital is Ct_0,

$$\text{then, } Ct_0 = \frac{ENR_1}{(1+r_1)} + \frac{ENR_2}{(1+r_1)^2} + ... + \frac{ENR_n}{(1+r_1)^n}$$

point 'B'

b. **The cost of new machinery:** In equilibrium the cost of the machine would just be equal to the present value of the expected stream of net revenues i.e. Ct_0 = PV. If present value were greater than cost then there would be an incentive for the firm to increase its stock of capital. If present value were less than cost than there would be an incentive for the firm to reduce its stock of capital.

$$Ct_0 = \frac{ENR_1}{(1+r_1)} + \frac{ENR_2}{(1+r_1)^2} + ... + \frac{ENR_n}{(1+r_1)^n}$$

For a given stream of ENR's, a rise in the cost of new machines (from Ct_0 to Ct_1) now means that Ct_1 is now greater than the present value of expected net revenues. The rate of interest needs to fall at each level of investment expenditure (the present value needs to increase) in order for the present value to be equal to Ct_1. Or, alternatively, there will be less investment at each rate of interest. In either case the curve will shift downwards (to the left).

Fig. 6.5 shows the effect of an increase in the cost of capital on the demand for investment.

If we start at II(Ct_0) and there is an increase in the cost of capital then II(Ct_0) would shift to the left to II(Ct_1).

c. **Expectations** (Confidence): If firms become more [less] optimistic about the level of future net revenues, then, at each rate of interest, there will be more [less] investment at each interest rate.

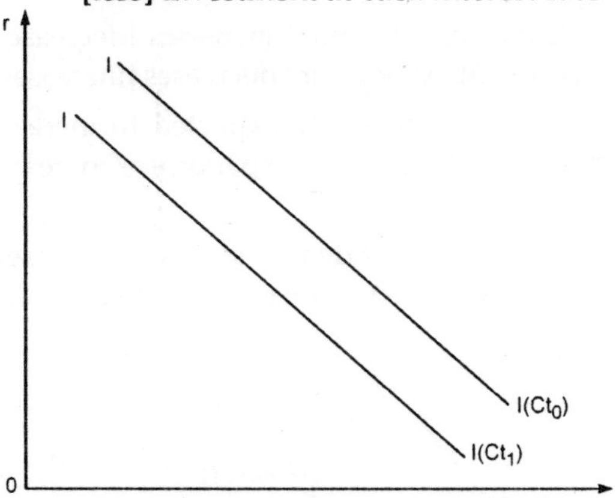

Fig. 6.5: An increase in the cost of capital and the investment demand schedule

Factors affecting business confidence.

i. **Expectations of changes in interest rates:** If interest rates are **expected** to increase this may lead to firms postponing investment expenditures as an increase in interest rates will lead to a fall in the present value of expected net revenues. The II schedule will shift to the left.

Expected cuts in interest rates will normally lead to increases in investment. However, expectations of large cuts in interest rates could panic the financial markets and weaken confidence not strengthen it. The argument between economists arguing for large cuts (the "slammers") and those arguing for a more gradual approach (the "tweakers") was taking place in the USA in 2003.

ii. **Political outlook of the government**: Some governments are perceived to be more sympathetic to the business community. In the UK this is **usually** governments led by the Conservative Party. An electoral defeat or an expected electoral defeat of the Conservative party may lead to businesses lowering their estimates of future net revenues and a reduction in investment expenditures. The investment schedule would then shift to the left.

iii. **The outlook for the income/output of an economy**: If the consensus of economic forecasters is that the income of the economy is going to increase then business can be fairly confident that expected net revenues are going to increase. This will increase the present value of investment projects and lead to increase in investment expenditures.

Fig. 6.6 shows the effect of an increase in business confidence. The investment schedule will shift to the right at each rate of interest (from IIo to II_1). If the 'credit crunch of 2007-08 leads to a fall in confidence (and an increase in interest rates) then less investment will take place. This can lead to a fall in aggregate demand and output/income and a rise in involuntary unemployment.

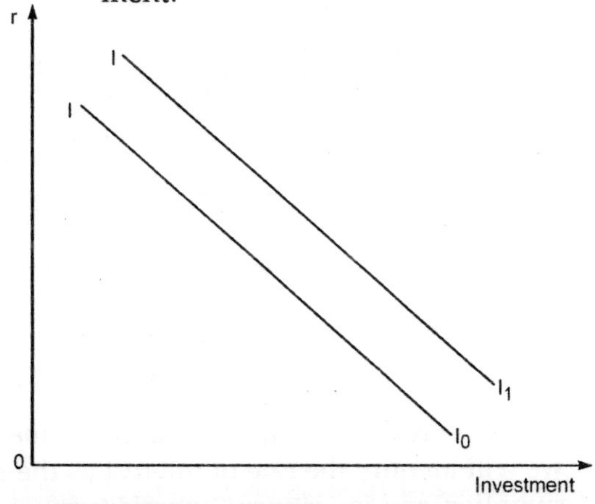

Fig. 6.6: Business confidence and investment schedule

YOU SHOULD REMEMBER

Real consumption (C) is determined by real income/output (**Y**), the rate of interest (**r**), the real stock of money (**M/P**) and consumer confidence (**CC**).

C = C(**Y**,**r**,**M/P**,**CC**)

If real income increases [decreases] real consumption expenditure increases [decreases].

If the rate of interest increases [decreases] real consumption expenditure decreases [increases].

If the real stock of money increases [decreases] real consumption expenditure increases [decreases].

Investment (I) is determined by the rate of interest (r), the cost of capital (C_t), net revenues expected in the years 1 to n (**ENR**$_i$): i = 1, 2..., n.

If consumer confidence increases [decreases] real consumption expenditure increases [decreases].

$I = I(r, C_t, ENR_i)$ i = 1, 2, ..., n

If the rate of interest increases [decreases] investment expenditure decreases [increases].

If the cost of capital increases [decreases] investment expenditure decreases [increases].

If net revenues are expected to increase [decrease] investment expenditure increases [decreases].

If business confidence increases [decreases] investment expenditure increases [decreases].

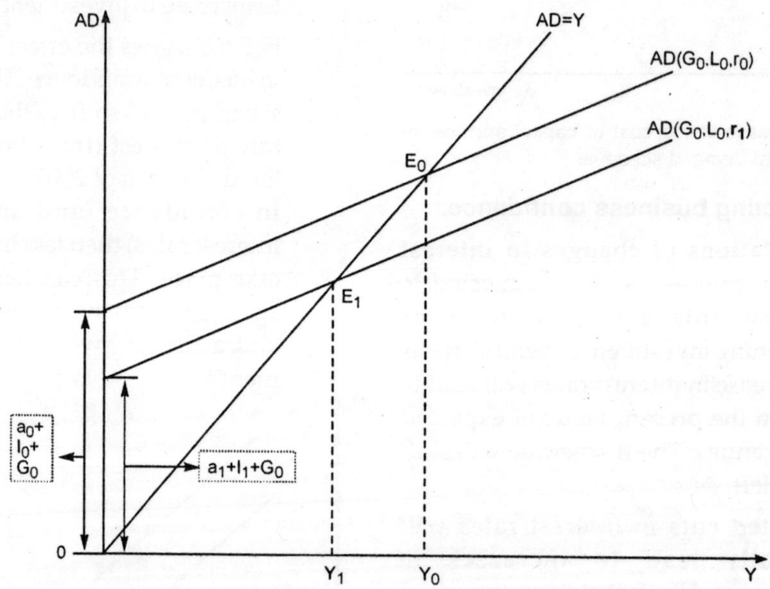

Fig. 6.7: An increase in the rate of interest and the aggregate demand schedule

YOU SHOULD REMEMBER

Although real consumption and investment expenditure are affected by several factors we will identify the rate of interest as the most important determinant of both real consumption and investment expenditure.

A change in the rate of interest and the level of real aggregate demand.

In Fig. 6.7 below, $AD(G_0,L_0,r_0)$ represents the level of real aggregate demand in an economy when the level of government expenditure is G_0, the real stock of money is L_0, and the rate of interest is r_0. The initial intercept is made up of a level of real autonomous consumption (a_0), initial real investment (I_0) and real government expenditure (G_0) (assume net exports are zero). The initial equilibrium position (E_0) is at the intersection of $AD(G_0,L_0,r_0)$ and AD=Y. Income/output is Y_0.

If interest rates are increased from, say, ro to r_1 then the price and value of bonds (Bd) will fall. Since bonds are part of the wealth of consumers their wealth falls. This encourages consumers to save more. Their real autonomous consumption expenditure will decrease.

The rise in the rate of interest will decrease both real autonomous consumption (the cost of borrowing rising) and real investment expenditure (the present value of expected net revenues decreasing).

Real autonomous consumption expenditure will fall (from ao to a_1) and real investment will fall (from $I_0$to I_1). $AD(G_0,L_0,r_0)$ will shift downwards to $AD(G_0,L_0,r_1)$ and bring about falls in induced consumption expenditure. Real income/output will fall to Y_1 from Y_0(point E_1).

APPENDIX I

The IS Curve

DEFINITION: The IS curve shows the relationship between the rate of interest and the level of real income/output in the goods market when the goods market is in equilibrium. Although the IS curve gives us no more information than the AD/Y diagram it will be useful in later analysis. Hence its derivation.

The derivation of the IS Curve

Fig. 6.8(a) shows the usual AD/Y diagram and figure 6.8(b) the space in which the IS curve will be constructed.

If we start at $AD(G_0,L_0,r_0)$ in Fig. 6.8(a) then the initial equilibrium level of real income/output is Y_0.

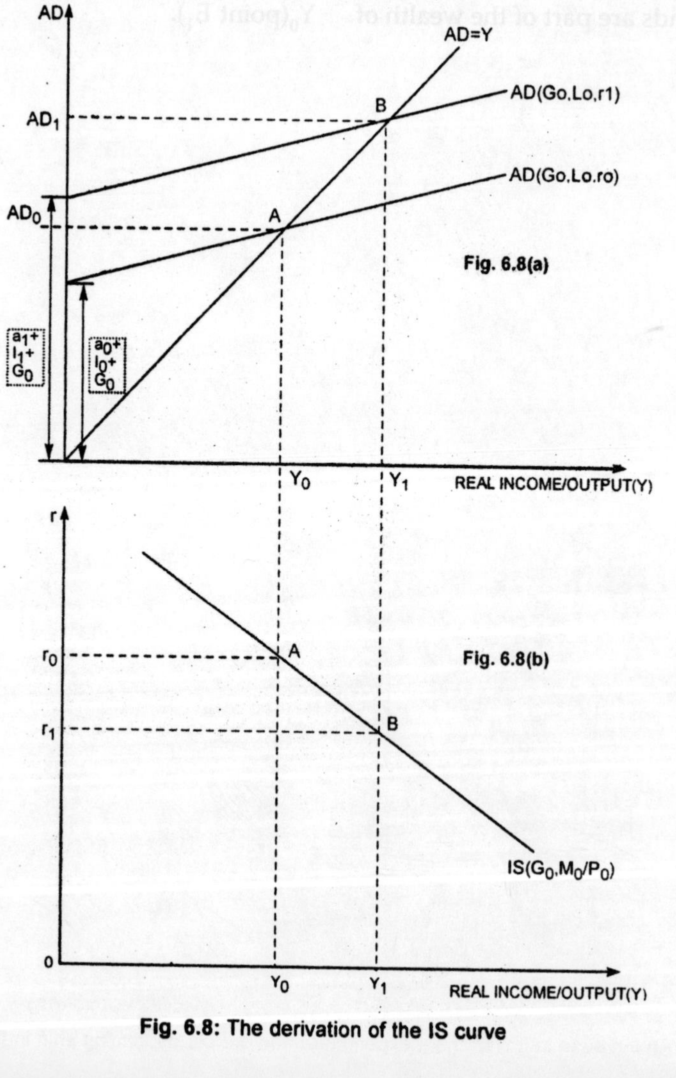

Fig. 6.8: The derivation of the IS curve

Since we have set the rate of interest to be ro we can mark that off on the vertical axis of Fig. 6.8(b) and, by marking off Y_0 on the horizontal axis, we can obtain a point (point 'A') on Fig. 6.8(b) at r_0, Y_0.

If the interest rate is now reduced to r_1 the level of aggregate demand will increase to $AD(G_0,L_0,r_1)$ and the new equilibrium level of output increases to Y_1.

We now have another point (point 'B') on Fig. 6.8(b) at r_1, Y_1.

For each rate of interest there will be a unique level of real income/output. Joining up these points will give us the IS curve, $IS(G_0,M_0/P_0)$—the IS curve drawn for the level of government expenditure equal G_0 and the real stock of money equal to M_0/P_0.

The IS curve will be shifted if government expenditure (G), the real stock of money (L_0 [$=M_0/P_0$]), autonomous consumption ('a'), investment (I), or net exports (NX) change.

Figs. 6.9(a) and 6.9(b) show the effect of an increase in government expenditure on the IS curve. Note: There would also be a similar rightward shift if the real stock of money ($L_0[=M_0/P_0]$), autonomous consumption ('a'), investment (I), or net exports (NX) increase.

An Increase in Government Expenditure and the IS Curve

If we start at $AD(G_0,L_0,r_0)$, Yo in figure 6.9(a) and r_0, Y_0 in figure 6.9(b). Then, by changing the rate of interest, we can derive the IS curve $IS(G_0,M_0/P_0)$ as in Figs. 6.8(a) and 6.8(b) above.

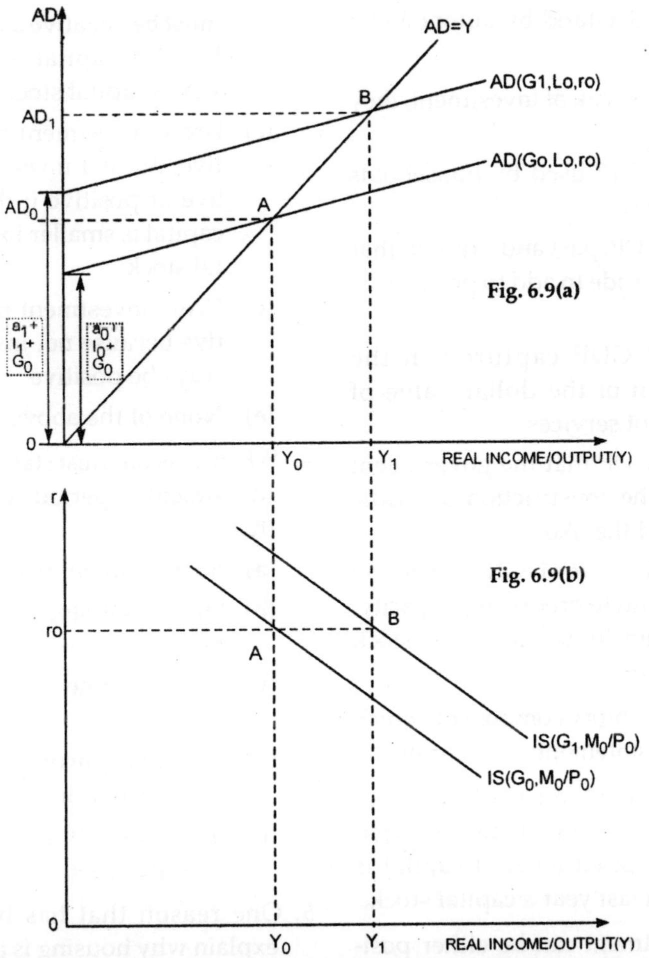

Fig. 6.9: An increase in government expenditure and the corresponding shift in the IS Curve

If we now increase government expenditure from G_0 to G_1 then AD(G_0,L_0,r_0) will shift upwards to AD(G_1,L_0,r_0) and equilibrium

In Fig. 6.9(b) output will increase to Y_1 at interest rate r_0 (point B).

If we now change the rate of interest we can trace out a new IS curve, IS(G_1,M_0/P_0) in Fig. 6.9(b).

The increase [decrease] in government expenditure will shift the IS curve to the right [left].

Note: There would also be a similar rightward shift if the real stock of money (L_0 [$=M_0/P_0$]), autonomous consumption ('a'), investment (I), or net exports (NX) increase.

QUESTIONS

1. What do you understand by autonomous consumption?
2. When economists speak of investment, they are speaking of
   (a) the part of GDP used by households for current use.
   (b) the part of GDP, past and present, that has been set aside to add to productive capacity.
   (c) the part of GDP captured in the computation of the dollar value of goods but not services.
   (d) the part of GDP that the government devotes to the construction of roads, airports, and the like.
   (e) the part of current GDP used by business to add to productive capacity, and by households to add to their stock of new houses.
3. Excluding the inventory component, which of the following statements is accurate?
   (a) Gross investment must be non-negative, but net investment must be negative if the desired level of capital is smaller than last year's capital stock.
   (b) Gross investment can be either positive or negative, but net investment must be negative as long as the desired level of capital is smaller than last year's capital stock.
   (c) Gross investment must be non-negative, but net investment can be negative or positive if the desired level of capital is smaller than last year's capital stock
   (d) Gross investment must be non-negative because net invest-ment must always be positive
   (e) None of the above.
4. When an economist states that Net National Investment in period A was zero, it means that
   (a) no investment was made in period A;
   (b) the capital stock was maintained intact;
   (c) new investment exceed capital depreciation;
   (d) new investment was significantly less than capital depreciation;
   (e) the productivity of the capital stock was increased.
5. One reason that has been proposed to explain why housing is a leading indicator of economic activity is that

(a) the demand for housing depends upon real GDP, and declines in real GDP always precede the onset of recession;

(b) the demand for housing depends upon the real interest rate, and real interest rates generally climb as economies begin to turn down into recession;

(c) the demand for housing depends at least indirectly on the prices of construction materials, and those prices always accelerate during the inflationary booms that precede re-cessions;

(d) the demand for housing depends critically upon nominal GNP, which always falls during the inflation that precedes recession;

(e) the demand for housing is affected by changes in real GNP abroad - one harbinger of changes in domestic activity.

6. Of the three major components of investment,

(a) non-residential fixed investment dominates, but inventory volatility gives inventory a primary role in driving the business cycle;

(b) residential fixed investment dominates and therefore plays a primary role in driving the business cycle;

(c) inventory holdings dominate, but the volatility of non-residential fixed investment is a primary source of business cycle fluctuation in GDP;

(d) only residential fixed investment depends on real GDP and thus has anything to do with the business cycle;

(e) None of the above.

7. 'An increase in the price of houses means that people who buy houses have to spend more on housing costs and have less to spend on other items. Therefore a rise in house prices leads to a fall in aggregate demand.' True or false?

8. Investment is generally sensitive to changes in the real interest rate because

(a) all three of the components of investment are sensitive to the interest rate;

(b) nonresidential investment increases as the interest rate climbs because the higher rental price of capital inspires substitution into the relatively less expensive employment of labor;

(c) residential investment increases as the interest rate climbs because the interest rate is a major component of the rental price of housing;

(d) inventories climb as the interest rate climbs because the interest rate is a major component of the holding cost of inventories;

(e) investor's expectations are irrationally linked to price inflation and thus to the real interest rate.

ANSWERS

1. Autonomous consumption is the part of consumption expenditure that is *not* affected by income. It is consumption affected by wealth, interest rates and consumer confidence.

2. (e) This is a question of definition. When economists speak of invest-ment, they are talking about activity that adds the capital stock of an economy-additions to the economy's stock of (new) housing, factories, equipment, and inventories. It is generally not for current use, but it is a current flow of new assets that add to productive capacity.

3. (c) Net investment equals gross investment (total expenditure on capital) minus depreciation. Total expenditure

can be, at worst, zero, so gross investment must be nonnegative. Net investment can, however, be either positive or negative or zero depending upon whether gross investment is larger, smaller, or equal to depreciation.

4. (b) Zero net investment means that new investment less depreciation is zero, and that the capital stock remains intact. Incidentally, this is not easily measured because the capital stock is valued at original cost.

5. (b) Increases in real interest rates are, as a matter of record, closely associated with downward turns in economic activity. Major compo-nents of aggregate demand, mostly captured within investment through inventories and housing, are strongly and negatively corre-lated with changes in the real interest rate. Higher real rates, therefore, work to reduce aggregate demand (shift the IS curve in) and slow the growth of real GDP. The workings of interest rates in housing demand are not mysterious. Most people borrow to purchase housing. When interest rates climb, the monthly cost of carrying a mortgage climbs, and the amount of money that people can comfortably borrow falls. They buy cheaper houses or no houses at all.

6. (a) Investment has three major components: residential fixed investment, nonresidential fixed investment and inventories. Nonresidential investment is the largest of the three in the UK as well as most developed economies, but inventories are the most sensitive to changes in the economic climate. The cost of carrying inventories is the cost of not carrying money (or borrowing money); i.e. it is the real rate of interest. Inventories are therefore extremely sensitive to changes in the interest rate. They are also sensitive to the aggregate demand, because inventories are the first to reflect excess demand or excess supply. A turn to recession, foretold as usual by an upturn in real interest rates, causes inventories to increase just when they are most expensive. It is no surprise that a quick production response (a contraction) is usually observed.

7. False. The number of people buying houses is small in relation to the overall size of the housing stock. An increase in house prices will lead to an increase in the value of the housing stock. This will increase the wealth of people. When wealth increases people tend to save less and consume more. The economy's average propensity to consume, autonomous consumption and aggregate demand will increase.

8. (a) All three components of investment are sensitive to different degrees and significance, to changes in the interest rate. The reasons provided in answers (b), (c), and (d) are the opposite; irrationality is not required to explain the sensitivity.

CHAPTER 7

FISCAL AND MONETARY POLICY IN A CLOSED ECONOMY

KEY TERMS

Crowding Out: An increase in government expenditure with the supply of money held constant will lead to crowding out.

Liquidity Trap: The liquidity trap occurs when the demand for money becomes perfectly interest elastic at a very low interest rate.

Pigou Effect or Real balance effect: With a general deflation of wages and prices, *ceteris paribus*, will ten to increase the real value of people's holding of money above their desired levels. Hence, they reduce their saving and increase their consumption in an attempt to reduce their saving and increase their consumption in an attempt to reduce their real balances. If there is unemployment in the economy, this will increase equilibrium level of income and employment.

Any change in government expenditure, taxa-tion (direct or indirect) or benefits will shift the aggregate demand schedule and hence the IS curve. Changes in the real stock of money (L = M/P) will, because of the real balance effect, also change the position of the IS curve and, as we have seen, the position of the LM curve. (Government expenditure, the rates of taxation, the benefit rates and the nominal supply of money are known as exogenous variables). Both fiscal and monetary policy affect the economy by changing aggregate demand. If aggregate demand increases [decreases] then output/income increases [decreases].

Fiscal Policy in a Closed Economy

1. **An increase in government expenditure when the economy is below full employment (there is some involuntary unemployment).**

   a. Consider Fig. 7.1. Start at an initial equilibrium position: $IS(G_0, M_0/P_0)$, $LM(M_0/P_0)$, Y_0, r_0. Income (Y_0) and the rate of interest (r_0) are simultaneously

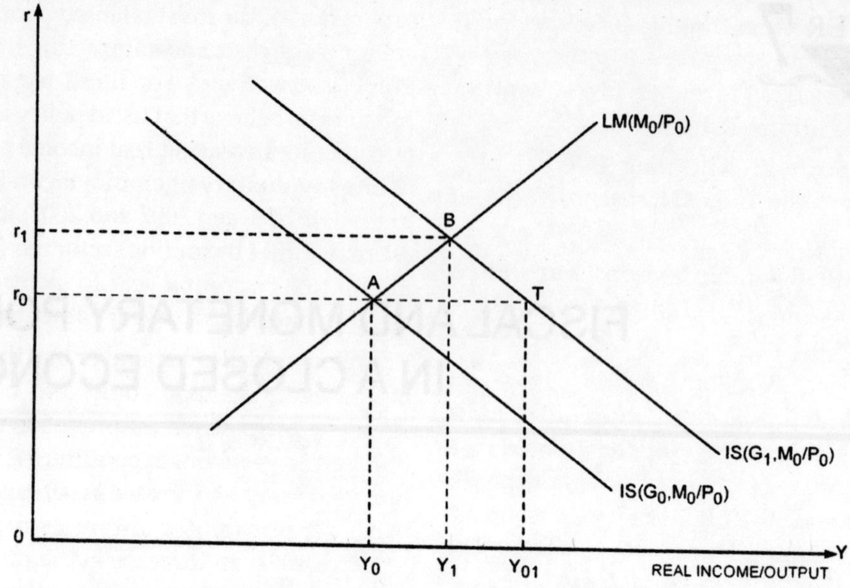

Fig. 7.1: An increase in government expenditure. No change in the supply of money

determined by the intersection of the IS and LM curves. They are determined within the model; they are **endogenous** variables. Any exogenous variable that changes the position of either the IS curve (government expenditure, taxation or the real stock of money) or the LM curve (the real stock of money) will change both real income/output (Y_0) and the rate of interest (r_0). The rate of interest is determined by the position of both the LM and IS curves – by monetary (M and M/P) and real factors (C, I, G, Td and Te). The rate of interest is not just determined by monetary factors.

b. If government expenditure (G) increases then $IS(G_0,M_0/P_0)$ initially increases to $IS(G_1,M_0/P_0)$. *Ceteris paribus*, real income/output would increase from Y_0 to Y_{01}.

G is assumed to be financed by selling bonds so there is no change in the supply of money. It will however increase any budget deficit. (It has been estimated that every one percentage point increase in the budget deficit's share of GDP will increase bond market rates by 0.66%).

c. There is, however, an effect in the monetary sector of the economy. The increase in income will increase the demand for money for transactions and precautionary balances. At r_0 there will be an excess demand for money which is equivalent to an excess supply of bonds. The price of bonds will fall and the rate of interest will increase.

This fall in bond prices and rise in the rate of interest will reduce aggregate demand because;

i. The wealth of consumers falls when bond prices fall. People save more and consume less out of a given income (to rebuild their stock of wealth). Autonomous consumption and the APC both decline.

ii. The cost of borrowing has increased which will also reduce autonomous consumption expenditure. This also decreases the APC of an economy.

iii. The rise in the rate of interest will reduce the present value of expected net revenues. Investment expenditure will fall.

Output will fall along $IS(G_1,M_0/P_0)$ (from point T) until it reaches Y_1 (point B).

d. The final equilibrium position will be at $IS(G_1,M_0/P_0)$, $LM(M_0/P_0)$, r_1, Y_1 – point B.

The fall in income from Y_{01} to Y_1 is **'crowded out'** by the rise in the interest rate. It has also been estimated that a 1% change in the rate of interest will lead to a £10 billion change in income/output per annum.

The increase in government expenditure, with a constant supply of money, has led to an increase in the rate of interest rate and a fall in consumption and investment expenditure.

The degree to which interest rates increase and the amount of 'crowding out' is a matter of argument between economists. The more 'right wing' economists believe that Y_0 to Y_1 is small or zero. (Y_{01} to Y_1 is large). It can also be argued that the state can absorb too large a proportion of the most talented people, pushing up wage costs and subtracting from entrepreneurial activity. For these reasons some economists believe that fiscal policy is not very effective in increasing real income and eliminating involuntary unemployment. However, in the UK between 2002 and 2007, it has been estimated that the public sector has been adding up to 1 per cent a year to increases in UK income/output (3% a year rather than 2%).

We should also remember that the increase in aggregate demand could also be brought about by increases in autonomous consumption ('a'), investment expenditure (I), or, in an open economy, an increase in net exports (NX). With an unchanged money supply there would also be an increase in the rate of interest.

2. **An increase in the level of government expenditure at a below full employment situation and the supply of money is increased sufficient to prevent an increase in the interest rate.**

   a. Consider Fig. 7.2. Start at an initial equilibrium position: $IS(G_0,M_0/P_0)$, $LM(M_0/P_0)$, Y_0, r_0. Increase government expenditure and the nominal

YOU SHOULD REMEMBER

1. With an unchanged supply of money interest rates will increase when aggregate demand and the real income/output of an economy are increasing.
2. An increase in government expenditure with the supply of money held constant will lead to 'crowding out'

   The degree to which 'crowding out' occurs depends upon two main factors:

   (a) The responsiveness of the rate of interest to an increase in the demand for money.

   If a small change in income leads to a large increase in the rate of interest then this is likely to lead to a large fall in aggregate demand and income. (The demand for money schedule is relatively steep). If this is the case then Y_1 to Y_{01} is likely to large.

   (b) The responsiveness of consumption and investment expenditure to changes in the rate of interest.

   If the interest elasticity of investment and consumption are large then small changes in the rate of interest will lead to relatively large changes in consumption and investment expenditure. If this is the case then Y_1 to Y_{01} is not likely to be small.

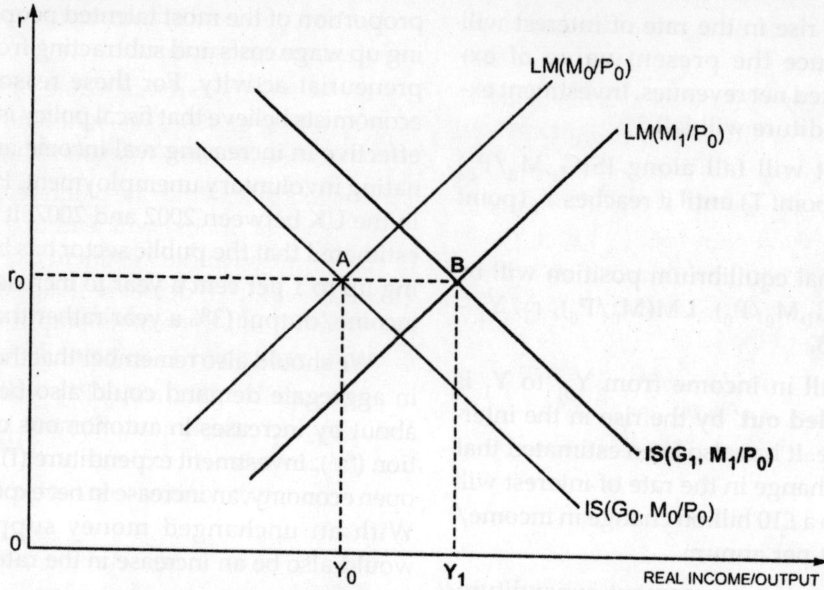

Fig. 7.2: An increase in government expenditure. The money supply being increased to prevent the interest rate rising

stock of money sufficient to prevent an increase in the rate of interest.

We have seen, above, that an increase in government expenditure with a constant supply of money will lead to an increase in the rate of interest.

If the monetary authorities do not wish for an increase in the rate of interest they can allow the money supply to increase sufficiently to maintain the rate of interest at r_0. The LM curve shifts from LM(M_0/P_0) to LM(M_1/P_0). The upward pressure on the interest rate will be offset by the increase in the nominal money supply from M_0 to M_1 (and the real money supply from $L_0=M_0/P_0$) to $L_1=M_1/P_0$).

The final equilibrium position will be at LM(M_1/P_0), IS(G_1,M_1/P_0)(note that the IS curve will be partially shifted to the right by the right by the real balance effect). Output will be Y_1 and the rate of interest will be unchanged at r_0.

There will be no 'crowding out' as there has been no change in the interest rate.

3. An increase in government expenditure at full employment.

a. Consider Fig. 7.3. Start at an initial equilibrium position: IS(G_0,M_0/P_0), LM(M_0/P_0), Y_f, r_0 – point A.

b. Increase government expenditure.

At all levels of income there will be an increase in aggregate demand. IS(G_0,M_0/P_0) will shift to the right to IS(G_1,M_0/P_0). If the

YOU SHOULD REMEMBER

1. Increasing the supply of money at the same time as increasing government expenditure leads to large increases aggregate demand and in real income/output.
2. Increasing the money supply may lead to inflation.
3. Also, research by the think-tank Open Europe shows that a cut of 10-points of GDP in public spending increases the annual rate of economic growth by one full percentage point. This means that after eight years, more money is available to be spent on public services than would have otherwise been the case.

economy were not at Y_f output would, initially, increase to T_0.

But, since aggregate demand is now greater than full employment output (Y_f), prices will start to rise.

As long as aggregate demand is greater than full employment output (Y_f) then prices will be increasing and the real stock of money will be falling. $IS(G_1,M_0/P_0)$ and $LM(M_0/P_0)$ will be shifting to the left.

Autonomous consumption will fall because of the real balance effect [wealth (Wh) falls]. This decrease in wealth, brought about by decrease in the real stock of money, will shift $IS(G_1,M_0/P_0)$ to the left to, say, $IS(G_1,M_0/P_1)$ – from point T_0 to point T_1.

Also, at r_0, there will be an excess demand for money, which is equivalent to an excess supply of bonds. The price of bonds will fall which is equivalent to a rise in the rate of interest.

The fall in the price of bonds will reduce autonomous consumption expenditure (wealth falls)

The rise in the rate of interest will

i. increase the cost of borrowing and lead to a decrease in autonomous consumption expenditure.

ii. reduce the present value of expected net revenues. This will lead to a decrease investment expenditure.

The increase in the rate of interest (and fall in the price of bonds) will lead to a decrease in consumption and investment expenditure. This will lead to a decrease in aggregate demand and a fall in income/output along the IS curve from point T_1 to point B.

Eventually, $IS(G_1,M_0/P_0)$ will shift to $IS(G_1,M_0/P_1)$ and $LM(M_0/P_0)$ to $LM(M_0/P_1)$. The interest rate will increase to r1. There will be no change in real income/output and employment.

The increase in government expenditure has led to a decrease in the real stock of money and a rise in the rate of interest. This reduction in the real stock of money and increase in the rate of interest has reduced consumption and investment expenditure by exactly the amount of the increase in government expenditure. There has been 100% 'crowding out'.

4. A decrease in the level of government expenditure at full (or below full) employment

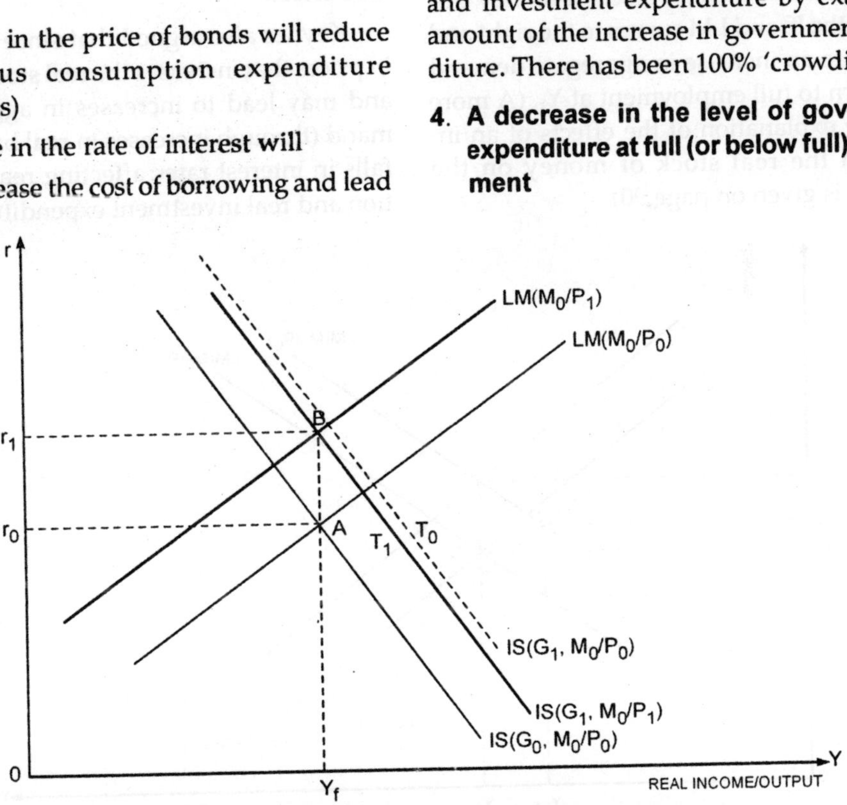

Fig. 7.3: An increase in government expenditure at full employment

a. Consider Fig. 7.4. Start at an initial equilibrium position: $IS(G_0,M_0/P_0)$, $LM(M_0/P_0)$, Y_f, r_0.

b. Decrease government expenditure from G_0 to G_1.

Aggregate demand will fall - $IS(G_0,M_0/P_0)$ will shift to the left to $IS(G_1,M_0/P_0)$. A new, temporary, equilibrium will be established at ro1, Yo1, $IS(G_1,M_0/P_0)$, $LM(M_0/P_0)$ – point To. There will be a lower budget deficit, a lower interest rate and an increase in (involuntary) unemployment. It has been estimated that every one percentage point reduction in the budget deficit's share of GDP will reduce bond market rates by 0.66%.

We will now slightly modify our assumptions and assume that **the involuntary unemployment brings about a fall in money wages and prices** (deflation).

Assuming that wage and price falls lead to an increase in the real stock of money this will shift the IS and LM curves to the right and will lead to an increase in aggregate demand and return to full employment at Y_f. (A more extensive explanation of the effects of an increase in the real stock of money on the economy is given on page 90).

The fall in government expenditure would have been fully been replaced by an increase in consumption and investment expenditure. Resources have been transferred from the public sector (the government) to the private sector (consumption, investment, exports and import substitutes). If resources are more efficiently allocated by the private sector then the overall productivity of the economy will increase.

There would also be the beneficial effect of downward pressure on nominal wages and the price level.

However, as J.M. Keynes pointed out, not only are cuts in money wages and prices very difficult to implement but they may not be effective in restoring full employment. Even if they are effective it may take many years (with long periods of high unemployment and low output) for the requisite price adjustments to take effect.

Keynes also argued that since it is the fall in prices that increases the real stock of money and may lead to increases in aggregate demand (through increases in real balances and falls in interest rates affecting real consumption and real investment expenditures) a sim-

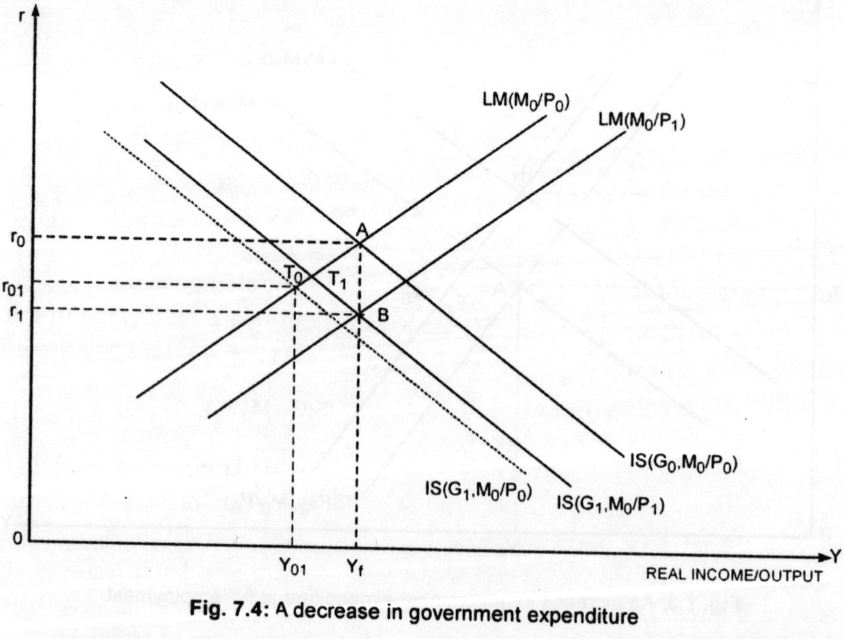

Fig. 7.4: A decrease in government expenditure

pler method of eliminating any involuntary unemployment is to increase the nominal supply of money with a constant price level the real stock will increase (though, in inflationary times, this may be difficult to implement).

It can also be argued that falling prices (deflation) will not lead to the establishment of an equilibrium but may destabilise a free market economy. Indeed, the new chairman of the Federal Reserve, B Bernanke, was so worried about deflation in the USA that he pressed for a cut in the short term interest rate right down to 1% in June 2003 (where it remained until to June 2004).

1. Falling wages and prices may not lead the rate of interest falling sufficiently for full employment to be attained. The rate of interest may reach a level so that everyone expects interest rates only to rise (bond prices to fall). Any extra real money balances will only be held and not exchanged for bonds (the liquidity trap). There will be no further fall in the rate of interest and hence no further change in real consumption or real investment expenditure. Unless the government increases its expenditure the economy may remain below full employment. Wages and price will fall indefinitely.
2. Real investment and real consumption expenditure may not respond sufficiently to falls in the rate of interest so that aggregate demand remains below its full employment level.

   i.e. Real investment and real consumption are interest inelastic.
3. Falls in the price level may increase the real rate of interest. (Remember, the percentage real rate of interest is equal to the percentage nominal rate of interest less [plus] any percentage increase [decrease] in the price level). An increase in the real rate of interest will reduce real consumption and real investment expenditure and hence aggregate demand.
4. Falls in the price level may lead to people thinking that prices may fall further. This may lead to the postponement of real consumption and/or real investment expenditure. There will be no increase in aggregate demand.
5. Falling prices lead to debts denominated in money terms increasing.
   a. This may lead more bankruptcies and to less borrowing by firms and less lending by the banking system (banks consider the prospective returns from lending as not being enough to compensate for the risks involved). This can lead to less investment.
   b. The real value of the National Debt will increase. This may result in taxation being increased which could undermine business confidence leading to less investment.
6. Falling asset prices (shares and futures and options based on them) reduce the value of collateral for bank loans, inducing weakened banks to engage in a fire sale of their loans and securities, leading to further asset price deflation.
7. We are also assuming that the nominal stock of money remains constant! If the money supply is **endogenous** then the nominal supply of money may fall along with the price level. There may be no change in the real stock of money and hence no change in the rate of interest or any real balance effect.
8. Falling prices will destroy jobs, damage growth and harm real investment.
   a. A falling price level will increase the risk associated with any assessment of future returns on an investment project. i.e. it reduces net revenues and hence real investment and the creation of new jobs.

b. A falling price level will make it difficult to distinguish between changes in *relative* price from changes in the *general* price level. As a result workers and employers find it more difficult to determine whether the decrease in their wage or product price is due to a fall in demand for their labour or product (and less should be produced and/or supplied) or whether it is due to a general fall in prices (and no more should be produced and/or supplied). Confusing the two can lead to a misallocation of resources.

c. A falling price level will force people to constantly relearn prices. It helps to destroy the information conveyed by relative prices.

9. It harms long-term contracts denominated in money terms. For example, people who bought long-term bonds that pay them a fixed amount each year will find that falling prices increase the real value of their returns. Of course, people who entered into long-term contracts that required them to pay a fixed amount each year will find that the real value of their payments will be increasing.

For the above reasons it can be argued that a fall in the price level will not lead to an increase in aggregate demand and hence no increase in income/output.

Post Keynesian economists argue that, in the real world, wages are inflexible downwards and it is this inflexibility that gives stability to a free market economy. It has also been argued that, the Roman Empires' decline was brought about by deflation.

Monetary Policy in a closed Economy

1. An increase in nominal stock of money at a below full employment initial equilibrium position.

At the beginning of the decade (2000's) former governor of the Bank of England, Sir E. George admitted (to the House of Commons Treasury Committee) stimulating the UK economy by lowering interest rates. This increased the supply of money and aggregate demand (especially consumption expenditure).

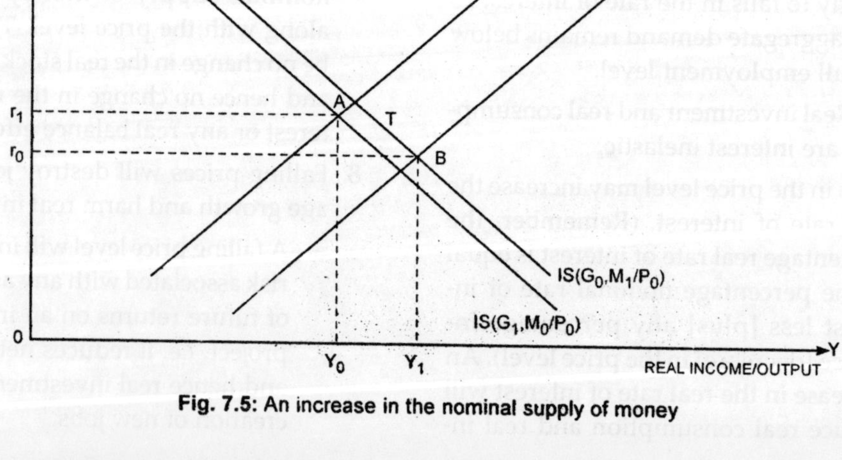

Fig. 7.5: An increase in the nominal supply of money

a. Consider figure 7.5. Start at an initial, below full employment, equilibrium position:

b. Increase the nominal stock of money from M_0 to M_1.

   i. With prices constant there will be an increase in the real stock of money. This will increase the wealth of consumers who will reduce their additions to their stocks of wealth by saving less and increasing their autonomous consumption (the real balance effect). This will shift the IS curve to the right from $IS(G_0,M_0/P_0)$ to $IS(G_0,M_1/P_0)$.

   ii. The increase in the supply of money will shift $LM(M_0/P_0)$ to the right to $LM(M_1/P_0)$. At r_0, there is now an excess supply of money, which is equivalent to an excess demand for bonds. The price of bonds will increase which is equivalent to a fall in the rate of interest.

The increase in the price of bonds will increase consumers' wealth and hence autonomous consumption expenditure.

Also, the fall in the rate of interest will;

Increase autonomous consumption expenditure; (the cost of borrowing has decreased) and,

Increase investment expenditure; (the present value of expected net revenues will increase).

It has been estimated that a 1% change in the rate of interest will lead to a £10 billion change in income/output per annum.

The final equilibrium position is at $IS(G_0,M_1/P_0)$, $LM(M_1/P_0)$, r_1, Y_1. Output and employment have increased and there has been a fall in involuntary unemployment (the increase in output is made up of a move from point A to point T due to the real balance effect and a movement from point T to point B due to the fall in the rate of interest and an increase in the price of bonds).

2. **An increase in the stock of money at full employment ($Y = Y_f$).**

   a. Consider figure 7.6. Start at an initial, full employment, equilibrium position: $IS(G_0,M_0/P_0)$, $LM(M_0/P_0)$, Y_f, r_0.

   Note: there is no involuntary unemployment but some voluntary unemployment.

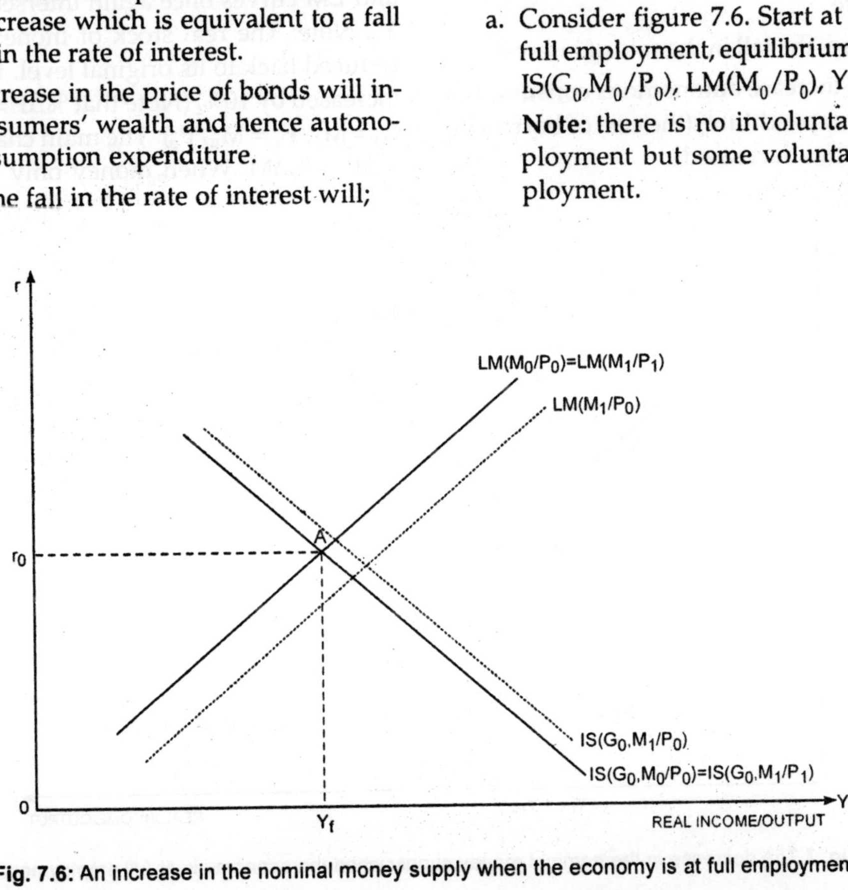

Fig. 7.6: An increase in the nominal money supply when the economy is at full employment

b. Increase the nominal stock of money (M_0) (say by 10%). With prices (P_0) constant the real stock of money L_0 ($=M_0/P_0$) will increase to $L_1(=M_1/P_0)$ (by 10%). Both the IS curve and the LM curve will shift to the right.

The increase in the real stock of money will increase the level of autonomous consumption expenditure (the real balance effect). This will shift the IS curve to the right.

At all levels of the interest rate there is now an excess supply of money which is equivalent to an excess demand for bonds. The price of bonds will increase which is equivalent to a fall in the rate of interest.

The increase in the price of bonds will increase consumers' wealth and hence autonomous consumption expenditure.

Also, the fall in the rate of interest will;

i. Increase autonomous consumption expenditure; (the cost of borrowing has decreased).

ii. Increase investment expenditure; (the present value of expected net revenues will increase).

The increase in autonomous consumption and investment expenditure will shift $IS(G_0,M_0/P_0)$ to $IS(G_0,M_1/P_0)$ and $LM(M_0/P_0)$ to $LM(M_1/P_0)$. Effectively the level of aggregate demand is greater than Y_f.

c. Since the economy is at a full employment position the price level will increase.

This will reduce the real stock of money. ($L_1 = M_1/P_0$). The reverse of (b) will occur.

As long as aggregate demand is greater than Y_f then prices will rise. This will reduce ggregate demand. Prices will continue to rise until aggregate demand is back equal to full employment income (Y_f); that is until the IS and LM curves once again intersect at r_0 and Y_0. Note: The real stock of money has been reduced back to its original level. Prices have increased by 10%. (Note that $\%\Delta P = \%\Delta M$ and $L_0 = M_1/P_1 = M_0/P_0$). The main change is that $\%\Delta P = \%\Delta M$. When money only affects the

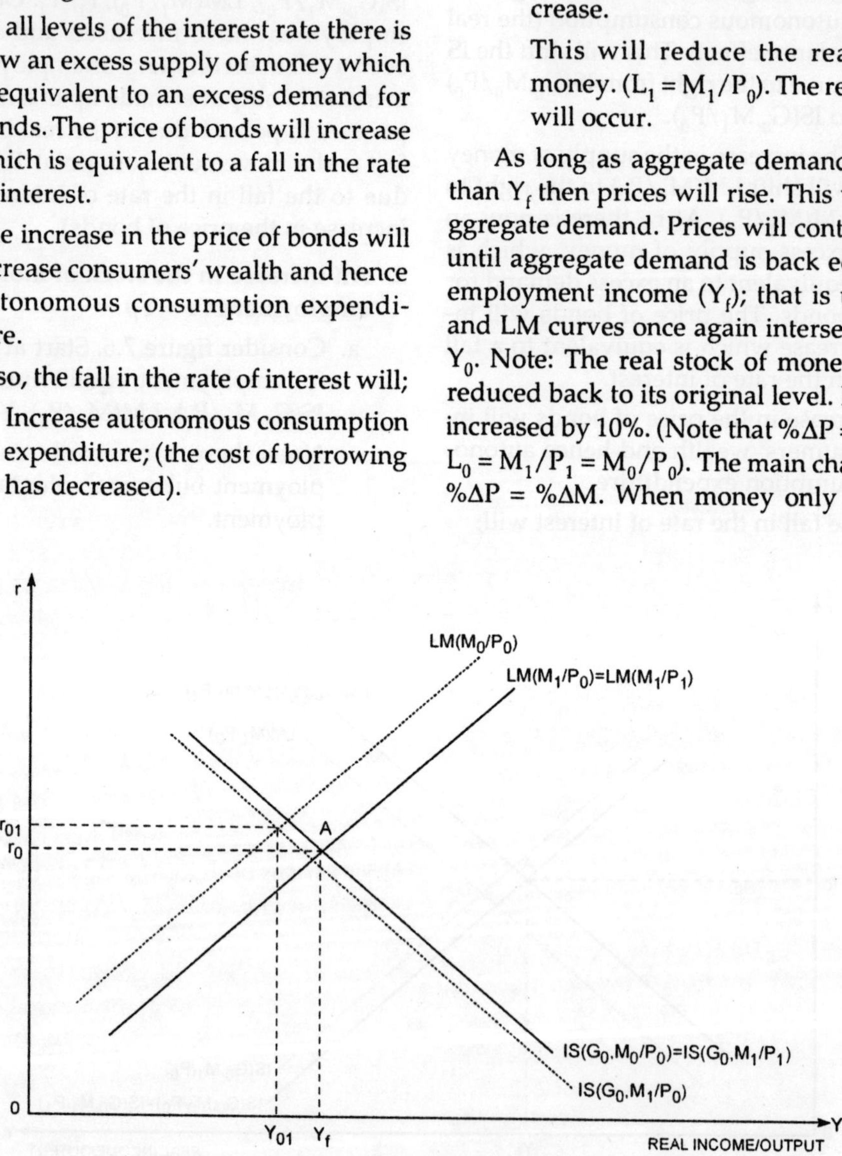

Fig. 7.7: A decrease in the nominal money supply when the economy is at full employment

price level it is said to be neutral. In this case it has no effect on real magnitudes (real income/output and employment). This analysis is behind the idea of what is known as the Quantity Theory of Money. See chapter 9.

3. **A decrease in the nominal stock of money at full employment.**
   a. Consider Fig. 7.7. Start at an initial equilibrium position: $IS(G_0, M_0/P_0)$, $LM(M_0/P_0)$, Y_f, r_0. Note: There is no involuntary unemployment but some voluntary unemployment.
   b. Decrease the nominal stock of money (M_0), say by 5%, to M_1. Both the IS and LM curves will shift to the left.

At r_0 there is now an excess demand for money and an excess supply of bonds. The price of bonds will fall and the interest rate will increase. Aggregate demand will fall and real income/output will fall to Y_{01}.

A new, temporary, equilibrium position will be at $IS(G_0, M_1/P_0)$, $LM(M_1/P_0)$, r_{01}, Y_{01}.

There will be an increase in (involuntary) unemployment.

Assume, as we did above, that the involuntary unemployment brings about a fall in money wages and prices. Theoretically, this will return the economy to full employment.

Note: $L_0 = M_1/P_1 = M_0/P_0$. The price fall of 5% has returned the economy back to full employment real income/output. The cut in the money supply has put downward pressure on the price level, but has not permanently changed the amount of involuntary unemployment.

The Derivation of the Aggregate Demand (Price) Schedule (ADp)

In this section we are going to derive three relationships between the aggregate price level (P) and the level of income/output (Y). The first thing to note is that we will call it the ADp schedule to distinguish it from the AD schedule (the relationship between AD and Y) derived in chapter 3. Once the ADp schedules are constructed we will combine them with two aggregate supply schedules (a long-run and a short run) to determine the aggregate price level and the level of output/income.

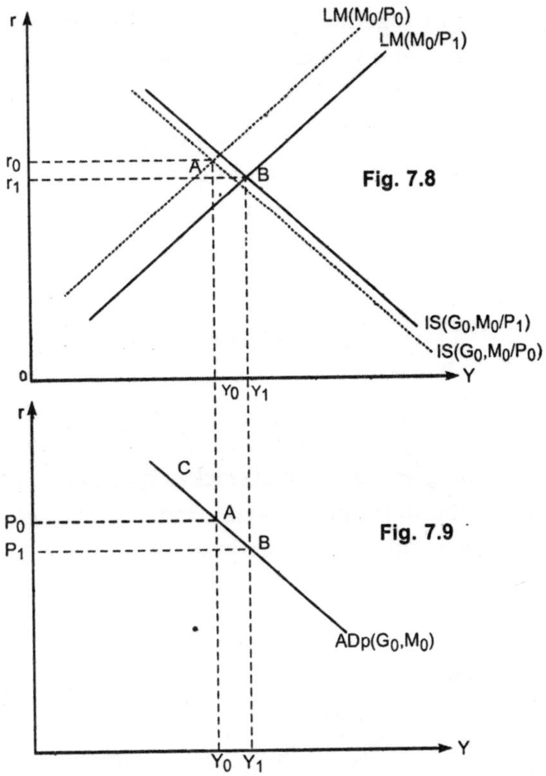

Fig. 7.8 and 7.9: The derivation of the ADp schedule

Consider Figs. 7.8 and 7.9. Start at an initial equilibrium position $IS(M_0/P_0)$, $LM(M_0/P_0)$, r_0. Point A in Fig. 7.8. P_0, Y_0 defines point A in Fig. 7.9.

Reduce the price level to P_1. The real stock of money increases from M_0/P_0 to M_0/P_1. *ceteris paribus* both $IS(M_0/P_0)$ and $LM(M_0/P_0)$ shift to the right to $IS(M_0/P_1)$ and $LM(M_0/P_1)$ respectively. The rise in real balances increases aggregate demand and output to, say, Y_1. This takes the economy to point B in Fig. 7.8.

In Fig. 7.9, the lower diagram, we can now mark off a point B corresponding to price level P_1 and output Y_1. In a similar way we can increase the price level. This will give us a point like C in Fig. 7.9.

Joining together the locus of points derived from different values of P will give the ADp schedule shown in Fig. 7.9.

We can now mark off a point 'B' on the lower diagram corresponding to price level P_1 and output Y_1. We will assume that the new equilibrium position is at 'B' the intersection of $IS(M_0/P_1)$

DEFINITION: The aggregate demand (price) schedule ($ADp(G_0,M_0)$ shows the relationship between the price level and the level of output, given a level of government expenditure (G_0) and a nominal stock of money (M_0), when the **both** the financial (money) market and the goods market are in equilibrium.

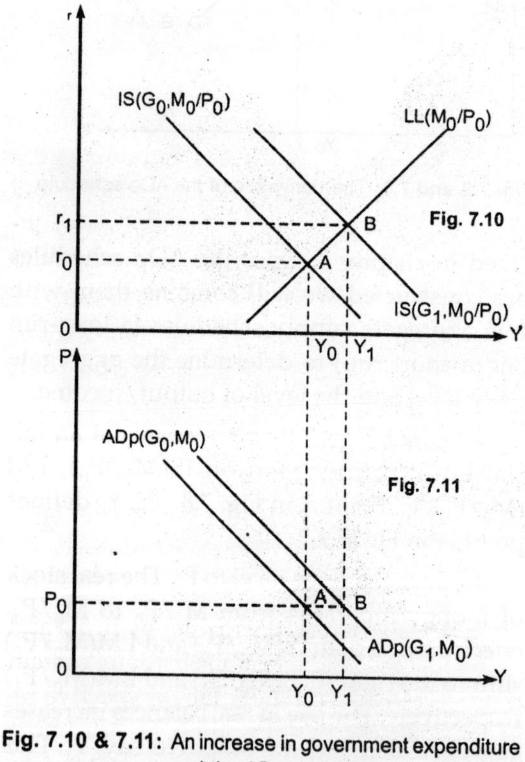

Fig. 7.10 & 7.11: An increase in government expenditure and the ADp schedule

Shifts in the IS or LM Curves and The ADp Schedule

1. Consider Figs. 7.10 and 7.11. Start at an initial equilibrium position (point A) $IS(G_0,M_0/P_0)$, $LM(M_0/P_0)$, r_0, P_0, Y_0 in Fig. 7.10. P_0, Y_0 defines point A in Fig. 7.11. If we imagine the price level changing we can derive $ADp(G_0,M_0)$.
2. If we now increase the level of government expenditure the IS curve will shift to the right and a new equilibrium will be established at point 'B' the intersection of $IS(G_0,M_0/P_0)$ and $LM(M_0/P_0)$. Point B in Fig. 7.11 will be at the intersection of P_0 and Y_1. If we again imagine the price level changing we can derive $ADp(G_1,M_0)$ which is to the right of and parallel to, $ADp(G_0,M_0)$.

The Post-Keynesian Aggregate Demand Schedule (assuming flexible wages and prices).

Consider Fig. 7.12. Start at an initial equilibrium position P_0, Y_0 that defines point A in

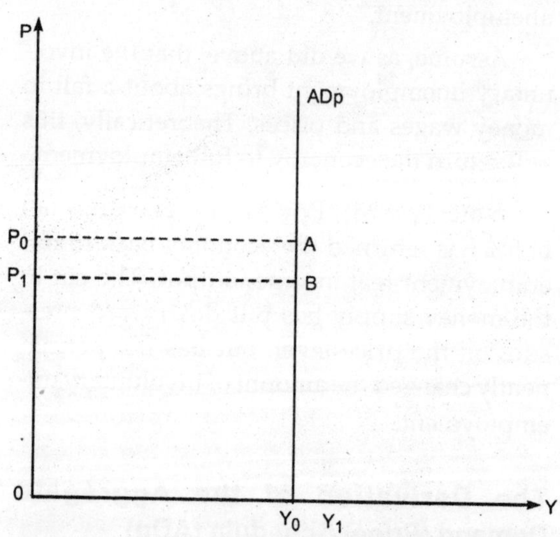

Fig. 7.12: A vertical aggregate demand (price) schedule

YOU SHOULD REMEMBER

Any variable that shifts the IS curve **and/or** the LM curve (OTHER THAN THE PRICE LEVEL) will shift the ADp schedule. If the price level changes there will be a movement **along** the ADp schedule.

Fig. 7.12. We will assume that Y_0 is less than full employment output Y_f. Since Y_0 is less than Y_f there exists some involuntary unemployment.

Assume that the involuntary unemployment leads to falls in the money wage and the price level. It can be argued that falling prices will not lead to an increase in aggregate demand and may even destabilise a free market economy.

1. Falling wages and prices may not lead the rate of interest falling sufficiently for full employment to be attained. The rate of interest may reach a level so that everyone expects interest rates only to rise (bond prices to fall). Any extra real money balances will only be held and not exchanged for bonds (this is known as the liquidity trap). There will be no fall in the rate of interest and hence no change in consumption or investment expenditure. Figs. 7.13 and 7.14 illustrate an economy with a liquidity trap.

   Start at $IS(G_0,M_0/P_0)$, $LM(M_0/P_0)$, r_0, Y_0, P_0. We will assume a negligible real balance (Pigou) effect. Why? In the USA, in the great depression, the real value of net private balances **rose** by 46% between 1929 and 1932, but real national income **fell** by 40% (D. Patinkin A.E.R. Sept. 1948).

   The negatively sloped part of the aggregate demand schedule corresponds to falling prices and increasing output.

   If we now assume that the rate of interest will not fall below r_0 (It reaches such a low level that everyone expects the interest rate to rise and bond prices to fall) any extra real money balances entering the economy will be held in speculative balances. This is known as the **liquidity trap**.

   If, when the interest rate reaches ro, the price level falls and the real stock of money increases. $LM(M_0/P_0)$ shifts to the right to $LM(M_0/P_1)$. But, because the extra real money balances are held in speculative balances then there are no bond purchases to increase the price of bonds and lower the rate of interest. Hence there are no wealth effects (ignoring the real balance [Pigou] effect) to increase consumption expenditure and no interest rate falls to increase consumption or investment expenditures. Aggregate demand will not change as the price level falls. It will be vertical at output Y_0.

2. Investment and consumption expenditure may not respond sufficiently to falls in the rate of interest so that aggregate demand remains below its full employment level.

   ie. Investment and consumption are interest inelastic.

3. Falls in the price level may **increase** the real rate of interest. (Remember, the percentage real rate of interest is equal to the percentage nominal rate of interest less [plus] any percentage increase [decrease] in the price level).

4. Falls in the price level may lead to people thinking that prices may fall further. This may lead to the postponement of consumption and/or investment expenditure.

5. Falling prices lead to debts denominated in money terms increasing.

   a. This may lead more bankruptcies and to less borrowing by firms and less lending by the banking system (banks consider the prospective returns from lending as not being enough to compensate for the risks involved). This can lead to less investment.

   b. The real value of the National Debt will increase. This may result in taxation being increased which could undermine business confidence leading to less investment.

6. Falling asset prices (shares and futures and options based on them) reduce the value of collateral for bank loans, inducing weakened banks to engage in a fire sale of their loans and securities, leading to further asset price deflation.

7. We are also assuming that the nominal stock of money remains constant! If the money supply is endogenous then the nominal supply of money may fall along with the price level. There may be no change in the real stock of money and hence no change in the rate of interest or any real balance (Pigou) effect.

8. Falling prices will destroy jobs, damage growth and harm real investment.

   a. A falling price level will increase the risk associated with any assessment of future returns on an investment project. i.e. it reduces net revenues and hence real investment and the creation of new jobs.

   b. A falling price level will make it difficult to distinguish between changes in *relative* price from changes in the *general* price level. As

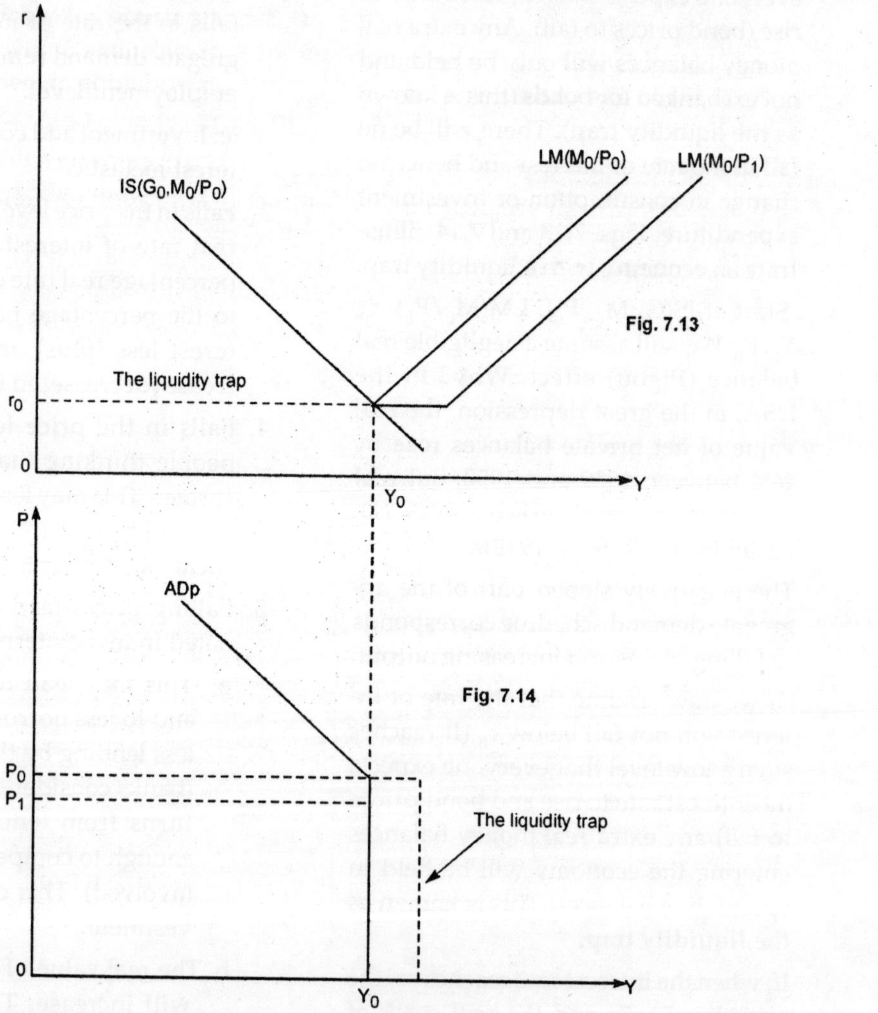

Fig. 7.13 and 7.14: The liquidity trap

a result workers and employers find it more difficult to determine whether the decrease in their wage or product price is due to a fall in demand for their labour or product (and less should be produced and/or supplied) or whether it is due to a general fall in prices (and no more should be produced and/or supplied). Confusing the two can lead to a mis-allocation of resources. The broadcast about relative prices is, as it were, being jammed by the noise coming from the deflation broadcast.

c. A falling price level will force people to constantly relearn prices. It helps to destroy the information conveyed by relative prices.

9. It harms long-term contracts denominated in money terms. For example, people who bought long-term bonds that pay them a fixed amount each year will find that falling prices increase the real value of their returns. Of course, people who entered into long-term contracts that required them to pay a fixed amount each year will find that the real value of their payments will be increasing.

10. Falls in wages will almost certainly be politically unpopular and could lead to popular discontent à la the UK poll tax riots. This could bring about an increase in the demand for money and no fall in interest rates.

Consider Fig. 7.15 and start at E_0. The fall in wages and prices will, ceteris paribus, and shift M_0/P_0 to the right to M_0/P_1 and lower the interest rate to r_{01}. However, if there is political unrest then this may lead to an increase in the demand for money and $LL_0(Y_0)$ will shift to the right. If $LL_0(Y_0)$ shifts to $LL_1(Y_0)$ then there will be no change in the rate of interest. The final equilibrium position will be at E_1.

For the above reasons it can be argued that a fall in the price level will lead to no increase in aggregate demand and hence no increase in income/output.

The implication of this is that the aggregate demand schedule is NOT negatively sloped but vertical. (Some economists argue that falling prices will lead to a *fall* in aggregate demand. They argue that the ADp schedule is *positively* sloped). In both cases there is no price level that will equate aggregate demand and aggregate supply. The economy is not ERGODIC—if it is

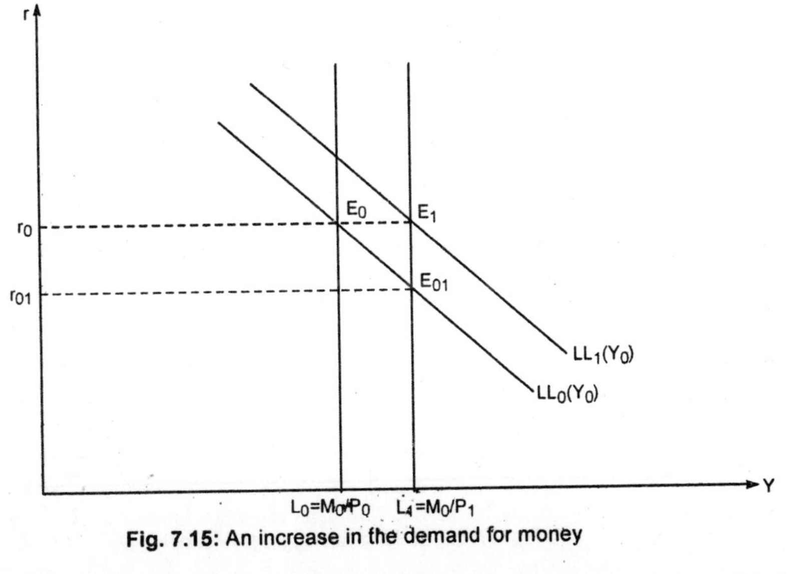

Fig. 7.15: An increase in the demand for money

destabilised then falling wages and prices will not return it to full employment equilibrium.

Post Keynesian economists argue that, in the real world, wages and prices (especially wages) are inflexible downwards and it is this inflexibility that gives stability to a free market economy.

The Aggregate Supply Schedule

Deriving aggregate supply schedules is beyond the scope of this book so we will just consider two of the accepted aggregate supply schedules - the long run and the short run aggregate supply schedules.

1. The long run aggregate supply schedule is drawn on the assumption that money wages are flexible upwards and downwards. If the demand for labour is greater than the supply of labour then money wages will quickly be bid upwards. If the demand for labour is less than the supply of labour then money wages will quickly be bid downwards
2. The short run aggregate supply schedule is drawn on the assumption that money wages are
   a. Flexible upwards—If the demand for labour is greater than the supply of labour then money wages will quickly be bid upwards, or
   b. Inflexible downwards—If the supply of labour is greater than the demand for labour then it will take the money wage a 'long time' to fall to the equilibrium level.

We assume that the price level is flexible both upwards and downwards.

1. **The long-run aggregate supply schedule**—This is assumed to be vertical above full employment income/output (Y_f) at all price levels. Y_f is, in the long run, determined by real factors—the real stock of capital, labour, raw materials etc. The employment of these factors of production is independent of the *aggregate* price level (P). Changes in P will not affect Y_f in the long run. Fig. 7.16 illustrates a long-run aggregate supply schedule (LAS).

   At a price level P_0 the level of output is Y_f. If the price falls to P_1 then, in the long-run, output is unchanged at Y_f.

2. **The short-run aggregate supply schedule (SAS(W_0) in Fig. 7.16).**

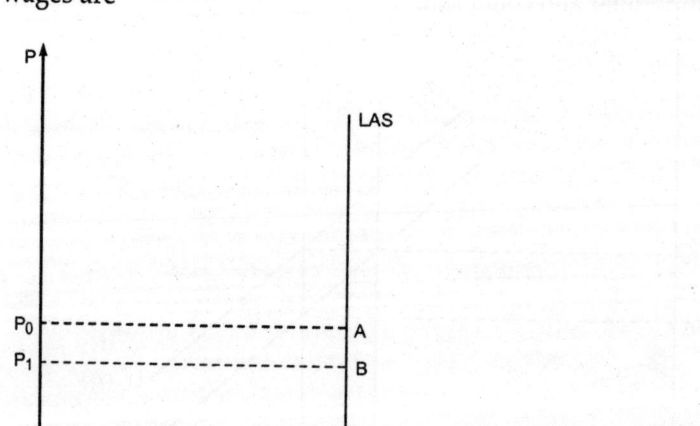

Fig. 7.16: The long-run aggregate supply

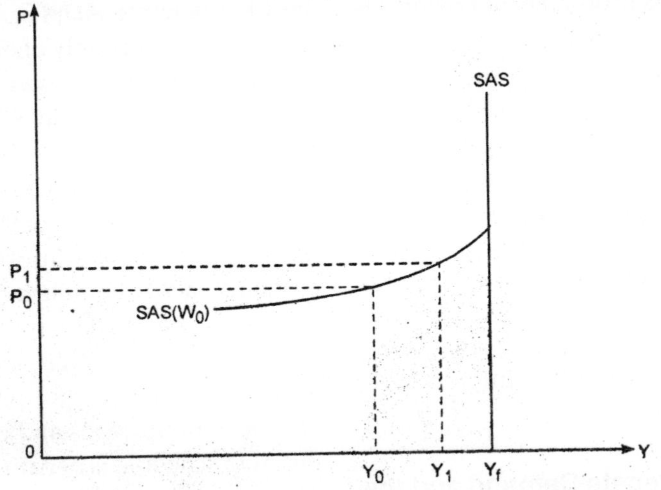

Fig. 7.17: A short-run aggregate supply schedule

This is assumed to be positively sloped (for a given money wage rate) up to full employment income/output (Y_f). An increase in the aggregate price level (P) will lead to the economy employing more labour and producing more income/output (as the price level increases, for a given level of the money wage the, real wage will fall and it is now profitable for the economy to employ more labour and produce more output). This can continue until there is no more involuntary unemployment to be employed. I.e. until the economy reaches full employment. At full-employment the SAS schedule becomes vertical. Each short-run aggregate supply schedule is constructed for a given level of the money wage. Fig. 7.17 illustrates a short-run aggregate supply schedule (SAS(W_0)) when the money wage rate is W_0. If the price level is P_0 then, with a money wage of W_0, the profit maximising output is Y_0. The economy (businesses) wish to produce output Y_0. If the price level increases

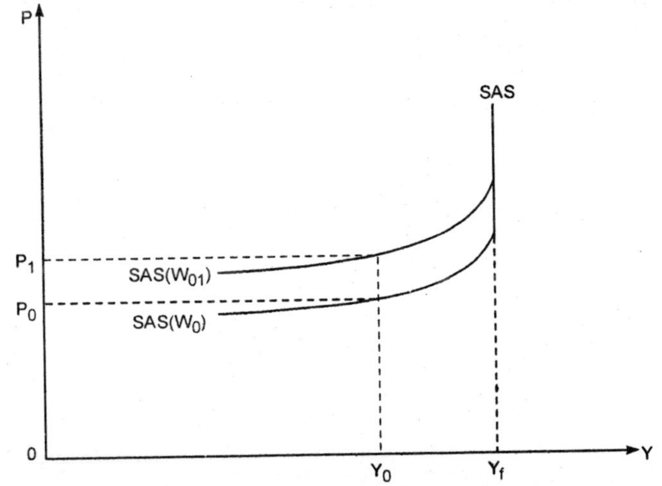

Fig. 7.18: A short-run aggregate supply schedule and the money wage

to P_1 then it is profitable for businesses to produce output Y_1.

If the money wage rate increases to Wo1 then the economy (businesses) need a higher price level to produce the same level of output. The short-run aggregate supply schedule will shift upwards to SAS(W_{01}). See Fig. 7.18. To continue to produce output Yo requires a higher price level P_{01}. You should note that the difference between P_{01} and P_0 is the same the difference between W_{01} and W_0.

A Change in Aggregate Demand and the Long-run Aggregate Supply Schedule

Fig. 7.19, point A, shows the long-run equilibrium situation in the economy – the intersection of the long run aggregate supply schedule (LAS) and the aggregate demand schedule (ADp(G_0,M_0)). The price level is P_0 and output is Y_f. At point 'A' the marginal productivity of labour ($mp_1(N_f)$) is equal to the real wage (W_0/P_0). **The aggregate price level P_0 and the level of full employment output (Y_f) are determined by the intersection of ADp(G_0,M_0) and LAS.**

If there is now a fall in the nominal stock of money (say %ΔM = -10%). ADp(G_0,M_0) will shift to the left to ADp(G_0,M_1). At P_0 there is now and excess supply of output (points A' to A). Prices (and money wages) will start to fall and aggregate demand will increase along ADp(G_0,M_1) from point 'A' towards point B. Once the price level reaches P_1 then aggregate demand will be back equal to long-run aggregate supply. The fall in prices has taken the economy back to equilibrium. Both prices and wages will have fallen by the same percentage (10%) so that W_1/P_1 is equal to mpl(N_f) (=W_0/P_0). If, wages and prices are perfectly flexible both upwards and downwards **AND** the ADp schedule is negatively sloped then it is assumed (by neoclassical economists) that the output of the economy will always be at full employment (Yf). The main change is that %ΔP = %ΔM. When money only affects the price level it is said to be neutral. In this case it has no effect on real magnitudes (real income/output and employment).

Since Y_f is determined by the supply side of the economy output is said to be **supply determined**. The faster that wages and prices fall then, the assumption is, the quicker will the economy return to full employment. Most economists (however, not Post-Keynesians) will go along with this analysis.

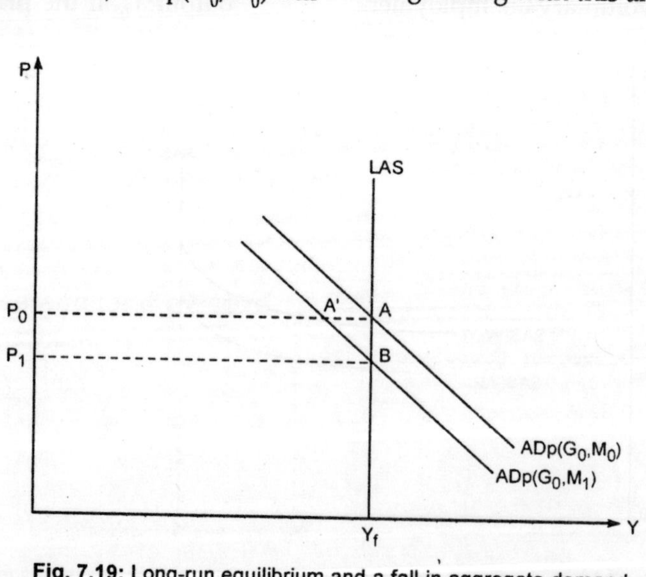

Fig. 7.19: Long-run equilibrium and a fall in aggregate demand

The Policy Implications of Neo-Classical Economics

The belief that falling wages and prices will take the economy to full employment has important implications for economic policy. If markets do not clear quickly then this will inhibit the attainment of full employment. Therefore, economists who think that price changes will take the economy to Y_f, will believe that prices should be as flexible as possible and, to facilitate this, all markets have to be made as 'efficient' as possible. The labour market has to be more competitive to enable wages to quickly adjust to their equilibrium positions and involuntary unemployment be eliminated. The product and financial markets have to be fully deregulated.

However, the deregulation of the financial markets led to housing and stock market bubbles that crashed in 2007-08. This has led to unprecedented troubles in the banking systems of different countries (the credit crunch) and the recession/depression of 2008 onwards.

A Change in Aggregate Demand and the Short-run Aggregate Supply Schedule

Fig. 7.20, point A, shows a long-run equilibrium situation in the economy—the intersection of the long-run aggregate supply schedule (LAS), the short-run aggregate supply schedule (SAS(W_0) and the aggregate demand schedule (ADp(G_0,M_0). The price level is P_0 and output is Yf. At point A the marginal productivity of labour ($mp_l(N_f)$) is equal to the real wage (W_0/P_0). The aggregate price level P_0 is determined by the intersection of ADp(G_0,M_0), SAS(W_0) and LAS.

If there is now a decline in the supply of money from M_0 to M_1 then ADp(G_0,M_0) will shift to the left to ADp(G_0,M_1). At Po there will now be an excess supply of output. The aggregate price will fall, say, to P_{01}. With money wages inflexible downward, in the short run, the real wage will increase to W_0/P_{01}. Now mpl(N_f) is less than W_0/P_{01} and it is now profitable for businesses, in the short-run, to employ less labour and produce output Y_{01}. There will now be some involuntary unemployment.

If we assume, **in the medium term**, that the involuntary unemployment will lead to a fall in the money wage then the money wage curve Wo will shift to the right (downwards). This will lead to an excess supply of output, a fall in the price level, an increase in the real stock of money and an increase in aggregate demand. Consider the effect on aggregate demand as prices fall.

The fall in the price level will increase the real stock of money. Since real money balances are part of the wealth of consumers then con-

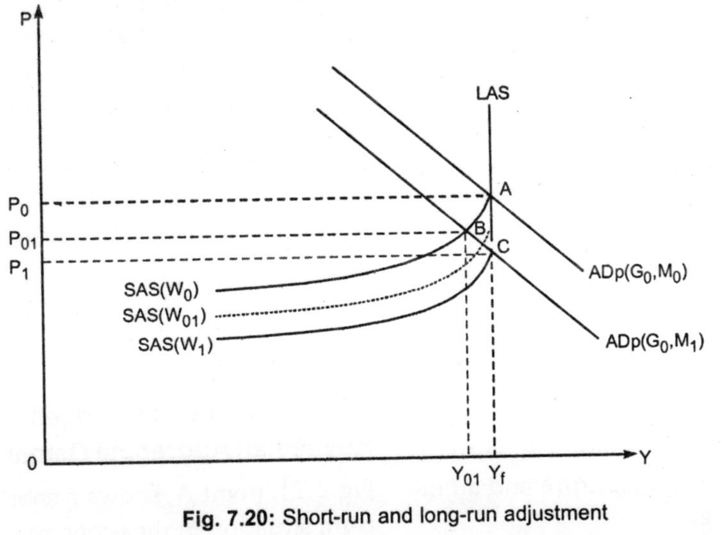

Fig. 7.20: Short-run and long-run adjustment

consumers' wealth increases. This encourages consumers to save less and consume more (in this case the Pigou effect). Their autonomous consumption expenditure will increase. As P_9 falls the real stock of money will increase, and there will now be an excess supply of money. This excess supply of money is equivalent to an excess demand for bonds. The increase in the price of bonds is equivalent to a fall in the rate of interest. Since bonds are part of the wealth of consumers then consumers' wealth increases. This encourages consumers to save less and consume more. Their autonomous consumption expenditure will increase.

The fall in the interest rate may

i. Lead to banks decreasing the size of their reserve deposit ratios ([see chapter 11] lower interest rates mean that it is less expensive for banks to borrow money from the central bank). This will increase the money multiplier and, directly, the supply of money.

ii. The fall in the rate of interest will increase autonomous consumption expenditure. (The fall in the cost of borrowing encouraging consumers to borrow more to finance a greater level of consumption expenditure out of a given income).

iii. Increase the present value of expected net revenues. This will, ceteris paribus, increase investment expenditure and also increase borrowing to finance investment expenditure.

iv. Reduce the costs of production as overdraft rates decrease.

v. Lead to an increase in revenues as demand is increased.

(iv) and (v) will usually lead to a rise in the expected net revenues of firms and lead to a rise in the present value of new investment projects. Ceteris paribus, there will be an increase in investment expenditure and an increase in borrowing.

As long as there is some involuntary unemployment the money wage and the price level will fall and the real stock of money and aggregate demand will increase.

The money wage and price level will fall, aggregate demand will increase until the economy reaches point C when the economy is back at full employment and there is no involuntary unemployment (only voluntary unemployment). This is, of course, assuming that the ADp schedule is negatively sloped.

Since Y_f is determined by the supply side of the economy (the production function and the demand and supply of labour) output is said to be **supply determined**. The faster that wages and prices fall then the quicker will the economy return to full employment (only voluntary unemployment). The main change is that $\%\Delta P = \%\Delta M$.

When money only affects the price level it is said to be neutral. In this case it reduces income/output in the short-run (Y_f toY_{01}) but has no effect on real magnitudes (real income/output, employment and involuntary unemployment) in the long-run. Money is said to be non-neutral in the short-run but neutral in the long-run.

In the UK (where an independent Bank of England prevents monetary policy being used for political purposes) if the rate of inflation (measured by the CPI – the consumer price index) falls below 2.0% and is expected to remain below 2.0%, then the Bank of England will cut interest rates and allow the supply of money to increase i.e. expand aggregate demand using monetary policy. As long as monetary policy is effective in changing aggregate demand then increases in income/output, employment and involuntary unemployment are not dependent upon the fall in the aggregate price level).

A Fall in Wages and Prices and the Post-Keynesian Aggregate Demand Schedule

Fig. 7.21, point A, shows a short-run equilibrium situation in the economy—the intersection of the short-run aggregate supply schedule (SAS(W_0) and the aggregate demand schedule (ADp(G_0,M_0). The price level is P_0, output is Yo and some involuntary unemployment. At point A, on SAS(W_0), the marginal productivity of labour (mpl(N_0) is equal to the real wage (W_0/P_0). The aggregate price level Po is determined by the intersection of ADp(G_0,M_0) and SAS(W_0).

If we assume that the involuntary unemployment will lead to a fall in the money wage then the money wage curve Wo will shift to the right (downwards), say, to SAS(W1).

This will lead to a fall in the real wage and encourage firms to increase the supply of output to, say, point A'(mpl(No)>W1/Po). However, at Po with aggregate demand at point A, there will be an excess supply of output (point A to point A'). This excess supply of output will lead to a fall in the price level.

It can be argued that falling prices (deflation) will not lead to an increase in aggregate demand and may even destabilise a free market economy. Indeed, the new chairman of the Federal Reserve, B. Bernanke, was so worried about deflation in the USA that he pressed for a cut in the short term interest rate right down to 1% in June 2003 (where it remained until to June 2004).

1. Falling wages and prices may not lead the rate of interest falling sufficiently for full employment to be attained. The rate of interest may reach a level so that everyone expects interest rates only to rise (bond prices to fall). Any extra real money balances will only be held and not exchanged for bonds (this is known as the liquidity trap). There will be no fall in the rate of interest and hence no change in consumption or investment expenditure. Figs. 7.22 and 7.23 illustrate an economy with a liquidity trap.

Start at IS(G_0,M_0/P_0), LM(M_0/P_0), r_0, Y_0, P_0. We will assume a negligible real balance (Pigou) effect. Why? In the USA, in the great depression, the real value of net private balances **rose** by 46% between 1929 and 1932, but real national income **fell** by 40% (D. Patinkin A.E.R. Sept. 1948).

The negatively sloped part of the aggregate demand schedule corresponds to falling prices and increasing output.

If we now assume that the rate of interest will not fall below ro (It reaches such a low level that everyone expects the interest rate to rise and bond prices to fall) any extra real money balances entering the economy will be held in

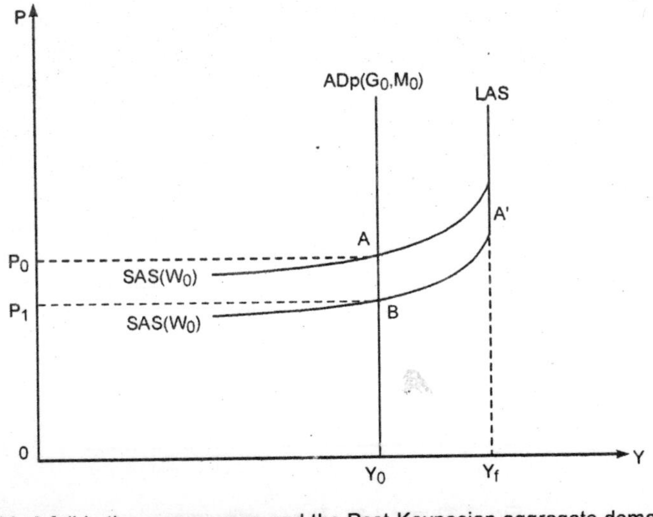

Fig. 7.21: A fall in the money wage and the Post-Keynesian aggregate demand schedule

speculative balances. This is known as the **liquidity trap**.

If, when the interest rate reaches ro, the price level falls and the real stock of money increases. $LM(M_0/P_0)$ shifts to the right to $LM(M_0/P_1)$. But, because the extra real money balances are held in speculative balances then there are no bond purchases to increase the price of bonds and lower the rate of interest. Hence there are no wealth effects (ignoring the real balance [Pigou] effect) to increase consumption expenditure and no interest rate falls to increase consumption or investment expenditures. Aggregate demand and involuntary unemployment will not change as the price level falls. The ADp schedule will be vertical at output Y_0.

2. Investment and consumption expenditure may not respond sufficiently to falls in the rate of interest so that aggregate demand remains below its full employment level.

   i.e. Investment and consumption are interest inelastic.

3. Falls in the price level may **increase** the real rate of interest. (Remember, the percentage real rate of interest is equal to the percentage nominal rate of in-

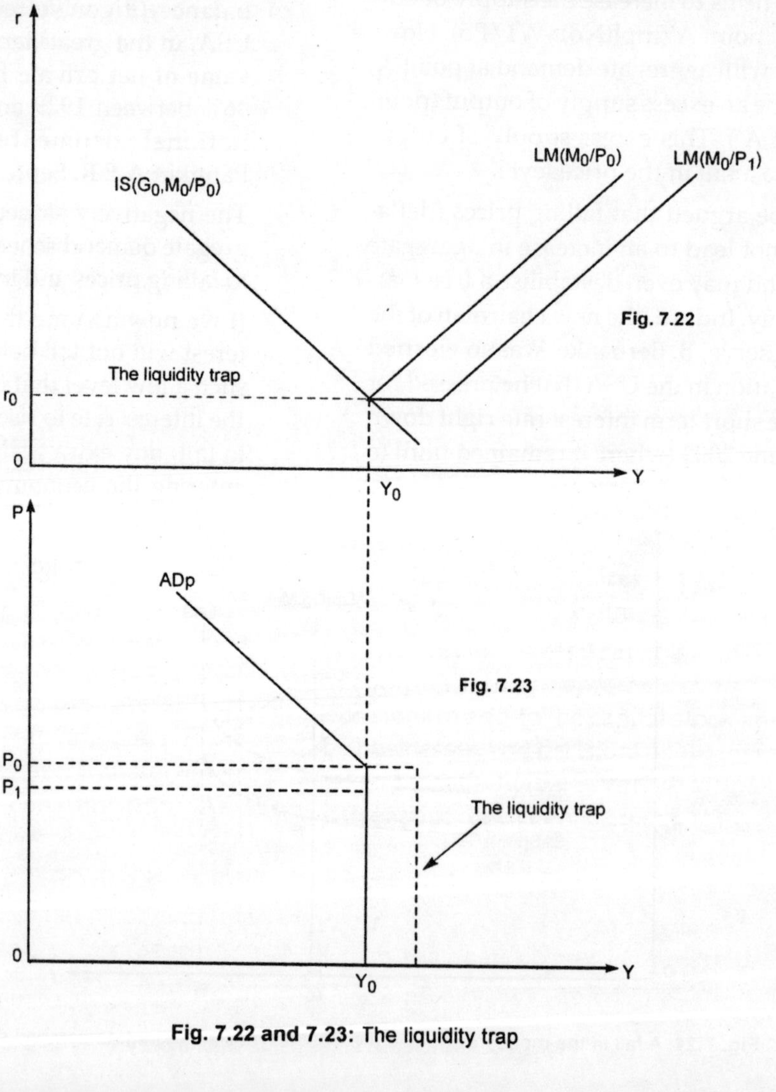

Fig. 7.22 and 7.23: The liquidity trap

terest less [plus] any percentage increase [decrease] in the price level).

4. Falls in the price level may lead to people thinking that prices may fall further. This may lead to the postponement of consumption and/or investment expenditure.
5. Falling prices lead to debts denominated in money terms increasing.
   a. This may lead more bankruptcies and to less borrowing by firms and less lending by the banking system (banks consider the prospective returns from lending as not being enough to compensate for the risks involved). This can lead to less investment.
   b. The real value of the National Debt will increase. This may result in taxation being increased which could undermine business confidence leading to less investment.
6. Falling asset prices (shares and futures and options based on them) reduce the value of collateral for bank loans, inducing weakened banks to engage in a fire sale of their loans and securities, leading to further asset price deflation.
7. We are also assuming that the nominal stock of money remains constant! If the money supply is **endogenous** then the nominal supply of money may fall along with the price level. There may be no change in the real stock of money and hence no change in the rate of interest or any real balance (Pigou) effect.
8. Falling prices will destroy jobs, damage growth and harm real investment.
   a. A falling price level will increase the risk associated with any assessment of future returns on an investment project. i.e. it reduces net revenues and hence real investment and the creation of new jobs.
   b. A falling price level will make it difficult to distinguish between changes in *relative* price from changes in the *general* price level. As a result workers and employers find it more difficult to determine whether the decrease in their wage or product price is due to a fall in demand for their labour or product (and less should be produced and/or supplied) or whether it is due to a general fall in prices (and no more should be produced and/or supplied). Confusing the two can lead to a mis-allocation of resources. The broadcast about relative prices is, as it were, being jammed by the noise

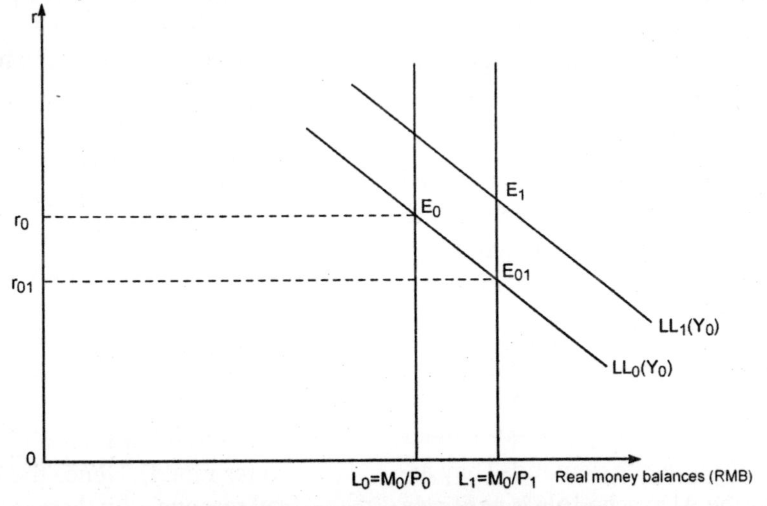

Fig. 7.24: An increase in the demand for money

coming from the deflation broadcast.

c. A falling price level will force people to constantly relearn prices. It helps to destroy the information conveyed by relative prices.

9. It harms long-term contracts denominated in money terms. For example, people who purchase long term bonds that pay a fixed amount each year will find that falling prices increases the **real** value of their returns. Of course, people who entered into long-term contracts that required them to pay a fixed amount each year will find that the real value of their payments will be increasing.

10. Falls in wages will almost certainly be politically unpopular and could lead to popular discontent à la the UK poll tax riots. This could bring about an increase in the demand for money and no fall in interest rates.

Consider Fig. 7.24 and start at E_0. The fall in wages and prices will, ceteris paribus, shift M_0/P_0 to the right to M_0/P_1 and lower the interest rate to r_{01}. However, if there is political unrest then this may lead to an increase in the demand for money and $LL_0(Y_0)$ will shift to the right. If $LL_0(Y_0)$ shifts to $LL_1(Y_0)$ then there will be no change in the rate of interest. The final equilibrium position will be at E_1.

For the above reasons it can be argued that a fall in the price level will lead to no increase in aggregate demand and hence no increase in income/output.

The implication of this is that the aggregate demand schedule is NOT negatively sloped but vertical. (Some economists argue that falling prices will lead to a *fall* in aggregate demand. They argue that the ADp schedule is *positively* sloped). In both cases there is no price level that will equate aggregate demand and aggregate supply. The economy is not ERGODIC-if it is destabilised then falling wages and prices will not return it to full employment equilibrium.

Post Keynesian economists argue that, in the real world, wages and prices (especially wages) are inflexible downwards and it is this inflexibility that gives stability to a free market economy.

SUMMARY

1. We have seen that an increase in aggregate demand brought about by monetary or fiscal policy or an increase in autonomous consumption expenditure, investment expenditure or net exports can reduce <u>involuntary</u> (cyclical) unemployment but that voluntary (structural) unemployment will be unchanged in the short run. There are disadvantages in the use expansionary of fiscal policy (crowding out) or expansionary monetary policy (inflation?). Both expansionary monetary and fiscal policy can lead to balance of payments problems (imports increase when income increases and exports may be diverted to the home market).

2. We have seen that there are *theoretical* reasons why the economy will (assuming that the ADp is negatively sloped and prices and wages that are flexible upwards and downwards) eliminate involuntary unemployment and return to the full employment real income/output level (Y_f) with only voluntary unemployment – output is supply determined. (However, if the ADp schedule is vertical then output is demand determined). Hence there are theoretical reasons why there is no need for an

active monetary or fiscal policy to expand aggregate demand and the economy (but see pages 89-90 oe 95-98 or 103-106). As J.M. Keynes pointed out, not only are cuts in money wages and prices very difficult to implement but they may not be effective in restoring full employment. Even if they are effective it may take many years (with long periods of high unemployment and low output) for the requisite price adjustments to take effect. i.e the fall in the price level needs to increase the real stock of money which needs to lead to a real balance effect and/or a fall in the rate of interest. The fall in the rate of interest needs to increase consumption and investment expenditure–ADp may be very steep. Keynes also argued that since it is the fall in prices that increases the real stock of money and may lead to an increase in the level of aggregate demand a simpler method of eliminating any involuntary unemployment is to increase the nominal supply of money—though, in inflationary times, this may be difficult to implement.

In the UK, if the rate of inflation falls below 2.0% and is expected to remain below 2.0%, then the Bank of England will cut interest rates and allow the supply of money to increase i.e. expand aggregate demand using monetary policy. In the UK the increase in real income/output of the economy is not dependent upon prices falling (deflation) to increase aggregate demand in the economy.

Economists generally accept the theoretical model that has been outlined. One of the things that they do disagree about is whether falling wages and prices can eliminate involuntary unemployment. Some economists argue that falling prices will destabilise an economy (see pages 89-90 or 95-8 or 103-6) and will not lead to an increase in aggregate demand. Indeed, the new chairman of the Federal Reserve, B. Bernanke, was so worried about deflation in the USA that he pressed for a cut in the short-term interest rate right down to 1% in June 2003 (where it remained until to June 2004).

Some economists disagree as to the time it takes for 'market forces' to eliminate any involuntary unemployment. Some argue that it will take so long for the economy to adjust to full employment that the government should use expansionary monetary and fiscal policies to eliminate the involuntary unemployment. Others argue that the economy returns so quickly to full employment that any government action would only destabilise the economy.

If governments accept that the dangers of expansionary fiscal and/or monetary policies outweigh their benefits and that 'market forces' within the economy will automatically eliminate any involuntary unemployment (and leave only voluntary unemployment), they then may conclude that their only responsibility is to attempt to reduce voluntary unemployment by implementing supply side policies. (However, in the UK, if the rate of inflation falls below 2.0% and is expected to remain below 2.0%, then the Bank of England will cut interest rates and allow the supply of money to increase i.e. expand aggregate demand using monetary policy. As long as monetary policy is effective in changing aggregate demand then increases in income/output are not dependent upon the fall in the aggregate price level [deflation]).

This takes us to policy measures to try shift the position of full employment real income/output level (Y_f) i.e. **'supply side'** measures that try to increase the productivity of an economy and reduce the level of voluntary (structural) unemployment.

QUESTIONS

1. What do you understand by 'crowding out'?

2. For the economy to have an unambiguous higher level of investment, given that the government is running a budget deficit, the proper monetary policy and fiscal policy mix would be
   (a) easy money and a government induced increase in personal income tax.
   (b) easy money and a government induced decrease in personal income tax.
   (c) tight money and reduced government spending.
   (d) tight money and increased government spending.
   (e) none of the above will affect investment.

3. Given the IS-LM construction illustrated in the figure above, an increase in government spending can be expected to
   (a) increase both interest rates and GNP.
   (b) reduce both interest rates and GNP.
   (c) reduce GNP and increase interest rates
   (d) increase GNP but cause an indeterminate, ambiguous effect on interest rates.
   (e) increase interest rates, but cause an indeterminate, ambiguous effect on GNP

4. Which of the following statements is consistent with the new classical theory?
   (a) If prices and wages are both flexible and expectations are rational, then policy is ineffective.
   (b) If prices but not necessarily wages are flexible and expectations are rational, then policy is ineffective.
   (c) If wages but not necessarily prices are flexible and expectations are rational, then policy is ineffective.
   (d) If expectations are rational, then policy is ineffective regardless of wage and price behavior.
   (e) If prices and wages are both flexible and expectations are rational, then monetary but not fiscal policy can be effective.

5. Given the IS-LM model, an unexpected increase in the price level, in the absence of any policy adjustment, will
   (a) increase both interest rates and GNP.
   (b) reduce both interest rates and GNP.
   (c) increase GNP but cause interest rates to fall
   (d) increase interest rates but cause GNP to fall
   (e) increase interest rates but cause an indeterminate, ambiguous effect on GNP.

6. A model that envisages price flexibility can explain recession only in terms of
   (a) increases in aggregate demand
   (b) decreases in aggregate demand
   (c) increases in the number of people looking for work without a corresponding increase in the number of Jobs
   (d) sudden surges in investment that cause the capital stock to increase too quickly
   (e) None of the above.

ANSWERS

1. 'Crowding out' is the fall in consumption and investment expenditure brought about by an increase in government expenditure and a relative shortage of money.

2. (a) Easy money would result in a larger supply of money and therefore lower interest rates. An increase in personal income tax will decrease the need for the government to borrow, again lowering the interest rates. Since investment (and consumption expenditure) is a function of the interest rate, investment (and consumption) will increase.

3. An increase in government spending is reflected by a rightward shift in the IS schedule. Equilibrium should therefore be expected to move up the LM curve to the right to support both a higher interest rate and a higher level of economic activity.

4. (a) The new classical theory requires both flexible prices and rational expectations*, flexible prices work to guarantee that aggregate supply is always set equal to potential GDP. Changes in aggregate demand, therefore, cause no change in actual GDP. Rational expectations undermine the ability of policy adjustments to change aggregate demand because people react to changes in a way that nullify its effect. Changes in policy, therefore, leave real wage and output unchanged.

5. (d) An increase in the price level functions just like a reduction in the real money supply, so the LM curve shifts up and to the left. Equilibrium therefore, moves along the IS curve to support a higher interest rate but a lower level of economic activity.

6. (e) With perfectly flexible prices, the aggregate supply schedule is vertical above a potential GDP (Y_f). Any change in aggregate demand results only in a corresponding change in the price with output being held fixed at a potential GDP; so, there is no recession. (An increase in aggregate demand creates the opposite potential for a boom, but again only prices move). Increases in either the number of people available to work or the capital stock, increase a potential GDP, but that results in lower prices, <u>not</u> unemployed resources.

*The theory of rational expectations assumes that people very quickly learn from their mistakes. They do not make systematic (the same) errors. On average, at the macroeconomic level, people do not make errors.

CHAPTER 8

SUPPLY SIDE ECONOMICS

KEY TERMS

Voluntary Unemployment: People who are in the labour force but do not want a job at the prevailing market real wage.

Involuntary Unemployment: People who are willing to work at the prevailing market real wage but can not find jobs.

Natural Rate of Unemployment: Is the percentage of the labour force that is unemployed when the labour market is in equilibrium.

Most Keynesians and Monetarists agree that the long-run the performance of an economy can only be improved by increasing the level of full employment output. This may involve reducing NAIRU (non-accelerating inflation rate of unemployment) or the natural rate of unemployment [the number of people voluntarily unemployed when the economy is at full employment]. If it were possible (and profitable) to employ some or all of the voluntary unemployed their employment would lead to a reduction in the NAIRU [natural rate] and a one off increase in the output of the economy.

The labour market and aggregate supply

1. **The demand for labour**: In the short-run, businesses, on aggregate, have a given stock of capital. We will assume that, on aggregate, businesses maximise profits and that labour is the only variable factor in the short-run.

DEFINITION: The (aggregate) marginal (physical) product of labour (mpl) when employment is 'N_0' (mpl(N_0) is the extra output produced by businesses from a given stock of capital when an additional unit of labour (a labour hour) is employed. ('N_0' labour input increases to N_{0+1}.

In the short-run it is the marginal product of labour in relation to the real wage (W/P = w) that determines the level of aggregate employment.

If mpl(N_0) is greater than the real wage (W/P = w) then businesses profits can

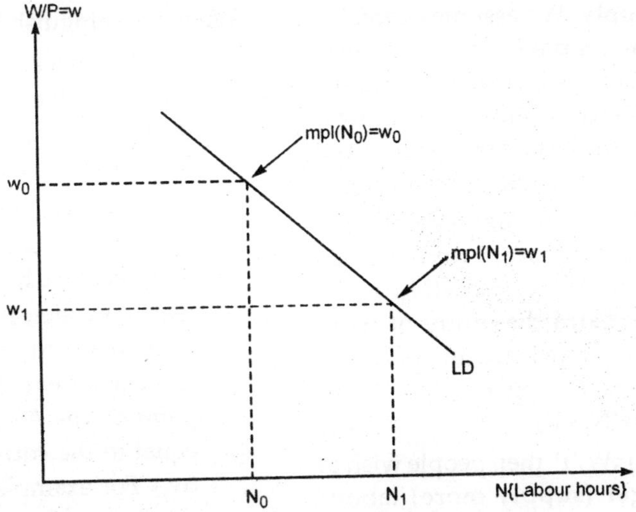

Fig. 8.1: The demand for labour at the macroeconomic level

be increased by expanding employment. The value of the extra output produced is greater than the cost of producing that extra output.

If mpl(N_0) is less than the real wage (W/P) then businesses profits can be increased by reducing the input of labour. The reduction in the cost of producing the lower output is greater than the reduction in the value of the lower output produced.

If the marginal productivity of labour (mpl(N_0) is equal to the real wage (W/P = w), (mpl(N_0) = W/P) then the profits of businesses are at a maximum. Increasing **or** decreasing labour input will reduce businesses profit.

Given a particular real wage, (W/P = w) there is only one level of employment that will maximise aggregate profit.

e.g. Consider figure 8.1: If the real wage is w_0 then, assume, that the optimum (profit maximising) level of (aggregate) employment is 'N_0' (mpl(N_0) = w_0).

We will assume that, with a fixed stock of capital, the marginal product of labour **declines** as more labour is employed. There is **diminishing marginal productivity of labour**. Consider Fig. 8.1 again. For labour input to increase from 'N_0' to 'N_1' requires 'N_1' labour to be paid a lower real wage than wo since mpl(N_1) is **less** than mpl(N_0). ie. N_1 labour can only be profitably employed if it can be paid a real wage lower than wo (say w_1).

Alternatively, if the real wage is below w_0, say w_1 (since w_0 = mpl(N_0) then w_1 is less than mpl(N_0)) it is more profitable to employ more than 'N_0' labour (say N_1). (At N_1, mpl(N_1) = w_1).

The aggregate demand for labour schedule is negatively sloped. On aggregate, an extra unit of labour will only be employed, ceteris paribus, if the real wage falls to compensate for the reduction in the marginal product of the next labour unit. (However, see question 1 at the end of the chapter). We are assuming that businesses are willing and able to provide more jobs (supply more labour hours) as the real wage falls.

Definition: The **LD** curve shows the aggregate profit maximising level of employment in an economy at a given real wage. We will assume it is negatively sloped as in Fig. 8.1.

2. **Labour supply**: We assume (unrealistically) that people do not like working; that there is increasing marginal dis-utility of work (**mdw**). The mdw is the value of the leisure being sacrificed in order to work another labour hour.

DEFINITION: The (aggregate) marginal dis-utility of work (mdw) when employment is 'N_0' (mdw(N_0) is the (aggregate) extra dis-utility of work produced when an extra unit of labour (a labour hour) is supplied. ('N_0' labour increases to 'N_0+1').

If mdw(N_0)<W/P then people wish to work longer (supply more) labour hours. If mdw(N_0)>W/P then people wish to work (supply) fewer labour hours. The equilibrium situation is when mdw(N_0)=W_0/P_0 (=w_0). People are willing to work exactly 'N_0' labour hours when the real wage is w_0. W_0/P_0 exactly compensates them for working the extra hour. Hence people need a higher real wage than W_0/P_0= w_0 to supply more labour hours.

We will distinguish between curves:

a. The **LF** curve: This shows the maximum possible size (in labour hours) of the labour force (we will assume that it does not vary with the real wage).

b. The **AJ** curve: This shows the aggregate number of labour hours willing to be worked at each real wage rate. As the real wage increases people are willing to increase their labour input (measured in terms of labour hours). At each point on the AJ curve the mdw(N_i) is equal to the corresponding real wage (w_i). For example, in Fig. 8.2, at a real wage of wo the number of labour hours supplied (willing to be worked) is 'N_0' (mdw(N_0) = w_0), where mdw(N_0) is the marginal dis-utility of work when employment is 'N_0'.

The horizontal distance AB are the registered unemployed at the real wage rate w_0. They are between jobs or do not wish to work at the wage rate wo; they are voluntarily unemployed.

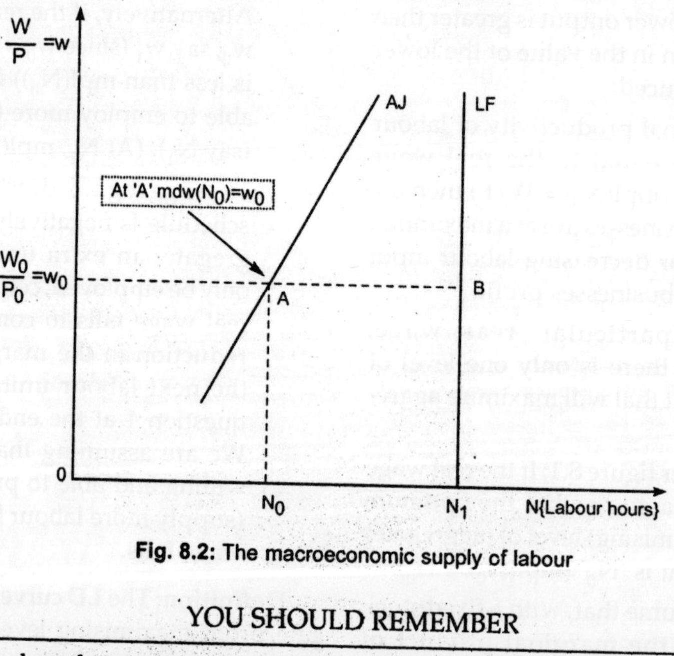

Fig. 8.2: The macroeconomic supply of labour

YOU SHOULD REMEMBER

A negatively sloped aggregate demand for labour curve assumes that **businesses are able, and willing, to provide more employment (jobs)** as the real wage falls.

LABOUR MARKET EQUILIBRIUM

The intersection of the demand for labour schedule LD and the supply of labour schedule AJ at point E in Fig. 8.3 determines a maximum possible level of full employment – Nfo. Below w_0 there will be less labour supplied than Nfo and above w_0 there will be less than Nfo labour hours [jobs] offered.

At 'E', $mdw(N_{f0}) = mpl(N_{f0}) = w_0$. Labour, Nfo, will produce the maximum output of an economy Y_{f0} that does not vary, in the short run, with aggregate demand or the price level. (See Fig. 8.7). Labour 'E' to 'F' are in the labour force but do not wish to work at the real wage w_0. They are voluntarily unemployed. We will also see that the economy may not be able to attain this maximum possible level of full employment due to taxes or excessively high real wages.

We will define the NATURAL RATE OF UNEMPLOYMENT as the percentage of the labour force that is unemployed when the labour market is in equilibrium. It is voluntary unemployment because people choose not to work at that wage rate. This is also known as the NAIRU (non-accelerating inflation rate of unemployment). The natural rate of unemployment (NAIRU) is EF in Fig. 8.3.

However, some "new Keynesian" economists argue that there is no natural rate of unemployment in the sense of a rate to which the actual rate tends to return. Instead, when actual unemployment rises and remains high for some time, the natural rate of unemployment rises as well. The dependence of the natural rate of unemployment on actual unemployment is known as the hysteresis hypothesis. One explanation for hysteresis in a heavily unionized economy is that unions directly represent the interests only of those who are currently employed. Unionisation undermines the ability of those outside the union to compete for employment. After prolonged layoffs employed workers inside the union may seek the benefits of higher wages for themselves, rather than moderating wage demands to promote the re-hiring of unemployed workers. The downside to the hysteresis hypothesis is that once unemployment becomes high—as it did in Europe in the recessions of the seventies—it is relatively impervious to monetary and fiscal stimulus, even in the short run.

Involuntary unemployment

If the real wage is above wo, say w_1 (as in figure 8.4), the number of labour hours (jobs)

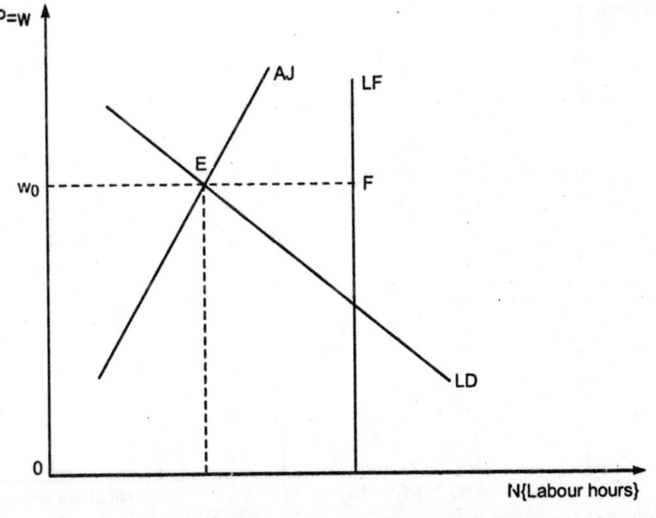

Fig. 8.3: Equilibrium in the labour market

employers are offering is N_A (point 'A' on the LD curve where mpl(N_A)= w_1). The number of labour hours people wish to work is N_B (point 'B' on the AJ curve is where mdw(N_B) = w_1 [note: mdw(N_A)< w1 at point 'A']). More people than N_A would like to work (or work longer hours) at the going wage rate, w_1, (A to B). 'A' to 'B' are involuntarily unemployed. 'B' to 'C' are in the labour force but do not wish to work they are voluntarily unemployed.

Some economists argue that, if wages and prices are perfectly flexible, any involuntary unemployment will quickly lead to an increase in aggregate demand and the elimination of that involuntary unemployment. The economy will, effectively, always be at the full employment level Nfo. This level of employment will produce full employment output, Yfo, in the real sector of the economy (see Fig. 8.7). This level of employment does not vary with the price level or aggregate demand. (We will, however, still have some voluntary unemployment).

Before considering specific supply side measures we will briefly discuss the background that led to the emergence of supply side economics.

SHOCKS TO THE SUPPLY SIDE: Both in 1973-74, 1978-79, 1980, 1990-91, 2002-03 and 2005-06 there were large increases in the price of oil and other commodity prices. In the 1970's high oil prices led to inflation and recession. At the time of writing this section (April 2006) the price of oil was over \$74 per barrel. However, for high oil prices to have the same effect on the economy as in the 1970s it needs to be adjusted both for the fact that real oil prices were higher in the past and that economies were more oil-sensitive. In 1980 it took £72 worth of crude oil to generate £1,000 worth of economic output; today the figure is £41. It has been calculated that it would need an oil price of just over \$200 (£110) to produce the same kind of inflationary and recessionary shocks as in the past. Others think that oil prices only need to rise to \$110.

A large rise in the price of oil leads to a fall in the demand for labour, an increase in voluntary unemployment, and a rise in the price level (a moderating factor is the lower price of manufacturing goods [brought about by globalisation?]). An increase in the real rate of interest will also shift LD to the left. The increase in the price of raw materials (including oil) reduces the productivity of labour. Effectively, the average and marginal productivity of labour will fall since each unit of labour produces less per unit of input. Consider Fig. 8.5.

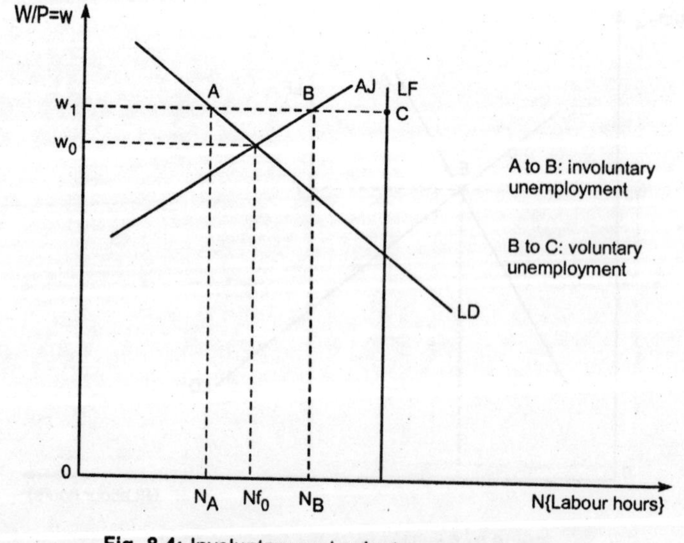

Fig. 8.4: Involuntary and voluntary unemployment

1. Start at LD_0, AJ, LF, Nf_0, w_0; $mdw(Nf_0)=mpl(Nf_0)$ = wo There is no involuntary unemployment but some voluntary unemployment (EF). The level of employment, Nf_0, produces Yf_0 full employment output (Fig. 8.6).
2. There is an increase in commodity (oil) prices. The demand for labour falls from LD_0 to LD_1 (mpl < w_0).
3. At w_0 there is an excess supply of labour. This will lead to a fall in the real wage (to w_1) and an increase in voluntary unemployment from EF to GH. The equilibrium level of employment is now Nf_1. Nf_1 level of employment produces Yf_1 (less than Yf_0) full employment output. There is, still, no involuntary unemployment. The rise in the price of oil will also increase the consumer price index and will reduce the purchasing power of the real wage when measured in terms of the price level associated with domestic consumer expenditure. We will assume that people will be less willing to work. Less labour will be supplied. The AJ curve will also shift to the left (not shown).

Consider the effect on the real sector of the economy. Start at $LM(M_0/P_0)$, $IS(G_0,M_0/P_0)$, Y_{f0} in figure 8.6 and let the demand for labour fall. Full employment output will be shifted to the left from Y_{f0} to Y_{f1}.

With an unchanged level of aggregate demand, aggregate demand will now be greater than full employment output (by an amount Y_{f1} to Y_{f0}). (However, in the UK from the 1 May 2006 gas bills are set to rise by 16.5% and electricity bills by 9.4%. Even before these latest rises, higher energy bills (gas, electricity and fuel for transport) and council taxes were set to soak up £3.7bn [€5.4bn, $6.6bn] of household spending – equivalent to 2p on the standard rate of tax. This will reduce real incomes and aggregate demand but probably not by the amount Y_{f1} to Y_{f0}). We have already seen what will happen if aggregate demand is greater than full employment output. The price level will increase, the real stock of money will fall. $LM(M_0/P_0)$, $IS(G_0,M_0/P_0)$ will, eventually, fall to $LM(M_0/P_1)$, $IS(G_0, M_0/P_1)$ respectively. The interest rate will increase and, *ceteris paribus*, aggregate demand and output will, eventually, fall to Y_{f1}.

There has been an increase in **voluntary** unemployment (EF to GH), a reduction in real

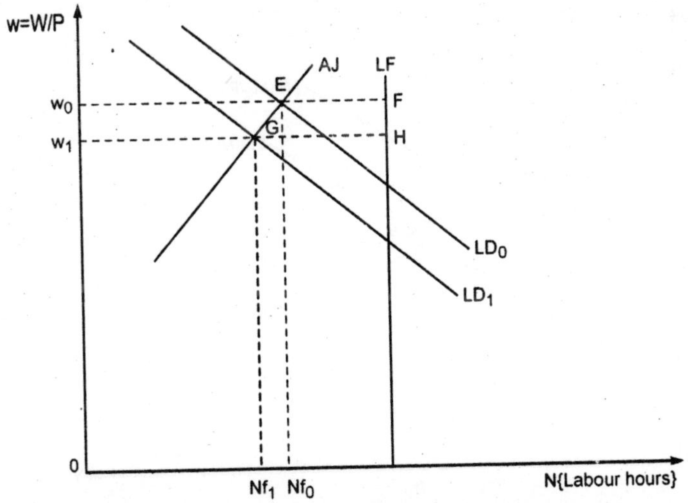

Fig. 8.5: A shock to the supply side and the demand for labour

incomes and aggregate demand and an increase in the price level (and, if the increase in the price level 'triggers off' an increase in inflation, a *positive* relationship between unemployment and inflation. This is known as stagflation) but no change in **involuntary** unemployment (since it was assumed that the economy was at full employment).

However, if the government thinks that the rise in unemployment is due to an increase in involuntary unemployment they may implement expansionary monetary and/or fiscal policies. As we have seen, when there is no involuntary unemployment, expansionary fiscal or monetary policies will lead to an increase in the price level but no increase in income/output. This may 'trigger off' or exacerbate an inflationary process.

Note, also, that the increase in raw material prices may lead to an upward pressure on the price level, which may 'trigger off 'an inflationary process.

In the UK the Bank of England has control over monetary policy with a remit to keep inflation (the CPI [consumer price index]) around 2.0%. In practice this means that if inflation is expected to rise above 2.0% (this could be because of a rise in import prices) then interest rates will be increased and aggregate demand will fall. Economic theory suggests that, if there is an increase in import prices and the domestic price level, then aggregate demand should be reduced. Giving control over monetary policy to the Bank of England ensures that, if inflation is expected to increase due to a rise in import prices, then interest rates will be increased and aggregate demand will be reduced. The IS and LM curves will be shifted to the left as in Fig. 8.6.

The Phillips curve purports to show that there is a *negative* relationship between unemployment and inflation. The *positive* relationship between unemployment and inflation in some of the years after 1973, and the belief, by some economists, that market forces will quickly eliminate involuntary unemployment led to the acceptance of policy measures that concentrate on the supply side of the economy and try to reduce the level of voluntary unemployment.

SUPPLY SIDE ECONOMICS

Supply side economics is the use of microeconomic incentives (that affect the macroeconomy) to reduce the level of voluntary unemployment (the NAIRU [the natural rate of unemployment]) and increase the level of full employment output (Y_f). Since more

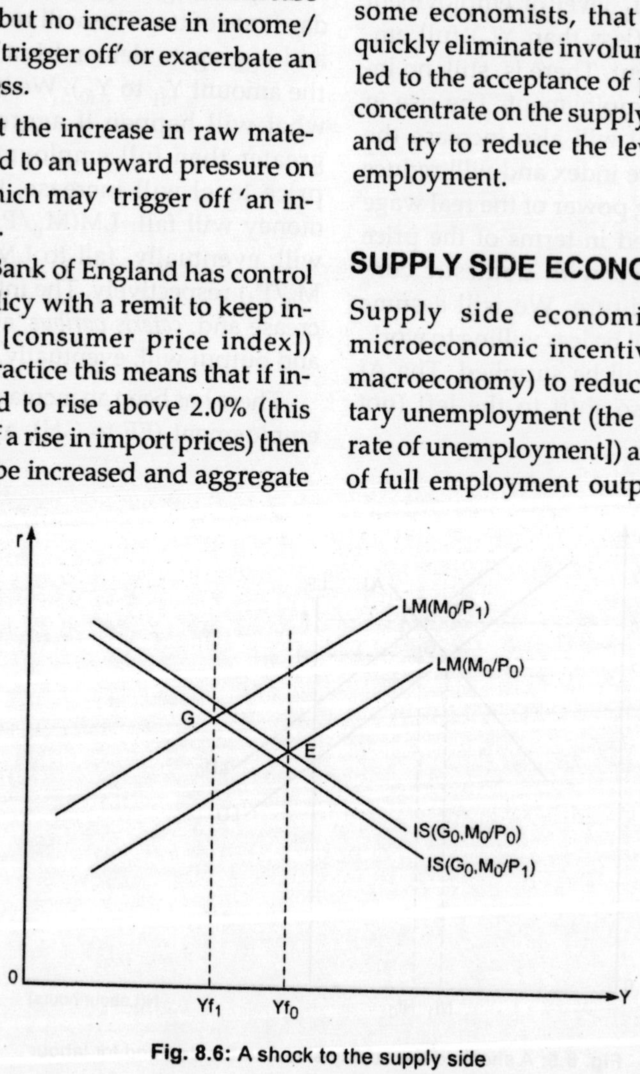

Fig. 8.6: A shock to the supply side

output is being produced with the same labour force then there will be a one-off increase in the productivity of the economy. Y_{f0} will be shifted to the right Y_{f1} as in Fig. 8.7.

The vertical dashed line above Y_{f0} (and Y_{f1}) indicates that, no matter the rate of interest (or the level of aggregate demand), output cannot g_0 above Y_{f0} (or Y_{f1}) in the short run. If the IS and LM intersected at a point above Y_{f0} then the level of aggregate demand (AD) is equal to Y_{f0}.

If Y_{f0} shifts to Y_{f1} then aggregate demand is now less than Y_{f1} — there will be some involuntary unemployment and downward pressure on money wages and prices.

SUPPLY SIDE MEASURES

Supply side economics will not change the number in the labour force but may encourage some of the voluntary unemployed to enter the ranks of the involuntary unemployed *or* may increase the productivity of the labour force. In either case Y_{f0} will be shifted to the right to Y_{f1} as in Fig. 8.7.

As we have seen any involuntary unemployment can, *theoretically*, be abolished by market forces. However, supply side measures are usually associated with the Neo-classical school of economics who assume that the economy is always close to, or at, full employment. Any change in supply side measures will be quickly incorporated into the economic system and the economy will quickly return to full employment.

The effectiveness of supply side measures depends upon a number of (doubtful?) assumptions.

1. It is usually assumed that any involuntary unemployment will lead to a fall in money wages and prices and that this will lead to an increase in aggregate demand and the elimination of any involuntary unemployment. We have, however, seen that this assumption is strongly challenged by the Post-Keynesian economists.

   However, the government may be able to expand aggregate demand using monetary and/or fiscal policies. A recent innovation (1997) in the UK is giving over the control of monetary policy to the Bank of England. The main responsibility of the Bank of England is an inflation rate (the CPI [consumer price index]) target of 2.0%. If inflation falls below 2.0% and is expected to remain below 2.0% (the economy is above NAIRU — there is a positive level of involuntary unemployment) then the Bank of England will cut in-

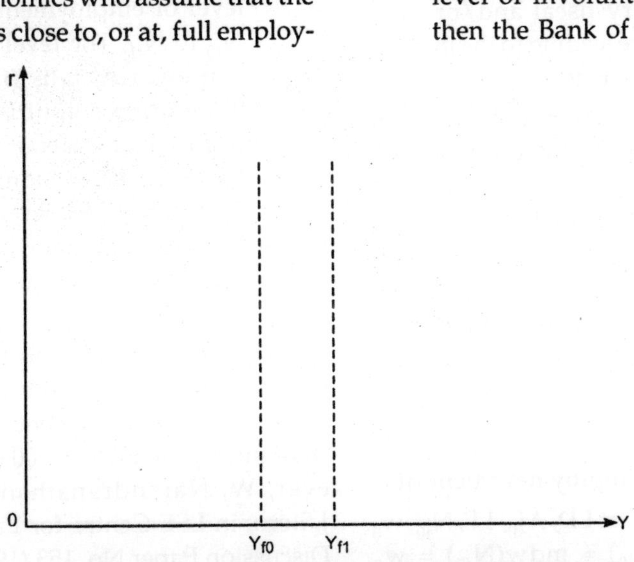

Fig. 8.7: An increase in full employment Income/output

terest rates and increase the money supply to increase aggregate demand and expand the economy. Conversely, if inflation is above 2.0% and is expected to remain above 2.0%, (the economy is below NAIRU) then the Bank of England will increase interest rates and decrease the money supply to contract the economy. As long as monetary policy is effective in changing aggregate demand the economy should always be close to full employment.

2. The (aggregate) demand curve for labour (the LD schedule) is usually assumed to be negatively sloped. A negatively sloped demand for labour curve implies that, for employment to increase, there must be a fall in the real wage. Any increase in aggregate demand must lead to a fall in the real wage. (However, see question 1 at the end the chapter).

   For this to happen either the money wage must fall faster than the fall in the price level (if market forces [falling wages and prices] are leading to the increase in aggregate demand) or the money wage must increase at a slower rate than the increase in the price level (if expansionary fiscal and/or monetary policies are leading to the increase in aggregate demand).

3. That sufficient new jobs (labour hours) will be supplied by the economy (the demand for labour will increase) if there is a fall in the real wage.

4. That the introduction of supply side measures will lead to significant changes in the behaviour of individuals and groups. I.e. there will be large shifts in the supply and/or demand curves for labour.

1. A reduction in unemployment benefit

a. Start, in Fig. 8.8, at LD, AJ_0, LF, N_{f0}, w_0. At w_0, $mpl(N_{f0}) = mdw(N_{f0}) = w_0$. There is no involuntary unemployment, but some voluntary unemployment ('E' to 'F'). N_{f0} level of employment produces Y_{f0} full employment output as in figure 8.7.

b. Cut unemployment benefit: The real wage will rise relative to unemployment benefit (the *replacement ratio* [the ratio of unemployment benefit to wages] has fallen). This encourages some of the voluntary unemployed to seek work. More people are now willing to work at each wage rate (there is a fall in the marginal disutility of work [$mdw(N_{f0})$ is now less than w_0]). Now, at the real wage w_0, the supply of labour is greater than the demand for labour by an amount 'E' to 'A' (at 'A' $mdw(N_A) = w_0$). The AJ_0 schedule shifts to AJ_1. There is now some involuntary unemployment (EA). The involuntary unemployment may reduce wages and prices, lead to an increase in aggregate demand (and a fall in the real wage) and a movement to the new full employment level (N_{f1}). If this occurs (or the relevant authorities increase the level of aggregate demand) the new, full employment, equilibrium level of employment increases from N_{f0} to N_{f1}; The level of voluntary unemployment falls (from AF to GH). Since more output is being produced from the same labour force, the productivity of the economy has increased. This is reflected in an increase in the level of full employment income/output (Y_f). Y_{f0} shifts to the right to Y_{f1} as in Fig. 8.7.

In his book *Unemployment – Cause and Cure* (1983). Professor P. Minford suggests that a 10% cut in unemployment benefit would reduce unemployment by 700,000 people. However, W. Narendranathan, S. Nickle and J.Stern, in LSE Centre for Labour Economics Discussion Paper No. 153 (1983), suggest that a 10% fall in benefits would only cut unemployment by 90,000 people.

2. Cuts in income tax or national insurance contributions

We have seen,, that cuts in direct taxation will lead to increase in disposable income, consumption expenditure, aggregate demand and income/output. Some economists think that tax changes have large effects the behaviour of people and large effects on the economy. Also, some economists think that, cuts in income tax may not even lead to an increase in any budget deficit or a reduction in any surplus.

We will consider a reduction in the marginal rate of income tax (the fraction of each extra pound the government takes in taxation); these tax cuts *theoretically* benefit the supply side of the economy.

There are two possible effects of a cut in taxation:

a. The increase in take-home pay derived from the last hour worked tends to make people substitute work for leisure. They work longer hours. This is known as the '*substitution effect*'.

b. People pay less in taxation: They need to do less work to obtain any given target living standard. They work fewer labour hours. This is known as the '*income effect*'.

The net effect is unknown - empirical work shows that tax cuts only lead to a small increase in the supply of labour. It is only if the substitution effect outweighs the income effect will a tax cut lead to an increase in the supply of labour.

However, the theoretical reasons for cuts in direct taxation are shown in the following diagrams (Figs. 8.9, 8.10 and 8.11).

Let AB be determined by the marginal rate of income tax (t), in this case t = 0.25 (25%). Let w_0 be the average wage paid by employers, say £8 per hour. At a wage of w_0 the demand for labour is N_{f0} ($mpl(N_{f0}) = w_0$ =£8).

Let (w_0-tx_0) be the after tax wage received, say £6 per hour. The tax take per hour worked is txo (equal to £2). At the after tax wage, N_{f0} labour hours are offered by the labour force ($mdw(N_{f0}) = w_0 - tx_0$ = £6).

The demand for labour is equal to the supply of labour. (= N_{f0}). This, of course, is not the maximum possible level of full employment. In Fig. 8.9 the maximum possible full employment level is N_{f1} which is the intersection of the LD and AJ schedules.

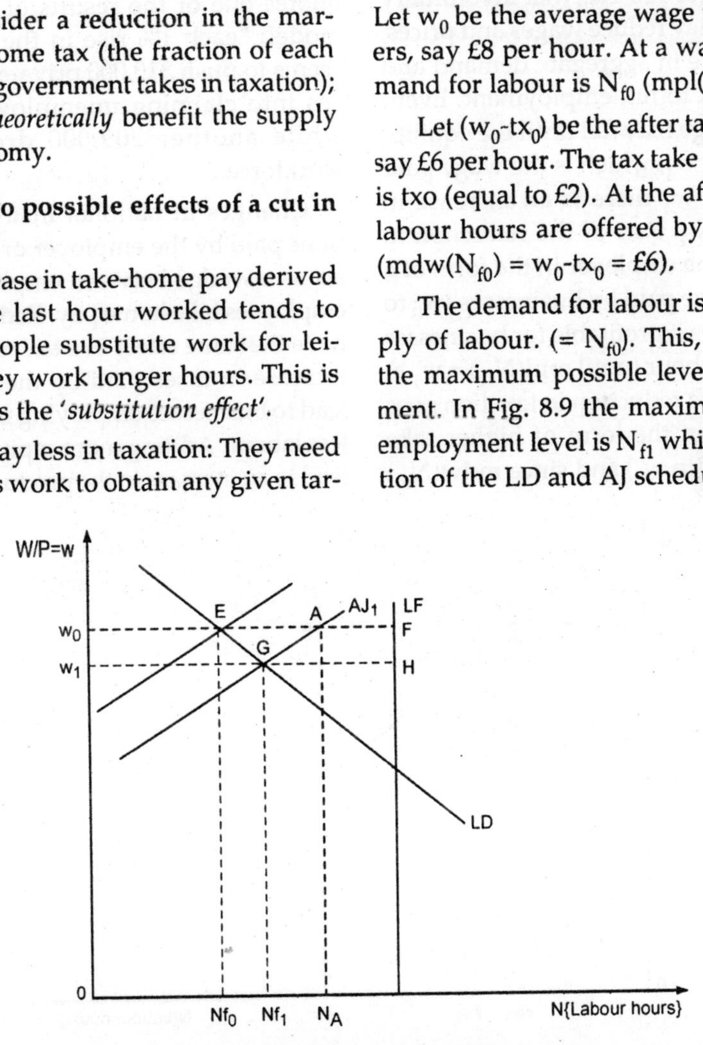

Fig. 8.8: A reduction in unemployment benefit

At Nfo there is no involuntary unemployment but some voluntary unemployment BC.

AB is known as the TAX WEDGE. It is the difference between the wage rate paid by the employer and the take home wage rate of the employee.

In the extreme case, if income tax is abolished, then the immediate effect is for the wage paid by the employer (w_0) to become the wage received by the employee. At w_0 the number of people willing to accept jobs is greater than the number of jobs offered (N_{f0}). There is, initially, an excess supply of labour (points A to D), which is involuntarily unemployed. We have seen, on pages 106-108, that involuntary unemployment may reduce wages and prices, lead to an increase in aggregate demand and a movement back to full employment. Eventually the real wage may fall until the equilibrium wage rate is w_1, which is the wage paid and received. At w_1 there is an increase in employment to N_{f1}. Part of the reduction in taxation goes to the employer in the form of a fall in the real wage paid by businesses (w_0 to w_1) and this makes it profitable for businesses to employ more labour (until $mpl(N_{f1}) = w_1$ at point E). Part of the reduction in taxation goes to the employee in the form of higher take home pay ($w_0 - tx_0$ to w_0) and since $mdw(N_{f0})$ is less than w_1 then employees are willing to supply more labour (until $mdw(N_{f1}) = w_1$ at point G).

Employment has increased from N_{f0} to N_{f1}. There is a reduction in voluntary unemployment from BC to GF. Effectively, in the real sector of the economy, Y_{f0} shifts to the right to Y_{f1}.

Of course an increase in income tax will take the economy further away from the maximum possible full employment position, in this case, N_{f1}.

D.B.Smith: *Is High Public Spending Good or Bad for You?* (Williams de Broe, 2002) page 17 quotes one of the results of his forecasting model; "each 1% rise in the UK tax *burden* seems to push 310,000 private sector employees into claiming unemployment benefits, while another 209,000 drop out of the workforce."

Changes in national insurance contributions paid by the employer or employee both act as a wedge between employers costs and employees take home pay. Reducing them will have the same effect as a tax cut. However, an increase in taxes paid by the employer may lead to businesses employing more capital and less labour. Adding more capital to labour will lead to an increase in the productivity of labour

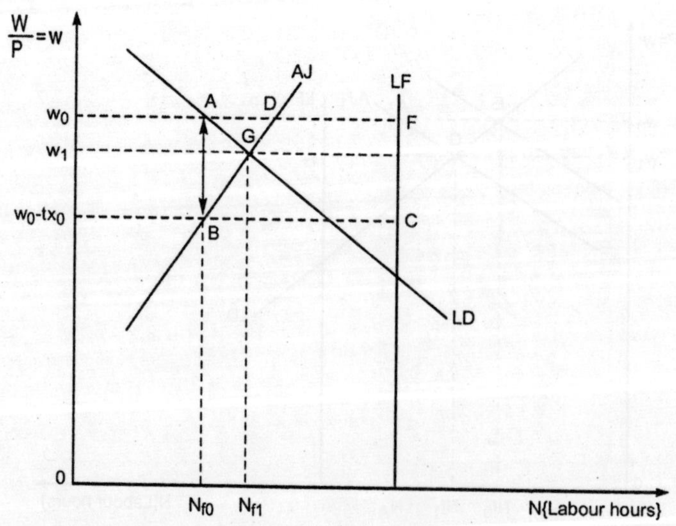

Fig. 8.9: A reduction in direct taxation

and shift the demand curve for labour (LD) to the right.

Start at LD_0, w_0, the full employment level of employment N_{f0} (producing Y_{f0} full employment income/output), point 'E' where $mdw(N_{f0}) = mpl(N_{f0}) = wo$. The level of voluntary unemployment is 'E to F'. Cuts in taxation have been especially aimed at reducing the income tax of the wealthy. (In the UK the highest rate of income tax was cut to 40% in 1988). Cutting the taxes of the wealthy will, *theoretically*, encourage these individuals to invest and set up new enterprises and businesses. Increasing investment will add more capital to a given stock of labour and, will, theoretically, increase the productivity of this labour. The demand for labour will increase. The $mpl(N_{f0})$ is now greater than the real wage, w_0. It is now profitable for firms to employ more labour than N_{f0}. LD_0 will shift to the right to LD_1 as in Fig. 8.10. At *real* wage wo there will now be an excess demand for labour. The real wage will be bid up to w_1. The new equilibrium will be at w_1; N_{f1} (producing Y_{f1} full employment output as in Fig. 8.7). Voluntary unemployment will be reduced from EF to GH.

These businesses, as well as producing more output, will then employ new workers who benefit from an increase in income. The benefits of a cut in taxation given to the wealthy will 'trickle down' to the less well off. In 1896 W.J. Bryan (interpreted by H. M. Littlefield as the Cowardly Lion in the Wizard of Oz), in his speech to the democratic convention made the following point. "There are those who believe that if you just legislate to make the well-to-do prosperous, their prosperity will leak through on those below."

The economy benefits because more output is produced, voluntary unemployment is reduced, there is downward pressure on the price level and the overall productivity of the economy is increased. People benefit through higher levels of employment (N_{f1}) and an increased real wage (w_1). However, if the real wage rises as fast as productivity (to w_{01} at point J), then there will be no increase in employment.

According to the Organisation for Economic cooperation and Development (OECD), every one percentage point increase in taxation as a proportion of GDP is associated with a reduction in output per head of about 0.6 to 0.7%. However M. O'Mahoney, who produced an exhaustive study of UK productivity, says that the underlying cause of poor productivity performance is low skills and that no

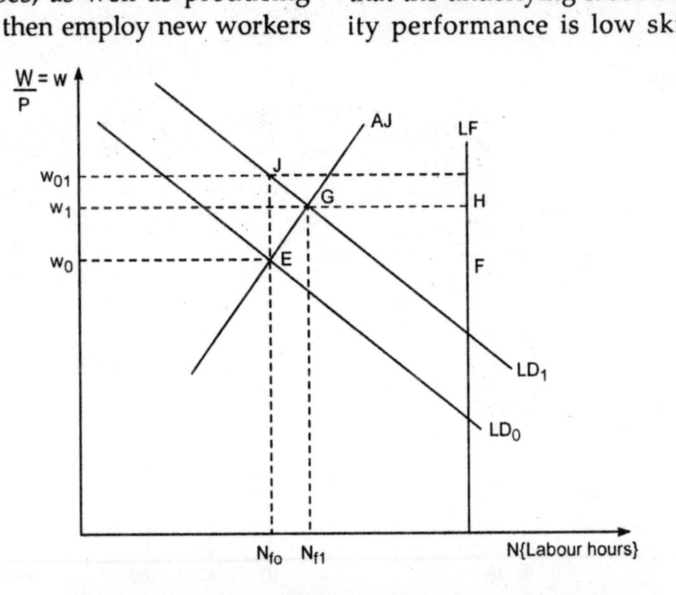

Fig. 8.10: An increase in the productivity of the labour force

amount of physical capital can make up for a poorly trained and educated labour force. Without it new machinery is of questionable value (*Britains Productivity Performance 1950-96*: NIESR., April 1999).

It is also argued that cuts in income tax may not lead to an increase in the budget deficit. Consider Fig. 8.11. The Laffer curve.

The tax revenue (tax take) of the government is measured on the vertical axis and the rate of taxation is measured on the horizontal axis.

At a tax rate of zero the tax take will be zero. At a tax rate of 100% no one would work and the tax take would again be zero. It is assumed (realistically?) that the curve is quadratic.

If the tax rate is **tC** then the tax take is **TTC**. Cutting the tax rate to **tD** will **increase** the tax revenue to **TTD**.

Supplysiders believe that a tax cut would lead to a large increase in both labour supply and investment, and hence to a large expansion in income/output. More income means more tax revenue for the government. It is also argued that a lower rate of taxation will discourage people from trying to evade taxation, hence increasing the tax take. This is the so called Gutmann effect.

However, if the tax rate is **tA** then the tax take is **TTA**. Cutting the tax rate to **tB** will **decrease** the tax revenue to **TTB**. Proponents of income tax cuts argue that the tax rate is **tC** rather than **tA**.

Even if tax cuts do not lead to an increase in tax take they may be of overall benefit to the economy. R A Mundell, who won the Nobel Prize in 1991 for his work on international economics, observed that an increase in government debt might represent an improvement in market efficiency, if it corresponded to an increase in incomes. That might occur if a reduction in taxes caused an increase in the deficit, while stimulating economic growth. In that case, Mundell argued, a tax cut would increase efficiency if the additional revenues assumed to be arising from the growth effect were larger than the interest on the bonds issued to cover the ensuing deficit.

Incidentally some economists believe that budget deficits are not important because people realise that the deficits need to be financed and that the level of their taxation will increase in the future. People will reduce their consumption expenditure and increase their

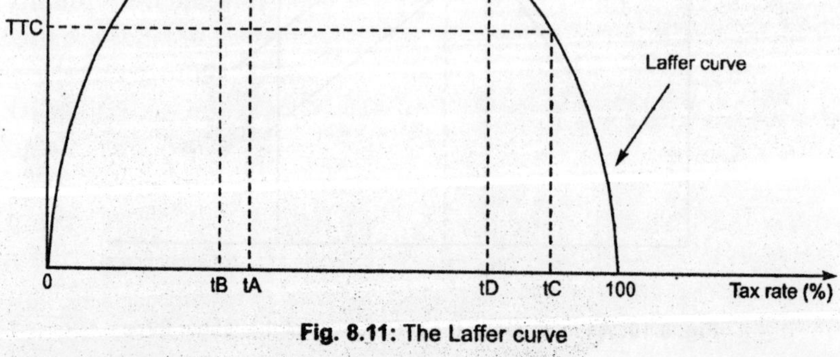

Fig. 8.11: The Laffer curve

saving to pay for future tax increases. In the jargon this is known as the Barro-Ricardo equivalence proposition or Ricardian equivalence.

In the UK, between 1979 and 1991, there were £31 billion in tax cuts. 27% of this went to the top 1% of income earners. 15% went to the lowest 50%. The average **real** income of the poorest 10% **fell** by 14% between the years 1979-91. Also, in February 1995, a report by the Joseph Rowntree Foundation said that there was no evidence of a trickle down effect in the UK.

There is also some evidence that tax cuts did not encourage the small business person to work harder, they may have had the opposite effect! (Understanding the Small Business Sector, by D.J. Storey: Routledge. 1994).

N. Isles's, Life at the Top: The Labour Market for FTSE-250 Chief Executives, published by The Work Foundation, quotes voluminous research to show CEOs are clever and talented but rarely exceptional. Despite the rhetoric of visionary leaders, for every talented individual there are 100 bureaucrats; stewards, not risk-takers. Most prefer deal making and mergers to boost short-term share price to the hard grind of managing their companies. There is no shortage of able people eager to do the job. But "the market" is their best excuse: here Isles lands his biggest blow. There is little global market in British managers. Overseas companies don't want ours and we don't often recruit from abroad: 86% of FTSE CEOs come from the UK, another 6% from the EU (many from Ireland) and 8% from the US and the rest of the world.

Also, most businesses don't even recruit their CEOs from outside their companies. Some two thirds of FTSE CEOs were home-grown from within their companies. So why is their pay rising when there is no strong market out there? US CEO salaries are 10 times higher than here. But French and German CEOs are paid less, although their companies' productivity is higher.

When all other arguments fail, apologists fall back on a blase view that CEO pay is such an infinitesimal part of a company's outgoings that it hardly matters. But it does. Isles accumulates research showing how dysfunctional it is. Managers set an example in their psychological contract with their staff: large pay differentials demotivate and demoralise. When differentials between top and bottom exceed 14:1, morale slides.

3. Classical unemployment and a reduction in the real wage

The argument of this section is that the real wage can be maintained above its equilibrium level either by the actions of trade unions (including increasing the cost of hiring and firing [the French economy?] *or* wages councils *or* minimum wage legislation. The resulting unemployment is known as classical unemployment (the unemployment can be regarded as the voluntary consequence of workers exercising their monopoly power – a monopoly power brought about by workers' bargaining strength or political power that established the labour market regulations).

However, it is difficult to understand how setting the money wage (W) can increase the real wage (W/P) above its equilibrium level when it is businesses that determine the price level (P).

a. If, in Fig. 8.12, we start at the *real* wage wo, the number of jobs (labour hours) offered by businesses are N_{fo}. As individuals, a number of workers, AB, will wish to work at w_0 but cannot find a job; they are **individually** *involuntarily* unemployed but are unwilling or unable to reduce the real wage level w_0. The argument is that AB are, **collectively**, *voluntarily* unemployed. AB is the classical unemployment. BC are the normal voluntary unemployed. There is Nfo employment and AC are voluntarily unemployed. There are no forces in the labour market acting to reduce the voluntary unemployed. In figure 8.12 the maximum possible full employment level is N_{f1} which is the intersection of the LD and AJ schedules. It should also be noted that any increase in the real wage will increase the number of individuals voluntarily unemployed. The number of registered unemployed will increase. The economy will move further away from the maximum possible full employment level (N_{f1}) which is the intersection of the labour demand schedule [AD] and the labor supply schedule [the accept job schedule—AJ].

b. Now there is a change in the law governing trade union activities *or* an incomes policy is introduced that reduces real wages *or* wages councils are abolished *or* legislation is introduced abolishing minimum wages. The collectively voluntarily unemployed AB are now individually involuntarily unemployed. The involuntary unemployment bring about a fall in wages and prices and an increase in aggregate demand.

We assume that the real wage wo falls to w_1. As the real wage falls it is profitable for businesses to employ more labour. Employment increases from Nfo to N_{f1} (assuming that new jobs are provided). Effectively, in the real sector of the economy, Y_f shifts to the right. Voluntary unemployment falls from AC to EF.

Changing industrial relations legislation, abolishing minimum wages or disbanding wages councils emphasises the need for labour to be a flexible commodity to be utilised as aggressively as possible. In an international economy the argument is that these changes will attract overseas investment (companies like Toyota, Nissan, LG and others have created over 1,000,000 jobs in the UK). However the OECD. report of July 1994 reports that, in the UK, foreign multinationals pay wages, on average, 15% higher than British companies, employ fewer part-time workers, have more collective bargaining arrangements and more consultation. These arrangements have *not* been at the expense of a reduction in productivity. The productivity of foreign multinationals is, on average, significantly higher than their British counterparts.

4. Other supply side policies

This school of thought advocates limiting the

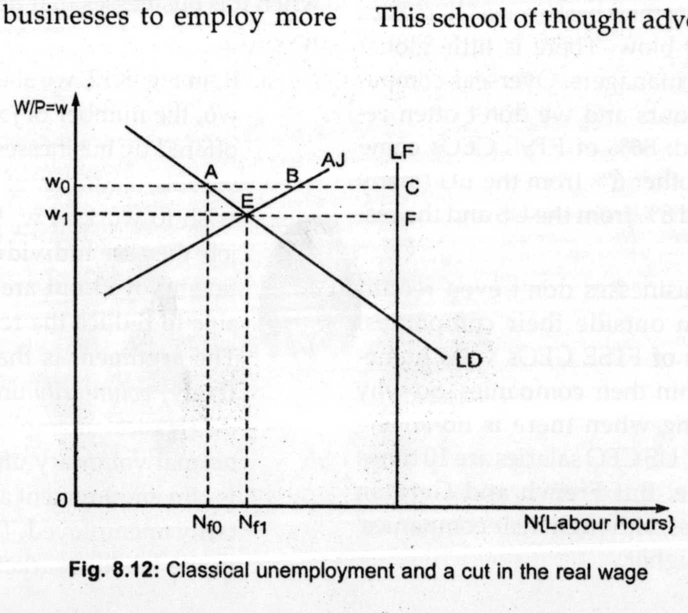

Fig. 8.12: Classical unemployment and a cut in the real wage

time for which the unemployed can draw benefit, in order to encourage them to search for work, while at the same time providing the long-term unemployed with counselling and other assistance to overcome both the obsolescence of their skills and pessimistic attitudes towards the chances of finding work. The underlying aim is to overcome the alienation of the long-term unemployed from the labour market, and thus to restore to it a force for wage moderation. Particular proposals connected with this school of thought involve tightening the conditions for payment of unemployment benefit, putting pressure on applicants for benefit to justify refusal to accept jobs offered, and withholding payment from those who will not undertake the training required. Other less sanction based proposals sought to tackle 'mismatches' between employment opportunities and the unemployed labour available ; this would be done by improving the information provided by the network of Employment Exchanges–re-christened as Jobcentres and by reducing constraints on the mobility of labour such as those applied by differential housing costs and the non-transferability of occupational pensions. A number of these ideas were drawn upon for the Labour Government's 'New Deal' programme, launched in 1998. Particular proposals connected with this school of thought involve tightening the conditions for payment of unemployment benefit, putting pressure on applicants for benefit to justify refusal to accept jobs offered, and withholding payment from those who will not undertake the training required. Other less sanction based proposals sought to tackle 'mismatches' between employment opportunities and the unemployed labour available ; this would be done by improving the information provided by the network of Employment Exchanges – re-christened as Jobcentres - and by reducing constraints on the mobility of labour such as those applied by differential housing costs and the non-transferability of occupational pensions. A number of these ideas were drawn upon for the Labour Government's 'New Deal' programme, launched in 1998.

a. Grants and allowances for retraining will improve the skills of the unemployed.

b. Measures to help school leavers develop skills and job experience. (a) and (b) improve the flexibility and productivity of the labour force.

c. (i) If the labour market is more flexible, then, as in Fig. 8.12, if the initial real wage (w_0) is above the equilibrium level (w_1) then it will fall faster to w_1.

(ii) Also, since more output can now be produced from the same labour input it is profitable for businesses to employ more labour. The demand for labour will increase. As in Fig. 8.10 above, LD_0 will shift to the right to LD_1.

The new equilibrium will be at w_1; N_{f1}. Voluntary unemployment will be reduced from EF to GH.

Employment will increase from N_{f0} to N_{f1}. In the real sector of the economy Y_{f0} will shift to the right (as in Fig. 8.7).

• The government is spending £2.5 billion on the New Deal programme to help the long-term unemployed. However, J. Heckman and J. Smith found that a similar scheme in the USA—the American Job Training Partnership Act-had made very little difference to participants' prospects and that in the case of younger men, those who took part in the programme were **less** likely to get jobs than those who did not! Schemes like the New Deal tend to help motivated workers who tend to find jobs anyway. An independent evaluation in 1999 found that most New Dealers who had found jobs under the scheme would have done so without it because of the improvement in the economy.

d. Planning agreements between industry, trade unions and the government. The argument is that an atmosphere of collaboration rather than confrontation best fosters economic growth.

e. Subsidies and grants to particular industries. e.g. microelectronic.

f. Policies aimed at underdeveloped, depressed or developing regions.

g. Monetary and fiscal policy: Some economists argue that increasing aggregate demand will, as well as reducing involuntary unemployment, stimulate economic activity, improve profitability and encourage productive investment. This will increase the productivity of the economy. Adding more capital to the stock of labour will increase the productivity of labour. The demand for labour will increase as in figure 8.10 above. In the real sector Y_f is shifted to the right (as in figure 8.7).

h. Deregulation of markets: This enables businesses, that, for some reason or other, were prevented from competing in a particular area of the economy, to offer their products in these particular areas. The extra competition should reduce the degree of monopoly in the economy, reduce prices and increase the real wage.

In a closed economy, with perfect competition, we have seen that the profit maximising amount of labour employed occurs when mpl = W/P. On aggregate, labour will be paid its marginal product. If we assume imperfect competition then the profit maximising amount of labour employed is when mpl.g = W/P.Where g = (1- Mp) and Mp is the average degree of monopoly in the system.

Since $0<Mp<1$, then $0<g<1$. Therefore the profit maximising real wage will be less than the marginal productivity of labour (mpl). Labour will be paid less than its marginal product. If Mp = 0 then g =1 and we are back to the purely competitive case (mpl = W/P). (The demand for labour [when g<1] will be to the left of the demand for labour curve when g=1).

If we start at wo, Nfo and reduce the average degree of monopoly in the system. (Mp falls and g increases), the demand for labour will increase from LD(g_0) to LD(g_0). The real wage will be bid up to w_1. The new equilibrium will be at w_1, N_{f1}. Voluntary unemployment will be reduced from EF to GH. In the real sector Y_f is shifted to the right (as in Fig. 8.7).

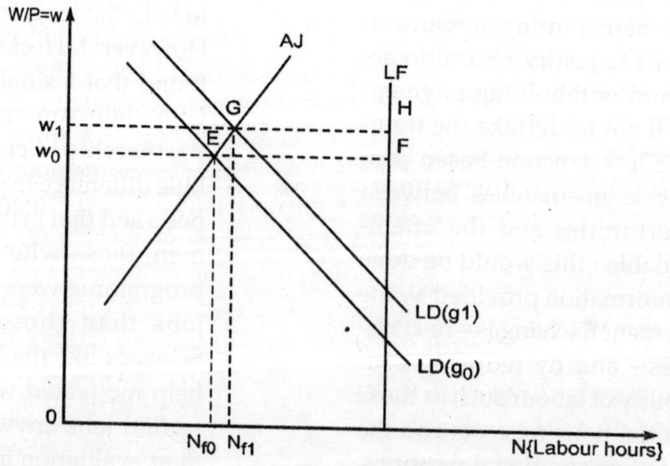

Fig. 8.13: A reduction in the degree of monopoly power in the economy

YOU SHOULD REMEMBER

1. An increase in aggregate demand (brought about by either monetary and/or fiscal policies) can reduce involuntary unemployment and may (Point **f**, above), reduce voluntary unemployment.
2. There are disadvantages both in the use of expansionary fiscal policy (crowding out and inflation?) or expansionary monetary policy (inflation?). They both can lead to balance of payments problems.
3. There are **theoretical** reasons why the economy will adjust to the new full employment level (Y_{f1}) and hence, some economists argue that there is no need for an active monetary and/or fiscal policy to expand the economy to reduce INVOLUNTARY unemployment. They argue that the economy must become more flexible (accept lower pay?) and dynamic (enjoy fewer in-work benefits?). Rigidities in the economy must be abolished (trade unions and welfare states?) so that the economy will quickly eliminate any involuntary unemployment and will become more competitive (companies can make bigger profits and pay less tax?) when facing the new global challenge. International organisations from the International Monetary Fund in Washington to the Organisation for Economic Cooperation in Paris and just about every finance minister and central banker believe that flexibility is the key to lower unemployment. They believe that those countries with flexible labour markets (ie lower rates of trade union membership, low non-wage costs, tough benefit rules) price marginal workers back into jobs. Countries with inflexible ones have high levels of youth unemployment and joblessness among those with low skills. The UK and the USA are examples of countries that have implemented supply side policies. Unemployment rates in the UK and the US were low in 2000 after two decades of structural reform, but not spectacularly so in comparison to other OECD countries. The Netherlands, Switzerland, Norway and Austria all had lower jobless rates, and none of those has signed up to Anglo-Saxon "flexibility". An alternative explanation is that unemployment in Britain and the US has come down due to higher levels of aggregate demand while staying high in some of the continental economies because of a demand deficiency. In 2003-04, John Schmitt and Jonathan Wadsworth, looked at a "flexibility is good for you in the end" strategy as the reason for British and American job success in the 1990s. The idea is that flexibility prices young people, the low-skilled and the long-term unemployed back into work, but Schmitt and Wadsworth found little to show that the US and the UK did any better with these than countries riddled with "rigidities".

   The cross-country data for youth unemployment in 2000 shows that the US and the UK were mid-table rather than league leaders. Ireland (4.7%), Switzerland (4.8%), the Netherlands (5.3%), Austria (6.3%), Denmark (6.7%), Germany (7.7%), Portugal (8.4%) and Japan (9.2%) all had lower youth unemployment rates than did the US (9.3%). Britain's rate was 11.8%, not that different from inflexible Sweden (11.9%). In 2003-04 David Howell and Friedrich Huebler investigated one of the other central claims for flexibility—that it is worth accepting more inequality in labour markets if it means lower unemployment. They found no such trade-off. They concluded, from the evidence, that the existence of trade unions and active government labour market policies are not to blame for high unemployment but have a profound effect on earnings distribution.
4. In the UK the Bank of England has control over monetary policy with a remit to keep

inflation (the CPI [consumer price index]) around 2.0%. In practice this means that if inflation is expected to fall below 2.0% then interest rates will be reduced and aggregate demand will increase. This policy ties in nicely with the government's supply side measures. If they are effective then there will be downward pressure on the inflation rate. This downward pressure will be brought about by either an increase in involuntary unemployment or by an increase in the productivity of labour. The Bank of England will then cut interest rates to expand aggregate demand and this will eliminate any involuntary unemployment and may reduce the level of voluntary unemployment. As long as monetary policy is effective the government is not relying on 'market forces' to take the economy to full employment.

5. Assuming that the economy is always at, or near to, full employment, the only effective policies that the government can introduce are supply side measures to reduce the level of voluntary unemploy-ment. I.e. policies to shift Y_f to the right (with the extra benefit of downward pressure on the price level).

The aim of supply side policies is to improve the economic performance of an economy. But an OECD report of 1994 reports that low labour market standards have little effect on either improving or worsening economic performance and job creation. It finds that employment growth is not a question of lax labour standards or deregulation of the labour market (the ease of hiring or firing, the regulation of daily or weekly working hours, the setting of minimum wage rates, and the representation of workers at the workplace) but it depends decisively on organisational and institutional structures. The OECD favours strong links between schools, employers and students that tend to raise skill levels. The OECD also recommends an economy to have a mix of large, medium and small companies with strong links between them.

Another OECD report of 26/5/97 concluded that the level of structural (voluntary) unemployment in the UK had fallen from 10.2% in 1986 to 7% in 1996.

QUESTIONS

1. Does the real wage have to fall for employment to increase?
2. Do changes in aggregate demand affect the supply side of the economy?
3. Will cuts in direct taxation lead to an increase in the supply of labour?
4. Does the Laffer curve show that cuts in taxation are self-financing?
5. Suppose that the number of people employed in an economy falls by 0.1% over the course of a single month. It is, in such a circumstance,
   (a) possible for the unemployment rate to fall if enough unemployed workers become too discouraged to look for a job
   (b) (b) possible for the unemployment rate to remain constant if the frictional component falls
   (c) impossible for the unemployment rate to do anything but fall
   (d) impossible for the unemployment rate to do anything but rise
   (e) possible for the unemployment rate to remain constant if the cyclical component falls.
6. A models that envisages perfectly flexible prices can explain recession only in terms of
   (a) increases in aggregate demand
   (b) decreases in aggregate demand
   (c) increases in the number of people looking for work without a corresponding increase in the number of jobs
   (d) sudden changes in investment expenditure that cause the capital stock to increase more quickly
   (e) none of the above.
7. Suppose that long-term labour contracts hold the real wage above equilibrium. Which of the following statements would then hold?
   (a) Fiscal policy stimulus would perversely increase the excess supply of labour.
   (b) Monetary stimulus would perversely increase the excess supply of labour.
   (c) Monetary stimulus would be totally ineffective to change the excess supply of labour.
   (d) Fiscal stimulus only would reduce the excess supply of labour.
   (e) Both fiscal and monetary stimulus could reduce the excess supply of labour.

ANSWERS

1. Given an unchanged, negatively sloped, demand for labour schedule the real wage needs to fall for employment to increase. However, if the productivity of labour is increasing, the real wage need not decline.

   If we start at point A where the economy is not at full employment. Normally the real wage will need to fall to w_1 for full employment to be restored at N_{f0}.

   However, if there is an increase in productivity, then the demand for labour schedule will shift from LD_0 to, say, LD_1 and the full employment level of employment will increase from N_{f0} to N_{f1}. To reach the new full employment output level N_{f1} does not now require a fall in the real wage. As long as there is an increase in aggregate demand then the economy will move to full employment.

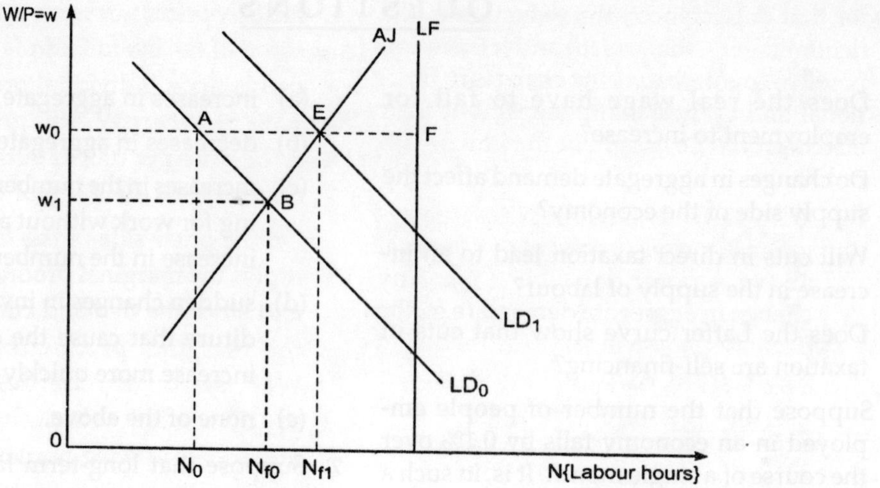

2. Infrastructure investment spending of the government will increase both the marginal products of labour and capital.(New Keynesianism and Aggregate Economic Activity by Assar Lindbeck – Economic Journal, 108, 1998 pp167-180). There will be an increase in the demand for labour at each wage rate. This will shift the LD schedule to the right, the production function upwards and shift the level of full employment output (Y_f) to the right.

3. There are two possible effects of a decrease in direct taxation.

   (a) The increase in take-home pay derived from the last hour worked tends to make people substitute work for leisure. People work longer hours. This is the substitution effect.

   (b) People pay less in taxation: They need to do less work to obtain any given target living standard. People work *fewer* labour hours. This is the income effect.

   The net effect is unknown - empirical work shows that tax cuts only lead to a small increase in the supply of labour.

4. No. It depends on the shape of the Laffer curve and the position of the initial tax position.

   We are assuming that the Laffer curve is quadratic. It may be a series of loops from 0 to 100 and the results of any tax change may be indeterminate.

   The initial tax rate also determines whether or not tax cuts will lead to increases or decreases in tax take. Starting at tA or tC will give opposite results.

5. (a)

   The unemployment rate is computed as

$$\frac{\text{number people unemployed}}{(\text{number of people unemployed}) + (\text{number of people employed})} \times 100\%$$

(number of people unemployed) + (number of people employed) where the number of people unemployed have to satisfy certain eligibility criteria. One criterion is that the individual actively looks for work —i.e. is a part of the labour force. Should an unemployed person become discouraged no longer to participate in the labour force. And that person is no longer unemployed. So, even if the number of people employed were to fall (thereby reducing the denominator and creating the likelihood that the rate will increase), the rate of unemployment <u>could</u> fall if the number of people unemployed fell by an amount sufficient to cause a reduction in the numerator that outdistanced the reduction in the denominator. Answers (b) and (c) mention possible counterbalancing changes in functional and cyclical components, but their effects would be caught in the initial—1% reduction.

6. (e) With perfectly flexible prices, the aggregate supply schedule is vertical above a potential GNP (Y_f). Any change in aggregate demand (e.g., the decrease shown in (**a**) of the following figure from ADp_0 to ADp_1) results only in a corresponding change in the price level (a reduction from P_0 to P_1 in part (**a**) with output being held fixed at a potential GNP; so, there is no recession. (An increase in the aggregate demand creates the opposite potential

7. Neither prices nor wage rates effect the position of the labour supply schedule; it depends upon individual preferences (mdw = W/P). Where W is the given wage, and P is the price per unit of output, and mdw is the marginal disutility of work.

On the other side of the labour market, if mpl is the marginal productivity of labour and since the demand curve for labour is the marginal product of labour, mpl= W/P, the equation that describes the quantity demanded for a given wage and a perfectly competitive market for output is: W/P = mpl. If this is an aggregate demand curve and contracts hold real wages constant, then, constant = [W/P] = mpl.

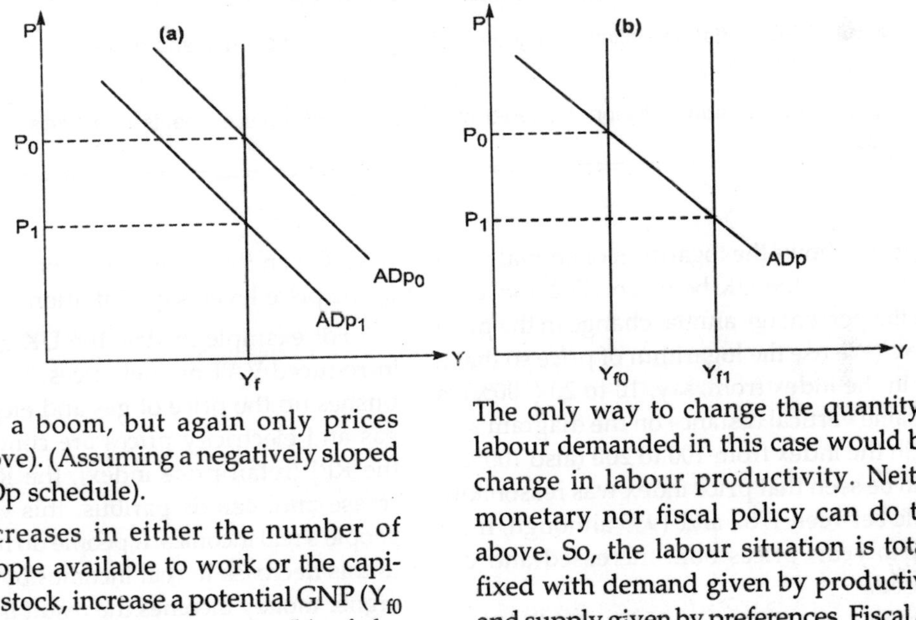

for a boom, but again only prices move). (Assuming a negatively sloped ADp schedule).

Increases in either the number of people available to work or the capital stock, increase a potential GNP (Y_{f0} to Y_{f1}), but (as shown in (b) of the above figure, that results in lower prices (P_0 to P_1), not unemployed resources (assuming a negatively sloped ADp schedule).

The only way to change the quantity of labour demanded in this case would be a change in labour productivity. Neither monetary nor fiscal policy can do that above. So, the labour situation is totally fixed with demand given by productivity and supply given by preferences. Fiscal and monetary policy can change neither, so they are ineffectual in address-ing any excess supply problem. Only answer (**c**) notes this intransigence correctly.

CHAPTER 9

INFLATION

KEY TERMS

Inflation: An increase in the price of goods and services over time.

Demand Pull Inflation: Inflation 'triggered off' when aggregate demand exceeds the potential output of the economy.

Cost Push Inflation: Inflation 'triggered off' when one or more elements of a firm's costs increase.

Fig. 9.1 shows the logarithm of annual price index for the UK between 1782 and 2002 and the percentage annual change in the price index. (We use the logarithm of price so that a rise in the index from, say, 10 to 20 (100%) is the same vertical distance on the diagram as a rise in the index from 100 to 200 (also 100%)). It can be seen that price index was reasonably stable between 1782 and 1939 although, from year to year, prices both increased and decreased.

It is only since the beginning of the Second World War that the price index has shown a substantial increase - with increases in the price index in every year but 1953. This post-1940 increase in prices is known as the great inflation. (It has also coincided with the introduction of Keynesian economics).

We will define inflation as an increase in the average price of goods and services over time. Given this definition a 'one off' increase in the price level is not inflation.

For example in 1994 the UK government introduced VAT on fuel prices. This of course pushes up the price of gas and electricity. As gas and electricity prices are components of the RPI (retail price index), the RPI will increase and, ceteris paribus, this will reduce people's real incomes. If people do not respond to this decrease in real incomes by asking for higher money incomes the result is a 'one off' increase the price level.

However, a 'one off' increase in the price level may lead to people demanding higher money incomes to compensate them for the fall in their real incomes. This rise in money income, will, generally, lead to an increase in the costs of production and an increase in the price level. Again money incomes rise costs rise and prices rise etc. Thus a 'one off' increase

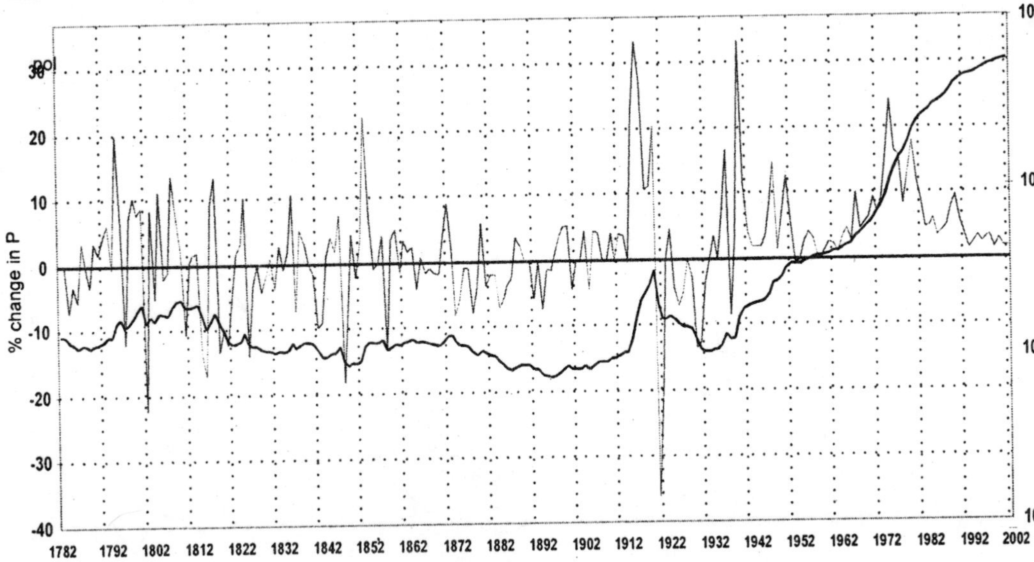

Fig. 9.1: The level and Parcentage change in the price level

in the price level may 'trigger off' an inflationary situation.

Why do economists wish to control inflation?

1. It is said to destroy jobs, damage growth and harm investment.
   a. A high and variable rate of inflation increases the risk associated with any assessment of future returns on an investment project i.e. it reduces expected net revenues and hence investment and the creation of new jobs. Figure 9.2 plots investment as a proportion of GDP, inflation, and unemployment for the years 1960-95. However, investment, inflation, and employment rose together from 1960-68, 1986-90 and fell together from 1991.
   b. A high and variable rate of inflation makes it difficult to distinguish between changes in *relative* price from changes in the *general* price level. As a result workers and employers find it more difficult to determine whether the increase in their wage or product price is due to an increase in demand for their labour or product (and more should be produced and/or supplied) or whether it is due to general inflation (and no more should be produced and/or supplied). Confusing the two can lead to a misallocation of resources. As M. Friedman stated "the broadcast about relative prices is, as it were, being jammed by the noise coming from the inflation broadcast".
   c. A high and variable rate of inflation forces people to constantly relearn prices. It helps to destroy the information conveyed by relative prices.
2. It harms long-term contracts denominated in money terms. For example, people who bought long term bonds that pays them a fixed amount of money each year will find that inflation erodes the **real** value of their returns. However, since the main issuer of bonds is the government, it is usually the government that benefits from inflation. Of course, people who entered into long-term contracts that required them to pay a fixed amount each

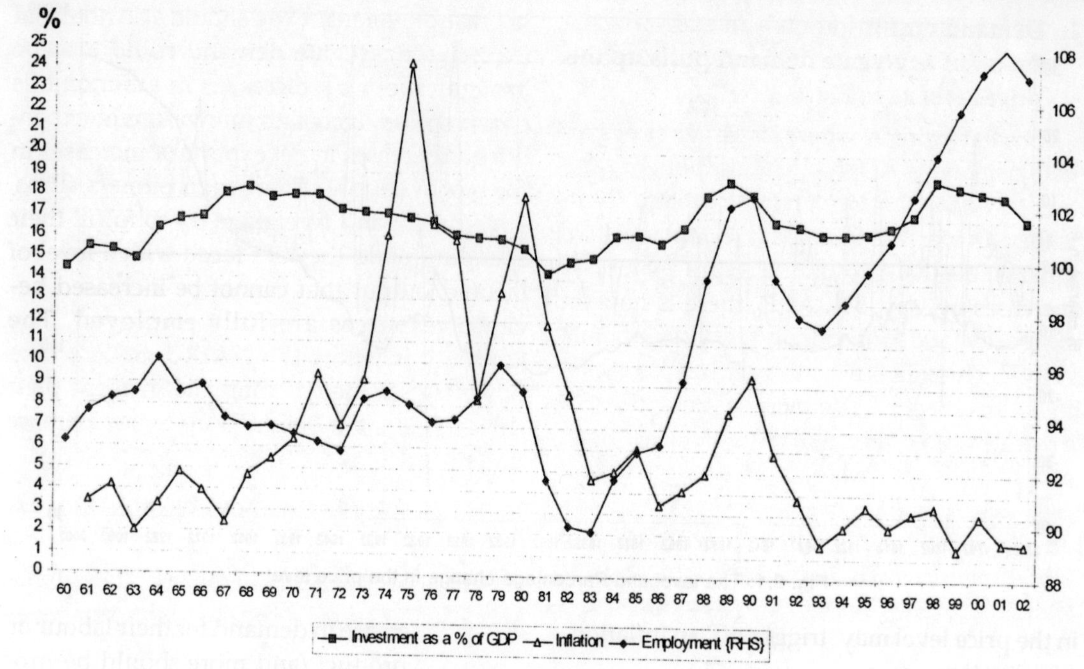

Fig. 9.2: UK-Investment, Inflation and Employment

year will find that the real value of their payments will be falling.

3. If tax thresholds are not increased in line with inflation then more people will pay more taxation as they are pushed into higher tax brackets. This is known as fiscal drag.

Are there any advantages of inflation?

1. Growth in the output of an economy involves structural change, and inflation is a natural accompaniment of a shift in resources from contracting to expanding sectors of an economy if costs and prices are more flexible upwards than downwards. In this sense, inflation is part of the growth process.
2. Real interest rates can be reduced by inflation. A fall in real interest rates will raise the prospective yields on investment and act as a stimulus to investment. There is nothing that discourages investment more than the anticipation by business that the monetary authorities or government will clamp down on demand as soon as there is any upward movement of the price level. (This is the unfortunate signal that the ECB has been transmitting in Euro-land for the years 2000-01, which is why growth there languishes below productive potential).
3. Another reason why inflation may be beneficial for growth is that it can give rise to a greater degree of real wage flexibility that is necessary for employment creation in activities subject to diminishing returns and rising marginal cost.

Sarel, IMF Staff Papers 1996, and Ghosh and Phillips, IMF Staff Papers 1998 — point to a non-linear relation between inflation and growth, with growth first positively related to inflation and then turning negative as the costs of inflation start to exceed the benefits.

THEORIES OF INFLATION

We will approach the different theories of inflation by considering the factors that could 'trigger off' an inflationary situation.

1. Demand Pull Inflation—an excessive increase in aggregate demand pulls up the price level as in Fig. 9.3

Start at point A where the level of aggregate demand is ADp(G_0,M_0), output is Y_f and there is no involuntary unemployment. There is then an increase in aggregate demand—we will assume that the nominal supply of money increases by, say, 5%. At P_0 there is now an excess demand for goods and services—points A to A'. This will pull up the general price level to, in this case, P_1. The increase in price, with a money wage of Wo, will reduce the real wage and make it profitable for businesses to employ more labour. Since the economy is at full employment there will now be a shortage of labour and this will bid up the money wage rate. The money wage will only stop rising when the economy returns to full employment—point B. Prices and wages have been pulled up by an increase in aggregate demand. M, P and W have all increased by 5%.

We will emphasise two broad categories of demand-pull inflation.

a. Inflation brought about by fiscal expansion

We saw that fiscal policy before could increase aggregate demand above the full employment output level (Y_f - which corresponds to the NAIRU [non-accelerating inflation rate of unemployment). (You should also note that excessive aggregate demand could also be brought about by increases in autonomous consumption, increases in investment expenditure, increases in net exports or increases in the money supply). Then, as consumers, firms, government and foreigners try to fulfill their spending plans they are faced with a level of income/output that cannot be increased because resources are fully employed. The economy is below the NAIRU. Sellers take advantage of the situation and increase their prices. Prices are PULLED up by an increase in demand

b. Inflation brought about by monetary expansion

The **quantity theory of money**. The emphasis is on increases in the supply of money as discussed.

The quantity theory of money can be represented by the following equation:

$$M \times V = P \times Y$$

The product (MV) is equal to the product (PY).

where M = nominal stock of money

V = velocity of circulation. The speed at which money circulates around the economy, or, put another way, the average number of times money changes hands. Techni-

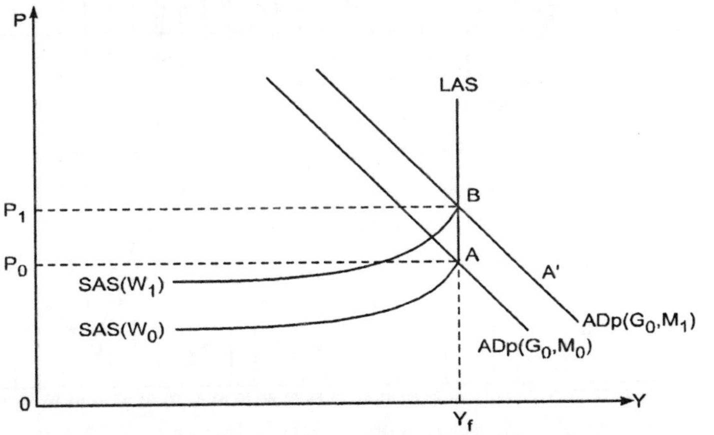

Fig. 9.3: Demand pull inflation

cally, it is measured as GNP divided by the money supply.

P = average price level.

Y = real income.

If the economy quickly returns to its full employment level then income/output (**Y**) can be regarded as being fixed at the full employment level Y_f. Also, if income (**Y**) is fixed at Y_f **and** the velocity of circulation (**V**) is constant, then the price level (**P**) is proportional to the supply of money (**M**), or $\%\Delta P = \%\Delta M$

The percentage increase in the price level is equal to the percentage increase in the nominal supply of money.

Hence, if the supply of money increases by 6% then the price level will increase by 6%. The percentage increase[decrease] in the price level is equal to the percentage increase [decrease] in the nominal supply of money. This is the result we found above Fig. 9.4 shows the growth in M4 and the RPI.

Over most of the period-considered (1964-2002) the growth in M4 has been well above the rate of inflation as measured by the RPI. (Another measure of the aggregate price level is the IPD [implicit price deflator of GDP]). This takes into account all of the prices of goods and services produced in an economy - not just the prices of goods and services covered by the RPI). However, in the USA, industry and agriculture, transport and power, and similar production and consumption expenditures account for less than 0.1 percent of the economy's flow of payments. The vast majority of transactions passing through the New York Clearing House and Fedwire are for stocks, bonds, packaged bank loans, options, derivatives and foreign currency transactions. The entire stock market value of many high-flying companies now changes hands in a single day, and the average holding time for currency trades has shrunk to just a few minutes. The value of these financial transactions each day exceeds that of the entire annual U.S. national income. It therefore seems absurd to relate the money supply only to consumer and wholesale prices, excluding asset prices.

Nor has the velocity of circulation remained constant. Fig. 9.5 shows that the ve-

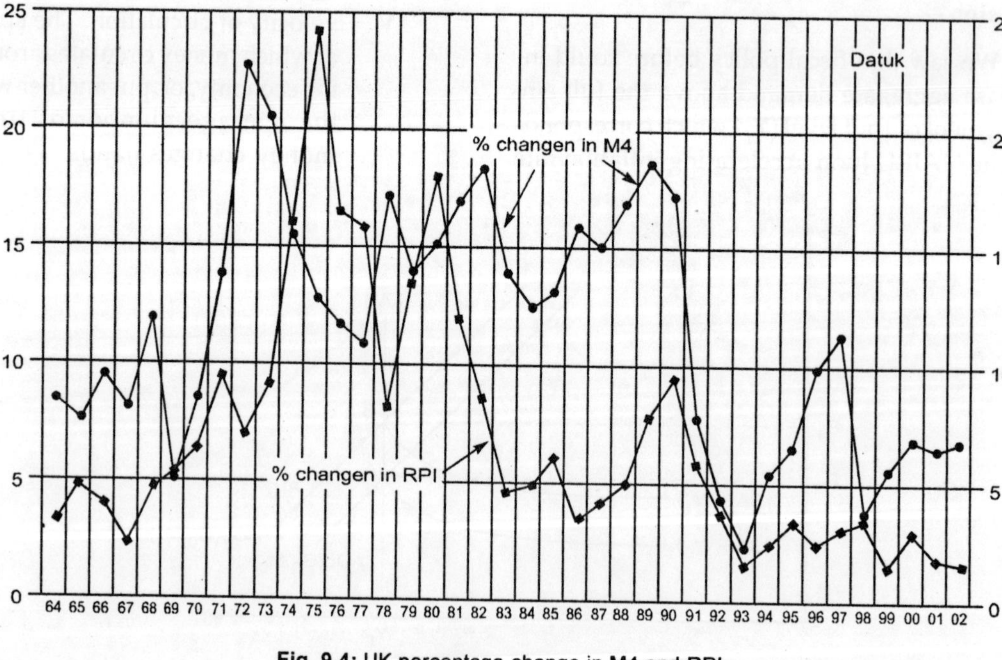

Fig. 9.4: UK percentage change in M4 and RPI

locity of circulation of M4 (nominal GDP/M4) has declined from 1980 onwards. (In appendix III we will examine the effect on the world economy, in 2007 onward, of a large decrease in the velocity of circulation and a 'credit crunch').

The main reasons velocity **increases** are:

a. **Increases** in Banking Efficiency: Credit cards, automatic tellers, and other bank innovations have made it easier for the public to obtain cash. This should **increase** velocity.
b. **Increases** in Nominal Interest Rates: These increase the opportunity cost of holding money causing velocity to **rise**.
c. **Increases** in Real Incomes: As people get richer they find it easier to economise on their holdings of money. This will increase velocity. Over the period 1983-95 both banking efficiency and real incomes have increased and the nominal rate of interest has only fallen from 8.5% to 5.75% after rising to over 14% in 1989.

2. Cost Push Inflation

If firms set their prices on the basis of their costs of production plus a mark-up for profit, then inflation is likely to occur when one or more elements of their costs have risen. Prices are then **PUSHED** up by an increase in costs. One example of this is shown in Fig. 9.6.

If we start at point A and assume that one element of cost, in this case money wages, increases (by 5%) from W_0 to W_1 (employees are trying to increase their real wage to W_1/P_0 – by 5%). SAS(W_0) will shift upwards to SAS(W_1) a vertical distance A to C. This increase in the money wage will increase the real wage to W_1/P_0 but will reduce the demand for labour. Businesses will wish to employ less labour and produce less output at price level P_0 – point A' on SAS(W_1). Since there is no change in the position of the ADp schedule there will be an excess demand for goods and services at P_0. This will lead to an increase in the price level to P_{01} and a new, temporary, equilibrium at point B. The real wage (W_1/P_{01}) will be less than W_1/P_0, output will fall to Y_{01} and there will be an increase in involuntary unemployment. If the authorities attempt to eliminate the involuntary unemployment by increasing aggregate demand then the economy will move to point C, but the real wage will decline to W_1/P_1 which is equal to the original real wage W_0/P_0. Wages and prices will be higher (by 5%).

If employees try to restore the real wage to W_1/P_0 by asking for, and receiving, a higher

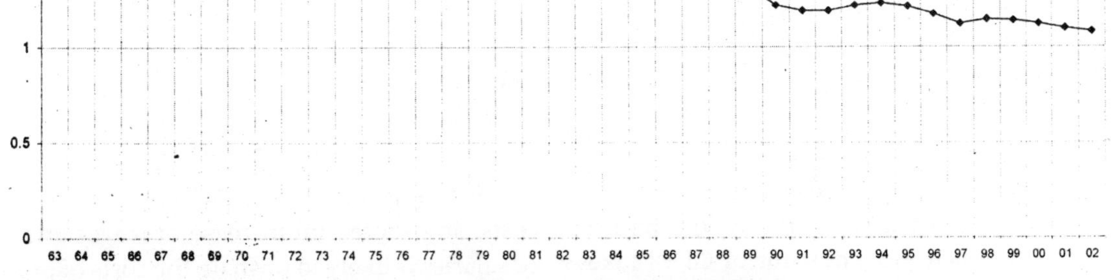

Fig. 9.5: UK-Velocity of circulation-GDP/M4

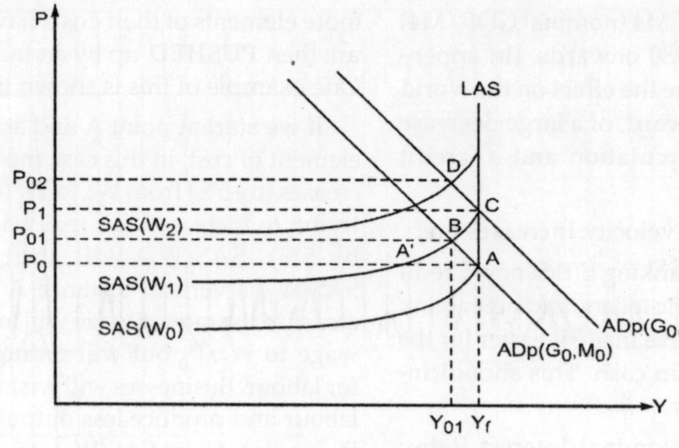

Fig. 9.6: Cost pull inflation

money wage, then W_1 will increase further and SAS(W_1) will shift upwards to, say, SAS(W_2). If there is no change in aggregate demand then output will again fall to Y_{01}, involuntary unemployment will increase; prices will rise to P_{02} and the real wage fall to W_1/P_{02}. If the authorities try to restore full employment then wages and prices will increase again. The increase in the money wage has 'triggered off' an increase in the price level.

Triggers to cost push inflation

a. **Wage costs**: Powerful trade unions are able to push up nominal wage costs which firms pass onto the consumer in the form of higher prices.

b. **Commodity (raw material) prices**: Since most UK raw materials (metals etc.) are imported then an increase in the price of raw materials on the world markets will probably push up the price level in the UK. Inflation can be imported. The two 'oil shocks' of 1972-73 and 1979 were precursors to the rise in the world-wide rate of inflation in the years after 1972-73 and 1979.

   Fig. 9.7 shows world commodity price increases, oil price increases and inflation (measured by the IPD). The IPD [implicit price deflator of GDP] takes into account all of the prices of goods and services produced in an economy —not just the prices of goods and services covered by the RPI).

c. **Other costs**: Interest rates and indirect taxes. These may increase because of government action; these will push up a business's operational costs.

   In the 1979 budget the government financed their cuts in direct taxation (the top rate was cut from 83% to 60%) by almost doubling the rate of VAT (from 8% and 12% to 15%). This, combined with the second oil shock, induced a price-wage spiral. The rate of inflation increased from 10% to over 20% before falling back.

Whilst any of the above demand pull or cost push measures can **'trigger off'** inflation, the process of inflation is likely to take a similar form.

Once prices have increased, real wages (W/P) fall. Money wages and salaries are likely to increase as employees try to defend their standard of living. They try to increase their money wages or salaries (W).

But, as wages form a large proportion of costs, any successful increase in wages and/or salaries is likely to push up the costs of production and again prices increase.

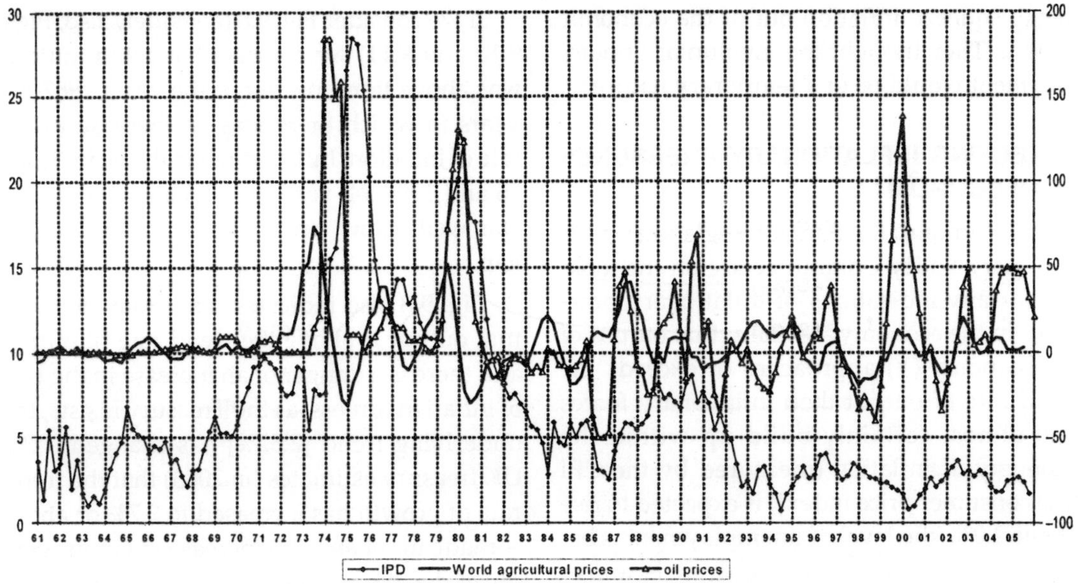

Fig. 9.7: % change in world agricultural prices (RHS), Oil (RHS), and IPD (LHS)

To try to restore the real wage, money wages will rise again; this again pushes up costs and prices. If the money supply is increased (or there is an increase in the velocity of circulation) and this continues the economy can enter an inflationary 'wage-cost-price spiral' where wages, costs and prices are accelerating upwards (See, also, Appendix III on page 151-152).

Another element common to all three theories of inflation is the importance of expectations. Large increases in fuel and food prices in 2007-08 threaten to 'trigger off inflation. The rise in the price level will reduce people's real incomes. If people ask for higher money wages (and they are granted) this will increase the costs to businesses, pushing up prices, reducing real wages etc etc. Once inflation takes hold, pay claims and price rises will begin to take into account the anticipated inflation. To the extent that such expectations become inbuilt, they will tend to be self-justifying and help to bring about the expected inflation. Workers will try to anticipate future price levels and try compensating for these in the current wage round. Instead of just catching up with past increases in the price level workers will ask for larger wage increases to prevent expected falls in real wages. The larger wage increases, if granted, will lead to a larger increase in costs and prices.

We have seen the effects of a reduction in the stock of money when the economy is below or at a full employment position. Involuntary unemployment increases and, theoretically, the economy (eventually) returns to full employment.

A similar process can occur in an inflationary situation when the nominal stock of money is not allowed to increase <u>or</u> it increases by a smaller percentage rate than the increase in the price level. The increase in the price level will reduce the real stock of money and bring about an increase in involuntary unemployment. The increase in involuntary unemployment will, eventually, reduce the rate of growth of wages and prices and inflation.

Theoretically, 'market forces' may then eliminate the involuntary unemployment and output will return to the full employment level Y_f.

Hence the government of 1979-87 allowed involuntary unemployment to increase in order to squeeze inflation out of the economic system. They thought the involuntary unemployment would be of a temporary nature.

DETECTING INFLATIONARY PRESSURES IN AN ECONOMY

The Governor of the Bank of England and the Monetary Policy Committee are on the look-out for any indications of inflationary pressures in the economy. As the actual output of the economy (Y) approaches or exceeds the trend rate of output then inflationary forces will almost certainly build up within the economy. If inflation (measured by the CPI [the consumer price index]) is expected to rise above 2.0% (the level of unemployment is below NAIRU and income/output is above trend) then interest rates will be increased and aggregate demand will fall. If inflation is expected to be below 2.0% (the level of unemployment is above NAIRU and income/output is below trend) interest rates will be reduced and aggregate demand will increase. This will, theoretically, keep the economy close to full employment.

If we consider Fig. 9.8 (consider, also, Figs. 9.10 and 9.11) we can see that actual output was above trend output in the years 1987-89; years in which there was an increase in the rate of inflation. Inflation fell in the years 1979-86 and 1990-94, years in which actual output was well below trend – there was an output gap.

Fig. 9.8 also indicates that, from 1996, actual output is above the trend rate of output and there is a danger of an increase in the rate of inflation (unless, as the Treasury insists, the underlying trend [2.52%] has changed). The UK treasury estimates (in 2003) that the trend rate of growth has increased to 2.7% or above —made up of an 0.7% increase in labour supply and a 2% annual increase in GDP.

With this in mind the controllers of economic policy closely monitor some or all of the following key statistics.

1. **Labour costs:** As wages and salaries contribute to about 60% of a firms costs any increase in earnings may soon be translated into higher labour costs and

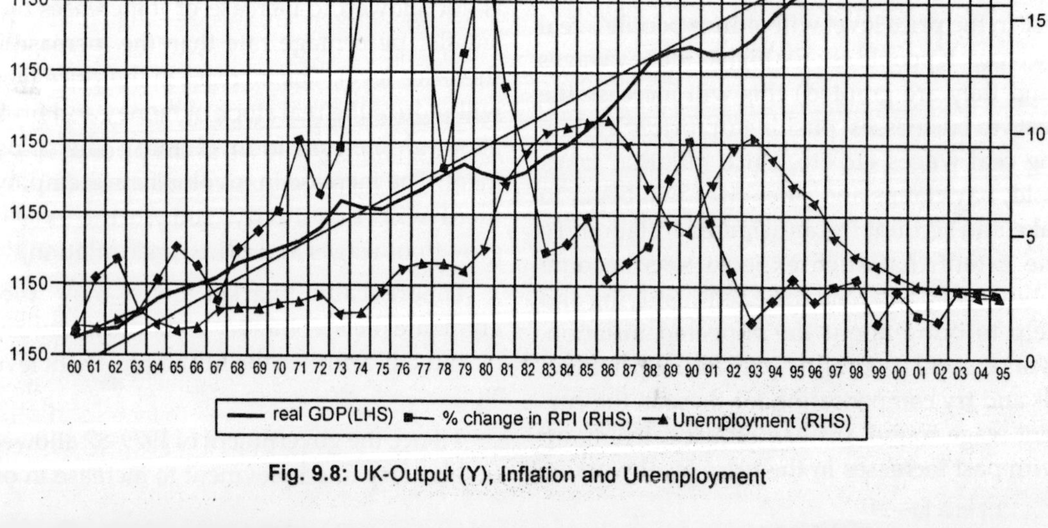

Fig. 9.8: UK-Output (Y), Inflation and Unemployment

prices (especially if productivity growth is low). We can think of price increases being linked to costs in the following way:

$$\%\Delta P = \%\Delta costs - \%\Delta productivity$$

The percentage change in the aggregate price level is equal to the percentage change in costs **less** the percentage change in the growth of productivity.

For example, if wage costs are increasing at 1.5% and productivity is growing at 1.5% then, if there is no redistribution of income from wages to profits or vice versa, there should be no increase in the aggregate price level.

More importantly, any rise in the rate of increase of earnings is an indication of the tightening of the labour market. An indication that the actual output of the economy is approaching the potential output of the economy (NAIRU).

2. **Commodity (raw material) prices:** As mentioned above (point 2) (b)) an increase in commodity prices can 'trigger off' an inflationary spiral. The authorities keep a close watch on the commodity price index (an indication of imported price pressure). One of the reasons for the increase in the interest rate on the 2/2/95 was that the non-oil commodity price index increased by 20% in the 12 months January 1994 to January 1995 (see Fig. 9.7). They feared that, without an increase in interest rates, the increase in costs would be translated into an increase in the price level.
3. **Input prices for manufacturing industry:** Increases in input prices for manufacturing industry are generally passed on in the form of higher output prices.
4. **House prices**: 'Excessive' increases in the price of property are an indication of loose monetary policy and a forward indicator of inflationary pressures in an economy.

In the past, especially the years 1986-89, increases in the prices of houses, have led to home owners either;

a. Borrowing against the increase in the value of the house.
b. Selling the property to realise the increase in the value of the property.

Both (a) and (b) can lead to home-owners increasing their autonomous consumption expenditure (usually buying 'big ticket' items such as cars, holiday's etc.). This increase in consumption expenditure will increase aggregate demand. Demand pull inflation may be 'triggered off'.

5. **Manufacturing and Producer Output Prices**: Gradual increases in these prices are an indication of inflationary pressures in an economy.
6. **The Regular Surveys of Industry's Intentions**: Surveys are conducted at regular intervals by bodies such as the CBI (the Confederation of Business Industry), the Treasury, Purchase Managers etc. These surveys provide information regarding manufacturing, distributive and service industries intentions with regard to price increases, wage increases, cost increases etc. This information can be an early warning of future price rises.
7. **The Exchange Rate**: As we will see (chapter 10), when exchange rates are allowed to float, an increase in the supply of money will lead, ceteris paribus, to a depreciation of the exchange rate and an increase in the price of imports – this may 'trigger off' an inflationary situation. Conversely, a depreciating exchange rate is an indication of loose monetary policy and a need for the monetary authorities to take action. Giving control over monetary policy to the Bank of England ensures that, if inflation is expected to increase[fall] due to a rise[fall] in import prices, then in-

terest rates will be increased [decreased] and aggregate demand will be reduced[increased].

8. **Monetary Aggregates**: Amongst the large number of monetary aggregates that are monitored is the growth of
   a. M0 (Notes and coin).
   b. M1 (Notes plus coin plus current account deposits).
   c. M4 (M0 plus current account and 'sight' deposits of both banks and other financial institutions).
   d. Borrowing by consumers.

   Excessive growth in any of these aggregates can be an indication of future inflationary pressures. The Quantity Theory of Money is one of the theoretical links between the growth in the amount of money in an economy and price increases.

ANTI-INFLATIONARY POLICY: The formulators of economic policy could use fiscal policy to reduce aggregate demand and moderate inflationary pressures. However

1. They are reluctant to increase taxation because:
   a. Direct taxation has supply side implications.
   b. Increases in indirect taxation (Te) may lead to inflation. Indirect tax increases may 'trigger off' an inflationary spiral.
2. Cuts in government expenditure may be politically difficult to introduce.
3. As we will see, in chapter 10, in an economy with floating exchange rates and a free flow of financial capital, monetary policy is much more effective than fiscal policy in increasing or decreasing the output of the economy.

The UK and other monetary authorities use interest rates, supply side measures and incomes policy as their main anti-inflationary weapons. If an international agreement could be arrived at then the wild fluctuations in commodity prices could be moderated by the introduction of 'buffer stocks'. This would help to moderate cost push inflation.

Interest rates: Although the government can, theoretically, directly control the growth of the stock of money by buying and selling government securities on the open market in practice the government use interest rates to affect monetary growth in an economy. Using interest rates means that the monetary authorities do not have to target one particular monetary aggregate. Interest rates, as well as directly affecting consumption and investment expenditure, are reduced to allow the supply of money will grow and increased to tighten monetary conditions:

Consider the effects of an increase in the rate of interest:

a. The price of bonds will fall (and all other forms of wealth inversely related to the interest rate)—wealth falls and autonomous consumption expenditure will fall.
b. The cost of borrowing increases and the present value of expected net revenues will decline. Both consumption and investment expenditures will fall.
c. The costs of production will increase (the cost of overdrafts will rise) and also there will be a fall in revenues as economic activity declines. The expected net revenues of firms (ENR's) will be reduced leading to a fall in the present value of new investment projects. *Ceteris paribus*, there will be a fall in investment expenditure.

   (b) and (c) will probably lead to a fall in the demand for new loans to finance consumption and investment expenditure and hence there will be a reduction in the growth of the supply of new money.

   (a), (b) and (c) will lead to aggregate demand falling and put downwards pressure on income/output and the price level. Involuntary unemployment will increase and put downward pressure on wage costs.

The Bank of England (*The Transmission Mechanism of Monetary Policy*: 1999) suggests that changes in interest rates will have their maximum effect on the price level after about 9 quarters. An increase in the rate of interest will initially affect the **income/output** of the economy; its full affect taking about 1 year. Paradoxically, in the early stages, an increase in the interest rate will **increase** business costs, overdrafts and the cost of borrowing and, initially, **increase** the rate of inflation. It has been estimated that a 1% change in the rate of interest will lead to a £10 billion change in income/output per annum.

d. An increase in the rate of interest will, generally, bring about an increase in the nominal and real exchange rate. Some economists argue that it is the change in the exchange rate that has the greatest effect on an open economy such as the UK.

   The increase in the exchange rate will reduce the price of imported raw materials and imported goods and services. This will help to reduce imported input costs and put downward pressure on prices.

   A fall in the price of imported goods and services will encourage domestic firms who compete with imports to be more cost conscious.

   It will also increase the relative price of domestic exports encouraging exporting domestic firms to be more cost conscious.

   However, the greatest impact on the economy is through changes in aggregate demand. Since the price of exports has increased and the price of imports has decreased, it is very likely that net exports will decline leading to a fall in aggregate demand.

   This will especially affect the sectors (such as manufacturing industry) more open to foreign competition.

e. A rise in interest rates may lead the banking system to review its future projections as to the level of risk associated with new loans. If commercial banks think that economic activity is going to decline they may only be willing to lend to, what they perceive to be, less risky projects. There will be a fall in the velocity of circulation. This will reduce the volume of new loans available and help to bring about a reduction in aggregate demand and economic activity. An extreme cut back in lending can lead to a very large fall in economic activity - a 'credit crunch'.

In the USA, for much of the 1990's, 'risky' borrowers had to pay only three percentage points over Treasury bond rates. By the beginning of 2002, the least creditworthy borrowers were having to pay eight percentage points above the US Treasury's cost of borrowing. Over the same period the credit worthiness of potential borrowers were also downgraded. At the end of 1999 there was a rating upgrade for every downgrade. In early 2002 there were three downgrades for every upgrade.

The rise in the cost of loans reduced borrowing by companies (In 2002 the balance of US loan officers reporting increased corporate demand for loans has fallen to a decade low of 60%). The downgrading of companies discouraged banks from lending to businesses.

After January 2001 the cost of Federal Reserve funds were cut from 6.5% to 1.75%. The commercial banks could borrow from the Federal Reserve (in June 2002) for 1.75%. The banks were borrowing from the Federal Reserve. However, they cut back lending from a peak of \$890bn in early 2001 to \$800bn in early 2002. What they did was purchase Treasury bonds which give a risk free return of at least 3.25% or they were buying 10 year bonds with a return of more than 5%. Their holdings of treasury bonds increased from around \$690bn to over \$800bn.

There was another large 'credit crunch' (a fall in the velocity of circulation) in the world in September 2007. The first extreme aspect of the crisis was a 'run' on a UK bank—the Northern Rock. People were queuing up to withdraw their cash. It was brought about because other banks chose not lend to Northern Rock (they preferred to hold onto their cash which reduced the velocity of circulation) and its individual depositors feared that the bank would go bankrupt. The Northern Rock crisis was only resolved when the banks deposits were guaranteed by the government and the bank was nationalised (the bank was taken into public ownership).

Using changes in interest rates to affect the money supply assumes that changes in the supply and demand for loans (new money) are inversely related to the rate of interest

The above points (a), (b), (c), (d) and (e) will, together, lead to an increase in involuntary unemployment and there will be downward pressure on wages and prices. Inflation will be squeezed out of the economic system, albeit at the cost of an increase in involuntary unemployment.

Supply side measures

We have seen, that the UK government has introduced several 'supply side measures' to try reduce voluntary unemployment and increase the productivity of the economy.

If the voluntary unemployed can be 'persuaded' to become involuntarily unemployed then the involuntary unemployment will put downward pressure on wages, costs and prices. This will help to moderate any inflationary pressures in the economy.

Productivity increases can lead to increases in income/output from the same resources (land, labour and capital) or, alternatively, the same income/output can be produced from fewer resources. In either case the average costs of production will fall enabling businesses (depending on the magnitude of the increase in productivity) to stabilise prices, reduce prices or moderate price increases.

As mentioned above we can think of price increases being linked to costs in the following way:

$$\%\Delta \mathbf{P} = \%\Delta \mathbf{costs} - \%\Delta \mathbf{productivity}$$

The percentage change in the aggregate price level is equal to the percentage change in costs **less** the percentage change in the growth of productivity.

For example, if wage costs are increasing at 3.5% and productivity is growing at 3.5% then, if there is no redistribution of income from wages to profits or vice versa, there should be no increase in the aggregate price level.

In the UK economy from 1979-2002, labour productivity increased, on average, by 1.9%. This includes the year 1989 when productivity fell (1991 was the depth of the recession) before increasing again, slightly, in 1990.

Firm's wage input costs increased between 1979-92 but actually fell in 1995. Money wage increases were positive in 1995, but were overtaken by increases in productivity in that year. Inflation fell from 1990 onwards.

Incomes policy

Without a formal incomes policy the economic authorities will implement an informal incomes policy involving increasing the level of unemployment whenever inflation looks likely to increase. This inflicts punishment on the entire economy but especially the unemployed and those people in insecure employment. Their aim, of course, is to run the economy around the NAIRU, say 7%. However this means that around 7% of the workforce will have to be unemployed (attempting to secure employment when unemployment is 7% will be self defeating - a fall in unemployment below 7% will lead to contractionary monetary and fiscal policies being introduced!). Of course, supply side measures aim to reduce the NAIRU.

If increases in money incomes and prices can be moderated at a given level of unemployment, then this will reduce the NAIRU, inflationary pressures and inflationary expectations without changing real incomes. This will allow the Government to expand demand a little more rapidly and soak up some of the unemployment (in Figure 9.10 the NAIRU would be less than 7%).

Although the voluntary incomes policy implemented by the labour government between 1974-79 was initially successful in moderating inflation it eventually broke down and, it is generally accepted, discredited voluntary incomes policies. (This has not prevented successive governments from implementing an incomes policy in the public sector of the economy!).

A market based approach to incomes policy that has been proposed by some Post Keynesian economists is one in which a firm's profit tax rate would vary according to its wage bill - a TIP or a *tax based incomes policy.* Firms employing a relatively large number of people (100+?) would pay extra taxation (a counter inflation tax) if their pay bill per employee rose by more than a government imposed norm. This norm would be based on average labour productivity increases within the economy. As average productivity grows in the economy, the average wages and salary bill would increase at the same pace.

A counter inflation tax would not be as inflexible a the tradition incomes policy as it would allow firms to pay more to some people and not to others or the firm can pay more but also pay the tax. The money raised by the tax would be handed back to firms in the form of lower labour taxes thus ensuring that firms did not merely pass on the cost of the tax in higher prices. Once instituted, TIP would have to be a permanent fixture if inflation is to be permanently kept under control. A constant reminder that inflating one's income at the expense of other is an anti-social activity.

A TIP would prevent wage increases in excess of productivity increases and price rises that inflict a cost on the entire society. Under TIP, it is those *individual* businesses that give into inflationary wage demands that would be penalised by having to pay higher taxes.

Those firms whose productivity exceeds the norm can afford to pay higher taxes in order to reward their employees and/or they can improve the quality of their product and/or lower their prices. This will make the firm more competitive and able to claim a greater market share. Thus, firms with above average productivity increases will grow faster than their competitors. As their market share grows they will hire more labour shifting, over time, labour into the most productive enterprises. As they grow total profits and returns to shareholders should also increase. The **main problem** with the tax is that it may discourage fast-growing firms offering big increases in pay to attract new staff. Also, if firms only paid the tax if they employed more than 100 members of staff, this would be an incentive to break up companies to avoid the tax.

Buffer Stocks

A buffer stock is nothing more than some commodity shelf inventory (such as oil or copper) that can be moved into and out of the spot market (by governments) to buffer the market from disruptions by offsetting the unforeseen changes in demand of supply. Buffer stocks helped to stabilise commodity prices during the period 1947 to 1972. When buffer stocks were dismantled (to save the cost of storage etc) the result was violent commodity price fluctuations in the 1970s and eighties. As we have seen in chapter eight, when oil prices and other imported commodities increase this leads to a detrimental effect on supply-side of the economy, an increase in the natural rate of unemployment, a rise in voluntary unemployment and upward pressure on the price level. This may trigger off an inflationary spiral. If an international agreement could be arrived at then wide fluctuations in commodity prices could be moderated thus reducing inflationary pressures within the world economy.

APPENDIX I

A Reduction in the Real Stock of Money to squeeze Inflation Out of the Economic System

a. Start at an initial equilibrium position: $IS(G_0, M_0/P_0)$, $LM(M_0/P_0)$, Y_f, r_0 – point A. Note: There is no involuntary unemployment but some voluntary unemployment. Assume that prices, money wages and the nominal stock of money are increasing at the same percentage rate (say 10%). Of course, there is no change in the **real** wage or the **real** stock of money.

   When there is no change in the real wage or the real stock of money there are no forces in the economy to push it away from the initial equilibrium position (in this case the NAIRU).

b. Decrease the growth of the nominal stock of money (M) to zero. With prices rising at 10% the real stock of money (L [=M/P]) will decrease (by 10%). The decrease in the real stock of money (L) will decrease the level of autonomous consumption expenditure (the real balance effect—the average propensity to consume (C/Y) falls). Both the LM and IS curves will shift to the left.

   At ro there is now an excess demand of money which is equivalent to an excess supply of bonds. The price of bonds will decrease which will bring about a rise in the rate of interest. The decrease in the price of bonds decreases the wealth of consumers and decreases autonomous consumption expenditure at all levels of income (C/Y falls).

The rise in the rate of interest will also;

a. Decrease autonomous consumption expenditure; (the cost of borrowing has increased).
b. Decrease investment expenditure; (the present value of expected net revenues will be reduced). The decrease in con-

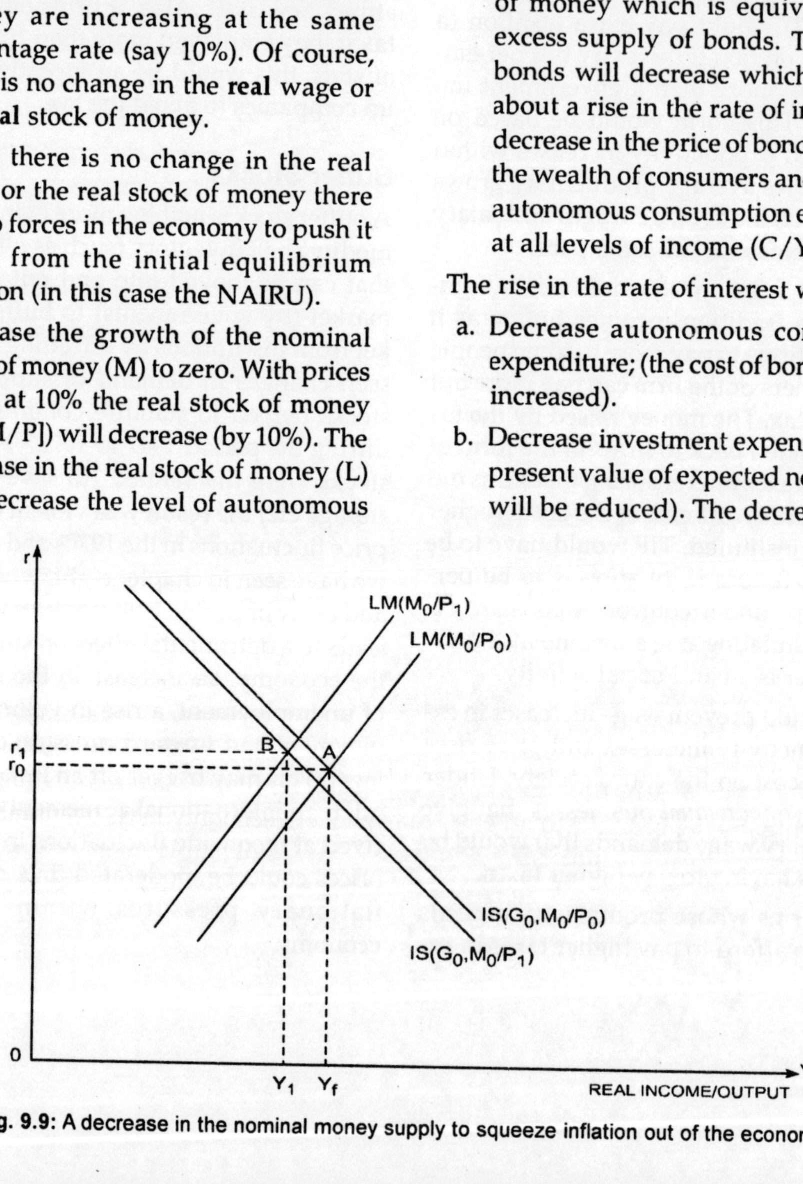

Fig. 9.9: A decrease in the nominal money supply to squeeze inflation out of the economy

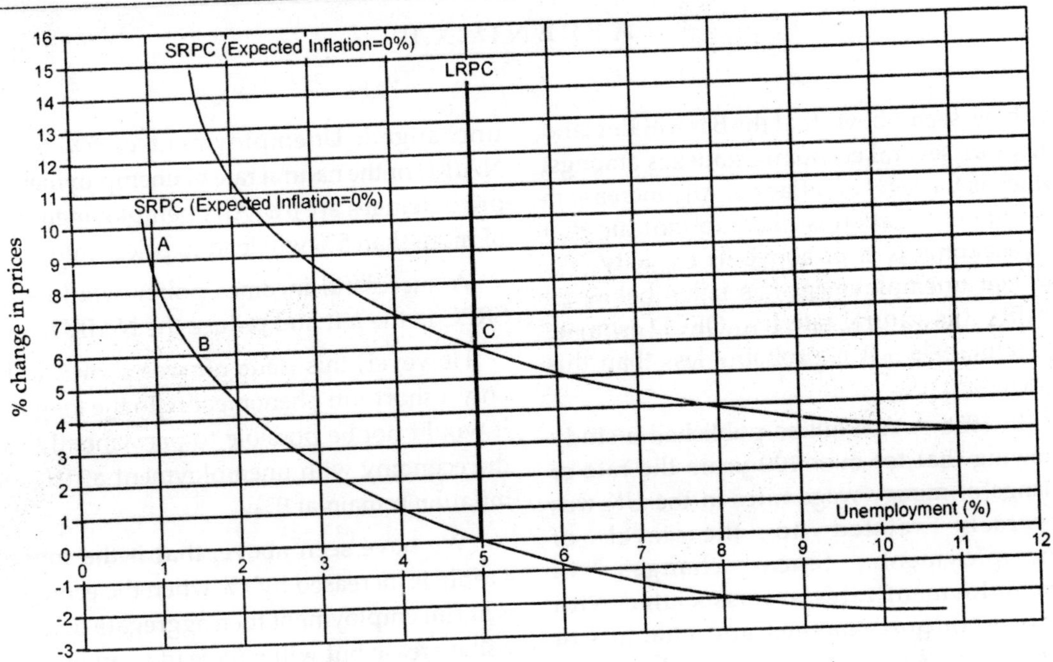

Fig. 9.10: The Philips curve

sumption and investment expenditure will reduce aggregate demand. Output falls and there is a fall in employment and an increase in involuntary unemployment (unemployment is greater than the NAIRU). As long as prices (P) are increasing faster than the nominal stock of money (M) the real stock of money ($L_0=M_0/P_0$) will be falling and involuntary unemployment will be increasing.

'Eventually' the level of involuntary unemployment will be such as to put downward pressure on wages and prices. The inflationary process will, eventually, be brought to an end. Assume that this is at point B when the real stock of money is M_0/P_1, the rate of interest is r_1 and the level of output is Y_1.

Theoretically, the involuntary unemployment will put further downward pressure on wages and prices and wages and prices will start to fall. The real stock of money will increase, aggregate demand **may** increase, the real wage fall and the economy return to full employment.

This theoretical model indicates that inflation can be eliminated from an economy by reducing the growth in the nominal stock of money and that the economy **may**, eventually return to its full employment output level.

APPENDIX II

We have seen, above, that the Bank of England monitors several economic statistics amongst which is the level of inflation. Any increase in the rate of inflation is likely to indicate that the economy is at or above its capacity (Y_f). i.e. that unemployment has fallen below its NAIRU (its natural rate [the OECD estimate is 7% in 1996 – it is probably less than this now]).

In 1958 A.W. Phillips published a study showing that for over 100 years the rate of change of money wage rates in the UK was inversely related to the level of unemployment. Since changes in unemployment rates are associated with income/output changes and changes in money wages rates are related to changes in prices then Phillips's research provided an easy explanation of inflation.

Inspection of Fig. 9.10 (SRPC is known as the 'Phillips curve' [SRPC stands for - short-run Phillips curve]) indicates that there is a trade off between inflation and unemployment. At an unemployment rate of 1% the rate of inflation is 9% (point 'A'), at unemployment of 1.5%, inflation is around 6% (point 'B') and at an unemployment rate of 5% prices are unchanged. Unemployment of 5% is the NAIRU or the natural rate of unemployment—price changes are 0%. An unemployment rate of more than 5% will lead to prices falling.

A successful incomes policy would shift SRPC to the left and reduce the NAIRU.

However, this trade off was shown to be only a short run phenomenon. In the long run it would not be possible to permanently run the economy with unemployment at 1% and inflation remain at 9%.

We have seen above, that if the money supply is increased by x% when the economy is at full employment then aggregate demand will increase but will only lead to an increase in the price level of x%: there will be no change in output.

If we relax assumption 8 then we can allow output to **temporarily** rise above Y_f and unemployment to temporarily fall below the NAIRU.

Consider Figure 9.10: A one off increase in the money supply of 2% will take unemploy-ment to 4%. But, as prices will increase by 2%, the real stock of money will

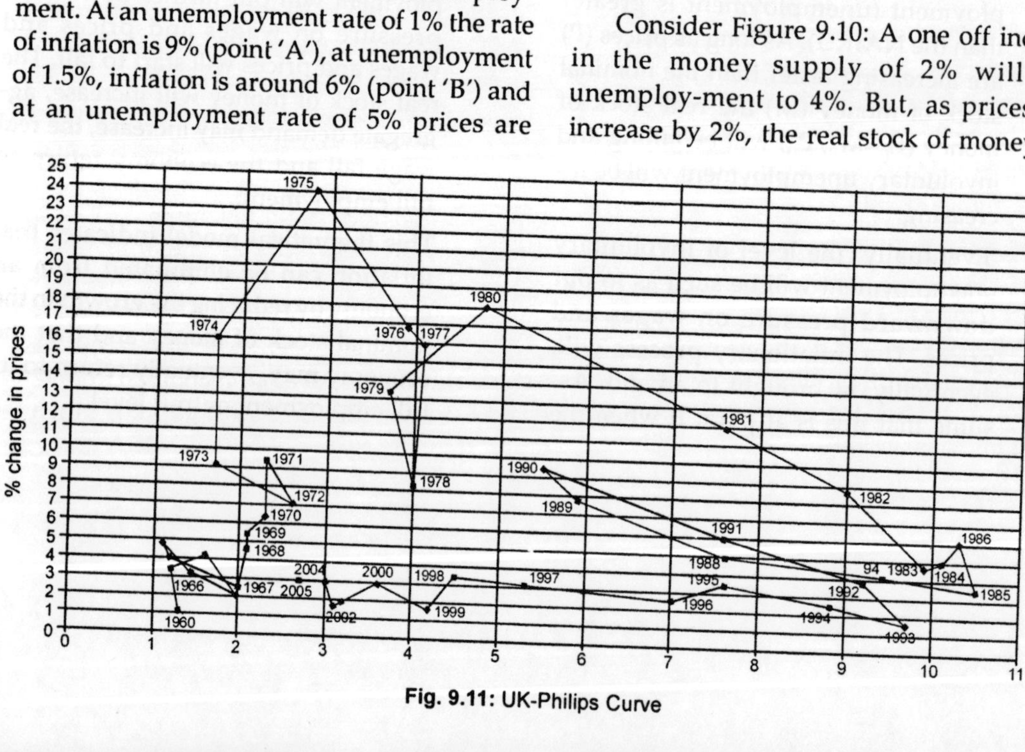

Fig. 9.11: UK-Philips Curve

fall taking the unemployment rate back to its natural rate of 5% and inflation back to 0%. To keep unemployment at 4% the money supply needs to continuously increase by 2% (to finance the 2% inflation).

The theoretical groundwork undermining the Phillips curve had already been laid by Milton Friedman when he argued that once workers expected future inflation (in this case 2%) they would build this anticipation into their wage demands. This would lead to wages and wage costs increasing by an extra 2%. Prices would need to increase by an extra 2% (i.e. 4%) at an unemployment rate of 4% (assuming the only costs of production are wage costs). If 4% becomes the expected rate of inflation then wage demands and costs will increase once again. Trying to maintain unemployment below NAIRU will lead to accelerating prices, wages and costs of production.

Friedman claimed that the long-run Phillips curve (LRPC) is vertical at the NAIRU (in our case 5%). We can have an equilibrium situation, as postulated in appendix I of this chapter, where prices, money wages and the nominal stock of money are increasing at the same percentage rate. When there are no change in real variables then there are no forces in the economy to push the economy away from the NAIRU.

One of the implication of this analysis is that there is not just one short-run Phillips curve but there are a whole series of short-run Phillips curves—one for each expected rate of inflation. The two illustrated in Figure 9.10 (SRPC) are drawn for expected rates of inflation of 0% and 6%.

If money wages, prices and the stock of money are growing at 6% a year and unemployment is 5% (the NAIRU) then the economy is on a short-run Phillips curve where the expected rate of inflation is 6% (running through LRPC at 'C') (There is no change in any real variables so there are no forces pushing the economy away from point 'C').

Any attempt to reduce unemployment below the NAIRU would merely exacerbate inflationary expectations.

To squeeze the 6% inflation out of the economic system requires unemployment to be increased above the NAIRU. This is what we demonstrated in appendix I of this chapter.

Another nail in the short-run Phillips curve was the data of the 1970's when the negative relationship broke down as **higher** unemployment rates were correlated with **higher** rates of inflation. This is known as **stagflation**.

Fig. 9.11 shows an estimated Phillips curve for the UK from 1971 to 2002.

As it can be seen both inflation and unemployment increased from 1974-75 and 1979-80. From 1980-86 unemployment substantially increased and inflation fell from 18% to below 4%.

As it the economy expanded from 1986 onwards inflation increased but never reached the levels of 1980. As unemployment rose from 1990 inflation once again fell. Inflation rose a little from 1993 onwards as unemployment fell. Looking at Fig. 9.11 it seems that the short run Phillips curve broke down in the 1960's and 1970's but since then there appears to be 3 short-run curves - 1980 to 1986, 1986 to 1992 and 1993-2005. The 1993-2005 curve is much flatter than the earlier two.

APPENDIX III

The Velocity of Circulation and the Credit Crunch

There was a large fall in the velocity of circulation in the UK from September 2007 onwards. A 'credit crunch'. The first extreme aspect of the crisis was a 'run' on a UK bank – the Northern Rock. People were queuing up outside to withdraw their cash. It was brought about because other banks chose not lend to Northern Rock (they preferred to hold onto their cash which reduced the velocity of circulation) and individual depositors feared that the bank would go bankrupt. The Northern Rock crisis was only resolved when the banks deposits were guaranteed by the government and the bank was nationalised (the bank was taken into public ownership).

However, this collapse was the precursor to a much wider world wide credit crunch with banks collapsing in different countries. The antecedents to this crisis were:

1. A relaxation in the regulation of the banking system.

   Various pieces of legislation passed over the years enabled the banking system to indulge in riskier projects and reduce the size of reserve deposit ratio (cash as a proportion of deposits – also known as the cash ratio. Up to 1981 the banking system had to keep a reserve deposit ratio of around 8%. The banking system could reduce the size their of reserve deposit ratios – in the UK this had fallen to about 0.15%! This enabled them to greatly expand their loans and other financial investments. Any large defaults on the loans would lead to the banks' cash reserves being compromised.

2. Unwise lending to the housing sector.

   In the UK the Northern Rock bank was lending up to 125% of the market value of a property. It assumed that rising property prices would be sufficient collateral for the loan in the case of any default in the repayments. When property prices started to fall retail depositors became worried about their deposits and queued up to withdraw them. There was a 'run' on the bank.

   The USA, because of its dominant economic position in the world, has been able to run large current account deficits. These deficits have been financed by inflows of financial capital from abroad and billions of dollars have entered into the financial sector. This, along with easing of bank regulation, led to the easy availability of credit. Aggressive mortgage lending in the housing market took place at below market rates of interest. These lower rates of interest have become known as 'teaser' rates (borrowers were essentially "teased" with an unrealistic expectation of what their mortgage interest rate would be). This encouraged people, who would not be able to finance mortgages at a higher rate of interest, to buy homes. This lending to riskier borrowers brought about what is known as the sub-prime market. One in five mortgages were of this type. These, and other less risky mortgages, were packaged into saleable financial assets which paid a relatively high rate of return. This rate of return depended on people being able to repay their mortgages.

   These financial assets were known as Collateralised Debt Obligations or CDO's, and some of them were (somehow?) given the top rated security rating, AAA, by the credit rating agencies. Some CDOs offered returns that were

2-3 percentage points higher than corporate bonds with the same credit rating.

These billions of dollars of CDO's were purchased (and insured) by banks and other financial institutions without, they admit, fully understanding the risks involved.

As opposed to regular CDOs, which contain actual bonds, synthetic CDOs provide income to investors by selling insurance against debt defaults, typically on a pool of a hundred or so companies or individual bonds. Given the size of the market, synthetic CDOs can have a large impact: By various estimates, they have sold insurance on the equivalent of between $1.25 trillion and $6 trillion in bonds.

3. A large increase in the price of oil and other commodity prices.

As we saw in previous chapter the increase in oil and other commodity prices will increase the amount consumers have to spend on heating, travel and food and reduce the amount of disposable income available for consumers to spend on other goods and services (including mortgage repayments). The large increase in the price of oil and food and the increase in interest rates occurred just as many of the subprime borrowers' two year fixed rate mortgages ended requiring large increases in mortgage repayments. (The US Federal reserve also increased short-term interest rates from 1.25% to 5.25%). People were now unable to repay their mortgages and defaulted on these and other loans. This led to an increase in the number of properties that people had to, or wished to, sell and a fall in property prices.

The above three points created the conditions for a 'meltdown' of the financial system. The returns on these financial assets were dependent upon home owners being able to repay their mortgages. A combination of the rising price of oil and rising interest rates along with the rise in some teaser rates, falling property prices (property prices have fallen by an estimated 6 trillion dollars) and mortgage defaults have undermined the value of these CDO's (they are now 'toxic assets'). Banks and other financial institutions have lost billions of dollars and this has led them to bankruptcy (Lehman Brothers) or to government guaranteed bailouts (American Insurance Group [AIG], Bear-Stearns).

The banks were so worried about running out of cash that they drastically reduced their lending.

The international nature of banking has led to a world wide credit crunch. Banks (rightly or wrongly) were unwilling or reluctant to lend, they were hoarding cash. There has been a fall in the velocity of circulation (V).

This reluctance to lend, and a fall in business and consumer expenditures (aggregate demand) led to a detrimental effect on the real output of the economy. Stock markets around the world fell. The fall in the US stock market alone led to eight trillion dollars being wiped off the value of US shares. The wealth effects of a six trillion fall in property prices and an eight trillion fall in share prices had a negative effect on consumer expenditure (autonomous consumption fell).

The fall in investment and/or consumption expenditure led to a fall in aggregate demand which lead to a fall in real income/output. Employment will declined, involuntary unemployment rose, and this led to further falls in aggregate demand and in real income/output. Throughout the world economies went into deep recessions. This led to the worry that prices would start to fall. We have seen above, the very real danger to the economy of falling prices (deflation).

The crucial nature of the banking system to the real economy led (over the week end of 11/12 October 2008) the countries of the European Union to back the banking system by guaranteeing deposits, new fund raising and guaranteeing unlimited liquidity to the banking sector. There were large increases in stock markets on the 13th. But these rises were more than wiped out by later falls!

The problems in the financial system have spilled over into the foreign exchange market. The Dollar has increased against the Euro and the Pound Sterling and fallen against the Yen. The fall against the Yen appears to be because of what is known as 'carry trade'. The term carry trade refers to currency carry trade: Investors borrow (Yen) in low interest rate countries (Japan) and, after changing into dollars, lend in relatively high-yielding countries (the USA).

The carry trade tends to increase with global financial and exchange rate stability, and decreases during global liquidity shortages. By early 2007, it was estimated that some US$1 trillion may be staked on the yen carry trade - much of it used to finance subprime lending in the USA. The credit crunch of 2007-8 reduced global liquidity and led to the unwinding of carry trades. This involves repaying the Yen loans. To do this people have to sell Dollars and buy Yen. Hence the Dollar falls and the Yen rises (and increases the prices of Japanese exports).

The fallout from the 'credit crunch' (the deep worldwide recession) has (2010) led to large budget deficits in many countries (in the UK the budget deficit as a percentage of GDP rose from less than 3% of GDP to over 11% of GDP) and uncertainty in the financial markets (stock markets throughout the world have fallen upwards of 10%). It is the fall in income/output that has led to falls in tax revenues and increases in government expenditures (investment and transfer payments [benefits]) and increases in budget deficits. In the UK tax revenues fell by approximately £52b. and government expenditures rose by around £88b. leading to the budget deficit rising by about £140b.(these figures are subject to revision but give an idea of the magnitude of the effect). Without the increase in government expenditure unemployment in the UK would undoubtedly be higher.

The budget deficits of countries (the PIIGS —Portugal, Ireland, Italy, Greece and Spain) within the European Union (EU) are seen as by the financial community.

Countries such as the UK and the USA cannot default on their obligations because they, unlike, for example, the PIIGS, control their own currencies. They can always 'create' more money to pay their debts.

Countries such as Greece, Spain etc do not have control their own currencies. They have borrowed in euros and have to pay their debts in euros. Greece etc cannot print euros. Some economists argue that in order to repay their debts these countries have to cut government expenditures in some form and increase taxes.

The problem with this analysis is that it may make things worse. Ireland's had five in less than two years. They announced spending cuts and tax rises for 2009 worth 5% of GDP. For perspective, if you undertook that kind of tightening in the UK you'd be taking £65bn out of the economy, in a single year. That's roughly what the chancellor has said he will do by 2015-16. The Irish government unveiled further cuts in December, of 2% of GDP in 2010.

Where's the money come from? The short answer is it has come from (almost) everyone. But public-sector workers have probably had it worst: many of them have seen a 20% cut in their net income. There's a new pension levy on public-sector earnings, worth an average of 7% of pay - in effect a new tax, to pay for the cost of their generous pensions. What has happened? The deficit was just over 11% of GDP in 2009, and even after all those cuts, it's going to be just over 11% of GDP in 2010 as well. That's because the economy is shrinking even faster than the budget! Ireland's national income has shrunk by more than 20% (output in the UK fell by 6.24%) since 2007 - and it's not growing yet. Economists agree that the recession has been made longer - and deeper - by the savagery of these cuts. And the weakness of the economy, in turn, has meant that, to some extent, the government is cutting to stand still. A similar situation has been seen in some Eastern European countries.

Other economists argue that a depressed economy (with a large amount of unemployed resources) needs increases in aggregate demand in order for more people and capital to be employed (paying more in taxation and costing less in unemployment benefits) to reduce the budget deficit. This is much more difficult for countries that in the euro zone – the increased deficit would require the ECB (European Central Bank) to finance the deficit, wholly or partially by printing euros.

The US and the UK can finance their deficits by printing dollars or sterling respectively. Once private sector expenditures start rising and the economy is approaching full employment then this may be time to cut G and increase taxation.

An interesting article on the implications of this analysis in J K Galbraith at [http://www.thenation.com/article/defense-deficits].

QUESTIONS

1. An economy operating at full employment enters a period of high-anticipated inflation. Which of the following statements accurately describes the likely result?
   (a) Most people increase saving to be better prepared for the higher prices that they know are coming, thereby increasing capital investment, stimulating the rate of economic growth, and supporting lower interest rates.
   (b) Most people decrease saving to increase current consumption and capital investment, thereby stimulating economic growth and supporting lower interest rates.
   (c) Most people decrease saving to increase current consumption, thereby slowing capital investment, slowing the rate of economic growth, and supporting lower interest rates.
   (d) Most people increase saving to be better prepared for the higher prices that they know are coming, thereby reducing capital investment, slowing the rate of economic growth, and supporting lower interest rates.
   (e) Most people decrease saving to increase current consumption, thereby slowing capital investment, slowing the rate of economic growth, and supporting higher interest rates.
2. If unemployment fell from 7.7% to 5.8% over the course of two years,
   (a) then inflationary concerns should be voiced, even if the natural rate of unemployment were 5.0%
   (b) then inflationary concerns should be voiced if the natural rate of unemployment were 6.0%
   (c) then concerns over a growth recession should be voiced, even if the natural rate were 6.0%
   (d) then concerns over a growth recession should be voiced if the natural rate were 5.0%
   (e) there would still be sufficient slack to reduce unemployment further without raising the spector of inflation even if the natural rate were 6.5%.
3. A logical extension of the Phillips curve relationship between inflation and the difference between actual and potential GDP is that

(a) the inflation rate and the unemployment rate should be positively related

(b) the inflation rate and the natural rate of unemployment should be positively correlated

(c) the inflation rate and the unemployment rate should be negatively correlated

(d) the inflation rate and the natural rate of unemployment should be negatively correlated

(e) the difference between actual and potential GNP should be negatively correlated with the difference between actual and full employment.

4. Why do some central banks target the rate of inflation?

5. Should the Bank of England's target be the CPI (the consumer price index) or some other measure?

ANSWERS

1. In response to anticipated inflation, people should be expected to increase consumption expenditures to take advantage of low current prices. The result, given full employment, is a reduction in capital expenditure as the production mix moves toward supplying the consumption surge. Additionally, the reduced saving decreases the supply of financial capital, thereby increasing interest rates and contributing to the reduction in investment in physical capital. The rate of economic growth must therefore be reduced.

2. (b) Inflation, by definition, becomes a potential concern as the unemployment rate approaches the natural rate from above. If the natural rate were 6%, then inflation should be a concern with unemployment falling so quickly from 7.7% to 5.8% < 6%. A growth recession refers to an economy that is growing, but not quickly enough to keep the unemployment rate from climbing over time; it does not apply to this question. Only answer (b) correctly applies to the definition of the natural rate.

3. (c) The Phillips curve relation asserts that inflation should be positively correlated with the difference between actual and potential GNP; e.g. should actual **GNP** climb above (fall below) potential GNP, then inflation should accelerate (decline). Since the unemployment rate increases (decreases) as actual GNP falls (increases) relative to potential, a negative correlation between the unemployment and inflation rates should be expected.

4. If inflation is expected to rise above, say, 2.0% (the level of unemployment is below NAIRU and income/output is above trend) then interest rates will be increased and aggregate demand will fall. This will take income/output back to trend. If inflation is expected to be below 2.0% (the level of unemployment is above NAIRU and income/output is below trend) interest rates will be reduced and aggregate demand will increase. This will take income/output back to trend.

5. Some economists argue that domestic output prices would be a better measure of inflation within the UK because the CPI is influenced by the price of imports, which, in turn, are affected by fluctuations in the exchange rate.

CHAPTER 10

OPEN ECONOMY MACROECONOMICS

KEY TERMS

Appreciation (Revalunation): When the value a nation's currency goes up such that it takes more of another nation's currency to purcahse it. This will make a country's exports moe expensive and a country's imports cheaper.

Depreciation (Devaluation): When the value of a currency goes down such that it takes less of another nation's currency to purcahse it. This will make a country's exports cheaper and a country's imports more expensive.

Fixed Exchange Rate: Governments agree to maintain their particular nominal exchange rate at a predetermined level.

Flexible Exchange Rate: A nominal exchange rate that is set by free market forces without government intervention.

Foreign Exchange Rate: The price of one country's currency in terms of another country's currency.

The Real Exchange Rate (R): measures the relative price of goods and services from different countries when measured in a common currency.

International Speculation: Is the flow of financial capital in search of the highest rate of return (both through interest payments and changes in foreign exchange rates).

Exports (X) and imports (Z) can account for a large proportion of an economy's gross national product (about 25% in the case of the UK). Foreign trade and capital flows must be taken into account in order to fully understand and complete any macroeconomic analysis.

The Balance of Payments

The balance of payments is a set of official accounts published annually. The accounts are a record of the transactions that have occurred between the residents of a country and the rest of the world over a one-year period. The accounts are divided into two main sections: The CURRENT and CAPITAL accounts.

The current account: The current account can be divided up into visible and invisible trade (see Table 10.1).

Visible trade refers to the export and import of physical items, namely goods such as machine tools, electrical goods, textiles etc.

Invisible trade is concerned with the trade in services. It includes:

a. Charges, fees and commission paid on current accounts held by foreign residents.
b. Earnings of insurance companies.
c. Earnings of civil aviation and sea transport.
d. Earnings of tourist visiting the UK.
e. Expenditure on military bases.
f. Interest, profit and dividends earned on foreign investment.
g. Expenditure on foreign embassies.
h. Transfer of money abroad by migrant workers.

Inflows of revenue from the above are invisible exports whereas outflows are invisible imports.

Taking the visible and invisible balance together the UK had a current account deficit of £18,425 billion in 2000 (since revised to a deficit of £19.1 billion).

The capital account: Capital account items arise through the international purchase and sales of foreign assets and deposits with overseas banks.

Transactions in UK assets and liabilities: This section includes the movement of short-term and long-term capital between countries.

Short-term capital flows refer to liquid funds held in bank accounts or short-term government securities such as Treasury bills.

Long-term capital flows refer to items such as private overseas investment in new plant and/or factories or the purchase of long-term government stock and/or shares.

The foreign exchange market: Is the international market in which one national currency can be exchanged for another. The price at which the two currencies exchange is called the exchange rate. (The nominal

Table 10.1: Summary of the UK balance of payments, 2000

		£ Million
Current account		
Visible trade		
Exports		187,656
Imports		–218,036
Visible balance (a)	–30,380	
Invisible trade		
Exports		225,228
Imports		-213,273
Invisible balance (b)	11,955	
Current balance (a)+(b)	–18,425	
Capital account		
Transactions in UK assets and liabilities		
UK external assets		-506,246
UK external liabilities	532,621	
Net transactions	26,375	
Capital account (balance)	1,973	
Balancing item		–9,923

exchange rate). For example, on the 25/01/05 the nominal pound.dollar exchange rate was \$1.8749 to £1 (0.5334 pence per dollar).

If government allow the currency to find its market value then the international demand and supply for the currency will determine its nominal price.

The demand for sterling (£'s) (or why do residents of overseas countries want pounds sterling?)

1. The medium of exchange within the UK economy is pounds sterling. Usually, UK firms require sterling in exchange for the goods and services that they produce. If foreign citizens wish to buy British goods or services they first have to purchase pounds sterling (£'s).
2. If foreign citizens wish to purchase British financial assets or deposit money in the UK banking system to earn UK interest rates they first have to exchange their foreign currency into sterling.

The supply of sterling (£'s)

If UK citizens wish to purchase overseas goods, services or financial assets they require foreign currency. They first have to exchange pounds for foreign currency (say dollars).

Consider Fig. 10.1. The demand for sterling is DD_0 and the supply of sterling is SS_0. The equilibrium rate (\$/£) is at E_0. It is determined by the intersection of the demand for, and the supply of, sterling in terms of dollars.

When the \$/£ exchange rate increases the pound sterling exchange rate increases (appreciates). There is an increase in the number of dollars received per pound.

When the \$/£ exchange rate decreases the pound sterling exchange rate decreases (depreciates). There is a decrease in the number of dollars received per pound.

Fixed exchange rate regimes: Governments promise to preserve the foreign exchange rate of the currency at a fixed exchange rate. They agree to buy or sell as much of the currency as people wish to trade at the fixed exchange rate (E_0). In the post second world war period, up to 1971, the pound sterling (£) was fixed against the dollar and other foreign currencies.

In Fig. 10.2, start at an initial equilibrium position DD_0, SS_0, E, E_0.

If there is a fall in the demand for the currency, (say DD_0 to DD_2) there is now an

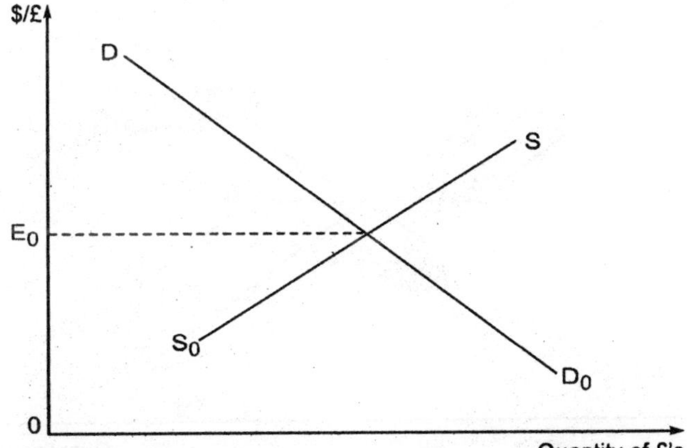

Fig. 10.1: The determination of the nominal exchange rate

excess supply of pounds at E_0 (A to E). To prevent a fall (depreciation) in the value of the currency the government uses its foreign currency reserves to purchase this excess supply 'A' to 'E' at the exchange rate Eo.

To purchase pounds the government has to reduce its holdings of foreign currency reserves.

The value of the foreign currency reserves fall by an equivalent monetary amount 'A' to 'E'.

Similarly an excess demand for pounds (DD_0 shifting to DD_1) leads to an increase in the foreign currency reserves 'E' to 'B'.

The Chinese Central Bank, which tries to maintain a fixed relationship between the Renminbi and the US dollar, is buying up dollars to prevent the Renminbi rising (the undervalued Renmimbi helps Chinese exporters). Its foreign exchange reserves have broken through the $875bn level and should hit $1 trillion by the end of the year (2006).

Other countries in Asia, who had fixed their (undervalued) currencies to the dollar, built up large dollar holdings. These were recycled into the US economy and helped to keep interest rates low. Indirectly this has led to the sub-prime crises in the US and the 'credit crunch'.

Many countries, from the Middle East to Asia, effectively tie their currencies to the US dollar. Others, such as Russia and Argentina, do not literally peg to the dollar but nevertheless try to smooth movements. As a result, whenever the Federal Bank cuts interest rates, it puts pressure on the whole "dollar bloc" to follow suit.

The Exchange Rate Mechanism (ERM) was a system where the pound sterling was fixed against the German Deutsche Mark, the French Franc and other European currencies. Prior to leaving the ERM in 1992 the UK authorities relied on high interest rates and the buying and selling of the currency to try maintain its value.

Flexible exchange rates: The value of the currency is determined by supply and demand. Any excess supply of the currency leads to a fall(depreciation) in the value of the currency. Any excess demand for the currency leads to an increase(appreciation) in the value of the currency.

There is, theoretically, no intervention in the foreign exchange markets.

There is no change in the foreign currency reserves. There are no net capital flows into or out of the country.

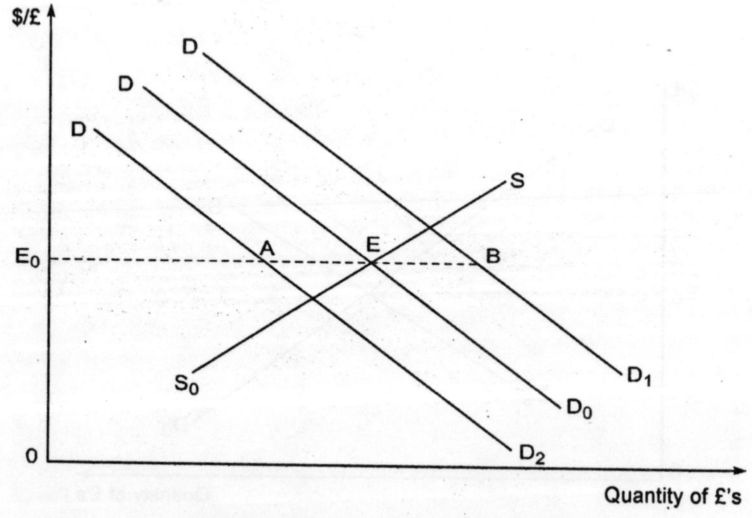

Fig. 10.2: A fixed, nominal, exchange rate

In Fig. 10.3 start at an initial equilibrium position E_0, 'A'.

An increase in the demand for pounds (say, DD_0 to DD_1) increases the exchange rate to E_1. The pound appreciates.

If there is a fall in the demand for pounds (DD_0 to DD_2) the exchange rate will fall to E_2. The pound depreciates.

The real exchange rate (R)

Up to now we have been discussing the nominal exchange rate.

Now consider whether or not a fall (depreciation) in the nominal exchange rate over a period of time will make domestic goods and services cheaper abroad.

The real exchange rate measures the relative price of goods from different countries when measured in a common currency. For example, the real exchange rate ($\mathbf{R}_{UK}$) between the UK pound sterling (£$_{UK}$) and the US dollar (\$$_{US}$) is

$$\mathbf{R}_{UK} = \frac{\pounds UK}{\$_{US}}$$

where: $\mathbf{R}_{UK}$ = the real exchange rate of UK goods and services

£$_{UK}$ = the pound sterling (£) price of UK goods

\$$_{US}$ = the dollar (\$) price of US goods.

\$/£ = the dollar, pound nominal exchange rate.

The data is from the OECD where, for the price indices, 1990 = 100.

Consider table 10.2. Between 1976 and 1981 prices in the UK rose by 88%, prices in the USA increased by 60%, and over this period of time the nominal value of the pound sterling appreciated by 12%. The combination of the increase in the exchange rate and the rise in the UK's price level relative to the price level in the USA led to an increase in the real exchange rate of 32.5%. Over the period 1976-81 UK exports became expensive relative to the prices of US goods and services and UK imports from the USA became relatively cheap.

Between '81 and '95, even though the UK inflation rate (99%) was greater than the USA inflation rate (67.5%), the pound fell(depreciated) sufficiently (by 18.8%) for the real exchange rate to fall (by 3.6%). UK exports are now cheaper and UK imports are more expensive than in 1981.

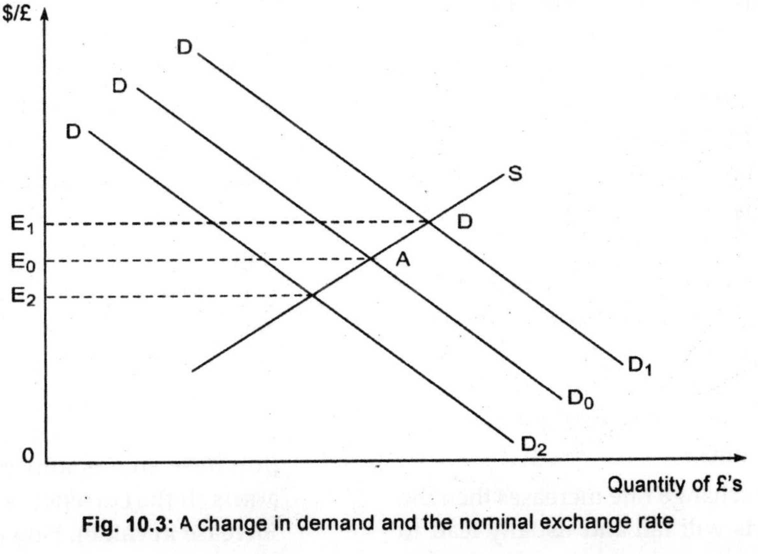

Fig. 10.3: A change in demand and the nominal exchange rate

Table 10.2: The nominal and real (R) exchange rate

	1976	% change '76-81	1981	% change '81-'95	1995
Nominal $/£	1.70	+12%	1.91	−18.8%	1.55
UK price level	31.6	+88%	59.3	+99%	118.2
US price level	43.5	+60%	69.6	+67.5%	116.6
Real $/£ ($R_{UK}$)	1.23	+32%	1.63	−3.6%	1.57

The data is from the OECD where, for the price indices, 1990=100

Determinants of the current account on the balance of payments

Exports (X) are determined by **WY** (world income) and **R** (the real exchange rate): (X=X(WY,R)).

If world income increases then, usually, there is an increase in exports. This will lead to an increase in demand for the domestic currency and will be recorded as a credit item in the balance of payments accounts.

If the real exchange rate increases then the price of exports will rise and usually lead to a fall in demand for domestic exports and corresponding fall in the earnings of these exporting countries. (It has been estimated that the a 10% rise of the Euro against the dollar reduces corporate Europe's earnings by 3.5%. Europe's car, energy and materials sector will have falls in earnings per share of 14.7%, 9.6% and 6.9% respectively). This will lead to a decrease in demand for the domestic currency and will be recorded as a debit item in the balance of payments accounts.

Imports (Z) are determined by **Y** (domestic income) and the real exchange rate (**R**): (Z = Z(Y,R)).

We have seen that an increase in domestic income will lead to an increase in the demand for imports. This will lead to an increase in demand for foreign currency and will be recorded as a debit item in the balance of payments accounts.

If the real exchange rate increases then the price of imports will fall and usually lead to an increase in the demand for imports. This will lead to an increase in demand for foreign currency and will be recorded as a debit item in the balance of payments accounts.

Capital account: determining the flow of short-term financial capital (speculation)

The total world stock of finance available for speculative movement is measured in trillions of dollars and can be freely moved in search of the highest rate of return. This movement of finance can have major effects at the macroeconomic level.

It has been estimated that, in 1970, 90% of foreign exchange transactions related to the real economy i.e. trade and investment. In 1998 this figure had fallen to 5%. The rest is speculative - 80% of which has a return time of 1 week or less (Noam Chomski, 'Power in the Global Arena' New Left Review, No.230, July/August 1998).

Where this finance goes depends on three factors.

1. The expected increase in the output of an economy.

   If the output of an economy is expected to increase then this will lead to people anticipating that profits will rise and shares and other financial assets will increase in value. Overseas finance will flow into the country in order to purchase shares and other financial assets (If the currency is floating it will increase in value). However, in 2003, a study from the US investment bank Merrill Lynch, demonstrated that there was no link between economic success and currency strength in a sample of 10 developed economies during the years 1992-2002.

2. The rate of interest that can be earned on the finance.
3. The **expected** change in the exchange rate.

Consider three situations, (**A**, **B**, and **C**) assuming that, at the beginning of, and throughout 2009, interest rates in two countries, Assumptia and Keteris, are known to be as follows: In Assumptia 10%: In Keteris 5%. The currency of Assumptia is the Assumptian pound (£A). The currency of Keteris is the Keterian dollar ($K). Ignore any transaction costs.

A. a. If £A1,000,000 were deposited in Assumptia for the year 2009 it would earn interest of £A100,000. The value of the deposit at the end of the year would be £A1,100,000. The return, in Assumptian pounds, would be 10%.

b. If £A1,000,000 is exchanged into Keterian dollars at the beginning of 2009 it would earn interest of £A50,000 over 2009. Changed back into Assumptian pounds the return, in Assumptian pounds, would be 5%.

Ceteris paribus, no sensible person (economically rational woman/man) would deposit finance in Keteris and earn 5% less than in Assumptia.

i. There would be a massive flow of finance from Keteris to Assumptia.

ii. With a freely floating exchange rate the £A would immediately rise until the £A reached such a level that it was expected to fall by 5% against the $K over 2009.

iii. This would equalise the returns (10%) an Assumptian could earn **both** in Assumptia **and** Keteris and equalise the returns (5%) a Keterian could earn in **both** Assumptia **and** Keteris.

(α) Assumptians would earn a **10% interest rate** return on funds deposited in Assumptia and earn a **10%** return on funds deposited in Keteris (a **5% interest rate** return <u>plus</u> a **5% currency return** (because of the 5% depreciation of the £A [equivalent to a 5% appreciation in the $K])).

(β) Keterians would earn a **5% interest** rate return on funds deposited in Keteris and earn a **5%** return on funds deposited in Assumptia (a **10% interest rate** return <u>less</u> **a 5% currency return** (because of the 5% depreciation of the £A [equivalent to a 5% appreciation in the $K])).

B. Consider point (A) again. At the beginning of 2009 the 'market obviously' <u>expected</u> the £A (Assumptian pound) to fall by 5% against the $K.

(α) Assumptians would then earn a **10% interest rate** return on funds deposited in Assumptia and earn a **10%** return on funds deposited in Keteris (a **5% interest rate** return **plus a 5% currency** return (because of the 5% depreciation of the £A [equivalent to a 5% appreciation in the $K])).

(β) Keterians would earn a **5% interest** rate return on funds deposited in Keteris and earn a **5%** return on funds deposited in Assumptia (a **10% interest**

YOU SHOULD REMEMBER

The return from overseas lending is equal to the foreign rate of interest **plus** (*minus*) any **appreciation** (*depreciation*) in the exchange rate of the foreign currency in terms of the domestic currency.

rate return **less a 5% currency** return (because of the 5% depreciation of the £A [equivalent to a 5% appreciation in the $K])).

C. a. At the beginning of 2009, £A1,000,000 are changed into $K's and deposited in Keteris.

b. **Contrary to 'market' expectations**, over 2009, the £A falls by 10% against the $K [equivalent to a 10% appreciation in the $K].

c. At the end of 2009, the £A1,050,000 worth of $K's are converted back into £A's.

The original £A1,000,000 would now be worth £A1,158,000.

The total £A return at the end of 2009 is 15%. This is made up of a **5% interest rate** return **plus a 10% currency** return (because of the 10% depreciation of the £A [equivalent to a 10% appreciation in the $K])).

N.B. In the foreign exchange market exchange rate changes can be much more important than a 1% or 2% interest differential.

Usually, countries with high interest rates have higher rates of inflation. In our example we would expect Assumptian inflation to be 5% more than Keterian inflation. The Assumptian real exchange rate would be rising by 5% per year relative to Keteris. Assumptian exports would be becoming less competitive relative to Keterian goods (by 5% a year, *ceteris paribus*). Imports to Assumptia would also be becoming cheaper (by 5% a year, *ceteris paribus*). To maintain competitiveness (a constant real exchange rate) the Assumptian **nominal** exchange rate would have to fall by 5%.

THE EXCHANGE RATE AND THE DOMESTIC MONEY SUPPLY

1. With a fixed exchange rate:

Any deficit or surplus on the balance of payments is financed by changes in the government holdings of foreign currency. This is known as official financing. This makes the balance of payments zero.

For example, if there is a balance of payments deficit of £20 billion pounds, foreign currency reserves will fall to finance the deficit (by £20 billion).

With a fixed exchange rate the domestic money supply will decrease[*increase*] by an amount equal to the size of the balance of payments deficit[*surplus*]. The foreign currency reserves will fall [rise] by an equivalent amount.

For example: A balance of payments deficit of £15 billion leads to individuals, within the domestic economy, purchasing the foreign exchange (say £15 billion worth of dollars) which will allow them to purchase these £15 billion worth of imports (net). Hence £15 billion has been withdrawn from circulation from the domestic economy.

The domestic money supply has fallen by £15 billion.

The Bank of England purchases this £15b., at the current exchange rate (to prevent the pound falling), and the foreign currency reserves fall in value by £15 billion. The Bank of England is now holding an extra £15 billion in sterling (£'s) *Ceteris paribus*, there is £15 billion less in the domestic economy. £15 billion in dollars flows to the USA.

YOU SHOULD REMEMBER

Both Assumptia and Keteris are following what is known as the **interest rate parity condition**. The **interest rate parity condition** states that:

The domestic return (the domestic interest rate) = overseas return = the foreign rate of interest **plus** (*minus*) any **appreciation** (*depreciation*) in the exchange rate of the foreign currency in terms of the domestic currency.

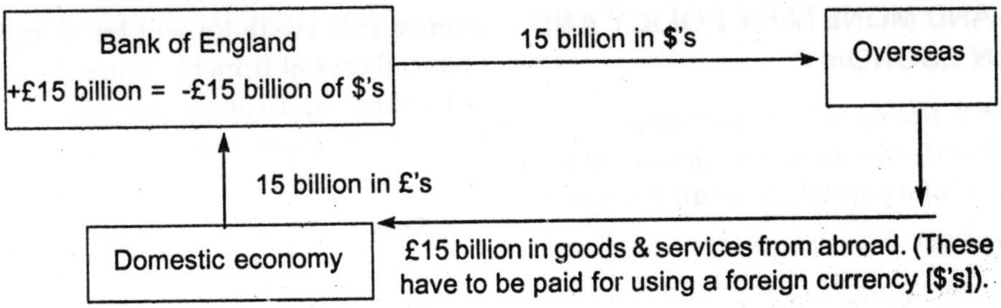

STERILIZATION is the neutralisation (by selling or buying bonds in the open market by the monetary authorities) of changes in the money supply brought about by a balance of payments surplus or deficit, e.g. with a fixed exchange rate a balance of payments deficit of £15 billion leads to a reduction in the domestic money supply of £15 billion.

Sterilisation is when the monetary authorities replace (sterilise) the £15 billion withdrawn from the economy. In this case the monetary authorities buy bonds in the open market and, through injections of cash, ensure that £15 billion is returned to the economy. As mentioned earlier, the Chinese Central Bank's policy of buying dollars and keeping the renminbi undervalued has helped Chinese exporters immensely, but it is also creating long-term problems. China lacks a well-developed government debt market, which means the government finds it difficult to sterilise its purchases of dollars by mopping up the excess renminbi it is forced to print in exchange.

2. With a flexible exchange rate

With a deficit [surplus] on the current account, there has to be a surplus [deficit] on the capital account. This is because, usually, the domestic currency is of no use outside the domestic economy – the US dollar is an exception as it is widely used throughout the world. (According to the Federal Reserve about $300bn in cash is circulating outside the USA). So, for example, if the UK has a current account deficit ($X<Z$) of £18 billion then the UK requires £18 billion of foreign currency to finance the current account deficit. Since £18 billion in sterling(£'s) is worthless outside the confines of the UK, then people/businesses must be found who will provide the £18 billion of foreign currency. ie people/businesses who want £18 billion of sterling to buy financial assets or earn UK interest on sterling (£'s) deposits with UK banks. If the £18 billion of foreign currency is not forthcoming at the current exchange rate then the nominal exchange rate will fall until the £18b of foreign currency is provided. Thus, if there is a deficit of £18 billion on the current account there is an £18 billion surplus on the capital account.

There is an automatic inflow [outflow] of financial capital equal to the deficit [surplus] on the current account. This has to occur whether at the current exchange rate or at a lower [higher] one.

If there is a surplus (say £18 billion) on the **capital** account (a deficit of £18 billion on the current account) then foreigners, on net, are acquiring assets (£18 billion) in the domestic (UK) economy.

YOU SHOULD REMEMBER

Under a fully flexible exchange rate regime the **current account plus the capital account is always equal to <u>zero</u>.**

FISCAL AND MONETARY POLICY AND AN OPEN ECONOMY

MONETARY Policy when exchange rates are FIXED and there is no restriction on the flow of financial capital between countries

1. Consider Fig. 10.4. Start at an initial, below full employment, equilibrium situation E_0. That is $r_0=r_w$, where ro is the original domestic rate of interest and r_w is the 'world' rate of interest. Y_0, $LM(M_0/P_0)$, $IS(G_0,M_0/P_0,R_0)$, where R_0 is the initial real exchange rate.
2. Increase the nominal stock of money (M), say by 10%.

With prices constant, the real stock of money ($L_0=M_0/P_0$) will increase to $L_{01}=M_1/P_0$ (by 10%). $LM(M_0/P_0)$ will shift to the right to $LM(M_1/P_0)$. At r_0 there is now an excess supply of money that is equivalent to an excess demand for bonds. The price of bonds will increase which leads to a fall in the rate of interest (to r_{01}). Since the domestic interest rate ro1 is now less than the world interest rate rw there will be an outflow of financial capital from the domestic economy. Individuals and companies will sell sterling (£'s) and buy foreign currency (in order to earn the higher overseas interest rates).

This sale of £'s would lead to a depreciation in the value of sterling *if* the government was not committed to maintaining a fixed exchange rate with other currencies.

To maintain the desired exchange rate the Bank of England will buy up the excess supply of £'s, running down its gold and foreign currency reserves. The pounds that are being sold are being taken from the domestic economy and are reducing the domestic money supply. (see page 165-166). M_1/P_0 will be shifted back towards M_0/P_0 and r_{01} will be returning to r_0 ($= r_w$).

As long as the domestic interest rate is below world interest rates sterling, £'s, will continue to be sold. Gold and foreign currency reserves will continue to fall and the domestic

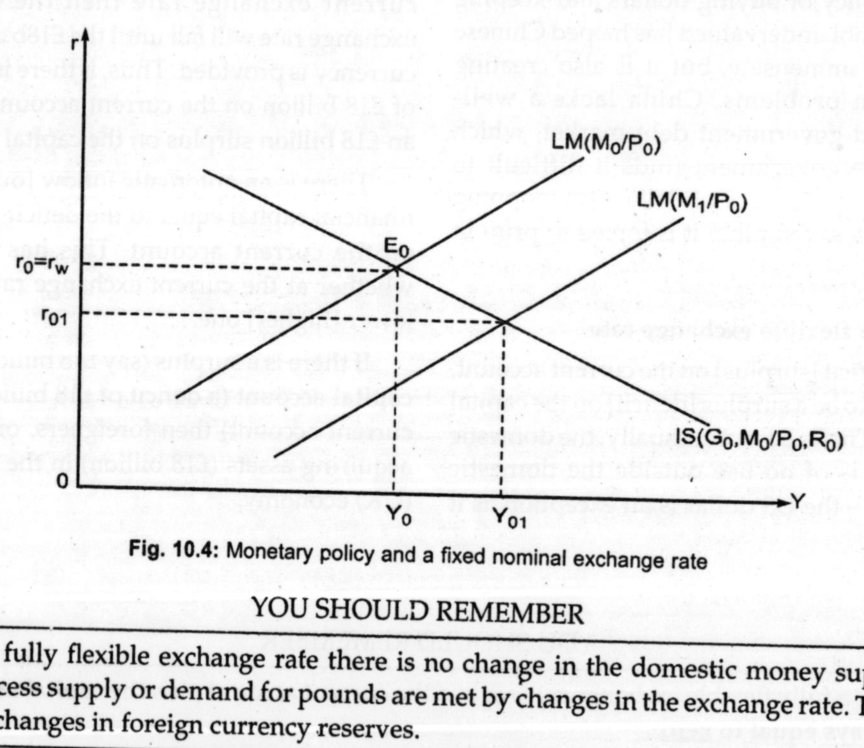

Fig. 10.4: Monetary policy and a fixed nominal exchange rate

YOU SHOULD REMEMBER

With a fully flexible exchange rate there is no change in the domestic money supply. Any excess supply or demand for pounds are met by changes in the exchange rate. There are no changes in foreign currency reserves.

money supply will continue to decrease. We will assume that the fall in the rate of interest will not last long enough to affect consumption or investment expenditure and hence aggregate demand. There will be no change in the position of $IS(G_0,M_0/P_0,r_0)$.

Any attempt by the Bank of England to sterilize the effects of the reduction in the money supply by buying bonds and putting money back into the economy will keep interest rates down, prolong the outflow of financial capital and the decrease in the foreign exchange reserves. Sooner or later the pressure on the reserves will force a change in policy.

During the sterling crises of September 1992 the pound was being sold. It was either sold short, people were selling sterling that they did not own and were only putting up a small percentage of the sterling they were selling, or they were borrowing from the UK banking system in £'s and exchanging it for foreign currencies. In both cases they hoped to buy it back at a cheaper exchange rate in the future to repay their debts. The massive loss of foreign currency reserves forced the UK government to leave the exchange rate mechanism in September 1992 and to devalue the pound against other European currencies.

FISCAL Policy when the exchange rate is FIXED and there is no restriction on the flow of financial capital between countries.

1. Consider figure 10.5. Start at an initial equilibrium, below full employment, situation E_0. That is $r_0=r_w$, Y_0, LM (M_0/P_0), $IS(G_0,M_0/P_0,R_0)$, where R_0 is the initial real exchange rate.
2. Increase the level of government expenditure. (A similar outcome will be observed if autonomous consumption, investment or net exports increase).

$IS(G_0,M_0/P_0,R_0)$ will shift upwards to $IS(G_1,M_0/P_0,R_0)$ and output will increase to Y_{01}

At r_0 there is now an excess demand for money which is equivalent to an excess supply of bonds.

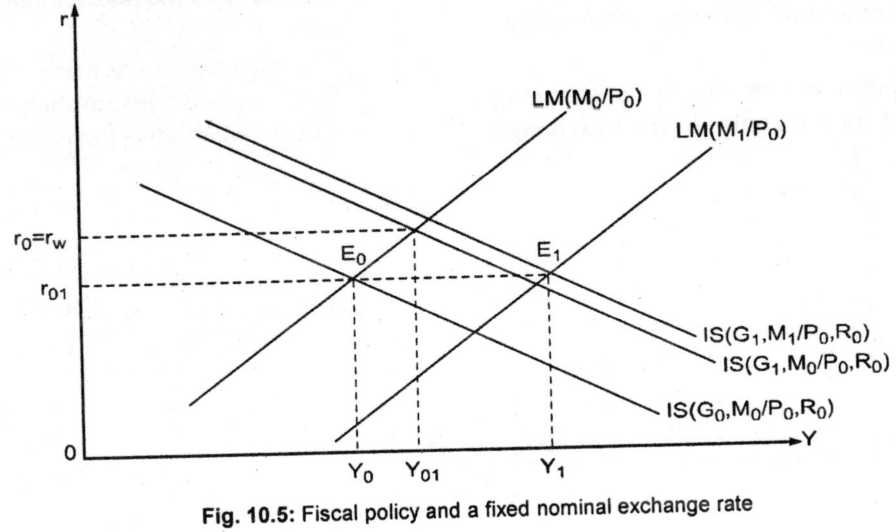

Fig. 10.5: Fiscal policy and a fixed nominal exchange rate

YOU SHOULD REMEMBER

With a fixed exchange rate the government loses control of the domestic money supply. With a *fixed* exchange rate monetary policy is ineffective. The government can control either the supply of money OR the exchange rate but not both.

The price of bonds will fall and the rate of interest will increase.

This increase in interest rates would, normally, 'crowd out' consumption and investment expenditure and lead to a reduction in aggregate demand. But, since the domestic interest rate is greater than the world interest rate (r_w), this will lead to an inflow of financial capital and an increase in the domestic money supply.

With a fixed exchange rate there will be an increase in the domestic money supply and, with a constant price level, an increase in the real stock of money. $LM(M_0/P_0)$ will start to shift to the right putting downward pressure on the interest rate.

As long as long as the domestic interest rate is greater than the world interest rate (r_w) there will be an inflow of financial capital, an increase in the domestic money supply and downward pressure on the rate of interest. This will continue until a new equilibrium is reached at E_1. That is $IS(G_1,M_1/P_0,r_0)$, Y_1, $L_1=M_1/P_0$. (Remember the increase in the real stock of money may increase autonomous consumption).

Fiscal policy is very effective in changing the level of income/output when exchange rates are fixed and there is a free flow of financial capital.

Monetary policy when exchange rates are Flexible and there are no restrictions on the flow of financial capital between countries.

1. Consider Fig. 10.6. Start at an initial equilibrium, below full employment, situation E_0. That is $r_0=r_w$, Y_0, $LM(M_0/P_0)$, $IS(G_0,M_0/P_0,R_0)$, where R_0 is the, initial, real exchange rate.
2. Increase the nominal stock of money (M_0). With prices (P_0) constant the real stock of money ($L_0=M_0/P_0$) will increase to $M_1/P_0=L_1$. $LM(M_0/P_0)$ will shift to the right to $LM(M_1/P_0)$.
   a. This will increase the level of consumption expenditure (the real balance effect). $IS(G_0,M_0/P_0,R_0)$ will shift to the right. At the rate of interest of ro there is now an excess supply of money, which is equivalent to an excess demand for bonds. The price of bonds will increase and the rate of interest will fall.

   The increase in the price of bonds will increase consumption expenditure (wealth has increased).

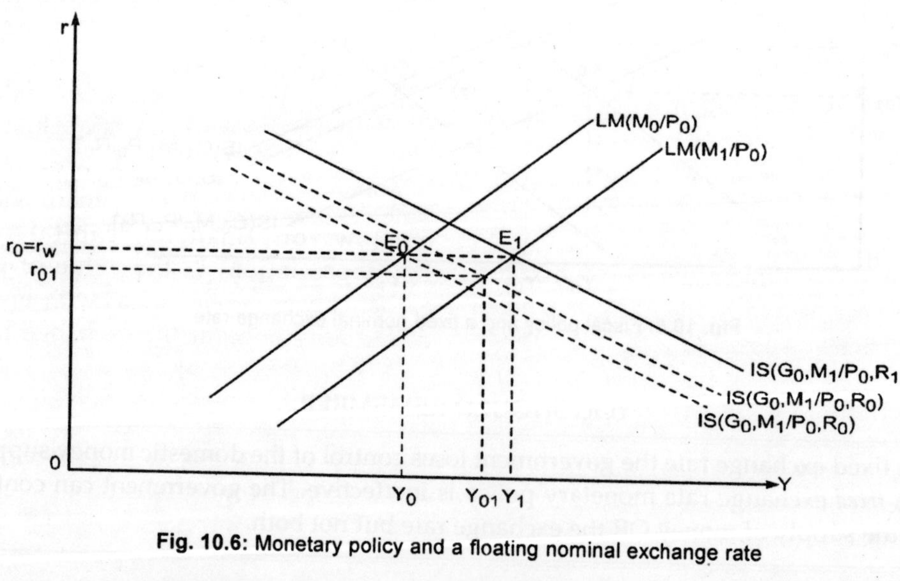

Fig. 10.6: Monetary policy and a floating nominal exchange rate

The fall in the rate of interest will:

i. Increase consumption expenditure; (the cost of borrowing has decreased).

ii. Increase investment expenditure; (the present value of expected future revenues will increase).

The increase in consumption and investment expenditure will increase aggregate demand. Income/output will increase and imports will increase.

b. The domestic rate of interest will fall relative to overseas interest rates. There will be an outflow of financial capital and downward pressure on the pound. The fall(depreciation) in the pound* (see Figure 10.7) will take the strain of the outflow of financial capital but the domestic money supply will be **unchanged** at its new level M_1/P_0.

Exports will be cheaper and imports will be more expensive. Exports will probably increase and imports fall. This will also increase aggregate demand and income/output.

Monetary policy is very effective in changing the level of income/output when exchange rates are flexible.

(a) and (b) together will lead to an increase in aggregate demand and income/output.

(a) will worsen the trade balance, (b) will improve it.

The net effect of (a) + (b) is small whichever way it goes.

NOTE: If the difference between r_0 and r_1 is 3% per year then the exchange rate will fall until it reaches a level where 'the foreign exchange market' ***expects*** it to increase by 3%, over the next year, back to its equilibrium value. The initial fall in the pound tends to *overshoot* its equilibrium level. This equalises the return in the domestic economy (r) vis-à-vis the world interest rate (r_w).

Consider figure 10.7: If the initial equilibrium exchange rate was at point 'A', and interest rates fell by 3%, then the exchange rate would fall(depreciate) past its equilibrium point 'E' to such a level where 'the foreign exchange market' ***expects*** it to increase (appreciate) by 3% over the next year. (back to its equilibrium level-E). This equalises the return in the domestic economy (r) vis-à-vis the world interest rate (r_w).

Fiscal policy when exchange rates are flexible and there is no restriction on the flow of financial capital between countries

1. Consider Fig. 10.8. Start at an initial equilibrium situation E_0. That is $r_0=r_w$, Y_0, $LM(M_0/P_0)$, $IS(G_0,M_0/P_0,R_0)$, where R_0 is the initial real exchange rate.

2. Cut government expenditure. (A similar outcome will result if there is an increase in taxation).

Aggregate demand will fall to $IS(G_1, M_0/P_0,R_0)$, leading to a fall in income to Y_{01}. At the rate of interest of r_0 there is now an excess supply of money, which is equivalent to an excess demand for bonds. The price of bonds will increase and the rate of interest will fall, say to r_{01}.

Since r_{01} is less than r_w there will be an outflow of financial capital and a fall(depreciation) in the value of the real exchange rate. We cannot say with any degree of certainty how far the exchange rate will

YOU SHOULD REMEMBER

The monetary authorities can control **either** the supply of money or the exchange rate—not both. (It should also be noted that an indication of loose [tight] monetary policy is a depreciating [appreciating] exchange rate).

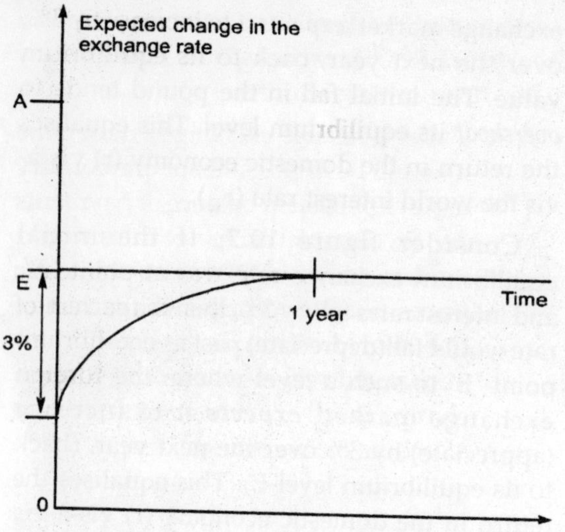

Fig. 10.7: An 'overshooting' exchange rate

fall(depreciate), but, if the difference between r_0 and r_{01} is 3% then the exchange rate will fall(depreciate) until it reaches a level where 'the foreign exchange market' ***expects*** it to increase by 3% over the next year (back to its equilibrium level) see Fig. 10.7. This equalises the return in the domestic economy (r) vis-à-vis the world interest rate (r_w).

There will be no change in the domestic money supply. Exports will be cheaper and imports will be more expensive.

Exports will probably increase and imports fall. Aggregate demand will increase. The increase in the price of bonds will increase consumption expenditure.

The fall in the rate of interest will;

i. Increase consumption expenditure. (The cost of borrowing will fall).

ii. Increase investment expenditure; (the present value of expected revenues will increase).

The increase in consumption and investment and the increase in exports and reduction in imports will increase aggregate demand and partially or wholly offset the decrease in aggregate demand brought about by the contractionary fiscal policy.

Cuts in government expenditure have led to interest rate reductions and the transfer of resources from the government sector to consumption, investment, exports and import substitutes.

2. Assume that, in the short-run, the economy ends up at IS(G_1,M_0/P_0,r_1), LM(M_0/P_0), Y_1.

Eventually the economy will return to Y_0 and $r_0=r_w$.

You should also note that an **increase** in government expenditure when the economy is below full employment will lead to an **increase** in the rate of interest and the

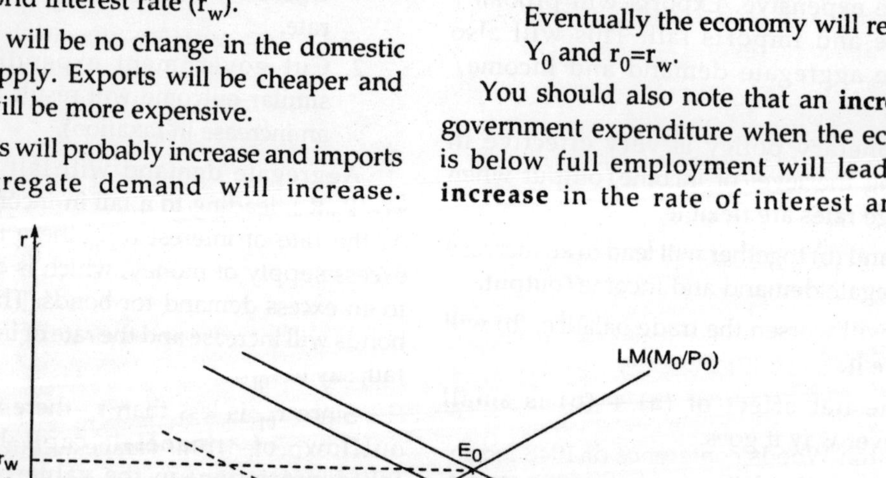

Fig. 10.8: Fiscal policy and a floating nominal exchange rate

exchange rate. Both the rise in the interest rate and the exchange rate will 'crowd out' consumption and investment expenditure.

Since monetarists believe that the price level is mainly determined by the nominal stock of money (and income is close to or equal to full employment income, Y_f), they favour flexible exchange rates where monetary policy is effective and the authorities have control over the nominal stock of money.

Keynesians, who think that fiscal policy is more effective, are more likely to prefer fixed exchange rates. With a fixed exchange rate fiscal policy is much more effective than monetary policy.

If the economy is at or near to a full employment position the price level will probably increase.

In a flexible exchange rate regime an increase in aggregate demand will lead to an increase in the rate of interest and a rise in the exchange rate. Speculators who think that an economy is 'coming out' of a recession will purchase that economy's currency before the interest rate increases and before the currency increases in value. If they anticipate correctly this will give them an increase in the value of their financial capital and a chance to earn above world interest rates when interest rates increase. The 'good' speculator will anticipate this inflow and buy the currency at the first sign of the 'green shoots' of recovery.

FIXED VERSUS FLEXIBLE EXCHANGE RATES

The Bretton Woods conference of 1948 led to the setting up of the IMF (International Monetary Fund) and the introduction of fixed (but *not* permanent) exchange rates. However, some economists were not happy over the workings of the fixed rate system and urged a return to a flexible exchange rate regime. They give the following reasons:

1. Under a flexible exchange rate regime it would be impossible for one country to run a persistent balance of payments deficit. Nominal exchange rates would tend to move in line with domestic prices relative to prices in the rest of the world. This is assuming an unchanged real exchange rate and no change in other 'fundamentals' that affect the real exchange rate.

   For example, if UK prices increased faster than prices in the rest of the world, then normally this would lead to a fall in exports and an increase in imports and a balance of payments deficit. However, with floating exchange rates, sterling would depreciate relative to other currencies to maintain sterling's real exchange rate and this should correct any balance of payments deficit.

   If there were any deviation from the real exchange rate then **stabilising** speculation would quickly take the exchange rate back to the real exchange rate. The argument is that speculation **must** be stabilising otherwise speculators would be selling when the currency is low in price and buying when the currency is high in price and hence be losing money.

   However, real exchange rates have been much more volatile than expected. This can be accounted for in several ways—

   a. Interest rates and exchange rates tend to adjust almost instantly whilst prices, output and the

YOU SHOULD REMEMBER

> Fiscal policy is not a very effective method of changing income/output when exchange rates are flexible

current account adjust much more slowly. Changes in the supply of money are likely to lead to an over adjustment in the exchange rate. See Fig. 10.7.

b. It usually takes a long time for changes in the exchange rate to have an effect on the trade balance. A decrease in the real exchange rate can lead to the value of the balance of trade deteriorating. The fall in the value of the currency usually leads, **initially**, to the **value** of exports falling (as foreigners are slow to increase their demand at the lower export prices) and the **value** of imports increase (importers have entered into contracts at the old exchange rate or are slow to cut back on their purchases). It is only when exports increase in volume and imports decrease in volume in the medium to long term that the balance of trade moves into surplus. (The 'J' curve).

We are assuming that the Marshal-Lerner condition is effective. The Marshal-Lerner condition predicts that if the sum of the price elasticities of demand for imports and exports is greater than 1 then the balance between the change in export earnings and import expenditure will be such as to improve the balance of payments. i.e. Net exports will increase.

We are also assuming that the economy is not at full employment and that resources are available to produce the extra exports and import substitutes.

c. Foreign exchange rate speculators may destabilise the currency by 'following trends' in the path of the currency. This reinforces the exchange rate trends, pulling the exchange rate away from equilibrium over extended periods (and giving insufficient time for, say, a devaluation to work).

d. If wage increases follow price increases then any fall(depreciation) in the exchange rate may 'trigger off' price increases in the domestic economy. Increases in money wages may lead to increases in costs and, again, prices. Increases in domestic prices will lead to an increase in the real exchange rate and require the currency to be devalued further. See, also, chapter 9.

e. In the modern world most of the financial markets are highly integrated. Nominal exchange rates (and real exchange rates) respond much more quickly to changes in interest rates rather than changes in current account deficits. It thus takes much longer for real exchange rates to return to their equilibrium levels.

But, since the oil shocks of 73, 79, 90 many Latin American countries (and the UK and the USA) have continued to run persistent balance of payments deficits.

2. Flexible exchange rates would enable a country to pursue independent macroeconomic policies.

a. Different countries needed different levels of unemployment to maintain the same rate of inflation. If there was a trade-off between unemployment and inflation (we are assuming that countries could have higher unemployment and lower inflation or lower unemployment and higher inflation) then, under a fixed exchange rate regime, countries would be forced to operate with a common world rate of inflation. Countries such as Germany would be exposed to imported inflation, whereas countries such as the UK may be forced to operate at a lower than preferred rate of inflation and require a higher level of unemployment.

Flexible exchange rates allowed countries to choose their own combinations of unemployment and inflation. This choice, it is argued, meant that countries would have to be better off.

But, by the late 1960's, economists had come to reject the notion of a 'trade off' between unemployment and inflation. Unemployment was seen to depend upon real magnitudes within the economy and only susceptible to supply side policies. Countries could, however, determine their inflation rates. This may or may not be a good thing! Overall, countries pursuing independent policies have not received the benefits of lower inflation and lower unemployment.

b. We have seen, above, that an economy with flexible exchange rates is not constrained by balance of payments imbalances and is able to use monetary policy to affect the level of domestic income, output and the price level.

   The authorities could control the rate of inflation by controlling the money supply. A flexible exchange rate regime would shelter the domestic economy from any external inflationary pressures as well as containing any domestic instability within the domestic economy and not allowing it to be transferred to the rest of the world.

   However swings in the monetary policy of the US in the years 1979-84 affected the European economies just as much as US monetary policy of the years 1968-72.

c. Since a flexible exchange rate regime does not require countries to hold reserve of gold or foreign currencies then all problems associated the provision of international reserves would be removed.

   This does not appear to be the case, as countries still require reserves to try to prevent large fluctuations in nominal exchange rates.

d. It was also assumed that flexible exchange rates would reduce protectionist tendencies. An economy with flexible exchange rates cannot improve its trade balance by implementing protectionist measures and also would quickly reduce misalignments in the currencies.

   This also does not appear to have happened. The USA, the EU and Japan are still in conflict over protectionism.

3. Encouraging the flow of capital from the rich creditor countries to poorer developing countries. This is based on the belief in the law of variable proportions that determine the real return on the factors of production. (More labour and less capital in the developing countries means that the marginal productivity of capital is higher in the developing countries attracting capital from overseas). The projects will be sufficient to repay the loan and interest and increase the standard of living in the developing country.

However, there has been a net flow of capital from developing countries to developed countries. World-wide inequalities have worsened. However, there has been a net flow of capital from developing countries to developed countries. World-wide inequalities have worsened. Two countries that weathered the global financial crisis very well were India and China. India's been having growth rate over the past decade of over 5%. China's growth rate has been faster. Neither of them followed the dictum of having capital market liberalisation. Indeed Newly Industrialized Countries (NICs) in Pacific-Asia have lifted millions out of poverty. However this development occurred despite 'globalisation' (freeing up markets, privatisation, reducing or abolishing trade barriers, freeing up their financial capital markets) ignoring central neo-liberal themes now institutionalised in the global economic structure. The NICs developed via massive state intervention in the market and illiberal controls on capital flows. Greater integration into the globalised market brought about the crash in 1997 that shattered the livelihoods of millions.

The UK and the Euro

In a speech in July 1997 Gordon Brown set five economics tests to determine whether the UK should adopt the Euro and give up the pound.

1. Are the business cycles and economic structures compatible, so we could live with Euro interest rates permanently?
2. If problems emerge, is there sufficient flexibility to deal with them?
3. Would joining the EMU create better conditions for firms making decisions to invest in the UK?
4. Would EMU entry have a positive impact on the competitiveness of the UK's financial services industry?
5. Will joining the EMU promote higher growth, stability and a lasting increase in jobs?

If, and when, these criteria are met the UK can then adopt the Euro.

QUESTIONS

1. A substantial fall in the price of the pound in foreign currencies (e.g., the price of the pound in euros) could be expected to affect physical quantities of exports from the UK and imports into the UK as follows:
   (a) increase both exports and imports.
   (b) increase exports, decrease imports.
   (c) decrease both exports and imports.
   (d) decrease exports, increase imports.
   (e) have no perceptible effect on either imports or exports.

2. Explain the effect on the business sector of the economy of a rise in the exchange rate for the country's currency.

3. Consider an outside shock on the value of the pound that causes it to depreciate. The policy makers could defend the pound by
   (a) increasing the money supply thereby lowering the LM curve and driving the interest rate up.
   (b) increasing government spending thereby raising the IS curve and driving the interest rate up.
   (c) reducing the money supply thereby raising the LM curve and driving the interest rate up.
   (d) increasing taxes thereby lowering the IS curve and driving the interest rate down.
   (e) simultaneously increasing government spending and the money supply so that GNP climbs with a fixed interest rate.

4. Suppose net exports were to become less sensitive to changes in the interest rate. You would then draw
   (a) A flatter IS curve.
   (b) A steeper IS curve.
   (c) A flatter LM curve.
   (d) A steeper LM curve.

5. Had net exports in the UK been reduced to zero by contractionary fiscal policy through the latter half of the 1990's, the UK economy would have
   (a) been producing output well above the full employment level of GNP.
   (b) been producing output slightly above the full employment level of GNP.
   (c) been producing output nearly equal to the full employment level of GNP.
   (d) been producing output slightly lower than the full employment level of GNP.
   (e) been producing output considerably lower than the full employment level of GNP.

6. A current account deficit
   (a) is never possible because the balance of payments must **always** balance.
   (b) can seldom be larger than 50% of a capital account surplus.
   (c) can be used to help finance a government deficit indefinitely.
   (d) can be used to help finance a government deficit if foreign lenders accumulate government bonds.
   (e) does not include investment earnings that are part of the capital account.

7. The US Treasury stated that the long-term capital inflow to the USA was $278 billion in the third quarter of 2005. This was $82 billion more than the very large current account deficit ($196 billion) for the same period and sent a reassuring message to the business community that the deficit could be easily financed. Since the dollar is allowed to float and there were no changes in foreign exchange reserves how can this be the case? I.e. How can the inflow of foreign capital be substantially greater then the current account deficit when the dollar is a floating currency?

ANSWERS

1. (b) A fall in the value of the sterling makes imports into the UK more expensive and exports out of the UK less expensive. As a result, exports should increase and imports should fall.

2. The price of exports will increase and the price of imports will decrease. We will assume that exports will fall and imports will increase. This will lead to a fall in aggregate demand and income/output. The price of imported goods and raw materials will fall leading to a fall in business costs and downward pressure on the price level.

3. When the value of the pound falls, protecting the currency requires that the policy makers consider doing something that will increase its demand overseas; i.e., it must somehow make some UK. assets (whose purchase requires foreign nationals to obtain pounds) more attractive abroad. Restricting the money supply so that domestic interest rates climb is the correct response (answer (c)). The real return to holding bonds denominated in pounds would then climb, making them more valuable to hold and increasing their demand. Since pounds would be required to purchase these bonds, the price of pounds (i.e., the exchange rate) would also climb according to the simple fundamentals of supply and demand analysis.

4. If net exports were to become less sensitive to changes in the interest rate then the IS curve would become steeper (answer (b). This is because an increase[decrease] in the rate of interest leads to an appreciation [depreciation] in the currency, a fall[rise] in net exports, a fall[rise] in aggregate demand and a fall[rise] in income/output . If net exports were to become less sensitive to changes in the interest rate then changes in aggregate demand and income/output would be less responsive to changes in interest rates. The IS curve would become steeper.

5. If net exports had been made to balance by contractionary fiscal policy, the UK would have suffered through a large demand deficiency recession. As in (e), the UK. economy would have been operating far below full employment.

6. (d) A current account deficit indicates a domestic economy's need for borrowing from abroad to finance excessive consumption (imports in excess of exports). Part of domestic consumption is a government component that may or may not indicate a government spending greater than the tax receipts. If a government is spending more than its receipts, then the government must borrow from someone by issuing bonds. If those bonds are purchased by foreigners as part of the balancing of a current account deficit, then foreign lenders are, in fact, helping to finance a domestic government deficit. This is what happened in the US in the first half of the 1980's.

7. As we have seen, with a flexible exchange rate regime the current account plus the capital account is *always* equal to zero.

   The main problem with the data is that the US Treasury only reports long term capital transactions in equities and bonds. It excludes bank deposits and lending as well as flows of net direct foreign investment.

   Thus the net **inflows** of long-term capital ($278 billion) must be equal to the current account deficit ($196 billion) plus any net **outflows** of short-term capital and direct investment ($82 billion).

The current account deficit = capital account surplus ($278 billion - $82 billion).

($196 billion) = net inflow of long term capital ($278 billion) less the net outflow of short term capital and direct foreign investment ($82 billion).

If the total net inflows were greater, then the US would be accumulating large reserves of foreign exchange. At this time this is not the case.

See the article by M. Feldstein in the Financial Times of the 10/01/06.

CHAPTER 11

BANKING AND THE CONTROL OF THE SUPPLY OF MONEY

KEY TERMS

Currency: Notes and coin (high-powered money [H]).

Reserve Deposit Ratio (rb = Rb/D): The currency held by the banking system (Rd) as a proportion of bank deposits (D).

Private Sectors Currency Reserve Ratio (c = Cp/D): The currency held by the private sector (Cp as a proportion of their bank deposits (D).

Money Multiplier (mm): The ratio of the increase in bank deposits to the increase in currency (high-powered money) that brought about the increase in deposits.

Monetary Base Control: Controlling the money supply (M) by controlling the amount of current in the economy (using open market operations).

Open market Operations: The purchase and sale of government stock to the private sector.

We have seen, in chapter 10, that, in an open economy with floating exchange rates and free flows of financial capital, fiscal policy is not as effective as monetary policy in changing the level of output and employment. With the prevalence of floating exchange rates many countries use monetary policy both to expand the economy in an attempt to increase output and employment and deflate the economy in an effort to control inflation. Usually the monetary authorities are trying to influence the growth of the supply of money. For example, if they wish to reduce the supply of money they will be trying to reduce the range of growth of the supply of money from, say, 10-12% to 6-8%. Theoretically, in the UK, the supply of money is under the control of the Bank of England. The nominal stock of money is said to be ***exogenously*** determined (determined outside of the economic system).

The Bank of England: The Bank of England is the central bank of the UK and implements, through the Monetary Policy Committee (MPC), an independent monetary policy to prevent monetary policy being used for political purposes. Ie it prevents the political authorities from increasing the money supply and aggregate demand prior to general elections in order to reduce unemployment and hence gain electoral advantage.

As well as implementing monetary policy the central bank also:

1. Issues note and coin (currency).
2. Keeps the accounts of the central government.
3. Administers the national debt.
4. Acts as banker to the commercial banks. A central bank holds deposits of commercial banks. In principal, commercial banks could hold currency reserves to cover currency withdrawals, but, in a multi-bank system most withdrawals arise because some people need to pay other people with accounts at other banks. To avoid the large scale transfer of currency between banks, almost all of which nets out at the end of the days business, the commercial banks deposit the majority of their reserves with the central bank which then settles any inter-bank indebtedness. Bank reserves thus include both currency at the central bank plus the currency in the banks' vaults.

THE SUPPLY OF MONEY

Most money in developed countries are bank (current account [sight]) deposits with commercial banks. Currency is only a small proportion of a country's money supply. In Feb. 2007, the notes and coins in circulation in the UK accounted for just 3.1% of the total money supply. The rest, £1.496 trillion are bank deposits.

Commercial banks (Barclays, Lloyds/TSB etc.) are profit maximising, deposit taking institutions; they make their profit by lending at a higher rate of interest than the interest they pay on deposits. (For simplicity we will assume that banks pay a zero rate of interest on their deposits).

In managing their portfolios, the commercial banks have two, possibly conflicting, aims.

1. Liquidity: Commercial banks settle their debts with other banks and individuals by transfers of currency (cash). Lack of sufficient currency reserves could lead to the bank going out of business (many banks do go out of business through a lack of currency). They have to keep a sufficient proportion of their deposits in the form of currency reserves (their reserve deposit ratio) in order to prevent bankruptcy. Although banks create money (current account bank deposits) they cannot create cash. The banking systems lack of currency has led to the 'credit crunch' of 2007-09 and many banks throughout the world requiring government funds to prevent them going out of business.
2. Profit maximising: In order to earn large profits banks use the currency that is deposited with them to create loans (or purchase financial assets) and in return are paid interest.

CREDIT CREATION (the creation of new bank [current account] money)

For ease of exposition we will assuming a closed economy with a single monopoly bank that maintains a currency reserve deposit ratio (rb) of 10%.

1. Initial position of the bank.

LIABILITIES		ASSETS	
Deposits	1,000	Currency	100
		Loans and Investments	900
	1,000		1,000

The currency reserve deposit ratio is 100/1,000 = 10%

Assume that 100, in currency, is now deposited into the bank (new customer deposits).

2. The new balance sheet is

LIABILITIES		ASSETS	
Deposits	1,100	Currency	200
		Loans and Investments	900
	1,100		1,100

The reserve deposit ratio is now 200/1,100 = 18.2%

Since the bank wishes to maximise profits it can do this by increasing its deposits by expanding the size of its loans and financial investments. To restore the reserve deposit ratio to 10% it increases loans and financial investments by 900 (the money supply increases by 900).

3. The final position

LIABILITIES		ASSETS	
Deposits	2,000	Currency	200
		Loans and Investments	1,800
	2,000		2,000

The reserve deposit ratio is now back to 10% (200/2,000).

The currency deposit of 100 has led to increase in loans and financial investments of 900. (For example, if one takes out a loan from a commercial bank then you would be given a cheque book and allowed to write cheques to the value of the loan). Money, in the form of current account deposits has increased by 900. Deposits have risen by 1,000.

A currency deposit of 100 has led to an increase in deposits of 1,000. We will call the ratio of the increase in deposits to the increase in the currency that brought the increase in deposits about the **money multiplier (mm)**.

In this (simple) case the money multiplier (**mm**) is 1,000/100 = 10.

Note: In this (simple) case, **mm** = 1/rb = (1/0.1) = 10.

This simple example gives the idea behind credit creation in an economy. Currency deposited with commercial banks is used as the basis of the creation of new money. (The creation of the new money enables the transfer of income/consumption from the future to the present). However, seven years ago, Britain's banks funded lending almost entirely out of customer deposits. By the first half of 2008 they had a funding "gap"; the amount they funded mainly from international wholesale money markets—of £740 billion. The difficulty of finding external funds has led to the credit crunch of 2007-10.

In the above example we were assuming that, on average, only 10% of the currency that is deposited with the banking system will be withdrawn from the banking system (most transfers of deposits will be done by people writing cheques drawn on their accounts [no withdrawals of cash are required, just a book-keeping entry]). 90% of their currency reserves will not be withdrawn and can be used, by the banks, as the basis of credit creation. In the 'real world' the value of **rb** is very much smaller (0.66%).

A slightly more sophisticated version allows for the fact that people (the private sector) hold a proportion of their bank deposits in the form of currency.

We will make the following assumptions.

1. Banks wish to hold currency reserves (**Rb**) in proportion (**rb** [their reserve deposit ratio – also known as the cash ratio]) to banks deposits (**D**).

   Therefore Rb = rb.D

2. The private sector wishes to hold currency to the value of (**Cp**) in proportion (**c**) to banks deposits (**D**). **c** = currency deposit ratio.

   Therefore Cp = c.D

High powered money (**H**) is the currency (notes and coin) with the private sector (**Cp**) plus the currency reserves held by banks (**Rb**). Remember, that, high powered money is the **currency** issued by the central bank.

$$H = Cp + Rb$$

or $H = c.D + rb.D = D(c + rb)$

rearranging $D = \dfrac{H}{(c+rb)}$

The money supply (M) equals currency in circulation (**Cp**) + banks deposits (**D**).

$$\mathbf{M} = Cp + D$$

or $M = c.D + D = \mathbf{D(c + 1)}$ (b)

Substituting (a) into (b) gives

$$M = \frac{(c+1)}{(c+rb)}.H \qquad (c)$$

In this case the money multiplier (mm) is

$$\frac{(c+1)}{(c+rb)} \qquad (d)$$

So M = mm × H: The amount of money in an economy (M) is equal to the money multiplier (mm) multiplied by the amount of high powered money (currency) (H).

Example: If c = 0.03 (3.0%) and rb = 0.01 (1.0%) then

$$\frac{c+1}{c+rb} = \frac{1.03}{0.04} = 25.75$$

In this case 100 extra units of currency entering the banking system leads to a 2575 unit increase in deposits. (made up of 100 in currency and 2475 of loans and financial investments).

In the UK the reserve deposit ratio is much smaller than 10%, leaving a larger proportion of the currency reserves deposited with the banking system as the basis for credit creation. With no other holdings of currency reserves this would lead to a very large money multiplier. If rb = 0.01 then the simple money multiplier is 100 (Of course, people holding a proportion of their bank deposits in the form of currency 'c' will reduce the size of the money multiplier).

N.B. If **rb** increases (decreases) then 'mm' will decrease (increase). If **c** increases (decreases) then 'mm' will decrease (increase).

THE CONTROL OF THE MONEY SUPPLY

The supply of money is, theoretically, under the control of the Central Bank (in the UK the Bank of England), which acts for the government.

The central bank can control the supply of money in four main ways:

1. By controlling the reserve ratio (**rb**): The central bank can (by legislation) determine the percentage of a banks' deposits that is held in the form of currency reserves (**rb**): If the central bank increases **rb** then the banks' ability to create new money is reduced or restricted. The size of the money multiplier (**mm**) is reduced (see equations **c**) or **d**) above).

   In practice the UK government does not directly change the fraction of deposits the banks wish to hold in the form of liquid assets (**rb**): It allows the banks to determine this ratio. However the Chinese and Indian monetary authorities do use changes in the reserve ratio to attempt to control the supply of money. In June 2008, the People's Bank of China raised its reserve ratio requirement for banks to a record 17.5%.

2. By using open market operations: Since the central bank is the ultimate source of currency reserves (H) it can, theoretically, control how the currency reserves are distributed between its own holdings and that with the private sector. It does this by buying and selling government stock.

   If the Bank sells stock on the open market then the individuals or institutions that purchase the stock pay by cheque drawn on their accounts. The Bank presents these cheques to the respective commercial banks. The commercial banks now owe the Bank an amount equal to the value of the cheques. Since the banks can only settle their debts by transferring currency, an amount of currency reserves equal to the value of the cheques will be transferred to the central bank. As a result the currency reserves (Rb) of the commercial banks will fall (as will H since H = Cp + Rb) and the banks will have to restrict or contract their loans and financial investments. The money supply (M) will fall since M = mm × H (equation **c**) above.

   If the Bank buys stock then this will increase H, and, ceteris paribus, through the money multiplier (mm) will increase M.

   An (extreme) example of where this relationship broke down was during the years 1929 and 1933 in the USA. Between August 1929 and March 1933 the stock of high powered money (H) increased by 17.5%. However, the combined effect of the increase in both the banks reserve deposit ratio and the currency deposit ratio led to an overall decline in the nominal supply of money (M) of 35%.

   Because the currency issued (H) is the base on which the money supply (M) is built, (M = mm × H) this approach is known as **monetary base control**.

   Selling government stock to the public will reduce H and restrict the growth of the supply of money. Buying government stock will increase H and ease the growth of the money supply. This ties in with the analysis given above as we have shown that the money supply was **exogenous** - under the control of the monetary authorities.

3. By moral suasion. This is a persuasion tactic used by an authority (i.e. the Bank of England) to influence and pressure, but not force, banks into adhering to policy. Tactics used are closed-door meetings with bank directors, increased severity of inspections, appeals to community spirit, or vague threats. At the time of writing the UK government is trying to persuade the UK banking system to be less restrictive in their lending policies.

4. By altering the cost of borrowing: The Bank of England, which is the lender of last resort, can control short-term interest rates. These are the interest rates that the financial system pays when borrowing from the Bank of England. If the Bank of England increases (decreases) its interest rates the financial system responds by putting up (reducing) its interest rates. It has been estimated that 1% increase in the rate of interest will lead to a fall in output of £10 billion per annum.

The Bank of England enforces a higher/lower interest rate by open market operations. If the Bank of England wishes to put up interest rates and there is not a shortage of money in the economy the Bank of England can reduce the supply of money by selling bonds on the open market. This will reduce the amount of money in the economy and push up interest rates.

Although the Bank of England can, theoretically, directly control the growth of the stock of money by buying and selling government securities on the open market in practice the government uses interest rates to affect monetary growth in an economy. Using interest rates means that the monetary authorities do not have to target one particular monetary aggregate.

Interest rates are reduced to allow the supply of money to grow and increased to tighten monetary conditions.

The effectiveness of monetary base control to affect the money supply of an economy depends upon the relative stability of the money multiplier. An unstable money multiplier (caused by fluctuations in **c**, **rb** or the demand for money schedule–the velocity of circulation) could lead to wide variations in the supply of money and interest rates. For these reasons the UK and US monetary authorities tend to favour interest rate targets.

Consider the possible effects of an increase in the interest rate: This may

a. Lead to banks increasing the size of their reserve deposit ratios; rb in equations (c) or (d) above (higher interest rates mean that it is more expensive for banks to borrow money from the central bank). This will reduce the money multiplier and, directly, the supply of money.

b. Increase the cost of borrowing, which will usually lead to a fall in borrowing and a fall in consumption expenditure. People (and businesses) who took out loans that charge a variable interest rate will find their repayments increasing. They will have less income to spend on other forms of expenditure.

c. Reduce the present value of expected net revenues. This will, ceteris paribus, reduce investment expenditure and also reduce borrowing to finance investment expenditure.

d. Push up costs of production as overdraft rates increase.

e. Lead to a fall in revenues as demand is cut back.

(**d**) and (**e**) will usually lead to a fall in the expected net revenues of firms and lead to a fall in the present value of new investment projects. *Ceteris paribus*, there will be a fall in investment expenditure and a reduction in borrowing.

f. Lead the banking system to review its future projections as to the level of risk associated with new loans. If banks think that economic activity is going to decline they may only be willing to lend to, what they perceive to be, less risky projects. There will be a fall in the velocity of circulation. This will reduce the volume of new loans available and help to bring about a reduction in aggregate demand and economic activity. An extreme cut back in lending can lead to a very large fall in economic activity—a 'credit crunch'.

In the USA, for much of the 1990's, 'risky' borrowers had to pay only three percentage points over Treasury bond rates. By the beginning of 2002, the least creditworthy borrowers were having to pay eight percentage points above the US Treasury's cost of borrowing. Over the same period the credit worthiness of potential borrowers were also downgraded. At the end of 1999 there was a rating upgrade for every downgrade. In early 2002 there were three downgrades for every upgrade.

The rise in the cost of loans reduced borrowing by companies (In 2002 the balance of US loan officers reporting increased corporate demand for loans has fallen to a decade low of 60%). The downgrading of companies discouraged banks from lending to businesses.

After January 2001 the cost of Federal Reserve funds were cut from 6.5% to 1.75%. The commercial banks could borrow from the Federal Reserve (in June 2002) for 1.75%. The banks were borrowing from the Federal Reserve. However, they cut back lending from a peak of $890 billion in early 2001 to $800 billion in early 2002. What they did was purchase Treasury bonds which give a risk free return of at least 3.25% or they were buying 10 year bonds with a return of more than 5%. Their holdings of treasury bonds increased from around $690 billion to over $800 billion.

There was another 'credit crunch' (a fall in the velocity of circulation) that began in the UK in September 2007. The first extreme aspect of the crisis was a 'run' on a UK bank—the Northern Rock. People were queuing up to withdraw their cash. It was brought about because other banks chose not lend to Northern Rock (they preferred to hold onto their cash which reduced the velocity of circulation) and its individual depositors feared that the bank would go bankrupt. The Northern Rock crisis was only resolved when the banks deposits were guaranteed by the government and the bank was nationalised (the bank was taken into public ownership).

g. Bring about an increase in the nominal and real exchange rate. Some economists argue that it is the change in the exchange rate through its impact on aggregate demand that has the greatest effect on an open economy such as the UK. Since the price of exports has increased and the price of imports has decreased, it is very likely that net exports will decline leading to a fall in aggregate demand.

This will especially affect the sectors (such as manufacturing industry) more open to foreign competition. This will reduce the revenues of firms, and, as unemployment rises, the confidence of consumers. Borrowing will fall.

Changes in the supply and demand for loans (new money) are inversely related to the rate of interest. The Post Keynesians, amongst others, would argue that the commercial banks can supply whatever new money they think is prudent at the market rate of interest. (the supply of money is not directly determined by the central bank but by the banking system. The supply of money is **endogenous**). An increase in the rate of interest will usually reduce the supply and demand for new loans for consumption and investment expenditures and hence there will be a reduction in the growth of the supply of new money.

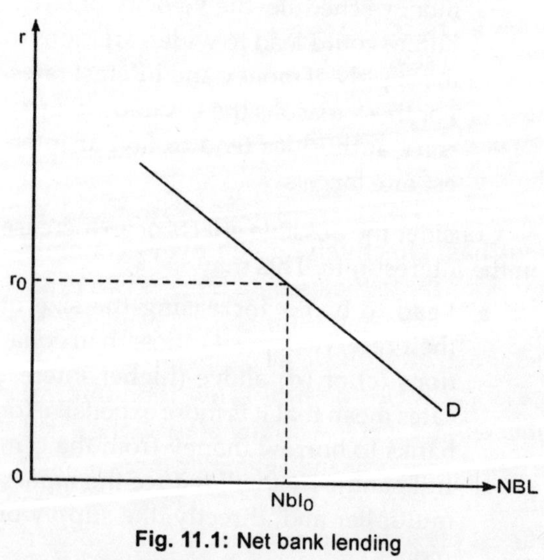

Fig. 11.1: Net bank lending

A similar process should work in reverse if the monetary authorities wish to reflate the economy. (but consider the affect of interest rate falls on the Japanese economy in the 1990's and the US economy in 2001-02 [see point (f) above]). Interest rates affect the supply of money indirectly by affecting the demand for new money (borrowing).

Setting the interest rate at r_0, and assuming that the banking system will supply the net lending required, the net bank lending (NBL) will be Nbl_0. If the interest rate falls [increases] then net bank lending will increase [decrease].

YOU SHOULD REMEMBER

Increasing interest rates will reduce borrowing (net bank lending), the money supply and aggregate demand: Reducing interest rates will lead to an increase in borrowing (net bank lending), an increase in the supply of money and an increase in aggregate demand.

The Bank of England (*The Transmission Mechanism of Monetary Policy*: 1999) suggests that changes in interest rates will have their maximum effect on the price level after about 9 quarters. An increase in the rate of interest will initially affect the **income/output** of the economy; its full affect taking about 1 year. Paradoxically, in the early stages, an increase in the interest rate will **increase** business costs, overdrafts and the cost of borrowing and, initially, **increase** the rate of inflation.

As we have seen an open economy with a floating exchange rate is more responsive to monetary policies. In giving the Bank of England control over monetary policy with a remit to keep inflation around 2.0% the government has, effectively, given over economic management to the Bank of England. In practise this means that if inflation is expected to rise above 2.0% (the level of unemployment is below NAIRU—'natural rate') then interest rates will be increased, monetary policy will be more restrictive and aggregate demand will fall. If inflation is expected to be below 2.0% interest rates will be reduced, there will be a loosening of monetary policy and aggregate demand will increase. (Incidentally, Ben Bernanke the new chairman of the Federal Reserve is considering the introduction an inflation target).

This policy ties in nicely with the aims of the UK government.

If supply side measures are effective then there will be downward pressure on the inflation rate. This downward pressure will be brought about by either an increase in involuntary unemployment or by an increase in the productivity of labour. The Bank of England will then cut interest rates, loosen monetary policy to expand aggregate demand and this will eliminate any involuntary unemployment and may help to reduce voluntary unemployment.

Economic theory suggests that, if there is an increase[decrease] in import prices and the domestic price level, then aggregate demand should be reduced[increased]. Giving control over monetary policy to the Bank of England ensures that, if inflation is expected to increase[fall] due to a rise[fall] in import prices, then interest rates will be increased[decreased] and aggregate demand will be reduced [increased].

As long as monetary policy is effective the government is not relying on 'market forces' to take the economy to full employment.

QUESTIONS

1. The simple money multiplier is 4, and the money creating potential of the banking system is £40,000,000. The legal reserve ratio and the excess reserves are
   (a) 40 percent and £4,000,000.
   (b) 40 percent and £10,000,000.
   (c) 25 percent and £2,500,000
   (d) 25 percent and £10,000,000.
   (e) 25 percent, but the excess reserves cannot be determined from the information provided.
2. What would happen to the money multiplier $\frac{(c+1)}{(c+rb)}$ if the reserve ratio (rb) increases?
3. What would happen to the money multiplier $\frac{(c+1)}{(c+rb)}$ if the proportion of deposits that the public holds in the of cash (c) increases?
4. If the central bank wished to "tighten" money it would
   (a) lower the discount rate.
   (b) sell government securities.
   (c) lower the legal reserve ratio.
   (d) lower the tax rate.
   (e) raise the tax rate.
5. The central bank controls money and credit with the exception of
   (a) controlling the money base through open-market operations.
   (b) controlling reserve requirements .
   (c) setting the discount rate of interest.
   (d) controlling the stock market.
   (e) applying moral suasion.

ANSWERS

1. (d) The simple money multiplier is 1/(rb) so 4 = 1/rb and 4.rb = 1; therefore the legal reserve ratio is 25% (1/4). The banking system can create money to the extent of its excess reserves multiplied by the money multiplier. Four times the excess reserves (£10,000,000) equals the money creat-ing potential of the banking system (£40,000,000).
2. If the reserve ratio (rb) increases then $\frac{(c+1)}{(c+rb)}$ will decline. A greater proportion of the cash entering the banking system will be held in reserves. There will be less lent out, there will be less cash to be redeposited; the size of the money multiplier will fall.
3. If the the proportion of deposits that the public holds in the form of cash (c) increases then $\frac{(c+1)}{(c+rb)}$ will decline. The banking system will have less cash deposited with it, less will be lent out; the money multiplier will fall.
4. (b) When the central bank sells government securities commercial banks and/or the public is exchanging money for the securities. If the central bank lowered the discount rate (a) member banks would likely borrow more from the central bank leading to monetary expansion. If the central bank lowered the legal reserve ratio,

(c) commercial banks would have to hold less reserves and the money multiplier would be increased. (d) and (c) are inappropriate because the central bank does not usually control tax rates.

5. (d) The central bank controls money and credit by using the reserve requirement, the discount rate of interest, open market operations, margin requirements, and moral suasion. The central bank does not control money and credit through the stock market.

APPENDIX 11A

The Ineffectiveness of Monetary Policy?

The inability to stimulate the Japanese economy by the use of monetary policy as led to some economists to review the whole workings of the 'free market' monetary system. We have seen, that, when the economy is in a liquidity trap, then an increase in the real stock of money (brought about by an increase in the nominal stock of money [M] or a decrease in the price level [P]) will not lead to an increase in real income/output. All the extra money is held in speculative balances. Consider figure 11A.1. The increase in the money supply from M_0 to M_1 does not increase real income/output (Y_0). In this situation the only policy option open to the authorities is fiscal policy.

Consider figure 11A.2. The increase in

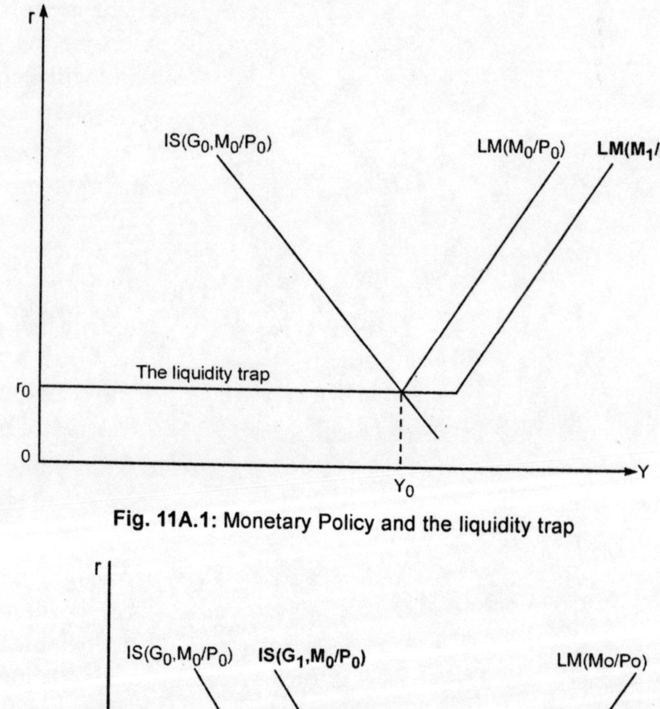

Fig. 11A.1: Monetary Policy and the liquidity trap

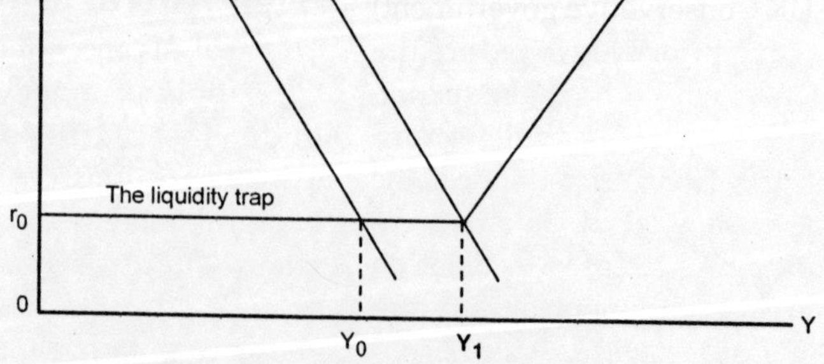

Fig. 11A.2: Fiscal Policy and the liquidity trap

government expenditure from G_0 to G_1 will shift the IS curve from $IS(G_0,M_0/P_0)$ to $IS(G_1,M_0/P_0)$ and increase real income/output from Y_0 to Y_1.

In a liquidity trap monetary policy is ineffective.

One of the arguments against fiscal policy is that increases in government expenditure or cuts in taxation have to be financed. It is financially constrained.The conventional argument is that fiscal policy requires more government borrowing and upward pressure on interest rates, and the crowding out of private expendi-tures. However, when a country, like the US or UK (but not Greece or Spain) has control over its own currency then its expenditure is not constrained by the ability to borrow.

Modern Monetary Theory (MMT)

We have seen, that an increase in the stock of money when the economy is at *full* employment will lead to an equivalent increase in the price level—the quantity theory of money. i.e. if the money supply increases by 5% then prices will increase by 5%.

In periods when unemployment is high and there is a large budget deficit then there are conflicting views on how to proceed.

One view is to assume that the unemployment is 'structural' i.e. is voluntary. This precludes the need to expand aggregate demand—expanding aggregate demand will only lead to inflation. The way to proceed is to introduce supply side measures.

Another view (and this is the argument accepted by the UK Conservative government) is that the overriding priority is to reduce the size of the budget deficit. Without a reduction in the budget deficit interest rates will rise and the deficit will be much harder to finance. The argument is that there needs to be a tightening of fiscal policy by increases in taxation and/or reductions in government expenditure and that these measures will lead to an increase in confidence and a decrease in the long-term interest rate. Although this will lead to a reduction in aggregate demand and a rise in unemployment (especially in the public sector) this will be offset by an increase in employment brought about by monetary policy, supply side policies and an increase in net exports.

1. Induced and autonomous consumption expenditure will increase. This will be brought about by falling real interest rates, by house price increases, increases in consumer confidence and the Barro-Ricardo equivalence (People will increase their consumption expenditure and reduce their level of saving because they realise that the reduction in the budget deficit will lead future tax cuts).
2. Private investment will increase. This will be brought about by falling interest rates, increases in confidence, by increases in profits and 'incentives' (supply side policies)—cuts in corporation and other business taxes.
3. Net exports will increase. This will be brought about by a decrease in the real exchange rate brought about by a falling rate of interest.

The Conservative government is expecting the above measures to lead to the creation of 2.5 million jobs.

This analysis recognises that most of the unemployment is involuntary but argues that there needs to be a rebalancing of the economy —towards more output being generated in the private sector and less in the public sector.

Another view: MMT

This analysis rejects the conventional view that the supply of money is exogenous, that is under the control of the central bank as explained in this chapter. The ability of the banking system to create money (via the money multiplier [mm]) relies upon amount of high powered money (H) that they are above to obtain. Since the amount of H is determined by the central bank then, theoretically, the supply of money (M) is determined by M = mm × H. MMT rejects this analysis. They say that commercial banks will lend to, what they consider to be, any credit worthy borro-wers. They will first create the deposits by extending loans (M) and then look for any requisite currency (H). In general, any shortage of money will lead to an increase in short-term interest rates and, since central banks usually target interest rates, then the central bank will, to prevent interest rates rising, ensure that there is no shortage of money. Thus, the relationship between M and H breaks down. The order of causation, according to MMT, is from M to H.

Another disagreement is over how any budget (positive net government expenditure [G+B > taxation]) needs to be financed. The conventional argument is that the financing of any budget deficit needs to be done by issuing government debt (bonds). Since the supply of money is assumed to be exogenous and fixed at any moment in time, then by issuing government debt (bonds) the stock (supply) of money will be exactly equal to the money injected into the economy by the positive net government expenditure. MMT argues that a country that issues its own sovereign currency—countries such as the USA, Japan or the UK (but not countries in the Euro area such as Portugal, Greece or Ireland)—can never 'run out of money'. They have the (unlimited) ability to print their own fiat (any money declared by a government to be legal tender) currency.

MMT argues that, **as long as there are unemployed resources**, governments do not need to be constrained, by the lack of ability to borrow to finance government expenditures—expenditures that will lead to an increase in aggregate demand, an increase income/output and the elimination that will lead to an increase in aggregate demand, an increase income/output and the elimination of any involuntary unemployment. Any financing of a budget deficit, when there are unemployed resources, can be done by the government creating new money, circumventing the need to borrow. As long as there are unemployed resources, can be done by the government creating new money, circumventing the need to borrow. As long as there are unemployed resources any increase in aggregate demand will not lead to excessive price inflation. Indeed, in an economy that runs close to capacity in income/output that will lead to falling average costs. This will put downward pressure on the price level.

MMT also argues for floating exchange rates. We have seen, that an economy with fixed exchange rates and a balance of payments deficit will lose any foreign exchange reserves and contract the domestic money supply. If the deficits continue the country could run out of foreign exchange and the ability to purchase essential imports (this was the threat in 1992 when the UK was a member of the ERM [exchange rate mechanism]). With floating exchange rates there are no foreign exchange reserve constraints. A positive or negative balance on the current account will not affect the domestic money supply.

MMT also takes a different view on trade to that outlined in mainstream economics textbooks. Imports are benefits to a nation while exports are a cost. The mainstream position is that imports are somehow bad too many of them is worse and exports are virtuous. Exports involve a nation giving up its resources to another nation so the citizens in the latter can enjoy them. That is a cost. Imports are the opposite.

The UK trade position (deficit) is actually a boost to their standard of living. By denying the UK citizens access to the cheapest possible imports the UK government would be compounding the consequences of their failure to implement fiscal policy of sufficient magnitude and jobs focus as private demand collapsed. The so called "huge trade deficits" are benefits to the United Kingdom and Europe.

One problem could be a large fall in the exchange rate (brought about by speculators who are worried about the value of the currency when governments create a large amount of fiat currency). This could, in an economy that imports (and exports) a large proportion of its GDP, lead to an upward to an upward pressure on costs and prices. With the economy running close to full employment this has possibility to 'trigger off' inflation (especially when the money supply is endogenous).

However, as mentioned above, there may be downward pressure on costs due to increasing investment and returns to scale. Any residual price increases due to rises in import prices may have to be tackled by the use of some form of incomes policy to prevent any cost plus inflation.

The fall in the exchange rate could also increase net exports, threatening to take the economy passed fully capacity. However, if the fall in the exchange rate leads to the elimination of the current account deficit, then there is no requirement for an inflow of finance on them capital account. This, along with increasing investment and returns to scale, may stabilse the exchange rate.

The government would have to be ready to increase taxation or restrict the supply of money (usually by direct controls on lending) in order to prevent aggregate demand exceeding the full employment level of output and 'triggering off' inflation continue, as we have above.

SYMBOLS

Symbols used

1. **In the <u>goods</u> market {the real sector of the economy [AD=Y]}**

Y = value of real income or output

AD = aggregate demand {at market prices} $= C + I + G + X - Z$

AD = Y : The equilibrium condition in the real sector of the economy {the sector where goods and services are produced}

Y_f {$= Y_p$} = potential output of the economy. {full employment output – no involuntary unemployment}

Y_d = disposable income {$= Y + B - T_d$}

a = autonomous consumption

b = marginal propensity to consume {mpc}

C = value of real consumption expenditure

S = saving {$Y_d - C$}

I = value of real investment expenditure {the purchase of new capital assets}

G = value of real government expenditure current and capital

X = real value of exports

Z = real value of imports

Wd = withdrawals

J = injections

m = marginal propensity to import: $0 < m < 1$

NX = net exports = X – Z

T_e = taxes on expenditure: e.g. indirect taxation, {VAT, specific taxes etc}

T_d = direct taxation: {income tax, national insurance payments, profit tax etc.}

B = Benefits: {transfer payments, subsidies etc.}.

NT = Net taxes: {Td less B [$NT = T_d - B$]}

T = Total net tax income of the government = NT + Te

C = C(Y,r,M/P,CC): Consumption expenditure is determined by the level of income, Y

{positively}; the rate of interest, r {negatively}; the real stock of money, M/P {positively}, and the level of consumer confidence, CC, {positively}.

I = I(r,Ct,ENR): Investment expenditure {I} is determined by the rate of interest, r {negatively}; the cost of capital, Ct {negatively}; and the level of expected net revenues, ENR {positively}.

$$PV = \frac{ENR_1}{(1+r)} + \frac{ENR_2}{(1+r)^2} + ... + \frac{ENR_n}{(1+r)^n}$$

X = X(WY,R): Exports {X} are determined by the level of world income WY {positively}; and the real exchange rate, R {negatively}.

Z = Z(Y,R): Imports {Z} are determined by the domestic country's real income, Y {positively}; and the real exchange rate, R {positively}.

$T_e = T_e(Y)$: The amount of indirect taxation Te is determined by the indirect tax rate {determined by the government} and the level of real income, Y. As Y increases T_e increases.

$T_d = T_d(Y)$: The amount of direct taxation Td is determined by the direct tax rate {determined by the government} and the level of real income Y. As Y increases Td increases.

NOTE: All the above are measured in **real** terms.

2. In the *financial* {money} market {L = LL}

M = nominal stock of money

V = velocity of circulation

P = an average price of all the goods and services produced in the economy

L = real stock of money = M/P

LL = demand for real money balances

L = LL: the equilibrium condition in the financial {money} market

r = the nominal rate of interest

r_0 = original rate of interest

r_w = the 'world' rate of interest

D = banks deposits

r_b = banks reserve deposit ratio

R_b = currency reserves of banks {= r_b.D}

c = the currency deposit ratio {the private sectors proportion of the value of their bank deposits held in the form of currency}.

Cp = currency held by the private sector {= c.D}

H = high powered money {= Cp + R_b}

mm = money multiplier

LL = L(Y,r): The demand for money {LL}, measured in real terms, is determined by the level of real income, Y {positively} and the rate of interest, r, {negatively}.

3. In the *labour* market {LD=AJ}

W = nominal wage

w = real wage = W/P

N = labour input {labour hours}

Mdw = the marginal disutility of work.

4. Others

K = stock of capital

Wh = stock of real wealth

Ct = cost of new capital goods

Pb = price of bonds

Qb = quantity of bonds

Bd = real value of bonds:

Bd = Pb x Qb

ENRi = expected **net** revenue in year i: i = 1 , 2,...n

ENR = expected revenue - expected costs

R = real exchange rate.

r_w = the 'world' rate of interest

INDEX

MICROECONOMICS

INDEX

MACROECONOMICS